CENTURY JETS

USAF Frontline Fighters of the Cold War

CENTURY JETS

USAF Frontline Fighters of the Cold War

General Editor
David Donald

AIRtime Publishing Inc.

United States of America • United Kingdom

Published by AIRtime Publishing Inc.
USA: 120 East Avenue, Norwalk, CT 06851
Tel (203) 838-7979 • Fax (203) 838-7344
email: airpower@airtimepublishing.com
www.airtimepublishing.com

ISBN 1-880588-68-4

Editors
  David Donald, John Heathcott and Jim Winchester

Authors
  Larry Davis (F-105)
  Robert F. Dorr (F-101, F-102 and F-106)
  John Fricker (F-104)
  Paul Jackson (F-104 operators)
  Jon Lake (F-100)

  Additional material by David Donald, Robert F. Dorr, John Heathcott,
  Terry Panopalis and Jim Winchester

Artists
  Mike Badrocke, Chris Davey, Keith Fretwell, Tim Maunder,
  Mark Rolfe, John Weal, Tony Wicks, Iain Wyllie

Jacket Design
  Zaur Eylanbekov

Controller
  Linda Deangelis

Publisher
  Mel Williams

PRINTED IN SINGAPORE

To order more copies of this book or any of our other titles call toll free
within the United States 1 800 359-3003, or visit our
website at: *www.airtimepublishing.com*

Other books by AIRtime Publishing include:
  United States Military Aviation Directory
  Carrier Aviation Air Power Directory
  Superfighters The Next Generation of Combat Aircraft
  Phantom: Spirit in the Skies Updated and Expanded Edition
  Tupolev Bombers
  Black Jets
  Russian Military Aviation Directory (spring 2004)

Retail distribution via:

Direct from Publisher
AIRtime Publishing Inc.
120 East Ave., Norwalk, CT 06851, USA
Tel (203) 838-7979 • Fax (203) 838-7344
Toll-free 1 800 359-3003

USA & Canada
Specialty Press Inc.
39966 Grand Avenue, North Branch
MN 55056
Tel (651) 277-1400 • Fax (651) 277-1203
Toll-free 1 800 895-4585

UK & Europe
Midland Counties Publications
4 Watling Drive
Hinckley LE10 3EY
Tel 01455 233 747 • Fax 01455 233 737

INTRODUCTION

This unique book is based on four highly detailed reports first published during the 1990s in *Wings of Fame*, and two reports published later in *International Air Power Review*. These profile the development, service history and technical aspects of the F-100, F-101, F-102, F-104, F-105 and F-106 programmes, which together make up the acclaimed 'Century Series' of classic Cold War jet fighters. Where appropriate, the text has been updated to reflect developments since the original article was published.
For ease of reference, a comprehensive index is provided.

CENTURY JETS

CONTENTS

North American
F-100
Super Sabre

First of the 'Century Series', the F-100 ushered in the supersonic era. Rapidly superseded by more capable types in its original fighter role, the 'Hun' found its true calling in the less glamorous world of fighter-bombers. As well as providing the backbone of the USAF's Cold War tactical nuclear forces in the late 1950s, it dominated the 'in-country' war in South Vietnam. The F-100 was also the platform which pioneered the defence suppression role.

A bomb-armed 'alert bird' coughs into life at Tuy Hoa in 1967, the J57 engine being started by cartridge. As well as pre-planned sorties, the F-100 force maintained several aircraft on alert so that they could provide rapid close air support if troops came into contact and required extra firepower. Tuy Hoa was the busiest of the four main F-100 bases in Vietnam (the others being Bien Hoa, Phan Rang and Phu Cat), and among the squadrons assigned to the resident 31st TFW was the 308th Tactical Fighter Squadron 'Emerald Knights', whose 'SM' tailcode is worn by this F-100D.

Top: Born in the Cold War, the F-100 achieved fame in the very 'hot' war in Vietnam. Here a 306th TFS F-100D with a full bomb load heads to its target. The 306th was assigned to the 31st TFW at Tuy Hoa, which had five F-100 squadrons assigned during the period 1967-70, making it the most important of the Super Sabre bases in southeast Asia.

Above: Of all the Cold War projects, few were as visually impressive as the ZELL programme, in which F-100s (and later F-104s) were to be blasted into the air from a shelter or, as here, a towed trailer. In the event of a nuclear exchange, recovering the aircraft was left to the discretion of the pilot to find whatever landing strip he could – but once the Mk 7 bomb had been delivered to its target, the continued usefulness of the aircraft had all but expired.

North American's F-100 Super Sabre was designed as the replacement for the uncontested 'top dog' of the fighter world of the early 1950s, the F-86 Sabre, and even echoed the name of its illustrious forebear. The original Sabre had claimed a 12:1 kill:loss ratio over the MiG-15 in Korea and became the standard fighter of leading Western air forces. The Super Sabre took on this mantle, and at first seemed to be repeating the earlier aircraft's incredible success. The F-100 was the USAF's first operational aircraft capable of exceeding the speed of sound in level flight. It was the first in a glamorous, glittering and famous 'Century series' of fighters which used F-10x designations. The aircraft enjoyed a relatively long service life (by the standards of the day) and gained an enviable combat record in Vietnam. The Super Sabre was the aircraft of the USAF's elite 'Thunderbirds' aerobatic team for several years. The F-86 had looked merely 'pretty', whereas the F-100 was good-looking in an altogether sleeker, more business-like and shark-like manner.

Following the success of the P-51 Mustang and F-86 Sabre, North American Aviation hoped that its first supersonic fighter would repeat the success of its progenitors. Insofar as the aircraft was built in bigger numbers than any of the other 'Century Series' fighters, the company succeeded, though its production total of 2,294 aircraft was barely one-quarter of that of the F-86 Sabre/FJ Fury family.

Although the Mustang and Sabre together brought NAA the status of America's premier fighter-builder, the F-100 lost the company its lead and, indeed, NAA never built another production fighter after the Super Sabre. Moreover, while the Sabre had dominated Tactical Air Command in the fighter and fighter-bomber roles, and had been pressed into service as a dedicated all-weather fighter interceptor,

the F-100 aircraft failed to become the single, dominant fighter in the USAF inventory, being augmented by a number of other types, several of which demonstrated greater suitability or effectiveness in particular roles. In fact, the Super Sabre became something of a low-cost makeweight in TAC's inventory: a good, versatile foot soldier which could usefully augment the more powerful F-105 Thunderchief in the air-to-ground role, but whose fundamental weaknesses in even this role led the Air Force to the almost unprecedented step of acquiring the US Navy's A-7 Corsair to replace it.

Nor was the F-100 a great export success for NAA in the way that the Mustang and Sabre had been (let alone the F-84), and saw service only with the Republic of China Air Force, and in Denmark, France and Turkey.

Genesis of the F-100

While other fighter manufacturers worked on more ambitious designs, some of which went far beyond what was then realistically achievable, NAA's plans for a replacement for its highly successful F-86 Sabre were rather more modest and more feasible, and the company hoped that its new fighter would be rapidly developed and would therefore be in service long before its bolder competitors. In the event, development of the fairly conservative F-100 was not appreciably less protracted than that of its rivals, and a host of faster, bigger and more useful fighters was soon in service alongside it.

NAA's initial hope was that it could produce a supersonic Sabre by doing little more than sweeping back the wing more sharply (to 45°) and adding a new turbojet engine. North American Aviation's Raymond Rice and Edgar Schmuel began work on a series of company-financed design studies in February 1949. They first proposed an area-ruled, 45°-winged, Mach 1.03 'Advanced F-86D', powered by a General Electric 'Advanced J47', which was rated at 9,400 lb st (41.80 kN) dry and 13,000 lb st (57.81 kN) with afterburning. The USAF rejected it and asked instead for a new day fighter. NAA then submitted a similar 'Advanced F-86E', with a new, slimmer fuselage and a new nose intake. It soon became clear that any gains in performance would be modest, thanks to the steep rise in aerodynamic drag that takes place as near-sonic speeds are reached.

NAA's next proposal was known simply as the NA-180 Sabre 45, (the '45' indicating the wing sweep), which combined features of the 'Advanced F-86D' and the 'Advanced F-86E'. It bore little resemblance to the F-86 Sabre except in basic configuration and structural design, and was significantly larger, faster and more powerful than the original aircraft, with different controls and a revised tail surface layout.

The Sabre 45 was to be powered by the new Pratt & Whitney J57-P-1 turbojet. This new axial-flow engine was slimmer than the centrifugal-flow engines then in common use, and thus allowed a narrower, lower-drag fuselage. It was also considerably more powerful, rated at 15,000 lb st (66.71 kN) with afterburner. By comparison with contem-

North American tested the 45° sweepback wing and low-set tailplane of the 'Sabre 45' on the first prototype YF-86D.

porary British axial-flow turbojets such as the Rolls-Royce Avon and Bristol Siddeley Sapphire, the J57 was heavy, crude and under-powered; however, it was reliable and cheap, and was being procured in huge numbers for a wide range of programmes, including the lumbering B-52 Stratofortress. Its afterburner was more advanced, efficient and reliable than those fitted to British engines, restoring the balance somewhat. When engaged, the afterburner delivered about 50 per cent extra thrust in an instant, giving the pilot a real 'kick in the back' and producing an impressive torch of gold and lilac flame and 'shock diamonds'.

These features gave the Sabre 45 an estimated maximum speed of Mach 1.3 (860 mph; 1384 km/h) at 35,000 ft (10668 m) and a respectable 580-nm (667-mile/1074-km) combat radius at an estimated combat gross weight of 23,750 lb (10773 kg). The aircraft was originally perceived as a radar-equipped fighter interceptor to replace the F-86D, but this role was given to the new F-102, and NAA was directed to draw up the Sabre 45 as a simple day fighter, without radar and with an armament of four T-130 (later redesignated as M39) 20-mm (0.787-in) cannon. This suited NAA down to the ground, since dispensing with radar allowed it to use a large, unobstructed nose intake to feed the new J57 engine, which, like all early axial-flow turbojets, was more vulnerable to disturbed airflow.

Priority for a Sabre follow-on

With the Korean War raging, the Sabre 45 was the right aircraft at the right time. The F-86 was achieving an astonishing degree of air superiority over the MiG-15, but it was clear that this was due more to pilot training and quality and to tactics than it was to any superiority of the aircraft. Indeed, the technical parity of the MiG-15 was a real worry, making a Sabre replacement an urgent priority for the USAF.

In October 1951, the USAF Council decided to press for the development of the Sabre 45 proposal, although some key figures believed that the design would be too costly and complex to fulfil the basic day fighter role. NAA had hoped that the USAF would order two Sabre 45 prototypes, one for aerodynamic testing and one for armament trials. However, the Air Force Council wanted the Sabre 45 in service much sooner than a conventional procurement process would have allowed, believing that two prototypes would not be enough to achieve early operational status. Accordingly, on 1 November 1951, the USAF issued a Letter Contract for two Sabre 45 prototypes, plus 110 NA-192 production aircraft. Ten of the latter were to be 'production test' aircraft. Full production was to be initiated even before initial flight testing was completed. This approach subsequently became known as the Cook-Craigie plan, after the two USAF generals who spearheaded it. The NA-180 prototypes were therefore built on definitive production jigs and

52-5754 was the first Super Sabre, one of two YF-100A prototypes. In initial configuration it had a pitot probe mounted on top of the intake, with a short probe underneath. The positions were subsequently reversed, as featured in the photograph below.

This fine portrait of the first YF-100A over Edwards AFB captures the simple lines and (for its day) dramatic sweepback of the wing. NAA revised the F-100's fin to the unfortunate short design, but it was too late to test it on either of the prototypes, which both had a fin shape more akin to that of later aircraft.

Right, top: 55-5756 was the first production F-100A. Series aircraft appeared soon after the second of the two prototypes, and the first were pitched into the flight test campaign while others were being built. Seventy aircraft had been completed with the inadequate short fin before the necessary alterations could be introduced to the line.

Above right: The arrival of the sixth production F-100A at Nellis AFB generated considerable interest among Air Force personnel. The Nevada base was later to play host to the F-100 weapons and tactical evaluation unit, and the 'Thunderbirds' display team.

With examples of its illustrious forebear – the F-86 Sabre – in the background, an F-100A sits on the ramp at Nellis AFB, Nevada. The Research and Development Unit conducted operational evaluation of new TAC aircraft, later evolving into the Air Warfare Center.

tooling, and large stocks of components began to be stock-piled for mass production. One month later, the new aircraft was designated the F-100.

The Sabre 45 mock-up had been inspected on 9 November, when more than 100 configuration change requests were received. In response, North American Aviation reshaped the fuselage with an even higher fine-ness ratio and provided an extended clamshell-type cock-pit canopy, while the horizontal tail was moved to a position below the extended chord of the wing. It was hoped that this would improve controllability at high angles of attack and would help to prevent pitch-up following the stall. The latter was a common and often deadly phenom-enon in many early swept-wing aircraft, and had even been dubbed the 'Sabre dance' after numerous accidents in the F-86. One YF-86D (50-577) was modified with a similar low-set horizontal tail arrangement, and proved its efficacy.

Subsequently, on 23 June 1952, NAA was directed to make provision for external weapons racks and to replace existing bladder tanks with non-self-sealing tanks in order to achieve a 400-lb (181-kg) weight saving. Additional changes were approved on 26 August 1952, at the conclu-sion of the final design stage. The air intake lip was given a sharp edge in order to improve airflow to the engine at supersonic speeds, and the nose was lengthened by 9 in (23 cm). The decision was also made to reduce the thick-ness/chord ratio of the horizontal and vertical tails to 0.035, by shortening them and increasing their chord. This final change came too late to be incorporated on the two YF-100 prototypes, then nearing completion, but was incorporated on production aircraft, 250 more of which were ordered at the same time.

Super Sabre takes to the air

The extent of these design changes was sufficient to warrant the prototypes being redesignated YF-100As. The first of these (52-5754) was completed at NAA's Los Angeles factory on 24 April 1953, and was then moved in great secrecy to Edwards AFB. Company test pilot George S. 'Wheaties' Welch made the type's maiden flight there on 25 May 1953, exceeding the speed of sound on this first 55-minute flight and then again on the second (20-minute) flight later that day. Subsonic at low level, the F-100 could exceed Mach 1 above 30,000 ft (9144 m) even in level flight, and on 6 July 1953 the YF-100A achieved a speed of Mach 1.44 in a long dive from 51,000 ft (15545 m). The two prototypes were powered by Pratt & Whitney J57-P-7 engines, then nominally rated at 9,220 lb st (41.00 kN) dry and 14,800 lb st (65.82 kN) with afterburner, although they were de-rated in the prototype aircraft.

The second prototype (52-5755) followed the first into the air on 14 October 1953, and five days later the aircraft was formally shown to the press. George Welch flew the aircraft past the press grandstand just feet from the ground and around Mach 1, creating a sonic bang which left broken windows in the airport administration building at Palmdale.

The first production aircraft (F-100A, 52-5756) flew on 29 October 1953. On the same day, Colonel F.K. ('Speedy Pete') Everest flew the first YF-100A to set a world speed record of 755.149 mph (1215.26 km/h) over a 15-km (9.3-mile) course, whose entry and exit gates were marked by columns of smoke from piles of burning vehicle tyres. This was the last world speed record set at less than 100 ft (30 m). Everest had previously flown the F-86D chase aircraft for the YF-100's first flight, and had won a beer from Welch by correctly predicting that the aircraft would achieve Mach 1 during its maiden flight. Everest had previ-ously averaged 757.75 mph (1219.45 km/h) on the required four runs over a 3-km (1.86-mile) course – beating the record set by the Douglas F4D Skyray, but not by the required 1 per cent margin.

NAA immediately claimed to have produced the world's first aircraft capable of breaking the sound barrier in level flight, as previous swept-wing contemporaries had managed supersonic flight only in a dive. This was proba-bly true, since MiG's SM-9 (forerunner of the MiG-19) did not break the sound barrier in level flight until 5 January 1954. NAA's claim to have produced the world's first in-service supersonic fighter are open to doubt, however, since the F-100's introduction to service was disrupted by technical problems.

Service test pilots who flew the YF-100As found that the aircraft outperformed the Air Force's existing types by a handsome margin, though they noted a number of short-

comings that might affect the introduction into service. Visibility over the nose during take-off and landing was rated as poor, the touchdown speed was too high, low-speed handling was 'rather poor' (with a marked tendency of the YF-100A to yaw and pitch near the stall, and an uncontrollable wing drop), and longitudinal stability in high-speed flight was considered inadequate. Without afterburner the rate of climb was considered too slow, taking 16 minutes to reach 40,000 ft (12192 m). Everest himself considered that the aircraft should not be released for service until some of the deficiencies had been rectified, but he was overruled.

Catastrophic problems

During early test flights, some rudder flutter problems had been encountered, but the installation of hydraulic rudder dampers from the 24th aircraft solved this. (A pitch damper was installed in the 154th and subsequent aircraft.) Worse was to come. Unfortunately, the aircraft's testing had not been fully completed before these early deliveries and the directional stability of the aircraft had been miscalculated: four aircraft were lost during the first year of testing due to inertia roll-yaw coupling – which was directly attributable to the short tail fin. The problem proved especially serious when underwing drop tanks were carried. On 12 October 1954, NAA test pilot George Welch was killed when his aircraft disintegrated while carrying out a maximum performance test dive followed by a high-*g* pullout in the ninth production F-100A (52-5764). The loss of Welch, who had shot down four enemy aircraft at Pearl Harbor and 14.5 more during the remainder of World War II, was felt keenly by North American.

A senior RAF evaluation officer, Air Commodore Geoffrey D. Stephenson, Commandant of the Central Fighter Establishment, was killed when his F-100A crashed at Eglin under similar circumstances. Another aircraft was lost on 9 November, although pilot Major Frank N. Emory was able to eject safely. The entire fleet was grounded on 12 October 1954, with 68 aircraft accepted or in service and 112 more completed and awaiting delivery.

Despite this, and even while the F-100 fleet was still grounded, NAA's 'Dutch' Kindleberger received the prestigious Collier Trophy from President Eisenhower. The

Fixing the fin

trophy was awarded by the National Aeronautic Association to recognise 'the greatest achievement in aviation in America' during the preceding year.

The decision was quickly made to reshape the fin and rudder, lengthening it to a form that resembled the original YF-100A surfaces, and adding about 27 per cent more vertical tail area. The F-100's large length:span ratio led to huge yaw excursions during rolling pull-out manoeuvres, producing aerodynamic loads sufficient to break the tailfin. A larger, stronger tailfin ensured adequate stability to Mach 1.4 and prevented these yaw excursions. The artificial feel systems for the aileron and stabiliser powered controls were also modified.

Service deliveries

At the end of November 1953, Tactical Air Command's 479th Fighter Day Wing at George AFB started equipping with short-finned F-100As, and initially all went well. The unit became operational on 29 September 1954. Deliveries of the modified F-100As began from the Los Angeles factory in the spring of 1954. From the 184th F-100A (e.g., the last 19 aircraft) these modifications were incorporated on the line, before the aircraft even flew, but all surviving F-100As (starting with the 34th aircraft and a random trial batch of 11 jets) were quickly brought up to the same standard. The grounding order was rescinded in February 1955 (by which time the MiG-19 was entering service) and the final F-100As were delivered in July 1955. The 479th Fighter Day Wing at George AFB finally achieved Initial Operational Capability with the modified F-100A in

Above: The short fin of the initial production F-100A provided insufficient directional stability, resulting in a series of roll-yaw coupling crashes. In December 1954 NACA modified an F-100A from the High-Speed Flight Station with a lengthened fin, the aircraft being seen at Edwards with a standard F-100A from the Air Force Flight Test Center.

Left: North American also schemed a larger fin – adding 27 per cent more area – to cure the F-100A's problems. This became the standard design, and was retrofitted to short-finned aircraft as well as being adopted on the production line. This aircraft, the 12th F-100A and second Block 5 aircraft, served with the Wright Air Development Center.

Seen in September 1954, this short-finned aircraft was designated EF-100A, and was used for tests by the Wright Air Development Center. The 'E' prefix, not to be confused with the present-day 'electronics', stood for 'exempt' and was changed to 'J' in 1955 to signify temporary assignment for test duties.

The first F-100 unit was the 479th Fighter Day Wing at George AFB. Its first aircraft were short-finned, but modified aircraft were later supplied.

Enough F-100As were made available to equip three ANG squadrons, which operated Sidewinder-equipped 'Huns' in the air defence role. Arizona's 152nd FIS (right) at Tucson converted from F-84Fs in May 1958 as an ADC-gained air defence squadron. Other ANG F-100A recipients were Connecticut's 118th TFS at Windsor Locks (below, summer 1960 to January 1966) and New Mexico's 188th FIS at Kirtland (April 1958 to the spring of 1964).

September 1955, although Project Hot Rod conducted by the USAF Air Proving Ground Command at Eglin AFB to evaluate the suitability of the F-100A for operational service revealed that the type still suffered from major operational deficiencies.

Most F-100As were phased out of the active inventory in 1958, some being transferred to the Air National Guard, and the rest being placed in storage at Nellis AFB.

The first Air National Guard unit to receive the F-100A was New Mexico's 188th FIS, which converted in April

1958, followed by the 152nd FIS (Arizona ANG) and the 118th TFS (Connecticut ANG). By 1960 the ANG had reached a peak inventory of 70 F-100As, and many of these returned to active service during the Berlin crisis of 1961, when Air National Guard and Air Force Reserve units were mobilised and called to active duty. Some of these F-100As were retained by the USAF even after the ANG personnel had been released from active duty in early 1962, and were used for aircrew training.

Some 118 F-100As (more than 58 per cent of total F-100A production) were transferred to the Chinese Nationalist Air Force, which used them until 1984. The aircraft had been withdrawn from USAF service by 1970.

The F-100A had a poor safety record, even after the tail modifications. About 50 F-100As were lost in USAF service, and Taiwan lost 49 more in accidents. F-100 landings were often described as 'controlled crashes' and one senior USAF F-100 pilot opined that the aircraft's optimum role was static display.

Early aircraft were powered by the 9,700-lb st (43.14-kN) Pratt & Whitney J57-P-7 engine (15,000 lb st/66.71 kN with afterburning), and the final 36 F-100A aircraft (from the 167th aircraft on) were built with the J57-P-39 engine, which produced 1,000 lb (4.45 kN) more thrust. From the 101st aircraft, the F-100As were also delivered with the extended wings originally intended for the F-100C fighter-bomber. Production of the F-100A eventually totalled 203 aircraft, although the USAF had increased its order to 273 aircraft (plus one static test example) on 26 August 1952. The last 70 aircraft were actually delivered as F-100Cs.

Design features

The final F-100As were broadly representative of the definitive F-100 design, since all further revisions and modifications were relatively minor, and all further production versions shared the same basic structure and configuration.

The Super Sabre's low-mounted 45° wing was dramatically swept, by the standards of the day, but, less obviously, was also extremely thin. The wing had a thickness:chord ratio of 0.082, compared to that of 0.10 for the F-86, and the wing leading-edge glove reduced the overall ratio to 0.07. This made it exceptionally thin and helped reduce drag at transonic speeds. With no room in the blade-like wing, the mainwheels retracted inwards into wells in the centre fuselage.

Like the F-86's wing, the Super Sabre's wing leading edge featured five-segment automatic slats. These increased the lift at take-off, delayed wing buffet, improved lateral control at low speeds, and permitted tighter turns. The ailerons were mounted inboard on the wing in order to reduce the tendency of the wing to twist during aileron deflection at high speeds, thereby preventing aileron reversal.

No fuel was carried in the wing of the F-100A, being accommodated instead in five non-self-sealing bladder tanks inside the fuselage. They had a total capacity of 750 US gal (2839 litres). Two 275-US gal (1041-litre) underwing drop tanks could be carried.

Behind and below the wing was a one-piece, powered, geared slab tailplane, activated by a pair of independent, irreversible hydraulic systems, with artificial 'feel' provided via springs and bungees. The rudder was unusually short, its height constrained by the position of the fuel dump pipe (which had been near the top of the short-finned F-100A's

Pratt & Whitney J57

The J57 (JT3C civil designation) was a landmark engine which ushered in a new era of fuel economy, reliability and pressure ratio. Pratt & Whitney built over 15,000, while Ford Motor Company production topped 6,200. The engine was adopted for numerous fighter types, as well as the B-52, KC-135, 707 and DC-8 large aircraft. It also directly spawned the JT3D/TF33 turbofan and the larger JT4A/J75 turbojet. The J57 was a two-spool axial-flow engine, with the inner low-pressure spool and outer high-pressure spool combining to provide a pressure ratio of 12.5.

Versions of the J57 installed in the F-100 were the J57-P-7 and J57-P-39 (both of 14,800 lb/65.86 kN thrust with afterburner), and the J57-P-21/21A (16,000 lb/71.2 kN). Many aircraft were later modified with the afterburner section from the F-102, while some received the afterburner section of the F-106's J75.

Today it is standard practice to design aircraft so that the engines slide out, but in the 1950s it was the vogue to remove the entire rear fuselage on a trolley, as demonstrated by a QF-100D drone on Tyndall's 'Death Row'.

tailfin, but was now about halfway down the tail). Despite its small size the rudder was extremely powerful. The final control surface was a retractable 'barn door' speed brake, which was mounted below the rear fuselage.

Unlike many of its contemporaries, the F-100 was not area-ruled and the humped, shark-like fuselage was relatively simple. The F-100 retained a plain pitot intake in the nose, like that of the F-86. This allowed a straight-through airflow to the compressor, without the complication of bifurcated intakes on the fuselage sides or in the wing roots. Unlike the F-86's intake, that fitted to the F-100 was broad and flat, somewhere between a rectangle and an oval in cross-section, allowing a broad, flat intake duct to flow easily under the pilot's cockpit and over the nose-wheel bay and cannon bays.

Cannon armament

The Super Sabre's armament consisted of four 20-mm (0.787-in) Pontiac M39 cannon, mounted in pairs on each side of the fuselage below the cockpit. The M39 had been tested in Korea on modified F-86Fs as the T-160, and had proved extremely effective. The weapon, like the British ADEN cannon and the French DEFA 552, was a belt-fed revolver-type cannon derived from the German Mauser MG 213C. While the British and French opted for a 30-mm (1.18-in) cannon, the US designers (from the Illinois Institute of Technology, working under contract for General Electric's Pontiac division) chose 20-mm to give a faster rate of fire. The M39 could fire up to 1,500 rounds per minute at a muzzle velocity of 3,300 ft (1006 m) per second.

In the F-100, ammunition capacity was usually limited to 200 rounds per gun in order to reduce the risk of rounds 'cooking off' in their ammunition boxes, though some F-100Ds could carry 257 rpg. The F-100F two-seater carried just 175 rounds for each of its two cannon. These powerful weapons were aimed using a lead-computing A-4 ranging gunsight. Lead was computed automatically, using ranging information from the ranging radar whose antenna was mounted inside the upper part of the engine inlet lip, covered by a flush-mounted dielectric panel.

The F-100's J57 engine was closely cowled in the rear fuselage – with so little room around it that the rear part of the F-100 proved almost impossible to paint. Early USAF F-100s had their 'Buzz' numbers on the rear fuselage, but they kept burning off and eventually had to be moved. Camouflaged aircraft soon became heavily weathered in this area. The F-100's rear fuselage culminated in a crude but effective variable-area afterburner nozzle, with petals

Superficially similar to the late F-100A, the C model was far more capable, having a 'wet' wing and underwing hardpoints for the carriage of tanks and weapons. It also had 'universal' (i.e. nuclear) wiring.

RF-100A – Slick Chick

The most mysterious of the 2,294 Super Sabres were the six RF-100A Slick Chick aircraft converted for the reconnaissance mission. Few details have emerged regarding their operations, from either the USAF (in Germany and Japan) or the RoCAF (from Taiwan). The camera installation entailed the removal of the guns and the installation of a bulged bay for five cameras. The advent of the faster and more capable RF-101 Voodoo put an end to the prospect of any further RF-100 conversions.

An F-100C from the 336th TFS/4th TFW leads two 333rd TFS F-100Fs. The aircraft formed the '9th AF Firepower Team'.

Below: F-100Cs went to Europe in 1956, equipping the 36th Fighter-Day Wing headquartered at Bitburg, West Germany. The role was tactical nuclear strike, the aircraft carrying a single Mk 7 'Blue Boy' on the left intermediate pylon and three drop tanks in the '1-E' configuration. The wing maintained a daytime nuclear-armed Victor alert status, whereas the later F-100D units had round-the-clock capability. The 36th had five squadrons scattered around several bases: this snow-dusted aircraft is from the 53rd Fighter-Day Squadron, seen at its Landstuhl base in January 1958.

opening and closing to vary the jetpipe diameter. This nozzle was only the visible portion of a 20-ft (6.1-m) long, 5,000-lb (2268-kg) structure which was fastened to the back of the 14-ft (4.28-m) long J57 engine.

The F-100 was even more innovative under the skin. The aircraft made extensive use of new manufacturing and construction techniques, and of new materials, particularly heat-resistant titanium. This was the first time that this metal had been used in large quantities in an aircraft, and North American actually used 80 per cent of all the titanium produced in the United States until 1954 in the manufacture of the Super Sabre. Titanium is an extremely strong and light metal and is more resistant to heat than aluminium, but is more brittle and more difficult to machine, and therefore costs more to work with. The aircraft made greater use of automatically machine-milled components, increasing machine tool costs but allowing the use of simpler sub-assemblies with smaller parts counts. Thus, while the F-86 wing box had used 462 parts and 16,000 fasteners, the integrally-stiffened F-100 wing box used 36 components and only 264 fasteners. Wing skins were tapered from root to tip and were machined into integrally-stiffened components. Massive single-alloy sheets were transformed into fuselage sides in a huge stretch press.

This use of advanced materials and manufacturing techniques was made possible by massive industry-wide invest-

ment which fed into a whole range of aircraft programmes. In Britain or France, where there might be only one or two simultaneous projects, such investment was virtually impossible. Nor could the Europeans draw upon the same range of research programmes, having had no direct counterparts to the succession of X-planes, high-speed wind tunnels and the like.

Strategic reconnaissance

Small numbers of F-86s had been successfully converted to high-speed tactical reconnaissance aircraft, and it was always likely that the F-100's sheer speed performance would make it a candidate for a similar conversion. Sure enough, in late 1953, NAA received a request to modify six F-100As as RF-100A reconnaissance aircraft, each carrying five Chicago Aerial Survey cameras. The F-100's supersonic capability promised to give it a degree of immunity from interception, and the new cameras, although not as advanced as the Hycon being developed for the U-2, could resolve golf balls on grass from 53,000 ft (16154 m).

A seven-man team under Don Rader began detailed design work immediately, and in September 1954 six F-100As (53-1545 to -1548, 55-1551 and 55-1554) were taken from the production line to be modified as unarmed RF-100A photographic reconnaissance aircraft under what became (on 7 December 1954) Project Slick Chick. Even with the removal of the cannon armament, the cameras and reconnaissance systems could not fit inside the existing fuselage, and a distinctive bulge had to be added under the fuselage belly, extending back from Station 80 below the cockpit to Station 267, almost at the wing trailing edge. The aircraft was also bulged on the forward fuselage sides, below the cockpit.

Together these fairings covered the camera stations which accommodated split vertical K-38 cameras (with their 36-in/91.4-cm lenses laid horizontally along the belly, on each side of the nose gear bay, each having a periscopic device to look down), and with a triple arrangement of oblique K-17s and a K-17C vertical camera roughly level with the wing leading edge. The camera ports were covered by electrically-powered doors to protect the expensive optics. Avionics systems were revised and relo-

Right: An F-100C from the 4th TFW takes off from Seymour-Johnson in 1959. The standard underwing store was the 275-US gal (1041-litre) supersonic 'banana' tank on the intermediate pylons, but a 200-US gal (757-litre) tank was available for carriage on inboard or outboard pylons. The F-100D introduced even larger tanks: a 335-US gal (1268-litre) 'banana' tank and a 450-US gal (1703-litre) subsonic tank.

Left: Seen in 1963, these F-100Cs are from the 166th TFS, Ohio ANG. During the Pueblo Crisis the squadron was deployed to Kunsan.

Below: Armed with napalm and bombs, a 152nd TFTS F-100C makes a dive attack. The Arizona unit trained F-100 pilots for the ANG, having earlier been an ADC fighter unit. It had the distinction of operating all four F-100 versions: A, C, D and F.

F-100Cs in the Air National Guard

At its peak the F-100C served with 11 ANG squadrons: 110th/MO, 119th/NJ, 120th/CO, 121st/DC, 124th/IA, 136th/NY, 152nd/AZ, 166th/OH, 174th/IA, 184th/KS (below) and 188th/NM. The first units to receive the type were the DC and New York squadrons, which began flying F-100Cs in mid-1960, and by the end of 1962 a further five had been equipped. The rundown of the C fleet began in June 1970 when the New Jersey Guard gave up its aircraft for F-105Bs. The last ANG F-100C squadron was Iowa's 124th TFS at Des Moines, which flew the type until mid-1975 before upgrading to F-100Ds.

cated – the gun ranging radar gave way to a new navigation system – and there was provision for the pilot to wear a pressure suit for very high altitude flying. The former aft electronics bay accommodated a new 830-US gal (3142-litre) fuel tank, giving the Slick Chick an endurance of up to 5½ hours.

The mission profile called for a lot of high-speed flight using afterburner, so the RF-100A carried four drop tanks rather than the usual two. New inboard pylons sway-braced to the fuselage carried a pair of 200-US gal (757-litre) tanks, and there were 275-US gal (1041-litre) tanks outboard.

Secret ops

A thick shroud of secrecy still covers the RF-100As that participated in politically-sensitive reconnaissance missions over Soviet and Soviet-occupied territory during the Cold War. It is known that the aircraft sometimes carried spurious serial numbers (one was photographed masquerading as 53-2600, actually an F-89 Scorpion).

Three of the Slick Chicks were shipped to Europe aboard the USS *Tripoli*, being flown from Burtonwood to Bitburg on 16 May 1955 to form Detachment 1 of the RB-57-equipped 7407th Support Squadron. The remaining trio joined the 6021st Reconnaissance Squadron at Yokota, Japan on 2 June 1955.

The aircraft's engines were replaced frequently in an effort to obtain the best possible high-altitude performance. The original J57-P-39 engines were initially tweaked to give an afterburning thrust of 16,000 lb st (71.16 kN), before being replaced by F-100D-type J57-P-21s. They then reverted to the J57-P-39, which proved better above 40,000 ft (12192 m), before being fitted with J57-P-21As in 1957.

The European Slick Chicks flew from Bitburg, Rhein Main, Hahn, Fürstenfeldbruck and Incirlik, accelerating to supersonic speed over West Germany before crossing the border with the East. They then flew in a straight-line reconnaissance run before starting a climbing turn, gaining

altitude before starting to dive (still in the turn) and then heading into a return run. The aircraft thus flew keyhole-shaped flight plans, accounting for the 'Keyhole' name applied to the missions. 53-1551 was abandoned by its pilot near Bitburg in October 1956, and the unit then used an unmodified F-100C for training before the Detachment disbanded on 1 July 1958.

In the Far East, the Yokota-based aircraft flew similar missions. One aircraft (53-1548) was lost on 23 June 1955 and the surviving one returned to Inglewood in June 1958.

The four surviving RF-100As were then transferred to the Nationalist Republic of China Air Force on Taiwan, arriving in December 1958 and January 1959 and equipping the 4th Squadron at Taoyuan. It has generally been believed that these aircraft flew operational overflight missions over the People's Republic of China, but recent reports suggest that this may not have been the case and that the aircraft suffered problems which prevented their operational use. They were supposedly retired in December 1960.

Two aerobatic display teams flew the F-100C – the 'Thunderbirds' between 1956 and 1963, and USAFE's 'Skyblazers' (illustrated) from late 1958 to early 1962. In the F-100 era the latter team was provided by the 36th TFW at Bitburg, operating seven aircraft which were additional to the wing's operational inventory.

Inside the Super Sabre

F-100 specifications

Dimensions
Wingspan: YF-100A – 36 ft 7 in (11.15 m); F-100A/C/D – 38 ft 9 in (11.81 m)
Length: YF-100A – 46 ft 3 in (14.10 m); F-100A/C – 47 ft 1¼ in (14.36 m); F-100D – 50 ft 0 in (15.24 m); F-100F – 52 ft 3 in (15.93 m)
Height: YF-100A – 16 ft 3 in (4.95 m); F-100A – 13 ft 4 in (4.06 m); F-100A modified 15 ft 8 in (4.77 m); F-100C – 15 ft 6 in (4.72 m); F-100D/F – 16 ft 2¾ in (4.95 m)
Wing area: YF-100A – 376 sq ft (34.93 m²); F-100A/C 385 sq ft (35.77 m²); F-100D/F 400 sq ft (37.16 m²)

Weights
Empty: YF-100A – 18,135 lb (8226 kg); F-100A – 18,185 lb (8249 kg); F-100C – 19,270 lb (8741 kg); F-100D – 20,638 lb (9361 kg); F-100F – 21,712 lb (9848 kg)
Gross: YF-100A – 24,789 lb (11244 kg); F-100A – 24,996 lb (11338 kg); F-100C – 27,587 lb (12513 kg); F-100D – 28,847 lb (13085 kg); F-100F – 31,413 lb (14249 kg)
MTOW: F-100C – 32,615 lb (14794 kg); F-100D – 34,832 lb (15800 kg); F-100F – 39,122 lb (17746 kg)

Powerplant
YF-100A – one Pratt & Whitney XJ57-P-7 rated at 8,700 lb st (38.71 kN) dry, or 13,200 lb st (58.74 kN) with afterburning
F-100A/C – one Pratt & Whitney J57-P-7/39 rated at 9,700 lb st (43.16 kN) dry, or 14,800 lb st (65.86 kN) with afterburning
F-100C/D/F – one Pratt & Whitney J57-P-21 rated at 10,200 lb st (45.39 kN) dry, or 16,000 lb st (71.2 kN) with afterburning
F-100D/F – one Pratt & Whitney J57-P-21A rated at 10,200 lb st (45.39 kN) dry, or 16,920 lb st (75.29 kN) with afterburning

Fuel
Fuel capacity (internal): YF-100 – 1,307 US gal (4947 litres); F-100A/F – 1,294 US gal (4898 litres); F-100C – 1,702 US gal (6443 litres), F-100D – 1,739 US gal (6583 litres)
Fuel capacity (total): F-100C/D – 2,139 US gal (8097 litres)

Armament
Internal: F-100A/C/D – four 20-mm Pontiac M39 cannon with 200 rpg, or 257 rpg (some F-100D); F-100F – two 20-mm Pontiac M39 cannon with 175 rpg
External: F-100A – 2,000 lb (907 kg); F-100C/F – 5,000 lb (2268 kg); F-100D – 7,040 lb (3193 kg)

Performance
Maximum speed at 35,000 ft (10668 m): YF-100A – 634 mph (1020 km/h); F-100A – 740 mph (1191 km/h); F-100C – 803 mph (1292 km/h); F-100D – 765 mph (1231 km/h); F-100F – 760 mph (1223 km/h)
Initial climb rate: YF-100A – 12,500 ft (3810 m) per minute; F-100A/F – 23,800 ft (7254 m) per minute; F-100C – 21,600 ft (6584 m) per minute; F-100D – 19,000 ft (5791 m) per minute
Service ceiling: YF-100A – 52,600 ft (16032 m); F-100A/F – 44,900 ft (13685 m); F-100C – 38,700 ft (11796 m); F-100D – 36,100 ft (11003 m)
Combat ceiling: F-100A/F – 51,000 ft (15545 m); F-100C – 49,100 ft (14966 m); F-100D – 47,700 ft (14539 m)
Combat radius: YF-100A – 422 miles (679 km); F-100A/F – 358 miles (576 km); F-100C – 572 miles (920 km); F-100D – 534 miles (859 km)
Maximum range: YF-100A – 1,410 miles (2269 km); F-100A/F – 1,294 miles (2082 km); F-100C – 1,954 miles (3144 km); F-100D – 1,995 miles (3210 km)

The four 20-mm cannon were easily accessed through panels in the lower fuselage, and the breech assembly hinged out for maintenance (above right). Ammunition was held in tanks located either side of the cockpit, feeding rounds to the staggered guns via side-by-side belts (above). These scenes of ground crew servicing and arming the weapons were recorded during combat operations in Vietnam.

North American F-100D cutaway

1 Pitot tube, folded for ground handling
2 Engine air intake
3 Pitot tube hinge point
4 Radome
5 IFF aerial
6 Ranging radar
7 Intake bleed air electronics cooling duct
8 Intake duct framing
9 Cooling air exhaust duct
10 Cannon muzzle port
11 UHF aerial
12 Nose avionics compartment
13 Hinged nose compartment access door
14 Inflight refuelling probe
15 Windscreen panels
16 A-4 radar gunsight
17 Instrument panel shroud
18 Cockpit front pressure bulkhead
19 Rudder pedals
20 Gunsight power supply
21 Armament relay panel
22 Intake ducting
23 Cockpit canopy emergency operating controls
24 Nosewheel leg door
25 Torque scissors
26 Twin nosewheels
27 Nose undercarriage leg strut
28 Philco-Ford M39 20-mm cannon (four)
29 Kick-in boarding steps
30 Ejection seat footrests
31 Instrument panel
32 Engine throttle
33 Canopy external handle
34 Starboard side console panel
35 Pilot's ejection seat
36 Headrest
37 Cockpit canopy cover
38 Ejection seat guide rails
39 Cockpit rear pressure bulkhead
40 Port side console panel
41 Cockpit floor level
42 Control cable runs
43 Gun bay access panel
44 Ammunition feed chutes
45 Ammunition tanks, 200 rounds per gun
46 Power supply amplifier
47 Rear electrical and electronics bay
48 Cockpit pressurisation valve
49 Anti-collision light
50 Air conditioning plant
51 Radio compass aerial
52 Intake bleed air heat exchanger
53 Heat exchanger exhaust duct
54 Secondary air turbine
55 Air turbine exhaust duct, open

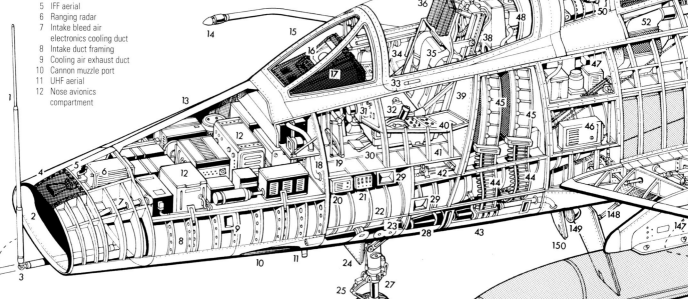

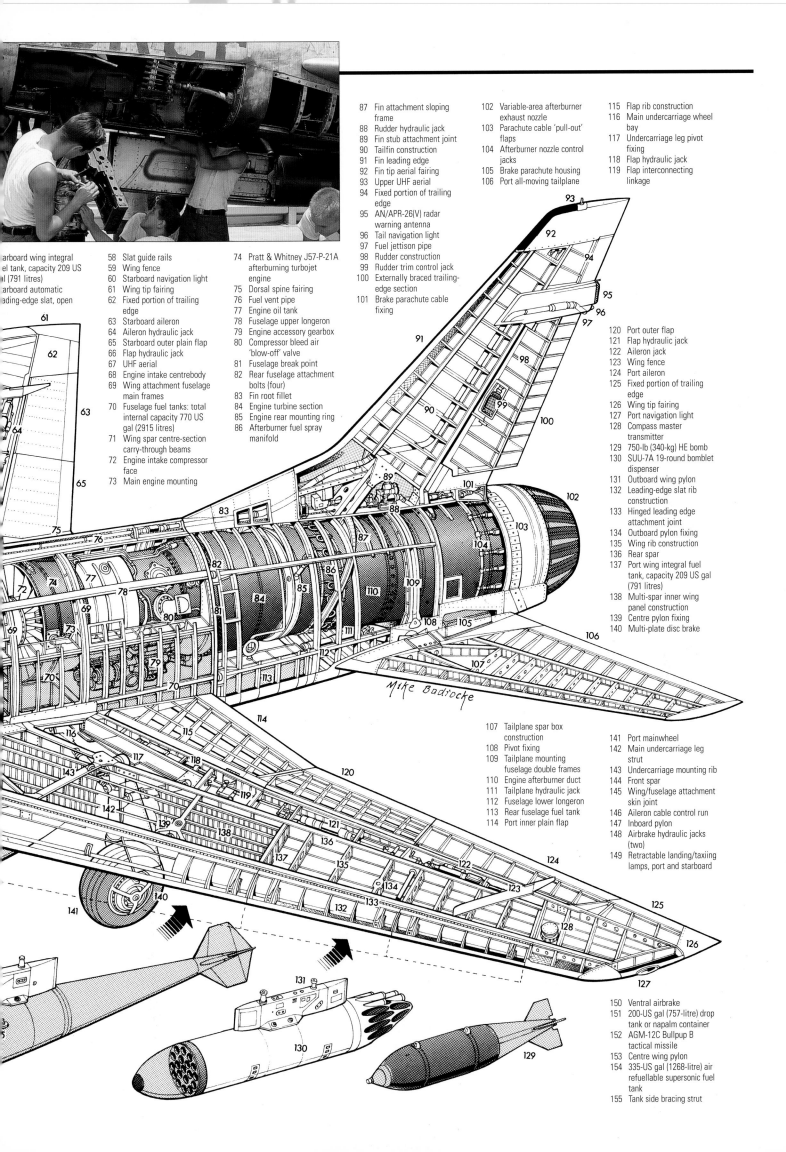

87 Fin attachment sloping frame
88 Rudder hydraulic jack
89 Fin stub attachment joint
90 Tailfin construction
91 Fin leading edge
92 Fin tip aerial fairing
93 Upper UHF aerial
94 Fixed portion of trailing edge
95 AN/APR-26(V) radar warning antenna
96 Tail navigation light
97 Fuel jettison pipe
98 Rudder construction
99 Rudder trim control jack
100 Externally braced trailing-edge section
101 Brake parachute cable fixing

102 Variable-area afterburner exhaust nozzle
103 Parachute cable 'pull-out' flaps
104 Afterburner nozzle control jacks
105 Brake parachute housing
106 Port all-moving tailplane

115 Flap rib construction
116 Main undercarriage wheel bay
117 Undercarriage leg pivot fixing
118 Flap hydraulic jack
119 Flap interconnecting linkage

58 Slat guide rails
59 Wing fence
60 Starboard navigation light
61 Wing tip fairing
62 Fixed portion of trailing edge
63 Starboard aileron
64 Aileron hydraulic jack
65 Starboard outer plain flap
66 Flap hydraulic jack
67 UHF aerial
68 Engine intake centrebody
69 Wing attachment fuselage main frames
70 Fuselage fuel tanks: total internal capacity 770 US gal (2915 litres)
71 Wing spar centre-section carry-through beams
72 Engine intake compressor face
73 Main engine mounting

74 Pratt & Whitney J57-P-21A afterburning turbojet engine
75 Dorsal spine fairing
76 Fuel vent pipe
77 Engine oil tank
78 Fuselage upper longeron
79 Engine accessory gearbox
80 Compressor bleed air 'blow-off' valve
81 Fuselage break point
82 Rear fuselage attachment bolts (four)
83 Fin root fillet
84 Engine turbine section
85 Engine rear mounting ring
86 Afterburner fuel spray manifold

Starboard wing integral fuel tank, capacity 209 US gal (791 litres)
Starboard automatic leading-edge slat, open

120 Port outer flap
121 Flap hydraulic jack
122 Aileron jack
123 Wing fence
124 Port aileron
125 Fixed portion of trailing edge
126 Wing tip fairing
127 Port navigation light
128 Compass master transmitter
129 750-lb (340-kg) HE bomb
130 SUU-7A 19-round bomblet dispenser
131 Outboard wing pylon
132 Leading-edge slat rib construction
133 Hinged leading edge attachment joint
134 Outboard pylon fixing
135 Wing rib construction
136 Rear spar
137 Port wing integral fuel tank, capacity 209 US gal (791 litres)
138 Multi-spar inner wing panel construction
139 Centre pylon fixing
140 Multi-plate disc brake

107 Tailplane spar box construction
108 Pivot fixing
109 Tailplane mounting fuselage double frames
110 Engine afterburner duct
111 Tailplane hydraulic jack
112 Fuselage lower longeron
113 Rear fuselage fuel tank
114 Port inner plain flap

141 Port mainwheel
142 Main undercarriage leg strut
143 Undercarriage mounting rib
144 Front spar
145 Wing/fuselage attachment skin joint
146 Aileron cable control run
147 Inboard pylon
148 Airbrake hydraulic jacks (two)
149 Retractable landing/taxiing lamps, port and starboard

150 Ventral airbrake
151 200-US gal (757-litre) drop tank or napalm container
152 AGM-12C Bullpup B tactical missile
153 Centre wing pylon
154 335-US gal (1268-litre) air refuellable supersonic fuel tank
155 Tank side bracing strut

Mike Badrocke

Under Project Rough Rider, a specially instrumented JF-100F, 56-3744, of the Wright Air Development Center was used to record the intensity of thunderstorms and lightning strikes in the vicinity of Oklahoma between 1960 and 1967. The aircraft was specially instrumented with gust vanes on the nose boom, temperature and hail probes on the underside, electrical field measuring equipment on the wing tips, hail erosion protection strips on the leading edges, and cameras on the left wing tank to photograph water droplets or ice crystals.

Two views show the Rough Rider JF-100F. The bucking bronco badge was picked as the project logo as an apt characterisation of the experience of flying through thunderstorms. Note the modified port wing tank which was used to house some of the recording equipment.

Below right: This Nellis-based aircraft was used to test the GAM-83A (later AGM-12) Bullpup missile, which led to the modification of 65 F-100Ds to carry the weapon.

Below: This gaudily striped F-100D was assigned to the commander of the 474th TFW at Cannon AFB, the markings representing the colours of the constituent squadrons. In May 1962 the 474th sent one of its squadrons on TDY to Takhli, initiating deployments to Thailand in the face of growing fighting in Laos. The wing's 428th TFS was the first to lose an aircraft in combat in southeast Asia, on 18 August 1964 while escorting an Air America ResCAP mission over Laos.

Fighter-bomber

Failing to set the world on fire in the day fighter role, and enjoying only modest success as a reconnaissance platform, the F-100 was still an aircraft in search of a role when the F-100A entered front-line service. During late 1953, slippages in the Republic F-84F Thunderstreak programme led Tactical Air Command (TAC) to recommend that a version of the Super Sabre should be developed with a secondary fighter-bomber capability. The use of the term fighter-bomber was perhaps slightly misleading, since what was actually required was a tactical nuclear strike aircraft; it would be used to blunt any Soviet armoured advance into western Europe and would employ small, low-yield nuclear weapons, providing the US and its allies with a measure of flexible response to Soviet aggression. The USAF hoped to gain an interim fighter-bomber capability pending full availability of the F-84F and of aircraft like the F-105. This fighter-bomber-capable Super Sabre version became the F-100C.

It was not then apparent that providing such a capability would save the Super Sabre from an ignominious early retirement, since the type's poor performance in its designed role had not then been exposed.

The groundwork for the F-100's successful adaptation as a fighter-bomber had begun in October 1952, even before the YF-100A had made its maiden flight. Mindful of the F-86's poor radius of action and of its successful use in the fighter-bomber role in Korea, the USAF requested that NAA should examine the possibility of developing 'wet' wings for the Super Sabre. It followed this up in July 1953 with a request that the new wing should also be strong enough to carry ordnance.

On 31 December 1953 the USAF directed that the last 70 F-100As on the order be modified as NA-214 (F-100C)

fighter-bombers. The importance of the fighter-bomber programme was underlined on 24 February 1954, when the Air Force ordered an additional 230 F-100Cs. The F-100C would become the first version of the Super Sabre to serve with the USAF in significant numbers, and manufacture eventually totalled 476 production aircraft. On 27 May, orders had been increased to 564 F-100Cs, though this was subsequently amended on 27 September so that many of the aircraft were completed as F-100Ds.

The fourth production F-100A (52-5759) was taken out of the flight test programme and modified to serve as the YF-100C prototype. This aircraft flew for the first time on 26 July 1954. It was not possible to incorporate integral fuel tanks in this fully-finished airframe, which also initially featured the short stubby fin common to early F-100s. The aircraft did, however, receive other modifications planned for the production F-100C.

The F-100C's wing was extensively modified with four additional hardpoints for either fuel tanks or weapons. The six underwing stations could together accommodate up to 5,000 lb (2268 kg) of stores including bombs, up to 12 5-in (12.7-cm) high-velocity air rockets, fuel tanks, napalm, and even 'special stores' in the form of the Mk 7 nuclear bomb.

Both wingtips were extended by 12 in (30.5 cm); this increased the wing area from 376 to 385.21 sq ft (34.93 to 35.79 m²), improving the roll characteristics and reducing the stalling speed. The wingtip extensions proved so useful that they were also incorporated into the F-100A production line, beginning with the 101st example.

The first production F-100C (53-1709) rolled off the line on 19 October 1954 and was conditionally accepted by the USAF on 29 October, though all Super Sabres were then still officially grounded. The aircraft (still fitted with an F-100A-type short tailfin) made its maiden flight on 17 January 1955 in the hands of Al White. This aircraft had the wet wing with integral fuel tanks. In this new leak-proofing system, all bolts that fastened the wing skin to the spars were specially sealed with injected material; this turned the wing into a 451-US gal (1707-litre) tank and brought total internal fuel capacity to 1,602 US gal (6064 litres).

The F-100C also had provision for a removable, non-retractable inflight-refuelling probe below the starboard wing and for single-point pressure refuelling. The F-100A had relied on individual gravity refuelling of its five fuselage tanks.

On 20 August 1955 USAF Colonel Harold Hanes flew the first production F-100C in two runs over a 15- to 25-km (9.3- to 15.5-mile) course laid out on the Mojave Desert. In doing so, he established a new world speed record of 822.135 mph (1323.062 km/h). This was the first record set at high altitude (the aircraft flew the course at 40,000 ft/12192 m) and also marked the first 'official' supersonic speed record. Chuck Yeager's flight in the Bell X-1 had been excluded because the aircraft had been dropped from a mother ship rather than taking off under its own power.

The first few F-100Cs were powered by the J57-P-7 engine, rated at 9,700 lb st (43.14 kN) dry and 14,800 lb st (65.82 kN) with afterburner. The next aircraft used the similarly-rated J57-P-39. From the 101st F-100C, the chosen powerplant was the J57-P-21, rated at 10,200 lb st

(45.36 kN) dry and 16,000 lb st (71.16 kN) with afterburner. The -21 engine also produced more thrust at high altitude, increasing the aircraft's speed at altitude by about 40 mph (64 km/h) and reducing the time taken to climb to 35,000 ft (10668 m) by about 10 per cent.

Deliveries of the F-100C to TAC's 450th Fighter Day Squadron at Foster AFB in Texas began in April 1955, and this unit became fully operational on 14 July 1955. On 4 September 1955, Colonel Carlos Talbott flew his F-100C the 2,325 miles (3742 km) across the USA from coast to coast, achieving an average speed of 610.726 mph (982.841 km/h). Colonel Talbott was awarded the Bendix Trophy for this flight.

The F-100C served only relatively briefly with the USAF's front-line fighter-bomber wings (including units in Japan and at Bitburg, Fürstenfeldbruck, Hahn and Landstuhl in West Germany, Camp New Amsterdam in the Netherlands, and Sidi Slimane in Morocco) before being superseded by the F-100D. The ex-USAF F-100Cs were then passed to the Air National Guard, whose first squadrons began receiving the F-100C during mid-1959.

ANG F-100C units were among those mobilised on 1 October 1961 in response to the Berlin Crisis, some deploying to Europe to reinforce NATO, others remaining within ConUS. All were demobilised in August 1962. Four ANG F-100C squadrons (from Colorado, New York, Iowa and New Mexico) were subsequently called up for service in Vietnam.

Although its front-line service was relatively brief, the F-100C was at least a success in its new role, unlike the F-100A. The Super Sabre was, at last, a good advertisement for NAA and the USAF and, accordingly, the type was chosen to equip the USAF's 'Thunderbirds' flight demonstration team. The team operated F-100Cs from 19 May 1956 until 1964, when they were replaced by F-105s; this, however, lasted only six shows until a major accident grounded the team and forced a conversion back to the F-100D. Successively designated the 3600th, 3595th and 4520th Air Demonstration Flight, the 'Thunderbirds' flew a seven-aircraft team and used 14 F-100Cs. The team's Super Sabres were modified with simple smoke-generating equipment that injected diesel oil into the jet efflux. This oil was carried from the modified rear fuselage tank in thin pipes which ran along the rear fuselage, beside the fin root. They also had their cannon, gun camera, gunsight, ranging radar and autopilot removed, and the 'slot' aircraft had a stainless steel fin leading edge and a relocated VHF antenna under

F-100Ds equipped numerous Fighter-Bomber Wings at CONUS bases, all of which were redesignated as Tactical Fighter Wings on 1 July 1958 (as were the Fighter-Day Wings). This aircraft was assigned to the 356th TFS of the 354th TFW, and is seen at Aviano, Italy, in 1959 during a regular reinforcement exercise deployment. In 1965 the wing deployed its aircraft to Ramey AFB, Puerto Rico, and San Isidro AB, Dominican Republic, during the crisis in the latter country.

ZELL – Zero Length Launch

By the mid-1950s the vulnerability of allied airfields to enemy attack was becoming a cause for some concern. Few USAF tactical aircraft were more reliant on having a long stretch of concrete available from which to take off than the F-100. Under the Zero Length Launch (ZELL) programme, the F-100 would be provided with a means of getting airborne from dispersed sites or from an airfield with damaged runways; it consisted of a simple mobile wheeled launch platform, with cradles which supported the aircraft's main undercarriage units and held the F-100 in the selected launch attitude. The aircraft was fitted with a massive 130,000-lb st (578.15-kN) Rocketdyne M-34 solid fuel rocket booster that burned for four seconds, propelling the aircraft to its climb-out speed of 275 kt (509 km/h) at an acceleration of up to 4 g. The booster was then jettisoned. It was found that the F-100D could be attached to its ramp and prepared for take-off by a five-man team well within two and a half hours (90 minutes, according to some sources). This capability was demonstrated during the 1958 Air Force Fighter Weapons Meet, when the test F-100D was fitted to and launched from its trailer in front of the press at Nellis AFB's Range 1 complex at Indian Springs.

NAA actually modified two F-100Ds for ZELL testing, 56-2904 and 56-2947. The first (-2904) made the first launch on 26 March 1958 in the hands of NAA's test pilot, Al Blackburn. The second launch went less well: the M-34 refused to jettison throughout Blackburn's one-hour flight, which he eventually had to end by ejecting. Blackburn flew 14

more launches, at different weights and with different combinations of stores, including the final launch on 26 August 1959, which was made at night from a simulated hardened shelter at Holloman AFB, New Mexico. Many of these launches were made with a Blue Boy Mk 7 'shape' under the port wing and a fuel tank to starboard, reflecting the system's deadly purpose, which was to ensure that the USAF could get its retaliatory nuclear strike airborne after an enemy attack. Four more launches were made by the

Several ZELL launches were made with a dummy Mk 7 nuclear bomb on the port wing, reflecting the 'real-world' scenario for which ZELL was proposed.

USAF project pilot, Captain Robert F. Titus (who went on to become a MiG-killer in Vietnam, though not in the F-100). It was concluded that any combat-ready pilot would be competent to make a ZELL launch, and the last 48 F-100Ds (148 according to some sources) were delivered with ZELL provision.

The second ZELL-equipped aircraft, 56-2947, launches from a mock-up of a nuclear hardened shelter, built at Holloman AFB, New Mexico, as part of the ZELL studies.

If the ZELL idea had been adopted, the trailer would have allowed the F-100 force to be dispersed widely. Here a complete ZELL rig is on display at Nellis AFB in 1960.

Little John *was an F-100D assigned to the 531st TFS, which was parented by the 39th Air Division at Misawa AB, Japan. The primary role of this unit was to stand nuclear alert, including a forward deployment at Kunsan in Korea.*

were known as NA-222s to the company and used NH rather than NA block designations. Twenty-five F-100Cs were built at Columbus, the first (55-2709) making its initial flight on 8 September 1955. They were followed by 221 F-100Ds.

Rewinged heavyweight

The final single-seat F-100 variant was by far the best, featuring a host of improvements that addressed most of the shortcomings of the earlier variants. This was the F-100D, which went under no fewer than four separate company design numbers (NA-223, -224, -235 and -245). It was built in the largest quantities, with 1,274 aircraft following the 203 F-100As and 476 F-100Cs off the Inglewood and Columbus production lines.

The F-100D was an improved fighter-bomber variant with internal electronic countermeasures (ECM) equipment, an AN/APS-54 tail warning radar on the trailing edge of an enlarged fin, an AN/AJB-1 low-altitude bombing system (LABS) to allow for nuclear toss-bombing, and a 1,200-lb (544-kg) increase in maximum take-off weight. The landing speed of an even heavier Super Sabre would have been nothing short of dangerous and, as a result, the F-100D also featured a redesigned wing.

The new wing had increased chord at the root, expanding the total wing area to 400.18 sq ft (37.18 m²). This resulted from the installation of flaps on the trailing edge, which were slightly less swept than the rest of the trailing edge and gave a slight kink to the aircraft's planform. To

PACAF had three nuclear-capable F-100 wings in Japan in the late 1950s: the 8th TFW at Itazuke (above), 18th TFW at Kadena (right) and the 21st TFW at Misawa. The 18th TFW aircraft, carrying a practice bomb dispenser, is from the 67th Tactical Fighter Squadron.

Two wings operated F-100Ds from bases in eastern England. The 20th Fighter-Bomber Wing (TFW from 1958) received F-100Ds at Wethersfield in 1957 (below). It was joined in January 1960 by the 48th TFW (below right) at Lakenheath, a refugee from the withdrawal of US nuclear forces from France. The principal role was tactical nuclear strike, and the aircraft would have deployed forward to the continent in time of tension.

the nose. 'Thunderbird' Super Sabres were painted primarily in natural metal, but had a huge 'Thunderbird' motif on their bellies plus red, white and blue markings on the nose, wingtips and tail units.

F-100Cs were also used by another aerobatic display team, this one being the 36th FDW's 'Skyblazers', a four-aircraft team that flew displays throughout Europe. Its aircraft were modified in just the same way as the 'Thunderbirds' aircraft and wore a similar scheme, with jagged nose, tailplane and wingtip stripes in red, white and blue, a blue tail bedecked in white stars, and a red-and-white candy-striped trailing edge.

With Super Sabre orders at last being placed in quantity, the decision was taken to find a second production source and North American's Columbus, Ohio, plant was chosen on 11 October 1954. Although they were no different to the Inglewood-built F-100s, Super Sabres built at Columbus

The 'Hun' in Europe

Nowhere was the F-100 more important than in Europe, where it equipped five fighter-bomber wings during the peak period of 1957 to 1961. They were initially based in France (48th FBW at Chaumont, 388/49th FBW at Etain-Rouvres and 50th FBW at Toul-Rosières), West Germany (36th FDW at Bitburg) and England (20th FBW at Wethersfield). All US nuclear-capable forces were removed from French soil in 1959/60, the F-100 wings redeploying to the UK and West Germany under Operation Red Richard.

Right: Two fighter-bomber wings moved from France in 1959 to West Germany: the 49th relocated to Spangdahlem in August and the 50th TFW (illustrated) moved to Hahn in December. Although the 49th was moved to Holloman AFB in 1968, it remained committed to NATO.

Below: In West Germany the Super Sabre was initially assigned to the 36th Fighter-Day Wing at Bitburg, which operated F-100Cs in the nuclear strike role. The wing transitioned to the F-105D from May 1961.

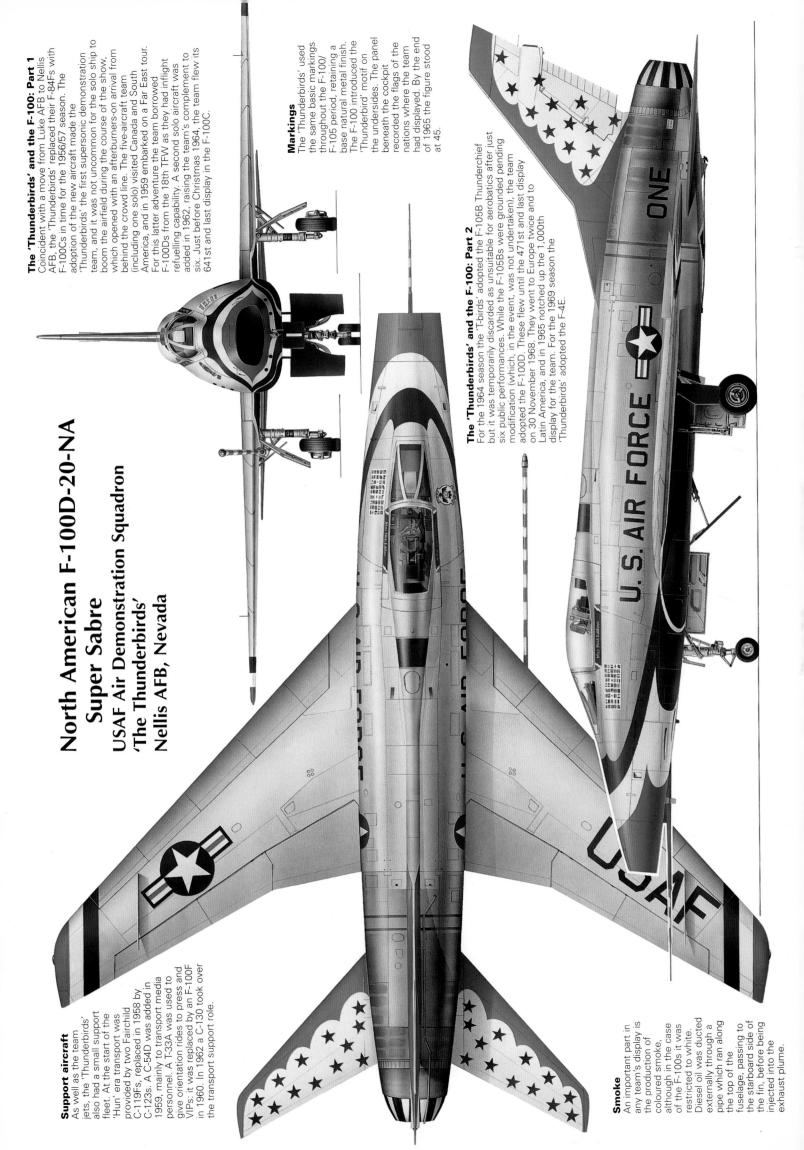

North American F-100D-20-NA Super Sabre
USAF Air Demonstration Squadron 'The Thunderbirds'
Nellis AFB, Nevada

The 'Thunderbirds' and the F-100: Part 1

Coincident with a move from Luke AFB to Nellis AFB, the 'Thunderbirds' replaced their F-84Fs with F-100Cs in time for the 1956/57 season. The adoption of the new aircraft made the 'Thunderbirds' the first supersonic demonstration team, and it was not uncommon for the solo ship to boom the airfield during the course of the show, which opened with an afterburners-on arrival from behind the crowd line. The five-aircraft team (including one solo) visited Canada and South America, and in 1959 embarked on a Far East tour. For this latter adventure the team borrowed F-100Ds from the 18th TFW as they had inflight refuelling capability. A second solo aircraft was added in 1962, raising the team's complement to six. Just before Christmas 1964, the team flew its 641st and last display in the F-100C.

Markings

The 'Thunderbirds' used the same basic markings throughout the F-100/F-105 period, retaining a base natural metal finish. The F-100 introduced the 'Thunderbird' motif on the undersides. The panel beneath the cockpit recorded the flags of the nations where the team had displayed. By the end of 1965 the figure stood at 45.

The 'Thunderbirds' and the F-100: Part 2

For the 1964 season the 'T-birds' adopted the F-105B Thunderchief but it was temporarily discarded as unsuitable for aerobatics after just six public performances. While the F-105Bs were grounded pending modification (which, in the event, was not undertaken), the team adopted the F-100D. These flew until the 471st and last display on 30 November 1968. They went to Europe twice and to Latin America, and in 1965 notched up the 1,000th display for the team. For the 1969 season the 'Thunderbirds' adopted the F-4E.

Support aircraft

As well as the team jets, the 'Thunderbirds' also had a small support fleet. At the start of the 'Hun' era transport was provided by two Fairchild C-119Fs, replaced in 1958 by C-123s. A C-54D was added in 1959, mainly to transport media personnel. A T-33A was used to give orientation rides to press and VIPs: it was replaced by an F-100F in 1960. In 1962 a C-130 took over the transport support role.

Smoke

An important part in any team's display is the production of coloured smoke, although in the case of the F-100s it was restricted to white. Diesel oil was ducted externally through a pipe which ran along the top of the fuselage, passing to the starboard side of the fin, before being injected into the exhaust plume.

54-1966 began life as a standard F-100C, but was loaned to North American for conversion into the TF-100C two-seater. It had an F-100D-style fin, and was lengthened by 36 in (0.91 m). It lacked any combat equipment as the original intention was for an austere conversion trainer.

Prior to flying with the thrust-reverser fitted, the NF-100F was tested in the 40 x 80-ft (12.2 x 24.4-m) wind tunnel at NASA Ames (Moffett Field, California). The aircraft later became a DF-100F drone director, and was one of three Super Sabres to use the NF-100F designation.

make room for the flaps, the ailerons were moved outboard. The flaps reduced landing speeds considerably, but increased pilot workload, since they had to be raised immediately upon touchdown to increase the 'weight on wheels' and maximise the F-100's braking efficiency. The flap normally extended to a full-down 45° position, though some aircraft had an intermediate 20° setting for take-off.

Other minor changes included provision of explosive jettison for the underwing pylons, which had previously relied on gravity for emergency separation. The aircraft could carry six M117 750-lb (340-kg) bombs, four 1,000-lb (454-kg) bombs, or a single Mk 7, Mk 28EX, Mk 28RE or Mk 43 nuclear weapon. Air-to-air missile armament, previously tested and demonstrated on a batch of six modified F-100Cs, was added from the 184th F-100D with accommodation for four GAR-8 (later AIM-9B) Sidewinder infrared-homing AAMs. This aircraft also introduced a new centreline hardpoint for nuclear weapons carriage, avoiding the asymmetry problems associated with the port intermediate pylon used previously. The same F-100D was originally planned to introduce an improved autopilot, but this was not ready in time, and did not make its debut until the 384th F-100D, although earlier aircraft were subsequently retrofitted with the new equipment.

The first F-100D made its maiden flight (in the hands of Dan Darnell) on 24 January 1956, and the first Columbus-

Reverse-thrust

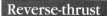

56-3725 was the first F-100F two-seater to be built, and after its initial test duties were completed, it was modified for a research programme and assigned the designation NF-100F. Wright Air Development Center removed the afterburner section and replaced it with a thrust reverser. Blown flaps were installed, as was an enlarged airbrake. The aircraft was used for research into steep approaches and high-speed landings in support of the North American X-15 and Boeing X-20 Dyna-Soar programmes.

Below: Wearing AFSC and WADC badges, this is the NF-100F thrust-reverser testbed. Note the massive airbrake which is deployed for display, and the fairing under the intake.

built example (NA-224 55-2734) followed on 12 June. Deliveries to front-line units began in September 1956, initially to the 405th Fighter-Bomber Wing at Langley AFB, Virginia. The new variant rapidly replaced the F-100C in most USAF Super Sabre wings.

Like the F-100A and the F-100C before it, the F-100D suffered teething problems, particularly regarding an inaccurate fire control system, an unreliable electrical system, and poor integration of LABS with the autopilot. There were also engine bearing and afterburner fuel system problems, inadvertent and uncommanded bomb releases, and inflight-refuelling probes that sometimes fell off the wing during high-g manoeuvres.

The response was a series of *ad hoc* in-service modifications that led to almost immediate loss of fleet-wide configuration control, so that no two F-100Ds on a typical flightline were quite identical. From 1962, 700 F-100Ds and F-100Fs were modified and standardised under Project High Wire, also gaining a spring-loaded airfield arrester hook. Modified aircraft were given new block numbers, so that, for instance, an F-100D-25-NA would become an F-100D-26-NA after High Wire modifications.

In service, 65 F-100Ds were modified to carry the Martin GAM-83A Bullpup optically-guided air-to-surface missile. The first GAM-83A-equipped F-100D squadron made its operational debut in December 1960, but the weapon proved problematic and was withdrawn after combat experience in Vietnam revealed its shortcomings. NAA went to great expense to develop a buddy refuelling pod for the F-100D, and although such a device was built, tested and cleared, it was never used in service.

Most F-100Ds did feature a redesigned refuelling probe, which kinked upwards closer to the pilot's natural eye-line in order to make refuelling slightly easier. This was perhaps just as well, since the F-100D made greater use of the technique than any previous fighter during its support of a number of long-range deployments. In November 1957, 16 F-100Cs and 16 F-100Ds undertook Operation Mobile Zebra, flying from George AFB, California, to Yokota in a gruelling 16 hours. Subsequent F-100Ds were delivered to the Fifth Air Force by less direct means. They were first flown to McClellan AFB, California, where they were partially dismantled and cocooned, and then towed 15 miles (24 km) on public roads to the Sacramento river, from where they were barged to NAS Alameda, where they were transferred to a US Navy carrier which conveyed them to Yokosuka, where they were moved to lighters which ferried them across Tokyo Bay to Kisarazu AB, where they were de-cocooned, re-assembled and then flown to Itazuke!

When the Lebanon crisis blew up in May 1958, F-100Ds from Myrtle Beach AFB, South Carolina, were immediately deployed to the region, arriving there the same day on which the order to deploy was received.

The F-100D saw extensive service in Vietnam, after which some 335 were transferred to the ANG. After a false start in which the team's original F-100Cs were briefly replaced by wholly unsuitable F-105s, the 'Thunderbirds' used the F-100D from July 1964 until November 1968, when they began to transition to the F-4E Phantom. On 21 October 1967 an air show accident at Laughlin AFB in Texas resulted in a 'Thunderbirds' F-100D (flown by future Chief of Staff Captain Merrill A. McPeak) disintegrating after a fatigue failure of the wing. The 'Thunderbirds' were temporarily grounded and a 4-g manoeuvre limit was imposed in Vietnam, where there had been several unexplained losses. A modification to the wing box solved the problem.

Two-seat trainer

The previous generation of jet fighters had been relatively benign, allowing a young pilot to transition from a P-51 Mustang, an F-80 Shooting Star or a T-33 jet trainer to an F-86 without undue difficulty. Thus, no two-seat trainer

F-100B and F-107A

The USAF's F-100 fighter-bombers performed an invaluable deterrent role during the Cold War, but the first time the aircraft looked as though it would be needed for a real 'shooting war', it was as a fighter interceptor.

The F-86 had spawned a number of highly successful dedicated all-weather fighter interceptor derivatives, and NAA hoped to produce a similar version of the Super Sabre. Work on a faster follow-on to the F-100A began in 1952, under the company designation NA-212. The new variant was expected to retain the F-100A's original swept wing planform but to have a much thinner wing cross-section and a 5 per cent thickness/chord ratio, while the fuselage was to have an increased fineness ratio and was to be area-ruled to reduce drag. Despite its thin section, the wing contained integral tanks, and there was to be no provision for the carriage of external fuel tanks. The aircraft was to be powered by an upgraded 16,000-lb st (71.15-kN) J57 engine with a variable-area inlet duct and a convergent-divergent afterburner nozzle. This was expected to confer a maximum speed of about Mach 1.8 at high altitude.

Interestingly, the F-100B (as the NA-212 was already tentatively designated) was expected to operate from primitive and unprepared forward airfields, and dual-wheel main landing-gear units were to be provided. This basic F-100B day

North American built three YF-107A prototypes, this being the first. One of the primary roles envisaged for the type was tactical nuclear strike, for which its 'special weapon' was carried semi-recessed in a central fuselage bay.

fighter formed the basis of a further derivative, the F-100I or F-100BI all-weather interceptor. It had an all-rocket armament and an AI radar in a new nose radome, and a forward fuselage redesigned with a variable-area air intake under the nose.

In November 1953, North American began adapting this evolution of the NA-212 back to the fighter-bomber role, adding six underwing hardpoints, providing single-point pressure refuelling capability, and redesigning the windshield and canopy to improve the pilot's view over the nose. In the face of continuing indifference from the USAF, the NA-212 programme was scaled back on 15 January 1954, when NAA president Lee Atwood abandoned plans for full production, reducing the programme's scope to a simple comprehensive engineering study. When interest in the project was revived, it was clear that the USAF was interested in the fighter-bomber configuration of the NA-212, and all work on the F-100B interceptor project was terminated, though the nose radome and chin intake of the interceptor version were retained.

The resulting F-100B gained an order on 11 June 1954, when the USAF authorised a contract for 33 F-100B fighter-bombers. On 8 July 1954, the designation of the aircraft was changed to F-107A. Further development of the F-107A, which became a dual-role interceptor and fighter-bomber, resulted in an aircraft considerably removed from the F-100 (with novel features such as over-fuselage variable-flow intake and one-piece tailfin), though it is worth noting that the aircraft flew successfully in prototype form before losing out to the Republic F-105 Thunderchief.

This view of the second YF-107A shows the type's derivation from the F-100, although the road from the initial NA-212 design to the eventual F-100B/F-107A hardware saw a great many changes being introduced. By the time the aircraft first flew on 10 September 1956, only the general wing structure design remained from the F-100.

versions of the F-84 and F-86 entered service, and the accident rate remained acceptable, if high.

From the beginning, however, the Super Sabre suffered a worrying accident rate. With its highly swept wing, tricky handling characteristics, and alarmingly high landing speed, it soon became clear that a two-seat trainer version would be useful in helping pilots convert to the aircraft. North American completed a private-venture design study for a supersonic trainer version of the F-100 day fighter on 10 May 1954, and on 2 September 1954 the USAF offered to loan the company a standard F-100C (54-1966) for conversion to TF-100C trainer configuration. Before this aircraft could fly in its new guise, the USAF's requirement for the trainer had firmed up, and in December 1955 a contract was issued for 259 TF-100Cs. The TF-100C was seen as a conversion trainer, pure and simple, and was expected to lack all operational equipment.

NAA test pilot Alvin S. White made the TF-100C (NA-230) prototype's first flight in its new configuration on 3 August 1956. The aircraft had the enlarged F-100D-type tailfin, but retained the C model's flapless wing. It was subsequently lost on 9 April 1957, when it failed to recover during a spinning test. 54-1966 was destined to be the only NA-230, since the USAF changed its mind about the TF-100C and decided that it needed a rather different trainer, one that would retain full operational capability in order to teach pilots weapons aiming and delivery and that

would be useful for standardisation and continuation training, not just type conversion. In the event, the resulting trainer's operational capability even extended to the carriage of nuclear weapons, and the only concession made was to reduce the cannon armament from four to two and ammunition capacity from 200 to 175 rounds per gun in order to save internal volume and weight.

Production two-seater

North American accordingly designed the F-100F (NA-243), closely basing the new trainer on the latest F-100D configuration. The short-lived TF-100C was felt to have proved the aerodynamic changes to the two-seat Super Sabre, and the first F-100F to fly was the first production aircraft (56-3725), which made its maiden flight in the hands of Gage Mace on 7 March 1957. An early F-100F was used by Major Robinson Risner (a Korean War ace) to retrace Lindbergh's journey from New York to Paris to cele-

An F-100F from the 356th TFS refuels in 1960 during a deployment to Europe. The squadron was part of the 354th TFW, home-based at Myrtle Beach, South Carolina. Two-seaters had full combat capability – including nuclear wiring – although they had two instead of four guns. The early, straight refuelling probe, as fitted to this aircraft, was later replaced in the F-100F and most Cs by the kinked probe introduced during F-100D production.

F-100 type conversion was concentrated at Luke and Williams, within the Phoenix suburbs. The two units operated a large number of F-100Fs between them.

Left: 'Thunderbird Nine' was part of the team's support organisation. Three F-100Fs were assigned to the team between 1960 and 1968 and were mainly used to give lucky VIPs and reporters a chance to experience the thrill of flying in the Super Sabre.

F-100As and F-100Fs line up on a Taiwanese base early in the type's RoCAF career. The aircraft in the foreground still wears its USAF 'buzz' number and has yet to receive Nationalist Chinese insignia. The As had all been hastily modified prior to delivery, including the fitment of F-100D fins.

brate the 30th anniversary of the historic flight of 'Lucky Lindy'. Deliveries began in January 1958.

At the specific request of the Pacific Air Forces, the final 29 two-seaters (F-100F-20-NA company designation NA-255) were built to a revised standard. They were fitted with an enhanced navigation system including an AN/ASN-7 dead-reckoning computer, and a PC-212 Doppler. The aircraft also featured modified flaps with a span-wise duct built into the leading edges, which directed air from the lower surface of the wing over the upper surface of the flap. This primitive 'flap-blowing' increased efficiency and reduced buffeting during landing. The modified flaps were limited to a full deflection angle of 40°, instead of the usual 45°.

F-100 production ended in October 1959 with the delivery of the last of 339 F-100Fs. This brought total Super Sabre production to 2,294 aircraft, including the 359 F-100Cs and F-100Ds built at Columbus.

Against Communist China

Tension between the Communist mainland People's Republic of China and the Nationalist Republic of China on the island of Formosa (Taiwan) erupted into conflict in August 1958. Communist Chinese forces bombarded the

Chinese Super Sabres

Nationalist China became the first foreign recipient of the Super Sabre as a result of the 1958 Qemoy crisis, when Communist China threatened to invade Taiwan. Four squadrons' worth of F-100As, plus F-100Fs, were handed to the RoCAF in some haste to bolster the island's defences. The last of these survived in service until 1984, and a number were preserved. The immaculate F-100F above wears the markings of the 2nd TFW at Hsinchu, and is spuriously marked with the serial number of a single-seat F-100A.

Nationalist enclave of Qemoy (a small island just off the mainland) and air battles raged above the Formosa straits. The AIM-9B-equipped RoCAF F-86s fared well against the Communist MiG-15s and MiG-17s, but were out-numbered. They were also too slow to cope with the MiG-19s then entering service with the PLA or to operate in the reactive interceptor role. When it became clear that the mainland was planning to invade Qemoy as a preliminary to the 'liberation' of Taiwan itself, the USA intervened.

USAF units in the area (including the F-100D-equipped 511th TFS at Ching Chuan, Taiwan, and the 354th TFW at Kadena, on Okinawa) were placed on higher states of alert, and six F-100Fs and 80 F-100As were hastily supplied to the RoCAF from August 1958, allowing the immediate conversion of four squadrons to the new type. In that year, the RoCAF also received the four surviving Slick Chick RF-100A reconnaissance aircraft. Thirty-eight more F-100As and eight more two-seaters were supplied from 1970-71.

All but four of the Taiwanese F-100As (53-1569, 53-1581, 53-1651 and 53-1662) were heavily modified before delivery, receiving a new F-100D-type tailfin with AN/APS-54 tail warning radar, a radio compass, an arrester hook, and new inboard pylons wired for the carriage of GAM-83A (AGM-12) Bullpup ASMs or twin AIM-9 Sidewinder AAMs. In this form, the aircraft were broadly equivalent to the F-100D, albeit without flaps and integral wing tanks, and were sometimes known as 'F-100A Rehabs'.

Details of the F-100's combat use by the RoCAF remain secret, though it is understood that the RF-100As suffered such poor availability that they flew no operational overflights, and were scrapped in 1960.

Other foreign users

The available stock of surplus F-100As went to Nationalist China, so other foreign recipients of the F-100 received later versions of the aircraft. All three remaining foreign F-100 users received their aircraft under the terms of the US Military Assistance Program (MAP), under which aircraft were effectively donated free of charge to selected NATO allies.

The first of these MAP Super Sabres went to France, where the first of 12 F-100Fs was received on 1 May 1958, and the first of an initial batch of 68 F-100Ds followed on 18 May. These 80 aircraft equipped Escadre de Chasse 11 at Luxeuil and Escadre de Chasse 3 at Reims. Many were

From 1961 to 1966 the French Super Sabre force was based in West Germany, armed with US-owned and controlled nuclear weapons. The nuclear commitment was lost when the aircraft returned to France. The disbandment of EC 3 allowed a third squadron to form at Toul: EC 3/11 'Corse'.

MAP F-100s for France

The initial batch of 80 F-100D/Fs for France was divided between EC 1/3 'Navarre', EC 2/3 'Champagne' at Reims, and EC 1/11 'Roussillon' and EC 2/11 'Vosges' at Luxeuil. In early 1961 all four squadrons moved to West Germany as part of 4th ATAF, the EC 3 units going to Lahr while EC 11 moved into Bremgarten. EC 3 transitioned to the Mirage IIIE shortly before it returned to France in 1967, while EC 11 brought its F-100s back to Toul-Rosières, where it absorbed the aircraft from EC 3. This led to the formation of a third squadron, EC 3/11 'Corse'. Serving for some years in a natural metal finish (above), most French Super Sabres were later painted in tactical camouflage, as demonstrated by the EC 1/11 example below. A flight of seven F-100Ds and one F-100F was established in Djibouti on 1 January 1973 as EC 4/11 'Jura'. The unit's aircraft sported a desert-style camouflage, and later adopted a large sharkmouth. One of the aircraft is seen at its Djibouti base in January 1974 (below right).

Turkey's F-100 force went to war twice in Cyprus, in 1964 and again 10 years later. Having received its first aircraft in 1958, the Turkish air force was – amazingly – still adding to its F-100 fleet in the early 1980s, and the type remained in THK service until 1987.

drawn from France-based F-100 units, but all were overhauled, modernised and upgraded in Spain before delivery to the Armée de l'Air.

The French Super Sabres were soon in action. In Algeria, French forces made extensive use of close air support aircraft in their war against the Armée de la Liberation Nationale, but increasingly sophisticated rebel weapons soon made the piston-engined T-6s vulnerable. From 1959, therefore, Super Sabres of EC 1/3 flew missions against pre-planned targets, taking off from their base at Reims and recovering to Istres to refuel on their return journey.

The two French Super Sabre wings moved to Lahr and Bremgarten in West Germany in February and June 1961, respectively, where they undertook nuclear strike duties for the 4th Allied Tactical Air Force using US Mk 7 bombs. Despite the delivery of 20 more F-100Ds as attrition replacements, EC 3 re-equipped with Mirage IIIs in September 1966, allowing the addition of a third Escadron within EC 11.

When President Charles de Gaulle pulled France out of NATO's military command structure in 1967, USAF units in France were withdrawn. The remaining West Germany-based Armée de l'Air units moved back to the vacated air bases on French soil and lost their strike commitment.

Turkish 'Huns'

Turkey was the largest foreign operator of the Super Sabre, and used the type for longer than any other. From 1958, the Türk Hava Kuvvetleri (THK) received some 270 Super Sabres, including 111 F-100Cs, 106 F-100Ds and 53 F-100Fs. Turkey was thus the only overseas operator of the F-100C, but was also the most important operator of the two later versions, as well. The THK received 14 F-100Cs and nine F-100Fs in 1958, allowing 111 Filo at Eskisehir to convert. Thirty-two F-100Ds and two more F-100Fs were delivered in 1959, followed by three F-100Ds and two F-100Fs in 1960. 113 and 112 Filo received these aircraft, settling at Erhac and Eskisehir.

On 8 August 1964, Turkey's F-100s went to war, attacking Greek Cypriot National Guard units and EOKA terrorists after attacks against Turkish villages in the north of Cyprus. One 111 Filo F-100D crashed while attacking a landing craft, and the pilot was captured and killed after ejecting. Between October 1965 and 1969, 112 Filo had to revert to the F-84F due to a shortage of Super Sabres, but re-converted following the delivery of 16 more F-100Ds and two F-100Fs, which also allowed 182 Filo at Erhac to convert.

Some 20 more F-100Ds and two F-100Fs arrived in 1970. In 1972 Turkey received 36 F-100Cs, and 47 more followed in 1973, with 28 more being taken on charge in 1974. 113 and 182 Filos at Erhac were redesignated as 171 and 172 Filos, and three new F-100 units formed with the new aircraft: 181 Filo at Diyarbakir, and 131 and 132 Filos at Konya.

The final MAP F-100 recipient was Denmark, which received F-100Ds and Fs to replace its two three-squadron wings of ageing straight-winged Republic F-84G Thunderjet fighter-bombers in the close air support, air defence and maritime attack roles. Danish pilots had evaluated the F-100 in 1957, and in August 1958 a small group of pilots and ground crew was trained on the aircraft at Myrtle Beach, though F-100s were not formally offered until 1959.

Esk 727 at Skrydstrup took delivery of three F-100Fs and 17 F-100Ds from May 1959, and 31 F-100Ds and seven F-100Fs followed in 1960 to re-equip Esk 725 at Karup and Esk 730 at Skrydstrup. The Danish F-100s were extensively modified in service, gaining Martin-Baker Mk DE5A ejection seats, a Decca Type 1664 Roller Map, and a Saab BT-9J bombsight. Attrition was heavy, a full one-third of the fleet

A Turkish pilot runs to his F-100D during a practice scramble. In the fighter role the aircraft could be fitted with inverted 'Y' racks for the carriage of four AIM-9 Sidewinders.

Denmark's F-100s were initially flown in natural metal finish, but subsequently received an all-over dark green scheme. Even the aft fuselage was painted, although the paint rapidly burnt through to form a characteristic pattern. During the 1960s the Danes had three squadrons of F-100s, but in 1970 one converted to the more capable Saab Draken, leaving Esk 727 and 730 at Skrydstrup.

TF-100F – Danish two-seater

The TF-100F designation covered the second batch of 14 two-seat aircraft delivered to the Danske Flyvevåbnet, which differed in some respects from the original 10 F-100Fs received by Denmark. Like the single-seaters, they were fitted with Martin-Baker seats.

Seen in 1960, this F-100D served with the 510th TFS, part of the 405th TFW at Clark AB in the Philippines. A year later, the squadron sent the first operational F-100 detachment to southeast Asia, six aircraft arriving at Don Muang airport (Bangkok) on 16 April 1961. The detachment lasted until late in the year, and was officially for air defence purposes, but in reality was more of a sabre-rattling exercise against growing Communist actions in the region.

reconnaissance missions. The war in southeast Asia was, however, probably the most important event in the aircraft's long career, and was the only large-scale conflict in which it was involved.

At its peak, the Super Sabre equipped a total of 16 USAF wings and four of those saw service in Vietnam, operating there between 1966 and 1971, and flying over 360,000 missions. This notable figure was all the more impressive when compared with the 259,702-mission total clocked up by 16,000 P-51 Mustangs during World War II. Those F-100s deployed to Vietnam averaged 1.2 sorties per day and the type demonstrated an 80 per cent readiness rate. The aircraft were hard-worked, and by 1969, the average flight time per surviving aircraft was 5,100 hours. Some 198 F-100s were lost in combat and 44 more in in-theatre accidents, with the loss of 87 pilots killed, five missing in action and five prisoners of war.

By the time the US involvement in Vietnam began, the F-100 was firmly established as a fighter-bomber, its weaknesses in the day fighter role having been widely recognised and acknowledged. Even in the fighter-bomber role, the aircraft's career was seen as coming towards an end, and five front-line wings had already converted to the F-104 and F-105 during 1959-62. The remainder seemed set to follow fairly rapidly.

It was therefore slightly ironic that the F-100D was one of the first US combat aircraft deployed to southeast Asia, and that (at least nominally) it did so as an air defence fighter. Following a string of events in disintegrating Laos, six F-100D/Fs from the 510th TFS at Clark AB, Philippines, were deployed to Don Muang airport in Thailand on 16 April 1961 under Operation Bell Tone. The aircraft were nominally there to provide air defence for the Thai capital, though the air threat was negligible and the F-100 was ill-

being lost in accidents. With insufficient aircraft to equip all three squadrons, Esk 725 converted to the Draken in 1970. Fourteen more ex-USAF F-100Fs were delivered from March 1974; they were fitted with Martin-Baker seats and redesignated as TF-100Fs in order to differentiate them from Denmark's original F-100Fs.

At war in Vietnam

US sources have often (wrongly) stated that the Super Sabre made its combat debut in Vietnam: F-100s had already flown combat missions in RoCAF service, and Armée de l'Air Super Sabres had flown live bombing missions over Algeria. Vietnam was not even the first combat use of the USAF's Super Sabres, since the Slick Chicks had come under hostile fire during their secretive

F-100 vs. MiG-17

The F-100 Super Sabre's history is a saga of superlatives. The 'Hun' flew faster, higher, and farther than its predecessors. It set speed records. It flew more individual sorties in the Vietnam war than any other fighter. It guarded against Soviet attack during tense moments in the Cold War. In fact, the F-100 Super Sabre did almost everything a modern fighter could do – except shoot down an enemy aircraft. Incredibly, despite its decades on the cutting edge of combat aviation, the F-100 was never credited with a single air-to-air victory. Since the high priests of the fighter profession regard an aerial 'kill' as sacred on the altar of their religion, the Super Sabre's other achievements can never compensate for the fact that it was never a MiG killer.

Or was it?

As far as official records are concerned, the facts are clear. No F-100 ever shot down an enemy aircraft. No enemy aircraft ever shot down an F-100, either. But veterans of the earliest days in Vietnam – a brief interval when the F-100 was employed as an escort fighter before being relegated to air-to-ground duty – say the official records are wrong. They say US Air Force Captain Donald L. Kilgus (pictured in his MiG-killing aircraft, below) shot down a North Vietnamese

MiG-17 on 4 April 1965. They also say Kilgus was denied credit for an aerial victory that should have placed it in his record, not because the MiG didn't fall out of the sky, but because errors were made.

Kilgus, a fighter pilot with the 416th Tactical Fighter Squadron at Da Nang, South Vietnam, flew the first mission on 2 March 1965 when the United States launched Operation Rolling Thunder – a campaign against North Vietnam that eventually lasted more than three years. "In those early days, we were just beginning to see heavy air fighting in the region around Hanoi," Kilgus said in an interview in 1990. "Big air battles would become familiar to us later, but in the beginning it was all new."

Just a month into the Rolling Thunder campaign, the first air-to-air engagement of the Vietnam war took place on 3 April 1965 when Soviet-built MiG-17 fighters of the North Vietnamese Air Force fired on a US Navy F-8 Crusader with no result. The next day marked a series of air-to-air battles, a tragic setback for the US, and a controversial dogfight for Kilgus.

On 4 April 1965, numerous air strikes went into North Vietnam. The setback occurred when North Vietnamese MiG-17s popped out of heavy clouds and shot down two Air Force F-105 Thunderchiefs piloted by Captain James A. Magnusson and Major Frank E. Bennett. Both F-105 pilots lost their lives. Both were members of the 354th Tactical Fighter Squadron, 355th Tactical Fighter Wing, flying from Korat Air Base, Thailand, operating that day as ZINC flight. Magnusson, at the controls of F-105D 59-1764, apparently was killed almost immediately, perhaps by cannon fire that struck his cockpit. Bennett, however, who was piloting F-105D 59-1754, should have survived. He nursed his crippled aircraft out to the Gulf of Tonkin and ejected safely. For a moment, he appeared to be safe on the surface of the Gulf, ready to be picked up, but somehow Bennett got tangled in his parachute and drowned before help could arrive.

North Vietnamese gunfire also downed an A-1H Skyraider (bureau number unknown), killing Captain Walter Draeger. Another F-105 pilot, Capt. Carlyle 'Smitty' Harris, at the controls of aircraft 62-4217 (from the 44th TFS 'Vampires', 18th TFW at Korat) was shot down, survived, and became one of the earliest American prisoners of war. He pioneered the 'tap code' later used by prisoners to communicate from one North Vietnamese cell to another.

Because there were certain things the outside world did not know that day, the air battle was reported as a stunning defeat for the United States. Americans simply were not accustomed to coming out second best in fighter-versus-fighter combat. Press reports focused on the dramatic loss of the two F-105s to MiGs.

Many years later, when North Vietnam's records became available, it became known that the North Vietnamese lost three MiG-17s that day. It appears that the North Vietnamese actually shot down two of their own MiGs with their own ground fire – possibly the same two MiGs that bagged the F-105s. Neither side has ever confirmed the circumstances of the loss of the third MiG listed as a casualty in Hanoi's records. The press did not immediately report a dogfight that day, between F-100 Super Sabre pilot Kilgus – assigned to escort the F-105s – and a MiG-17 Kilgus was certain he shot down.

"We saw something come up out of the haze," Kilgus said. "And one thousandth of a second later … it's a MiG. I turned into him, jettisoned my auxiliary fuel tanks, and in that instant he turned 90 degrees to face me." Kilgus spotted a second MiG. The first overshot and missed him. Kilgus shook off the second, manoeuvred abruptly, and found himself behind the first.

"I said, 'I'll get in range.' I pulled my nose up. All four guns are in the belly of the airplane, so I pulled up the nose and just fired enough so he'd see those 20-millimetre cannons winking." The F-100 was armed with four 20-mm Pontiac M39E cannons with 1,200 rounds, although most aerial victories in Vietnam were achieved with air-to-air missiles.

"Knowing I was in an advantageous position because I was above him, I allowed him to get a little separation on me. I went on afterburner and saw 450 knots on my air speed indicator. He was now going straight down and I was thinking, 'He's playing chicken,' knowing that because his plane is lighter he can pull out of a dive faster than I can. I was preoccupied with my gunsight. This was while going straight down and turning the gun switch to hot. My mind was saying, 'When are we going to pull out?'

"I fired a burst. Now, training comes into play. I tried to remember everything I'd learned, and began shooting seriously at him at [an altitude of] 7,100 feet. I said to myself, I wouldn't worry about how

suited to deal with it. It did, however, place a flight-strength unit of the USAF's principal jet fighter-bombers in the area. The deployment increased to squadron size from 18 May 1962, with 18 aircraft manned by rotational Saw Buck deployments from Cannon and England AFBs.

Following the shoot-down of an RF-8 over Laos on 22 May 1964, eight F-100Ds from the 615th TFS redeployed to Da Nang and mounted the first retaliatory strike on 9 June 1964, against targets in the Plaines des Jarres in Laos. Colonel George Laven led the mission in 54-2076, an aircraft he had hand-picked because its 'last four' matched those of the P-38 he had flown during World War II, when he had become an ace.

Eight F-100Ds from the 615th TFS deployed to Da Nang again after the Gulf of Tonkin incident, and began flying intensively, mainly in the escort role. The Super Sabre force suffered its first recorded combat loss soon afterwards, when an F-100D (56-3085) was shot down on 18 August 1964 over Laos. The aircraft were increasingly committed to close air support and AAA-suppression missions, and losses began to mount.

From 14 December 1964, the F-100s flew Barrel Roll sorties against NVA forces just across the border in Laos, often operating in squadron strength. The longer-ranged F-105 (which carried a heavier load than the Super Sabre) increasingly displaced the F-100 as the focus of attacks switched to North Vietnamese targets during Flaming Dart,

though the F-100s usually accompanied the Thunderchiefs to provide fighter cover and flak suppression. Operation Rolling Thunder began in March 1965. The Vietnamese People's Air Force began flying combat missions on 3 April, and the following day, MiGs tangled with USAF F-100s for the first time. Captain Donald Kilgus fired on one MiG-17, observed strikes on the enemy aircraft and claimed a probable kill. Other aircraft engaged more MiGs with AIM-9s, without apparent success (though post-war research revealed that three MiGs failed to return), and the F-100 was withdrawn from the fighter cover role. 4 April marked the only occasion on which F-100s encountered enemy fighter opposition.

From November 1965, the F-100s were camouflaged, losing their gaudy unit colours and receiving two-letter squadron tailcodes in their place. Nose art remained, however, and increasingly began to flourish.

F-100Ds from the 416th TFS are seen at Da Nang (above) and Tan Son Nhut (above left). The 'Silver Knights led something of a nomadic existence in southeast Asia, deploying as part of Operation Sawbuck to Clark and on to Da Nang in March 1965, and then to Bien Hoa in mid-June. In November 1965 they went to Tan Son Nhut, then Phu Cat in April 1967, and finally to Tuy Hoa in May 1969. Having been in the warzone since the start, the unit finally returned to England AFB, Louisiana, at the end of September 1970.

---

much ammo I was using because this was my last chance to hit him. I saw puffs and sparks on the vertical tail of the MiG, and very shortly thereafter I didn't see anything. I could have been at 580 knots. I won't embroider the story by saying I got spray from the Gulf of Tonkin on my windshield, but I pulled out at the last minute." Kilgus said he saw "sparks" on the MiG and "major pieces coming off it." There was no other action, that day, which could explain the North's confirmation that a third MiG was shot down.

Don McCarthy, a Waterford, Conn., historian who has studied both American and North Vietnamese accounts of the battle, is "absolutely certain" Kilgus's

cannon shells brought down the MiG-17. "The Air Force only credited Kilgus with a 'probable' kill," McCarthy said in a telephone interview. "The reason has never been clear." The Air Force has never released an official list of aerial victories intended for public consumption. Kilgus's claim was also supported by Capt. (later Lt. Col.) Ralph Havens, another member of the F-100D flight that day.

Kilgus died in a traffic mishap in the Washington, D. C. area in 1995. In all he flew three tours in Vietnam, in the O-1 Bird Dog, F-100D Super Sabre, and F-105 Thunderchief. He never made an issue of his claim to have downed a MiG-17, but he believed

the MiG went down and all available evidence – including North Vietnamese records – seems to confirm it. Shortly after those early Rolling Thunder missions, the F-100 was shifted to air-to-ground duties.

Robert F. Dorr

After its brief flirtation with the escort fighter mission in the first few weeks of Rolling Thunder, the 416th TFS – and the F-100 community in general – became embroiled in 'mud-moving'. This 'Silver Knights' aircraft, seen on a mission in mid-1965, carries a typical mix of iron bombs and napalm tanks.

Right: The escalating seriousness of the war in southeast Asia was mirrored in the adoption of warpaint in 1965. Officially called T.O.1-1-4, the three-tone SEA camouflage scheme spread rapidly through the USAF's tactical forces. This is a 416th TFS aircraft, parked next to another which retained its natural metal finish.

Virtually all targets in South Vietnam were 'soft', which usually meant Viet Cong forces. Area weapons such as cluster bombs, 'daisy-cutters', napalm and 2.75-in rockets were used. This shot captures the dispersal of a full rocket salvo.

USAF F-100 squadrons remained in the USA. Despite some maintenance issues, the F-100D briefly gained the best maintenance record of any aircraft in the Vietnam combat zone, and always enjoyed a better availability rate than most fast jets in-theatre.

Although the F-105 and F-4 could carry a heavier bomb load farther than the F-100, the Super Sabre's ability to drop from low altitudes brought it a reputation for accuracy, and the type was preferred by many forward air controllers for precision strikes in support of troops in contact. After 1966 the F-100 was the only USAF aircraft in-theatre using probe-and-drogue refuelling, and it became increasingly difficult to find tanker support, since most tankers were fitted with the boom system. These factors together led to the F-100D fighter-bombers generally operating in South Vietnam.

By October 1966, one F-100 unit served with the 27th TFW at Tan Son Nhut, three squadrons of F-100s formed the 35th TFW at Phan Rang, and three more squadrons formed the 3rd TFW at Bien Hoa. Additional F-100Ds were based with the 37th TFW at Phu Cat from 1 March 1967, and an eventual total of five squadrons served with the 31st TFW at Tuy Hoa from November 1966. Many of these units were manned by ANG squadrons on rotational deployment, and flew F-100Cs. By June 1967, only five regular

The F-100s were gradually withdrawn from combat as attrition took its toll and increasing numbers of newer aircraft (especially F-4E Phantoms) became available, and the last F-100Ds finally left Vietnam in July 1971. By then, the Super Sabre had proved its mettle in two more specialised roles, both of which required the use of the two-seat F-100F.

Misty FAC

The use of airborne forward air controllers (FACs) to direct and correct the efforts of fast jet close air support aircraft had proved invaluable in Vietnam, although their piston-engined O-1s and O-2s were slow and vulnerable. The obvious solution was to put a FAC in the back seat of a fast jet, and in 1967 the Commando Sabre programme was instituted to do just that.

Led by Major George 'Bud' Day, the Misty FAC F-100Fs were assigned to Det 1 of the 612th TFS, borrowing four F-100Fs from the 416th TFS. Trial missions from Phan Rang began on 15 May 1967, before operations proper commenced (flown from Phu Cat) on 28 June. The aircraft were crewed by a pair of volunteer pilots, both of whom had to have logged 25 combat sorties and 1,000 flying hours before joining the programme. The back-seater carried a comprehensive set of detailed maps, a handheld 35-mm 'strike camera' (actually an SLR with a telephoto lens), and handled communications with the fighter-bombers. The front-seater found the targets and marked them, using the Misty F-100F's armament of two seven-shot white phosphorus rockets.

Pueblo Crisis – Air National Guard F-100Cs in Vietnam

When the North Koreans seized the USS *Pueblo* on 24 January 1968, US active-duty forces were too stretched to react to this new crisis, so President Johnson mobilised a number of ANG squadrons two days later. Included were eight units with F-100Cs. Of these, two were deployed to Myrtle Beach to conduct F-100 training, two went to Kunsan in Korea, and the remaining four were sent to join the fray in Vietnam (120th to Phan Rang, 174th to Phu Cat, 136th and 188th to Tuy Hoa).

Right: Arriving at Phan Rang on 3 May 1968 to augment the 35th TFW, the 120th TFS of the Colorado ANG was the first Guard unit to fly combat missions, mounting its first sortie on 8 May. The squadron's 5,905th and last was flown on 8 April 1969.

Below: Iowa's 174th TFS ('HA' tailcode) deployed from Sioux City to Phu Cat in May 1968, flying as part of the 37th TFW. The other two F-100C units joined the 31st TFW at Tuy Hoa.

The DC ANG's 121st TFS was one of two units (along with the 119th TFS/New Jersey) which formed a wing at Myrtle Beach during the Pueblo mobilisation to augment the active-duty training effort.

Misty pilots were an elite group, their number including two future USAF Chiefs of Staff (Ronald Fogleman and Merrill McPeak) and the round-the-world record breaker, Dick Rutan. The mission was hazardous, and many aircraft were hit by ground fire as they orbited the target area at low level. Seven Misty FAC pilots were killed in action and four more became POWs. Thirty-four aircraft were lost between August 1967 and May 1970, when they were replaced by Wolf FAC, Stormy FAC and Tiger FAC F-4s. The Misty FAC F-100Fs also flew reconnaissance and ResCAP missions, acting as on-scene controllers and co-ordinators during combat SAR missions. Missions often involved inflight refuelling and could last up to six hours, with four inflight refuelling contacts.

Wild Weasel

Arguably the most hazardous missions flown by the Super Sabre were those flown by the Wild Weasel F-100Fs. The first Vietnamese SA-2 SAM sites had been found and identified by USAF reconnaissance aircraft in April 1965, and by July, seven had been identified. An F-4C was shot down by an SA-2 on 24 July 1965, and only then were attacks against them authorised. Such attacks were hampered by sanctuary areas around Hanoi, Haiphong and Phuc Yen, and by the insistence that sites first be positively identified by low-level reconnaissance photos. If a missile was deployed outside the huge 'off limits' areas, it could be moved by the time any attack was mounted.

One response was to provide individual strike aircraft with ECM equipment that would blind the enemy radar, and podded ECM equipment was quickly developed and deployed. It soon became clear that the best way to defeat the surface-to-air missile threat would be to destroy the guidance radars on which they relied (or force them to shut down), not least because each such radar could control several missiles.

The best way of achieving this would be to send out pathfinder aircraft, equipped with both the radar-homing sensors necessary to detect and locate the enemy radars, and the armament to destroy them. This tentative conclusion had been reached in 1964, when a number of F-100Fs equipped with QRC-253-2 homing equipment were used against HAWK SAMs during Exercise Goldfire. A task force led by General K.C. Dempster, formed on 3 August, rapidly reached the same conclusion, and directed Bendix and Applied Technology Inc. (ATI) to come up with solutions.

Suitable self-protection had been available for larger aircraft for some years, but it was too large, too heavy and too expensive for tactical aircraft. ATI had already developed smaller, lighter equipment for the U-2, using the new-fangled transistor, and was given a contract (chalked on a blackboard and photographed, according to legend) to produce a suitable radar warning receiver, missile launch detector and tuned radar intercept receiver for installation on a test F-100F (58-1231).

North American quickly installed hand-built equipment in four F-100Fs (58-1221, -1226, -1227 and -1231). It included an AN/APR-25 radar homing and warning receiver, which was capable of detecting and locating the SA-2 fire control radar's standard S-band signal (as well as the C-band signal emitted by upgraded SA-2 systems and the X-band signals emitted by AI radars). Its output was

displayed on a threat panel and a 3-in (7.62-cm) diameter CRT display. An AN/APR-26 tuned crystal receiver could detect the power change in the L-band Fan Song guidance radar which would indicate an imminent launch, illuminating a red light in the F-100F's cockpit.

Finally, an IR-133 receiver was fitted, having greater sensitivity than the APR-25 and thus offering longer range

Phan Rang operations: an F-100D and an F-100F from the 612th TFS drop 'daisy-cutter' bombs (top), while a 352nd TFS F-100F lands back at the base (above). Phan Rang's F-100s were parented by the 35th TFW.

Commando Sabre – fast FAC over Vietnam

Under the project name Commando Sabre, and using the callsign MISTY, Det 1 of the 612th TFS flew F-100Fs on dangerous fast-FAC missions. The detachment started and ended its career at Phan Rang, but for the most part operated from Phu Cat. Although the unit had its own tailcode allocated ('HS'), it often flew 'HE'-coded aircraft from the co-located 416th TFS (above). The duration of the fast-FAC missions required much use of inflight refuelling (left). The aircraft carries the standard Misty load of two seven-round pods with white phosphorus 'Willie Pete' rockets for marking targets.

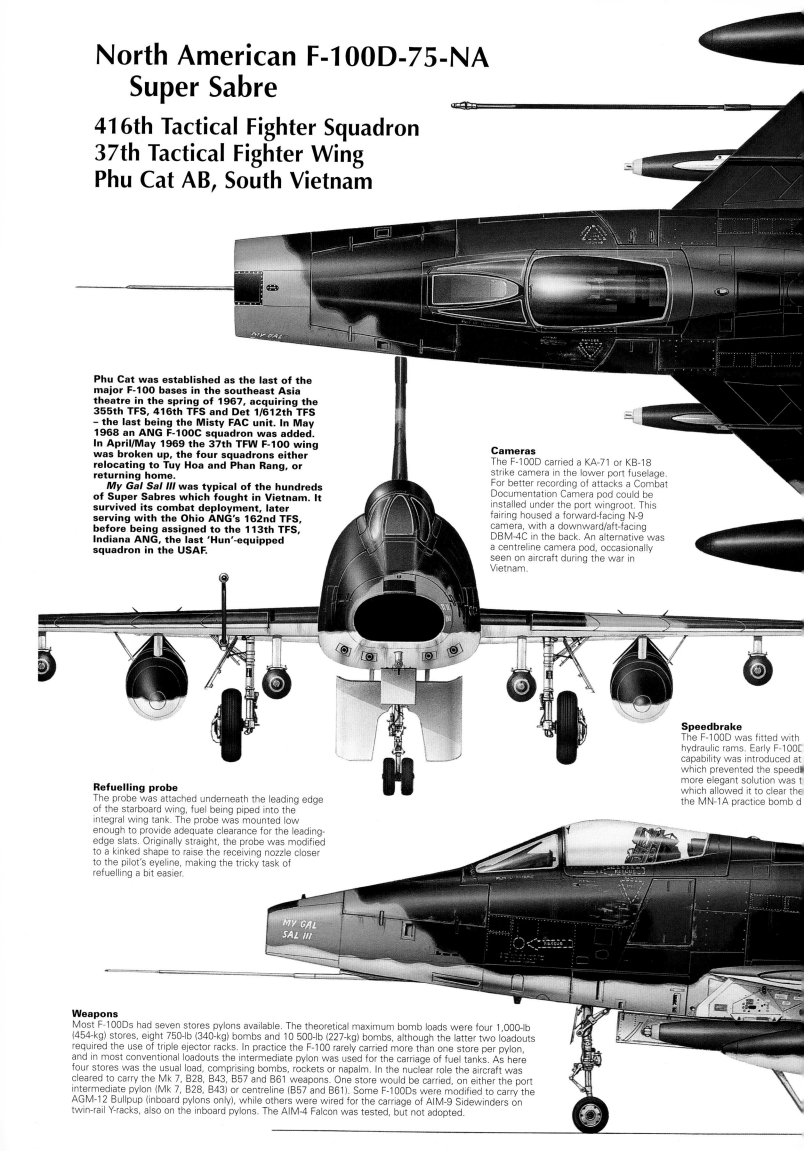

North American F-100D-75-NA Super Sabre

416th Tactical Fighter Squadron
37th Tactical Fighter Wing
Phu Cat AB, South Vietnam

Phu Cat was established as the last of the major F-100 bases in the southeast Asia theatre in the spring of 1967, acquiring the 355th TFS, 416th TFS and Det 1/612th TFS – the last being the Misty FAC unit. In May 1968 an ANG F-100C squadron was added. In April/May 1969 the 37th TFW F-100 wing was broken up, the four squadrons either relocating to Tuy Hoa and Phan Rang, or returning home.

My Gal Sal III was typical of the hundreds of Super Sabres which fought in Vietnam. It survived its combat deployment, later serving with the Ohio ANG's 162nd TFS, before being assigned to the 113th TFS, Indiana ANG, the last 'Hun'-equipped squadron in the USAF.

Cameras
The F-100D carried a KA-71 or KB-18 strike camera in the lower port fuselage. For better recording of attacks a Combat Documentation Camera pod could be installed under the port wingroot. This fairing housed a forward-facing N-9 camera, with a downward/aft-facing DBM-4C in the back. An alternative was a centreline camera pod, occasionally seen on aircraft during the war in Vietnam.

Speedbrake
The F-100D was fitted with hydraulic rams. Early F-100D capability was introduced at which prevented the speed more elegant solution was t which allowed it to clear the the MN-1A practice bomb d

Refuelling probe
The probe was attached underneath the leading edge of the starboard wing, fuel being piped into the integral wing tank. The probe was mounted low enough to provide adequate clearance for the leading-edge slats. Originally straight, the probe was modified to a kinked shape to raise the receiving nozzle closer to the pilot's eyeline, making the tricky task of refuelling a bit easier.

Weapons
Most F-100Ds had seven stores pylons available. The theoretical maximum bomb loads were four 1,000-lb (454-kg) stores, eight 750-lb (340-kg) bombs and 10 500-lb (227-kg) bombs, although the latter two loadouts required the use of triple ejector racks. In practice the F-100 rarely carried more than one store per pylon, and in most conventional loadouts the intermediate pylon was used for the carriage of fuel tanks. As here four stores was the usual load, comprising bombs, rockets or napalm. In the nuclear role the aircraft was cleared to carry the Mk 7, B28, B43, B57 and B61 weapons. One store would be carried, on either the port intermediate pylon (Mk 7, B28, B43) or centreline (B57 and B61). Some F-100Ds were modified to carry the AGM-12 Bullpup (inboard pylons only), while others were wired for the carriage of AIM-9 Sidewinders on twin-rail Y-racks, also on the inboard pylons. The AIM-4 Falcon was tested, but not adopted.

Stopping the F-100
In addition to wheel brakes, the F-100 was fitted with a brake chute. It was housed in a compartment under the port side of the tail section, covered by double doors. As part of the High Wire programme, F-100s were fitted with a spring-loaded airfield arrester hook. Initially this did not have a point guard, but one was fitted later following a number of accidental hook engagments. The guard was a simple triangualar piece of metal bolted to the underside of the aircraft alongside the stowed hook The F-100 also had a retractable tail skid which was linked into the undercarriage extension system. This prevented rear fuselage damage in the event of over-rotation.

Engine nozzle
The F-100's afterburner nozzle was an iris-type structure with 24 segments. The nozzle enlarged automatically when afterburner was selected, activated by air pressure. However, it was common for not all of the segments to open concurrently, leading to momentary asymmetric thrust deflection. Air National Guard aircraft were fitted with the rod-actuated flap-type nozzle from the F-102 to cure the problem.

orake which was actuated by two
y centreline stores, but when this
ylon was fitted with a connection
when a store was being carried. A
a larger cut-out in the speedbrake
centreline stores – a camera pod,
e B57 tactical nuclear bomb.

warning. It also provided a degree of threat classification through signal analysis. The modified aircraft were also fitted with a KA-60 panoramic strike camera and a dual-track tape recorder.

Combat deployment

The four modified Wild Weasel I F-100Fs were used to form the basis of a new unit, the 6234th TFW, staffed with five volunteer F-100 pilots, five back-seaters drawn from B-52 and B-66 EWOs, and 40 support staff. The unit deployed to Korat RTAFB on Thanksgiving Day, 1965, where it came under the control of the 388th TFW.

The first Wild Weasel F-100F combat mission was flown on 3 December 1965, with two F-100Fs accompanied by four F-105s. Using the codename Iron Hand, the F-100Fs identified and marked the radar site, which was then attacked by the accompanying F-105Ds. These early Wild Weasels were armed with a pair of 12-shot LAU-3 rocket pods, although they were soon replaced by bombs. Subsequent missions tended to use a single F-100F, and sometimes involved fighter top cover and an accompanying reconnaissance aircraft. The mission was extremely hazardous, and an F-100F was lost to AAA on 20 December. The first confirmed kill of an SA-2 radar was achieved on 22 December, using 304 high-explosive armour-piercing rockets and 2,900 rounds of 20-mm (0.787-in) ammunition. A number of SA-2 missiles were attacked at the same time, still under their camouflage netting. The attack was one of those which won Captain Alan Lamb, who later destroyed two more SAM radars, a well-deserved (but much-delayed) Silver Star; all six crews were awarded DFCs.

Three additional Wild Weasel I F-100Fs were deployed to southeast Asia on 27 February 1966, and the aircraft were soon leading every strike against targets in North Vietnam. From the spring of 1966, the F-100Fs carried AGM-45A Shrike anti-radiation missiles, which could passively detect enemy radar emissions and follow them all the way back to their source. The first combat use of the Shrike was made on 18 April 1966.

Many potential targets for the Wild Weasel F-100Fs were deep inside the areas which USAF aircraft were forbidden to attack without individual specific permission. The extent to which the war was then being micro-managed was soon clear to one F-100F pilot, Major Donald L. 'Buns' Frazier, who requested permission to attack one particularly troublesome SAM site near Hanoi. His request went up the chain of command and, to his astonishment, he received a personal phone call in response from the then-President, Lyndon Johnson, authorising the attack. This really was clearance from what the troops called the HMFIC ('Head Motherf***er in Charge'), and the mission was flown the next day.

A second Wild Weasel F-100F was lost to AAA on 23 March 1966. In return for the programme's two losses, F-100F Wild Weasel Is claimed nine confirmed SAM radar kills, and an unknown number of other enemy radars were forced off the air long enough for strike packages to get through unmolested. Having proven the Wild Weasel concept, the F-100F Wild Weasel I was replaced by Wild Weasel III conversions of the F-105F and later by the F-4-based Wild Weasel IV.

At war over Cyprus

Turkey's newly expanded F-100 fleet (strengthened between 1972 and 1974 by the addition of 111 F-100Ds and 20 F-100Fs) went to war again in July 1974. Following the overthrow of the Greek Cypriot leader Archbishop Makarios, Turkish residents of the island came under increasing pressure, and on 20 July Turkey acted to protect them. Six F-100 squadrons (111, 112, 131, 132, 171 and 172 Filos) supported the Turkish invasion of northern (Turkish) Cyprus, flying ground attack missions against Greek Cypriot National Guard positions on the first day of the operation.

F-100s from 111, 112 and 181 Filos (and a handful of F-104Gs) scored an unfortunate 'own goal' when they attacked and sank a Turkish Navy 'Gearing'-class destroyer, mistaking it for a similar Greek vessel. Eight F-100s were lost during the Cyprus operation, one in a take-off accident, two to engine failures, and at least two to hostile ground fire. The fate of the remaining three aircraft lost was not officially confirmed, but all eight pilots survived.

Prospective F-100 versions

NAA had hoped to export much larger numbers of Super Sabres, and there were a number of design studies for new versions of the aircraft. Although the F-100E, F-100G, F-100H, F-100M, F-100P, F-100Q and F-100R designations were never assigned, other versions were allocated new designation suffixes. The F-100J, for example, was a projected all-weather interceptor version offered to Japan

Wild Weasel – hunting radars

Although only seven aircraft were involved, Project Wild Weasel was one of the most important tasks undertaken by the F-100, as it pioneered the use of fighter aircraft in the anti-radar, defence suppression role – now known as SEAD and an integral part of combat operations. The seven F-100Fs were fitted with equipment to detect and locate hostile radars, which could then be attacked with rockets and bombs carried by the F-100 itself, or by accompanying attack aircraft (notably the F-105). Later, the F-100Fs acquired the capability to fire the AGM-45 Shrike missile, which homed on radar emissions. The Wild Weasel force operated from Korat, Thailand, as a separate and secretive detachment from the Tactical Air Warfare Center at Eglin AFB, Florida, although it reported to the 6234th TFW. Combat operations (officially an 'evaluation') lasted from 20 December 1965 to July 1966, at which time the F-105F Wild Weasel III took over the Iron Hand anti-radar mission.

'Huns' in the Guard

through the Foreign Military Sales programme, while the F-100K and F-100L designations were applied to J57-P-55-powered versions of the F-100F and F-100D, respectively. The F-100N was intended as a simplified export version of the F-100D, having no nuclear capability and less advanced electronics. The aircraft was aimed at NATO's smaller, poorer nations.

The F-100S designation was applied to an ambitious 1964 proposal to re-engine F-100Ds and F-100Fs with a Rolls-Royce RB.168-25R Spey turbofan, as used in the British Phantom versions. It was hoped that this would produce a low-cost fighter-bomber that would have 50 per cent more payload than the basic Super Sabre, 30 per cent longer range, a shorter take-off distance and an improved climb rate. North American had hoped to convert existing USAF aircraft during their regular Inspect and Repair As Necessary (IRAN) maintenance, and had planned to establish a production line in France for 200 new-build examples of the F-100S for the Armée de l'Air. As an alternative, NAA also proposed using an afterburning Allison TF41 engine, but this was no more successful in winning customers, and the advanced F-100S, which could have given the Super Sabre a new lease of life, remained on the drawing board.

The final rundown

Without major modernisation, the F-100D and F-100F were looking increasingly anachronistic by the 1970s, and the type entered a rapid decline. USAFE retired its last F-100s in April 1972, when the 48th TFW at Lakenheath,

England, completed conversion to the F-4D. The last front-line F-100s in USAF service were those of the 524th TFS at Cannon AFB, New Mexico, the last of the 27th TFW's squadrons to convert to the F-111D.

The Air National Guard's four F-100 squadrons in southeast Asia had returned home from Vietnam in 1969. All 26 ANG F-100 squadrons quickly converted to other, newer types between 1969 and 1979. The F-100 finally flew its last operational mission with the ANG on 10 November 1979, when First Lieutenant Bill Layne of the 113th TFS, 181st Tactical Fighter Group flew a sortie in 56-2979 *City of Terre Haute* at Hulman Field, Indiana. This aircraft was subsequently flown to the MASDC 'boneyard' by Brigadier General Frank Hettlinger, CO of the 122nd TFW.

33

Above: The 27th TFW at Cannon AFB was the last active-duty wing to operate Super Sabres, withdrawing its last aircraft (from the 524th TFS, illustrated) in late 1972. By that time the wing had been flying F-111s for three years.

control, but plans to retain a handful of aircraft for target towing came to nothing. Four F-100Ds flew to Alconbury and Woodbridge for crash rescue training and fire practice, and to Lakenheath and Wethersfield (former USAF F-100 bases) for display, and 36 more flew to Sculthorpe for storage and disposal. Nine were saved for preservation at UK museums, but the rest were scrapped by the 7519th Combat Support Squadron.

At one time, Denmark had hoped to replace all of its F-100s with Drakens, but funding was not available and the Danish F-100s were retained until replaced by F-16s in the early 1980s. The aircraft by then were showing their age, and a succession of technical problems led to them being grounded several times. Some aircraft were fitted with F-102-type Project Pacer Transplant afterburners, and some even received wingtip-mounted ALR-45D/APR-37D RHAWS, with distinctive wingtip pods. The RDAF made its last F-100 flight on 11 August 1982. Three TF-100Fs were retained for display, and six TF-100Fs went to Flight Systems Inc. (FSI). Some 20 surviving F-100Ds went to Turkey, together with two F-100Fs. One more F-100D became unserviceable in Italy en route to Turkey, eventually becoming Aviano's gate guard.

Surviving French Super Sabres were withdrawn from service in 1976-78 as EC 11 re-equipped with the Jaguar. The last in service were the seven F-100Ds and single F-100F of EC 4/11 'Jura' at Djibouti. These aircraft wore huge gaudy sharkmouths, and four were specially equipped for the reconnaissance role.

Having been supplied under MAP provisions, the surviving Armée de l'Air Super Sabres were returned to American

The last F-100As retired from service in late 1984 when Taiwan finally grounded its last Super Sabres, which by then equipped only two squadrons. The last of these ageing aircraft made its final flight on 5 September 1984. Taiwanese plans to pack the surplus aircraft with explosive and launch them at China as crude cruise missiles were quietly discouraged by the USA.

More 'Huns' for Turkey

The withdrawal of the last ANG and Danish F-100s allowed Turkey's F-100 force to be reinforced and, while everyone else was busy retiring the F-100, Turkey actually strengthened its Super Sabre fleet. Fifteen ex-ANG F-100Ds arrived in 1977-78, and 20 ex-RDAF F-100Ds and two F-100Fs were delivered in 1981-82. Thus, in 1980 182 Filo actually converted to the F-100 – the last new Super Sabre squadron to form anywhere in the world.

By 1983, 65 F-100Ds and 30 F-100Fs equipped two front-line units (181 and 182 Filos at Diyarbakir) and a tactical weapons training unit at Konya, which consisted of 131 and 132 Filos, giving basic 'academic' weapons training to pilots destined for front-line units flying the F-100 and the F-104. With a glut of F-104s available as NATO nations re-equipped with the F-16, Turkey's remaining front-line units re-equipped during March-April 1985, but 35 F-100Ds and 20 F-100Fs remained in use at Konya until 1 November 1987, when 132 Filo flew its last Super Sabre sortie. This marked the end of the F-100 in front-line military service,

In Europe the F-100 lived on into the 1980s. France returned its aircraft to US ownership in 1978, and most ended up at Sculthorpe in England (above) where they were scrapped. Denmark's fleet (right) served until 1982, the single-seaters being passed on to Turkey, which flew the type until 1987. Most of the two-seaters went on to another career as target tugs.

QF-100 – drone conversion

With large numbers of aircraft available, the Super Sabre was a natural choice to satisfy the growing demands of the USAF's FSAT (Full-Scale Aerial Target) programme, resulting in a total of 310 aircraft being converted to QF-100 status for consumption in missile trials and live-firing exercises. As well as radio control equipment, the QF-100s were fitted with a scoring system, countermeasures as required, and – for IR-guided missile shots – wingtip burners which attracted the missile away from the aircraft's engine in an attempt to enhance its survivability and so prolong its useful life. The aircraft above has a burner fitted, and other modifications such as a 'sugar-scoop' IR shield over the exhaust and blacked-out canopy. The red star was an obvious addition for an aircraft destined to be shot down by a USAF fighter.

but the aircraft continued to fly in important military support roles.

Target drones

Between 1973 and 1981, Sperry Flight Systems had converted 215 redundant F-102s to QF-102A and PQM-102A/B unmanned target drone configuration under the Pave Deuce programme. These were used for missile trials, but also as realistic targets for front-line pilots during William Tell weapons competitions and in other exercises. It was always planned that the Delta Dagger drones would be followed by similar drone conversions of the F-106 Delta Dart from 1986, but the rapid expenditure of QF-102s led to a requirement for another interim target drone.

In March 1982, therefore, Sperry received a contract for an initial trial batch of nine F-100 drone conversions. Two 'manned' YQF-100D prototypes (56-3414 and 56-3610) were produced at Sperry's Litchfield Airport facility, followed by six QF-100Ds and a two-seat QF-100F. The trials batch was followed by 89 more QF-100Ds and two more QF-100Fs. Unmanned operations by the 82nd Tactical Aerial Targets Squadron (part of the 475th Weapons Evaluation Group) began from Tyndall AFB from 19 November 1981.

The Sperry QF-100s were followed by 169 QF-100Ds and 41 QF-100Fs converted by FSI at Mojave. The conversion of 14 additional aircraft was cancelled in December 1990, by when the QF-4 drone conversion programme was well underway. Six F-100Fs flew back to the 'boneyard', and five more were returned there by road. FSI bought in spares from other former F-100 operators, and even purchased three ex-Turkish aircraft for possible modification. They were ferried to Mojave in 1989, but remained unconverted.

The take-off of the QF-100 was handled by two controllers sitting in a telemetry van positioned at the end of the runway. One controlled the aircraft in pitch and managed the throttle, while the other controlled the ailerons and rudder. Once airborne, the drone was handed off to a third controller sitting in a fixed-base ground station. A dual redundant system was used to get the drone to the mission area and to select from a variety of pre-programmed manoeuvres. If the drone survived the

mission, it was flown back to the handover point, where the two take-off controllers brought the aircraft back in.

QF-100s were usually engaged using missiles with inert warheads, and had a digital Doppler system to measure miss distances. This allowed the aircraft to have a useful average life of six or seven drone target missions, since an attacking fighter could score a theoretical kill without destroying the drone. One drone survived 15 missile shots. The QF-100s could carry ECM, chaff and flares in order to enhance their value as a 'realistic target'. If a drone was too badly damaged to be recovered safely, it could be destroyed by remote control, and the same self-destruct system was used if contact with the drone was lost for more than six minutes. The aircraft could be flown by a pilot, conversion back to manned configuration being achieved by the flick of a switch on later conversions.

The 475th Weapons Evaluation Group expended its last QF-100 in 1992, though a handful remained in use with the 6585th Test Group at Holloman, supporting US Army programmes (including the HAWK SAM) after that date. The last two US military F-100Fs and a single F-100D were finally withdrawn in August 1994.

Target towing

During the 1950s and 1960s, many units used their own front-line aircraft to provide such target-towing support

Above left: Mojave's ramp groans under the weight of freshly modified QF-100s at the height of the FSI drone conversion programme in the late 1980s. Of the 198 aircraft whose fate has been published, 84 were shot down by AIM-9 Sidewinders, 63 by AIM-7 Sparrows, 22 by AIM-120 AMRAAMs and three by AIM-4 Falcons. Twenty crashed – mostly on take-off and landing – and six were destroyed by their operators.

With blacked-out canopy, a QF-100 lands in 'no live operator' mode. Many of the QF-100s were fitted with a Drone Formation Control System (DFCS), which enabled several to be flown together to stage multi-bogey engagements.

This view from September 1963 shows the 7272nd Fighter Training Wing's ramp at Wheelus, populated by target-towing F-100Cs. In the foreground are 335-US gal (1268-litre) supersonic tanks for the Super Sabres. Following a military coup led by Colonel Muammar Ghadaffi, US forces left Libya. Wheelus was subsequently renamed Okba ben Nafi air base, and played host to Soviet Tu-22s and MiG-25s.

Flight Systems Inc. (subsequently Tracor Flight Systems, then BAE Systems) operated five TF-100F target tugs in Europe, initially on a USAFE contract from Hurn in England and then on a Luftwaffe contract. For the latter the aircraft were fitted with Dornier Sk 10 darts, as seen on this aircraft at Wittmund, the main operating base in Germany. After retirement in 2001 their place was taken by ex-Israeli A-4 Skyhawks.

duties as was necessary, usually towing basic banner targets from a simple lug or hook, which was often fitted at base or squadron level. Many units adapted one or two F-100s in just this way. Dedicated F-100C target tugs were used by the 7272nd Fighter Training Wing at Wheelus AFB, Libya, from January 1958 until 1965, to provide target facilities for USAFE units visiting Wheelus for gunnery training. Similarly-equipped F-100Cs and F-100Fs were used by the 4758th Defense Systems Evaluation Squadron at Biggs AFB, Texas, from July 1962, and then from April 1966 until October 1970 at Holloman AFB, New Mexico.

Flight Systems Inc. had been a long-term provider of contract target-towing services to the US armed forces using F-86 Sabres, and when Denmark retired its last F-100s the company took the opportunity to acquire six of them for conversion as target tugs. These promised to be able to tow heavier targets than the F-86s, and more quickly, and spares support for the aircraft (especially in the light of the company's participation in the QF-100 programme) would be easier.

The company therefore purchased six TF-100Fs (N414FS (ex-56-3826, RDAF GT-826), N415FS (ex-56-3844, RDAF GT-844), N416FS (ex-56-3916, RDAF GT-916), N417FS (ex-56-3842, RDAF GT-842), N418FS (ex-56-3996, RDAF GT-996), and N419FS (ex-56-3971, RDAF GT-971)) from the Royal Danish Air Force, and converted them to target-towing configuration. A target-towing winch and its associated controls were installed, and the J57 engine was modernised and modified, gaining the afterburner of the (F-106-type) J75 engine.

One aircraft (N415FS (ex-56-3844, RDAF GT-844) was retained in the USA to service a contract at Holloman AFB, but the remainder were based at Bournemouth's Hurn airport to provide target-towing support for USAFE units. Funding constraints meant that this contract was not renewed in 1988, but FSI (by then Tracor Flight Systems Inc.) was able to gain a replacement contract to provide similar services to the Luftwaffe. The Luftwaffe had previ-

Target tugs at Wheelus

Until the USAF was ejected from Libya in 1965, the 7272nd Fighter Training Wing was based at Wheelus AFB. The location offered large unpopulated areas, excellent year-round flying weather, and the extensive El Uota live bombing range. It was used by USAFE units for armament practice. To provide targets for aerial gunnery the wing used F-100Cs modified to tow banners. They were first allocated to the task in 1958.

ously used its own F-4Fs and F-104Gs to tow targets, but FSI was able to offer a more cost-effective service. The TF-100Fs moved to Wittmund, home of JG 71 'Richthofen', from where they flew sorties over the North Sea ranges. They also supported Luftwaffe deployments to Decimomannu.

The TF-100Fs carried a Dornier DATS-3 target pod below the port inboard station, in place of the original USAF Model 15 A/A37U-15 target system. This consisted of an RMU-10 target winch and a Dornier Sk 10 target dart. The TF-100Fs also usually carried a 200-US gal (757-litre) tank to port, with a huge 335-US gal (1268-litre) tank to starboard. Unlike the original TDU-10 target dart, the new dart was fitted with miss distance recorders and a transponder which allowed it to change its radar signature.

N414FS was lost in a fatal accident at Cuxhaven on 11 July 1994 and the Holloman-based aircraft (N415FS) was sold to a private owner after its contract came to an end, but the four remaining F-100s flew on. They were finally retired from the target-towing role in June 2001, and BAE Flight Systems' final four aircraft flew back to Mojave from Wittmund. At least two of the aircraft remained there, maintained and ready for reactivation if required until 2003.

Warbirds

The only F-100s still flying are a trio of civilian-owned jet warbirds in the USA. Two were among the three ex-Turkish Air Force jets that had been sold to FSI for possible drone conversion and ferried to Mojave in August 1989. They were not needed, however, and were sold on to private owners. The two-seater (F-100F N2011V 56-3498) was delivered to Thomas J. Hickman of Addison, Texas, in August 1992, before being sold to Dean F. 'Cutter' Cutshall (or to his company, American Horizons) of Fort Wayne, Indiana, in July 1996. The aircraft has been beautifully restored and now flies in the striking red and white colours of the 354th TFW.

For several years the only other flying F-100 was another two-seater. TF-100F N26AZ (56-3844) was a former FSI aircraft, N415FS, which was owned and operated by David Tokoph's El Paso, Texas-based Grecoair in New Mexico ANG colours until sold (with an asking price of $US700,000). The aircraft is now decorated in 'Thunderbirds' livery.

Flight Systems Inc. – civilian target-towing

From its Mojave base Flight Systems Inc. operated a number of Super Sabres on various government target facilities contracts through the 1980s. Left is Hilda, an ex-Massachusetts ANG F-100F, while at right is an F-100D (56-3022) which had flown with Connecticut ANG before being acquired by FSI in late 1979.

NACA/NASA 'Huns'

Right: 53-1709 (NASA 703) was designated JF-100C and was flown by NACA/NASA from Moffett (Ames) and Edwards (Dryden). It was fitted with a variable-stability system which allowed it to perform inflight simulations of different control systems, effectively allowing it to mimic other aircraft types.

Below: F-100A 52-5778 was operated by the High-Speed Flight Station (Edwards) from 1954 to 1960, investigating various phenomena which affected supersonic fighters, including pitch-up. Between 1957 and 1961, NACA (which became NASA in July 1958) also flew F-100C 53-1717 on basic research duties.

Alias NASA-200, this F-100A was used to test take-off performance improvements. By a combination of blown boundary layer control across the leading- and trailing-edge flaps, and the deflection of the leading-edge flaps to 60°, a 10 percent improvement was achieved. Note the enlarged intake fitted to the aircraft.

F-100D-50-NH (55-2888) was the second ex-Turkish F-100 flown to Mojave, where it was registered to Global Aerospace of Diamond Bar, California, as N2011U in 1993. The aircraft (by then partly cannibalised for spares) was sold to jet warbird restorer Greg Forbes of Sacramento in 1998, who spent three years restoring the aircraft to flying condition. The F-100D was ferried to the former McClellan AFB near Sacramento for a full restoration on 1 November 2001, which took another 18 months. Test pilot Lee Holcomb of El Dorado Hills, California, flew the aircraft on its first post-restoration flight on an unrecorded day in April 2003, but because the weather was so poor on that day, the event officially took place on 10 May 2003. Forbes reportedly plans to paint his F-100D in the colours of the 'Thunderbirds' team, and it will then join his stable of warbirds, which includes a T-33, six Drakens, and an F-86.

The third of the ex-Turkish FSI jets was an F-100C (54-2091 N2011M), which passed into the hands of Al Hansen and Mojo Jets before being sold (reportedly on eBay) in June 2002. The status of this sale is doubtful, however, and most sources suggest that the aircraft remains in Mr Hansen's hands. The oldest and most 'tired' of the trio, the F-100C was the last of the aircraft to find a new owner. Its restoration to full flying condition would seem unlikely, but cannot be ruled out.

Perhaps the most likely F-100 to return to the air will be one of the BAE Flight Systems TF-100Fs, several of which are stored at Mojave and still have FAA airworthiness certifi-

cates. Lynn High, owner of the Fightertown Aviation FBO 60 miles (96 km) north of Dallas, partnered with Mike Menez, a former ANG F-100 pilot and now a commercial pilot with Cathay Pacific, to form Heritage Jets; the sole aim is acquiring an F-100 Super Sabre and getting out on the air show circuit – originally hoping to do so in time for the 50th anniversary of the aircraft in 2003. Menez confirmed in 2002 that Heritage Jets had submitted a bid to BAE and had hired a professional marketing firm to market sponsorship opportunities, but things then went quiet. The four surviving TF-100Fs were recently sold, with the FAA recording a change of ownership on 12 June 2003 to Big Sky Warbirds LLC of Belgrade, Montana

Nevertheless, with three F-100s able to make their own unique and noisy contribution to the US air show circuit, it is unlikely that the Super Sabre will be forgotten just yet.

And the F-100 is an aircraft which should not be forgotten. Unfairly dubbed the 'Not so Super Sabre' by some writers and journalists, the F-100 may not have been much of an air-to-air fighter, and its all-weather fighter variant may have been stillborn, but the aircraft did give useful service as a fighter-bomber. Although the aircraft had never been intended for the air-to-ground role – a role other aircraft performed with greater facility – the F-100 was in the right place at the right time, and its dedicated and highly skilled pilots worked wonders in it, earning a formidable reputation in combat over southeast Asia.

Jon Lake

In 1989 FSI purchased three Turkish air force aircraft for potential QF-100 drone conversions. The trio was sold on to private owners, and two of them are flying in 2003 on the airshow circuit. This is the third aircraft, F-100C N2011M, which may yet be restored to airworthy condition. The other flyer was another ex-FSI aircraft, a Danish TF-100F which had been used by FSI for a contract at Holloman AFB.

F-100 Operators

UNITED STATES AIR FORCE

In July 1958 the USAF dispensed with the 'Fighter Day' and 'Fighter Bomber' unit designators in favour of 'Tactical Fighter'. This affected many F-100 units.

3rd TFW
Operated F-100Ds and F-100Fs from England AFB, LA, from June 1964. Deployed to Bien Hoa AB, South Vietnam, on 8 November 1965. The 3rd TFW was unmanned and unequipped, existing only on paper after its withdrawal from southeast Asia on 31 October 1970. The wing moved to Kunsan AB, South Korea, on 15 March 1971, where it re-equipped with F-4 Phantoms. While in Vietnam the wing included squadrons operating other aircraft types such as the B-57.
90th Tactical Fighter Squadron 'Pair o' Dice': assigned 9 June 1964 – 19 November 1965 and 3 February 1966 – 31 October 1970, tailcode 'CB', light blue colours. With 401st TFW in interim
307th Tactical Fighter Squadron: assigned 21 November – 6 December 1965, on TDY
308th Tactical Fighter Squadron: assigned 2 December 1965 – 25 December 1966, on TDY
416th Tact. Fighter Squadron 'Silver Knights': assigned 16 June 1964 – 8 November 1965 and 16 November 1965 – 15 April 1967, blue colours
429th Tactical Fighter Squadron: assigned 21 November – 14 December 1965, on TDY
510th Tactical Fighter Squadron: assigned 16 March 1964 – 15 November 1969, tailcode 'CE', purple colours
531st Tactical Fighter Squadron: assigned to the 3rd TFW 16 June 1964 – 19 November 1965 and 7 December 1965 – 31 July 1970, tailcode 'CP', red colours

4th FDW/TFW
Formed by re-numbering the 83rd FDW. Operated F-100Cs from Seymour Johnson AFB, NC, from early 1958 until conversion to the F-105B began on 16 June 1959. Plain broad bands encircled the nose and the tailfin.
333rd Fighter Day Squadron 'Lancers': assigned December 1957 – 1960, red colours
334th Fighter Day Squadron 'Eagles': assigned December 1957 – 1960, blue colours
335th Fighter Day Squadron 'Chiefs': assigned December 1957 – 1960, green colours
336th Fighter Day Squadron 'Rocketeers': assigned December 1957 – 1960, yellow colours

8th TFW
Operated F-100Ds and Fs from Itazuke AFB, Japan, from late 1956 until conversion to the F-105F began in May 1963. Unit markings consisted of three chevrons on the fin, in squadron colours, with a squadron badge in centre of middle chevron.
35th Tactical Fighter Squadron: assigned 1956 – 1963, blue colours
36th Tactical Fighter Squadron 'Flying Fiends': assigned 1956 – 1963, red colours
80th Tactical Fighter Squadron 'Headhunters': assigned 1956 – 1963, yellow colours

18th TFW
Operated F-100Ds and Fs from Kadena AB, Okinawa, Japan, from 1957 until

conversion to the F-105D/F began in October 1962. Unit markings consisted of diagonal stripes around the nose in squadron colours, and a three-pronged red white and blue arrowhead on the fin.
12th Tactical Fighter Squadron 'Bald Eagles': assigned 1957 – 1963, yellow/black colours.
44th Tactical Fighter Squadron 'Vampires': assigned 1957 – 1963, blue/white colours
67th Tactical Fighter Squadron 'Fighting Cocks': assigned to the 18th TFW 1957 – 1963, red/white colours

20th TFW
The 20th TFW converted to the F-100D and F-100F from the F-84F from 16 June 1957, initially based at RAF Wethersfield and RAF Woodbridge (79th FS). The 79th FS moved to Upper Heyford on 15 January 1970, and the Wethersfield units moved on 1 June 1970. The wing converted to the F-111E from September 1970. Unit markings consisted of a lightning flash down the fin and repeated on the fuselage, in squadron colours, with squadron and wing badges superimposed to starboard and port. A three-coloured lightning flash was applied on the tail alone after 1961.
55th Tactical Fighter Squadron 'Fighting Fifty Fifth': assigned June 1957 – 1970, blue colours
77th Tactical Fighter Squadron 'Gamblers': assigned 1957 – 1971, red colours
79th Tactical Fighter Squadron 'Tigers': assigned 1957 – 1971, yellow colours

21st TFW
The 21st TFW converted to the F-100D and F at Misawa from July 1958, but deactivated in June 1960, its squadrons being reassigned to the 3rd TFW and 39th AD. Unit markings consisted of two overlapping chevrons on the fin, with bands encircling the intake. These were in squadron colours. The intake bands were edged with blue bands and white stars.
416th Tactical Fighter Squadron 'Silver Knights': assigned July 1958 – June 1960 colours blue
531st Tactical Fighter Squadron: assigned July 1958 – June 1960, colours red

27th TFW
The 27th TFW became an operator of the F-100D and F at Cannon AFB, NM, in February 1959 by the renumbering of the 312th TFW. The wing maintained a Detachment at Takhli from 13 December 1962 – 1 June 1963, before moving to Da Nang until 6 May 1964. The 27th flew the F-100 until 1972. Unit markings consisted of a huge area of colour on the upper half of the tailfin. This was bisected diagonally, with colour above the diagonal which ran from the fin fillet on the leading

edge to the trailing edge above the RWR. This was replaced by a smaller 'Arrowhead' chevron high on the fin.
481st Tactical Fighter Squadron: assigned February 1959 – 1972, tailcode 'CA', green colours
522nd Tactical Fighter Squadron 'Fireballs': assigned February 1959 – 1972, tailcode 'CC', red colours
523rd Tactical Fighter Squadron: assigned February 1959 – November 1965, blue colours, to the 405th TFW, November 1965
524th Tactical Fighter Squadron 'Hounds of Heaven': assigned February 1959 – 1972, tailcode 'CD', yellow colours.

31st TFW
The 31st TFW converted to the F-100D and F in mid-1957 at Turner AFB, with the 31st, 306th, 307th, 308th and 309th TFSs. The wing's assets were transferred to the 354th TFW at Myrtle Beach on 15 March 1959, but the wing and squadron designations were then taken over by the units of the 413th TFW at George AFB. The wing moved to Homestead AFB in mid-1960, then deployed to Tuy Hoa between December 1966 and 15 October 1970. Thereafter, the wing returned to the USA as a paper unit only. In Vietnam, the wing included a number of ANG F-100Cs. Unit markings originally consisted of a broad coloured band going up the tailfin, with a squadron coloured nose. At George AFB the 31st TFW's aircraft wore two broad parallel bands across the tailfin and one around the nose.
136th Tactical Fighter Squadron, NY ANG 'Rocky's Raiders': assigned June 1968 – May 1969, tailcode 'SG'
188th Tactical Fighter Squadron NM ANG 'Enchilada Air Force': assigned June 1968 – May 1969, tailcode 'SK'
306th Tactical Fighter Squadron: assigned 1957 – 1970, tailcode 'SD', red colours
307th Tactical Fighter Squadron: assigned 1957 – April 1966, reassigned to Torrejon. Blue colours
308th Tactical Fighter Squadron 'Emerald Knights': assigned 1957 – 1970, tailcode 'SM', green colours
309th Tactical Fighter Squadron: assigned 1957 – 1970, tailcode 'SS', yellow colours
355th Tactical Fighter Squadron: assigned May 1969 – September 1970, tailcode 'SP'
416th Tactical Fighter Squadron 'Silver Knights': assigned May 1969 – September 1970, to 4403rd TFW. Tailcode 'SE', blue colours

35th TFW
The 35th TFW formed as an F-100 unit by the exchange of designations with

the 366th TFW, which became an F-4 wing at Da Nang. The wing was based at Phan Rang AB, from October 1966 until July 1971.
120th Tactical Fighter Squadron, Colorado ANG: assigned April 1968 – April 1969, tailcode 'VS' when 612th at Phu Cat
352nd Tactical Fighter Squadron: assigned October 1966 – July 1971, tailcode 'VM', yellow colours
612th Tactical Fighter Squadron, Det 1 'Misty FAC': assigned October 1966 – January 1967 and April 1969 – 1971, tailcode 'VS', blue colours
614th Tactical Fighter Squadron 'Lucky Devils': assigned 1966 – 1971, tailcode 'VP', red colours
615th Tactical Fighter Squadron: assigned 1966 – 1971, tailcode 'VZ', green colours

36th FDW/TFW
The 36th FDW converted to the F-100C in 1956, mainly at Bitburg but with single squadrons at Ramstein/Landstuhl, Hahn and Soesterberg. The wing was re-designated as a TFW after 1 July 1958, and its surviving squadrons converted to F-105s from May 1961. Unit markings consisted of three broad diagonal stripes on the tailfin, with a chevron tapering back from the intake.
22nd Tactical Fighter Squadron: assigned May 1956 – 1961. Red colours
23rd Tactical Fighter Squadron: assigned April 1956 – 1961. Blue colours
32nd Tactical Fighter Squadron: assigned July 1956 – August 1960 at Soesterberg. To F-102. Green colours
53rd Tactical Fighter Squadron: assigned June 1956 – 1961, at Ramstein. Yellow colours
461st Tactical Fighter Squadron: assigned 1956 – August 1959, at Hahn. Deactivated. Black colours
'Skyblazers': assigned September 1956 – 1961

37th TFW
The 37th TFW activated as an F-100 unit at Phu Cat AB, Vietnam, on 1 March 1967, and remained there until May 1969.
174th Tactical Fighter Squadron: assigned May 1968 – May 1969, tailcode 'HA'
355th Tactical Fighter Squadron: assigned February 1968 – May 1969, tailcode 'HP'
416th Tactical Fighter Squadron 'Silver Knights': assigned April 1967 – May 1969, tailcode 'HE', blue colours
612th Tactical Fighter Squadron Det 1 'Misty FAC': assigned June 1967 – April 1969, tailcode 'HS'

39th Air Division
In 1958 the 39th AD briefly had the 418th TFS allocated with F-100Cs at Clark AB, Philippines. Later, the 356th TFS was directly assigned to the 39th Air Division at Misawa, but was not part of the 21st TFW. It was responsible for maintaining four F-100s on nuclear alert at Kunsan, Korea (supported by the 6175th Air Base Group) and would have deployed forward to Korea in the event of hostilities. When the 21st TFW deactivated in 1960, the 531st TFS was reassigned to the 39th AD. The 27th TFW provided F-100s from June 1964 – June 1965, the 401st TFW from June 1965 – August 1965, and the 3rd TFW from August 1965 – June 1966, before the 401st TFW took over. The 39th AD at Misawa converted to F-4s in June 1967, though these did not immediately

F-100D, 90th TFS/3rd TFW, Bien Hoa AB, South Vietnam, May 1969

F-100D, 20th TFW at Nouasseur AB, Morocco, June 1958. 79th TFS – yellow tail, 77th TFS – red tail

F-100D, 492nd TFS/48th TFW, RAF Lakenheath, England

take over the nuclear alert duty at Kunsan.

418th Tactical Fighter Squadron: assigned 1958 at Clark AB

356th Tactical Fighter Squadron 'Green Demons': assigned April 1964 – June 1966. Then to Det 1 475th TFW

531st Tactical Fighter Squadron: assigned 1960 – 1964 at Misawa AB

48th FBW/TFW

Transitioned from the F-86F at Chaumont AB, France, in late 1956. Transferred to RAF Lakenheath as the 48th TFW, by 15 January 1960. Converted to F-4D Phantoms from February 1972. Unit markings consisted of alternating stripes across the tailfin in squadron colours, with a shadowed 'V' shaped chevron on the nose added from 1959. A more subdued chevron on the tail replaced stripes when the wing moved to England.

492nd Tactical Fighter Squadron 'Bolars': assigned September 1956 – April 1972, tailcode 'LR', blue colours

493rd Tactical Fighter Squadron 'Roosters': assigned 1956 – 1972, tailcode 'LS', yellow colours

494th Tactical Fighter Squadron 'Panthers': assigned 1956 – 1972, tailcode 'LT', red colours

---

49th FBW/TFW

Formed at Etain-Rouvres AB, France on 10 December 1957 by renumbering the 388th FBW. Transferred to Spangdahlem as the 49th TFW during 1960. Converted to F-105 from October 1961. Unit markings included a broad band on the fin and a chevron on intake in squadron colours with white four-angled lightning bolt on fin.

7th Tactical Fighter Squadron: assigned December 1957 – 1962, blue colours

8th Tactical Fighter Squadron 'Black Sheep': assigned December 1957 – 1962, yellow colours

9th Tactical Fighter Squadron 'Iron Knights': assigned December 1957 – 1962, red colours

---

50th FBW/TFW

Transitioned from the F-86F at Toul-Rosières AB, France, in 1957. Transferred to Hahn as the 50th TFW, by 10 December 1959. Converted to F-4C and F-4D Phantoms from October 1966. Unit markings consisted of starred bands across the fin.

10th Tactical Fighter Squadron: assigned December 1957 – 1967, blue bands with white stars

81st Tactical Fighter Squadron: assigned July 1958 – 1966, yellow bands with black stars

417th Tactical Fighter Squadron: assigned 1958 – 1966, red bands with white stars

---

57th Fighter Weapons Wing

Formed by re-numbering the 4525th FWW at Nellis AFB in October 1969. Its F-100 element was inactivated 31 December 1969.

65th Fighter Weapons Squadron: the former 4525th FWS was assigned to the 57th FWW October 1969 – 31 December 1969, tailcode 'WB', yellow and black colours

---

58th Tactical Fighter Training Wing

Formed by re-numbering the 4510th CCTW at Luke AFB in October 1969. Its F-100 elements were inactivated during 1971. 'LA' tailcodes were worn by all squadrons.

310th Tactical Fighter Training Squadron: assigned Oct 1969 – 1971

311th Tactical Fighter Training Squadron: assigned 18 January 1970 – 21 August 1971

426th Tactical Fighter Training Squadron: assigned 18 January 1970 – 13 September 1971

4511th Combat Crew Training Squadron: assigned October 1969 – 18 January 1970, replaced by 311th TFTS

4514th Combat Crew Training Squadron: assigned October 1969 – 15 December 1969 became A-7 training unit

4515th Combat Crew Training Squadron: assigned October 1969 – 18 June 1970 became 426th TFTS

4517th Combat Crew Training Squadron: assigned from October 1969

67th Tactical Reconnaissance Wing

The 67th TRW was activated on 25 February 1951 and inactivated on 8 December 1960. It briefly parented the 6021st Reconnaissance Squadron with RF-100As, though at other times they were assigned to the 6000th Operations Wing.

6021st Reconnaissance Squadron: attached to the 67th TRW 1 July – 8 December 1957.

83rd FDW

Perhaps the shortest lived F-100 unit was the 83rd FDW at Seymour Johnson AFB. The unit moved to Seymour Johnson in July 1956, and converted to the F-100 in August 1957. It was re-numbered as the 4th FDW in December 1957.

448th Fighter-Day Squadron: assigned August 1957 – December 1957

532nd Fighter-Day Squadron: assigned 1957 – December 1957

533rd Fighter-Day Squadron: assigned 1957 – December 1957

534th Fighter-Day Squadron: assigned 1957 – December 1957

95th Bombardment Wing

The ADC-assigned 4758th Defense Systems Evaluation Squadron came under the control of the 95th Bombardment Wing while operating from Biggs AFB, TX. The squadron moved to Holloman AFB and was officially inactivated on 26 June 1966. Its aircraft wore a small squadron badge on the tail and often carried dayglo orange fuel tanks.

4758th Defense Systems Evaluation Squadron

113th TFW

The 113th TFW formed at Myrtle Beach in March 1968 to act as an RTU for ANG F-100 aircrew deploying to Vietnam, with two ANG squadrons being called to active duty to man it. It closed in June 1969. The wing tailcode 'XD' was sometimes worn.

119th Tactical Fighter Squadron, NJ ANG: assigned March 1968 – June 1969, 'XA' tailcode

121st Tactical Fighter Squadron, DC ANG: assigned March 1968 – June 1969, 'XB' tailcode

---

312th FBW/TFW

The 312th FBW was another short-lived F-100 user, converting from the F-86H in late 1956, but then re-designating as the 27th TFW in February 1959. The 312th itself went from FBW to TFW on 1 July 1958. Its aircraft wore a small wing badge on the fin, later coloured fins, leaving the fintip and a triangular portion of the rear, from the trailing edge tapering down to the fin leading edge, unpainted.

386th Tactical Fighter Squadron: assigned late 1956 – February 1959, red colours

387th Tactical Fighter Squadron: assigned late 1956 – February 1959, blue colours

388th Tactical Fighter Squadron: assigned late 1956 – February 1959, yellow colours

477th Tactical Fighter Squadron: assigned October 1957 – February 1959, green colours

F-100D, 81st TFS/50th TFW, at Wheelus AFB, Libya, on weapons practice camp

316th Air Division

The 45th FDS was a conversion training and transition unit for USAFE F-100 units, briefly based at Sidi Slimane AB, French Morocco. The squadron's aircraft had a black edged scalloped yellow nose band and a yellow tailfin, with black/yellow chevrons superimposed.

45th Tactical Fighter Squadron: assigned March 1956 – 8 January 1958

322nd FDW

Though it was TAC's first F-100 operator, the 322nd FDW at Foster AFB, TX, was short-lived, converting from the F-86F in mid-1955 but passing its aircraft on to the 4th and 36th FDWs in late 1957. Its aircraft wore a broad band on the fin with playing cards insignia superimposed.

450th Fighter Day Squadron: assigned 1955 – 1957, red colours

451st Fighter Day Squadron: assigned 1955 – 1957, yellow colours

452nd Fighter Day Squadron: assigned 1955 – 1957, green colours

323rd FBW

The 323rd FBW at Bunker Hill AFB initially used a few F-100As with the 323rd FBG, before equipping the 386th FBG with the F-100D. The unit's aircraft wore a band on the tail, and around the nose, edged with small black checkers.

453rd Fighter Bomber Squadron: assigned March 1956 – May 1957

454th Fighter Bomber Squadron: assigned March 1956 – May 1957

454th Fighter Bomber Squadron: assigned March 1956 – May 1957

552nd Fighter Bomber Squadron: assigned late 1956 – August 1957

553rd Fighter Bomber Squadron: assigned late 1956 – August 1957

553rd Fighter Bomber Squadron: assigned late 1956 – August 1957

325th Fighter Weapons Wing

The 325th Fighter Weapons Wing was reformed on 17 Jun 1981. It included the 82nd TATS with QF-100 drones.

82nd Tactical Aerial Target Squadron: assigned 1 Jul 1981 – 15 Oct 1983

354th FBW/TFW

The 354th FBW/TFW had two incarnations as an F-100 operator. The wing formed at Myrtle Beach AFB, SC, in early 1957, taking over the assets of the deactivated 31st FBW, under the command of WWII and Korean ace Francis S Gabreski. It became the 354th TFW on 1 July 1958. Its squadrons were reassigned to units in Vietnam by June 1968 and it began a new existence as the controlling wing for two ANG squadrons deployed to Kunsan AB, Korea.

127th Tactical Fighter Squadron, KS ANG: assigned at Kunsan, 5 July 1968 – 10 June 1969, 'BO' tailcode, blue colours

166th Tactical Fighter Squadron, OH ANG: assigned at Kunsan, 5 July 1968 – 10 June 1969, 'BP' tailcode, red colours

352nd Tactical Fighter Squadron: assigned September 1957 – August 1966, yellow colours. To 366th TFW

353rd Tactical Fighter Squadron 'Black Panthers': assigned September 1957 – April 1966, red colours. To F-4E, designation to A-7 unit 1970

355th Tactical Fighter Squadron: assigned September 1957 – April 1968, blue colours. To 37th TFW

356th Tactical Fighter Squadron 'Green Demons': assigned September 1957 – November 1965, green colours. To F-4C November 1967

366th TFW

The 366th FBW converted from the F-84F to the F-100D in late 1957, but deactivated at England AFB, LA, in early 1959. The wing subsequently reactivated in Vietnam in April 1966, operating there between April and October 1966, when it swapped identities with the 35th TFW at Da Nang. The wing's early markings consisted of a candy striped nose band and alternating diagonal strips across most of the tailfin.

352nd Tactical Fighter Squadron: assigned at Phan Rang August 1966 – October 1966

389th Tactical Fighter Squadron: assigned at England AFB, LA, September 1957 – January 1959

390th Tactical Fighter Squadron: assigned at England AFB, LA, September 1957 – January 1959

391st Tactical Fighter Squadron: assigned at England AFB, LA, September 1957 – February 1959

480th Fighter Bomber Squadron: assigned at

F-100C, 45th FDS/316th Air Division, based at Sidi Slimane AB, Morocco

England AFB, LA, September 1957 – March 1959
614th Tactical Fighter Squadron: assigned at Phan Rang July 1966 – October 1966
615th Tactical Fighter Squadron: assigned at Phan Rang July 1966 – October 1966

388th TFW
The 388th FBW converted from the F-86F at Etain-Rouvres in late 1956, but re-numbered as the 49th FBW in December 1957. The wing subsequently reactivated at McConnell AFB on 1 October 1962, with a single F-100 unit but converted to the F-105D in mid-1963. As an F-105-equipped wing at Korat, the 388th subsequently parented the Wild Weasel I F-100 unit.
560th Tactical Fighter Squadron: assigned at McConnell, 1 October 1962 – mid-1963
561st Tactical Fighter Squadron: assigned at Etain-Rouvres late 1956 – December 1957, yellow colours
562nd Tactical Fighter Squadron: assigned at Etain-Rouvres late 1956 – December 1957, blue colours
563rd Tactical Fighter Squadron: assigned at Etain-Rouvres late 1956 – December 1957, red colours
6234th Tactical Fighter Squadron 'Wild Weasel 1': assigned at Korat November 1965 – May 1966

401st TFW
The 401st TFW converted from the F-84F at England AFB, LA, in late 1957. It lost most of its squadrons on TDY to wings in Vietnam, having only one remaining unit when it transferred to Torrejon in Spain in April 1966. The wing converted to the F-4 Phantom in 1970.
90th Tactical Fighter Squadron: assigned December 1965 – February 1966
307th Tactical Fighter Squadron: assigned at Torrejon April 1966 – June 1971
353rd Tactical Fighter Squadron 'Black Panthers': assigned at Torrejon April 1966 – June 1971
531st Tactical Fighter Squadron: assigned November 1965 – December 1965
612th Tactical Fighter Squadron 'Screaming Eagles': assigned September 1957 – November 1965. Blue colours. To 366th TFW
613th Tactical Fighter Squadron 'Squids': assigned September 1957 – 1970. Yellow colours
614th Tactical Fighter Squadron 'Lucky Devils': assigned September 1957 – April 1966. Red colours. To 35th TFW
615th Tactical Fighter Squadron: assigned 1957 – April 1966. Green colours. To 35th TFW

402nd FDW
The 402nd FDW operated F-100Cs for only six months in late 1956. Its aircraft wore two bands high on the tailfin.
320th Fighter Day Squadron: assigned to the 402nd FDG – 1956
442nd Fighter Day Squadron: assigned to the 402nd FDG – 1956
540th Fighter Day Squadron: assigned to the 402nd FDG – 1956

405th FBW/TFW
The 405th FBW was TAC's first F-100D unit, converting from the F-84F in late 1956 at Langley AFB, VA. The wing

deactivated on 1 July 1958, but reactivated at Clark AFB on 9 April 1959 with a single F-100 unit. The wing's aircraft wore a broad fin band in the squadron colour, edged in dark blue/black, with a stylised white bird, and there was a checkerboard around the nose intake in the squadron colour and white.
508th Fighter Bomber Squadron: assigned 1956 – March 1958. Yellow colours
509th Tactical Fighter Squadron: assigned April 1959 – August 1964, and November 1965 – 1967. Red colours
510th Tactical Fighter Squadron: assigned at Langley 1956 – April 1958. Assigned at Clark AB 9 April 1959 – March 1964. Purple colours. To 3rd TFW
511th Fighter Bomber Squadron: assigned 1956 – May 1958. Blue colours
522nd Tactical Fighter Squadron: assigned August 1965 – November 1965
523rd Tactical Fighter Squadron: assigned November 1965 – 1967
531st Tactical Fighter Squadron: assigned November 1964 – February 1965
612th Tactical Fighter Squadron: assigned at Langley 1956 – 1958. Assigned February 1964 – June 1964
615th Tactical Fighter Squadron: assigned 4 – 6 June 1964

413th FDW/TFW
The 423rd FDW at George AFB converted to the F-100C from the F-86H in late 1957. It transitioned to the F-100D in 1958, becoming the 413th TFW. The wing was redesignated as the 31st TFW on 15 March 1959. The wing's aircraft wore a squadron coloured fin band containing the squadron badge, and a coloured nose band
1st Fighter Bomber Squadron: assigned October 1957 – 15 March 1959, red colours
21st Fighter Bomber Squadron: assigned October 1957 – 15 March 1959, blue colours
34th Fighter Bomber Squadron: assigned October 1957 – 15 March 1959, green colours
474th Fighter Bomber Squadron: October 1957 – March 1959, yellow colours

450th FDW/TFW
The 450th FDW converted from the F-86F to the F-100C at Foster AFB in 1955, but deactivated in December 1958. The wing's aircraft wore an approximation of the stars and stripes, with seven red and six white stripes on the trailing edge, and three stars in white on the blue forward portion of the fin. They also used a coloured, scalloped nose chevron.
720th Fighter-Day Squadron: assigned 1955 – July 1958
721st Fighter-Day Squadron: assigned 1955 – July 1958, red colours
722nd Fighter-Day Squadron: assigned 1955 – July 1958
723rd Fighter-Day Squadron: assigned 1955 – August 1958

474th FBW/TFW
The 474th FBW converted from the F-86H to the F-100D at Cannon AB, NM

F-100D, 355th TFS/354th TFW, refuelling during deployment to Aviano, February 1959

in late 1957. The unit converted to the F-111 in 1968. The wing's aircraft wore a thick band on the tail containing a double-headed 'Machbusters' shockwave device, and later used alternating chevrons covering most of the fin. Three of the wing's constituent squadrons were sent to Vietnam on TDY.
428th Tactical Fighter Squadron 'Buccaneers': assigned 1957 – September 1965. Blue colours
429th Tactical Fighter Squadron 'Black Falcons': assigned 1957 – December 1965. Yellow and black colours
430th Tactical Fighter Squadron 'Tigers': assigned 1957 – September 1965. Red colours
478th Tactical Fighter Squadron: assigned 1957 – September 1965. Green colours, but later black and white

475th TFW
The 475th TFW activated on 21 December 1967, but was a 'paper' unit which borrowed assets from other wings in SEA. The 475th TFW's Det 1 (rotated between F-100 and F-4 units) took over the Korean nuclear alert commitment from the 39th AD, despite the presence of ANG F-100s at Kunsan. The wing's three squadrons converted to F-4s later during 1968.
67th Tactical Fighter Squadron 'Fighting Cocks': assigned 15 January 1968 – 15 March 1971
356th Tactical Fighter Squadron 'Green Devils': assigned 15 January 1968 – 15 March 1971
391st Tactical Fighter Squadron: assigned 22 July 1968 – 28 February 1971

475th Weapons Evaluation Group
The 475th WEG parented the QF-100s at Tyndall AFB after the re-designation of the 325th FWW. Det 1 of the 475th WEG looked after the QF-100 drones at Holloman AFB.
82nd Tactical Aerial Target Squadron: assigned October 1983-1992

479th FDW/TFW
The 479th FDW at George AFB converted from F-86F to F-100A in 1954. The wing subsequently received F-100Cs, becoming TAC's first F-100C unit, before converting to the F-104A in 1958, when it also became the 479th TFW.
434th Fighter Day Squadron: assigned September 1954 – 1959, red colours
435th Fighter Day Squadron: assigned September 1954 – 1959, green colours
436th Fighter Day Squadron: assigned September 1954 – 1959, yellow colours
476th Fighter Day Squadron: assigned 8 October 1954 – 1959, blue colours

506th TFW
The 506th FBW transitioned from the F-84F at Tinker AFB in September 1957. After a number of deployments to West Germany, the wing deactivated on 1 April 1959. The wing's F-100s wore markings reminiscent of those briefly used by the 450th TFW, with an approximation of the stars and stripes, with four coloured and three contrasting stripes on the trailing edge and two stars on the forward portion of the fin. Coloured, scalloped nose chevron.
457th Fighter Bomber Squadron: assigned 1957 – December 1958, red/white colours
458th Fighter Bomber Squadron: assigned

1957 – December 1958, yellow/black colours
462nd Fighter Bomber Squadron: assigned 1957 – December 1958, blue colours
470th Fighter Bomber Squadron: assigned 1957 – December 1958, green colours

3525th CCTW
The 3525th Combat Crew Training Wing was a pilot training unit based at Williams AFB. When responsibility for advanced training passed from Air Training Command, the 3,000 series CCTWs were redesignated, and new basic training units were formed using the old designations. The 3525th CCTW became the 4530th Combat Crew Training Wing. When it was redesignated in July 1958 it had both F-86 Sabres and F-100s on charge.

3595th CCTW
The 3595th Combat Crew Training Wing was based at Nellis AFB, and used F-86s and F-100s between 1954 – July 1958, when it became the 4520th Combat Crew Training Wing. The 3595th CCTW's most famous F-100 element was the 'Thunderbirds' display team, which moved to Nellis AFB in 1956, becoming the 3595th Air Demonstration Flight.

3600th CCTW
The 3600th Combat Crew Training Wing was based at Luke AFB, and used F-86s and F-100s between December 1957 – July 1958. It was redesignated as the 4510th Combat Crew Training Wing when training passed to TAC. The 'Thunderbirds' display team was originally based at Luke as the 3600th Air Demonstration Flight.

4403rd TFW
The 4403rd TFW was a provisional unit established at Homestead to parent F-100 units returning from SEA before re-equipment. The unit operated F-100Ds and F-100Fs from England AFB, La, from 1970-1972.
68th Tactical Fighter Squadron: assigned 1970 – 1972, 'SD' tailcode, yellow colours
416th Tactical Fighter Squadron: assigned September 1970 – 1972, 'SE' tailcode, blue colours
431st Tactical Fighter Squadron: assigned 1970 – 1972, 'SM' tailcode, red colours

4510th CCTW
When responsibility for advanced training passed from Air Training Command to TAC in July 1958, the 3600th Combat Crew Training Wing at Luke AFB was re-designated as the 4510th CCTW. 'LA' tailcodes were used from July 1968, and the wing was re-designated as the 58th TFTW in October 1969.
4511th Combat Crew Training Squadron: assigned July 1958 – 18 January 1970
4512th Combat Crew Training Squadron: assigned July 1958 – 1970
4514th Combat Crew Training Squadron: assigned July 1958 – 15 December 1969
4515th Combat Crew Training Squadron: assigned 1 September 1966 – 18 June 1970
4517th Combat Crew Training Squadron: assigned 1 September 1966 – October 1969

4520th CCTW
The 3595th Combat Crew Training Wing at Nellis AFB was redesignated as the 4520th CCTW in July 1958 when TAC

F-100D, 614th TFS/401st TFW, at Langley AFB, Virginia

F-100D, 429th TFS/474th TFW, combat deployment to Bien Hoa, July to November 1965

took responsibility for advanced training. The F-100 originally served with two squadrons, though these aircraft transferred to Luke AFB in 1962. The remaining F-100s at Nellis were then concentrated with the 4536th FWS of the 4525th CCTW.

4523rd Combat Crew Training Squadron: assigned July 1958 – 1960/1961
4526th Combat Crew Training Squadron: assigned July 1958 – 1960/1961

4525th CCTW/FWW
The 4525th CCTW was a Nellis-based advanced and weapons training unit. The wing was redesignated as the 57th FWW in October 1969, and then on 15 October, as the 57th TTW.
4536th Fighter Weapons Squadron: assigned to the 4525th FWW September 1966 – October 1969

4530th CCTW
The 4530th CCTW was formed by the re-designation of the 3525th CCTW at Williams AFB in July 1958. The wing ceased F-100 operations in October 1960.

6000th Operations Wing
The 6000th Operations Wing parented the 6021st Reconnaissance Squadron with RF-100As, though at other times they were assigned to the 67th TRW.
6021st Reconnaissance Squadron: attached 2 June 1955 – June 1958

6200th Air Base Wing
The 6200th ABW parented the 72nd Tactical Fighter Squadron (formerly the 418th FBS) at Clark AB, Philippines. The unit subsequently became the 510th

FBS with the 405th FBW. The squadron's markings comprised a red fin band, edged in white, with white chevron superimposed, with a white-edged red nose band.
72nd Tactical Fighter Squadron: assigned 1 July 1958 – 9 April 1959
418th Fighter Bomber Squadron: assigned May 1958 – 30 June 1958

6585th Test Group
The 6585th Test Group supported activities at the White Sands missile range, and included Det 1 of the 82nd Tactical Aerial Targets Squadron from Tyndall.

7272nd Flying Training Wing
The 7272nd FTW supported training

F-100C, 436th FDS/479th FDW, first unit with F-100A and F-100C

detachments by USAFE combat wings to use the ranges in Libya. It was based at Wheelus AFB, Libya, from January 1958 until 1965. Its F-100 target tugs wore red and yellow markings originally, but these were replaced by dark blue bands on the tail and around the nose, with white arrows superimposed.
7235th Support Squadron: assigned 1959 – January 1970

7499th Support Group
The 7499th SG parented the 7407th Support Squadron with RF-100As. They were replaced by six RB-57Fs from 9 June 1959, which were detached from the 4080th SRW.
7407th Support Squadron: assigned May 1955 – 1 July 1958

AIR NATIONAL GUARD

102nd TFG, Massachusetts ANG
The 101st TFS briefly operated the F-100D from Logan Airport between May 1971 and the spring of 1972, when F-106s were received.
101st Tactical Fighter Squadron: assigned June 1971 – June 1972

103rd TFG, Connecticut ANG
The 118th TFS converted from F-86Hs to F-100As during the summer of 1960, at Bradley Field, re-designating as the 118th FIS on 1 September 1960 and becoming ADC-gained. F-100As gave way to F-102As in January 1966, but F-100Ds were received in June 1971, when the squadron became the TAC-gained 118th TFS again. Early aircraft wore a coloured nose band, edged in white, but markings on the F-100D were limited to a 'CT' tailcode.
118th Tactical Fighter Squadron: assigned to the 103rd TFG October 1959 – September 1960, to the 103rd FIG September 1960 – January 1966, and to the 103rd TFG April 1971 – mid-1979

104th TFG, Massachusetts ANG
The 131st TFS converted from F-84Fs to F-100Ds in June 1971, at Barnes Field, and to the A-10A in July 1979. These aircraft wore a red/white/red fin stripe, and sometimes used 'MA' codes.
131st Tactical Fighter Squadron: assigned June 1971 – 1979

107th TFG, New York ANG
At Niagara Falls MAP the 136th TFS's F-86Hs gave way to F-100Cs in August 1960. The squadron was called to active duty between 1 October 1961 – 24 August 1962 during the Berlin Crisis (but remained at Niagara Falls MAP), and then again between 26 January 1968 – 11 June 1969 during the *Pueblo* Crisis, deploying to Tuy Hoa, where it became known as 'Rocky's Raiders', and wore the tailcode 'SG'.
136th Tactical Fighter Squadron: assigned to the 107th TFG 1960 – 1971, and to the 31st TFW June 1968 – May 1969

113th TFG, DC ANG
The 121st TFS converted from F-86Hs

to F-100Cs in mid-1960, becoming TAC-gained in July. The unit was called to active duty 1 October 1961 – 24 August 1962 during the Berlin Crisis, but remained at Andrews AFB. The squadron was called to active duty again between 26 January 1968 – 18 June 1969 during the *Pueblo* Crisis, forming part of the F-100 CCTW at Myrtle Beach using the 'XB' tailcode. F-100Cs gave way to F-105s in July 1971. Early aircraft wore a dark fin stripe containing five white stars on natural metal aircraft.
121st Tactical Fighter Squadron: assigned to the 113th TFG mid-1960 – 1971, and to the 113th TFW March 1968 – June 1969

114th TFG, South Dakota ANG
The 175th TFS converted from the F-102 to the F-100D at Sioux Falls in the spring of 1970. These remained in use until 1977 when they gave way to A-7Ds. The squadron's F-100s often wore a stylised white line drawing of a wolf's head on the fin cap.
175th Tactical Fighter Squadron: assigned to the 114th TFG May 1970 – 1977

116th TFG, Georgia ANG
The 128th Military Airlift Squadron at Dobbins AFB gained a new aircraft type and a new role when it converted from the C-124C Globemaster to the F-100D, becoming the 128th TFS in April 1973. The F-100s gave way to F-105s in late 1979. They wore a yellow fin cap, with a blue fin stripe lower on the fin.
128th Tactical Fighter Squadron: assigned to the 116th TFG April 1973 – mid 1979

121st TFG, Ohio ANG
The 166th TFS traded F-84Fs for F-100Cs at Lockbourne AFB during August 1962. The squadron was called to active duty 26 January 1968 – 18 June 1969 during the *Pueblo* Crisis, deploying to Kunsan, where it wore the 'BP' tailcode, and red colours. The squadron gained F-100Ds in November 1971 and converted to the A-7 in December 1974.
166th Tactical Fighter Squadron: assigned to the 121st TFG August 1962 – July 1968 and June

1969 – 1974, and to the 354th TFW at Kunsan, 5 July 1968 – 10 June 1969

122nd TFG, Indiana ANG
F-84Fs gave way to F-100Ds in June 1971. The 122nd TFG disbanded on 9 December 1974, and the F-100s were assigned directly to the 122nd TFW. The squadron converted to the F-4Cs in early 1979. The aircraft wore a yellow fin band, edged in white.
163rd Tactical Fighter Squadron: assigned to the 122nd TFG June 1971 – 1979

127th TFG, Michigan ANG
RF-101As gave way to F-100Ds with the Selfridge-based 107th TFS in the summer of 1972. They were replaced by A-7Ds in the summer of 1978. The squadron's F-100s wore a thin red fin band with 'MICHIGAN' superimposed in white.
107th Tactical Fighter Squadron: assigned to the 127th TFG June 1972 – October 1978

131st TFG, Missouri ANG
The 110th TFS replaced its F-84Fs with F-100Cs at Lambert Field in August 1962, and replaced these with F-100Ds in December 1971. The F-100 gave way to the Phantom in early 1979. The unit's Super Sabres were decorated with a thin red fin band, thinly outlined in white, with 'Missouri' superimposed in white.
110th Tactical Fighter Squadron: assigned to the 131st TFG fall 1962 – 1979

132nd TFG, Iowa ANG
The 124th TFS converted from F-84Fs to F-100Cs in April 1971, at Des Moines MAP, and then gained F-100Ds in 1975, replacing what were the ANG's last C-models. The unit converted to the A-7D in January 1977.
124th Tactical Fighter Squadron: assigned to the 132nd TFG April 1971 – July 1978

138th TFG, Oklahoma ANG
The 125th ATS relinquished its C-124Cs in January 1973, gaining F-100Ds and becoming the 125th TFS. The Tulsa-based unit flew these until July 1978, when it converted to the A-7. The unit's F-100s wore a red fin band, thinly outlined in white, with 'Oklahoma' superimposed in white.
125th Tactical Fighter Squadron: assigned to the 138th TFG January 1973 – July 1978

140th TFG, Colorado ANG
The 120th TFS exchanged F-86Ls for F-100Cs on 1 January 1961, switching from ADC to TAC. The unit was called to active duty on 1 October 1961 during the Berlin Crisis, but remained at Buckley ANGB until stood down on 24 August 1962. The unit was called to active duty again between 26 January 1968 – 30 April 1969 during the *Pueblo* Crisis, deploying to Phan Rang and flying 5,905 combat sorties. The unit returned to state control on 30 April 1969 and converted to F-100Ds in October 1971. These gave way to A-7s in April 1974. Its early aircraft wore a

F-100C, 121st TFS/113th TFG, District of Columbia ANG, Andrews AFB, April 1963

F-100D, 122nd TFS/159th TFG, Louisiana ANG – three F-4 'kill' markings

F-100D/Fs, 113th TFS/181st TFG, Indiana ANG, Hulman Field – last F-100 operator

large chevron on the tailfin, while camouflaged aircraft had a red mountain lion's head on nose gear door and sometimes on the tailfin in Vietnam.

120th Tactical Fighter Squadron: assigned to the 140th TFG January 1961 – April 1974, and to the 35th TFW at Phu Cat April 1968 – April 1969, tailcode 'VS'

149th TFG, Texas ANG
The 182nd TFS traded F-84Fs for F-100Ds in the spring of 1971, at Kelly AFB. These were used until spring 1979, when the unit converted to the F-4C. The squadron's Super Sabres wore a thin red fin band, thinly outlined in white, with 'TEXAS' superimposed in white.

182nd Tactical Fighter Squadron: assigned to the 149th TFG April 1971 – mid-1979

150th TFG, New Mexico ANG
Ancient F-80Cs gave way to F-100As with the 188th FIS at Kirtland AFB in April 1958. The unit became TAC-gained in 1960, and converted to F-100Cs in spring 1964. The squadron was called to active duty 26 January 1968 – 4 June 1969 during the *Pueblo* Crisis, deploying to Tuy Hoa as the 'Enchilada Air Force'. Returning to Kirtland, the 188th TFS finally converted to the A-7 in late 1973. Camouflaged aircraft wore a small yellow roadrunner on the fin, together with a Distinguished Unit Citation ribbon. Natural metal and ADC grey aircraft carried yellow-edged black chevrons on the fin, and a yellow-edged black flash on the fuselage. In Vietnam the squadron used the tailcode 'SK'.

188th Tactical Fighter Squadron: assigned to the 150th FIG/TFG April 1958 – June 1968 and May 1969 – 1973, and to the 31st TFW June 1968 – May 1969

159th TFG, Louisiana ANG
At NAS New Orleans, the 122nd TFS converted from F-102s to F-100Ds in late 1970, and used these until F-4Cs arrived in April 1979.

122nd Tactical Fighter Squadron: assigned to the 159th TFG July 1970 – April 1979

162nd TFG, Arizona ANG
The group's 152nd FIS converted from the F-84F to the F-100A in May 1958, and transitioned to the F-102A from February 1966. The F-102 was replaced by the F-100C in 1969, when the 152nd became a training unit. F-100Ds arrived in June 1972. The F-100 was phased out in March 1978. Natural metal aircraft had a yellow fin chevron and intake band, both thinly outlined in black.

152nd Tactical Fighter Squadron: assigned to the 162nd FIG at Tucson IAP from mid 1958 – 1964, and to the 162nd TFTG September 1969 – 1978, as the 152nd TFTS

177th TFG, New Jersey ANG
At Atlantic City, the 119th TFS converted from F-86Hs to F-100Cs in September 1965. The unit was called to active duty 26 January 1968 – 17 June 1969 during the *Pueblo* Crisis, going to Myrtle Beach to form part of the F-100 CCTW there, using the 'XA' tailcode. The unit began conversion to the F-105 in June 1970.

119th Tactical Fighter Squadron: assigned to the 177th TFG 1964 – June 1970, and to the 113th TFW March 1968 – June 1969

178th TFG, Ohio ANG
The 162nd TFS at Springfield traded F-84Fs for F-100Ds in April 1970. They were replaced by A-7Ds in April 1978. The aircraft wore a red or green fin band, thinly outlined in white, with 'Ohio' superimposed in white.

162nd Tactical Fighter Squadron: assigned to the 178th TFG April 1970 – 1977

179th TFG, Ohio ANG
The F-84F-equipped 164th TFS converted to F-100Ds in February 1972, at Mansfield-Lahm airport. The squadron converted to the C-130B Hercules during the winter of 1975. The unit's F-100s wore a white-edged yellow tail band.

164th Tactical Fighter Squadron: assigned to the 179th TFG February 1972 – 1975

180th TFG, Ohio ANG
The 112th TFS at Toledo Express Airport swapped its F-84Fs for F-100Ds in October 1970, and flew these until late 1979, when it converted to the A-7. The squadron's Super Sabres wore a black and white checkerboard fin band, thinly edged in yellow.

112th Tactical Fighter Squadron: assigned to the 180th TFG October 1970 – 1979

181st TFG, Indiana ANG
The 113th converted from RF-84Fs to F-100Ds in September 1971, at Hulman Field, Terre Haute, but converted to the F-4C in the summer of 1979. Its aircraft had a fin cap divided into red, white and blue horizontal bands, with 'Indiana' superimposed on the white stripe.

113th Tactical Fighter Squadron: assigned to

the 181st TFG September 1971 – November 1979

184th TFG, Kansas ANG
The 127th TFS converted from the F-86L to the F-100C in April 1961, at McConnell. The unit was called to active duty 26 January 1968 – 18 June 1969 during the *Pueblo* Crisis, deploying to Kunsan where they used 'BO' codes. The squadron converted to F-100Ds in March 1971, and then to F-4D Phantoms in October 1979.

127th Tactical Fighter Squadron: assigned to the 184th TFG April 1961 – March 1971 and to the 354th TFW at Kunsan, 5 July 1968 – 10 June 1969

185th TFG, Iowa ANG
The 174th converted from the RF-84F to the F-100C during the summer of 1961, at Sioux City MAP. The squadron was called to active duty 26 January 1968 – 28 May 1969 during the *Pueblo* Crisis, and deployed to Phu Cat. The squadron converted to the F-100D in June 1974, and then to the A-7 in December 1976. The squadron's early aircraft wore a yellow chevron on the fin, a curved flash on the fuselage and a yellow nose. In Vietnam the unit used the tailcode 'HA'.

174th Tactical Fighter Squadron: assigned to the 185th TFG June 1961 – 1968, and 1969 – July 1977 and to the 37th TFW May 1968 – May 1969

188th TFG, Arkansas ANG
The 184th TFS converted from the RF-101C to the F-100D in June 1972, and retained the Super Sabre until 1979, when it converted to the F-4 Phantom. The aircraft carried a red fin band, thinly outlined in white, with 'ARKANSAS' superimposed in white.

184th Tactical Fighter Squadron: assigned to the 188th TFG June 1972 – mid-1979

MISCELLANEOUS UNITS

A number of units used small numbers of F-100s in support, test and training roles. These units included:

Armament Development Test Center (ADTC), previously the Air Proving Ground Command
Air Force Logistics Command (AFLC) at McClellan AFB (Sacramento Air Materiel Area/SMAMA)
Air Force Flight Test Center (AFFTC), Edwards AFB
Air Force Special Weapons Center (AFSWC), Kirtland AFB
Aerospace Medical Division (AMD) at Brooks and then Kelly AFBs
Air Research and Development Command (ARDC)
NACA and NASA – mostly at Ames (Moffett) and Dryden (Edwards)
Wright Air Development Center (WADC)
1708th Ferrying Wing, MATS, which trained ferry pilots for the F-100
4925th OMS at Kirtland AFB
4758th DSES at Holloman AFB, which provided target facilities for ADC units and the White Sands missile range, until replaced in 1970 by an element of the New Mexico ANG
US Army operated QF-100s at Holloman AFB in support of missile activities at nearby White Sands

F-100D, Sacramento Air Material Area, McClellan AFB, California

F-100F, Air Force Special Weapons Center, Kirtland AFB, New Mexico.

QF-100D, US Army/FSI, Holloman AFB, New Mexico for HAWK SAM trials

OVERSEAS OPERATORS

DENMARK – KONGELIGE DANSKE FLVEVÅBNET

Danish aircraft wore colourful markings until they were camouflaged, when large areas of colour gave way to small and discreet unit badges. Danish F-100s wore serials consisting of the prefix G- or GT- (Fs) followed by the last three numerals of the original USAF serial.

Esk 725: operated F-100s from Karup from April 1961 to September 1970, when the squadron converted to the F35 Draken.
Esk 727: operated F-100s from Karup from May 1959 to April 1974, then from Skrydstrup until conversion to the F-16 in April 1981. Esk 727's aircraft initially had a red nose chevron, thinly outlined in black, and had a red RWR antenna on the fin trailing edge.
Esk 730: operated F-100s from Skrydstrup from July 1961 to August 1982. Esk 730's aircraft

originally had a dark green nose, edged with white and dark blue diagonal bands, and had green/white/green stripes on the RWR antenna.

Denmark's F-100s were delivered from May 1959, and initially retained a natural metal finish, with squadron markings applied on the fin. This aircraft also wears the red nose flash of Eskadrille 727.

FRANCE – ARMÉE DE L'AIR

3ème Escadre de Chasse
EC 1/3 'Navarre': F-100s replaced F-84Fs in January 1959 at Reims. Redeployed to Lahr 1961 – 66, transitioning to the Mirage III. Returned to Nancy-Ochey September 1967. Codes '3-IA' to '3-IZ'.
EC 2/3 'Champagne': F-100s replaced F-84Fs in January 1959 at Reims. Redeployed to Lahr 1961 – 66, transitioning to the Mirage III. Returned to Nancy-Ochey September 1967. Codes '3-JA' to '3-JZ'.

11ème Escadre de Chasse
EC 1/11 'Roussillon': F-100s replaced F-84Fs and Gs in May 1958 at Luxeuil-St Sauveur. Redeployed to Bremgarten June 1961 – September 1967. Returned to France (Toul-Rosières) September 1967. Converted to Jaguar October 1975. Codes '11-EA' to '11-EZ'

EC 2/11 'Vosges': F-100s replaced F-84Fs and Gs in May 1958 at Luxeuil-St Sauveur. Redeployed to Bremgarten June 1961 – September 1967. Returned to France (Toul-Rosières) September 1967. Converted to Jaguar late 1976. Codes '11-MA' to '11-MZ'.
EC 3/11 'Corse': formed at Bremgarten in April 1966, returning to France (Colmar and Toul) in late 1967. Became the F-100 conversion training unit. Converted to Jaguar late 1976. Codes '11-RA' to '11-RX'.
EC 4/11 'Jura': activated at Djibouti 1 January 1973. Ended F-100 operations 12 December 1978. Aircraft carried large sharkmouth from March 1978. Codes '11-YA' to '11-YZ'

Esc. de Convoyage EC 070
This escadrille was responsible for ferrying AdA aircraft, and transported the remaining F-100s to RAF Sculthorpe in 1977-78. Codes 'MA' to 'MZ'.

France's Super Sabres had two 'lives': as NATO-controlled nuclear strikers based in Germany, and as nationally-controlled conventional fighter-bombers in France.

TAIWAN – REPUBLIC OF CHINA AIR FORCE

All Taiwanese Super Sabres (except a handful of camouflaged jets) wore the RoCAF's standard blue and white rudder stripes, and most also wore colourful squadron markings. Hsinchu aircraft usually wore the 2nd FBW badge on their tailfins. Taiwanese F-100s wore sequential four-digit serials.

2nd FBW
The 2nd Fighter Bomber Wing at Hsinchu had three F-100 units.
41st Fighter Bomber Squadron: formerly the 17th FBS from Chiayi. Assigned 1959 – 1983. The squadron's F-100s had a red lightning flash on the nose. Transitioned to the F-104G
42nd Fighter Bomber Squadron: assigned 1959 – 1984. Its aircraft had blue nose markings like those of the 23rd FBS. Transitioned to F-104G 1983-1984
48th Fighter Bomber Squadron: assigned 1959 – 5 September 1984. Red, white and blue 'Skyblazer' type nose marking. Last Taiwanese F-100 operator. Transitioned to the F-104G

4th FBW
The 4th FBW at Chiayi had a maximum strength of three F-100 units, one transferring to Hsinchu after forming.
17th Fighter Bomber Squadron: transferred to Hsinchu and became the 41st FBS
21st Fighter Bomber Squadron: assigned 1960 – 1978. 21st FBS aircraft wore a red fin chevron and nose markings. Transitioned to the F-5E
22nd Fighter Bomber Squadron: assigned 1960 – 1978. Squadron had a yellow fin chevron and nose markings. Transitioned to the F-5E
23rd Fighter Bomber Squadron: assigned 1960 – 1979. Markings comprised a blue fin chevron and nose markings. Transitioned to the F-5E

5th/401st Tactical Combined Wing
The 5th Wing at Taoyuan parented the four RF-100A Slick Chick reconnaissance aircraft of the 4th Squadron.

This F-100A is preserved in 2nd TFW markings

4th Reconnaissance Squadron: assigned 1 January 1959 – December 1960. No squadron markings were carried

TURKEY – TÜRK HAVA KUVVETLERI

1nci Ana Jet Ussu
Between 1958 and 1979 the First Main Jet Base at Eskisehir included three F-100 squadrons.
111 Filo 'Panter' (Panther): assigned November 1958 – 1979. 111 Filo aircraft carried a black panther nose badge and coloured bands around the nose
112 Filo 'Seytan' (Devil): assigned 1962 – 1965 and 1969 – 1974.
113 Filo 'Isik' (Light): assigned 1959 – 1972, became 171 Filo. 113 Filo aircraft carried a black skull and crossbones superimposed on a black edged yellow lightning flash on nose, and had a black edged yellow flash on the fin

3ncu Ana Jet Ussu
The 3rd Main Jet Air Base at Konya had two F-100 squadrons.
131 Filo 'Ejder' (Dragon): assigned 1974 – 1978
132 Filo 'Hancer' (Dagger): assigned 1974 – 1987

7nci Ana Jet Ussu
The 7th Main Jet Air Base at Malatya had two F-100 squadrons.
171 Filo: assigned 1972 – 1977, ex 113 Filo
172 Filo: assigned 1972 – 1979, ex 182 Filo.

8nci Ana Jet Ussu
The 8th Main Jet Air Base at Diyarbakir had two F-100 squadrons.

181 Filo 'Pars' (Leopard): assigned 1972 – 1986
112 Filo 'Atmaca' (Sparrowhawk): assigned 1969 – 1986

Turkey's F-100s mostly wore standard SEA camouflage. The national insignia changed from this square to a roundel.

Conceived as a long-range fighter to accompany Strategic Air Command bombers, the F-88 never reached production status, yet did provide the basis for the later F-101 Voodoo. This aircraft was also initially designed as a strategic fighter, yet it saw service in three other major roles: nuclear bomber, tactical reconnaissance platform and defender of North American airspace. In the latter tasking, the Voodoo survived into the 1980s in the hands of the Canadians. Difficult to fly and maintain, the Voodoo's sleek looks and blistering performance were nevertheless guaranteed to generate excitement.

The McDonnell F-101 Voodoo evoked superlatives. It was bigger, faster. Pilots who took the RF-101C to Hanoi flew higher and faster than anything around them, challenged formidable air defences, and succeeded at high-risk, daytime combat reconnaissance. Crew chiefs who fussed over the F-101B interceptor assailed by Arctic winds on an icy, outdoor flight line cursed the aircraft for being nearly impossible to work on, but became

excited when both afterburners were lit and the huge Voodoo was hurtling skyward. The F-101 Voodoo was also, arguably, the most dangerous, difficult-to-fly aircraft ever admitted into squadron service. From the beginning of its career to the end, the Voodoo had a reputation for forgiving no one, ever.

Coming from a manufacturer which excelled with Banshee and Phantom fighters, the Voodoo gave new meaning to the notion of

Although it was unsuccessful, the XF-88 was instrumental in establishing McDonnell as a major supplier of fighters to the Air Force. Here the very first Voodoo is parked outside the St Louis works – later to become the birthplace of the world-beating F-4 Phantom and F-15 Eagle. The XF-88 exhibited state-of-the-art features for a late 1940s jet fighter, such as lateral wingroot-mounted intakes, bulbous fuselage and wings swept at 35°. Speed performance was poor: the two engines did not provide nearly enough power.

McDonnell F-88/F-101 Voodoo Variant Briefing

Main picture: **Of the weapons associated with the F-101, the most impressive was the AIR-2 Genie. Often called a missile, it was unguided and was thus more correctly a rocket. Its mission was to destroy enemy aircraft, especially incoming bombers, and it made up for its lack of guidance by way of a 1.5-kT yield nuclear warhead. This was exploded in the general proximity of the bombers, the aim being to place it in the centre of a formation. The explosion and resulting shock waves were lethal over a wide radius, necessitating immediate evasive action by the F-101 once the Genie was on its way.**

brute force. Conceived as a 'penetration fighter', a post-war term for the escort function in which P-51 Mustangs excelled over Berlin, the Voodoo became not just a tactical reconnaissance collector and long-range strategic interceptor, but also an atomic bomber, supersonic propeller testbed, and crew trainer. For all that, Voodoo's imprint on our world was perhaps less than it might have been. The aircraft is remembered today with respect but without universal fondness.

Only the RF-101C 'recce' version got into combat, consistently flying the fastest combat sorties ever flown (with the special exception of the SR-71 Blackbird), daily challenging North Vietnam's missiles, MiGs and Triple-A at speeds greater than those of the F-4, F-8 or F-105. In its interceptor version, the Voodoo wore both 'stars and bars' and Canada's maple leaf, and evolved with difficulty into an exceedingly

potent weapon. The interceptor never won the accolades men bestowed on the prettier, more manoeuvrable (and slightly later) Convair F-106A Delta Dart. Furthermore, the interceptor Voodoo was worth having only after protracted difficulties with its fire-control and weapons systems were resolved.

In all of its versions, the Voodoo had a pitch-up problem caused by the manner in which air flowed over its wings and under its high tail.

There was no prototype of the second-generation Voodoo as such, but this F-101A (53-2418) was the first of the production aircraft and served as an evaluation airframe along with other early machines. Weapon systems were not carried initially, and the nose mounted a long air data probe for the duration of the aerodynamic trials. Here it is seen during its 29 September 1954 first flight from Edwards AFB, with Robert Little at the controls. On this sortie the F-101 became the first aircraft type to achieve supersonic flight on its maiden voyage.

The tendency to jerk into a nose-high attitude, unexpectedly and at the worst of times, killed several pilots, among them air ace Major Lonnie Moore who repeatedly prevailed over the MiG-15 in Korea but, like many, could not win out over the F-101 Voodoo in America. A pitch inhibitor, or 'stick knocker', installed in mid-life, did little to resolve the problem.

We have to remember that the F-101 Voodoo was "not just big", as one pilot described it, "but seriously big." An F-101B,

From 1961 the CF-101 provided Canada's main contribution to NORAD's defensive shield. The survivors of the initial batch of 66 were swapped for a second similarly-sized batch in 1971, and these veterans served until replacement by the CF-188 in 1984/85.

fully-armed, standing alert with a load of fuel tanks topped off, ready to launch against Soviet bombers streaming down from the polar north, swayed the scales at 54,650 lb (24790 kg). Its twin J57 turbojet engines on full afterburner kicked back a combined thrust of over 32,000 lb (142.34 kN), a figure without precedent. With an internal fuel capacity of 2,341 US gal (8862 litres), the Voodoo held five times the 435 US gal (1647 litres) of an F-84D Thunderjet. The fuselage of an F-101B with its length of 71 ft 1 in (22.02 m) was almost 10 ft (2 m) longer than a DC-3 transport. Designer Edward M. ('Bud') Flesh and others who created the F-88 and F-101 series at the McDonnell Aircraft Company in St Louis were thinking big

The F-101's first true mission was a nuclear bomber with the 81st TFW (an aircraft of the 92nd TFS being depicted here). The single nuclear weapon was usually released in a LABS Immelmann, the bomb being lobbed upwards to about 22,000 ft (6705 m), thus giving the Voodoo time to escape. From about 1963 the LADD (low-angle drogue delivery) supplanted the LABS profile, using parachute-retarded weapons.

from the start. They had no choice because their aircraft was conceived for the purpose of accompanying B-36 bombers deep into Soviet territory.

For James S. McDonnell, a pioneer in both aviation and business, the F-101 marked a turning point because it was his company's first sale to the US Air Force.   **Robert F. Dorr**

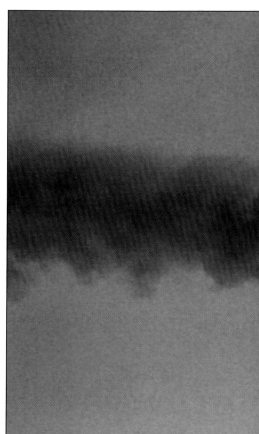

Above: Photographed from its wingman, an RF-101C makes a high-altitude dash across the North Vietnamese MiG base at Kep. The RF-101C, popularly called the 'Long Bird', was the only Voodoo variant to see combat.

Right: Gear down and brakes out, an F-101B of the 29th FIS crosses the Missouri as it prepares to land at its base at Malmstrom AFB, Montana.

Below: The Canadian government officially neither confirmed nor denied the existence of nuclear weapons in its inventory, but this spectacular Genie shot from a CF-101B during a William Tell exercise certainly proves the capability.

McDonnell F-88/F-101 Voodoo Variants

XP-88

On 1 April 1946, McDonnell Aircraft Company in St Louis, Missouri began design work on the company's Model 36 to meet a US Air Force requirement for a 'penetration fighter' to escort long-range bombers to their targets. The US Army Air Forces were planning to fight as they had during World War II, with fighters accompanying bombers and guarding them deep inside enemy territory. Early efforts to develop escort

fighters combining the speed of jet propulsion with the endurance of piston-engined warplanes, like the Consolidated Vultee XP-81 with a turboprop engine in the nose and turbojet in the tail, produced disappointing results. Consequently, in 1946, the USAAF levied a requirement for a pure-jet fighter with a combat radius of 900 miles (1450 km) and performance over the target good enough to cope with anticipated enemy opposition. USAAF planners knew nothing of the MiG-15, which made its first flight on 30 December 1947, but realised the Soviets were developing jet-propelled

aircraft. They anticipated serious air opposition.

On 20 June 1946, the USAAF awarded McDonnell a contract for two XP-88 pursuit aircraft (serial nos 46-525/526). In September 1946, before the P-88 design was finalised, McDonnell's tentative concept looked like the ship which finally emerged but had a butterfly, or Vee-shaped tail.

The XP-88 was first submitted to the US Air Force (which became a service branch on 17 September 1947) with the butterfly tail. The objective was to reduce the number and improve the nature of tail intersections

where compressibility effects were likely to give trouble. Early in wind tunnel tests, however, engineers encountered adverse rolling moments due to rudder action and insufficient longitudinal stability near the stall. A conventional tail was tested in the tunnel and was chosen when found largely free of aerodynamic faults. The V-tail remained in vogue for some years (successful on the Beech Bonanza, it was tested on the Republic XF-91), but McDonnell engineers dropped it early in their design work.

XF-88

On 1 July 1948, nine months after gaining its independence, the US Air Force changed its 'P' for pursuit designation to 'F' for fighter. The first of two McDonnell fighters then nearing completion was redesignated XF-88. The second became the XF-88A and is described separately. The nickname 'Voodoo', consistent with McDonnell's tradition of spirit-like apparitions, was given to the F-88 series.

Rolled out on 11 August 1948, the single-seat XF-88 (48-525) was a low/mid-wing aircraft characterised by 35° swept wings and tail surfaces and a lengthy fuselage to house fuel for its penetration mission. Powerplant was two 3,000-lb (13.35-kN) thrust Westinghouse XJ34-WE-13 turbojet engines mounted in the lower centre fuselage.

McDonnell chief test pilot Robert M. Edholm made the first flight of the XF-88 on 20 October 1948 at Muroc Dry Lake, California. Phase II flight tests were carried out 15-25 March 1949. Tests showed that the XF-88 was disappointingly slow, and led to the decision to add afterburning to the second Voodoo built, which became the XF-88A (below). The sole XF-88 was itself brought up to XF-88A standard with 52-in (130-cm) afterburners. Later, this ship was converted to become the XF-88B turboprop testbed.

Early test-flying at Lambert Field and Muroc Dry Lake revealed that, despite its ultra-thin swept wing, the XF-88 Voodoo was too slow for its intended mission. This was largely due to the low power rating of the engines and the bulky fuselage.

After exhaustive studies into a butterfly tail, the XF-88 finally emerged with a standard tail unit, albeit with the tailplane held part way up the fin to keep it in undisturbed airflow. The wing-sweep of 35° was largely determined by the result of German wartime research, most of which involved data at this setting. Any less was considered at the time as being not worth the effort: any more would be too risky. Originally McDonnell planned the F-88 with engines carried in the wingroots, but this proved unfeasible, and they were located in the lower fuselage where they could be easily reached and dropped out for maintenance. The fuselage was necessarily long and bulky to accommodate sufficient fuel for the escort fighter mission.

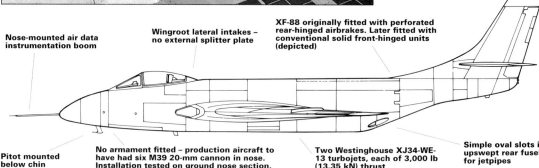

Nose-mounted air data instrumentation boom

Wingroot lateral intakes – no external splitter plate

XF-88 originally fitted with perforated rear-hinged airbrakes. Later fitted with conventional solid front-hinged units (depicted)

Pitot mounted below chin

No armament fitted – production aircraft to have had six M39 20-mm cannon in nose. Installation tested on ground nose section.

Two Westinghouse XJ34-WE-13 turbojets, each of 3,000 lb (13.35 kN) thrust

Simple oval slots in upswept rear fuselage for jetpipes

XF-88A

he second of two 'penetration fighter'
rototypes from McDonnell, the XF-88A (46-
26) made its first flight at St Louis on 26
pril 1949. This fighter was identical to the
arlier XF-88 except that it was equipped
vith afterburners for improved J34-WE-22
ngines. In its 318-hour test flight
rogramme, the XF-88A exceeded Mach 1
n dives and otherwise performed well, but
he programme was curtailed by funding
roblems. This was a major disappointment,
ecause the XF-88A was the winner in a
igorous 'penetration fighter' competition
vith the Lockheed XF-90 and North
merican YF-93A (F-86C).
This original XF-88A ended up at Langley
\FB, Virginia where it was used for parts for
he turboprop XF-88B, described separately.
Both aircraft in the F-88 series were
ventually scrapped at Langley. The original
F-88A was turned over to base salvage on
July 1958. The designation XF-88A also
pplies to the first XF-88 when it was
elatedly modified with afterburners, and
efore it was further modified to become
he XF-88B.
KF-88A serial: 48-526

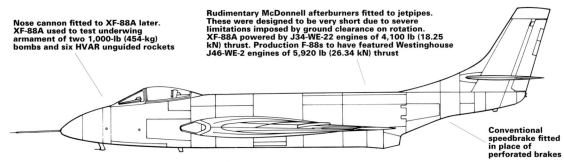

Nose cannon fitted to XF-88A later.
XF-88A used to test underwing
armament of two 1,000-lb (454-kg)
bombs and six HVAR unguided rockets

Rudimentary McDonnell afterburners fitted to jetpipes.
These were designed to be very short due to severe
limitations imposed by ground clearance on rotation.
XF-88A powered by J34-WE-22 engines of 4,100 lb (18.25
kN) thrust. Production F-88s to have featured Westinghouse
J46-WE-2 engines of 5,920 lb (26.34 kN) thrust

Conventional
speedbrake fitted
in place of
perforated brakes

*In this configuration the XF-88A was
representative of the intended
production fighter, lacking the nose
instrumentation boom and featuring
the cannon and afterburners. The
first machine was also brought up to
a similar standard, and both set
impressive performance figures,
including a level speed some 20 mph
faster than the contemporary
absolute speed record (held by a
Sabre).*

XF-88B

he XF-88B was the XF-88 (the first
irframe, which meanwhile had been
rought up to XF-88A standard) modified to
ecome a research testbed for high-speed
ropellers. The USAF ordered this
nodification on 25 July 1949. McDonnell
onverted the aircraft between August and
Jovember 1952. The XF-88B 'tri-motor' first
ew on 14 April 1953.
A 2,500-shp (1875-kW) Allison XT38, or
ompany Model 501 F-1, turboprop engine
vas installed in the nose. Fuel tanks in the
orward fuselage were removed, leaving
bout 300 US gal (1135 litres) for the two
34 turbojet engines with afterburners, plus
he turboprop, making for very short flights.
he engine installation also required that the
ose landing gear be mounted about 18 in
45 cm) off centre, but this did not affect
round handling. Because the XT38's
urbine was directly behind the pilot's seat,
rmour plate was installed under the seat.
Propeller gearbox ratios provided three
rop speeds of 1,700, 3,600, and 6,000 rpm.
he design was be compatible with
ropellers of 4, 7 and 10 ft (1.2, 2.1 and 3.0
n). With the largest of these, ground
learance was a paltry 6.7 in (17 cm). The
F-88B was designed to take off with the
ropeller feathered and in an 'X' position to
eep it from hitting the ground.
The USAF's Air Research and

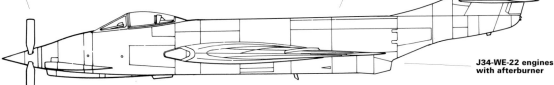

Three supersonic propeller
configurations tested in flight,
consisting of four-bladed
(illustrated), three-bladed and
three-bladed with 'turnip'
spinner. Sensor rigs often carried
either side of nose

Allison XT38 turboprop mounted
in nose, using fuel from main
system. Nosewheel redesigned to
accommodate engine

Standard XF-88 airframe
used (after upgrading to
XF-88A configuration with
standard airbrakes and
afterburner

J34-WE-22 engines
with afterburner

Development Command (ARDC) embarked
on tests of the XF-88B in early 1953 in
collaboration with the US Navy's Bureau of
Aeronautics and the National Advisory
Committee for Aeronautics. The XF-88B's
maiden flight was revealed only months
after it happened. An Air Force pilot first
flew the XF-88B on 23 June 1953 following
16 test flights by McDonnell pilots.
The XF-88B was flown by Capt. John M.
'Fitz' Fitzpatrick to NACA's Langley AFB,
Virginia, facility where it was flown with
various propeller configurations by NACA
project pilots John P. (Jack) Reeder and
William L. Alford. The XF-88B made 43 test
flights.

Fitzpatrick remembers of the XF-88B that
"one obvious test objective was to see how
fast it would go. After accelerating to
maximum speed, about 0.91 Mach, with full
power on both jets and the turboprop, I
would put it into a slight dive. On each flight
I steepened the dive angle. The Mach meter
would get to about 0.96 and stick there. The
McDonnell engineers tried to convince us
that with their airspeed corrections I was
actually supersonic. I may have been, but
we had a rule in the Fighter Section that
unless you actually indicated supersonic
speed, with the accompanying altimeter
jump, you could not claim to have done so."
On 27 June 1953, Fitzpatrick exceeded

Mach 1.0, possibly the first measured
supersonic flight by a propeller aircraft.
The USAF later pursued its fascination for
the supersonic turboprop with the Republic
XF-84H, although it is hard to see why. A test
pilot recalls that, "the propeller lab people
were running our R&D programme." These
aircraft produced so much noise and vibration
that ground crewmen became ill. The XF-88B
contributed significantly to aeronautical
knowledge, but its successor the XF-84H
flew only a few hours. Eventually, the XF-88B
was flown by NACA at Langley Field. It was
turned over to salvage crews to be scrapped
on 16 September 1958.
XF-88B serial: 46-525

**een prior to its first flight in June 1953, the XF-88B stands outside the St
ouis factory, displaying the initial four-bladed propeller installation.**

*The XF-88B often had to be towed to the runway to conserve fuel, as all three
engines ran off the fuel system, which itself was much reduced by the
fitment of the turboprop. After take-off with the propeller feathered, it was
started for about 20 minutes for tests.*

F-88

everal versions of the F-88 Voodoo were
roposed by McDonnell engineers:
Navy F-88: On 30 June 1948, McDonnell
roposed a US Navy carrier-based XP-88
edesignated XF-88 the next day. At the
ame time, the company made changes in
'S Air Force XF-88 to make it more
ttractive for naval operations: these
cluded deleting the 350-US gal (1325-litre)
ingtip tanks integral to the type's design,
vhich were fitted on the second ship (the
F-88A) prior to its first flight, but were

never flown because wind tunnel tests
predicted stall problems. The fuselage nose
forward of the cockpit pressure bulkhead
was equipped with hinges to rotate the
nose section. Wing-fold mechanism and
hinges and a strengthened undercarriage for
carrier operations were added. The US Navy
chose to proceed with the carrier-based
McDonnell XF2D-1 Banshee (later XF2H-1)
instead, neither the first nor the last time
the Navy selected a straight-wing aircraft,
and delayed getting into the swept-wing jet
fighter business.
Two-seater: In 1948, a concept by
McDonnell's H. N. Cole sketched out a

production F-88 with a two-man crew in
tandem seats. No contemporaneous
documents have survived, but it is likely the
manufacturer was still thinking of the escort-
fighter role. The design was not proceeded
with, but a two-seat configuration evolved
separately for the F-101B/F interceptor.
Production USAF version: The
production F-88 was to be powered by two
5,920-lb (26.33-kN) Westinghouse J46-W-2
engines. This is the thrust rating of the
Westinghouse engine without afterburning
(the company's J34, J40, and J46 were
used in a series of aircraft deemed
underpowered). The production warplane

would have had reheat, although its burner
cans still would have been limited to 52 in
(130-cm) in length, lest the aircraft scrape
the ground when rotating on take-off.
RF-88A: Not an official designation, RF-88A
was McDonnell's term for a version with an
interchangeable nose which would enable a
single airframe to be quickly field-modified,
flying as a fighter on one mission, a photo-
gatherer on the next. Studies on an F-88A/
RF-88A which could shift roles on short
notice contributed to the manufacturer's
later work on the YRF-101A.

F-101A

The F-101 was conceived as an escort fighter but the first model to appear, the F-101A, enjoyed only a brief career in different job status as a one-way, single-mission atomic bomber. The F-101A and C fighters were also known as Weapon System WS-105A in Pentagon jargon of the mid-1950s, though the practice of assigning a 'WS' designation to tanks, ships and aircraft lasted only a couple of years.

After determining that the Westinghouse J46 powerplant of the mooted production F-88 offered insufficient thrust, the McDonnell design team under Edward M. ('Bud') Flesh contemplated the Allison J71 as powerplant for the twin-engined F-101. Instead, the aircraft was completed with two Pratt & Whitney J57-P-13 turbojet engines rated at 10,200 lb (45.38 kN) thrust, a figure which rose to 15,000 lb (66.73 kN) with afterburning. The '-13' version of the engine propelled all Voodoo models except the F-101B.

Fed by enlarged and redesigned air intakes in the wingroots, the P&W engines were expected to be more powerful than other engines tried or considered, but also to offer better fuel consumption. Still, the aircraft was designed with its enormous 2,341 US gal (8862-litre) fuel capacity.

Because of delays in the flight test programme, the USAF's goal of having an airframe able to withstand 7.33 g could not be met in initial production machines. Numerous remedies were pondered but in the end the USAF opted, in June 1956, to take delivery of 6.33-g airframes until structurally improved models could be built: the USAF decreed that the 'A' suffix would denote 6.33-g airframes while the 'C' suffix would identify 7.33-g airframes. This distinction was preserved with reconnaissance Voodoos which had an 'RF' prefix.

The F-101A drew heavily on the F-88 design and was a low/mid-wing aircraft with the familiar elongated fuselage and swept wings and tail surfaces. The F-101A fuselage offered sufficient ground clearance for afterburner cans of reasonable length. The aircraft was a remarkable 67 ft 4 ¾ in (20.54 m) long, some 14 ft (4.33 m) more than the F-88, yet its wing span remained unchanged at 39 ft 8 in (12.09 m). Because of an increase in chord, wing area rose from 350 sq ft (32.52 m²) to 368 sq ft (34.19 m), yet there remained a rather flimsy appearance to the wing structure and,

Above: Proudly wearing its name on the nose, the first F-101A rests on Rogers Dry Lake at Edwards AFB. In this early form the derivation from the F-88 is clearly visible.

Right: The sixth F-101A was part of the trials fleet, seen here with a full load of three external tanks. The F-101's armament was reduced to four M39 cannon from the F-88's six.

indirectly, the pitch-up problem which was to plague the aircraft throughout its career. The most obvious change from the earlier F-88 was a higher-mounted horizontal stabiliser, almost a T-tail.

McDonnell test pilot Robert C. Little remembers that, "without question, the F-101A at the time had the highest thrust-to-weight ratio and the highest wing loading of any fighter aircraft ever built." Little made the maiden flight of the first F-101A at Edwards AFB, California on 29 September 1954. It was the first time a new aircraft went supersonic on its debut and Little outran two chase planes, a T-33 trainer and an F-100, which could not keep up even on full afterburner.

Like the F-101C to follow, the F-101A was armed with four 20-mm M39 cannons aimed through a K-19 gunsight. World War II experience had shown that bombers could not campaign effectively against a nation's military and industrial infrastructure unless

accompanied by fighter escort, provided in Europe by the North American P-51 Mustang. Strategic Air Command's chief, General Curtis E. LeMay, remained unconvinced that 'little friends' were needed. Although SAC fielded squadrons of Republic F-84F Thunderstreak and F-84E/G Thunderjet fighters, LeMay never lost his misgivings.

Flight tests and minor modifications to the F-101A resolved an early problem with engine compressor stalls. The F-101 Voodoo's pitch-up problem was never overcome. As described by Brigadier General Robin Olds, who commanded a

Voodoo wing, "It didn't take much for the F-101 to go into pitch-up, even in cruise. Reason: the angle of attack needed to achieve lift at, let's say, 34,000 ft [10350 m] with full flaps, drop tanks and internal fuel was awfully close to the pitch-up stall point where the flow of air over the wings created a downflow over the slab, which the slab could not accommodate." On 10 January 1956, Major Lonnie R. Moore, a Korean War ace with 10 MiG-15 kills, was lost in an F-101A Voodoo pitch-up mishap at Eglin AFB, Florida. Installation of an inhibitor, known to pilots as a 'stick knocker', helped some, but not much. Also never resolved was the problem of retracting the Voodoo's nosewheel, designed to be hoisted forward into the airstream. Beyond a speed of about 90 mph (144 km/h), the wheel would not go up.

SAC operated the F-101A, but for a scant two months. On 1 July 1957, two months after the first deliveries of the F-101A began far behind schedule, the 27th Strategic Fighter Wing at Bergstrom AFB, Texas, was transferred to Tactical Air Command and became the 27th Fighter-Bomber Wing. The wing (consisting of the 481st, 522nd and 523rd FBS) had previously operated the F-84F Thunderstreak. The Voodoo's original mission was forgotten and it was assigned to deliver a centreline nuclear bomb to a target. It was capable of little else and, although designated a 'fighter', would have acquitted itself poorly in any air-to-air duel. Some F-101As later served with the 81st TFW in England (as noted in the separate entry on the F-101C).

An F-101A was assigned to Project

Above: The F-101 was destined to never serve in its intended escort fighter role, but was instead used initially as a nuclear bomber. This trials aircraft carries a test 'shape' for a Mk 7 device on the centreline. During Operation Redwing, an F-101A was flown supersonically through an H-bomb mushroom cloud, although the Voodoo was never used to drop a live weapon.

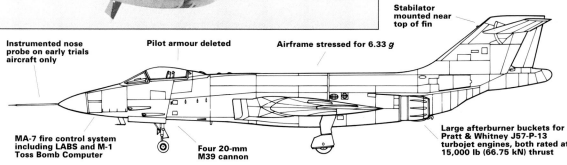

Instrumented nose probe on early trials aircraft only

Pilot armour deleted

Airframe stressed for 6.33 g

Stabilator mounted near top of fin

MA-7 fire control system including LABS and M-1 Toss Bomb Computer

Four 20-mm M39 cannon

Large afterburner buckets for Pratt & Whitney J57-P-13 turbojet engines, both rated at 15,000 lb (66.75 kN) thrust

Above: An F-101A on a pre-delivery flight displays the type's fine lines. An attempt to area-rule the F-101A was made by adding bulges around the afterburner region, but these were unsuccessful.

Right: F-101As served alongside the strengthened C model in both the 27th FBW and the 81st TFW in England. The latter's aircraft were initially marked with a double fin-stripe in the squadron colours.

Redwing, the detonation of hydrogen bombs at Eniwetok Atoll in the Pacific in 1957. By late 1958, however, after less than 18 months of operational service, the 27th FBW began converting to F-100 Super Sabres and F-101As were retired.

NACA acquired two F-101A Voodoos, 53-2434 which was ferried from Edwards to Langley by Jack Reeder on 22 August 1956

and 54-1442 which was taken on charge by NACA on 18 April 1958. Of 77 F-101As accepted by the USAF, 50 reached service and the remainder were used for tests and special projects. Long after their bombing mission was history, 29 F-101As were converted to RF-101G.
F-101A serials: 53-2418/2446, 54-1438/1485.

JF-101A

The sole JF-101A – the 'J' prefix signifying a temporary change in configuration for test purposes — was the ninth F-101A bailed to Pratt & Whitney to evaluate the more powerful J57-P-53 engines chosen for the F-101B interceptor. This required little internal modification, but did require a large extension of the jetpipe to accommodate the much longer afterburner section. The afterburner section of the JF-101A was different to that fitted to production F-101Bs, and incorporated additional air scoops for afterburner cooling.

In Operation Fire Wall on 12 December 1957, Major Adrian Drew of the 27th FBW flew the JF-101A to a world speed record of 1,207.6 mph (1943.43 km/h), taking the record from the British Fairey Delta 2.
JF-101A serial: 53-2426

The 'Fire Wall' aircraft was an engine test-ship, but the chance to shatter the world speed record could not be passed over. After the record run at Edwards, Drew immediately flew to Los Angeles International Airport to receive the DFC from General McCarty, commander of 18th Air Force.

Air data instrumentation boom retained

Airframe of early evaluation F-101A – no armament or weapon system fitted

Extended jetpipe for large afterburner

Undernose pitot

Pratt & Whitney J57-P-53 engines fitted of 16,000 lb (71.2 kN) thrust in afterburner

Air scoop for additional cooling air

NF-101A

The NF-101A – the 'N' prefix indicating a permanent change in configuration for test purposes – was the first F-101A bailed to General Electric as a platform for the J79-GE-1 turbojet engine, apparently in connection with design and development work on McDonnell's F4H-1 Phantom II fleet interceptor for the US Navy. The sole NF-101A eventually ended its life as a ground maintenance trainer at Amarillo AFB, Texas, but apparently was not assigned a GF-101A designation as would have been appropriate.
NF-101A serial: 53-2418.

The J79 Voodoo featured a different extended afterburner section to the JF-101A. This aircraft flew trials in support of the Phantom programme.

McDonnell F-88/F-101 Voodoo Variants

YRF-101A

The YRF-101A was the service-test prototype for the 'recce' Voodoo, also known to the Pentagon was Weapon System WS-105L. The 'YRF' had the same configuration as the 6.33-*g* RF-101A and 7.33-*g* RF-101C which followed.

On 11 October 1953, the USAF contracted McDonnell to rebuild the 16th and 19th F-101As on the production line and complete them as YRF-101As. The USAF considered but rejected a design with an interchangeable nose to carry guns on one sortie and, after a quick ground change, cameras on the next. On 13 January 1954 during a mock-up inspection it was decided to incorporate the bulky KA-1 camera which dictated the long, wedge-shaped configuration of the camera nose. The first YRF-101A flew on 30 June 1955. **YRF-101A serials:** 54-149/150

54-0149 was the first of two YRF-101As converted on the production line and was delivered without cameras. The drag chute was housed in the tailcone behind a hinged cap.

The second YRF-101A was fitted with cameras, a mixture of Fairchild KA-1 and KA-2 units. The large KA-1 which faced obliquely forward through the nose dictated the characteristic chisel-shaped nose.

RF-101A

The RF-101A reconnaissance Voodoo followed the pair of service-test ships. The RF-101A was originally intended for SAC, but years were to pass until the command picked up a dedicated reconnaissance aircraft (the SR-71); in a last-minute change, the RF-101A went to Tactical Air Command. Thirty-five were built.

All reconnaissance versions of the Voodoo could carry up to six cameras. The RF-101A's initial 'fit' consisted of one 12-in focal length Fairchild KA-2 framing camera shooting forward, three 6-in focal length KA-2s in a forward tri-camera station shooting downward, and a pair of larger KA-1s farther astern. A KA-18 strip camera could also be carried. A VF-31 viewfinder allowed the pilot to look through the tri-camera station. The RF-101A offered redundant receptacles for air refuelling (flying boom for KC-97 and KC-135, probe and drogue for the KB-50J).

The RF-101A's nose camera system had a battery-operated elevator to lower the camera to retrieve the film packs. When the cameras were not installed, the forward regions of the wedge nose provided excess stowage space for cargo or personal belongings.

Although the aircraft design was mature, development of camera systems for the RF-101A was still occurring (with the 3241st Test Squadron at Eglin AFB, Florida) when the first aircraft were delivered to the 17th Tactical Reconnaissance Squadron (and, soon afterward, the 18th TRS), 363rd Tactical Reconnaissance Wing, at Shaw Air Force Base, South Carolina on 6 May 1957, replacing the RB-57A/B Canberra.

On 26 November 1957, an RF-101A Voodoo flown by Gustave B. Klatt set a West Coast (Los Angeles to New York to Los Angeles) transcontinental record of six hours 42 minutes 6.9 seconds. On the return leg, Klatt set an east-west record of three hours 34 minutes 8.6 seconds.

RF-101As served briefly with the Air National Guard's 154th TRS (Fort Smith, Arkansas) and 127th TRG (Selfridge ANGB, Michigan).

In Operation Boom Town culminating in October 1959, approximately eight RF-101As were transferred to the Republic of China air force on Formosa (as Americans called Taiwan, then), which used them for reconnaissance operations over the Chinese mainland. Peking claims to have shot down two RF-101As, one of them in March 1965. **RF-101A serials:** 54-1494/1521; 56-155/161

Chisel nose containing camera installation

Retractable refuelling probe in upper nose

Airframe based on F-101A – 6.33 *g* stressing

Pratt & Whitney J57-P-13 engines

Above: The first USAF unit to receive the Voodoo was the 363rd Tactical Reconnaissance Wing at Shaw AFB, which acquired its first RF-101A on 6 May 1957. This aircraft wears the marks of the 18th TRS.

Below: RF-101As were all delivered in a natural metal finish, with a dark anti-glare panel on the upper forward fuselage.

Right: During the mid-1960s several RF-101As were tested with complicated camouflage patterns. These were shelved in favour of the standard T.O. 114 three-tone 'Southeast Asia' camouflage.

Below right: The RF-101 fleet was given a light grey paint scheme in the mid-1960s to protect against corrosion. Many aircraft did not wear unit markings, although this machine wears the TAC badge.

Below: A 363rd TRW F-101A flies by at speed. The 363rd controlled the 432nd TRG which, when elevated to wing status, took over control of the four RF-101A squadrons in 1958.

F-101B

The F-101B (originally, F-109) was the two-seat, long-range interceptor. The aircraft was also known to the manufacturer as the Model 36 AT, and to the USAF as Weapon System 217A. Its forward fuselage had tandem pressurised and air-conditioned cockpits under a single clamshell-style plexiglass canopy. With 479 examples built for the Air Defense Command, or ADC (Aerospace Defense Command after January 1968), the F-101B was the most numerous Voodoo model. It was heavier than single-seat variants and employed larger tyres with a beefed-up undercarriage and bulges in the lower gear doors and undersides of the fuselage to accommodate the tyres. The F-101B was powered by two 10,700-lb (44.47-kN) thrust Pratt & Whitney J57-P-55 turbojet engines, the only Voodoo not using

After service evaluation by the 60th FIS at Otis AFB, the F-101B entered service with 17 Air Defense Command squadrons, all equipped by December 1960. This aircraft flew with the 29th FIS at Malmstrom.

the -13 version of the engine. The F-101B had extended afterburner cans about 24 in (60 cm) longer than those on other Voodoo models. Afterburning raised the thrust rating to about 15,000 lb (66.73 kN).

The F-101B was compatible with the Semi-Automatic Ground Environment (SAGE) system which was the USAF's standard method of ground-controlled intercept in the 1950s. Its Hughes MG-13 fire-control system handled both nuclear and non-nuclear air-to-air rocket missiles and projectiles. Armament initially comprised two Hughes GAR-8 (originally XF-98, later AIM-4) Falcon infra-red air-to-air missiles. The F-101B acquired additional teeth when it was configured in a 1961 modification programme to carry two MB-1 (later AIR-2A) Genie unguided rockets with atomic warheads. The latter was designed to scatter incoming Soviet bomb formations and was tested 'live' on 19 July 1957 when a Genie was fired from an F-89J Scorpion over Yucca Flat, Nevada and detonated a 1.5-kT blast. The F-101B was also configured to carry a number of tow targets, principally the Hayes TDU-25/B. The F-101B's fire control system initially was the Hughes MG-11, replaced in retrofit by the MG-13.

Above: Early F-101Bs were assigned to trials duties and often had metal noses housing test equipment rather than the radar. This aircraft was the fifth B model.

McDonnell F-88/F-101 Voodoo Variants

Above: A common sight on F-101Bs, particularly at Tyndall AFB, was the 'Rummy 8', more formally known as the RMU-8A target system. A centreline mounted pod could reel out a dart target on up to 49,000 ft (14935 m) of cable on 'Super Tow' missions. Different darts could undertake missile or Genie test scoring, and contained radar signature enhancers and infra-red sources.

Above: Another view of 56-0236 portrays the twin carriage of AIR-2A Genies during the early B test programme. At the time the rocket was designated MB-1.

Right: With missile bays empty and airbrakes out, an F-101B of the 437th FIS breaks from the camera. The 437th was based at Oxnard AFB, California.

The F-101B entered service with the 60th Fighter-Interceptor Squadron at Otis AFB, Massachusetts on 5 January 1959 while still testing its compatibility with the SAGE system. Early users of the B model from June 1959 included the 84th (Hamilton AFB, California), 98th (Dover AFB, Delaware) and 322nd (Klamath Falls, Oregon) squadrons, joined before the end of 1959 by the 2nd (Suffolk County, New York), 13th (Glascow AFB, Montana), 49th (Griffiss AFB, New York), and 62nd (K. I. Sawyer AFB, Michigan). By June 1960, a third stage of readiness had been attained when the F-101B reached initial operating capability with the 15th (Davis-Monthan AFB, Arizona), 18th (Grand Forks AFB, North Dakota), 29th (Malmstrom AFB, Montana), 87th (Lockbourne AFB, Ohio), 437th (Oxnard AFB, California), 444th (Charleston AFB, South Carolina) and 445th (Wurtsmith AFB, Michigan). The F-101B was flown by the 4570th Test Squadron, the operational suitability test unit for ADC, at Tyndall AFB, Florida and by the 4756th CCTS (later redesignated the 2nd Fighter-Interceptor Training Squadron) at the same location. ADC F-101Bs were withdrawn from service over the period 1969-72.

The ANG began operating the F-101B

interceptor in November 1969. ANG squadrons included the 111th (Ellington AFB, Texas), 116th (Spokane, Washington), 123rd (Portland, Oregon), 132nd (Bangor AFB, Maine), 136th (Niagara Falls, New York), 178th (Fargo, South Dakota), 179th (Duluth, Minnesota) and 192nd (Reno, Nevada). The final operator of the F-101B was the 111th FIS at Ellington, which operated the F-101B/F briefly as a part of Tactical Air Command after ADC was inactivated on 1 April 1980. In 1981, after the base itself had changed from an AFB to an ANGB, Ellington gave up its Voodoos for the F-4C Phantom. Also in 1981, Colorado State University flew a civil-registered F-101B fitted with special instrumentation as part of a weather research programme. Production of the F-101B interceptor ended on 24 March 1961. Subsequently, a major update of the fire control system,

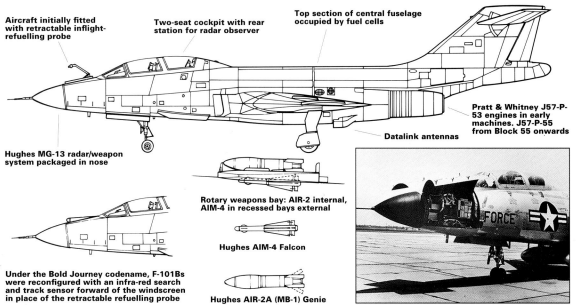

Aircraft initially fitted with retractable inflight-refuelling probe

Two-seat cockpit with rear station for radar observer

Top section of central fuselage occupied by fuel cells

Pratt & Whitney J57-P-53 engines in early machines. J57-P-55 from Block 55 onwards

Datalink antennas

Hughes MG-13 radar/weapon system packaged in nose

Rotary weapons bay: AIR-2 internal, AIM-4 in recessed bays external

Hughes AIM-4 Falcon

Under the Bold Journey codename, F-101Bs were reconfigured with an infra-red search and track sensor forward of the windscreen in place of the retractable refuelling probe

Hughes AIR-2A (MB-1) Genie

The Hughes MG-13 fire control system was integrated with the SAGE system. It was hard to master but was capable of hands-off Genie launches, including automatic launch of rocket, turning the airplane into the escape manoeuvre, and detonating the nuclear warhead at the appropriate time.

Above: After its active-duty days were over, the F-101B served with the Guard. These aircraft are from the 136th FIS, New York ANG. Note the searchlight below the rear cockpit.

Below: An F-101B displays the striking markings of the 437th FIS. Between 1960 and 1964 the F-101 was ADC's most numerous aircraft, but by 1971 all operational aircraft had passed to the ANG.

Above: The Tyndall-based Air Defense Weapons Center was the final USAF user of the F-101B, operating the type on target-towing and EW (note ECM pod) duties until 20 September 1982. The final ANG F-101B user was the 111th FIS, Texas ANG, which gave up Voodoos earlier in the year.

ccomplished in the latter half of 1961 and nown by the codename Kitty Car, brought arlier production F-101Bs up to the final lock 120 standard. Other post-production nprovements were introduced between 961 and 1966 in project Bold Journey, also nown as the IIP (Interceptor Improvement rogram). This long-running programme nhanced the resistance of F-101B rframes to electromagnetic pulse and stalled an improved MG-13 fire-control ystem for use especially against targets ying at low level. The distinguishing feature Bold Journey was the infra-red detection canner in the nose space formerly ccupied by an inflight-refuelling probe.

Delivered in bare metal, F-101Bs were ter painted grey to reduce corrosion. Of 79 F-101Bs manufactured, 79 were ompleted as 'two-seat dual-control aircraft' nd 152 more retrofitted to dual-control onfiguration. In the first batch of 79, 58 vere initially completed as TF-101B aircraft . ll dual-control aircraft were eventually esignated F-101F. Serials are listed in the -101F entry.

Some 112 F-101B interceptors were ansferred to Canada along with 20 dual-ontrol CF-101Fs.

-101B serials (including two-seat ircraft): 56-0233/00328, 57-0247/0452, 8-0259/0342, 59-0391/0483

he AIM-4 Falcon was fired from a ail which deployed down from the otary door. Ahead of the port nissile was a baffle to deflect hot air om a cooling exhaust away from he infra-red sensor.

CF-101B

CF-101B was the Canadian designation for F-101Bs supplied from USAF inventory to the Canadians in two batches on separate occasions. Under Operation Queens Row, the US provided 66 Voodoos, including 56 F-101Bs and 10 dual-control ships which were handed over with a nose inflight-refuelling probe just forward of the pilot's windscreen even though air refuelling was never used tactically by RCAF Voodoos. It must be assumed that arrangements existed for the US to release to Canada the nuclear warhead for the AIR-2A Genie missile, which the Canadians employed. The first batch was in service on 1 February 1968, the date of integration when the RCAF (Royal Canadian Air Force) became the CAF (Canadian Armed Forces/Forces Armées Canadiennes). The arrival of the bilingual era saw French titles appearing alongside English on Voodoos.

The second batch of 66 Voodoos reaching Canada from US inventory contained a

retrofit also found on their American counterparts, namely a nose-mounted infra-red sensor ball used for target detection.

RCAF squadrons operating the Voodoo were Nos. 409 'Crossbow' (later 'Nighthawk') (Comox, Cold Lake), 410 'Cougar' (Uplands, Bagotville), 414 'Black Knights' (North Bay), 416 'Black Lynx' (Uplands, Bagotville, Chatham), and 425 'Alhouette' (Bagotville). No. 410 Squadron at Uplands was the Operational Training Squadron for the type. No. 414 Squadron at North Bay was the final operator of the CF-101B/F.

CF-101B serials from the first batch delivered to Canada (not including 10 dual-control aircraft designated CF-101F in Canadian service, serials of which are listed separately): 59-391/392 (RCAF 17391/17392); 59-394/399 (17394/17399); 59-401/411 (17401/17411); 59-433/436 (17433/17436); 59-438/442 (17438/17442); 59-444/448 (17444/17448); 59-450/453 (17450/17453); 59-445/457 (17455/17457); 59-459 (17459); 59-461 (17461); 57-463/465 (17463/17465); 59-467/471 (17467/17471);

Above: Initial deliveries went to Namao, Alberta, in October 1961, the first Canadian crews having undergone training at Hamilton AFB, California. Squadron colours were carried on the rudder.

Above: This CF-101B is in the interim scheme, retaining the natural metal but having adopted the 'band-aid' maple leaf flag. Note the datalink under the starboard engine.

Below: From 1 July 1982, 425 Sqn CF-101Bs began Cold Shaft operations, holding at one-hour readiness to augment other squadrons at five-mninute alert. This trio of 425 aircraft includes two CF-101Fs.

Above: Temporary camouflage was applied to a 425 Sqn CF-101B for a Maple Flag exericse held at CFB Cold Lake. The paint was soluble and easily washed off.

59-475/477 (17475/17477); 59-479/483 (17479/17483).

CF-101B serials from the second batch delivered to Canada (not including 10 dual-control CF-101Fs listed separately): 56-260 (CAF 101002); 57-268, 57-273, 57-286, 57-289, 57-293, 57-296, 57-298/299, 57-303, 57-305/306, 57-314/315, 57-321

(101008/101021); 57-323 (101023); 57-334, 57-340/341, 57-346, 57-351, 57-354, 57-358/360, 57-362/364, 57-366, 57-368/369, 57-373/375, 57-380/382, 57-384, 57-388, 57-391, 57-395/396, 57-398 (101025/101051); 57-418, 57-420, 57-424, 57-426, 57-429, 57-431/434, 57-441/444, 57-451 (101053/101066).

Initial markings consisted of the original Canadian flag on the fin, 'Royal Canadian Air Force' titles and a large maple roundel on the nose on an unpainted aircraft. The legend 'RCAF' appeared ahead of the roundel with the last-three of the serial behind. The 'RCAF' was soon dropped, as shown here. A considerable period of transition then occurred, the first markings to change being the flag, which became the current 'band-aid' maple leaf, and the roundel, which remained large but with the maple leaf becoming much smaller in side the white circle. The second batch of aircraft featured silver aluminium paint with small-size roundels. Fuselage titles reflected the integration of the services with 'Canadian Armed Forces' to port and 'Forces Armées Canadiennes' to starboard. This scheme subsequently gave way to anti-corrosion light grey paint, with 'Canada' fuselage titles and small roundels flanked by 'Armed Forces' and 'Forces Armées'.

Fuel

Five fuel cells in the upper fuselage and three in each wing combined to give an internal capacity of 13,546 lb (6144 kg). This could be augmented by two 450-US gal (1703-litre) drop tanks, which were short large-diameter units on the first batch of aircraft and longer, more streamlined tanks on the second batch. The first batch of aircraft also retained the retractable refuelling probe in the nose but was not used. The second batch replaced the probe with the infra-red search and track sensor.

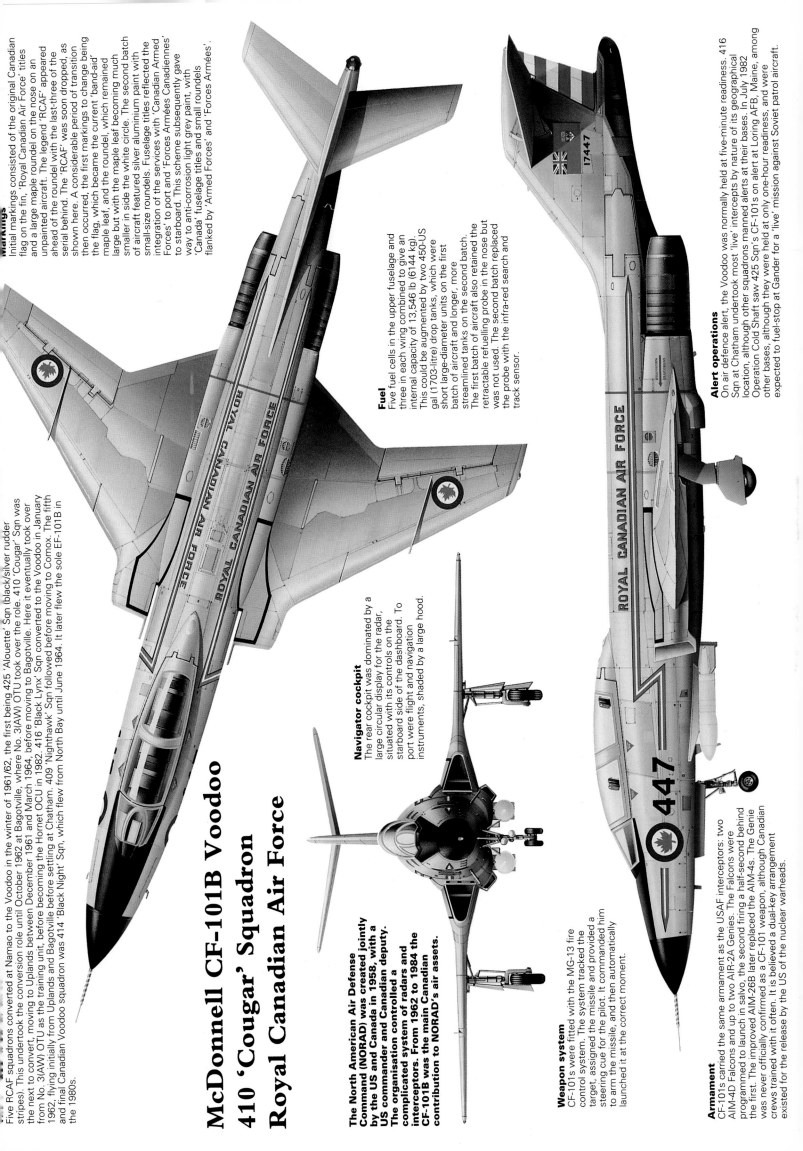

McDonnell CF-101B Voodoo
410 'Cougar' Squadron
Royal Canadian Air Force

Five RCAF squadrons converted to the Voodoo in the winter of 1961/62, the first being 425 'Alouette' Sqn (black/silver rudder stripes). This undertook the conversion role until October 1962 at Bagotville, where No. 3(AW) OTU took over the role. 410 'Cougar' Sqn was the next to convert, moving to Uplands between December 1961 and March 1964, before moving to Bagotville. Here it eventually took over from No. 3(AW) OTU as the training unit, before becoming the Hornet OCU in 1982. 416 'Black Lynx' Sqn converted to the Voodoo in January 1962, flying initially from Uplands and Bagotville before settling at Chatham. 409 'Nighthawk' Sqn followed before moving to Comox. The fifth and final Canadian Voodoo squadron was 414 'Black Night' Sqn, which flew from North Bay until June 1964. It later flew the sole EF-101B in the 1980s.

The North American Air Defense
Command (NORAD) was created jointly by the US and Canada in 1958, with a US commander and Canadian deputy. The organisation controlled a complicated system of radars and interceptors. From 1962 to 1984 the CF-101B was the main Canadian contribution to NORAD's air assets.

Navigator cockpit

The rear cockpit was dominated by a large circular display for the radar, situated with its controls on the starboard side of the dashboard. To port were flight and navigation instruments, shaded by a large hood.

Weapon system

CF-101s were fitted with the MG-13 fire control system. The system tracked the target, assigned the missile and provided a steering cue for the pilot. It commanded him to arm the missile, and then automatically launched it at the correct moment.

Armament

CF-101s carried the same armament as the USAF interceptors: two AIM-4D Falcons and up to two AIR-2A Genies. The Falcons were programmed to launch in salvo, the second firing a half-second behind the first. The improved AIM-26B later replaced the AIM-4s. The Genie was never officially confirmed as a CF-101 weapon, although Canadian crews trained with it often. It is believed a dual-key arrangement existed for the release by the US of the nuclear warheads.

Alert operations

On air defence alert, the Voodoo was normally held at five-minute readiness. 416 Sqn at Chatham undertook most 'live' intercepts by nature of its geographical location, although other squadrons manned alerts at their bases. In July 1982 Operation Cold Shaft saw 425 Sqn's CF-101s on alert at Loring AFB, Maine, among other bases, although they were held at only one-hour readiness, and were expected to fuel-stop at Gander for a 'live' mission against Soviet patrol aircraft.

McDonnell F-88/F-101 Voodoo Variants

EF-101B

Canada leased the sole EF-101B, or 'Electric Voodoo', from the US Air Force and flew the aircraft with 414 'Black Knights' Squadron at North Bay. Not among Canada's two batches of 66 F-101B interceptors, the EF-101B served as an electronic target aircraft, simulating the radar signature of an incoming Soviet bomber. Retired in 1987 (and relegated to a museum in Minneapolis-St Paul), the EF-101B was the final Voodoo in service with any air arm.
EF-101B serial: 58-0300 (CAF 101067)

The EF-101B entered service with 414 Sqn in 1983, having been stored at Davis-Monthan. Originally delivered in grey, it was the only Canadian Voodoo to never receive a fuselage cheat line. Note the additional antennas below and behind the cockpit.

NF-101B

The NF-101B was the two-seat prototype for the long-range F-101B/F interceptor series. The aircraft was retained at Edwards AFB, California after its 27 March 1957 first flight (which also qualifies as the first flight by an F-101B). This was the only B model built with an A-model airframe limited to 6.33 *g*. It remained a test ship because teething troubles demanded a more rigorous flight-test programme than originally foreseen.

A second ship was later given the 'N' prefix, which indicates a permanent change for test purposes. This aircraft had a one-of-a-kind pointed nose configuration and was used to test systems for surface-to-air drones as targets at Tyndall.
NF-101B serials: 56-232, 57-409.

The prototype two-seater was designated NF-101B in respect of its permanent test status. The aircraft had the low-strength airframe, and had test equipment in the nose instead of the fire control system and radar.

Another view of '232 during an early test flight, carrying dummy Falcon missiles. The NF-101B could be distinguished by having much shorter jetpipes instead of the lengthened burner cans of production aircraft.

RF-101B

The RF-101B became the final reconnaissance version of the Voodoo and the only version with a backseat crew member. On their return from Canada, the US Air Force converted 22 ex-CAF F-101B interceptors to RF-101B standard. Under a 30 December 1968 contract, the aircraft had their fire control systems removed and flying boom refuelling receptacle added. The work was accomplished between September 1971 and January 1972 by Ling-Temco-Vought in Greenville, South Carolina. A 23rd RF-101B (57-301), actually the first to be flown, was a developmental test airframe and did not come from Canada.

The reconnaissance package for the RF-101B included three KS-87B cameras in forward, left split vertical, and right split vertical configurations, plus two AXQ-2 television cameras in forward-looking and downward-looking positions. The pilot's panel was equipped with a TV viewfinder control indicator. Most instruments in the rear cockpit were removed during the modification.

The RF-101B was assigned to the 192nd TRS, Nevada ANG, at Reno 1971-72. Upon its arrival, Reno sent its RF-101Hs to Louisville, while the Kentucky ANG transferred its RF-101Gs to Arkansas.
RF-101B serials (all but the first converted from CF-101B): 57-301, 59-391, 59-397/398, 59-402/404, 59-410, 59-434, 59-436, 59-441, 59-447/448, 59-450, 59-453, 59-457, 59-459, 59-463, 59-467, 59-477, 59-481/483.

A total of 23 RF-101B conversions was undertaken for the ANG, and the only user was the 192nd TRG at Reno. The aircrafts' career was relatively short, replacing RF-101Gs in November 1971 and giving way to RF-4C Phantoms in July 1975. The type was produced to cover a perceived shortfall in tactical reconnaissance assets, but proved to be a very costly programme compared to the results achieved, while the aircraft required several fixes in their short lives to maintain an acceptable operational standard.

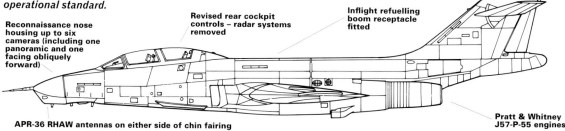

Reconnaissance nose housing up to six cameras (including one panoramic and one facing obliquely forward)

Revised rear cockpit controls – radar systems removed

Inflight refuelling boom receptacle fitted

APR-36 RHAW antennas on either side of chin fairing

Pratt & Whitney J57-P-55 engines

TF-101B

The TF-101B designation was applied at the factory to the first 58 'two-seat dual-control airplanes', all of which (79 from new production and 152 from conversions) were eventually designated F-101F. Serials are listed in the F-101F entry.

F-101C

The F-101C was virtually identical to the F-101A. The variants were used interchangeably, and both relied on the same 'Dash One' (pilots manual) and 'Dash Thirty-Four' (weapons manual). Much of the time, a pilot did not even notice whether his mount was an A model or a C.

The F-101C was, however, 500 lb (227 kg) heavier to accommodate structural improvements which increased its maximum g tolerance from 6.33 to 7.33. The F-101C also had different fuel pumps and fuel feed and control systems, increasing its maximum available afterburner time from six minutes (F-101A) to 15. The F-101C had very minor changes in its pressurisation system. The aircraft never had any mission except to fly – probably one way – and to deliver a centreline atomic bomb. Except for tolerance to g-forces which was increased in the C model, the F-101A and F-101C were interchangeable. The F-101C also began its operational career with the 27th FBW at Bergstrom. Fighter-bomber wings were redesignated tactical fighter wings on 7 July 1958, and the first Voodoo operator became the 27th TFW. F-101A/C Voodoos of the 27th deployed to Formosa during heightened tensions in 1958.

In a move in part for economy reasons and largely to bring the Voodoo's striking power closer to targets in the Soviet Union, the men and equipment of the 27th TFW were transferred to the 81st Tactical Fighter Wing at RAF Bentwaters/Woodbridge. Here, the F-101C replaced the F-84F. The 81st TFW operated three squadrons, the 78th TFS 'Bushmasters', 91st TFS 'Blue Streaks' and 92nd TFS 'Avengers'.

The mission of the F-101C was to fly out to a distance as great as 1,000 miles (1610 km) and drop a single, tactical nuclear weapon on a Soviet or Eastern European target. In the F-101C, field refinements were made of systems built into both F-101A and C models, including the all-weather, low-level nuclear delivery system using the Voodoo's gun-ranging radar which had a ground-mapping mode. The F-101A/C's Low Altitude Bombing System (LABS) and its later Low Angle Drogued Delivery (LADD) systems were a maze of gyros, timers and computers designed to permit the aircraft to drop its atomic bomb after making a run-in top target at an altitude as low as 50 ft (17 m). LABS employed a Mergenthaler Linotype M-1 Toss Bombing System (TBS-1), enabling the pilot to deliver his weapon by lining up the target on the crosshairs of his K-19 gunsight and pushing a button which computed an automatic release. Pilots were briefed that they were flying a one-way mission, and received training in E & E (escape and evasion) techniques to be used after ejecting and parachuting behind Soviet lines.

The 81st TFW operated the F-101C Voodoo until 3 January 1966 when the wing

Seen in 1964, this 81st TFW clutches a pair of fuel tanks to its belly. The tanks were not attached to pylons, but directly to attachments on the fuselage itself. This eased the problem of ground clearance.

finished replacing the type with the McDonnell F-4C Phantom. Forty-seven F-101Cs were built, of which 32 were later converted to RF-101H reconnaissance models. An additional 96 aircraft originally scheduled to be built as F-101Cs were

Nose of F-101C showing refuelling probe extended

completed as RF-101C reconnaissance aircraft.
F-101C serials: 54-1486/1493; 56-001/039

Above: The star-studded fins of this line of F-101Cs identify the aircraft as serving with the 27th TFW at Bergstrom AFB. Fins were marked by colour according to squadron (481st TFS – green, 522nd TFS – red, 523rd TFS – yellow, 524th TFS – blue).

Right and below: When the Voodoos moved to Bentwaters, the markings changed to a double stripe. Again these were in squadron colours (78th TFS – red, 91st TFS – blue, 92nd TFS – yellow).

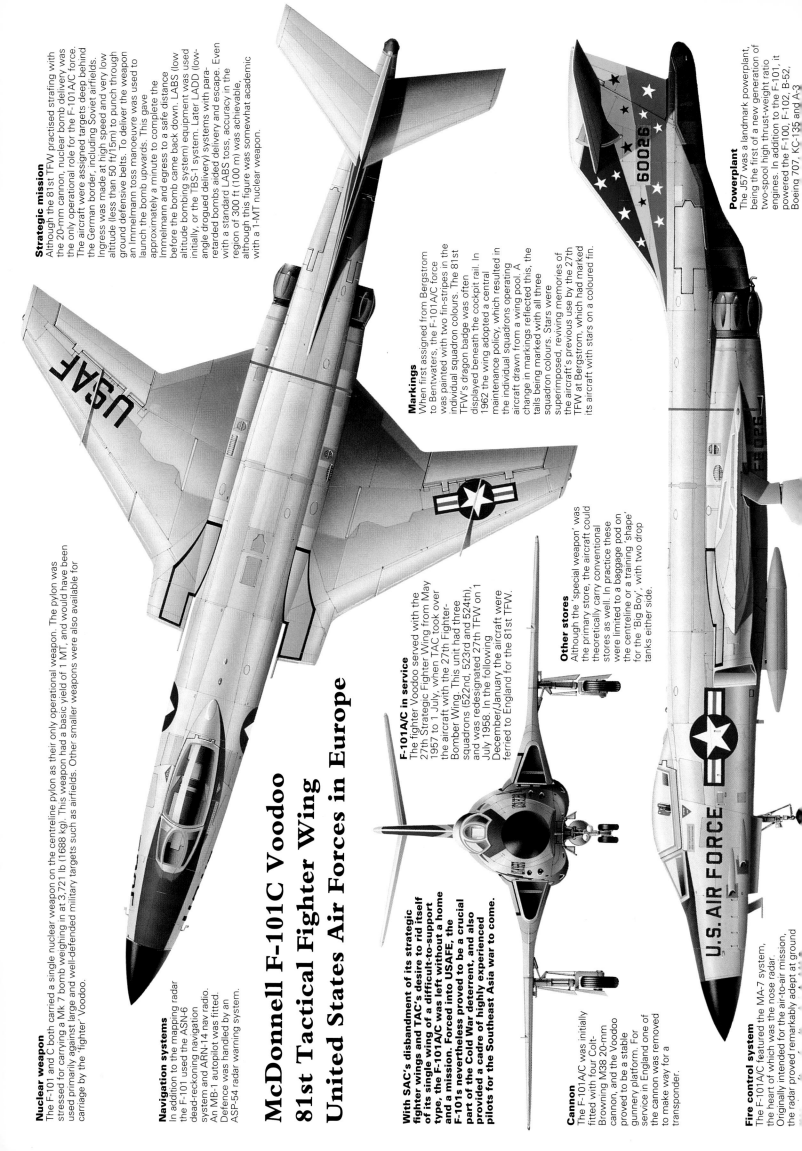

Nuclear weapon

The F-101 and C both carried a single nuclear weapon on the centreline pylon as their only operational weapon. The pylon was stressed for carrying a Mk 7 bomb weighing in at 3,721 lb (1688 kg). This weapon had a basic yield of 1 MT, and would have been used primarily against large and well-defended military targets such as airfields. Other smaller weapons were also available for carriage by the 'fighter' Voodoo.

Navigation systems

In addition to the mapping radar the F-101 used the ASN-6 dead-reckoning navigation system and ARN-14 nav radio. An MB-1 autopilot was fitted. Defence was handled by an ASP-54 radar warning system.

Strategic mission

Although the 81st TFW practised strafing with the 20-mm cannon, nuclear bomb delivery was the only operational role for the F-101A/C force. The aircraft were assigned targets deep behind the German border, including Soviet airfields. Ingress was made at high speed and very low altitude (less than 50 ft/15m) to punch through ground defensive belts. To deliver the weapon an Immelmann toss manoeuvre was used to launch the bomb upwards. This gave approximately a minute to complete the Immelmann and egress to a safe distance before the bomb came back down. LABS (low altitude bombing system) equipment was used initially, or the TBS-1 system. Later LADD (low-angle drogued delivery) systems with para-retarded bombs aided delivery and escape. Even with a standard LABS toss, accuracy in the region of 300 ft (100 m) was achievable, although this figure was somewhat academic with a 1-MT nuclear weapon.

McDonnell F-101C Voodoo
81st Tactical Fighter Wing
United States Air Forces in Europe

With SAC's disbandment of its strategic fighter wings and TAC's desire to rid itself of its single wing of a difficult-to-support type, the F-101A/C was left without a home and a mission. Forced into USAFE, the F-101s nevertheless proved to be a crucial part of the Cold War deterrent, and also provided a cadre of highly experienced pilots for the Southeast Asia war to come.

Cannon

The F-101A/C was initially fitted with four Colt-Browning M38 20-mm cannon, and the Voodoo proved to be a stable gunnery platform. For service in England one of the cannon was removed to make way for a transponder.

F-101A/C in service

The fighter Voodoo served with the 27th Strategic Fighter Wing from May 1957 to 1 July, when TAC took over the aircraft with the 27th Fighter-Bomber Wing. This unit had three squadrons (522nd, 523rd and 524th), and was redesignated 27th TFW on 1 July 1958. In the following December/January the aircraft were ferried to England for the 81st TFW.

Other stores

Although the 'special weapon' was the primary store, the aircraft could theoretically carry conventional stores as well. In practice these were limited to a baggage pod on the centreline or a training 'shape' for the 'Big Boy', with two drop tanks either side.

Markings

When first assigned from Bergstrom to Bentwaters, the F-101A/C force was painted with two fin-stripes in the individual squadron colours. The 81st TFW's dragon badge was often displayed beneath the cockpit rail. In 1962 the wing adopted a central maintenance policy, which resulted in the individual squadrons operating aircraft drawn from a wing pool. A change in markings reflected this, the tails being marked with all three squadron colours. Stars were superimposed, reviving memories of the 27th TFW at Bergstrom, which had marked its aircraft with stars on a coloured fin.

Powerplant

The J57 was a landmark powerplant, being the first of a new generation of two-spool high thrust-weight ratio engines. In addition to the F-101, it powered the F-100, F-102, B-52, Boeing 707, KC-135 and A-3

Fire control system

The F-101A/C featured the MA-7 system, the heart of which was the nose radar. Originally intended for the air-to-air mission, the radar proved remarkably adept at ground

RF-101C

The RF-101C was the definitive reconnaissance Voodoo, combining the wing structure of the F-101C with the camera installation of the RF-101A. It was the only Voodoo to see combat in American hands. The RF-101C first flew on 12 July 1957 and (corresponding to the F-101C in the 'bomber' world) was improved over the A model in being stressed to handle 7.33 g and was modified to carry a centreline nuclear weapon.

The beginning of RF-101 operations at Shaw AFB, South Carolina is cited in the entry for the RF-101A, which served beside the RF-101C for a brief time but was quickly replaced by it. In June 1958, the 4414th Combat Crew Training Squadron became operational with Shaw's 363rd TRW as the RTU (replacement training unit) for Voodoo reconnaissance pilots.

In May 1958, the RF-101C-equipped 17th and 18th TRS were transferred from Shaw AFB, South Carolina to join the 66th TRW at Laon AB, France. The Laon-based wing also

Below: The RF-101C was the first USAF jet to fly missions in Southeast Asia, the 15th and 45th TRS manning detachments at Saigon (Pipe Stem) and Don Muang (Able Mabel) from November 1961. Camouflage swiftly appeared on these aircraft, and the national insignia were reduced in size.

included the 32nd and 38th TRS which relinquished RF-84F Thunderstreaks for the RF-101C. The 38th changed location to Ramstein AB, Germany when Laon grew desperately short of ramp space and facilities, and the entire wing moved in 1965 to RAF Upper Heyford, England, ending RF-101C operations when it was inactivated on 1 April 1970.

The RF-101A/C had a critical role in the Cuban missile crisis: Voodoos from Shaw deployed to Florida and flew 82 combat sorties between 26 October and 15 November 1962.

Only RF-101C models reached Vietnam. Beginning in 1958, the RF-101C Voodoo was operated by the 432nd Tactical Reconnaissance Wing, which initially was responsible for the 20th and 29th TRS and later acquired the 17th and 18th (from Shaw AFB, SC). The wing was formed at Shaw in February 1958 and detached to the Far East two years later. From 1965, the wing operated at Udorn RTAFB, Thailand, where

Right and above right: Operation Sun Run was conducted on 27 November 1957 using six RF-101Cs to shatter US coast-to-coast records. These included a west-east time of 3 hours 7 minutes 43 seconds (Lt Gustav Klatt), east-west of 3:36.32 and round-trip of 6:46.36 (both by Captain Robert Sweet).

Above: RF-101Cs were delivered in natural metal, but adopted light grey anti-corrosive paint. Several camouflage schemes were tested before the standard T.O.114 scheme was settled upon.

McDonnell F-88/F-101 Voodoo Variants

Above: RF-101Cs were delivered to the 432nd TRG at Shaw from the end of 1957. The following year the RF-101s were put under the control of the 363rd TRW, in whose markings this aircraft is seen. The wing controlled two operational squadrons (20th and 29th TRS), and the training unit (4414th CCTS). The Shaw wing flew 82 combat reconnaissance flights during the Cuban missile crisis.

it acquired the 20th TRS, by now nicknamed 'Green Pythons', which carried out the bulk of combat operations credited to the Voodoo. The 15th TRS 'Cotton Pickers' at Kadena AB, Okinawa began operating RF-101Cs in Southeast Asia as early as 1960. These began with temporary deployments to Don Muang airfield in Thailand and Tan Son Nhut in South Vietnam. The 45th TRS 'Polka Dots', originally at Misawa AB, Japan and later at Tan Son Nhut, also joined the fighting.

In Southeast Asia, RF-101Cs were modified to carry photo flash cartridges and TLQ-8 jammers. The Toy Tiger update was a retrofit of cameras introducing a new nose panoramic and 4.5 x 4.5-in format KA-45s on side and vertical gyro stab, including night cameras using flash cartridges, as well as Hycon KS-72 cameras and automatic controls designed for the RF-4C Phantom. The 45th TRS ended a decade of Voodoo combat operations when the last RF-101C Voodoo, replaced by the RF-4C Phantom, departed Saigon on 16 November 1970. The last Tactical Air Command RF-101C was phased out by the 31st TRTS, a replacement training unit at Shaw, on 16 February 1971. RF-101Cs later served with several Air National Guard squadrons alongside RF-101As.

Of 166 RF-101Cs completed, 96 had originally been scheduled for production as F-101C airplanes.
RF-101C serials: 56-40/135, 56-162/231

Above: The RF-101C was the first USAF type to don tactical warpaint.

Right: In Europe the 66th TRW and its four squadrons (17th, 18th, 32nd and 38th TRS) were very active along the German border, flying from Laon and a detachment at Ramstein. Unofficial reports talk of RF-101s employing maximum afterburner turns to escape from MiGs. In the early 1960s the 66th crews were qualified in the delivery of nuclear weapons.

Six ANG squadrons flew the RF-101C in the early 1970s: 154th (illustrated) and 184th TRS/AR ANG, 107th and 171st TRS/MI ANG, 165th TRS/KY ANG and 153rd TRS/MS.

The RF-101C largely replaced the RF-101G/H and RF-84F in Guard service, this being a Kentucky aircraft. Mississippi's 153rd TRS had the distinction of flying the last USAF RF-101 mission on 13 January 1979.

McDonnell RF-101C 66066

45th Tactical Reconnaissance Squadron 'Polka Dots'

Pacific Air Forces

reconnaissance asset when it entered the Southeast Asia war in 1961, and the type served with distinction until replacement by the slower but better-equipped RF-4C was completed in November 1970. Around 35,000 combat sorties were flown, including 10,000 over North Vietnam and 9,000 over Laos.

Mission profile

When the RF-101C began SEA operations, the type usually flew medium-altitude single-ship missions, although two-ship missions were flown into heavily-defended areas. From mid-1965 the SAM threat dictated a change in tactics, the Voodoos using a low-altitude ingress followed by a pop-up to about 10,000-15,000 ft. About two or three minutes were available at this altitude for the photo-run before SAM operators could lock up and launch. After the pop-up, the aircraft dived back down to the safety of low altitude. This tactic continued until April 1967, when improved ECM equipment (in the form of up to four ALQ-71 pods on each aircraft allowed a return to medium-altitude operations. However, the pods seriously damaged the RF-101's blistering speed, making them easier to catch by MiGs (which were otherwise not a serious threat). Consequently, fighter escorts became more prevalent.

Cameras

RF-101Cs were initially fitted with a 12-in Fairchild KA-2 camera facing forward, three 6-in KA-2s in a tri-sensor station behind, and two 36-in Fairchild KA-1 cameras facing downwards. In order to give a night capability, some RF-101Cs were reconfigured with four KA-45 cameras in the forward station and two 12-in KA-47s replacing the KA-1s. These 'Toy Tiger' aircraft carried up to 80 M123 photo-flash cartridges in a centreline ejector pod. In 1964/65 many RF-101Cs were given the Mod 1181 improvment, which replaced the KA-2 cameras with Hycon KS-72 sensors, and added an automatic control system as developed for the RF-4C. Initial operations were not encouraging, but later proved to be effective after some modification.

Nuclear weapons

Unlike the RF-101A, the C was capable of carrying a single centreline nuclear bomb, principally for European service. McDonnell had originally proposed a quick-change radar nose but this was rejected owing to the complexity of the camera installation.

Cockpit

The instrument panel of the RF-101C was dominated by a large circular scope for the VF-31 viewfinder. This provided a vertical view as seen from the tri-camera station.

RF-101C losses

During the Southeast Asia war, the RF-101C fleet suffered 44 losses. Of these 31 fell to AAA guns, five to SAMs, one to a MiG, one in an airfield attack and six to operational causes.

RF-101C in PACAF

RF-101Cs were initially delivered to the 15th TRS 'Cotton Pickers' at Kadena and the 45th TRS 'Polka Dots' at Misawa. These units manned the initial SEA Pipe Stem and Able Mable deployments on rotation. Aircraft were occasionally drafted in from Shaw, and in 1965 the 20th TRS 'Green Pythons' was moved in to replace the 15th TRS, which converted to RF-4Cs. The 20th operated for most of its career from Udorn, and took the lion's share of northern North Vietnam missions. The 45th TRS was based at Tan Son Nhut, covering the south.

Individual aircraft

This aircraft wears the polka dot fin-cap of the 45th TRS, based at Tan Son Nhut. The 'Luv Bug' nose art was worn only briefly. Earlier the aircraft had achieved fame as one of the six Sun Run record-breakers, painted with the nickname 'Cin Min'. Flown by Captain Ray Schrecengost, it was the first away and briefly held the round-trip coast-to-coast record before being beaten by a following aircraft. The aircraft is now preserved in the Air Force Museum, after 6,604.9 flying hours.

McDonnell F-88/F-101 Voodoo Variants

F-101F

The designation F-101F was assigned on 3 February 1961 to all 'two-seat dual-control aircraft' which were otherwise identical to the F-101B interceptor. Seventy-nine of these were manufactured from the outset as 'two-seat dual-control aircraft' and 152 more were originally completed as F-101Bs but, rather than being upgraded with the rest of the F-101B fleet, were retrofitted to dual-control configuration.

F-101F serials (for the 72 aircraft built as dual-control ships): 56-274/275, 56-277, 56-289, 56-294, 56-299, 56-304, 56-308, 56-312, 56-316, 56-320, 56-324, 56-328, 57-263, 57-267, 57-271, 57-275, 57-279, 57-283, 57-287, 57-292, 57-297, 57-302, 57-307, 57-312, 57-317, 57-322, 57-327, 57-332, 57-337, 57-342, 57-347, 57-352, 57-357, 57-365, 57-372, 57-379, 57-386, 57-393, 57-400, 57-407, 57-414, 57-421, 57-428, 57-449, 58-262, 58-269, 58-276, 58-283, 58-290, 58-297, 58-304, 58-311, 58-318, 58-324, 58-331, 58-338, 59-393, 59-400, 59-407, 59-413, 59-419, 59-425, 59-437, 59-443, 59-449, 59-454, 59-460, 59-466, 59-472, 59-278, and two others.

At the start of 1970 the 11th FIS/Texas ANG adopted the Guard training role for the F-102, and added the same CCTU function for the interceptor Voodoo in May 1971, acquiring several dual-control F-101Fs. The CCTU task was relinquished in April 1976, but the 111th continued as a regular interceptor unit with its original F-101B/F aircraft.

Right: Dual-control aircraft were widespread throughout the fleet, and retained combat capability. A sizeable proportion were concentrated in the training units, with a handful assigned to each operational interceptor unit. Reconnaissance Voodoo squadrons were also assigned a handful of F-101Fs to assist with their conversion/continuation training programmes. This aircraft wears the muted markings of the 154th TRS/Arkansas ANG, based at Little Rock AFB.

TF-101F

Twenty-four 'two-seat dual-control aircraft' based on the F-101B interceptor were initially designated TF-101F. These were later redesignated F-101F and are listed in the entry for the latter.

CF-101F

This designation was applied to the dual-control aircraft supplied to Canada, of which there were 10 in each batch. Serial numbers are as follows:
1st batch: 59-0393 (17393), 59-0400 (17400), 59-0407 (17407), 59-0437 (17437), 59-0443 (17443), 59-0449 (17449), 59-0460 (17460), 59-0466 (17466), 59-0472 (17472), 59-0478 (17478)

2nd batch: 56-0253 (101001), 56-0260 (101002), 56-0262 (101003), 56-0277 (101004), 56-0304 (101005), 56-0324 (101006), 56-0328 (101007), 57-0322 (101022), 57-0332 (101024), 57-0400 (101052)

The rear seat of the F/CF-101F had only rudimentary controls, and could not operate flaps, afterburner, landing gear or brake chute. This CF-101F is from 425 'Alouette' Sqn.

RF-101G

The RF-101G was a conversion of the 29 F-101A airframes to become a single-seat reconnaissance aircraft (corresponding to the RF-101C conversion made from F-101C models). Accomplished by Lockheed Aircraft Services, the modification work entailed removal of integral cannon armament and its replacement by cameras, a revised nosecone featuring camera ports being fitted at the same time.

The first RF-101G conversions went to the Kentucky Air National Guard (165rd TRS/123rd TRW) at Standiford Airport in Louisville. Kentucky received its first RF-101G in July 1965, replacing the RB-57B Canberra. Kentucky Guardsmen were activated during the 1968 *Pueblo* crisis in Korea. While the group did not deploy to Korea, it carried out operations in Alaska, Panama and Japan while on active duty. In 1969, the Louisville unit came off active duty, transferred its RF-101G aircraft to Fort Smith, Arkansas, and converted to the RF-101H model.

The RF-101G was also employed by the Arkansas ANG (154th TRS/189th TFG) from July 1965 as a replacement for the RB-57B, with a *Pueblo*-era active-duty stint intervening) concluding in 1972 when the unit converted to RF-101Cs.

RF-101G serials (converted from F-101A): 54-1445, 54-1449, 54-1451/1455; 54-1457, 54-1459/1464; 54-1466, 54-1468, 54-1470, 54-1472/1473, 54-1475/1477, 54-1479, 54-1481/1482, 54-1484/1485, plus two other aircraft from among 54-1456, 54-1469, and 54-1516.

When the F-101As and Cs in England were replaced on the nuclear strike role by F-4C Phantoms in 1965-66, they became available for conversion to the reconnaissance role. The camera fit included a pallet of cameras mounted aft of the front fuselage bulkhead, and a new nose housing a forward-facing camera. The nosecone slid forward on rails to allow technicians to maintain the cameras and load film. Large hinged panels allowed access to the pallet and avionics bay to the rear. Lockheed undertook about half the conversions, with McClellan AFB performing the rest to speed up the process.

New nosecone with window for forward oblique camera

F-101A airframe – 6.33 g stressing

Pratt & Whitney J57-P-13 engines

Camera pallet mounted in forward fuselage with fan mounting and panoramic window

RF-101Gs and Hs initially served alongside each other with the three ANG units, but in 1971 were rationalised into RF-101B (Nevada), RF-101G (Arkansas) and RF-101H (Kentucky) units. This RF-101G is seen shortly after delivery in 1965 to Kentucky's 165th TRS. All three units undertook deployments to Itazuke during 1968/69.

RF-101H

In a conversion similar to the RF-101G, 32 F-101Cs were given reconnaissance systems to become RF-101Hs. The only difference between the two was the strengthened airframe of the H. The RF-101H was employed by the Nevada Air National Guard from October 1965, and also served alongside Gs with Arkansas and Kentucky Guards. All three units were called to active duty during the *Pueblo* crisis in 1968/69. In 1971 the ANG fleet was rationalised, with all RF-101Hs being assigned to the 165th TRS, Kentucky ANG. These were replaced by RF-101Cs in 1972.

RF-101H serials (converted from F-101C): 54-1486/1488, 54-1491, 54-1493, 56-0001/0004; 56-0006, 56-0010/0012; 56-0014, 56-0016, 56-0018/0020; 56-0022/0023; 56-0025/0027, 56-0029/0036, 56-0039

The H was outwardly identical to the G, and could only be distinguished by serial number.

F-109

The only aircraft ever assigned the designation F-109 by the US Air Force was the ship which was quickly redesignated F-101B and, as a long-range interceptor, became the most numerous Voodoo model. Contrary to published accounts, the F-109 nomenclature was never assigned to the tail-sitter Ryan vertical take-off aircraft (completed as the X-13 Vertijet) or to a Bell horizontal V/STOL proposal. The F-109 concept was redesignated F-101B in August 1955.

Convair F-102 Delta Dagger

Evolved from wartime German research, the Convair F-102A (and the two-seat TF-102A) was the first pure delta-winged fighter to enter service. Initial problems, including an unwillingness to go supersonic, delayed its introduction and forced a complete redesign. Its front-line career was brief, but three times as many 'Deuces' were built than its successor, and it saw service with far more units, including two foreign customers.

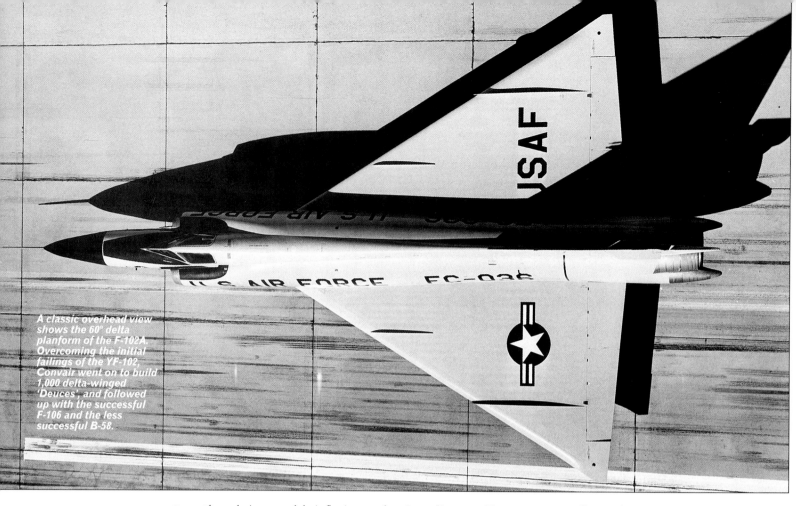

A classic overhead view shows the 60° delta planform of the F-102A. Overcoming the initial failings of the YF-102, Convair went on to build 1,000 delta-winged 'Deuces', and followed up with the successful F-106 and the less successful B-58.

The first powered delta-winged aircraft to fly was Convair's Model 7-000, or XF-92A. Based on research by Alexander Lippisch in wartime Germany (who only got as far as testing gliders), the XF-92A was scaled up to produce the ultimately unsuccessful YF-102.

Though it served briefly in combat in a distant foreign clime, the Convair F-102 Delta Dagger left a mark on history because of its long service with the US Air Force and Air National Guard on the home front. Among several fighters in the 'Century series' (those with designations beginning with 100 or more), the F-102A guarded North America during the years when an atomic attack was a real and immediate possibility.

The F-102 had a long and costly development that taught the world a great deal about supersonic flight and about integrated weapon systems. Once it began to reach operational squadrons, it developed a cult of pilots and maintainers who shrugged off its minor faults, revelled in its spectacular performance, and never lost the thrill of performing, seeing, or hearing an afterburner take-off with that J57 engine sending a plume of flame into the exhaust.

To repeat an appellation that pilots use too often for their mounts, many who flew this aircraft dubbed it 'the Cadillac of the skies'. Once teething troubles lay behind, it was stable, reliable, and lethal — and it gave pilots a trip like nothing they had experienced in the slower, clunkier aircraft it replaced.

For a time, it was one of the most advanced fighters in the world — and one of the most difficult to maintain. With its delta wing, it was the penultimate success in a story of technological progress that started with the XF-92, XF-92A, F2Y Sea Dart and B-58 Hustler and later culminated in its successor, the F-106 Delta Dart. It was the F-102 that introduced the area-ruled 'wasp waist' for sustained flight at supersonic speed. And the F-102 was a giant leap forward with many of its features, from radar to afterburner, from its weapons integration concept to its advanced missiles.

In addition to 14 prototype and pre-production specimens, 875 examples of the definitive F-102A single-seater were built, and no fewer than 111 TF-102A two-seaters, for a total population of precisely 1,000 airframes. The 'Deuce' (for no-one ever called it the Delta Dagger, a name which in any event came late in its career) and the two-seat 'Tub' were star performers at air shows and in mock air battles for two decades. In real air fights in Southeast Asia, in conditions for which it had never been designed, the glamour faded. Like the US itself, after Vietnam the F-102 was less a shiny ideal and more a maturing, practical entity that soldiered on in a less innocent world. And by the 1980s, the only F-102s left were those flying as drones.

History

On 8 October 1948, a US Air Force board of senior officers at Muroc AFB, California recommended that the USAF organise a competition for a new, all-weather interceptor, to be operational in 1954. From the beginning, before the size, shape or builder of the aircraft was known, it was dubbed as the '1954 interceptor'. The USAF announced approval of the board's recommendations on 4 February 1949 and ordered that the design competition be held in 1950. Searching for a new way to do business, in November 1949 the USAF decided that the 'weapons system' method would be used in developing the new interceptor. First, an appropriate FCS (fire-control system)

The F-102's most important role was probably providing 'top cover for America' from bases in Alaska, Canada, Greenland and Iceland. After the disbandment of the 31st FIS, the 317th FIS (seen above) became one of the largest fighter squadrons ever, with nearly 50 aircraft detached to locations all over the largest state in the Union.

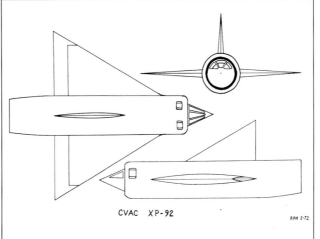

CVAC XP-92

RPH 2-72

Left and below:
Convair's delta-winged fighters, bombers and seaplanes originated with the 1946 XP-92 design for a short-range supersonic interceptor. The XP-92 contained so many radical features, including a compound rocket/ramjet engine, trolley take-off and a single control surface on each wing (dubbed the 'elevon'), that it was deemed sensible to develop a cheap low-speed test aircraft – the XF-92A – first. The XP-92 got as far as the mock-up stage.

would be designed. Then, an airframe compatible with the FCS would be developed. At the time, the USAF was fielding 'interim' jet interceptors to guard North America against atomic attack, namely the F-86D Sabre, F-89 Scorpion and F-94, which was later nicknamed Starfire only in its subsequent F-94C variant. A considerable portion of the air defence commitment was still being handled well into the 1950s, however, by day fighters such as the F-86A Sabre.

In January 1950 USAF Air Materiel Command (AMC) invited 50 firms to submit bids for the new interceptor. Some 18 of these companies responded, and a proposal submitted by one manufacturer had a price tag 10 times the amount proposed by another, a sign that the American aircraft industry was stepping into uncharted territory.

In May 1950 the AMC shortened its list of potential manufacturers to six. At the Pentagon, a board headed by Major General Gordon P. Saville looked at proposals for the FCS and farmed out some of its deliberations to an Air Defense Engineering Committee headed by Dr George E. Valley. After review of the recommendations of the Valley committee, the Saville Board narrowed FCS bidders to Hughes and North American by June 1950. Work on the new interceptor continued to be a top-priority item in the Pentagon despite the outbreak of war in Korea later that month. After a visit to the west coast, the Valley committee felt that the best answer was to award FCS developmental contracts to both Hughes and North American. The Saville board disagreed and declared that Hughes was the chosen contractor.

Convair (the name created by the merger of Consolidated and Vultee, later formalised in April 1954) had already done considerable work on delta-winged aircraft that might be applicable to the interceptor mission, among them two wholly different aircraft designated P-92. But Convair was no certainty for a contract award. On 2 July 1951, three winners were named for the airframe proposals. Convair, Lockheed and Republic were authorised to proceed through the mock-up stage. The most promising design of the trio was to be awarded a production contract and dubbed Project MX-1554. As it turned out, Lockheed dropped out, Republic continued through the mock-up stage, and Convair was given a contract for a '1954 interceptor' designated XF-102.

Convair F-102 Delta Dagger

XF-92A

Convair's biggest and smallest products are seen here brought together for a photo shoot. The XF-92 was built in Nashville and San Diego, and the B-36 at Fort Worth. The Fort Worth factory was later to create the B-58 Hustler, which owed much to the aerodynamic principles proved by the XF-92.

In the 1950s, the Convair company was equally busy with a range of civil aircraft products. Another shoot was arranged with the XF-92 and the prototype CV-240, first of a long series of 'Convairliners'. The CV-240 was borrowed back from General Motors which, in 1951, had converted it to turbine power with Allison T-38s as the Model 240-21 Turbo-Liner.

The aerodynamic test vehicle built as the Convair Model 7-002 took shape at Vultee Field near Nashville in late 1946 and early 1947. With the closure of the Vultee plant in the summer of 1947, the partially finished airframe was sent to San Diego for completion. After a long period of ground runs and high-speed taxying tests at Muroc, the 7-002 made its first flight there on 18 September 1948. E.D. ('Sam') Shannon became the first pilot to fly a true delta-winged powered aircraft. At the time, the design was still expected to lead to a mixed powerplant (turbojet-rocket) interceptor, but this requirement was dropped while the 7-002 was undergoing further tests in 1949. The engine fitted, a J33-A-23 of 5,200 lb st (23.15 kN) thrust was not powerful enough to push the 7-002 past the sound barrier, but the aircraft's performance was impressive enough to suggest that this would not be a problem given more thrust. The USAF cancelled the P-92 but adopted the 7-002 as a pure research vehicle, designated XF-92A with the serial 46-682. The XF-92A was re-engined with an afterburning 5,900-lb st (26.24-kN) Allison J33-A-29 with water/methanol injection increasing static thrust to 7,500 lb (33.36 kN). The aircraft could now be dived through the sound barrier, but performance and reliability were generally disappointing. A further change of engine, to the J33-A-16 of 8,400 lb st (37.37 kN) was made and the aircraft passed to NACA. A nosewheel collapse ended its flying career in October 1953.

ready in time for the F-102A, so the USAF decided that a simpler FCS, dubbed the E-9, would be employed in the F-102. Already, before any F-102 had taken to the sky, on 7 January 1953 the Air Defense Command requested development of an MRIX (Medium Range Interceptor, Experimental) to replace the F-102A and F-102B (later F-106A) by October 1959. As it would turn out, the MRIX would not proceed and, as a result, the F-106A would become the last warplane built in the USA solely for the interceptor mission.

For all Convair's experience, as late as 1953 when the supersonic interceptor was supposed to be far advanced in its development, the company's work had little to commend itself to the Pentagon or anyone else. Indeed, the company produced the wrong aircraft, whose performance in its initial version was described by one expert as "abysmal", and the prototype was destroyed within a week of its first test flight. The goal of an interceptor capable of sustained flight at supersonic speed seemed out of reach, to say nothing of the ultimate goal of a fully supersonic, round-the-clock, all-weather interceptor created as a complete integrated weapon system with advanced radar and missiles. At one point progress on the original YF-102 design – also known as the Model 8-82, the version that was wholly inadequate in every respect – was so discouraging that D. E. Thompson of Hughes Aircraft, maker of the fire-control system, scribbled a note to his boss: 'This is not looking good for early resolution...'

The cancellation of the unpromising YF-102 – its 'Y' prefix signifying service-test duty – hung in the balance and it was obvious that the fighter would need to be completely redesigned if it was to have any chance of saving its San Diego, California manufacturer by winning a lucrative production contract. Another Convair document of the era shows an unnamed company member noting that, 'We are in serious trouble here'.

XP-92 design

The story really begins not in the mid-1950s but in the late 1940s, when Convair drew the task of exploiting wartime German delta-wing research to create a supersonic interceptor using mixed jet and rocket power. This P-92 'pursuit' aircraft (always accompanied by an 'X' for 'experimental' prefix so that it was first the XP-92 then the XF-92) resulted from Convair consultations with Dr Alexander M. Lippisch, German delta-wing pioneer, and from exhaustive wind-tunnel work.

The XP-92, also known by the company designation Model 7, combined internal rocket and ramjet power with an external rocket and was, as a Convair document in

Before any metal was cut, it had already been decided (though it did not exactly work out that way) that the XF-102, powered by the 10,000-lb st (44.48-kN) Pratt & Whitney J57 turbojet engine, would be an interim interceptor pending the advent of the ultimate interceptor, which would be the F-102B with the J67 engine, based on a British engine, the Bristol Olympus. The latter aircraft (with a different engine) became the F-106 Delta Dart and is the subject of a separate history in *Wings of Fame* No. 13.

There now began a seemingly endless series of problems with the fire-control system. The FCS being developed by Hughes and known as the MX-1179 was not going to be

Convair publicity photos show the Model 7-002 in its initial form, left, and after modification with an afterburner and other improvements as the XF-92A. The 7-002 first arrived at Muroc (later Edwards) in April 1948 and conducted a long period of taxi runs while pilots 'Sam' Shannon and Bill Martin got used to the sensitive handling characteristics. One short 'hop' was made in June 1948, three months before the official first flight. In 1951 the afterburning J33-A-29 engine was installed at San Diego. For a period, the aircraft remained in natural metal before receiving the overall white finish seen here.

August 1947 asserted, 'designed for the purpose of destroying attacking enemy aircraft and airborne missiles'. The pilot of this arrow-shaped aircraft sat inside a 'spike' to the round air inlet, looking out through a flush windscreen at air rushing into the ramjet engine around him. There were numerous unconventional features, to put it mildly, on the XP-92 design, and these included the 'take-off and alighting gear': the XP-92 was supposed to go aloft from a 'four-wheel, take-off cart, which is not an integral part of the airplane'. It seemed that 'when the airplane reaches a take-off angle of 18°, the cart is automatically disengaged'. After

the XP-92 was aloft, the cart would automatically stop itself. The XP-92 was also equipped with a manually retractable, internal tricycle arrangement which gave new meaning to the term 'landing gear': it really was to be used for landing only.

Before returning to the XP-92, it should be noted that Convair was also creating other delta-winged fighters on its drawing boards. A 28 October 1948 proposal for a 'Class VA long-range special attack airplane' described a triangle-shaped aircraft intended for operation on the US Navy's forthcoming aircraft-carrier, the USS *United States* (CVA-58), which was later cancelled amidst bad blood in Washington over the merits of carriers versus bombers. This Convair delta was clearly meant for the nuclear mission at a time when the aircraft-carrier had not yet been ruled out as part of the US strategic nuclear force. Convair also intended the aircraft to be capable of launching from 'Midway'-class carriers and landing on 'Essex'-class carriers. For a while the US Navy's dream of a new class of carriers was still alive – the *United States* was a smooth-looking warship indeed, lacking the 'island' associated with most carriers, and the Convair aircraft shared this sleekness.

Below: The Howard Hughes-produced movie Jet Pilot is not regarded as a classic by film buffs or aviation enthusiasts. It might have been more memorable if the 'MIG 23', as played by the XF-92A, had not wound up on the cutting room floor. Although the film was completed in 1950, arguments between Hughes and the USAF over security issues helped delay its release for seven years.

Left: Majors 'Pete' Everest and 'Chuck' Yeager (seen here) did most of the test flying on behalf of the Air Force. Yeager also did some of the flying for Jet Pilot.

Convair F-102 Delta Dagger

What was not immediately obvious from the slick illustration on the cover of the 1948 report was that the 'Class VA long-range special attack airplane' was actually two flying machines – a small, dart-like mother craft otherwise known as the 'return component', and a droppable pod. The return component featured a 60° delta wing and vertical tail, and a single turbojet engine with afterburner. The enormous pod (the ordnance to be dropped by this aircraft) had three separate engines of its own. The big

'Class VA long-range special attack airplane' would also require six JATO (jet-assisted take-off) units to enable it to get aloft from the carrier deck. The composite aircraft had a take-off weight of 96,260 lb (43664 kg), but weighed only about half as much after dropping its powered load. (VA, it should be noted, was the US Navy's term for a heavier-than-air attack aircraft). The composite concept may have contributed later to the design of the B-58 Hustler bomber at a different facility (Fort Worth, Texas), but the US Navy never proceeded with the 1948 proposal. After briefly hitching its nuclear star to the Lockheed P2V-3C Neptune, which weighed only a little more than the Convair proposal and was strictly a 'one-way' aircraft able to launch from, but not land on, a carrier, the US Navy eventually settled after a series of attack aircraft on the submarine-launched ballistic missile as its contribution to the US nuclear force.

Power for the XP-92 was to have consisted of a combined ducted rocket/ramjet installation: 'Fifteen 50-lb [0.22-kN] thrust rockets discharge into a duct which is also the ram-jet combustion chamber. In addition to the main powerplant section, three 4,000-lb [17.79-kN] thrust unducted rockets are employed for high-power, short-period operation at take-off, in climbing, and for accelera-

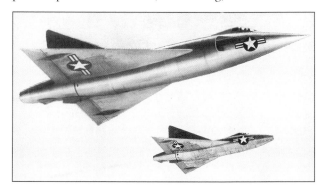

This Convair montage shows the XF-92A with an early F-102 concept. The faired, almost NACA-type intake design contrasts with that actually used, while everything from the wing root aft is a simple scale-up of the XF-92A.

YF-102

With the principles of delta-winged jet flight proved by the XF-92, Convair's designers decided to take a low-risk approach and scale up the design to carry the MX-1179 weapons system (including the as-yet-unbuilt Falcon missile). The two YF-102 prototypes were essentially the XF-92A scaled up by a factor of 1.22, with lateral intakes, a lowered wing and an afterburning J57-P-11 turbojet giving 14,800 lb (6713 kg) maximum thrust. Dick Johnson flew the first example on 24 October 1953, but only nine days later it was written off when the engine flamed out on take-off, Johnson being unhurt. Testing continued with the second aircraft, but when the transonic region was probed, severe instability and buffeting occurred, and the YF-102 simply refused to accelerate past Mach 1.

Below: The crash landing of the first YF-102 on 2 November 1953, caused by an engine stall on take-off, delayed the flight test programme until January the following year. More importantly, it delayed the discovery that the design was difficult to fly at transonic speed and incapable of going subsonic.

The second YF-102 first flew on 11 January 1954 and, before long, proved that the design had been based on inaccurate or over-optimistic wind-tunnel calculations.

Model 8-82

After flight-testing with the second YF-102 had proved the need for a complete redesign, Convair was left with a second batch of eight aircraft on the production line too advanced to be completed to the new design. The company set out to see what could be done to squeeze some extra speed and improve the handling of the YF-102. A revised wing incorporating conical camber and a new elevon-fuselage junction was added, which reduced buffet and improved handling, but this revised version (Convair Model 8-82) remained subsonic in level flight, only being coaxed to Mach 1.29 in a steep dive.

The third of the eight reconfigured YF-102s (53-1779/1786) sits forlornly on the Muroc dry lakebed, apparently after a nosewheel collapse.

tion to supersonic speed'. A close look at detailed plans of the XP-92, which resembled the Flash Gordon rocket ships of 1930s motion picture serial fame, reveals absolutely no space anywhere on the 18,850-lb (8550-kg) aircraft which could have been used to accommodate radar, armament or, for that matter, sufficient fuel to travel very far. However, the company blithely asserted that the XP-92 – if it got off the ground at all – would have an armament 'of four 20-mm cannons installed in the forward section of the fuselage' with 824 rounds of ammunition.

Mercifully for Convair test pilots, as well as citizens residing on the slope above Lindbergh Field, the airport at the factory which even in the 1940s was situated amidst urban growth, the XP-92 was never completed as a design, let alone built or flown. After the 'P' for 'pursuit' designation had been changed to 'F' for 'fighter' on 5 June 1948, the USAF took the unusual step of reissuing the number 92 and assigning it to a totally different, far simpler – but in the end equally ineffectual – Convair delta-winged fighter.

Below left: This unusual view shows the heavily-framed mult-part windscreen of the YF-102s. The pilot preparing for a test flight here is Air Force Major Fitzhugh 'Fitz' Fulton who later was heavily involved in testing the Convair B-58.

Enter the XF-92A

The XF-92A (company Model 7-002 or, in some documents, 7002) was a completely different aircraft. It began as a mock-up cobbled together from parts of five other aircraft to save time and money. The aircraft itself was rolled out of the San Diego factory in September 1948. Powered by a 4,800-lb st (21.35-kN) Allison J33-A-23 centrifugal-flow turbojet engine borrowed from an F-80 Shooting Star (and none of the fancy rocket and ramjet gadgetry foreseen for its predecessor), the XF-92A (46-682) was now intended to be only a one-of-a-kind 'dogship' to furnish data from flight tests that would aid in the development of future aircraft, including the future F-102. Orders for two further aircraft (46-683/684) were cancelled before the sole example ever saw the light of day.

The XF-92A boasted a cigar-shaped fuselage housing the jet engine with the cockpit positioned just in front of the powerplant. The engine air inlet was a circular hole in the nose, no longer interrupted by the enormous spike that would have distinguished its predecessor. The XF-92A, initially flown in natural metal with no paint except for markings etc., had a delta wing spanning 31 ft 3 in (9.525 m) with an area of 230.0 sq ft (21.37 m²). The XF-92A sat astride a rather intricate tricycle landing gear: the nose unit's leg (from a Bell P-63 Kingcobra) retracted forward, while the two main units' legs (from a North American

This line-up shows three of the Model 8-82 YF-102s and the surviving original Model 8-80, third from front, which seems to have been fitted with a longer nose cone during tests. When the decision was taken to completely redesign the F-102, 20,000 of the 30,000 tools already purchased had to be discarded, an inevitable result of the early gearing up for production stipulated under the Cook-Craigie Plan.

Below: 53-1784 was the sixth of eight YF-102s. Some vestiges of the XP-92 design remained by this stage in F-102 development, but the production F-102A was to be a very different machine.

After the failure of the YF-102s to go supersonic, Convair put a lengthened model with a relocated fin and wing through wind-tunnel testing. When this also fell short of expectations, they accepted Richard Whitcomb's theories of area rule, further extending and 'wasp waisting' the fuselage. Faced with the prospect of the entire programme being cancelled, Convair worked feverishly to build and fly this new design, the 8-90, in a record 117 days. This, the YF-102A, dubbed the 'Hot Rod', first flew on 19 December 1954.

This head-on view of the 'Hot Rod' illustrates the conical camber (downturned leading edge) that was used on all subsequent F-102s.

Back to the drawing board

Above: The YF-102A (left) was over 16 ft (4.9 m) longer than the YF-102. Other changes included a V-shaped windscreen and new canopy.

Right: Photographed during extensive taxi tests at Lindbergh Field, the first YF-102A, displays its 'Marilyn' fairings. which reduced drag in the transonic flight regime.

After its ground tests, the first YF-102A was taken to Edwards, where it made its first flight on 19 December 1954. Dick Johnson took it through the sound barrier on its second flight two days later. Early the following year, the Air Force rescinded its production hold order and by June the required altitude and speed figures had been met or exceeded.

FJ-1 Fury) pivoted inward about halfway up their struts before retracting outward into the wings. Other dimensions, including a height of 17 ft 8 in (5.38 m), were very similar to those of the earlier, more complex delta-wing design.

Convair had developed considerable sensitivity to the urban 'sprawl' growing on the mesa above Lindbergh Field, so the XF-92A departed San Diego not by air but by truck for the Mojave Desert. E. D. 'Sam' Shannon, a youthful 40 with 20 years of test-pilot experience, took the XF-92A aloft for its maiden flight at Muroc Air Force Base, California (soon to be re-named Edwards) on 18 September 1948. Shannon was sitting in an ejection seat that had been originally designed for the Convair XP-81 compound jet/propeller fighter.

After about 80 test flights at Edwards (and after being publicised along with other Convair products such as the B-36 bomber built in Fort Worth, Texas), the XF-92A was re-engined with a 5,200-lb st (23.13-kN) Allison J33-A-29 equipped with both an afterburner and a water/methanol

injection system which increased thrust to 7,500 lb st (33.36 kN). The afterburner increased fuselage length to 42 ft 5 in (12.93 m), significantly altering the appearance of an aircraft that had previously looked puggish and blunt.

The XF-92A reached 590 mph (949 km/h) but apparently was not supersonic, even with the afterburner or even in a dive. USAF test pilot Major Charles E. Yeager praised it as one of the first jet aircraft with workable hydraulic flight controls. Long after Convair was proceeding with its subsequent F-102 – and making a host of mistakes in the initial design of the new fighter – the XF-92A continued to perform flight test duties for the USAF and in a gleaming cream-white paint scheme for NACA (National Advisory Committee for Aeronautics). Long before there was any Soviet fighter with such a designation, the XF-92A was filmed in matte-grey with the name 'MIG 23' painted in huge letters on its tail for the Hollywood epic *Jet Pilot* starring John Wayne – but, alas, this celluloid villain ended up on the cutting-room floor and the movie was released without it. Today preserved at the Air Force Museum in Dayton, Ohio, the XF-92A provided an enormous amount of aerodynamic data for the future F-102 but, ironically, some of the data may have been wrong and thus may have contributed to the tribulations that went into revising the F-102 design to make it supersonic.

Developing an interceptor

In January 1951, Convair entered the USAF's design competition by submitting its specifications for a delta-winged fighter that eventually became the YF-102A. Convair was selected to carry out Phase I of a development programme, and in August 1951 entered into a contract for the F-102.

At this juncture, not distracted by the Korean War and focused strongly on the likelihood of war with the USSR, the USAF established the Cook-Craigie plan for the production and development of new combat aircraft such as the future F-102A. The plan was formally dubbed the ADTP (Accelerated Development Test Program) and called for two prototypes and the first 40 production aircraft to carry out all phases of development testing which had, in the past, been carried out by a maximum of six aircraft in a typical test programme. Convair saw two motives behind this scheme: firstly, the advent of sustained supersonic flight would require an almost total reinvestigation of all established criteria for testing aircraft, and secondly the ADTP would shorten the development of a new aircraft by a substantial period of time. The latter goal, especially, was to prove elusive, but it seemed a way towards getting the new interceptor into operational service more rapidly.

Accelerated production plans

More to the point, a slow initial production rate parallel to an intensive test programme would work the 'bugs' out of the new aircraft before hundreds had been built, while at the same time preserving the capability for higher-rate production once that happened. The USAF called for tooling that would produce 10 aircraft per month but could later accelerate to a production rate of 50 aircraft per month. Convair made a counter-proposal which called for a progressive tooling policy that would bring the manufacturer up to the capability for 50 aircraft monthly at a gradual pace. As part of these negotiations, Convair acquired Plant II in San Diego to manufacture the F-102, with A. P. Higgins as works manager.

For the engineering team, the creation of the new aircraft posed numerous challenges as it was designing a new aircraft around a new engine that was, itself, still in the design stage. When they sat in meetings with plant engineers, the designers did not yet know that their delta-winged aircraft would eventually introduce a modified cockpit, fuselage length and shape, wing tips, leading edges, and exhaust. All of these changes to the early F-102

concept were to occur while Convair was building a factory that could accommodate the planning and tooling peculiarities associated with the aerodynamics surface tolerances and contour control requirements inherent to supersonic flying.

The first two YF-102 (company Model 8-80) aircraft (52-7994/7995) began flight tests on 24 October 1953, when Richard L. Johnson took the first aircraft (52-7994) aloft. On 2 November 1953, during its seventh flight, a flame-out occurred during take-off and the YF-102 rose a scant 10 ft (3.05 m) or so, wallowed through the air briefly, then smashed into the runway, seriously injuring Johnson and itself being damaged beyond repair. The cause was later identified as a fuel system failure.

'Sam' Shannon (not Johnson, as often reported) first flew the second YF-102 (52-7995) on 11 January 1954, losing relatively little time as a result of the loss of the first machine. It quickly became evident that wind tunnel tests had been unduly optimistic. This aircraft went supersonic for the first time on 27 January 1954, achieving Mach 1.06, but only with difficulty and then in a dive. Even with the highly regarded 10,900-lb st (48.49-kN) Pratt & Whitney J57-P-11 axial-flow turbojet, which offered 14,000 lb st (62.28 kN) with afterburning, the YF-102 lacked the performance that had been predicted, which included the ability to sustain supersonic speed in level flight. A much-healed Johnson returned to the programme in April, and his experience with the original YF-102 design was summed up in the remark, "Performance found lacking". On 28 April 1954, Major General Albert Boyd became the first military pilot to fly the F-102: Boyd flew many types, and there is no evidence that the F-102 especially impressed him.

Wasp waist

The 'wasp waist' or 'Coke bottle' fuselage of the final YF-102A was the result in part of tests conducted on models and mock-ups in the transonic and supersonic ranges in June 1952 by NACA at Langley Field, Virginia. Richard T. Whitcomb of NACA showed Convair

With its distinctive original short fin, this is the first of four YF-102As, now preserved in New Orleans. The YF-102A was weapons-capable and met a particular milestone on 8 July 1955 when six Falcons and 24 rockets were fired in the space of 10 seconds.

The second YF-102A, 53-1788, reverted to the original heavily-framed YF-102 canopy for a period. Here it is seen partially painted in the grey scheme that was to be worn by the majority of Convair fighters to follow. It was preserved at the now-defunct Florence Air and Missile Museum in Florence, South Carolina. More recently it has moved to the Carolinas Aviation Museum in Charlotte, North Carolina.

One of the most visible improvements incorporated on the YF-102A was a two-panel canopy and a V-shaped windscreen. This latter item reduced drag but took some getting used to for pilots. Later a 'vision splitter' (a black sheet of metal) was added behind the leading edge of the screen to cut down reflections.

This is 53-1791, the first of 1,000 'Deuces'. It is seen here some time after its first flight while testing 230-US gal (871-litre) fuel tanks. These purely subsonic wing tanks were designed to increase the interception range, and were to be jettisoned along with the pylons when combat began. A later design made the tank independently jettisonable.

The second YF-102 posed with a block 60 F-102A (below) to show the many changes between the prototype and a late-production F-102A. Immediately obvious are the differences in fuselage cross section, the tall tail and the cockpit glazing. The intake splitter plates and airbrake were among the many other external changes. The YF-102 is fitted with an elongated nose section that contrasts with the stubby unit of the other early 'Deuces'.

F-102A

The first production Model 8-10 F-102A followed the 8-90 (YF-102A), making its first flight on 24 June 1955. By this time around 190 aircraft had been ordered, even though YF-102A testing was incomplete. The F-102A had a number of detail changes, including a larger airbrake and redesigned intakes with external splitter plates.

engineers his area-rule principle. Wind tunnel tests showed that the original constant-taper fuselage could lose a tremendous amount of configuration drag – making the aircraft faster and more fuel-efficient – when revised with a pinched mid-section. This meant a design change (in contrast to the original F-102 design, which flew as the YF-102) with an extension of approximately 7 ft (2.13 m) to the rear of the fuselage with a corresponding movement of the vertical tail and an approximately 3-ft 3-in (0.99-m) rearward movement of the delta wing to maintain balance. In blunt words, the original fuselage was too bulky. Yet it would not be until August 1953 that Convair would accept the implications of area rule – while in the meantime manufacturing 10 almost useless YF-102 aircraft with the unwaisted fuselage.

While this was going on, Convair was becoming tooled up to produce the original F-102 design (as flown in YF-102 form) but a company document reported that, 'The performance gains with the J57 engine in the transonic speed range and in high speed at altitude [offered by the redesign of the aircraft] were sufficient to warrant serious consideration of a change in the F-102 configuration in as early in the production program as was feasible. Since this change would have an appreciable effect on the flight test program, [Convair] reviewed the change with all affected

Air Force agencies in an effort to obtain a decision as to whether this change [area rule] should be incorporated. It was decided that the change would not have adverse effect' on the goal of having the new fighter in squadron service by early 1956. Nor would the change to the fuselage design jeopardise the ongoing development of the fire-control system.

In May 1954, the USAF decided that the F-102 needed a fire-control system more advanced than the E-9, which was already in service on the Northrop F-89H Scorpion, so the decision was taken that the Hughes E-10 system, soon redesignated as the MG-10, should be prepared for the F-102.

Early operations

Rarely, if ever, had a warplane design seen so many changes as those which differentiated the YF-102 from the subsequent YF-102A, or Model 8-90. The outside observer could have been forgiven for thinking that the latter was a wholly new aircraft. On both aircraft, the 'Y' prefix indicated a service-test role, although the original YF-102 was in reality more of an experimental research vehicle.

On 20 December 1954, test pilot Johnson performed the first flight of the first YF-102A (53-1787), dubbed the 'Hot Rod' by some. This much-revised version employed the new area-rule technology and in its external shape closely resembled the production configuration of the new fighter. This aircraft also introduced a cleaned-up cockpit and canopy design, a lengthened fuselage and a modified exhaust area, all of which were retained on production machines, and the changes gave the YF-102A a look distinctly different from that of the YF-102 aircraft that had been flying for more than a year. The YF-102A had an interim powerplant in the form of the J57-P-41 turbojet

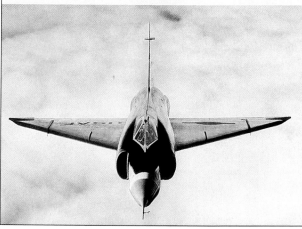

Convair also issued these comparison images of a YF-102 (top) and a YF-102A, showing the tubular fuselage of the YF-102 and the 'Coke bottle' area-ruled fuselage of its successor. Note also the extra wing fences on the YF-102A.

and also the small fin associated with early 'Deuce' aircraft, and was one of the few aircraft in the series to fly in natural metal finish. 'CONVAIR UNVEILS NEW PLANE', headlined the *San Diego Evening Tribune* two weeks later on 5 January 1955.

The new aircraft also behaved differently: Johnson discovered that it needed less runway for take-off, could achieve Mach 1.2 in level flight, and was still climbing when the altimeter read 51,600 ft (15727 m).

While the YF-102A was being tested, Convair was exploring other ideas. In 1955, the company briefly explored the possibility, for the US Navy, of a carrier-based version of its new fighter, using laboratory models based on the original YF-102 design and studying the concept's use with the C-7 and C-11 American adaptations of the British-developed steam catapult. The company studied variations in catapult attachment point, catapult bridle length and other features. Had it been built, the US Navy version would presumably have been designated F3Y-1. Convair was later to go to even greater effort in mooting a carrierborne version of the subsequent F-106A, but neither the 'Deuce' nor the 'Six' ever came close to flying in naval livery.

Service test batch

Convair eventually turned out four YF-102A (53-1787/1790) service test aircraft. For reasons never made clear, the second of these retained the 'prison bar' braced canopy of the earlier YF-102 aircraft, while the other three adopted the new canopy shape. Phase I performance testing was conducted from 20 December 1954 through to the end of February 1955, and confirmed performance expectations for the new YF-102A configuration. The first aircraft achieved a speed of Mach 1.20 at 35,000 ft (10668 m) on 21 December 1954, on 29 December exceeded an altitude of 52,000 ft (15850 m), and on 21 January 1955 flew to the highest altitude yet reached, namely 55,130 ft (16804 m).

Right and below: A series of publicity photos was taken of a quartet of early F-102s shortly before delivery to the Air Force in April 1956. FC-792, and -794 were F-102A-5s and FC-795 and -796 were -10s. There were only four of the first block and three of the latter produced, indicating the high number of modifications requested and incorporated after early testing.

Phase II testing of the early 'Deuces', covering flying qualities, stability and control, lasted until March 1956. Thereafter, the first YF-102A was modified with the tailpipe shape intended for the F-106A interceptor and was flown until 25 April 1956 to evaluate this feature. The flight test programme for the YF-102A was completed on 2 October 1956. Fully a decade later, the first YF-102A would briefly reappear in a new role. In the mid-1960s, apparently after it was no longer airworthy, the aircraft became the first 'Deuce' to be painted in the T.O.114 camouflage scheme adopted during the years of the Vietnam War. It wore an early version of the 'camo' scheme which left the radome white and the radio call number (serial number) in white lettering on the tail. All F-102 warplanes that eventually acquired the green, brown and tan warpaint received it at Convair's Plant 2 in San Diego and were flown back to operational units from Lindbergh Field.

Seen turning finals for Wright Field, this early F-102A, the last of five F-102A-15s, was assigned to trials work with Air Research and Development Command. On this particular test, a KB-50 tanker had been spraying water over the 'Deuce' at high altitude as part of investigations into the type's icing characteristics. A small residue of ice is just visible on the underside of the nose.

F-102 Details

The two YF-102s sported a heavily-framed cockpit windscreen and canopy design (far left), soon abandoned in favour of the YF-102A's smaller canopy, with less framework (left). Note also the redesigned engine air intakes which, on production F-102As, were again altered to include a splitter plate.

Below: The IRST, installed in F-102As from 1963 under Project Big Eight, was fitted immediately in front of the windscreen.

Convair F-102A Delta Dagger cutaway drawing

1 Pitot head
2 Radome
3 Radar scanner
4 Scanner tracking mechanism
5 ILS glideslope aerial
6 Radar mounting bulkhead
7 Radar pulse generator and modulator units
8 Nose compartment access doors
9 Static port
10 Lower IFF aerial
11 Angle of attack transmitter
12 TACAN aerial
13 MG-10 fire control system electronics
14 Nose compartment longeron
15 Infra-red detector
16 Electronics cooling air duct
17 Windscreen panels
18 Central vision splitter
19 Instrument panel shroud
20 Rudder pedals and linkages
21 Cockpit front pressure bulkhead
22 Air conditioning system ram air intake
23 Boundary layer splitter plate
24 Electrical system equipment
25 Port air intake
26 Nosewheel door
27 Taxiing lamp
28 Nosewheel, forward-retracting
29 Nose undercarriage leg strut
30 Torque scissor links
31 Intake duct framing
32 Nose undercarriage pivot mounting
33 Cockpit pressure floor
34 Port side console panel
35 Engine throttle lever
36 Two-handed control grip, radar and flight controls
37 Pilot's ejection seat
38 Canopy handle
39 Starboard side console panel
40 Radar display
41 Optical sight
42 Cockpit canopy cover, upward-hingeing
43 Ejection seat headrest
44 Boundary layer spill duct
45 Sloping cockpit rear pressure bulkhead
46 Air conditioning plant
47 Canopy external release
48 Canopy jack
49 Air exit louvres
50 Equipment bay access hatches, port and starboard
51 Canopy hinge
52 Radio and electronics equipment bay
53 Forward position light
54 Intake trunking
55 Missile bay cooling air duct
56 Missile bay door pneumatic jacks
57 Canopy emergency release
58 Liquid oxygen converter
59 Electrical system equipment bay

60 Fuselage upper longeron
61 Upper IFF aerial
62 Wing front spar attachment bulkhead
63 Pneumatic system air bottles
64 Bifurcated intake duct
65 Close-pitched fuselage frame construction
66 Engine bleed air duct
67 Anti-collision light
68 Starboard wing forward main fuel tank, total internal capacity 1,085 US gal (4107 litres)
69 Inboard wing fence
70 Fuel system piping
71 Centre-section wing dry bay
72 Wing pylon mountings and connectors
73 Starboard main undercarriage pivot mounting
74 Dorsal spine fairing
75 Intake duct mixing chamber
76 Engine intake centre-body fairing
77 Wing main spar attachment bulkheads
78 Intake compressor face
79 Forward engine mounting
80 Pratt & Whitney J57-P-23A afterburning turbojet engine
81 Engine oil tank, capacity 5.5 US gal (21 litres)
82 Oil filler cap
83 Starboard wing aft main fuel tanks
84 Fuel feed and vent piping
85 Ventral actuator fairing
86 Outboard wing fence
87 Cambered leading edge
88 Wing tip camber wash-out
89 Starboard navigation light
90 Fixed portion of trailing edge
91 Starboard outer elevon
92 Elevon hydraulic actuator
93 Trailing-edge dry bay
94 Fin leading-edge rib construction
95 Aerial tuning units
96 Fin attachment joints
97 Tailfin construction
98 Artificial feel system pitot intakes

103 VOR localiser aerial
104 Rudder
105 Honeycomb core rudder construction
106 Split airbrake panels
107 Airbrake pneumatic jacks
108 Airbrake, open position
109 Variable-area afterburner exhaust nozzle
110 Aft fuselage aerodynamic (area-rule) fairing
111 Exhaust nozzle control jacks (eight)
112 Tailcone attachment joint frame (engine removal)
113 Rear position lights
114 Afterburner duct
115 Engine bay internal heat shield
116 Brake parachute housing
117 Rudder hydraulic actuator
118 Rudder trim and feel force control units
119 Afterburner fuel manifold
120 Rear engine mounting
121 Inboard elevon hydraulic actuator
122 Engine turbine section
123 Bleed air connections
124 Bleed air blow-off valve
125 Engine accessory equipment gearbox
126 Wingspar/fuselage frame pin joints
127 Wing root rib
128 Port wing aft integral fuel tanks
129 Fuel tank dividing rib
130 Rear spar
131 Trailing-edge ribs
132 Runway emergency arrester hook, lowered
133 Elevon spar
134 Inboard elevon
135 Elevon rib construction
136 Outboard elevon
137 Trailing-edge honeycomb
138 Wing tip fairing construction

144 Twin main spars
145 Main undercarriage side strut
146 Hydraulic retraction jack
147 Main undercarriage leg pivot mounting
148 Drag strut and pneumatic brake reservoir
149 Landing lamp
150 Port wing dry bay
151 Wing pylon mountings and connectors
152 Main undercarriage leg door
153 Port mainwheel
154 Torque scissor links
155 Port wing forward integral fuel tank
156 Inboard wing fence
157 Mainwheel door
158 Hydraulic reservoirs
159 Position of ram air turbine on starboard side
160 Missile bay aft section doors

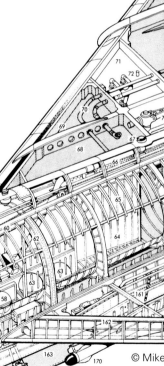

© Mike

99 Sloping front spar
100 Upper fin multi-spar construction
101 Fin tip aerial fairing
102 UHF aerials

139 Port navigation light
140 Cambered leading-edge rib construction
141 Outboard wing fence
142 Wing rib construction
143 Main undercarriage mounting rib

e over-run barrier probe
spar
e bay doors
hic action missile
ent gear
ent gear hydraulic jack
unch rail
y door integral rocket launch

The F-102's massive nose cone (above left) contained its Hughes MG-10 fire control system (FCS) comprising a radar scanner (above) and associated electronics. Originally Hughes' E-9 FCS (later known as MG-3), as fitted to the Northrop F-89, was selected for the 'Deuce', but an aircraft with the performance of the F-102 demanded a better system and the MG-10 was chosen. MG-10 was effectively MG-3 with a addition of an AN/ARR-44 datalink, MG-1 automatic flight control system and AN/ARC-34 miniaturised communications set.

Mike Badrocke

These views of the YF-102A (below) and a production F-102A (above) show the aerodynamic fairings either side of the tail pipe, introduced when the fuselage was 'area-ruled' to reduce drag. Note also the smaller speed brake on the YF-102A. In the upper a Technical Sergeant packs the aircraft's braking parachute.

The F-102 sported a single pylon beneath each wing, used exclusively for the carriage of a 215-US gal (814 litre) drop tank.

ssile bay door
-cm) FFAR folding-fin rockets

alcon air-to-air missile (6)
fuel tank pylon
al (814 -litre) external fuel

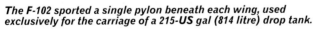

Ejection seat

Unlike the later F-106 seat, there was no official requirement for the F-102 escape system to cope with ejection at high altitude and high Mach. A conventional explosive cartridge-fired seat manufactured by Weber was fitted, although there had been a proposal for an elaborate capsule system. F-102A ejection seat testing required the use of one of the first supersonic rocket sled tracks in existence, at the Air Force Flight Test Center at Edwards AFB. The TF-102 trainer offered particular challenges, being the first supersonic aircraft with side-by-side seating.

Space normally used for the weapons system on the TF-102 was used to mount test recording equipment on the nose section used in ejection tests. The high-speed test track was dubbed 'The Edwards and Western Supersonic Railroad'.

While the 'Deuce' was still a service-test type, Stanley Aviation developed a pilot capsule that would permit bail-out from the new interceptor at supersonic speed. A mock-up was completed using the braced YF-102 canopy configuration. The capsule enabled the pilot to eject upwards in a pressurised, air-tight and water-tight cocoon designed to shield him from wind blast and, if necessary, to keep him afloat at sea. Stanley hoped to sell the system not only for the F-102 but for other fighters in the 'Century'

series. A working example was never built, and the idea was then abandoned in favour of a conventional ejection seat.

It is worth noting as a footnote regarding the earlier 'Deuce' prototypes that, at some point in the test programme, 52-7995 (the second YF-102 and oldest surviving aircraft in this series) was modified with the nose associated with the very different YF-102A, possibly to serve as a test ship for the MG-10 system. The new nose section was apparently painted in Dayglo colours. This aircraft did not, of course, have the area-ruled fuselage and other features found on the YF-102A, and retained the braced canopy found only on the YF-102 aircraft and a single YF-102A, but the new nose made it look more like the 'new' F-102 than the old.

F-102A model

When 53-1791 made its maiden flight on 24 June 1955, the 'Y' prefix vanished like a hot potato. Convair announced that this was the first production fighter in the series even though it was nothing of the sort. In fact, the

Service entry

The F-102A entered service with the 327th Fighter Interceptor Squadron at George AFB, California in April 1956. Even this date was seven months behind the revised delivery schedule agreed in March 1954. A month before this date, the USAF and Convair had decided on further design revisions, including enlarging the vertical fin, and the 327th was to be the only operational unit to use the 'small tail' F-102s.

Air Defense Command was eager to publicise its hot new interceptor and staged a series of fine publicity pictures, showing the 327th FIS at full strength and conducting a practice 'scramble'.

'weapon system' was nowhere near finalised as the FCS was still being refined and other production-standard features had not yet been installed. Flight testing for the F-102A, as distinguished from the YF-102A, began on 24 June 1956. Initially, 53-1791 and the airframes that followed soon after it still had the interim J57-P-41 engine, Case X wing with cambered leading edges and wing tips, an area-ruled fuselage and a small vertical tail surface.

During flutter tests 53-1791 demonstrated some unsatisfactory handling qualities above Mach 1.20. This led to extensive flight testing between July 1955 and January 1956 to determine corrective modifications. The result was an extended engine inlet ramp, beef-up of the engine inlet duct inter-wall, and bifurcation of the inlet duct wedge. After these modifications, the first F-102A demonstrated

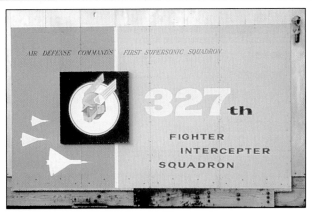

Left: The 327th was equally proud of its new supersonic interceptors, although the smart signage masked a number of frustrating teething problems. These included landing gear defects and disintegrating speedbrakes.

Left and below: The 327th's early F-102As were smoothed and polished and proudly wore the squadron's iron mask badge. Variations in markings, even on the very first aircraft, included the position of the national insignia and of the 'U.S. Air Force' titles. The squadron commander's aircraft received the one-off chequered tail pattern seen below.

An F-102A-41-CO shows off the exceptionally clean lines of the early 'Deuce'. The internal weapons bay, a feature that has returned on the latest US fighters for 'stealth' reasons, was the main reason for this purity of form. Later upgrades added external fuel tanks, an arrester hook, anti-collision beacons and an infra-red search-and-track sensor. This aircraft has the large fin, but retains the original small airbrake.

Perrin AFB, Texas was the home to USAF interceptor pilot training for many years under the auspices of the 4780th Air Defense Wing, whose 1959 markings are seen here.

The 327th FIS came up with this colourful tail marking after it received its tall-tailed F-102s. It was short-lived as the 327th soon exchanged California for Greenland and arctic red trim.

satisfactory performance up to the Mach 1.5 that had been part of the original specification. On 18 January 1956, the aircraft reached Mach 1.535.

Tank tests

Following Phase IV tests (operational suitability), 53-1791 was modified in September 1956 for the carriage of external tanks. External fuel tank testing was conducted in November and December 1956, and on 27 December 1956 a test pilot successfully jettisoned the tanks simultaneously at an altitude of 36,515 ft (11130 m) at the speed of Mach 0.953. The remainder of the programme so far as 53-1791 was concerned came to an end on 31 July 1957 after tests that were not related to performance.

On 10 December 1955, the 23rd example of the F-102A (53-1813) made the first flight with the larger fin (described below) that later became standard. The test programme consisted primarily of stability and control and flutter testing. The programme ended on 18 April 1956, and the large tail was adopted for the final production configuration. A later F-102A (54-1380) was assigned the task of powerplant and components development for the production J57-P-23A engine which replaced the interim J57-P-41. Engine tests were started on 13 June 1956 and concluded on 2 April 1957.

Evaluation of the Case XX wing was conducted with yet another F-102A (54-1317). Testing began on 28 June 1957 and continued through to 19 November 1957. This wing then became the production standard. The new wing appeared on all F-102 aircraft leaving the factory after October 1957, and was retrofitted on all others in operation. With it, the interceptor was capable of reaching 55,000 ft (16765 m), and also had much improved stability, especially at lower speeds.

The 64th FIS at McChord AFB, later Paine Field, Washington, was one of 16 ADC squadrons to equip with the 'Deuce' during 1957. One of the squadron's 'Tubs' is seen at McChord in September of that year.

TF-102A: the 'Tub'

In July 1954, while the F-102A was still undergoing modification to 'hot rod' configuration, the USAF ordered 20 of the Model 8-12 or TF-102A. Previous interceptors such as the F-86, F-89 and F-101 had been built only in single-control versions to that point. Neither ADC nor Air Training Command believed that pilots could safely transition to the delta-winged fighter directly from conventional jet trainers. At the time, flight training was mainly conducted on the T-33 and radar training in specially equipped B-25s. Following successful initial testing of the revised F-102A, a production 'hold' order was rescinded, and a further 28 TF-102As were ordered in early 1955. Eventually, one in every nine of all 'Deuces' was built as a two-seater, or 'Tub', for a grand total of 111. The side-by-side seating arrangement was chosen, despite the likely performance loss, to simplify radar training in particular. Unfortunately, severe buffeting problems proved impossible to solve by revising the canopy and windscreen design. In the end, rows of inelegant vortex generators provided a cure, but not until after another production 'hold' and a cut in the air force order. The similarly configured English Electric Lightning trainers (also colloquially known as 'Tubs') appeared somewhat later, design of the first, the T.Mk 4, beginning in 1957.

The prototype TF-102A takes shape among the single-seaters at San Diego. The mock-up forward fuselage, which was approved in early 1954, was constructed at Convair's Fort Worth facility.

Cold weather

In March 1956, the 11th example of the F-102A (53-1801) went to Ladd AFB, Alaska to undergo Arctic climate testing. The evaluation under real-life conditions had been preceded by artificial Arctic tests in an indoor climate hangar at Eglin AFB, Florida. This machine was probably the first 'Deuce' to wear brilliant Arctic red colours on rear fuselage and outer wing panels.

By June 1956 Convair was preparing for series production of three versions of the new aircraft, namely the F-102A single-seat interceptor, the TF-102A two-seat version with full combat capabilities (later to be called the 'Tub' by crews), and the F-102B (Convair Model 8-24, originally 8-21, also dubbed Weapon System WS-201B) with the more powerful J75 engine, inspired by the appearance of the Soviet Myasischyev M-4 'Bison' turbojet-powered long-range strategic bomber. On 17 June 1956, however, the F-102B was redesignated as the F-106A (see *Wings of Fame* No. 13).

The October 1955 debut of the TF-102A combat proficiency trainer, or Model 8-12, was not a rollout so much as a rollover – over the freeway, that is. San Diego was belatedly joining the rest of California in sprouting obscene, six-lane thoroughfares. Newly-built 'Deuces', mounted atop a large truck trailer, had to be transported past the main gate at Plant 2 (where a guard post had to be moved to make room for it to pass), then taken over a small

Below: The first flight of the TF-102A on 8 November 1955 was five months behind schedule. Buffeting problems were not sorted out until the third aircraft, by which time the USAF had decided to cut its order by nearly 70 aircraft.

narrow bridge which was the only way to cross the broad Pacific Highway (today's Interstate No. 5). The sight of a jet aircraft passing above freeway traffic eventually became routine, since this became the way all 'Deuces' began their travels, but at this juncture it drew considerable comment from press and public. The first TF-102A (54-1351) was

Above: A cynic might say that this classic 1950s publicity shot was an attempt to equate the portly lines of the TF-102A with those of a more popular two-seater, a Ford Thunderbird. Compared to the F-102A, the TF was no 'sports car', being more commonly referred to as a 'sled'.

Below: This view across the cockpit of a TF-102A shows the roomy interior. The pilot is Mercury astronaut Gordon 'Gordo' Cooper on a proficiency flight with a NASA-assigned TF-102A. The new nose was 6 in (15.25 cm) higher than that of the A, and it increased the overall fuselage width by 11 in (27.9 cm).

then taken by land to Edwards AFB where, on 31 October 1955, tests began with the performance of the first flight by Dick Johnson.

The 'Tub' was viewed as the answer to the knotty problem of familiarising an interceptor pilot with flying and fighting a complex supersonic weapons system. Initially, it was also billed as the solution to the criticism of the one-man all-weather fighter, because this version could be flown as a full tactical weapon by either one or two men. In fact, although it was fully capable of operating with the basic missile armament, the TF-102A lacked the MG-10 system fitted to the F-102A. In practice after the type became operational, the TF-102A was not used interchangeably with the F-102A on interceptor duties. And indeed it was not interchangeable, being marginally slower than the needle-nosed variant with one-man accommodation.

The very first TF-102A started out with the production J57-P-23A engine but had pre-production Case X wing with cambered leading edges and tips, the small tail and no vortex generators on the large canopy.

The two-seat model used a nose section manufactured at Convair's other factory in Fort Worth, Texas and trucked overland to San Diego to be mated to a fuselage in Plant 2. Early test flying revealed a problem not found in the single-seater, namely a buffet condition at Mach 0.85 to 0.90. Various fixes were tried, including balsa wedges on the aircraft's exterior in the canopy area, boundary-layer plough slats and many configurations of vortex generators. In April 1956, the USAF conducted a comparative flight evaluation of the original canopy configuration on the first aircraft and a cut-down canopy shape on the third (53-1353), of which the latter has apparently never been seen in surviving photos. The tests validated the original canopy configuration and this, with vortex generators installed, was selected

for the production configuration. Buffet testing was completed on 28 November 1956 and the TF-102A was considered satisfactory to move ahead to service evaluation.

An early TF-102A (54-1380) was used for powerplant development work from 13 June 1956 to 2 April 1957, resulting in minor changes to the production engine. A subsequent TF-102A (54-1390) was the first with the large fin. The test programme for this configuration included stability and control, flutter and landing gear structural tests, and ran from 27 August 1956 to 23 October 1957. External fuel tank testing was performed with another TF-102A (54-1398) from 21 September 1956 to 9 April 1958, and this aircraft was also used to test some F-106A landing gear structural features.

The F-102 was very slow in development, flight test and deployment, and began to reach USAF squadrons only in April 1956, when the first arrived to join the 327th Fighter Interceptor Squadron (FIS) at George AFB, California.

By the time the 'Deuce' became operational, the development of the new interceptor had taken so long, and had involved so many airframes, that the USAF was littered with flying machines that were only partly up to the production standard. The effort to convert these ships from test versions to the tactical configuration was carried out by Convair in Fort Worth. It included changes to the radar system, missile bay doors, air inlet ramp and automatic flight control system. The 'Test to Tactical' programme added every feature, no matter how minor, that was now part of the definitive production standard. And, after all the years of work, the production warplane was a spectacle to behold.

A footnote to the story of a warplane that had in essence only two variants, namely the single- and two-seat versions, is that though the USAF assigned the designation F-102C, no operational aircraft ever took to the air as a 'C' model.

Rockets and missiles

The F-102 was designed as the airframe portion of the MX-1179 weapons system, of which the MG-10 was to become the fire control system (FCS) and the AIM-4 Falcon was to be the primary air-to-air weapon. These latter two elements were designed in parallel with the F-102 itself, but at the time Convair won the airframe contract, all they knew about the rest of MX-1179 was the maximum dimensions of the components. In the end, weapons system integration proved to be one of the least troublesome aspects of the programme and the F-102 was soon demonstrating the ability to fire all four AIM-4s and 24 rockets within seconds. The rockets, initially of both 2-in and 2.75-in types, were the 'Deuce's secondary armament, providing a 'shotgun' capabilty against targets that escaped the missiles.

Below: The F-102's rockets were mounted inside the missile bay doors. There were three tubes in each of four doors, into which pairs of rockets could be loaded, one behind the other. The aft pair was not usually loaded in peacetime for safety reasons, and later the capacity was reduced by half in order to accommodate the larger Nuclear Falcon in the weapons bay. This sequence, covering 'perhaps two-tenths of a second' according to Convair, shows a launch of all 24 rockets from one of the earliest production F-102As.

Convair proposed to use an upgraded J57 turbojet engine, the J57-P-47 with a titanium compressor, in an installation that would have extended the tail cone by 7 in (0.178 m), and the other major change would have been the revision of the missile bay to include provision for one MB-1 Genie unguided rocket projectile with a nuclear warhead. A number of F-102A aircraft were used in special tests, and one F-102A (53-1806), was photographed at Sheppard AFB, Texas marked as a 'YF-102C'.

F-102A described

The F-102A Delta Dagger interceptor, or Model 8-10, viewed from outside, was nothing less than a miracle of the pre-microchip industrial age. The powerplant was based on one J57-P-23A axial-flow turbojet engine rated at 10,200 lb st (45.37 kN) on military power at sea level and at 16,000 lb st (71.17 kN) with afterburning. Although it was considered an interim engine when it was introduced on the production 'Deuce', the J57 became the standard not only for the F-102 fleet but for most of the aircraft entering service in the late 1950s. The engine weighed 5,045 lb (2288 kg) and was equipped with an automatic, two-

Above: A 329th FIS F-102 flicks open its weapons bay and fires a salvo of AIM-4s. Infra-red and radar-guided missiles were usually fired in pairs, but firing all six at a single target in wartime might have been considered overkill.

Wearing a partial pressure suit, a USAF pilot looks longingly at an infra-red-guided AIM-4C. Behind him is a radar-guided AIM-4A. There were endless variations of this pose in 1950s Hughes publicity photos, which at least gave a good idea of the missile's size.

F-102 Colours

Vermont ANG

0·70869

U.S. AIR FORCE

The Green Mountain Boys

This F-102A of 'The Green Mountain Boys' has various items of green trim over its basic colours, including green wing fences. At different times, the 134th FIS marked flight assignment with coloured chevrons and/or fin tips.

California ANG (196th FIS)

0·61391

U.S. AIR FORCE

Most F-102s were painted in overall 'Air Defense Command Gray': Federal Standard Colour 16473, like this one. The 196th FIS and a couple of other units operated 'natural metal' F-102s for some years. These appear to have been silver painted rather than bare metal.

Hawaii ANG

53357

U.S. AIR FORCE

In their 15-year career with the 199th FIS, Hawaii ANG, the squadron's F-102s markings varied little. One addition to the basic scheme was red trim on the wing fences and fin tip.

Minnesota ANG

0·61323

U.S. AIR FORCE

In common with F-102s and other interceptors based in Alaska, Canada, Greenland and Iceland, 179th FIS 'Deuces' were trimmed in Arctic red. The letter 'B' on the air brake of this example may have been a flight assignment or an individual code letter.

Florida ANG

USAF·O·61122

13

Some ANG F-102 units, such as Florida's 159th FIS, had all-camouflaged aircraft in their later years. Some of these had seen service in Vietnam, while others had been repainted for USAFE units.

Turkey

0·53404

Türk Hava Kuvvetleri (Turkish Air Force) F-102s retained their basic USAF colour schemes and even their serials. In the latter part of their service, the circular roundel replaced the earlier white-bordered red square.

Greece

0·61238

Elliniki Polimiki Aeroporia (Hellenic Air Force) F-102s were mainly supplied from USAFE stocks, and included both camouflaged and ADC grey airframes. Like the Turkish AF aircraft, they wore their old USAF serials.

The 'silver bullet' in the Deuce's armoury from 1963 was the 'Falcon Model Y52A' or AIM-26 Super Falcon, in its nuclear tipped AIM-26A form also known as 'Nuclear Falcon'. Around half of the F-102 fleet was equipped to carry the missile at a modification cost of $10,000 per aircraft.

Above: As may be seen from this view of members of the Hughes Falcon AAM family (from left: AIM-26A, AIM-4C, AIM-4A, AIM-4G and AIM-4F), a typical AIM-4 was between 78 in (1.98 m) and 86 in (2.18 m) in length. The white leading edges on some of the missiles' fins are fuses to detonate the warhead.

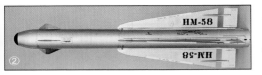

Above: More than 450 F/TF-102As were modified prior to 1963 under T.O. 1F-102A-620 to carry one or a pair of SARH AIM-26A (GAR-11) nuclear-capable AAMs in the centre bay. AIM-26A Super Falcon employed the same 1.5kT warhead as Douglas AIR-2 (MB-1) Genie and was proximity fused. AIM-26B (GAR-11A) was the nuclear Super Falcon's conventionally-armed equivalent. Though Convair proposed an 'F-102C' (originally 'F-102X') armed with a single Genie (and four Falcons), the unguided nuclear-tipped air-to-air rocket never formed part of the Deuce's arsenal, though F-102A 53-1797 was used to test the weapon at Holloman AFB, New Mexico in mid-1957.

The F-102's primary air-to-air weapon was the Hughes AIM-4 Falcon AAM (known as XF-98 in its prototype form and later redesignated GAR-1). Up to six missiles, usually three each of an IR- and radar-guided variant, were carried in pairs on rails in the aircraft's three weapons bays. The main AIM-4 models with which the F-102 was armed were, initially, the SARH AIM-4A (GAR-1D) ① and the IR-guided AIM-4C (GAR-2A, or HM-58 when exported) ②. These were superseded by the SARH AIM-4E (the first of the so-called Super Falcons, developed for use in the F-106 and originally known as GAR-3) and IR AIM-4F (GAR-3A) ③, respectively. Two other IR-guided Falcon variants saw limited use in the F-102. The AIM-4D (GAR-2B, middle right) was the last production Falcon, tailored for anti-fighter combat, while the AIM-4G (GAR-4A) was an AIM-4F derivative with a new IR seeker able to lock-on to smaller targets at greater distances. The other F-102A weapon option was up to 24 2.75-in (70-mm) folding-fin aerial rockets (FFARs) located in tubes in the missile bay doors. Aircraft modified to carry AIM-26 carried only 12 rockets, those on the two centre bay doors being deleted. Eventually the FFARs were removed altogether from F-102s.

Right: Each weapons bay contained two Falcon launch rails, each of which carried a single missile. During the firing sequence, the launch rails were hydraulically extended into the slipstream

Above: Typical of the IR-guided Falcons, AIM-4D was 79½ in (2.02 m) in length, 6⅜ in (0.163 m) in diameter, had a 20-in (0.508-m) span and a launch weight of 134 lb (61 kg). With a range of six miles (9.7 km), it had a top speed of Mach 4.

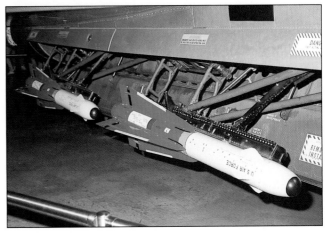

At the peak of Air Defense Command F-102 operations at the end of 1958, 25 squadrons were equipped with the type. Six squadrons had formed or transitioned in 1956 and 15 the following year. By 1959, the 'Ultimate Interceptor', the F-106, was coming on line, and the 'Deuce' was being handed down to ANG squadrons.

Above: The 482nd FIS from Seymour Johnson was one of the squadrons that worked up on the F-102 in 1956. It kept its mounts for a relatively long period – until 1965, but was then inactivated.

Above: The 11th FIS at Duluth, Minnesota was one of the earliest F-102 users (August 1956) and one of the first to pass them on in favour of the F-106, in 1960.

Below: The 27th FIS had an even briefer career with the 'Deuce', transitioning from the F-94C in June 1957 and receiving F-106s in February 1959.

Above: The 48th FIS at Langley AFB, Virginia was proud of its new delta-winged interceptors, and emblazoned them with a 48-starred tailfin design. Within three years of accepting the F-102, the 48th transitioned to slightly less gaudy F-106s.

Above right: The 332nd FIS, initially at McGuire AFB, New Jersey, operated the F-102 for nearly eight years, inactivating in mid-1965 at Thule, Greenland.

position tailpipe first introduced on the first YF-102A. The afterburner nozzle unit was manufactured by another company headquartered in San Diego, subcontractor Rheem.

Fuselage and armament

The needle-nosed and area-ruled fuselage of the F-102A was 68 ft 1½ in (11.62 m) in length including the nose probe, while the TF-102A two-seater was a fraction of an inch longer. The fuselage structure of the F-102A was largely of light alloy construction but utilised titanium alloy frames around the area of the powerplant. The fuselage's central section was manufactured in left and right front and rear quarters. The final canopy design was of knife-edged windscreen glazed with stretched plastic which could not

Cuba occupied ADC for a number of years. F-102s were first directed towards the island during Operation Southern Tip in 1961 and again in October 1962 during the Missile Crisis. This 326th FIS F-102A shows its planform over the Gulf of Mexico on a detachment to Key West.

be shattered by impact, manufactured at different times by Beech and Goodyear. The pilot sat in a roomy cockpit on a lightweight Weber ejection seat. The ejection sequence could supposedly be completed in two seconds – first the cockpit depressurised, then the canopy unlocked and jettisoned, and finally the seat was fired. For normal cruising flight the cockpit was pressurised to 7.2 lb/sq in (0.5 bar), but USAF regulations required that for flight above 50,000 ft (15240 m) the MC-1 pressure suit was to be worn. The suit appeared on many recruiting posters in the 1950s and was frequently worn during test flying, but in an operational setting it was rarely, if ever, worn.

Immediately aft and below the canopy was the first of three missile bays, which in total carried six Hughes GAR-1 Falcon semi-active radar homing missiles (originally designated F-98, developed under Project MX-904, and later redesignated AIM-4 in 1962), designed to home on a target illuminated by the fire control radar of the MG-10 FCS. This early missile was soon supplanted by the improved GAR-1B (AIM-4B) version. Both of these radar-homing variants were later made interchangeable with the GAR-2A (AIM-4C) missile with infra-red homing. The Falcons were mounted on short rails which were extended into the airstream before the missiles were fired in a fraction of a second. The secondary armament on the F-102 was initially intended to be an unspecified number of 20-in (508-mm) T214B unguided air-to-air rocket projectiles. After developmental work on the T214B was abandoned at an early stage, the F-102A initially carried a secondary armament of twenty-four 2¾-in (70-mm) FFAR (Folding

Below: A latter-day 'Rosie the Rivetter' manoeuvres an F-102A windscreen frame into position on a forward fuselage section.

Above: The F-102 line is seen on the night shift somewhere about one-third of the way through the production run. In all, exactly 1,000 aircraft were produced in just over three years, with F-106 production gearing up in the same period

Below: The 'wing primary line' began with the basic structure panels, which were integral fuel tanks. By the end of the line, the wings were ready for attachment, with leading edges, doors, landing gear, wiring and elevons all fitted.

F-102 factory

Convair's Plant 2 at Lindbergh Field, formerly used for B-24 production, was transformed from an empty building to an F-102 factory in 16 months. Initial production was exactly on schedule, but Convair admitted that they were delivering an "80 per cent weapon", rather than the fully-equipped fighter the new production line was designed to produce. Peak monthy deliveries were in June 1956, when 51 aircraft were accepted by the USAF. The peak year was FY57 when 372 (more than the total number of F-106s produced) were handed over. The Convair Service Center, also at San Diego, did a degree of refurbishment work and repainting of aircraft for the Air Force.

Although most overhaul work was conducted at Sacramento, the San Diego factory did some work on the 'Deuce'. In September-October 1965, aircraft destined for Vietnam arrived from Travis AFB for painting in the T.O.114 camouflage. This pair is seen leaving for Travis in late October, while others await their turn in the paintshop in the background.

North to Alaska

Deployment of the F-102 to Alaska (and to Europe) had to wait for the installation of TACAN equipment. The Alaska-bound aircraft were prepared first and two squadrons, the 31st and 317th FISs, were transferred to Alaskan Air Command (AAC) in August 1957. After a reorganisation in 1960, the 31st was disbanded and the 317th took over its aircraft, basing them at Elmendorf with detachments at Galena, King Salmon, Ladd and Eielson. Despite this dispersal of operations, the F-102s were hard pressed to defend Alaskan airspace and a number of Soviet intruders came too close for Washington's comfort. The 317th served with F-102s until 1969, but from 1963 they shared alert duties with rotating White Shoes/College Shoes deployments of the higher-performing F-106.

Top: The 31st FIS only served in Alaska from August 1957 to October 1958, when it disbanded and was absorbed into the 317th. The two squadrons were the first to be sent 'overseas' as Alaska was not yet a US state in 1957.

Above: This 317th FIS F-102A, seen at Galena Airport in August 1960, later served with the New York ANG and eventually became a PQM-102B drone.

Fin Aircraft Rocket) projectiles, which were replaced in later versions by the AIM-26 Nuclear Falcon. One F-102A (53-1797) was used to test the MB-1 Genie nuclear projectile at Holloman AFB, New Mexico in mid-1957, but the Genie never became an operational weapon aboard the 'Deuce'.

The Hughes MG-10 system was an extension of the interim MG-3 rocket and missile FCS which went into production in mid-1955. MG-3 development was initiated in late 1952 when it became apparent that the MA-1 system (then being developed under Project MX-1179 for use in the future F-102 and Republic F-103) would not be ready in time for delivery for the early production units of the F-102. The MG-10 system included, in addition to the basic MG-3 components, an automatic flight-control subsystem and a datalink subsystem. These gave the MG-10 capabilities approaching those of the more ambitious MA-1.

Defence of the Distant Early Warning line and the Alaskan pipeline was part of the mission of the AAC F-102s.

In addition to internal fuel, the F-102A and TF-102A were each capable of carrying two 215-US gal (179-Imp gal; 814-litre) or 230-US gal (191.5-Imp gal; 871-litre) external fuel tanks which, as the USAF cautioned its pilots, were 'solely to increase the subsonic range capabilities of the airplane'. The design limit speed of the tanks was Mach 0.95, and the tanks were to be jettisoned before combat.

Flying surfaces

The F-102A employed a delta wing swept at 60° 6' with a cambered leading edge extending from wing root to wing tip, and typified by a root chord of 29 ft 9¾ in (8.87 m), span of 38 ft 1 m (11.62 m) and area of 661.50 sq ft (61.45 m²). The only other flying surface was the triangular vertical tail surface. The control surfaces, comprising two-section elevons on each half of the wing's trailing edge and a rudder inset into the trailing edge of the fin, were power operated. Convair referred to the wing employed on the YF-102 prototypes as the Case X wing, and this lacked the cambered leading edge. The YF-102A and a few early

Below and left: As in Europe, pilots sat long hours of alert in four-bay 'Zulu' hangars (these are at Elmendorf), ready to be airborne in five minutes. The 317th FIS boasted a three-minute reaction time from alert warning to aircraft airborne.

F-102A aircraft also had a Case X wing in a form revised with cambered leading edges and tops. Most production examples of the F-102A and TF-102A had what Convair called the Case XX wing, which was simply the same wing, with the same dimensions, but incorporating minor improvements.

The camber was the direct result of flight tests. Modifications to install cambered wing leading edges with reflexed tips were completed on 14 April 1954, and minor handling problems were resolved. After testing throughout June 1954 which went up to Mach 1.29 (a speed attained on 2 May 1954), the decision was made to change the wing tips to full camber without reflex. In subsequent flying, Mach 1.33 was attained.

Enlarged fin

Early in the production of the F-102A and TF-102A, Convair changed and enlarged the shape of the fin, which was manufactured by Rheem. The original fin of the F-102 had been virtually the same as the triangular vertical tail on the XF-92A, and had left the aircraft vulnerable to roll-coupling. Rheem redesigned the larger fin design that became standard for this aircraft type. The original fin, found on early production aircraft, stood 8 ft 8 in (2.64 m) above the fuselage line by comparison with the figure of 11 ft 6 in (3.51 m) for the larger version. The original fin gave the aircraft an overall height of 17 ft 11⅔ in (5.47 m), a figure increased to 21 ft 2½ in (6.45 m) by the adoption of the larger fin. The smaller fin measured 15 ft 0⅛ in (4.57 m) in chord at its base, while the larger fin had a chord of 15 ft 10 in (4.81 m). The adoption of the larger fin resulted in a minor reduction in performance, but improved flight safety. The fin and portions of the wing made extensive use of resin-bonded honeycomb.

The landing gear of the F-102A and TF-102A was of the tricycle type with a single wheel on each unit. Each of the units was hydraulically actuated, the mainwheel units retracting inward into the underside of the wing roots and the nosewheel unit retracting forward into the underside of the fuselage.

In service with Air Defense Command

In the early 1950s, the US role in the defence of North America was divided among Alaskan Air Command, Continental Air Command and Northeast Air Command, the latter also responsible for operations outside the USA in locations like Goose Bay, Labrador and Thule, Greenland. This arrangement proved cumbersome, and at about the time the F-102 was coming on line the job was integrated

The 317th FIS was headquartered at Elmendorf, but dispersed its aircraft around the state. It was part of the 21st Composite Wing under Alaskan Air Command. Apart from a squadron badge, which was not always worn, the 317th usually carried distinctive fuel tanks marked with a lightning bolt, as seen here.

Left: An Alaska-based pilot is handed his helmet to top off his winter flying ensemble. Note the thick gloves – which must have made it hard to manipulate the smaller switches and controls – and the radar scope, which dominated the instrument panel.

Below: One concession to the environment at the various auxiliary fields used by the F-102 detachments in Alaska was the provision of 'nose hangars'. These allowed the weapons bays to be loaded and unloaded with reasonable protection from the elements.

Convair F-102A-75-CO Delta Dagger
317th Fighter Interceptor Squadron
21st Composite Wing
Alaskan Air Command
Elmendorf Air Force Base, Alaska
1968

Fuel tanks

As designed, the F-102A had no provision for external fuel, absolute 'cleanliness' of the airframe being seen as a priority for a supersonic interceptor. When 'Deuces' were based in Alaska, Iceland and Europe, it became clear that extra range was essential. Convair developed an external tank design which was fitted to all F-102As from 1958. The original design of the 215-US gal (814-litre) F-102 tank featured an integral pylon which was jettisoned along with the tank. In late 1966, the USAF flight-cleared a Convair-designed tank that could be hung from the standard Aero-7A rail, and this was put into production in July 1967. Convair also produced the refuelling probe kits needed for deployment to Japan, Vietnam and elsewhere. Internal fuel was contained in four wing tanks with a total capacity of 1,085 US gal (4107 litres).

F-102A-75-CO Delta Dagger 56-1279

56-1279 was delivered new on 15 September 1957 to the 31st FIS at Wurtsmith AFB, Michigan, the unit moving to Elmendorf AFB, Alaska, the following month. On 8 October 1958 the aircraft was handed over to the 317th FIS with whom it flew until 15 December 1969, when it was passed to the Wisconsin ANG (176th FIS) at General Mitchell Field, Milwaukee. The New York ANG (102nd FIS) at Suffolk County Airport, Westhampton Beach was the next unit to operate the aircraft, from 11 October 1974, though within six months it had been retired from active service and allocated to the 4950th Test Wing at Wright-Patterson AFB, on 18 March 1975. On 6 January 1976 the aircraft was written-off.

Radar

Like the F-86D/L that preceded the 'Deuce' in many ADC squadrons, but unlike most other 'all-weather' fighters of the day, the F-102A had a single crewman to fly the aircraft and operate the weapons system. In order to fly the interception (when not under remote control from the ground), the pilot had his face inside a rubber hood watching the radar display, flying the aircraft with the (fixed) right-hand grip of the control stick and directing the radar with the left, moveable, grip. The throttle was left alone, set to full military power. Rocking the left grip from side to side scanned the radar and tilting it forward focused the beam on a target; lock-on was automatic. Holding down a trigger armed the Falcon missiles and released them in a chosen sequence when correct range was achieved. Disengagement from the collision-course flightpath was then automatic.

Stopping the 'Deuce'

Mounted at the base of the fin was a clamshell-type speed brake. As well as slowing the aircraft in flight and on landing, the brake, in its retracted position, provided extra keel area, and thus stability in the yaw plane. As the fin area of the F-102A was increased after the earliest examples, so an upper fairing was added to increase the speed brake area and to strengthen the unit, which was prone to failures above 350 kt (403 mph; 642 km/h). Touchdown was usually made at 140 kt (161 mph; 259 km/h) although landings could comfortably be made at speeds as low as 90 kt (104 mph; 167 km/h).

On the ground, the 'Deuce' was further slowed by holding the nose high for aerodynamic braking, using the wheel brakes, and by a relatively small drag chute which was neatly housed in a compartment between the two speed brake petals. Use of the speed brake and chute reduced the landing roll from about 2,450 ft (747 m) to about 1,780 ft (543 m) for a point defence (no external fuel) mission. Moisture leaking through the housing onto the parachute could cause the chute to freeze at high altitude, and it would fail to open on deployment.

As a 'last resort', the 'dog pecker' barrier engagement hook came into play. Fitted on the F-102 fleet by 1958, this device deployed from beneath the centre fuselage when the drag chute handle was pulled. Its function was to grab the runway-end barriers which were installed at most ADC bases. The barrier was flicked up by the nosewheel of an overrunning aircraft, but would normally fall back to the ground before catching the main gear, hence the barrier hook. From 1960, a Sheaffer runway arrester hook, as developed for the F-106, replaced the barrier probe on most 'Deuces'.

Fin

Testing of the initial batch of F-102As revealed lateral instabilty and a tendency for roll-coupling (roll coupled with yaw, leading to departure from controlled flight). One month before the F-102A entered service, the decision was taken to introduce a larger fin to counter this. After the 65th F-102A, 55-3356, a new fin was introduced on production Block 41 and later retrofitted to the earlier aircraft. The larger unit was 95 sq ft (8.8 m²) in area compared to the 68 sq ft (6.3 m²) of the original. Comparative heights were 11 ft 5 in (3.48 m) and 8 ft 8 in (2.64 m), respectively. While increasing the stability, maximum speed was reduced by about Mach 0.1 with the addition of the larger fin. The fintip was made of a dielectric plastic material, and along with the horizontal aerial contained IFF and UHF antennas.

Structure and powerplant

The F-102 made more use than hitherto of heavy-pressed forgings. Complete fuselage frames, wing spars and longitudinal members were designed to be pressed from single large forgings. The main contractors for this work were Wyman-Gordon and Alcoa, and the use of the eight types of component these companies produced saved over 100 lb (45.3 kg) in weight, 273 components and 3,200 rivets. When the YF-102 failed to go supersonic, and it was deduced that the problem was failure to conform to the 'area rule', the nature of the Cook-Craigie production plan meant that changing the entire fuselage structure was considered impractical. A longer nose was fitted to improve the fineness ratio and large fairings were fitted to bulk out the rear fuselage. These were called 'Marilyns' in a tribute to the charms of a certain contemporary film star. Although these changes greatly improved the YF-102's performance, the air force called for further redesign. The resulting YF-102A was 14 ft (4.26 m) longer than the original YF-102 and was substantially different in most structural respects; two-thirds of the 30,000 tools purchased by October 1953 were discarded.

Other structural changes made to reduce transonic and supersonic drag included adding partial conical camber to the wing, which reduced high-altitude drag and improved handling at high angles of attack. During the enforced halt in the programme, Convair engineers took the opportunity to increase the accessibility of the engine and other internal components, improve the pilot's view by drooping the nose and making many other minor changes. These improvements, made possible by the original design's performance failings, transformed the F-102A into a much better weapon than would have otherwise resulted had production progressed based on the YF-102 airframe.

The F-102A's powerplant was a Pratt & Whitney J57-23A or -25 turbojet rated at 11,700 lb (114.7 kN) static 'dry' thrust and 17,200 lb (168.7 kN) with afterburner. At the same time as the new, enlarged fin was added, intake splitter plates were introduced. This was a 'buzz fix' intended to reduce vibration, and cockpit noise levels rather than to smooth or regulate airflow into the engine.

Wings

The original wing fiited to the F-102A was known as the 'Case X' ('Case 10') wing. It was fitted to aircraft up to 56-1316, and could be distinguished by the squared-off tip to the wing, which was also slightly upswept, as seen here on 56-1279. The 'Case XX' ('Case 20') wing was tested in May 1957 and had been introduced into production by the end of the year. The new wing, with its downturned, pointed tips and leading-edge camber, increased the F-102A's ceiling, and improved manoeuvrability, glide angle and low-speed stability. Top speed was also increased by Mach 0.06. However, despite these benefits, the 'Case XX' wing was not retrofitted to earlier examples.

The 'Deuce' was the first delta-winged fighter put into series production, and thus pioneered many of the features used on aircraft of this configuration today. It was in fact a scaled-up descendant of the very first powered pure delta, Convair's own XF-92A. Excluding the rudder, all control surfaces were mounted on the trailing edge of the wing. These comprised four elevons of primarily honeycomb construction, all hydraulically actuated, as were the missile bays and landing gear doors.

The wings were manufactured to a very close tolerance and were considered interchangeable between aircraft. Each contained two integral fuel tanks which were coated internally with Scotchweld sealant and assembled with Convair's patented Straylor rivets, which were then milled flush with the surface. The tanks were pressure tested to 7.5 lb/sq in (51.7 kPa) before installation. At least in early service, they were regarded as leak-proof, with no leaks or ruptures outside catastrophic aircraft accidents.

Canopy and windscreen

The F-102A was not built with conventional dogfighting in mind, and thus all-around pilot view was sacrificed for greater aerodynamic cleanliness. With interception designed to be mostly 'automatic', with the pilot directing parts of the procedure head-down in the cockpit, the view provided was judged sufficient to take-off, land and fly the aircraft in formation, rather than to visually acquire and track a target. The knife-edged windscreen featured prominent heating elements on each facet and the line of its central pillar followed on to a central canopy bar, allowing the canopy to be constructed in two halves. These were manufactured from stretched plastic, rather than cast acrylic, which proved shatter-proof when tested against 0.30-in calibre bullets, though the F-106, with an almost identical unit, was later retrofitted with a single-piece 'bubble' unit. 'A vision splitter', as found on the F-106, was refitted to F-102As, reducing internal reflections. The prototype YF-102A had a heavier 'birdcage' unit than those that followed, although the second through fourth YF-102s briefly reverted to this original canopy during testing.

Weapons

An MB-1 Genie (then known as 'Ding-Dong') nuclear rocket was test fired from a YF-102 in May 1956, and consideration was given to equipping the F-102A fleet with this unguided air-to-air weapon, but this project was cancelled in early 1957, the Genie going to the F-101 and F-106 instead. The Dagger was to be equipped with the AIM-26A Nuclear Falcon. Originally known as GAR-11, Nuclear Falcon was designed by Hughes specifically for the F-102A, but provision for its use was not incorporated from the start, this being included in the modernisation phase by the fitting of kits to the centre missile bay, a process that was not completed until 1953, and then only to 450 aircraft (including trainers). The AIM-26A had semi-active radar homing (SARH) and essentially the same sub-kiloton warhead as used in the much larger Genie. Later modifications allowed interchangability of conventional and nuclear Falcons in the centre bay.

As a back-up to the relatively untried Falcon missiles, the Delta Dagger was able to fire up to 24 unguided rockets from launchers in the weapons bay doors. Aircraft delivered prior to December 1956 were capable of firing the 2-in and 2.75-in rockets, but after this, the USAF standardised on the larger weapon for the Delta Dagger, and teams from SAAMA modified up to 170 aircraft in the field. Nuclear Falcon-equipped 'Deuces' had the rocket tubes deleted from the centre bay doors, but could carry two rockets per tube in the other doors. Later, rocket capability was deleted altogether.

A typical weapons load was three semi-active radar homing GAR-1D/AIM-4A and three GAR-2A/AIM-4C or AIM-4G IR-guided missiles. This mix of radar-homing and infra red-guided missiles, fired in pairs consisting of one of each type, was pioneered in the F-102A and was later adopted as standard practice by most Soviet fighters.

For training, a Falcon-shaped device called a Weapons Evaluation System Missile (WESM) was often carried in the centre bay. This would remain attached to the weapons cradle which would pop up out of the bay just long enough for the WESM to photograph the target aircraft. The addition of an infra-red search-and-track sensor under Project Big Eight, from 1963, assisted the Falcon in reliably locking on in heavy cloud and rain, which otherwise drastically reduced missile capability. As delivered, the weapons system contributed $219,876 to the $1.2 million flyaway cost of each Delta Dagger.

317th FIS

The badge of the 317th (approved in 1951) depicted sunshine, clouds, lightning, stars and rain, illustrating the all-weather, day-and-night role of the squadron, which had been formed as a day-fighter unit at Mitchell Field, New York in August 1942. Initially equipped with P-40s and forming part of the 325th Fighter Group, the squadron took part in combat in Algeria and Tunisia, before moving to Italy with P-47s and later P-51s. Known as the 'Checkertail Clan', the 325th produced 27 fighter aces. Inactivated in October 1945, the squadron reformed in August 1947 as the 317th Fighter Squadron (All-Weather) in May 1948 operating P-61 Black Widows until 1948 when F-82s arrived, followed by F-94s, F-86Ds and, finally, F-102s from 1956. Based in Washington state from 1948, at first as part of the 325th Fighter-All Weather/Fighter-Interceptor Group, then the 4704th Defense Wing, and eventually the 567th Air Defense Group, the 317th became part of the 325th Fighter Group once again in August 1955.

From August 1957, the squadron was detached to Alaska as part of the 10th Air Division, then the 5070th Air Defense Wing. The squadron became permanently subordinated to Alaskan Air Command (AAC) in October 1961. The 317th FIS was the primary interceptor asset of AAC, supplemented by 'White Shoes' rotations of CONUS-based F-106s from 1963 when it became clear that the F-102A had inadequate range to see off Soviet bombers probing the far reaches of Alaskan airspace. The 31st FIS served alongside the 317th in Alaska for only 13 months before its aircraft were handed over to the 317th, which became one of the largest fighter squadrons in USAF history with 46 aircraft, based in various locations including Elmendorf, Galena, King Salmon and Ladd AFB. The squadron was inactivated on New Year's Eve 1969. AAC itself was stood down in 1990 and its assigned units became part of 11th AF, in turn subordinated to Pacific Air Forces (PACAF).

Convair F-102 Delta Dagger

In order to practise interceptions against ECM-equipped Soviet bombers, Alaskan-based F-102s regularly flew with EB-57E Canberras acting as 'electronic aggressors'. The EB-57E pictured belonged to the 5041st Tactical Operations Squadron (until 1963 the 504th Radar Evaluation Squadron). It was lost in a collision with an F-102A during a practice intercept on 13 June 1969. All three crewmen involved ejected safely.

into ADC (Air Defense Command), which was itself a component of the joint US-Canadian NORAD (North American Air Defense Command). ADC enjoyed top priority, along with the Strategic Air Command, when the Pentagon handed out people and equipment. An Air Force hero of World War II and the Korean War, General Earle E. Partridge, was the boss at ADC when the F-102A was being developed. He summed up his own priorities in five words "Nothing's too good for ADC."

Partridge meant, of course, that he wanted the best for his men. But the remark also hints at a willingness to be patient with a seemingly endless series of technical bugs. Although it was known by various terms during its gestation (but not the Delta Dagger, a term that was retrospectively applied only many years later), the F-102A had

always been regarded as the '1954 interceptor', and when it finally went on duty it was two years late.

Still, there were a lot of handshakes when the first true production example of the F-102A was formally accepted in June 1956 by Captain Alexander Butterfield, the assistant

Above: One of the deployments to South Vietnam was in anticipation of a coup against President Diem in October 1962. When it occurred, there was little the F-102s could do.

Left: A 509th FIS F-102A purges liquid oxygen (LOX) into the morning air at Don Muang in January 1962.

Right: Nose art was almost unheard of on F-102s and squadron markings tended to follow set patterns. The 509th was an exception, at least for a while, with the leaping tiger on the noses of its F-102. The pilot here is Captain Tom Halley.

Thailand

In 1961 F-102s of the 509th FIS were sent to Don Muang airport in Thailand to support the SEATO allies and the kingdom of Laos which was increasingly being drawn into the Vietnam conflict. From then on, a minimum of four USAF interceptors was kept on alert in Thailand. Rotations to Tan Son Nhut near Saigon began in March 1962. After May 1963, when the rotations were stopped, Thai-based aircraft were sent on a number of 'no-notice' exercises to test the ability of the F-102s to deploy quickly to Tan Son Nhut and Da Nang.

Camouflage

Technical order (T.O.) 114 issued in 1964 laid down a whole new system of camouflage for aircraft engaged in tactical operations in southeast Asia. It stipulated a pattern of tan, light green and medium green over light grey for each type of tactical fighter. Soon, the glossy 'ADC gray' colours of the F-102s vanished under the so-called 'SEA' or 'Asia Minor' camouflage. In Europe, camouflage was applied as aircraft went through major overhauls, the first appearing in 1965.

A freshly-painted F-102A, ready for Vietnam service, is seen outside outside the maintenance hangar at McClellan AFB, California. The Sacramento Air Material Area (SAMA) was responsible for overhauling F-102s for Vietnam, including bringing them up to the latest modification standard. The IRST sensor on this aircraft indicates upgrade to at least FIG-8 status.

When camouflage came in Europe, squadron markings disappeared, and the 'Deuce' left USAFE before tailcodes became widespread. These aircraft from the 526th FIS illustrate old and new schemes.

USAF plant officer in San Diego and project pilot on the 'Deuce'. In that same summer F-102A production aircraft began to reach the ADC's 327th FIS located at George AFB, California, and commanded by Lieutenant Colonel Charles E. Rigney, who rated the type "the easiest plane to fly I've ever been in". Rigney soon demonstrated the capabilities of the F-102A by flying from George to Oklahoma City, Oklahoma, a distance of 1,120 miles (1802 km) in 1 hour 22 minutes, beginning with a climb without afterburner and averaging a cruise of 711.7 kt (819.5 mph; 1318 km/h) at about 41,000 ft (12496 m). Rigney's 327th FIS forwarded to the USAF a proposal which had actually originated at Convair's Plant 2, which was the huge, rectangular building in San Diego that had once churned out B-24 Liberators and was now the assembly location for the F-102A. The suggestion was that the new warplane be given the popular name Lancer. The idea was rejected by the Pentagon for reasons that are difficult to fathom today, particularly since the name has subsequently been allotted to the Rockwell (now Boeing) B-1B bomber.

Good neighbours

In a community relations effort aimed at convincing taxpayers that the noisy J57 turbojet, which was always operated in afterburning mode during the take-off roll, was in fact the sound of freedom, citizens living near F-102A bases were given a free tour of ADC headquarters at Colorado Springs and a two-day instructional course at San Diego.

As if to compensate for the two-year delay in attaining operational status, the F-102A force expanded rapidly after the first arrival. The 11th FIS at Duluth, Minnesota was the second unit to get the delta-winged fighter, and many others followed so that by 31 December 1956 some 97 examples of the F-102A were in the inventory. The first

airframes resulting from the Fort Worth 'Test to Tactical' programme were delivered to the 438th FIS at Kinross AFB, Michigan in July 1957 and by the end of that year the number of F-102A and TF-102A fighters in the ADC inventory had risen dramatically to 428. The ADC's highest number of 'Deuces' (the nickname assigned by pilots long after the USAF had rejected the name Lancer and before the appellation Delta Dagger was introduced) was 651 on 31 December 1958. Patience was a virtue, however: the downside was that, as of that date, ADC had sustained 62 accidents which resulted in 28 aircraft destroyed. By the end of the 1950s the ADC had already begun to equip with the F-106A – the former F-102B later named as the Delta Dart – and started to transfer some of its F-102A warplanes elsewhere. On 31 December 1959 the ADC mustered some 482 'Deuces', which now represented about 40 per cent of the ADC fighter force.

The first operational loss of a 'Deuce' occurred on 25 February 1957 when an aircraft (56-0976) of the 317th FIS

Left: The 509th FIS was headquartered at Clark in the Phillipines, but maintained detachments in South Vietnam, Thailand and Taiwan. This is one of the squadron's two-seaters, topping up its liquid oxygen supply before a sortie somewhere in southeast Asia during 1962.

Below: The 16th FIS at Naha, Okinawa played host to the first of many Phantoms deployed to Asia in December 1964. The 555th TFS, later to become famous for Vietnam MiG-killing, shared the base until March 1965.

Refuelling

Designed as a point-defence interceptor, the F-102 was built without provision for aerial refuelling. As the Vietnam conflict escalated, inflight refuelling was seen as a necessity to allow quick deployment of additional interceptors to southeast Asia. Convair developed a bolt-on refuelling probe kit that allowed refuelling from the same tank that was supplying the engine. The first F-102 units to make an air-refuelled deployment were the 64th and 82nd FISs who flew from California to Okinawa in January 1966 in Operation Thirsty Camel, but it appears to have been little used subsequently. Inflight refuelling was specified for a proposed RF-102 reconnaisance version which was never produced.

William Tell

The ADC launched its much-celebrated air-to-air weapons competition, dubbed William Tell, at Tyndall AFB, Florida during 1958 and had an F-102A category from the start. A team from the 326th FIS at Richards-Gebaur AFB, Missouri, won the first meet. The F-102 competitions at William Tell continued until 1974. Thereafter, William Tell saw the F-102A aircraft only as a drone. In a total of eight William Tell meets, 34 F-102A teams competed.

As the F-102A pressed on in its career, the USAF and Convair began a series of upgrades which brought minor changes and improvements, including the Configuration 5 modification programme which ended in December 1959 and the Configuration 6 programme that was completed in September 1960. Even as F-102A strength in ADC began to decline – there were 15 F-102A and TF-102A squadrons in the ADC on 30 June 1960 – a new milestone was reached when the first Air National Guard (ANG) squadron took delivery of the fighter on 1 July 1960.

Also in 1960, Convair began the Configuration 7 modification programme which added the GAR-11 missile, an improved version of the Falcon later to evolve into the AIM-26 Super Falcon. At the end of that year the ADC's F-102A and TF-102A squadron strength had declined to nine.

Above and right: the Convair-designed refuelling installation was a fairly unsophisticated affair, with the probe raised high and forward by a large external brace for pilot visibility and to prevent intake fuel ingestion. As late as 1964, PACAF relied solely on hose-and-drogue refuelling (with KB-50s), and most TAC aircraft used the same method until well into the Vietnam war.

at McChord AFB, Washington suffered an engine failure and crashed. On 24 June 1957, two F-102A interceptors of the 327th FIS from George AFB, California, flew through the atomic mushroom cloud created by the 'Priscilla' shot in the Operation Plumbob series of nuclear tests in the Pacific. The fighters used in the tests were piloted by Major Budd Butcher and 1st Lieutenant Richard Satterfield.

Right and below: The overcrowded nature of US air bases in South Vietnam and the lack of effective low-level radar made them tempting targets to the North Vietnamese Air Force. The US commanders believed they would have as little as one minute's warning of an attack on Da Nang. Aircraft were kept on five-minute alert at four bases in South Vietnam and Thailand with the rest of the F-102 force on one-hour alert. The 509th FIS F-102s at right were seen at Tan Son Nhut in May 1969. Below, a 64th FIS 'Deuce' taxis in at a typically busy US airfield in South Vietnam.

Above: Pilots of the 509th FIS chat with an NBC reporter in the alert trailer at Da Nang in 1968.

Left: 'C' Flight of the 509th was usually based at Bien Hoa with four aircraft and eight pilots. They had a more permanent structure as an alert pad.

The exact meaning of this very unofficial 'C' Flight, 509th FIS patch is obscure, but said to be unprintable.

This neat line of parked 64th FIS interceptors at Bien Hoa in December 1968 would not have been possible at Da Nang and some other bases, where Viet Cong mortar attacks took their toll on US aircraft, including F-102s.

Vietnam

Involvement in the Vietnam conflict for the F-102 began in 1962, long before US airpower was generally employed in combat in Southeast Asia. The Tactical Air Control System (TACS) radar network set up by the US in South Vietnam was picking up targets in the central highlands and four F-102s were dispatched from Clark to Tan Son Nhut on 22 March. The 'Deuces' rotated with Navy EA-1F Skyraiders every six weeks, but no targets were ever intercepted. Further F-102s were sent to Da Nang as soon as President Johnson authorised the US buildup following the Gulf of Tonkin incident in August 1964 under the codename Water Glass. During the war, the F-102s were primarily used for base defence at a number of locations. By the end of 1968, there were six aircraft on alert at Bien Hoa and six at Da Nang, with another 10 in Thailand (Udorn and Don Muang).

On 12 April 1961, the USAF began Exercise Southern Tip using the F-102A to counter possible nuisance raids by the Cuban regime under the communist Fidel Castro against the area of Miami, Florida, where many of Castro's domestic opponents had found asylum. In retrospect, it is impossible to separate this exercise from the catastrophic Bay of Pigs invasion of that month, but no connection can be proven. Six F-102A interceptors from Tyndall AFB were positioned at Homestead AFB, Florida (closer to Cuba) on two- to five-minute alert at all times. Following the failed landings at the Bay of Pigs, the Joint Chiefs of Staff directed that Southern Tip continue indefinitely, and as a result Homestead became home to a permanent detachment of interceptors.

The F-102 was employed at the start of the 1960s to judge the performance of a new, delta-winged bomber against air defences. Launched on 23 October 1961, Project

Below left: Seeing a need for air-to-ground firepower greater than the 12 2.75-in rockets in the weapons bay doors, Det. 3 of the 509th FIS conducted fit trials with a minigun pod hung from a TER on the drop tank mounting point. San Antonio Air Material Authority, the approving authority, was not happy with the installation's ability to withstand gun recoil and there were other practical reasons for its non-adoption. Only one was ever mounted on an F-102 and it was never fired as it was not wired to the aircraft's systems.

Below: 509th FIS F-102As fly over the defoliated and bomb-blasted terrain of South Vietnam. With little air threat, the F-102 was used as a B-52 escort and even in a limited ground attack role. A contemporary Aviation Week account, quoting the Air Force Times, credited the 509th with the destruction of 106 buildings (with damage to 59 others), 16 sampans and one bridge in 199 sorties in a 45-day period.

An F-102A from Det 1 of the 82nd FIS, then at Suwon, sees off an inquisitive Antonov An-12 'Cub-B' in June 1970.

Right: A fully-armed F-102A starts up in an alert hangar somewhere in South Korea, February 1971.

Above right: A trio of 82nd FIS 'Deuces' is seen high over South Korea during a deployment in 1970.

The 64th FIS was based at Clark AB in the Phillipines, but rotated aircraft in and out of the war zone as needs dictated. This F-102A was photographed at Yokota, Japan on 23 March 1969.

Korea

North Korean seizure of the spy-ship USS *Pueblo* in January 1968 led to the activation of several reserve units and the transfer of a number of active-duty units to South Korean bases. One of the first was the Naha-based 82nd FIS, which deployed to Osan before the end of the month. It was replaced by the first College Cadence deployment of F-106s at the end of February. Although the *Pueblo* crew was released in December 1968, F-102s made occasional deployments to Korea until 1971.

Dry Martini pitted defending F-102A and TF-102A warplanes of the 326th FIS against attacking Convair B-58 Hustler supersonic bombers. Lessons learned as a result of these intercepts helped both the bombers and the fighters to improve their tactics. The bottom line of the project, which ended on 5 January 1962, was that a big bomber with a configuration similar to that of the 'Deuce' was extremely difficult to stop.

At the turn of the year, on 31 December 1961, there had been 10 F-102A and TF-102A squadrons assigned to the ADC. Soon the ADC was operating the 'Deuce' even farther from home when the 57th FIS 'Black Knights' stood up in Iceland in July 1962. The squadron's claim to

fame, long after Goose Bay and Thule had ceased to be familiar names in the air defence lexicon, was that it was the only ADC unit in a foreign country.

Flying the F-102

At air defence bases the F-102A was kept in the alert barns that had been built originally for North American F-86 Sabres, Northrop F-89 Scorpions and Lockheed F-94 Starfires. These barns were flimsy metal structures, barely strong enough to protect an aircraft from the elements and usually housing four aircraft, two on each side of an alert facility where pilots could lounge in flying gear while pulling alert duty. When the klaxon went off, the pilots were supposed to step smartly to their F-102A warplanes (there was no need to run) while ground crew assisted them in quickly starting up and taxiing out. All pre-flight checks were already finished. The job was to get the aircraft from the barn (located near the end of the runway) into the sky within three minutes. Lieutenant General Robert M. Lee, who commanded the ADC from 1 March 1961, is reported to have told an aide, "I want to hear afterburners [signifying a take-off roll] within three minutes of the klaxon. Any squadron that can't do that is going to have a new commander, and the old commander is going to be in charge of the Purple Water Fountain." This last is located in the basement of the Pentagon and while it exists for drinking purposes, in USAF jargon it signifies being demoted to the lowliest, most miserable desk job an officer can hold.

Below: When the 82nd FIS deactivated in May 1971, 18 of the squadron's 26 F-102s which had severe wing cracks and corrosion were scrapped at Naha. The remainder were flown back to the USA to join ANG squadrons.

Right: Two-seat 'Deuces' carried missiles and rockets (in the yellow trolley) in Vietnam alongside the single-seaters. In ADC units, a proportion of TF-102s were not equipped with the weapons system or had it removed, and were only used as 'hacks'.

Convair TF-102A-45-CO
82nd Fighter Interceptor Squadron
Naha, Okinawa 1968

The 82nd FIS was one of the first F-102 users, becoming operational in July 1957. It became part of PACAF in June 1966. Its main role was providing air defence for Okinawa until it was deactivated in May 1971. Later, as the 82nd Tactical Aerial Targets Squadron (TATS), it was the last US F-102 user, flying PQM-102 Full-Scale Aerial Targets (FSATs).

This TF-102A-45-CO, the 17th-to-last two-seater built, has all the main features of a late F-102, including the 'Big Eight' IRST sensor and the Case XX wing. New antennas and external lights continued to appear on F-102s up to 1972. The aircraft was delivered on 25 May 1958 to the 326th FIS at Richards-Gebaur AFB. It subsequently served with the 4756th ADW at Tyndall AFB (from 24 August 1962), 325th FIS at Truax Field (from 1 April 1966), 326th FIS at Richards-Gebaur (from 13 June 1966) and 4780th ADW at Perrin AFB (from 23 November 1966). It then transferred to PACAF for service with the 82nd FIS at Naha from June 1970. It was scrapped there after the 31 May 1971 inactivation of the 82nd FIS.

New nose
The new two-place nose on the TF-102A reduced the overall length by 55 in (140 cm) compared to the F-102A. The two-seater was about 250 lb (113.5 kg) heavier in an unloaded condition. Noses were produced at Convair's Fort Worth factory and mated to the rest of the airframe at San Diego.

War role
With little actual threat from North Vietnamese bombers, the F-102s were underemployed in their design role. They were sometimes used to escort B-52s flying 'Arc Light' missions over the south. On occasion, they went out at night searching for heat-emitting targets with the IRST and sometimes launched IR Falcons at them. Results are unknown, but it was an expensive way to destroy a truck or a campfire.

Canopy and windscreen
The new wide cockpit section with its extensive glazing caused severe buffet problems when first flown. Tuft tests found that the airflow just aft of the canopy was actually moving forward. After some different canopy shapes were trialled, the solution chosen was to add two rows of vortex generators, one across the windscreen-canopy bow, and another across the midpoint of the canopy. This rather inelegant modification proved a satisfactory 'fix'.

Performance
The 'Tub' was supersonic like the single-seater, but only just. Maximum range was nominally the same, as there was no loss of fuel tankage, but climb rate and ceiling were slightly reduced due to the higher weight.

Quite early in the F-102's career, one aircraft was bailed to General Electric for use as an engine testbed. 54-1398, an F-102A-35, had a large pylon fitted in its forward weapons bay to which was attached a podded J85 turbojet (right). The testing, which took place at Edwards AFB in mid-1959, was conducted with an F-102 presumably because of the lack of supersonic wind tunnels at the time. The J85 was the engine used on the Northrop T-38 and N-156 (F-5), and the McDonnell AQM-20 Quail decoy missile. The aircraft above carries a J85 fitted in an AQM-20 fuselage, minus control surfaces.

After 1961 the F-102A was flown by pilots trained at Perrin AFB, Texas by the 4780th Air Defense Wing (Training) in a programme aimed at producing 120 'Deuce' flyers per year. Although the training course underwent numerous changes over the years, it was typically a 26-week combination of academics and flying which included 93 sorties totalling 146 hours 30 minutes of flying plus 293 hours of ground briefing, debriefing and simulator work. A shorter course retrained some pilots who had earlier flown the McDonnell F-101 Voodoo. Perrin was very much in the business of producing combat pilots, and the men who emerged from its classes were unlikely to be relegated to desk clerk duties by General Lee or his successors.

The F-102A did not intercept just any 'unknown' that appeared anywhere. The type was scrambled only when an unknown appeared in an Air Defense Identification Zone (ADIZ), one of several dozen regions around the US sea coast and land border that overlapped the likely approach route of Soviet bombers or, indeed, Cuban intruders. The F-102A did not carry wing tanks on alert status, and inflight-refuelling was not part of the scenario in the ground-to-air interception role. With a total internal fuel capacity of 1,085 US gal (903.5 Imp gal; 4107 litres) carried by four internal tanks in the spacious delta wing, an F-102A carrying three Falcon and one Super Falcon missile was able to get airborne in about 3,800 ft (1014 m) and climb to 17,400 ft (5305 m) in the first minute of flight. By this time, of course, the F-102A and the approaching intruder were like bullets fired at each other: when they converge, two objects come together at the speed of one plus the speed of the other.

Although the USA would soon field an automated system known as Semi-Automatic Ground Environment (SAGE) to decrease the human element in the interception process, the F-102A was guided to its targets in the old-fashioned Ground-Controlled Intercept (GCI) way. From a radar site, usually in a location quite separate from their air base, Delta Dagger pilots were fed information on the target's location, bearing, speed and altitude by the voice of a GCI operator bent over a radar screen and following a 'blip' with his eyes. It was expected that an F-102A would climb to 35,000 ft (10670 m) in about three minutes, and if

Sperry, which was the contractor on the Pave Deuce drone conversion programme, painted one QF-102 in its house colours and used it as a demonstrator. It is seen right, in 1978 and below, with its eventual successor in many squadrons, the F-16. The two generations of fighter were both built by General Dynamics (the F-102 by the Convair Division and the F-16 at Fort Worth), but share little in common except being single-engined.

Five-minute alert

The F-102 was designed for point defence (taking off and landing at the same base) and area defence (landing at another base). To this end, ADC and ANG squadrons were based in or detached to the majority of US states, as well as Canada, Greenland and Iceland for interception and identification of intruders approaching US airspace. Typically, a 25-aircraft squadron would have four flights with pilots on an eight-day cycle, two days on day alert (0800-1700) and two on nights in the 'Zulu' hangar, two days continuation training and two rest days. A scramble call would have the doors open and the engines started before the pilots reached the aircraft. As little as seven minutes after the call, the F-102s could be passing through 40,000 feet (12192 m) on a collision-course interception path with the unidentified aircraft or 'Zombie'.

Right: For many years, the 199th FIS at Hickam AFB provided the Hawaiian Islands' only air defence unit. This pair of 'Deuces' is seen in November 1976, in the twilight of the type's career.

Above: At established ADC bases, open-ended hangars of a variety of designs were built to allow a quick getaway. Usually there was room for four F-102s, such as these 482nd FIS examples at Seymour Johnson, South Carolina in 1965.

necessary reach maximum practical operating altitude of 54,000 ft (16460) in about 10 minutes. With fuel and armament, the 'Deuce' was capable of about 716 kt (825 mph; 1328 km/h) or Mach 1.25 in level flight at an altitude of 40,000 ft (12190 m). The expectation was that the interceptor would be fast enough, and its GCI guidance accurate enough, to allow a realistic interception of any bomber – even the new jet-powered Myasischyev M-4 'Bison' and Tupolev Tu-16 'Badger', of which US officials had become cognisant in 1955.

Heading upstairs on an intercept mission was not necessarily the most exciting flying in the world, but 'Deuce' pilots quickly became fond of their mount and celebrated both its merits and its quirks. Those who had flown Sabres, Scorpions and Starfires found that they had not only better performance but more cockpit space and, for the most part, greater ease of handling using the two-handled control stick that was a feature of Convair delta-winged fighters. One pilot called it "a real kiddycar to fly". The F-102A was not an aircraft to manoeuvre, however, and with its delta wing the type bled off energy at a dizzying rate when turning.

The ADC strategy was to send the interceptors up in what amounted to the shortest, straight-line route to the target. Pilots have different memories, today, of when and at what distance their on-board radar was capable of detecting and locking on to the target, the general impression being that it was useful only when the 'Deuce' closed to within 40 to 50 miles (64 to 80 km). While a first engagement from abeam was much preferred, it was neither expected nor assured, speed of interception being regarded as a higher priority. A speedy intercept might begin, however, with a 'lead-in pursuit pass' – a direct nose-to-nose collision course.

Only thereafter, and here the manoeuvrability and airspeed of the F-102 were deemed sufficient, might the Delta Dagger re-engage from the side following the initial, head-on engagement. The ADC wanted to catch the foe some 520 to 695 nm (600 to 800 miles; 966 to 1287 km) off shore. In later years, when air-launched cruise missiles became a factor in the bomber-versus-fighter equation, the ADC did not believe the air-to-air radar on the F-102 would detect a cruise missile after launch. Guided to a GCI intercept, the F-102 would attack first with several Falcons or a single Nuclear Falcon, depending on the circumstance, and would attempt to re-engage if possible.

SAGE compatibility

In later years, the addition of datalink capability made the F-102A compatible with the SAGE system for which its successor, the F-106A, had been equipped from the outset. Late in its service life, the F-102A also acquired an IR seeker whose sensor protruded from in front of the windscreen.

Landing in the F-102A was easy, even if adrenaline churned when it was being done at night, in a rain squall,

Crews of the 326th FIS run for their aircraft at Grandview AFB, Montana, 1960. By this time, ADC had over 25 squadrons of F-102s with numerous detachments spread around the USA.

The aircraft marked 'YF-102C' and seen at Shepherd AFB in 1960 remains a bit of a mystery, as no such designation actually existed. The proposed F-102C with the J75 engine and the MB-1 Genie missile armament of the F-102B (F-106) was never built, although some F-102As were used for related trials.

57th FIS 'Black Knights'

Probably the most famous 'Deuce' user was the 57th FIS at Naval Station Keflavik, Iceland which converted to the F-102 in July 1964. The 'Black Knights' of the 57th saw more 'trade' (unidentified aircraft) than any other ADC squadron. Mostly these were Soviet Tu-95 'Bear' bombers and reconnaissance aircraft, some of which were en route to Cuban or Angolan bases. In the latter days of their service, the F-102s were given datalink equipment, allowing them to make interceptions guided by ground radar or by EC-121 Constellations. Air Defense Command awarded the 'Black Knights' the Hughes Achievement Award for the outstanding interceptor unit in 1970, and the USAF flying safety award for 1968-71. The last regular squadron to operate the F-102, the 'Black Knights' returned their F-102s to the USA in July 1973. The last 'Bear' intercepted by the F-102 had been in June, when the squadron was in the process of transitioning to the F-4C.

As seen from a 57th FIS TF-102, one of the squadron's single-seaters banks over the hostile terrain. The 57th was the last active-duty F-102 operator in the USAF.

Above: The 57th participated in William Tell 1972 having already been to Combat Pike, a live-firing exercise at Tyndall. Here, an F-102A breaks away after a Falcon shoot. It wears the later markings with 15 black/white squares on the rudder. Up to late 1969, the rudder markings were smaller blue/white chequers.

Right: International orange flight suits were a necessary accoutrement for flying over the desolate terrain of Iceland. The pilot carried his parachute on his back, unlike most later fighters where the 'chute was integrated into the seat.

The 57th FIS received its F-102s in 1962. By 1972, more than 1,000 'Bear' intercepts inside Iceland's Military Air Defense Identification Zone (MADIZ) had taken place. At particularly busy periods, over 100 were recorded in a single month. This intruder is a Tu-95K 'Bear-B' cruise missile carrier. The F-102A in the foreground was lost off the Icelandic coast on 22 January 1973.

by radar control. The big delta planform was in most respects an assurance of good handling at low speed in the airfield pattern. Although the pilot often experienced an excessive sink rate just before touchdown, the ground effect smoothed out the landing nicely. The F-102A also suffered little effect from crosswinds. It was necessary to put the nose down quickly after initial impact when in a crosswind, but otherwise a landing in the 'Deuce' was virtually second nature, and the landing run was shortened by use of the drag chute located in a housing at the base of the fin's trailing edge.

Pilots complained that the knife-edge or inverted-V windscreen was a bar to good visibility, especially when

taxiing in the rain. The pilot could not see his wing tips, so had to use dead reckoning to avoid any ground object that loomed too close to the taxiing warplane. Groundcrew also griped that the pneumatic brakes were a persistent maintenance problem.

Cuban missile crisis

The F-102A was an important part of the rapid build-up of US military strength that occurred during the Cuban missile crisis in October and November 1962. While the USA went 'eyeball-to-eyeball' with the USSR, to use the expression coined by Dean Rusk, President John F. Kennedy's Secretary of State, 'Deuce' squadrons, which had

spent so much of their time preparing to defend North America from the north, now stood ready to mount a defence against attacks from the south. In the end, Moscow backed down from its plan to install nuclear missiles and Ilyushin Il-28 'Beagle' bombers on Cuban soil, the crisis was resolved without war, and Rusk concluded that, "The other fellow just blinked."

On 30 June 1963, with American attention beginning to shift from Cuba to Vietnam, the count was nine ADC squadrons equipped with the 'Deuce'. During that year F-102A interceptors and Lockheed RC-121 Warning Star airborne warning and control aircraft worked together in Exercise Cashew Tree, a readiness rehearsal in the Panama Canal Zone.

Cold War

By September 1961 the 'Deuce' was entering ANG service and the USAF decided to equip six ANG and ADC squadrons with the new GAR-11 nuclear-armed missile. This was the Super Falcon or, more commonly and to avoid confusion with other variants enjoying the 'Super'

An advantage of the delta wing is that it remains controllable at low speeds. This was useful when trying to formate on a slow target such as a No. 202 Squadron, RAF, Hastings Met.Mk 1 on a weather reconnaissance flight over the GIUK gap. The 57th FIS 'Deuce' seen here is now displayed in the USAF Museum.

appellation, the Nuclear Falcon. The initial version gave way at an early stage to a model designated GAR-11B, which was shortened by about 1 ft (0.3 m) to facilitate accommodation in the weapons bay of the 'Deuce'. On 1 October 1962, the two missile types were redesignated as the AIM-26A and AIM-26B respectively.

Although they were developed primarily to carry a nuclear warhead, in effect using overkill to destroy an attacking bomber formation because the accuracy of non-nuclear missiles was still inadequate, the AIM-26A and AIM-26B were also widely used with conventional warheads. In its conventional guise, the AIM-26 was also sold to Sweden and Switzerland for use as the Rb 27 and HM-55, respectively, on the Saab 35F Draken and Dassault Mirage IIIS fighters equipped with Hughes Taran radar. The AIM-26B was 6 ft 11.6 in (2.07 m) long and had a fin span of 2 ft 0.4 in (0.62 m), at launch weighed 262 lb (119 kg), and used semi-active radar homing for an effective range of 6 miles (9.7 km).

In order to operate nuclear weapons, the ADC had to create and manage a PRP (Personnel Reliability Program) to exercise control over who had access to 'nukes'. Throughout the USAF anyone who dealt with 'nukes' had to be screened for PRP and the access was made a part of the individual's medical records. Midway through its career, when it became an ANG type, the F-102A retained its Nuclear Falcon capability. The decision to use an atomic

The 57th had two 'Tubs'. This one, pictured in September 1969, wears a large unit citation ribbon above the national insignia.

Far left: The 230-US gal (871-litre) external tanks were essential for the missions flown by the 57th and made a suitable canvas for this artwork representative of the squadron's business – a jet-borne black knight chasing a Russian bear.

Less well known than the 57th FIS, which occupied Keflavik for 40 years, are the various other squadrons who operated in the even harsher climate of Thule AB, Greenland. This trio is seen above the partly-frozen Wolstenholm Fjord in August 1958.

Nearly 170 F-102As and TF-102As served with six squadrons in Europe between the years 1959 and 1970. The first aircraft arrived at Saint-Nazaire aboard a converted wartime escort carrier in January 1959. They were then towed to Sud-Aviation's facility at Montoir Air Base where their protective cocoons were removed and the aircraft were prepared for flight. By the end of 1960, three United States Air Forces Europe (USAFE) squadrons in West Germany, two in Spain and one in the Netherlands were equipped with the 'Deuce'. The three Germany-based squadrons formed the 86th Air Division (Defense) under the Fourth Allied Tactical Air Force (4 ATAF). They comprised the 496th FIS at Hahn, the 525th at Bitburg and the 526th at Ramstein. Spain had the 431st FIS at Zaragoza and the 497th at Torrejon under the 65th AD. The Soesterberg-based 32nd FIS was part of 2 ATAF, under the operational control of the Royal Dutch Air Force. Twenty-one USAFE F-102s were lost in over a decade of service, about 12 per cent of the inventory. This compared with the overall loss rate (F-102As only) of 14 per cent.

Uniquely, the 32nd FIS at Soesterberg was under tactical control of the Royal Netherlands Air Force. Here, the 'Wolfhounds' 'Tub' completes a line-up of Dutch airpower of the early 1960s. The relative size of the F-102, just shorter than a B-17 bomber, is evident here.

F-102s of the 32nd FIS (right) and the 526th (far right) line up on the ground and in the air circa 1963. F-102 squadrons of the period were large by modern standards, with up to 25 aircraft, including two or three two-seaters. The view at far right shows the runway arrester hook, developed for the F-106 and installed on USAFE F-102s from April 1961.

The great strength of the F-102 in Europe was its all-weather capability. This picture of an unidentified unit's F-102A can be dated to after the 1963/64 time frame by the IRST ahead of the windscreen which was added under project Big Eight at that time.

weapon on board an interceptor reflected the thinking of the time: under today's rules, nuclear weapons would not be released to ANG personnel. Release of nuclear weapons in wartime requires an order from the NCA (National Command Authority), meaning the President or Secretary of Defense. Moreover, there are no nuclear-tipped air defence missiles in today's USAF inventory.

By this juncture, the ANG was very much a part of the Total Force, to use a term coined in the Pentagon, and ANG personnel played a direct role in the air defence of North America and in deployments overseas. By 1964, the F-102A and TF-102A were in service with 10 ANG squadrons and, at the peak of this interceptor's ANG career in the late 1960s, no fewer than 22 squadrons were equipped with the type. This level was maintained until 1970, when the ANG began slowly decreasing its 'Deuce' force in favour of newer aircraft, including the F-106A. At

least 500 Delta Daggers, or half of those built, served with the ANG.

The ANG story would in itself fill volumes. Guardsmen are much like military folk of a past era – bonded to a particular unit for decades, if not for life – part of a local community as well as trustees of a national mission. Offering both full- and part-time slots, with some assurance of the permanency not provided by active-duty military life, the ANG readily attracted former active-duty members with a wealth of experience for the F-102A cockpit and for the maintenance shops. A visitor to any ANG squadron in 1970 – a period coinciding with a time of civil unrest at home and a war in Vietnam – would have quickly detected that the unit was alert, neat and proud. In competitions, F-102A ground and flight crews of the ANG routinely beat the socks off active-duty folk.

In Europe

It was decided at an early stage that the 'Deuce' would have an air defence role in Europe, where NATO confronted the risk of a westward push on the continent by Soviet and Warsaw Pact forces. The US Air Forces in

A pair of 526th FIS F-102As is seen blasting off from Ramstein during September 1965. Ramstein was the HQ of the 86th Air Division. By this period, USAF 'Deuce' markings were smart rather than flamboyant, with the squadron and air division badges on either side of the fin.

Above: It might seem that France adopted the basic design of the F-102A for its succesful Mirage series, but it would be more correct to say that the French built upon XF-92 research to follow its own path to similar ends. The first contract for research into a 'Mystère Delta' reached Dassault in early 1952 and the resulting Mirage I flew in June 1955. Today's Mirage 2000 bears superficial resemblance to the Convair deltas, but engine, materials and control technology, not to mention the radar, put the Mirage in an entirely different league. This 32nd FIS Delta Dagger was photographed at the 1965 Paris Air Show.

Europe (USAFE) eventually operated six fighter interceptor squadrons using aircraft made available by the ADC. The first two squadrons, the 525th FIS at Bitburg Air Base and the 496th FIS at Hahn AB, both in Germany, were operational by mid-1959. Eventually, the F-102A interceptors had a datalink system enabling them to use the NATO Air Defense Ground Environment (NADGE) system, the European equivalent of SAGE.

In Europe the F-102A enjoyed a relatively long period of service, aircraft in late service wearing the same camouflage as that employed in Vietnam. Details of squadron assignments appear in the operator's section.

In the Pacific

In Pacific Air Forces (PACAF) the F-102A became a fixture after 1959 at the very time Americans were taking their first tentative steps toward involvement in Vietnam. In 1959-60 the 4th, 16th, 40th, 68th and 509th FISs of PACAF converted to the Delta Dagger.

The long, slow descent into the hell of Vietnam had one of its early steps in Operation Water Glass, the temporary deployment of Delta Daggers to Vietnamese soil to guard against a perceived incursion by North Vietnamese aircraft, which were then of the propeller-driven type. Unidentified radar tracks over South Vietnam on 19-20 March 1962 led to deployment of four F-102A interceptors to Tan Son Nhut AB outside Saigon. In a quote that revealed how Americans were fooling themselves and would continue to do so throughout the 1960s, the hapless US commander in Vietnam at the time, General Paul Harking, announced that, "There is no air battle in Vietnam and there are no indications that one will develop."

The 'Deuces' deployed to Vietnam on 21 March 1962 and returned to Clark AB, Philippines a week later without making any active intercepts. Additional Water Glass deployments continued throughout the year, using two-seat TF-102A aircraft which were more effective against expected targets flying 'low and slow'. In July 1962 the mission was taken over by Douglas AD-5Q Skyraiders of the US Navy, but in November the TF-102A aircraft returned.

The temporary deployments continued until May 1963, and were then briefly resumed during November 1963 in Operation Candy Machine. F-102 pilots and ground crews

After the colourful 86th AD markings disappeared from the northern European 'Deuces', it was not long before squadron identity began to reassert itself. The wolfhound badge is prominent on this 32nd FIS aircraft, and a vestige of red, white and blue remains on the airbrakes.
The 32nd FIS won the F-102 portion of the 1965 William Tell fighter meet at Tyndall AFB.

Left: The 497th FIS at Torrejon was based alongside Spanish Air Force Sabres and stood alert under large blister hangars such as this one. Like the other USAFE F-102 squadrons, the 497th travelled to Wheelus AB in Libya for live weapons firing.

Although never based in the UK, the F-102 was a frequent visitor to Britain, especially for airshows. This 496th FIS, 86th Air Division 'Tub' was a visitor to RAF Lakenheath in May 1969.

Convair F-102 Delta Dagger

The Upper Heyford Air Day 1969 gave the British public the chance to see at close hand a newly-camouflaged F-102A of the 526th FIS in rare British airshow sunshine. The 526th's aircraft began to receive camouflage as they were overhauled by CASA, the first being delivered in 1965 and the last in 1968. Most of the 526th's aircraft were assigned to the Connecticut ANG in 1970.

In April and June 1964, over 40 F-102s were returned to the US. Most of these were from the 431st FIS and 496th FIS. The 431st and fellow Spanish-based unit, the 497th FIS, transitioned to the F-4C Phantom in early 1964, and the latter unit's aircraft were swapped with those of the 496th at Hahn. Operation Krazy Kat saw the 'Deuces' flown across the Atlantic via Prestwick, Scotland, where the first group is seen here. Just visible, second from right, is an aircraft from one of the Hanscom Field test units that had been assigned to trials with the 526th FIS.

became familiar with Vietnam as a place to come and go. Later that year, 'Deuce' operations throughout the Pacific reached a pause when inspections of Naha-based aircraft revealed structural defects in the air inlet ducts caused by severe corrosion. Over the next three months, PACAF grounded 28 airframes and made repairs.

There was a resumption of F-102A deployments to South Korea in 1963 under the programme name Bone Deep. In that year 12 four-aircraft deployments were made. North Korea had an entire air division of Il-28 light bombers, to say nothing of 300 or more Mikoyan-Gurevich fighters, and the F-102A represented the only all-weather interception capability that was readily available.

Candy Machine resumed on 26 June 1964 with a 10-day deployment of three F-102A interceptors to Da Nang. Within two months, the Gulf of Tonkin incident would lead to an American build-up in Vietnam, eventually to reach 545,000 troops, and the Vietnam story would overshadow everything else in the region.

But even at the height of the Vietnam conflict, Korea never ceased to be a trouble spot. On 28 April 1965, a Yokota-based Boeing RB-47 Stratojet was attacked by two North Korean MiG-17 fighters as it undertook a reconnaissance mission 50 miles (80 km) off the Korean coast. The crew returned fire but the bomber suffered severe damage.

F-102A interceptors of the 4th FIS scrambled to escort the crippled Stratojet back to Japan, but did not engage the MiGs.

The first inflight-refuelling of the F-102A and the deployment of the 'Deuce' to the Far East during the US build-up in Vietnam is described in detail in the entry for the 82nd FIS in the operators' section. Using the programme name Thirsty Camel, 'Deuces' of the 82nd FIS deployed to Okinawa where they arrived on 18 February 1966 and began alert duty five days later. At about the same time, beginning on 6 June 1966, the 64th FIS deployed from Hamilton AFB, California, to Clark Field, Philippines in a project dubbed Hot Spice.

When the spy ship USS *Pueblo* (AGER-2) was seized by North Korea on 23 January 1968, the 82nd FIS deployed its 'Deuces' from Naha to Osan AB, Korea, eventually being relieved there by the F-106A interceptors of the 318th FIS in one of the rare overseas deployments of the Delta Dart. The F-106A was rotated into South Korea until the last of the type departed on 12 May 1970, marking the end of the crisis period.

Vietnam

The F-102A and TF-102A were to become intermittent participants in the Vietnam War. In air-to-air combat, the

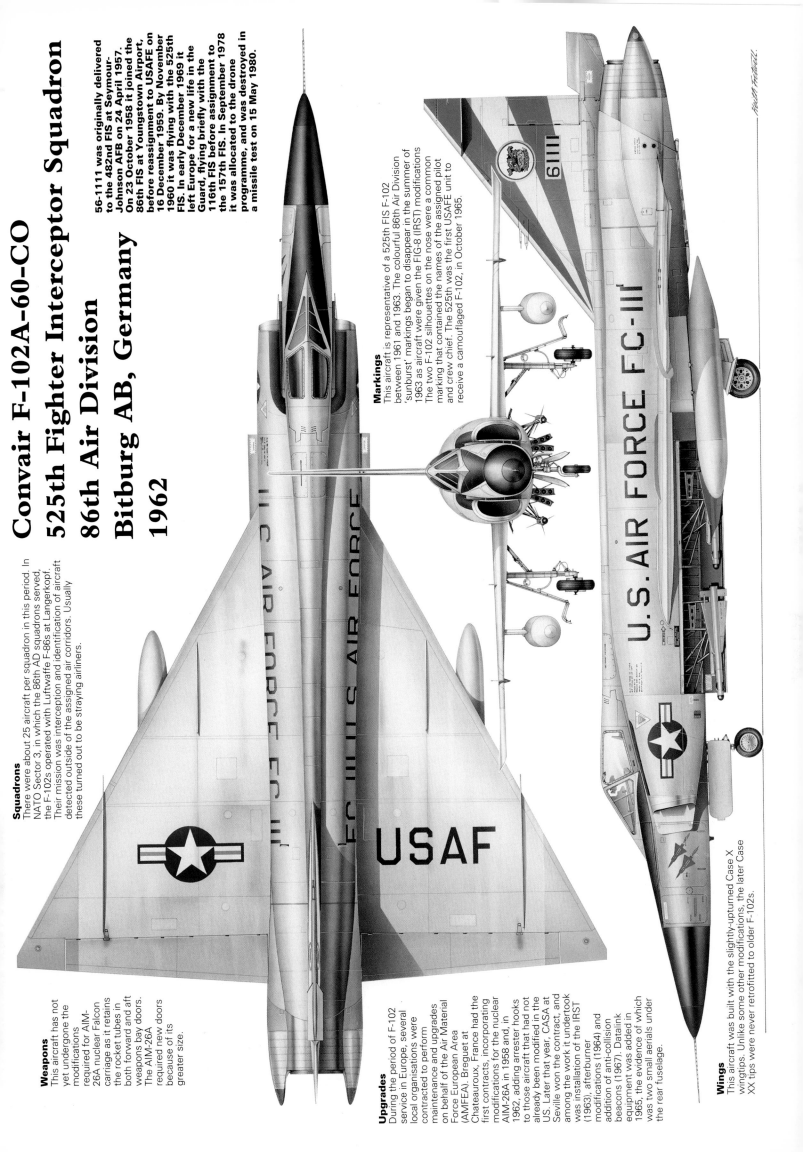

Convair F-102A-60-CO
525th Fighter Interceptor Squadron
86th Air Division
Bitburg AB, Germany
1962

56-1111 was originally delivered to the 482nd FIS at Seymour-Johnson AFB on 24 April 1957. On 23 October 1958 it joined the 86th FIS at Youngstown Airport, before reassignment to USAFE on 16 December 1959. By November 1960 it was flying with the 525th FIS. In early December 1969 it left Europe for a new life in the Guard, flying briefly with the 116th FIS before assignment to the 157th FIS. In September 1978 it was allocated to the drone programme, and was destroyed in a missile test on 15 May 1980.

Squadrons

There were about 25 aircraft per squadron in this period. In NATO Sector 3, in which the 86th AD squadrons served, the F-102s operated with Luftwaffe F-86s at Langerkopf. Their mission was interception and identification of aircraft detected outside of the assigned air corridors. Usually these turned out to be straying airliners.

Weapons

This aircraft has not yet undergone the modifications required for AIM-26A nuclear Falcon carriage as it retains the rocket tubes in both forward and aft weapons bay doors. The AIM-26A required new doors because of its greater size.

Upgrades

During the period of F-102 service in Europe, several local organisations were contracted to perform maintenance and upgrades on behalf of the Air Material Force European Area (AMFEA). Breguet at Chateauroux, France had the first contracts, incorporating modifications for the nuclear AIM-26A in 1958 and, in 1962, adding arrester hooks to those aircraft that had not already been modified in the US. Later that year, CASA at Seville won the contract, and among the work it undertook was installation of the IRST (1963), afterburner modifications (1964) and addition of anti-collision beacons (1967). Datalink equipment was added in 1965, the evidence of which was two small aerials under the rear fuselage.

Markings

This aircraft is representative of a 525th FIS F-102 between 1961 and 1963. The colourful 86th Air Division 'sunburst' markings began to disappear in the summer of 1963 as aircraft were given the FIG-8 (IRST) modifications The two F-102 silhouettes on the nose were a common marking that contained the names of the assigned pilot and crew chief. The 525th was the first USAFE unit to receive a camouflaged F-102, in October 1965.

Wings

This aircraft was built with the slightly-upturned Case X wingtips. Unlike some other modifications, the later Case XX tips were never retrofitted to older F-102s.

The Elliniki Polimiki Aeroporia (Hellenic Air Force) received 26 F-102s for use by the 114th Pterix at Tanagra in 1969. The aircraft comprised 20 F-102As and six TF-102As as follows: (F-102As) 56-0981*, 56-0988, 56-1001, 56-1007, 56-1011, 56-1016, 56-1024, 56-1025, 56-1031*, 56-1034, 56-1039, 56-1040, 56-1052, 56-1056, 56-1059, 56-1079, 56-1106*, 56-1125, 56-1232, 56-1233*. TF-102s: 55-4035*, 56-2326, 56-2327, 56-2334, 56-2335 plus one. Those marked * are believed preserved today. The Greek F-102s were phased out in favour of Mirage F1CGs in 1979.

None of the Greek F-102s was equipped with the IRST sensor. It appears that the units were removed prior to delivery. They were not fitted to Turkish 'Deuces' either, thus denying either of these potential adversaries a technological edge over the other.

Some of the Greek F-102s were delivered in southeast Asia camouflage, and retained this during their service.

This view of the flightline at Tanagra shows a quarter of the Greek Delta Daggers. Speculation about 'Deuce' vs 'Deuce' air combats in 1974 seems to be unfounded.

'Deuce' was to suffer the indignity of a final score of 0 to 1 against the MiG-21 – i.e. the type sustained one combat loss while never shooting down any enemy aircraft. There were numerous other losses to other causes as the conflict grew.

The first Southeast Asia loss occurred on 24 November 1964 when an F-102A (56-1159) of the 509th FIS suffered engine failure on a flight from Tan Son Nhut. On 1 July 1965 three more F-102A warplanes (55-0371, 56-1161 and 56-1182) were destroyed during a mortar attack on Da Nang airfield. Altogether, counting the one air-to-air combat loss, 15 Delta Daggers were lost in Vietnam. Of these, 12 were counted as operational rather than combat losses (including those wrecked by mortar fire), two more were lost to ground fire, and one was the sole air-to-air victim.

In the last six months of 1965, the 509th FIS's 'Deuces' at Tan Son Nhut participated in Project Stove Pipe. Using

its IR seeker, the F-102A (designed for nothing but interception) used 2¾-in (70-mm) FFAR projectiles and AIM-4D Falcon missiles against heat-emitting ground targets. When Project Stove Pipe ended in December 1965, the official finding was that the 'Deuce' could be used as a tactical air-to-ground weapon. But pilots who were there say that the results of this experiment were murky at best.

Pacific TDY

It was the strain on PACAF resources amidst the Vietnam build-up that brought ADC squadrons on temporary duty to the Pacific, beginning with the 82nd FIS and continuing with the 64th FIS, as noted above. Although these two squadrons initially 'backfilled' the alert commitment at Naha, Okinawa, they soon began pulling detachment duty at Da Nang. At the end of June 1966, no fewer than 22 F-102A interceptors were standing alert in South Vietnam and Thailand – a modest number of warplanes compared to the growing legions of Republic F-105

Turkey

The Türk Hava Kuvvertleri (THK - Turkish Air Force) operated at least 35 F-102As and eight TF-102As which were delivered during 1968. Known F-102A serial numbers include: 53-1814, 53-1815, 54-1377, 54-1379, 54-1380, 54-1382, 54-1383, 54-1384, 54-1386, 54-1403, 55-3380, 55-3383, 55-3384, 55-3385, 55-3386*,55-3389, 55-3390, 55-3392, 55-3395, 55-3396, 55-3400, 55-3401, 55-3403, 55-3404, 55-3405, 55-3408, 55-3409, 55-3410, 55-3412, 55-3413, 55-3416, 55-3421, 55-3425, 55-3426, 55-3429, 55-3443, 55-3452, 55-3455 and 54-3461. TF-102As were: 54-1360, 55-4033, 55-4053, 56-2325, 56-2342, 56-2355 and 56-2368*. Preserved F-102s are marked *. It has been said that Turkish F-102As may have shot down a pair of Greek F-5As during the short war over Cyprus in 1974, although F-102 involvement in the conflict was minimal. 182 Filo transitioned to the F-100C and 142 Filo to the TF-104G during 1979.

Above and above right: The 114th Filo at Mürted was the initial Turkish F-102 operator. It later split into two 18-aircraft units, the 142nd and 182nd Filos with the latter moving to Diyarbakir. The landings on Cyprus in July 1974 led to a US embargo on arms and military aid, including spare parts. The F-102 units were particularly hard hit, as there was no-one willing to provide spares in the way that a number of European F-5 and F-104 users did.

Thunderchiefs and McDonnell F-4 Phantom IIs that shared ramp space with them, but it was an important contribution nonetheless. The inclusion of the 'Deuce' in the Southeast Asian war effort was symbolised by the T.O.114 camouflage that adorned all PACAF F-102A and TF-102A aircraft by the end of 1966. In 1968, the three squadrons in the war zone acquired tail codes.

Air-to-air

The sole F-102A lost in air combat fell victim to the extraordinary success of the MiG-21 'Fishbed' fighter, which in 1967 and 1968 was prevailing against American fighters over North Vietnam with a success ratio of almost 4 to 1, at the very time American pilots were batting

MiG-17 'Fresco' fighters out of the air like flies. On 3 February 1968, Captain Allen Lomax and 1st Lieutenant Wallace Wiggins of the 509th FIS were launched to escort a flight of jamming aircraft over Laos. When the jammers failed to show as scheduled, Lomax and Wiggins fell into a trap. Apparently, they did not know they were being intercepted and ambushed by MiG-21F-13 'Fishbed-E' fighters until Wiggins radioed, "There's something wrong with my aircraft." That was when an AA-2 'Atoll' missile hit him, failed to detonate, but kinetically ripped his Delta Dagger (56-1166) to pieces. Lomax also thought he saw cannon fire from a MiG-21 arching through the air around them. Too distant from the fast-moving MiG-21s for a clear shot, Lomax rippled off three AIM-4D-8 Falcon missiles anyway, believing (correctly) that he was unlikely to hit anything. When he shifted his gaze back to the Wiggins fighter he saw "a fireball, and then debris, falling everywhere". In the only air-to-air engagement by the F-102A that resulted in an aerial victory, albeit for the other side, Wiggins apparently did not manage to eject, and thus became the only F-102A pilot ever to be killed in air-to-air action.

The wind-down of the F-102's role in Southeast Asia began when the 64th FIS ceased its alert commitment on 15 November 1969. Half a dozen of its aircraft reached the other two squadrons in the war zone, but in early 1970 the 509th FIS, too, began to discontinue its alert detachments in Southeast Asia. The 82nd FIS departed the Vietnam region for Naha and was inactivated on 31 May 1971, its

This TF-102A wears the post-1972 roundel insignia. The earlier red/white square, used since 1945, was thought to be mistakeable for a Soviet red star in certain conditions. This example is one of two 'Deuces' preserved at the Turkish Air Force Museum in Ankara.

Far left: When their operational days were over, 20 of the Greek Delta Daggers were 'put out to pasture' at their former base, Tanagra, and at Elefsis near Athens. All five Greek TF-102s were relegated to decoy duties at Elefsis. A small number of the total found their way to museums.

Convair F-102 Delta Dagger

An F-102A of the Wisconsin ANG's 176th FIS (sometimes known as the 'Bushy Badgers') takes off during an Operational Readiness Inspection (ORI).

F-102As of 'blue' and 'yellow' flights of the 134th FIS line up for a formation take-off.

'Deuces' being consumed by the scrappers' torches at Naha in a busy three-week period.

At several junctures during the Vietnam War, Convair attempted to sell the USAF a major programme to modify existing 'Deuces' into what the company called a 'close support all-weather interceptor'. With inflight-refuelling capability, an unrefuelled ferry range of 2,506 nm (2,885 miles; 4643 km), and a ready supply and maintenance infrastructure, the new, dual-role version would have had six external ordnance stations in addition to the standard missile bay, and would have retained the existing MG-10 fire-control system. The 'close support' version would also have been capable of carrying up to three reconnaissance cameras, which would be interchangeable with the

A pair of 'Deuces' of the Louisiana ANG flies over its home town of New Orleans during 1965. Deficiencies in NORAD's coverage of the southern sector of the US led, in 1971/72, to an increased alert role for the Louisiana Guard.

internally carried Falcon AAMs, and would have had wing pylons for two 750-lb (340-kg) and four 1,000-lb (454-kg) bombs, or alternatively for rockets. Possible weapon loads would have included the AGM-12 Bullpup ASM (by then determined by the USAF to be essentially useless but still being manufactured), 5-in (127-mm) Zuni rocket projectiles and fragmentation bombs. The general idea was that this proposal would offer a degree of flexibility deemed, by Convair at least, to be appropriate for the Vietnam setting. The USAF never bit, and there was never a 'Deuce' fighter-bomber.

The gradual weaning-down of the USAF's inventory of 'Deuces' continued into the 1970s. On 30 June 1971, Perrin AFB, Texas ended its long-standing role as Replacement Training Unit (RTU) for Delta Dagger pilots, and all F-102A and TF-102A training was transferred to the 111th FIS, Texas ANG.

In the late 1960s, a number of 'natural metal' F-102As appeared in ANG squadrons, mainly in the Oregon and Montana Guards and California's 196th FIS at Ontario (below). Fifty aircraft that passed through depot-level maintenance at Fairchild-Hiller's facility at Crestview, Florida from May 1969 were finished with a new silver acrylic lacquer paint. Although the resulting scheme was attractive and durable, it did not enter widespread service.

Above: Some TF-102s were not equipped with weapons or fire control equipment (or had it removed) and were mainly used for check-rides. Others, including this 199th FIS 'Tub', had a dual fire control system (FCS) fitted.

The Cold War and the American face-off with Cuba continued. On 26 October 1971, a Cuban Antonov An-24 'Coke' twin-engined transport 22 nm (25 miles; 41 km) from New Orleans radioed the control tower requesting landing instructions. It was a defector, and the call was the first inkling that a Cuban aircraft was in the area. The 'Coke' was allowed to land and the press went into a frenzy, demanding to know what had happened to the southern air defence of the USA. To augment and beef-up this defence, three F-102 alert detachments of the ANG were created in Louisiana, Texas and Arizona.

The end of the F-102A Delta Dagger era in the ADC, which had been redesigned Aerospace Defense Command on 15 January 1968, came on 1 July 1973 when the 57th FIS 'Black Knights' at Keflavik AB, Iceland surrendered its 'Deuces' and filled its alert barns with F-4C Phantoms. The previous year, however, new life had been breathed into the Delta Dagger with a plan to fly a version that carried no pilot.

PQM-102A/B

In 1972 the USAF asked six aerospace contractors to submit proposals for a drone conversation of the F-102. On 31 March 1973, Sperry won a contract to convert six airframes. The programme became known as Pave Deuce.

The 'Deuce' drone was intended to replace the Ryan BQM-34 (*née* Q-2C) Firebee I and II drones, then being employed as high-speed, manoeuvrable aerial targets. The PQM-102A (which should have been designated QF-102A under the existing system for naming aircraft) made its first flight on 13 August 1974. It was billed, inaccurately, as the first full-scale pilotless target with an afterburning engine and hence the first able to simulate warplanes that might be encountered in actual combat.

In fact, the USAF had ordered the PQM-102A in part because of its lack of foresight with a previous full-scale, afterburner-equipped target. Earlier, the USAF had operat-

A Wisconsin ANG TF-102A glistens after an April shower. About half of the two-seaters were equipped with AIM-26A Nuclear Falcon capability, although it is unlikely that any ANG 'Tubs' ever carried the weapon.

The Texas Guard was the first and the last Continental US ANG users of the F-102, although different squadrons introduced the 'Deuce' (182nd FIS, July 1960), and saw out (111th FIS, January 1975) the Delta Dagger. Seen here with its replacement is an aircraft of the 111th. Note that both the F-102A and the F-101F have the 'O' for 'obsolete' serial prefix.

Air National Guard phaseout

The first F-102 squadron gave up its 'Deuces' as early as 1964, but the bulk of the 23 units so equipped phased them out in the 1969-71 period. When the F-102As were retired from the ANG, the squadrons that operated them transitioned to a wide variety of different types. Most stayed, broadly, in the fighter business, but only three made the logical step to the F-106. Five went to the F-100, six to the F-101, two to the O-2, one to the F-4 and one to the RF-4. Single squadrons acquired the A-7, F-84, KC-97 and EB-57. One became an air rescue squadron with HC-130s and HH-3s. The very last US user of operational F-102s was the 199th Fighter Interceptor Squadron at Hickam AFB, which retired them in favour of F-4Cs in January 1977.

F-102 Colours

5th FIS

The tail markings of the 'Spittin' Kittens' changed from simple red and black lightning bolts to this design, with the squadron badge and stars. It was later adapted by the 526th FIS without the central badge.

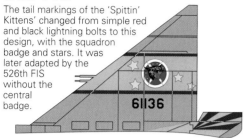

318th FIS

The 318th FIS's tail insignia was derived from the Chrysler Motors 'Way Forward' logo of the late 1950s. The squadron's dragon badge was often worn on the noses of its F-102s.

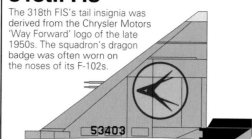

16th FIS

The 16th FIS at Naha also used a broad (black/white) chequered fin band, but distinguished itself from the 4th FIS with the squadron badge (a tomahawk splitting a stake) and the squadron designator.

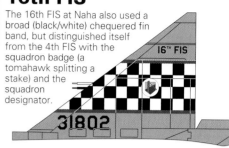

11th FIS

Some squadron commanders preferred to save on maintenance time by keeping the markings as small and as simple as possible. The 11th FIS charging bull badge and some red intake trim was all that 11th FIS F-102s carried.

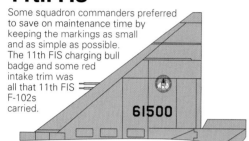

327th FIS

Most of the 'short-tail' F-102As of the 327th initially wore a simple badge on the nose. The commander's aircraft featured this chequered fin. 'Tall-tail' 'Deuces' briefly wore a different red and white design.

40th FIS

The 'Fighting Fortieth', based at Yokota, carried an especially large version of its regular squadon badge; a laughing devil's head.

48th FIS

The spectacular 48th FIS tail design featured 24 Kelly green stars on each side of the fin (for a total of 48). The squadron's badge featured a red and yellow flash with four stars above and eight below.

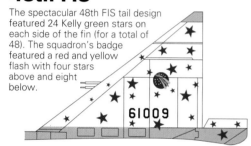

460th FIS

The tails of 460th FIS F-102s featured an enlarged squadron badge warning 'Beware of the Tiger'. The wing fences and, unusually, the wing tips were yellow on at least one squadron aircraft.

68th FIS

The famous knight insignia of the 68th, seen previously on F-61s, F-82s, F-94s and F-86s, appeared atop a large central red triangle on the squadron's F-102s.

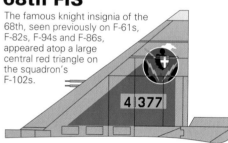

57th FIS

The 'Black Knights' (a nickname shared by the 525th FIS) wore the standard Arctic red wingtips and fins as had been seen on its F-89s. The F-102s added a chequered rudder to this pattern.

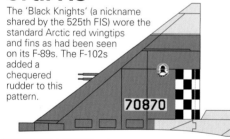

4780th ADW

The F-102A was the last of a long line of aircraft that trained interceptor pilots at Perrin AFB, Texas. This 'Deuce' had the 470th ADW's double chevron insignia, but no serial number on the fin.

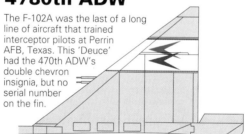

32nd FIS

The earliest markings of the 32nd FIS in Europe featured the colours of the Dutch flag over the whole fin. After mid-1963, the red, white and blue was restricted to the airbrake.

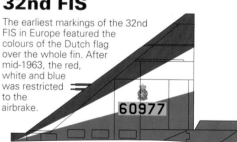

59th FIS

The 59th FIS was based at Goose Bay from 1952. Around the time it swapped its F-94s for F-102s, the unit also changed its dancing lion badge for the bat shown here.

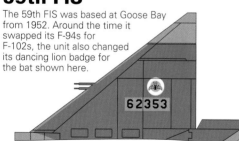

ADWC

In the latter period of Air Defense Weapons Center F-102 use, this red and blue chevron with red/white rudder pattern was introduced. It was later applied, with variations, on ADWC F-106s.

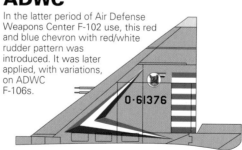

496th FIS

The sunburst marking of the 86th Air Division was seen on 496th aircraft from 1960 to mid-1963 when the general toning down began. In 1964, a broad band based on the 5th FIS markings appeared.

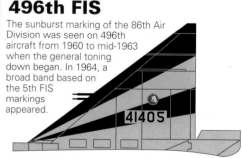

NASA

There was only one F-102 painted in full NASA colours with a NASA registration. The black of the central tail area continued along the fuselage to the air intakes.

4th FIS

The 4th FIS at Naha on Okinawa used a broad red and black chequered band as a unit identifier, with no squadron badge.

526th FIS

Flight assignment in the 'Black Knights' was denoted by the colour on the airbrake, either red, white or blue. The 526th was the first European unit to get camouflaged F-102s, in 1965.

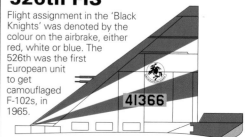

525th FIS

...s with the 526th, airbrake colour on ...Bulldogs' F-102s denoted Red, ...White or Blue flights. The ...markings were later toned ...own to a badge on a ...rey fin.

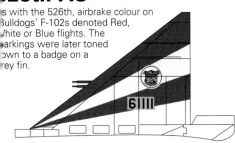

Texas ANG (111th FIS)

...he 111th FIS carried the ANG badge ...n both sides of its F-102 fins, as ...well as the squadron's star and ...laying card badge. The ...adge dates from 1933 ...when the 111th was a ...exas National ...uard ...observation ...quadron.

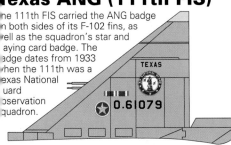

New York ANG

...he 102nd FIS was one of the few ...quadrons to add any colour to the ...O.114 tactical camouflage ...cheme, in the form of a ...tylised seagull on a blue ...nd white base.

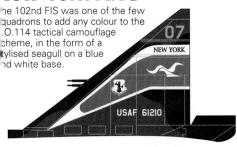

Connecticut ANG

...robably the cleverest design used on ...-102 tail fins was the black and ...white stylised gull applied by ...he 118th FIS based at ...radley ANG Station. The ...18th was an F-102 ...ser from 1966 ...o 1971.

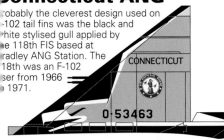

Oregon ANG

...ke most ANG squadrons, the 123rd ...IS, based at Portland Municipal ...irport, wore the ANG badge on ...he port side of the fin and ...he squadron badge on the ...tarboard side. The 'O' ...refix to the ...erial indicated ...n 'obsolete' ...pe.

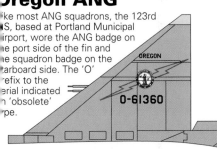

Vermont ANG

...he 134th FIS 'Green Mountain Boys' ...sed this simple green and yellow ...hevron on its aircraft. ...ometimes the fin tip was ...oloured to denote flights ...ithin the squadron.

Pennsylvania ANG

The 146th FIS at Pittsburgh airport was distinguished by this striking black fin with striped rudder. A small tactical code number was often worn on the fin.

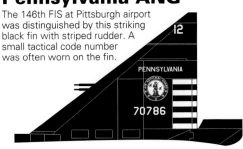

South Carolina ANG

Quite a few ANG F-102 users had variations of a band and stars, including the 157th FIS at McEntire which also had a coloured tail fin on some aircraft. Coloured air brake extensions were also seen.

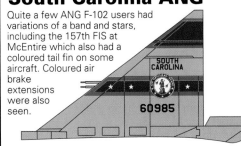

Florida ANG

The 159th FIS's F-102s wore this lightning flash in a blue band. The device was used, with variations, on the squadron's later F-106s, F-16s and F-15s. The abbreviated state name was unique to the 159th.

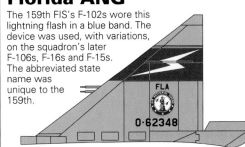

South Dakota ANG

The 175th FIS at South Dakota's Sioux City airport, which was one of the first ANG 'Deuce' squadrons, carried the state name on the fuselage (as S.DAK.AIR GUARD) rather than on the fin like other units.

Wisconsin ANG

Like Pennsylvania's 146th FIS, Wisconsin's 176th marked its Delta Daggers with a full-colour fin, in this case red, with a red and white striped rudder. Large tactical numbers were also carried.

North Dakota

The 'Happy Hooligans' are said to have been so named after a boisterous trainng camp. The tail band was to appear on 178th FIS F-101s, F-4Ds and F-16s. A state law was passed to allow it to be worn on the 'low-vis' F-16.

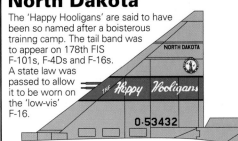

Minnesota

Although not an Alaska- or Arctic-based squadron, the 179th FIS at Duluth applied red tail and wing surfaces. The rudder was kept unpainted for balance reasons.

Montana ANG

Some ANG units used tactical code letters. The 'Big Sky Country' F-102s of the 186th FIS used an alpha-numeric system that had appeared on the F-89s previously used by the unit.

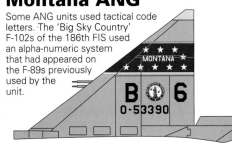

Idaho ANG

The 190th FIS was one of a small number of ANG units to have 'Deuces' in overall 'silver' finish. Its F-102s sometimes wore a numeric code on the rear fuselage.

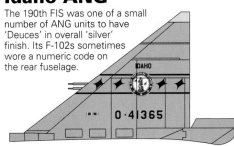

California ANG 196th FIS

The flamboyant stylised stars motif of the 196th FIS's F-102s reappeared on its later F-4 and RF-4 Phantoms. The 196th applied a natural metal finish to its F-102s for a period.

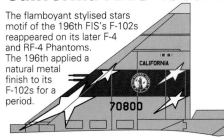

California ANG 194th FIS

In contrast to the 196th FIS, the 194th at Fresno used a simple small unit badge on its F-102s.

Hawaii ANG

The longest-lived ANG squadron, the 199th FIS F-102s wore a band based on a Hawaiian native basket design. It reappeared in reduced form on the later F-4Cs and F-15s.

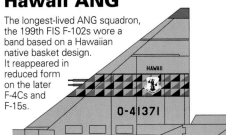

PQM/QF-102

Under a contract managed by the USAF at Eglin AFB, bidders were sought for the conversion of F-102s into unmanned targets. Bidders included Sperry Rand Flight Systems Division, Lear Siegler, Northrop, Celesco Industries, Lockheed and Hughes/Honeywell. The winner, in April 1973, was Sperry Rand, which, after converting and testing the first of six prototypes at Holloman AFB in August 1974, subcontracted Fairchild at Crestview Florida to do the remaining 24 conversions and maintenance. Following further contracts, conversion and maintenance was taken over by Sperry at a new facility at Litchfield Park near Davis-Monthan where large numbers of F-102s were stored

The first aircraft destined for conversion to PQM-102B standard is seen arriving at Litchfield Park. 56-1077 was an ex-Idaho ANG aircraft that had been delivered to AMARC in April 1975. The conversion process from 'boneyard' to drone took six months.

by the US Army. Fairchild described the conversion process as follows:

"Crews at Crestview remove most of the original avionics equipment. After that, there is extensive re-wiring and refitting to install the Sperry-designed autopilots, flight controls, and low-altitude radar.

"Technicians also install a smoke system, designed by Fairchild engineers, which allows ground observers to visually track the drone at high altitude, even with the afterburner on. They also install a destruct system which controllers can use to blow up the drone in the event it goes out of control."

After completion, the PQM-102A drones were flown to Tyndall AFB by civilian pilots employed by Sperry. At Tyndall, Sperry removed the ejection seat and installed 'black boxes' in the cockpit so that the PQM-102A could no longer be flown by a human pilot.

Four of the 65, or perhaps 89, PQM-102A aircraft did not receive the cockpit modification and remained, throughout their service lives, capable of being flown either remotely or by a pilot. These four were the only aircraft to be designated QF-102A. The first QF-102A was the first 'Deuce' to make an unmanned flight, in this instance at Holloman AFB on 13 August 1975.

The first unmanned flight of a production-standard PQM-102A was also accomplished at Holloman AFB, where testing was delegated to the USAF Special Weapons Center's 6585th Test Group. Operations also took place at Tyndall AFB where a new 7,000-ft (2133-m) runway for drone work was constructed 4 miles (6.4 km) east of the main base, the drones being towed to the launch site over a newly built taxi strip.

Sperry's Litchfield Park, Arizona plant began making the PQM-102B model in 1978. In the 'A' model the remote control equipment was located in the cockpit. In the PQM-102B that should, by rights, have been designated as the QF-102B, the equipment was moved to the nose, mak-

Flight Control Stabilisation System (FCSS) components replaced the F-102's old vacuum tube autopilot, while a manoeuvre programmer allowed evasive actions to be input by the ground controller.

Take-offs by drones were conducted by the mobile Ground Station (MGS). After five minutes' flight, the mission was handed over to a control centre on base and regained for landing (if the drone was recoverable) by the MGS about 10 miles (16 km) out.

ed the Lockheed QF-104 Starfighter, the drone target version of a fighter that had had a relatively lacklustre career in US service. But in a false economy move, the USAF had ordered only 22 QF-104 conversions and only very slowly, over a decade's time. It was a time of vigorous weapons testing, and the final QF-104 was shot down in July 1972.

The PQM-102A was purposely ordered in more robust numbers. Among other duties, the type was to serve as a realistic target for McDonnell Douglas F-15 Eagles in air-to-air engagements and, when flying from Holloman AFB, for US Army surface-to-air missiles launched from the White Sands Missile Range. Ultimately, by 1977, Sperry's Crestview, Florida facility transformed 65 former Delta Dagger interceptors into PQM-102A drones. Some 29 aircraft – it is unclear whether their number is included in the total of 65 or increased the total to 89 – were converted in Crestview by Fairchild. Of this number, 14 were owned

Control consoles in the MGS were a representation of the F-102's original instrument layout. Two pilots controlled the drone, one handled throttle and pitch, the other direction.

NACA and NASA

NASA and its predecessor NACA made less use of the F-102 than they did of its 'Century Series' stablemates, the F-104 and F-106. The XF-92A, a YF-102, six F-102As and two TF-102As served with various NASA centres between 1953 and 1974, although only one of these wore a NASA number.

Right: NASA 617 (56-998) was based at NASA Lewis at Cleveland Municipal Airport on chase duties for the NF-106B NASA 616 which was flying SST research missions over the Great Lakes. It was retired to AMARC in 1974.

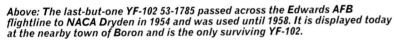

Above: The last-but-one YF-102 53-1785 passed across the Edwards AFB flightline to NACA Dryden in 1954 and was used until 1958. It is displayed today at the nearby town of Boron and is the only surviving YF-102.

Above: F-102A 56-1358 arrived at NASA Ames (Moffett Field, California) on 23 December 1957. It was used on explorations of 'fire control auto manoeuvres', until March 1960. Similarly, F-102A 56-1304 was used for 'auto attack evaluation'.

Left: Astronaut Alan Shepherd arrives at a NASA facility in F-102A 55-3391. This aircraft flew nearly 500 hours in the 22 months it was based at the Johnson Space Center.

After the Project Mercury astronauts had complained that they were being treated more like lab rats than test pilots, NASA's Manned Spacecraft Center at Houston acquired two F-102As (55-3391 and 55-3405) and two TF-102As (54-1338 and 54-1356) in September 1962. They were used for proficiency flying and for 'commuting' between various NASA and contractor sites. The 'Deuces' supplemented USAF-loaned T-33s, and were later replaced themselves by F-106s, the last being sent to Perrin AFB in August 1964.

Robert M. White is seen boarding NTF-102A 54-1354 in an MC-2 full-pressure suit

One of the original 'Mercury Seven', Virgil I. 'Gus' Grissom, stands by F-102A 56-1017 (not a NASA aircraft). Both he and Robert White died in the tragic Apollo I capsule fire.

Convair F-102 Delta Dagger

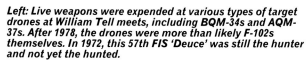

Above: The F-104 Starfighter was known as 'the missile with a man in it'. The F-102 became something of a missile without the man when converted to drone form. This is a (non man-rated) PQM-102A.

The last role of the F-102 included the indignity of being a target for its successor, the F-106. The 'Deuce' here, 56-1254, formerly with Wisconsin's 176th FIS, was one of the drones expended at William Tell 80. The 87th FIS F-106A in this picture was in turn converted to a drone and shot down, by an AMRAAM missile in May 1994.

Left: Live weapons were expended at various types of target drones at William Tell meets, including BQM-34s and AQM-37s. After 1978, the drones were more than likely F-102s themselves. In 1972, this 57th FIS 'Deuce' was still the hunter and not yet the hunted.

ing it possible for the aircraft to be flown manually by a pilot. Sperry produced about 145 examples of the latter version.

Operation of the drones was initially by Sperry under contract, and later by the RCA company. PQM-102A/B drones served the USAF for several years. The last PQM-102B mission was flown at Tyndall AFB on 14 July 1983 when such an aircraft (56-1175, call sign SPAD 793) completed the 500th mission in the programme. This aircraft and another were flown to Holloman AFB on 9 August 1983, and operations continued at Holloman AFB until 1986. It is believed that the final mission at Holloman AFB was flown by another PQM-102B (56-1072, call sign SPAD 800) in that year.

Civil 'Deuce'

The F-102A was so expensive to operate and to keep in flying shape that none is likely, ever, to appear as a restored museum piece on the warbird circuit. Indeed, although many are in museums, none survives today in a condition that even approaches being a candidate for restoration. There was, however, a civil F-102A for a six-month period.

An F-102A (57-0835) was given civil registry N300 and assigned to the Federal Aviation Administration (FAA) in

William Tell

The F-102 made its first appearance at the biennial William Tell Weapons Meet in 1958, the year the competition moved to Tyndall AFB. The F-102 was the first supersonic interceptor to appear. The William Tell competition had no overall winner as such, but each squadron competed with those flying the same type. The first ANG squadron to win the F-102 category was Pennsylvania's 146th FIS in 1963, and the 32nd FIS took the trophy for USAFE in 1965. Guard squadrons won again in 1970 (Minnesota), 1972 (Wisconsin) and 1974 (Idaho), but by that time the *only* F-102s were in the ANG. The F-102 was absent in 1976, but returned in 1978 – this time in the form of PQM-102 target drones.

The squadron scoreboard at William Tell '82 is flanked by the drones used in that competition, the PQM-102 and the 'newer' QF-100D. This was the last year the 'Deuce' took part, the Pave Deuce programme concluding the following year.

'Deuce' destruction

F-102As served for nearly a decade in the drone role at both Holloman, New Mexico, and Tyndall, Florida. The Tyndall-based drones were used for air-to-air engagements, while those at Holloman more frequently faced SAMs fired from the White Sands missile range. On average, a PQM-102 survived four missile engagements (including inert warhead missiles that passed within 'kill' distance). Some 'lucky' aircraft survived 16 or 20. The last F-102 built, 57-0909, was shot down in March 1982 by an AIM-7E fired by an F-4D Phantom of the Michigan ANG, but 17 aircraft of the 213 converted remained when the programme ended in 1983. Of the 200 or so remaining F-102s that were not converted to drones, 20 were given to the New Mexico Institute of Mining and Technology for explosive testing, others went to China Lake for weapons tests and over 100 went to a scrap company in Arizona in 1976-77. One (56-1515) remains at Davis-Monthan.

This sequence, recorded by a high-speed camera mounted on the tracking radar dish, shows the destruction of a PQM-102, possibly by a Stinger SAM (also a General Dynamics product). In the third image, hydraulic system damage appears to have caused the undercarriage to lower, precipitating the disintegration of the drone. The US Army were given the use of seven PQM-102s to expend in the Stinger and Patriot missile programmes.

Below: Over 60 'Deuces' are preserved in the USA alone, with further examples in Canada, Greece, Turkey, the Netherlands and Germany. This F-102A, late of the 'Green Mountain Boys', is displayed at Burlington International Airport, Vermont.

June 1970. The aircraft carried out a six-month flight research programme at Edwards AFB to provide information for the development of airworthiness standards for the SST (supersonic transport) then planned by Boeing but later abandoned. Tests were directed at evaluation of low-speed performance characteristics to determine a suitable performance base-line that could be used in lieu of a stall speed for the SST, because delta-winged aircraft do not stall in the same way as straight- and swept-winged aircraft.

With test pilot Richard F. LaSuer doing the honours, the F-102A was modified with a wooden tail skid in order to restrict take-off rotation attitude to that of the proposed SST. Take-off and climb thrust were also limited to simulate normal thrust/weight ratios of the SST. In addition, the landing gear remained extended during tests to simulate the performance characteristics of typical SST designs. Speed brakes were then used to create landing gear drag. The programme yielded a wealth of performance that assisted with Concorde operations. It was probably the only appearance of the Convair F-102 Delta Dagger on the civilian scene. **Robert F. Dorr**

F-102 Operators

Air Defense Command (ADC)

Between April 1956 and July 1973, ADC (Air Defense Command) operated 32 squadrons equipped with the Convair F/TF-102A. Midway through this era the interceptor acquired a nickname, the Delta Dagger, while ADC was redesignated Aerospace Defense Command. The aircraft and the mission remained little-changed throughout: the job was to defend North America against bombers and cruise missiles.

The focus was always on an attack from the Soviet Union, but during much of the 1960s, ADC was also preoccupied with Cuba, where the US sponsored a failed invasion by exiles in 1961 and forced the Soviets to remove missiles and bombers in 1962. From the very time Fidel Castro seized power, he had 'Deuces' aimed at him, and this condition persisted until 15 November 1969 when a longstanding alert detachment of eight F/TF-102As at Naval Air Station Key West, Florida, suspended operations. Even thereafter, a detachment of F-4 Phantoms was kept on alert for air defence against Cuba.

2nd FIS

The 2nd FIS at Suffolk County AFB, New York, operated the T/TF-102A from 29 January 1957 until 9 February 1960. The squadron was dubbed the 'Unicorns' but more frequently called the 'Horny Horses.' The emblem of a unicorn and the phrase 'Second to None' had previously adorned the F-86D/L Sabre. After the departure of the 'Deuce', the squadron continued in the air defence role flying the F-101B/F Voodoo.

55-3461 moved from the 5th FIS to the 2nd FIS in November 1958. Both squadrons were part of the 52nd FG.

5th FIS

The 5th FIS at Suffolk County AFB, New York, operated the T/TF-102A from 28 March 1957 until 21 March 1960. The F-86D/L Sabre had previously been the mount of the 'Spittin' Kittens' with their distinctive cat emblem and yellow/black trim. They progressed from the Delta Dagger to the next offering from Convair, the F-106A/B Delta Dart.

The 2nd and 5th FISs at Suffolk County wore 52nd FG colours rather than a squadron design.

11th FIS

The 11th FIS at Duluth International Airport, Minnesota, flew F/TF-102As from 27 August 1956 until 15 August 1960. One of at least two squadrons to use a charging bull as its emblem, the 11th FIS had previously operated the Northrop F-89H/J Scorpion. The squadron progressed in 1960 to the F-106A/B.

The 11th FIS CO's F-102A was marked with 'command stripes' over its otherwise plain finish.

18th FIS

The 18th FIS operated F/TF-102As from 27 August 1956 until 15 August 1960. Their emblem was a blue fox firing a machine-gun through the clouds. They were preceded at Wurtsmith AFB, Michigan by the F-89J Scorpion and replaced by the F-101B/F Voodoo, later becoming an Alaskan-based F-16 unit.

This F-102A of the 18th FIS, seen in 1958, has a band on the tail consisting of golden yellow and dark blue stripes, as well as a large squadron badge.

27th FIS

The 27th FIS, located during the 'Deuce' era at Griffiss AFB, New York, enjoyed the distinction of being the oldest fighter squadron in the Air Force, having been Frank Luke's unit in World War I. The 'Eagles' have operated everything from the Spad XIII to the F-15C/D Eagle.

The squadron began converting from the F-94C Starfire to the F-102A shortly after the first 'Deuce' arrived on 4 June 1957. The squadron remained an operator of the F/TF-102A until 18 February 1960. The F-102 was replaced by the F-106A/B.

When the 27th FIS transitioned to the F-106, it retained the yellow/black chequerboard and chevron markings used on its F-102s.

31st FIS

The 31st FIS at Wurtsmith AFB, Michigan had a brief interlude with the F/TF-102A from 1 December 1956 until 17 October 1957. The squadron employed a wolf emblem copyrighted by Walt Disney studios. The 31st dates to 1940 and was flying F-86 Sabres before the 'Deuce' came along. The squadron transferred to Alaskan Air Command, in 1957 and its further operations are noted in the section on AAC.

January 1957 at Wurtsmith gave the 31st a taste of the conditions they would soon find in Alaska.

37th FIS

The 37th FIS 'Green Mountain Boys' at Ethan Allen AFB, Vermont, flew the F/TF-102A from 3 January 1958 until 23 May 1960. The squadron derives its name not merely from the craggy peaks of Vermont, but also from a band of local patriots in the American war for independence. The 37th traces its origins to 1940 and was flying the F-86 Sabre prior to the 'Deuce'. The squadron later flew F-4D Phantoms and now flies the F-16C/D block 25 Fighting Falcon.

The 37th FIS was one of several ADC units to adopt arctic markings.

47th FIS

The 47th FIS at Niagara Falls International Airport, New York, was an F/TF-102A operator from 3 January 1958 until 25 May 1960. The squadron used a bumblebee or 'turnip termite' emblem, copyrighted by United Features Syndicate.

The squadron is one of only a couple to revert to an earlier aircraft. After flying the Delta Dagger in 1958-60, it reverted to the F-84F Thunderstreak.

Only the centre of these three 47th FIS 'Deuces' has the full squadron markings with the spade and dice insignia.

48th FIS

The 48th FIS at Langley AFB, Virginia flew F/TF-102As from 28 March 1957 until 28 September 1960. The Delta Daggers were replaced by F-106A/B Delta Darts. The squadron's symbol was a starburst broken by a bolt of lightning. Its history dates to 1917. It had F-94C Starfires before progressing to the 'Deuce'. Only after many subsequent years with F-106A/Bs and F-15A/B Eagles was the squadron eventually inactivated.

Seen at Langley in 1958, one of the 48th FIS's F-102As shows off its spectacular star-spangled tail markings.

57th FIS

The 57th FIS was the final ADC operator of the F/TF-102A, replacing its 'Deuces' with F-4C Phantoms on 1 July 1973. Before that happened, the squadron had a long and distinguished history flying the Delta Dagger. On 1 July 1962, the 57th FIS transferred from MATS (Military Air Transport Service) to ADC at Keflavik AB, Iceland. The following month, the squadron began converting from the F-89D Scorpion to the F/TF-102A. The squadron also operated T-33A Shooting Stars as 'hack' and electronic decoy aircraft.

One measure of the degree of activity in the 'GIUK Gap' (Greenland, Iceland, United Kingdom) was the enormous number of occasions when 'Deuces' from Keflavik intercepted and escorted Soviet bombers and reconnnaissance aircraft. In fact, on 15 September 1972, two F-102As of the 57th FIS made their 1,000th intercept of an unidentified aircraft. Sadly for those who gave their hearts to the 'Deuce,' on 1 July 1973 the F-4C Phantom replaced the F-102A on alert with the busy 57th. At this late date, the 57th FIS had the distinction of being the final active-duty unit to operate the Delta Dagger. The last F-102s left Iceland on 17 July 1973.

The squadron's emblem was a knight's head in a helmet. Its aircraft were frequently painted with black and white chequerboards.

A well-worn F-102A of the 57th FIS is seen on an interception mission in the 1966-67 period.

59th FIS

The 59th FIS was officially the 'Lions' for most of its existence, but informally dubbed the 'Black Bats' and also called the 'Black Watch' by troops. The squadron was located at Goose Bay, Labrador and transferred from Northeast Air Command to ADC when the former was disbanded and the latter took over the air defence role. The 59th FIS had been an operator of the F-94C Starfire when its first F-102A arrived on 24 May 1960. The 'Deuce' era lasted half a dozen years until 19 December 1966.

The squadron survives today as an operator of the F-15C/D Eagle at Eglin AFB, Florida with the 33rd FW.

One of the 'Black Bats' TF-102A proficiency trainers is seen on a visit to Andrews AFB in June 1965.

61st FIS

Located at Truax Field, Wisconsin, the 61st FIS flew the 'Deuce' only very briefly, from 9 October 1957 until 31 January 1958. The squadron emblem and mascot was an English bulldog.

The 61st began operations in 1941 and was flying F-89H/J Scorpions before graduating to the 'Deuce.' The ultimate fate of this squadron has proven elusive, but it is thought to have been retired following its F-102 era.

This 61st FIS F-102 has the arctic red trim extending along the spine.

64th FIS

The 64th FIS had the distinction of operating the F/TF-102A from two stateside locations before going overseas. The squadron is sometimes called the 'Scorpions' and has that creature as its emblem.

The squadron flew 'Deuces' at McChord AFB, Washington from 2 August 1957 until 7 June 1960, and at Paine Field, Washington from 8 February 1960 through 2 June 1966. That month, the squadron went temporarily to Hamilton AFB, California to prepare for overseas deployment. Its story is continued in the entry under Pacific Air Forces.

76th FIS

The 76th FIS at Westover AFB, Massachusetts flew the F/TF-102A from 3 March 1961 until 16 March 1963. The squadron's insignia of a tiger flanked by the Chinese characters meaning 'Vanguard,' relates to its origin as a follow-on to the American Volunteer Group, the 'Flying Tigers', of the China Burma India Theater in World War II.

The squadron had flown F-86D/L Sabres before the 'Deuce.' It subsequently flew the F-106A/B Delta Dart.

71st FIS

The 71st FIS at Selfridge AFB, Michigan operated 'Deuces' from 7 October 1958 to 22 November 1960. The squadron later flew the F-106A/B. Subsequently, on 1 July 1971, the 71st designation was transferred to Langley AFB, Virginia and the squadron lost its status as an air defence unit, becoming an F-15C/D Eagle outfit.

A simple squadron badge marked the F-102s of the 71st FIS at Langley. The aircraft otherwise wore completely standard ADC markings, with 'FC' buzzcodes and intake-mounted national insignia.

82nd FIS

ADC's 82nd FIS was stationed at Travis AFB, Calif. The squadron was a 'Deuce' operator from 3 July 1957. Almost a decade later, on 1 November 1965, as American attention became focused on Vietnam, the 82nd FIS ceased alert operations in preparation for a TDY (temporary duty) assignment which would transfer the unit from ADC to PACAF (Pacific Air Forces). The deployment overseas, because it would involve the 'Deuce' gobbling down fuel in mid-air for the first time, was given the programme name Thirsty Camel.

The 82nd flew its F-102A interceptors--camouflaged, and with angle-braced air refuelling probes installed – across the Pacific in 1966, and the squadron became a component of the 51st FIW at Naha. This was the first deployment of the 'Deuce' using aerial refuelling. The 82nd FIS assumed the air defence mission for Okinawa (which had then not yet reverted

to Japan) enabling the F-4C Phantoms of the 555th TFS 'Triple Nickel' to transfer to Udorn, Thailand. Twenty-three F-102As arrived at Naha on 19 February 1966 and three more on 22 February 1966. The story of this squadron's role in the Far East is

continued in the entry under PACAF.

With an unusual white-painted radome, this 82nd FIS 'Deuce' was a participant at a March 1964 airshow.

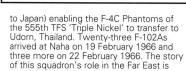

86th FIS

After operating the F-86 Sabre, the 86th FIS adopted the F-102 in 1957 and operated it until 1960 at Youngstown Municipal Airport, Ohio. Its Indian in the clouds squadron badge was officially approved in 1959.

The 86th FIS markings consisted of a tiny red lightning bolt on the rudder, as seen on this 'Tub' at Youngstown in May 1959.

87th FIS

The 87th FIS, symbolised by a Walt Disney insignia of a bee carrying a machine-gun, but apparently never given a nickname, was an ADC unit on a SAC base at Lockbourne AFB (known today as Rickenbacker AFB) near Columbus, Ohio. After flying the F-86D Sabre, the unit acquired its first F-102A on 26 August 1958. It operated 'Deuces' only until 22 June 1960, when it began conversion to the F-101B/F Voodoo.

317th FIS

In its capacity as a component of ADC, the 317th FIS flew the F/TF-102A at McChord AFB, Washington for just a year, beginning on 3 December 1956. The squadron was transferred to AAC (Alaskan Air Command) in a process that began on 15 August 1957 and was completed on 24 December 1957. The squadron's subsequent story appears in the AAC entry.

95th FIS

The 95th FIS, known as 'Mr. Bones' and sporting an emblem of a skeleton in a high-hat, operated all-weather Sabres before becoming an F/TF-102A user at Andrews AFB, Maryland on 9 January 1958. The squadron's brief Delta Dagger era concluded on 12 August 1960. From the 'Deuce,' the squadron moved on to the F-106A/B Delta Dart.

Photographs of 95th FIS F-102s are rare. This view was captured at a 1958 airshow.

318th FIS

The 318th FIS at McChord AFB, Washington flew the T/TF-102A from 6 January 1957 until 25 May 1960. The squadron graduated from the 'Deuce' to the F-106A/B.

This F-102A of the 318th FIS sports the squadron badge on the forward fuselage and the Chrysler 'Way Forward'-inspired tail marking.

325th FIS

The 325rd FIS operated the F/TF-102A at Truax Field, Wisconsin from 6 February 1957 until 13 June 1966. The squadron emblem is a stylised young bull butting against the moon. The squadron had previously operated the F-86 Sabre.

In 1963, when these 325th FIS F-102As were photographed at McEntire AFB, South Carolina, the squadron was using tail insignia similar to that used on 1st FIW F-106s. The Dayglo bands are of interest.

326th FIS

The 326th FIS operated F/TF-102As at Richards-Gebaur AFB, Missouri briefly from 25 March 1957 until 5 January 1958. The squadron emblem was a snarling wolf.

56-1383, seen at Forbes (formerly Salinas) AFB Texas in May 1964, was lost after a mid-air collision on 22 December 1966.

327th FIS

The 327th FIS at George AFB, California had the distinction of becoming the first operator of a Convair delta-wing fighter when it took delivery of its first F-102A in April 1956, much later than had been planned. Once initial delays in the 'Deuce' programme were ironed out, the squadron operated the type at George from 24 April 1956 until 17 June 1958. The squadron also

flew the Delta Dagger at Thule AB, Greenland. The squadron emblem was a medieval red iron mask.

The chequered tail, intake lips and command stripes on this early F-102A were unique to the 327th FIS commander's aircraft.

F-102 Operators

329th FIS

The 329th FIS operated the F/TF-102A at George AFB, California, from 22 March 1958 until 24 October 1960. The squadron progressed to the F-106A/B.

An even more stylised version of the 329th FIS's delta-winged aircraft insignia formed the basis of the squadron's F-102 markings.

331st FIS

The 331st FIS flew F/TF-102As at Webb AFB, Texas from 18 March 1960 until 21 May 1963. The squadron emblem was a stylised griffin.

Seen on Armed Forces Day 1960 at Peterson AFB ('Pete Field'), Colorado Springs, the markings of this 331st FIS 'Deuce' consisted of a blue-edged yellow 'swoosh' and star.

332nd FIS

The 332nd FIS is the only ADC operator of the F/TF-102A Delta Dagger to fly the aircraft at three locations. After graduating from the F-86D/L Sabre, the unit operated at McGuire AFB, New Jersey from 30 July 1957 until 30 October 1959, at England Air Force Base, Louisiana from 24 July 1959 until 25 August 1960, and from Thule AB, Greenland from 21 July 1960 until 16 April 1965. The squadron emblem was a white eagle.

Thule, Greenland was home to this 332nd FIS TF-102A in April 1964.

438th FIS

The 438th FIS at Kinross AFB, Michigan was an operator of the F/TF-102A from 4 March 1957 until 4 November 1960.

The squadron badge used Donald Duck, who is copyrighted by Walt Disney Productions. After its 'Deuce' period, the squadron continued delta-winged flying with the F-106A/B.

456th FIS

The 456th FIS operated F/TF-102As from Castle AFB, California from 15 April 1958 until 15 October 1960. The squadron emblem used a red octopus. The 'Deuce' was preceded by the F-86 Sabre and followed by the F-106A Delta Dart.

460th FIS

The 460th FIS operated F/TF-102As at Portland International Airport, Oregon, from 11 January 1958 until 25 February 1966. The squadron had a badge depicting a tiger. It went from the F-89H/J Scorpion to the 'Deuce.' The unit was inactivated after its F-102 era but was later activated to fly the F-106A/B.

The 460th FIS's large 'beware of the tiger' badge is seen here on an F-102A on 20 September 1962.

482nd FIS

The 482nd FS was stationed at Seymour Johnson AFB, North Carolina. The squadron flew the F/TF-102A beginning 24 April 1957.

In November 1961, reacting to tensions in the aftermath of the failed Bay of Pigs invasion of Cuba, the 482nd FIS established a permanent alert detachment at Homestead AFB, Florida. For a brief period prior to that date, the 482nd FIS operated at Miami International Airport while repairs to the Homestead runway were completed.

On 15 June 1963, the 482nd FIS moved its alert contingent from Homestead to Key West, Florida, the US city closest to Cuba. By then, the Bay of Pigs had been followed

by the Cuban missile crisis, and tensions had peaked and begun to decline. In 1 July 1965, the 482nd ceased alert operations. The last F-102A apparently departed on 17 August 1965. The squadron was inactivated

at Seymour Johnson on 8 October 1965.

A star of the Langley air show static park in 1960 was this F-102A of the 482nd FIS.

Air Defense Weapons Center

The ADWC at Tyndall operated F-102s from 1 January 1968 until June 1971. The centre had responsibility for developing Air Defense Command weapons and tactics, and operated all aircraft types in ADC inventory. Its constituent units included the Interceptor Weapons School.

4780th ADW

Located at Perrin AFB, Texas, the 4780th Air Defense Wing operated F-102s from 1 July 1962 until 29 June 1971. Perrin was the traditional training base for interceptor pilots for many years.

4756th ADW

The 4756th Air Defense Wing at Tyndall AFB, Florida was an F-102 operator for exactly a year, from January 1957 until January 1958. Its mission was primarily training rather than air defence.

Pilots and crew chiefs line up for an inspection with their 'Deuces'. Note the aircraft in the centre without markings or IRST sensor.

The double chevron insignia of the 4780th Air Defense Wing graced many interceptors, including this TF-102A 'Tub'.

Alaskan Air Command (AAC)

Alaskan Air Command remained separate from ADC and retained jurisdiction for its area of responsibility for decades longer than the short-lived Northeast Air Command. When the Convair F/TF-102A began operations (long before the belated Delta Dagger nickname was assigned), Alaska was still a territory of the United States, although it gained statehood two years later.

The F-102 was no stranger, having undergone arctic weather evaluation at Ladd AFB long before it returned to the region in a state of combat readiness. Serious F-102 business began when AAC became the 'gaining command' of the reassigned 317th FIS on 15 August 1957.

This was the first transfer of an ADC F/TF-102A unit to another US Air Force command. The second 'Deuce' squadron to be assigned to AAC was the 31st FIS from Wurtsmith AFB, Michigan on 20 August 1957. These squadrons fell under AAC's 10th Air Division until the division was inactivated on 25 August 1960. After that date, the sole AAC squadron, the 317th, was subordinate to the 5040th Air Base Wing. Much later, on 8 July 1966, it became a component of the 21st Composite Group.

AAC operated forward bases and alert detachments for the 'Deuce' at Eielson AFB, Galena, King Salmon and Ladd AFB. Ladd AFB ended its long association with the USAF when it was transferred to the US Army on 1 January 1961.

The 'Deuce' era in Alaska coincided with increased Soviet aerial reconnaissance in the region, beginning in March 1958. In September 1958, F-102s attempted without success to intercept and escort a Soviet aircraft. Not until 5 December 1961 did two 'Deuces' scramble from Galena to achieve the first successful intercept of a pair of Tupolev Tu-16 'Badger' aircraft off the northwest coast. And when the 317th FIS failed to intercept an intruder during an actual overflight, as described in the entry for the squadron, the result was an unprecedented uproar in Alaska and Washington, especially in the Pentagon. Indeed, the furore caused nine F-106 Delta Darts to be deployed to Elmendorf in July 1963 to augment the AAC 'Deuces' on a temporary basis.

31st FIS

The 31st FIS, the second 'Deuce' unit in Alaska, transferred from ADC and brought its first aircraft to Elmendorf AFB, Alaska on 16 September 1957.

The squadron brought along its wolf emblem copyrighted by Walt Disney studios. But just a year after the squadron began flying in the cold north, the USAF made a decision to disband the 31st and to combine its existing 'Deuce' holdings into a single squadron, the 317th. The 31st had operated 23 'Deuce' airframes and had lost none in mishaps, when it transferred the fighters. The 31st was then inactivated on 8 October 1958. It has never returned to the USAF order of battle.

The 31st passed its aircraft on to the 317th FIS upon its inactivation.

317th FIS

On 1 September 1957, the first 317th FIS F-102A landed at Elmendorf AFB, Alaska. The arrival gave meaning to the transfer of the 317th FIS from ADC, which apparently had been official on 15 August 1957. It also marked the beginning of 12 years of 'Deuce' operations in Alaska by the 317th, which had transferred from McChord AFB, Washington. The unit's beginning at that base is noted in the section on ADC.

After losing two aircraft in mishaps, the 317th FIS was left with 23. When it acquired 23 more 'Deuces' following the 8 October 1958 inactivation of the 31st FIS, also at Elemendorf, the 46-plane 317th FIS became the largest squadron in the history of the Convair fighter. The successful intercept of two 'Badgers' in 1961 by Galena-based fighters proved to be a high-water mark for the 317th which soon encountered problems.

On 15 March 1963, a Soviet reconnaissance bomber overflew Nunivak Island and the west coast of Alaska. The 317th scrambled two 'Deuces' from King Salmon but the fighters had to break off 20 miles (31 km) from the target because of low fuel. As noted above, this much-publicited failure resulted in the arrival of F-106A Delta Darts on a temporary status to augment the 317th FIS' inventory of 'Deuces.' In the years that followed, F-102As made 13 successful intercepts and F-106As made 17 more before the squadron was inactivated on 31 December 1969. Its strength reduced to 27 aircraft

earlier in the year, the squadron left behind only one (56-1282), which had a cracked wing spar and became a display at the Alaska Transportation Museum. During its years of operation, the 317th lost 14 Delta Daggers in mishaps.

The 317th's F-102s were decorated with squadron badges and lightning-flashed tanks in the latter part of their career.

US Air Forces in Europe (USAFE)

To confront the Soviet Union and the Warsaw Pact high above the plains of Europe, US Air Forces in Europe at one time operated six fighter-interceptor squadrons equipped with F/TF-102As. With one exception, namely the 32nd FIS (an F-100 Super Sabre outfit), all of these units were well prepared for air defence, having previously flown the F-86D Sabre.

The F-102s that reached Europe aboard US Navy carriers were ex-ADC ships that had gone through extensive maintenance at depots. Later, additional 'Deuces' reached Europe from the 317th FIS in Alaska. The first squadron in Europe to equip with the Convair fighter was the 525th FIS in West Germany. the last the 32nd FS in Holland.

In Europe, the F/TF-102A Delta Dagger began with plain markings, with only a squadron insignia on the tail. Markings became more colourful as the 1960s progressed, then went away altogether to be replaced by Vietnam-era T. O. 114 camouflage after 1965.

32nd FIS

The 32nd FIS 'Wolfhounds' arranged to be at Wheelus AB, Libya for initial training when it took delivery of its first F-102A fighters on 12 August 1960. With pilots who had no previous 'Deuce' experience (18 were checked out in the F-100C Super Sabre, four in the F-86D Sabre), the squadron operated temporarily under the mantle of the 86th FIW until a cadre of Delta Dagger-qualified flyers could be brought up to speed.

The squadron's usual home base was Soesterberg AB known to the Americans as Camp Amsterdam, Netherlands and the first eight F-102As arrived there from

Wheelus on 18 November 1960. The squadron came under direct operational control of the Royal Netherlands Air Force. The squadron emblem was a wolfhound designed by Walt Disney studios.

The squadron operated a T-33A Shooting Star (52-9833) to tow a Delmar target for live-fire training of F-102 crews over the North Sea. After being the last squadron from Europe to participate in a William Tell competition, the 32nd FIS gave up its last 'Deuce' on 3 July 1969 and became an operator of the F-4 Phantom.

After a period of relatively austere markings, the 32nd FIS and other USAFE units introduced coloured tail bands.

431st FIS

The 431st FIS at Zaragoza AB, Spain accepted its first F-102A (55-3447) on 28 September 1960. Known as the 'Satan' or 'Devil' squadron, the 431st FIS had the shortest F/TF-102A tenure of any squadron in Europe. The unit gave up its aircraft on 23 April 1964. On receipt of its new F-4Cs, it was redesignated as the 431st Tactical Fighter Squadron.

Below: The stars on the 431st FIS badge and tail marking depict the Southern Cross. The squadron was formed in Australia in 1943.

496th FIS

The 496th FIS was the second European squadron to receive 'Deuces,' taking delivery of its first two F-102As and two TF-102As at Hahn AB, Germany on 9 December 1959, eleven months after operations began at Bitburg. A decade later, the 496th went out of the F-102 business in December 1969 and relinquished its aircraft to the Air National Guard.

In full 86th AD markings with a black and yellow tail, this 496th FIS F-102A displays a bay full of Falcons.

497th FIS

The 497th FIS began F-102 operations with the receipt of its first aircraft at Torrejon AB, Spain on 26 April 1960.

This squadron was under control of the Strategic Air Command's 65th Air Division until transfer to USAFE on 1 July 1960. The 497th continued to operate the 'Deuce' until giving up its last aircraft on 3 June 1964, its F-102s going to other USAFE units.

Normally based in sunny Spain, F-102s were seen at German bases in November 1963 on a strategic mobility exercise.

525th FIS

The 525th FIS 'Bulldogs' at Bitburg AB, Germany became the first Europe-based USAF squadron to receive the F-102 Delta Dagger when it took three F-102As and two TF-102As on charge on 3 January 1959. Soon afterwards, the 525th used borrowed F-102s to participate in the 1959 William Tell competition and reached second place.

The 525th FIS operated the F-102 until October 1969 when it transitioned to the F-4E Phantom.

A 'Bulldogs' F-102A is seen at a rainy Bitburg Air Base airshow in 1960.

526th FIS

The 526th FIS at Ramstein AB, Germany took delivery of its first three F-102As on 7 June 1960. It was the fourth combat unit in USAFE to receive the 'Deuce.' It lasted longer than all the others in Europe and gave up its last aircraft on 16 April 1970 when it became an F-4E user and a Tactical Fighter Squadron.

In early-period markings, this 526th FIS F-102A flies high over Europe, 1961. External fuel tanks were normally carried by European F-102s.

Pacific Air Forces (PACAF)

In PACAF (Pacific Air Forces), the F-102A became a fixture after 1959 and even before Americans took their first tentative steps toward Vietnam. In 1959-60, five PACAF squadrons – the 4th, 16th, 40th, 68th and 509th FIS – converted to Delta Daggers. First was the 16th FIS at Naha, and last was the 509th FIS at Clark Field in the Philippines.

As the United States began sending small teams of advisors to South Vietnam and eyeing the Pathet Lao in Laos, indications of hostile air activity began to show up even though no potential adversary in the region, not even North Vietnam had yet built a real air force. On 19 March 1962, a radar station at Pleiku, South Vietnam picked up seven unknown flight tracks over the Vietnamese central highlands. The only 'friendly' that could be scrambled was a B-26 Invader propeller-driven bomber. No contact was made, and hostile radar tracks were detected the next day, with the same result. The ensuing frustration led to the deployment of four F-102As to Tan Son Nhut AB outside Saigon. Thereafter, as described in the main text, the 'Deuce' was involved in Vietnam intermittently well into the late 1960s.

F/TF-102A fighters in the Pacific briefly enjoyed somewhat colorful markings until 1964. That year, all PACAF 'Deuces' lost individual squadron markings while remaining in 'ADC gray' with the PACAF emblem on both sides of the fin. After 1965, Vietnam-era T.O.114 camouflage became standard.

4th FIS

The 4th Fighter-Interceptor Squadron at Misawa Air Base, Japan, had a long tradition of night- and all-weather fighting, having been an operator of the F-61B Black Widow (until 1949), F-82G Twin Mustang (until 1951), F-94B (until 1954) and F-86D Sabre. The squadron moved from Naha, Okinawa to Kadena in 1954 and converted from F-86D to F-102A Delta Dagger in 1960. The badge for the 4th FIS shows the Okinawan god of wind, better known as a 'big bug' to Americans, flying against a backdrop of storm cloud and lightning bolt.

The last F-86D in PACAF (Pacific Air Forces) inventory went out of service on 8 March 1960. At Misawa, the F-102A provided greater speed and range, and enhanced the defence of western Japan against potential Soviet intrusions. Although farther from Korea than other units in Japan, the 4th FIS also deployed on occasion to Korea in a temporary deployment program dubbed Bone Deep.

On 28 April 1965, a Yokota-based RB-47 Stratojet was attacked by two North Korean MiG-17s on a reconnaissance mission 50 miles off the coast of North Korea. The RB-47 crew returned fire but the aircraft was severely damaged. F-102As of the 4th FIS were scrambled to the scene and although they did not make contact with the MiG-17s, they escorted the RB-47 back to safety.

As part of Project Clear Water, an effort to restructure PACAF units, the 4th FIS at Misawa stood down in 1965 (together with the 40th FIS on Okinawa), bringing to an end the role of the F-102A in the air defence of Japan. The Vietnam war was now escalating and in the late 1960s the 4th designation reappeared as the 4th TFS became an operator of the F-4 Phantom in Southeast Asia.

Red Striped Rascal was a rare example of a named F-102. Seen at Naha, Japan, it was the CO's aircraft of the infrequently-photographed 4th FIS.

16th FIS

The 16th FIS, sometimes called the 'Tigers' or boasting the motto 'Every man a tiger' was located at Naha AB, Okinawa in 1959. The squadron had been one of the prime F-86 Sabre squadrons during the Korean War and had produced 16-kill air ace Captain Joseph McConnell. Now as the 1950s came to an end the 16th FIS converted from F-86D to F-102A.

The squadron received its first F-102A at Naha on 9 March 1959 and was declared operationally ready in September 1959. The squadron represented PACAF in the 1959 World-Wide Interceptor Weapons Meet at Tyndall AFB, Fla. The 16th FIS deployed its F-102As to Suwon AB, Korea for the first tiome on 18 December 1959 to participate in a local air defence exercise known as Bone Deep.

In 1964, in a reorganisation known as Project Clear Water, the 16th FIS was deactivated. The 'Deuces' belonging to the defunct 16th were transferred to the Hawaii Air National Guard.

The attractive chequered markings of the 16th FIS's F-102s are not often illustrated.

40th FIS

This PACAF squadron began to convert from F-86D to F-102A in 1960. For much of its existence, the 40th was located at Yokota Air Base near Tokyo, Japan. One of several squadrons to have a devil's face as an emblem, the 40th FIS was flying F-86 Sabres when it converted to the Convair interceptor.

The squadron stood down on 30 June 1965 when the air defence of Japan reverted to the JASDF (Japan Air Self-Defence Force). The withdrawal of the last F-102s from Japan marked the end of the reorganisation known as Operation Clear Water (see 68th FIS).

One of the 40th FIS's TF-102s, seen at its home base of Yokota, illustrates the squadron's devil's head and lightning bolt badge.

F-102As of the 64th FIS are seen during the 1966 Hot Spice transit to the Phillipines.

64th FIS

On 6 June 1966, the 64th FIS – which had been garrisoned at Paine Field, Washington and was unofficially dubbed the 'Scorpions' – made a deployment from Hamilton AFB, California, to Clark Field, Philippines in a project dubbed Hot Spice. The squadron was destined to keep Clark Field as it its permanent duty station, with temporary jaunts to Vietnam, until being inactivated in December 1969.

68th FIS

The 68th FIS at Itazuke AB near Fukuoka, Japan began receiving F-102A fighters in 1960, replacing F-86D Dog Sabres. In 1964, in a reorganisation known as Project Clear Water, Itazuke lost its flying squadrons and the 68th returned to the continental US beginning 12 May 1970.

Despite operating the F-102 for a decade, the 68th FIS, whose Crusader emblem was made famous on the F-82 Twin Mustang, was rarely photographed.

82nd FIS

The 82nd FIS (assigned the tail code NV in 1968) formally transferred from ADC to PACAF on 25 June 1966 at Naha, Okinawa – following its expedition from the US which marked the first use of air refuelling by the 'Deuce.'

The 82nd deployed to Korea after the spy ship USS *Pueblo* was seized on 23 January 1968, returning to home base at Naha on 18 February 1968.

The 51st FIW at Naha transferred its serviceable F-102As to the ANG early in 1971. The remaining 18 F-102As which had severe wing cracks and corrosion, were reclaimed in place during March 1971 and dropped from the records.The official inactivation date of 31 May 1971 marked the end of the F-102's role in the Pacific,

save only for those aircraft in Air National Guard service in Hawaii.

The 82nd FIS was the only squadron assigned to the 51st FIW at Naha, Okinawa.

509th FIS

The PACAF-based 509th FIS at Clark AB, Philippines (assigned tail code PK in 1968), began to receive the F-102A, replacing the F-86D, in 1960. The squadron was a component of the 405th TFW throughout its 'Deuce' period. The arrival of the last of the programmed F-102As at Clark on 3 March 1961 marked the end of the F-86D era in the Pacific region (three remaining 'Dog Sabres' went to the Philippine Air Force on 8 March 1961, the remainder into storage).

509th Delta Daggers deployed to Formosa (Taiwan) under Exercise Big Truck while the CNAF's F-104 Starfighters were grounded with engine problems. Big Truck terminated on 30 September 1961.

The 509th was apparently the first squadron to deploy F-102As to Tan Son Nhut AB, Vietnam in Operation Water Glass, a series of temporary movements that began in March 1962. It also sustained the first non-combat loss of a 'Deuce'. Later, the squadron maintained a detachment of F-102As at Bien Hoa until the practice was ended on 7 September 1968. The deployment had been a strain because the 509th was also making

frequent deployments to Thailand and Korea.

As part of a reduction programme known as Project 703, the squadron's detachments at Taiwan (Formosa) and Don Muang (Thailand) were withdrawn. At its home base, Clark AB, Philippines, the 509th was inactivated on 24 July 1970. The squadron's F-102As were all flown to Itazuke and

In the early days of the 509th FIS's involvement in South East Asia, its F-102s were decorated with a chequered rudder and a leaping tiger on the nose.

scrapped as this was cheaper than shipping them back to the US.

Air National Guard

By the time the F-102A Delta Dagger came on the scene, American air power was beginning its transition toward today's 'total force' concept in which members of the reserve component operate modern equipment and perform missions identical to those of active-duty airmen. This was a sea change from an earlier time when Air National Guard maintainers and flyers were dismissed as a useless cadre of 'weekend warriors.' In 1960, almost as much as today, it would have been inconceivable to conduct a military operation without the ANG being an integral participant. It should be noted that the same applies to the Air Force Reserve, although the latter was never an F-102 user.

So it was an important moment when, on 1 July 1960, the 182nd FIS at Kelly Air Force Base, Texas became the ANG's first F/TF-102A squadron. This was the result of a National Guard Bureau decision to build up four 'Deuce' squadrons beginning in fiscal year 1961 (which began on 1 July 1960). The four squadrons, beginning with the one in the Lone Star State, would take delivery

of aircraft from active-duty units converting to the F-101B Voodoo and F-106A Delta Dart. Ultimately, however, Texas may become better known not for being first in the Guard, but for having a pilot who flew the F-102A in its other ANG squadron, the 111th FIS at Ellington Field near Houston – the state's governor and presidential aspirant George W. Bush.

As for the initial plan which brought the Guard into the 'Deuce' business, it was ambitious indeed. Back in 1959, NORAD (North American Air Defense Command) planners had proposed 19 permanent ANG alert units at points along the northern and southern borders and in areas where there existed gaps in ANG interceptor coverage. The plan assumed that the 19 squadrons would be equipped with F-102s, a total of no fewer than 475 aircraft. At the time, F-102s were also slated for PACAF and USAFE, meaning there would be scarcely a

'Deuce' to spare if the ANG plan were implemented.

It turned out that there were sufficient aircraft, barely, to begin the plan as conceived and the 111th FIS and 122nd FIS soon began acquiring their 'Deuces'. Others followed. Ultimately, the Guard operated not 19 but 25 F-102 squadrons.

During the Berlin and Cuban tensions of 1960 and 1961, some ANG units were activated, but the only deployments of Guard F-102s were to Alaska for annual training.

In every instance where an Air National Guard (ANG) squadron flew the TF/F-102A Delta Dagger, it functioned as an 'ADC-gained' unit meaning that, when carrying out its national mission, it came under the Air Defense Command (later Aerospace Defense Command) and was employed in the defence of the North American continent.

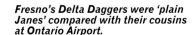

Arizona
152nd FIS

The 152nd FIS/162nd FG, Arizona ANG, flew F-102As, including TF-102A two-seaters, during a 43-month reign sandwiched between two periods when Tucson-based Guardsmen operated F-100 Super Sabres, these being the F-100A model until February 1966 and the F-100D version after 16 September 1969. A pristine 'Deuce' wearing the yellow tail blazer and yellow boundary layer fence, typical of 1966-69 operations, remains on display at the Tucson main gate today.

California
194th FIS

The 194th FIS/144th FIG, California ANG, flew F-102As from July 1964 until 11 July 1974. The earlier date marked the unit's transition from the F-86L Sabre to the F-102A, including the TF-102A model, at Fresno Air Terminal.

In January 1970, as part of an exercise dubbed Coronet East, the Fresno Guardsmen ferried 20 F/TF-102As from

Fresno's Delta Daggers were 'plain Janes' compared with their cousins at Ontario Airport.

Hahn Air Base, Germany to their home base. Even after equipping with newer Delta Daggers, the 194th members were planning to receive a new aircraft. The last F-102 departed in July 1974 and the 194th converted to the F-106A Delta Dart.

The 144th FIW also operated detachment 1 of the 194th FIS at Davis-Monthan AFB, Arizona from 1971.

California
196th FIS

The 196th FIS, 163rd FIG, California ANG, based at Ontario International airport near Los Angeles, was the second unit in the state to equip with the Convair delta-wing interceptors, flying them from May 1965 to 8 March 1975. The unit went directly from F-86A/L Sabres to the mighty F-102, and adorned its aircraft with white stars against a blue band on the fin, with the name of the state displayed prominently. Concern over

noise pollution, plus anti-military feelings coinciding with the end of the war in Vietnam, forced the 196th FIS to exchange its 'Deuce' interceptors for Cessna O-2As and to become a forward air control unit beginning on the 1975 date.

In common with a number of units, the 196th painted the wing fences of its otherwise naturally-finished F-102s.

Connecticut
118th FIS

The 118th FIS/103rd FG, Connecticut ANG, flew F-102As at Bradley Field in Windsor Locks near Hartford beginning on January 1966. The 'Flying Yankees' converted from the F-100A Super Sabre and operated F/TF-102A interceptors until the final aircraft departed on 11 June 71. The Delta Dagger era was something of a departure for this unit, which has spent most of its career performing the air-to-ground mission. The 118th went from the F/TF-102A to the F-100D/F Super Sabre, but is better known

in recent years as an operator of the A-10A 'Warthog.'

This F-102A of the Connecticut Guard was seen visiting Wright-Patterson AFB in September 1970.

Florida 159th FIS

The 159th FIS/125th FIG, Florida ANG located at the Thomas Cole Imeson Airport in Jacksonville, Florida, had briefly operated F-86L Sabres before converting to the F/TF-102A on 1 July 1960. The unit re-located to the Jacksonville International Airport on 24 October 1968. The Florida Guardsmen received upgraded Configuration 8 F/TF-102As in 1968 and continued to operate Delta Daggers until July 1974. Thereafter, the Jacksonville squadron flew the F-106A/B Delta Dart.

Detachment 1 of the 125th FIS kept F-102s on alert at NAS New Orleans, Louisiana, facing towards Cuba, from 1971 until 1974.

A small fintip lightning bolt and large tactical numbers identified Florida's Delta Daggers in June 1974, shortly before their retirement.

Hawaii 199th FIS

A ship carrying the first F-102As for the Hawaii Air National Guard docked at Fort Island, Pearl Harbor, on 5 December 1960. In Hawaii, the 'Deuce' was a replacement for the F-86L Sabre which had served the Guard for only three years. The first flight of a Hawaii ANG TF-102A occurred on 21 January 1961. F-102As replaced the F-86L on alert status at Honolulu's Hickam AFB in May 1961.

On 20 March 1965, Hawaii's 199th FIS received 20 newer F-102A fighters ('configuration 8' or 'Fig 8' standard, with infra-red devices, replacing aircraft of 'Fig 7' standard). These had been phased out by the deactivated 16th FIS at Itazuke AB, Japan.

On 31 March 1970, the same day the

Hawaii Army National Guard deactivated its Nike missile battery leaving the 'Deuce' as the sole defender of the Hawaiian islands, the UE (unit establishment – authorised strength) of the 199th was cut from 24 to 18 aircraft.

The 199th received its first F-4C Phantom on 31 October 1975 and began

the process of replacing its well-worn 'Deuces.' The last F-102A was phased out in October 1976.

In November 1975, when this F-102A was photographed at Hickam, the 199th FIS was phasing in the F-4C Phantom.

Idaho 190th FIS

The 190th FIS/124th FIG, Idaho ANG, flew F-102As from July 1964 to 19 November 1975. Located at Gowen Field in Boise, the unit had briefly operated the F-86L Sabre prior to the Delta Dagger's appearance on the scene. When its F-102 era ended, the Idaho Guard became a tactical reconnaissance unit and converted to the RF-4C Phantom.

This 190th FIS 'Deuce' was photographed at Williams AFB, Texas in June 1975.

Louisiana 122nd FIS

Known throughout much of its existence as the 'Coonass Militia,' a term reflecting local Cajun parlance and devoid of racial undertone, the 122nd FIS/159th FIG, Louisiana ANG, flew F-102As from July 1960 to 4 December 1970. Located at Naval Air Station New Orleans, the Louisiana Guard graduated into the F/TF-102A from the F-86L Sabre. A decade later, the 122nd converted to the F-100D/F Super Sabre.

This 'Deuce' was seen at Langley on 25 June 1970, in the last months of 122nd FIS F-102 operations.

Maine 132nd FIS

The 132nd FIS/101st FG, Maine ANG, flew F-102As from August 1969 to 17 November 1969. Located at Bangor International Airport, which had previously been the site of Dow Air Force Base (inactivated in June 1968), the 132nd FIS made the transition to the Delta Dagger from the F-89J Scorpion. Following the truncated, 15-month tenure of the Convair delta-winged fighter, the 132nd converted to the McDonnell F-101B/F Voodoo.

This F-102, which had previously served with the 32nd FIS in the Netherlands, was captured at Bangor in November 1969, the month the 132nd gave up its Delta Daggers.

Minnesota 179th FIS

The 179th FIS, 148th FIG, Minnesota ANG, flew F-102As from November 1966 until 15 April 1971. The 'Deuce' made its debut with the 179th FIS on the heels of the F-89J Scorpion, flying at Duluth Municipal Airport. The five-year Delta Dagger era came to an end when the Minnesota Guardsmen began receiving F-101B/F Voodoo interceptors.

In September 1974, this Minnesota ANG F-102A awaited conversion into a drone at MASDC at Davis-Monthan.

Montana 186th FIS

Up in 'Big Sky Country,' the 186th FIS/120th FIG, Montana ANG, flew F-102As from July 1966 until 5 April 1972. The location was Great Falls Municipal Airport. The F-89J came before the Delta Dagger and the F-106A/B followed it.

The 186th FIS was phasing its F-102s out in favour of the F-106 when this TF-102A in its markings was seen at Fresno on 16 April 1972.

New York 102nd FIS

The 102nd FIS/106th FG, New York ANG, flew F-102As from 2 December 1972 to 14 June 1975. Located at Suffolk County Airport in Westhampton Beach (since named for World War II air ace Francis S. Gabreski), the unit had previously been an air refuelling outfit operating KC-97L Stratocruisers. Following its Delta Dagger period, this New York Guard unit became a combat rescue as an operator of the HC-130H/P Hercules and HH-3E Jolly Green.

Unlike many other Guard F-102 squadrons, the 102nd FIS added a splash of colour to the tactical camouflage scheme, as illustrated by these examples at Suffolk County in September 1974.

North Dakota 178th FIS

The 178th FIS/119th FIG 'Happy Hooligans,' North Dakota ANG, flew F-102As from June 1966 until 17 November 1969. The squadron has always operated at Hector Field, Fargo Municipal Airport. The F-89J Scorpion preceded the F/TF-102A in 'Hooligans' livery and the F-101B/F Voodoo followed it. During its 'Deuce' era, the 178th FIS also operated a VC-131D Samaritan transport.

As seen in 1967, this 'Happy Hooligans' F-102A marked its flight assignment with yellow on the airbrake extension.

Oregon 123rd FIS

The 123rd FIS/142nd FIG, Oregon ANG, flew F-102As from January 1966 to 8 March 1971. The squadron, which has a 'Redhawk' emblem, operated F-89J Scorpions previously and F-101B/F Voodoos subsequently. The location was Portland Municipal Airport.

The 123rd FIS retained aircraft in 'natural metal' as late as 1970, while many other squadrons were adopting camouflage.

Pennsylvania 146th FIS

The 146th FIS/112th FIG, Pennsylvania ANG, located at the Greater Pittsburgh (Coreapolis) Airport, was an operator of TF/F-102A interceptors from November 1960 to 12 April 1975. The 'Deuce' replaced the F-86L Sabre and was, in turn, replaced in Pittsburgh by the A-7D attack aircraft (named the Corsair II in its US Navy variant).

The black tails of the 146th FIS's aircraft made their aircraft instantly recognisable.

South Carolina 157th FIS

The 157th FIS/169th FIG, South Carolina ANG, flew F-102As from June 1963 until 5 April 1975. The 'Swamp Foxes' previously flew F-104A/B Starfighters. The 'Deuce' was subsequently replaced at McEntire Air National Guard Base by A-7D attack aircraft.

The South Carolina ANG's 157th FIS was one of several units to restrict its markings to a coloured fin band.

Tennessee 151st FIS

The 151st FIS/134th FIG Tennessee ANG flew F-102As from March 1963 until 5 April 1964. Located at McGhee Tyson Airport, the squadron converted from the F-104A/B Starfighter. After a decade in the 'Deuce' and nearly three decades in fighters, the squadron became a tanker outfit and converted to the KC-97G Stratocruiser.

South Dakota 175th FIS

The 'Lobos' of the 174th FIS/114th FIG, South Dakota ANG, flew F-102As from October 1960 until 23 May 1970. Located at Sioux Falls Municipal Airport, the squadron went from the F-89J Scorpion to the F/TF-102A to the F-100D/F Super Sabre, all in the span of just over a decade.

A small number of F-102s were seen with Dayglo radomes, including this 175th FIS example.

F-102 Operators

Texas 111th FIS

The 111th FIS/147th FIG, Texas ANG, flew F-102As from August 1960 until 11 January 1975. When the active-duty force ceased F/TF-102A training on 30 June 1971, the 111th FIS became the RTU for F-102 pilots.

One pilot who flew F/TF-102As with this unit was Texas Governor George W. Bush, considered a likely presidential candidate in 2000. The unit at Ellington Air Force Base had previously flown F-86L Sabres and T-33A Shooting Stars, and retained the T-33As for jet instrumentation school. During the Delta Dagger era, the squadron's base changed status and became Ellington Air National Guard Base in July 1968.

On 1 January 1970, the unit became the 111th Combat Crew Training Squadron and

served as the Air National Guard's RTU (Replacement Training Unit) for the F/TF-102A, while also retaining the T-33A instrument training function. In May 1971, the unit added F-101B/F Voodoos and became the RTU for the latter type, while continuing as the Delta Dagger RTU. The F/TF-102As were phased out in January 1975 and the Voodoos remained.

The unit also operated detachment 1 of

The 1973 Patrick AFB air show saw an appearance by this F-102A of the 111th FIS.

the 147th FIW at Ellington. The detachment was apart from the squadron in that it maintained constant alert status whilst facing towards Cuba.

Texas 182nd FIS

The 182nd FIS/149th FIG, Texas ANG, flew F-102As from July 1960 until 16 September 1969. The squadron enjoyed the distinction of being the first 'Deuce' operator in the

ANG. Located at Kelly Air Force Base, Texas, like so many Guard units, the 182nd went from the F-86L Sabre to the F/TF-102A Delta Dagger.

'We ran the check-out program for other squadrons,' remembers group commander Colonel Charles Quist. The 182nd FIS temporarily became the training unit for Guard F/TF-102A operators and, for a time, remained on alert status in the F-86L while training Guardsmen from other units in the F-102. There was no gap when the F-102A took up the alert role. Throughout its F-102A period, the unit also operated three T-33A Shooting Stars for training duties and a Convair VT-29 transport for 'hack' duties. The squadron had two TF-102A two-seaters.

The squadron's subsequent conversion to the F-84F Thunderstreak, however, was unique among 'Deuce' units, even if it was only a temporary measure until F-100D/F Super Sabres could arrive.

Seen in April 1969 alongside one of the squadron's T-33s, this 182nd FIS 'Deuce' has the 'last three' of the serial number repeated in the airbrake.

Vermont 134th FIS

The 134th FIS, 158th FIG 'Green Mountain Boys' of the Vermont ANG, located at Burlington, flew F-102As from August 1965 to 9 June 1974. The squadron is apparently the only Guard unit to go into the Delta Dagger from the F-89D Scorpion without operating the F-89J in the interim. Following completion of their F/TF-102A era, the 'Green Mountain Boys' took on the defence systems evaluation job – acting as decoys for the North American air defence network. Among 'Deuce' units, they were thus unique in converting to the EB-57B/C/E Canberra.

These Vermont Guard 'Deuces' exhibit coloured fin tips denoting the flights to which they belonged.

Washington 116th FIS

The 116th FIS/141st FG Washington ANG flew F-102As from May 1965 to 1 December 1969. The 'Ace of Spades' unit, located at Geiger Field, Paine, Washington, had previously flown the F-89J Scorpion. Following the 'Deuce' era, the squadron converted to the F-101B/F Voodoo and later moved to Fairchild Air Force Base, Washington.

Wisconsin 176th FIS

The 176th FIS/115th FIG, Wisconsin ANG, flew F-102As from May 1966 until 9 November 1974. Informally dubbed the 'Raggedy Ass Militia' for a time, the 176th FIS had previously flown F-89J Scorpions at Truax Field (the former Truax Air Force Base) in Madison, Wisconsin. Like California's 196th FIS, the 176th converted to the O-2A.

In common with Pennsylvania's 146th FIS, Wisconsin's 'Deuce' unit adopted a bold single fin colour to distinguish its aircraft.

Miscellaneous users

Left: The 6520th Test Group at Hanscom AFB, Massachussetts operated a number of F-102s on test work. At least one wore 'HH' tailcodes signifying 'Happy Hanscom'. This preceded the official adoption of tailcodes during the Vietnam War. The 6250th also operated F-106 Delta Darts at the same time.

Above: Air Proving Ground Command at Eglin AFB operated a small number of early F-102s. APGC's job was to test weapons and weapons separation and maintaining the Eglin ranges. The name changed to the Air Force Development Test Center in July 1957, and today this reports to Air Force Materiel Command.

Below: A number of Delta Daggers wore the markings of the Sperry company, usually a small tail logo. The F-102As were used during QF-102/PQM-102 development to test the drone control equipment. The TF-102As (sometimes called QF-102Bs) were used for checkout flights for trainee drone pilots.

Left: The Federal Aviation Administration operated a single Delta Dagger as part of research into supersonic transports (SSTs). The aircraft, registered N300, flew approach paths simulating a large delta-winged aircraft, in a programme to develop procedures for air traffic controllers. As seen here, it joined ANG F-102s in the 'boneyard' at Davis-Monthan AFB when its trials tasks had been completed.

Above: NACA and NASA operated at least nine F-102s, including a YF-102 and a TF-102A . Only one, 56-998 seen here, carried a NACA or NASA number (N617NA), and this served for four years at the Lewis Research Center, mainly as a chase aircraft for the ejection seat testbed NF-106B. Other aircraft were used for shorter periods at Ames on fire-control evaluation manoeuvres and at Johnson for astronaut pilot proficiency.

Greece (Elliniki Polimiki Aeroporia)

Greece began training pilots for its F-102A Delta Dagger fighters in Project Peace Violet when six Greek instructors began training at Perrin AFB, Texas on 30 September 1968. It appears that Turkish pilots had completed their work at Perrin by then, making it unnecessary for flyers from the two countries, hardly friends, to serve together in Texas.

Greece received 24 F-102s. The HAF (Hellenic Air Force), or Elliniki Polimiki Aeroporia, flew 20 F-102As and four TF-102As (plus possibly one or two more of the latter) beginning in 1969. The HAF was the subject of a temporary embargo on arms sales to Greece by the United States when the time came to find a 'Deuce' replacement, so Greece ordered 40 Dassault Mirage F1CGs to fulfil the interceptor role.

114th Pterix (Wing) at Tanagra was the sole Greek F-102 operator, flying the Dart from 1969 until 1979.

Turkey (Türk Hava Kuvvetleri)

Turkey began training pilots for its F-102A Delta Dagger fighters in Project Peace Violet when six Turkish instructors began training at Perrin AFB, Texas on 20 November 1967.

Turkey's air force, the Türk Hava Kuvvetleri or THK, received 38 F-102s according to one source, 39 according to another (36 F-102As and three TF-102As, and 46 according to a third (39 As and seven TFs). After preparation and workups, these equipped two interceptor squadrons,

apparently 142 Filo at Murted and 182 Filo at Diyarbakir, both of which belonged to the THK's 1st Tactical Air Force, or Birinci Taktik Hava Kuvveti. The Turkish F/TF-102As had a relatively brief operational career and were replaced in the interceptor mission by the F-104G (142 Filo) and F-100C (182 Filo) in mid-1979.

Turkey's two F-102 squadrons had no distinctive identifying markings.

Lockheed F-104 Starfighter

Few aircraft have engendered such interest and excitement as Lockheed's pencil-slim Starfighter. At the outset of its career its space-age looks and blistering performance grabbed the public imagination, but later its popular image turned sour as it earned an unenviable reputation as the 'Widow Maker'. In service it operated as a super-quick interceptor, low-level camera platform, nuclear bomber and ground attacker. It was the backbone of NATO and no story of the Cold War can be written without its mention. With speed in abundance but always short-legged, the F-104 remained a potent weapon system long after it had been superseded by more modern types, and remains in limited service today. No aircraft was more worthy of the one nickname which endured throughout the type's career: 'Star'.

High over San Francisco harbour, a pair of F-104As from the 337th Fighter Interceptor Squadron passes the Bay Bridge. The Starfighter's arrival in Air Defense Command was much heralded, although the type proved less than ideal in the defence of the continental United States and enjoyed only a brief career in this role.

No group of aircraft represented the huge technological leaps made by the US aviation industry in the post-war period more than the fabled 'Century Series' of fighters. Here the first prototype XF-104 heads a line-up of F-100, F-102, F-101 and F-105, encapsulating the mid-1950s state of the art in fighter, interceptor and nuclear strike aircraft.

Far right: Seen on a test flight from Edwards AFB, the first prototype displays the salient features of the XF-104s: simple intakes and pen-nib exhaust. The nose and tail markings were Lockheed's own house logo.

Above: Developed under considerable secrecy, the F-104 finally emerged into the public glare on 17 April 1956, two years after the XF-104 had made its first flight. The publicity at the time highlighted the type's climb performance and amazingly thin wings.

'Flying Coffin', 'Jinx Jet', 'Zipper' and 'Widow Maker' – these were just some of the unflattering sobriquets applied to Lockheed's mould-breaking Starfighter at the peak of its career in the 1960s, mainly because of its unfortunate accident record in operations with the West German Luftwaffe and Marineflieger. In nearly 30 years of service, the German forces lost some 270 of their 917 F-104s, or just under 30 per cent in air and ground accidents, together with 110 pilots. This resulted in bitter public criticism and, at one stage, a political and military crisis with constitutional overtones. Although Germany's basic problem was that its reformed air element had expanded at a technically insupportable rate, in the long term German Starfighter accident losses were proportionately lower than in several other NATO air forces. Many of the accidents were attributed to poor maintenance, and the changeable weather conditions in Europe confronting inexperienced pilots having qualified under more predictable US climatic conditions. At the other extreme, Spain's Ejercito del Aire operated 21 CF-104Gs for seven years, from 1965 until 1972, without a single loss or accident.

Another of the F-104's more popular appellations was 'the missile with a man in it', resulting from its radical configuration, comprising a long needle-nosed fuselage with almost vestigial wings, each spanning only 7 ft 7 in (2.3 m), and of extreme thinness. A key feature of the Starfighter's sustained Mach 2 capability – the first of any operational combat aircraft – was its miniature razor-thin

mainplanes, only 4.5 in (11.43 cm) deep at the roots and with a gross area of a mere 196 sq ft (18.2 m²); they also gave the XF-104 the unprepossessing wing loading at maximum take-off weight of over 80 lb/sq ft (390.5 kg/m²). This compared with the 59 lb/sq ft (288 kg/m²) of the previous generation F-86F Sabre, and in the later F-104G was to increase to no less than 158 lb/sq ft (771 kg/m²), emphasising still further the Starfighter's previous power-off characteristics, and making it extremely unforgiving in emergency situations.

Design origins

Ironically, ease of handling was one of the main objectives when Clarence L. 'Kelly' Johnson, legendary leader of Lockheed's equally renowned 'Skunk Works' design group at Burbank, California, began studying follow-on designs for the F-80, F-94 and XF-90 in the early 1950s. USAF requirements for a new and higher-performance fighter with level supersonic capability had been accentuated by the first air-to-air jet combats against Chinese-supplied MiG-15s over the Yalu in North Korea, with the declared objective of 'establishing local air superiority in a given area by sweeping the skies of enemy aircraft'. Lockheed therefore abandoned work on its F-100-sized Project 207, with a thin, straight wing and dorsal air intake. In March 1952 Kelly Johnson turned his attention to achieving a quantum leap in performance from lighter-weight designs.

The final F-104 design formula was not achieved without exploring a wide range of mainly single-engine projects in close succession, starting with the low-wing Project 227-0-6, with a MiG-21-type centre-cone nose intake, followed by the more futuristic mid-mounted delta-wing 227-0-11 with a flush cockpit in the conical nose, lateral intakes and a high-set tail on a sharply-swept fin. In the following month, the 227-8-1 reverted to a conventional low/mid-wing layout but had a design weight of about 30,000 lb (13608 kg). This was to be succeeded within a few weeks by the similarly-configured (apart from a chin intake) 227-16-2, weighing only 8,000 lb (3629 kg). The Model 227-16-2 was significant in introducing the ultra-thin minuscule straight wing, which featured in all subsequent design studies, except for the

Prototypes

Lockheed produced two XF-104 prototypes to validate the Starfighter concept, both powered by a a Curtiss-Wright XJ65 turbojet (licence-built Sapphire) in the absence of the intended General Electric J79. Even with this low-rated powerplant the XF-104 immediately showed itself to be a 'hot ship' – not for the faint-hearted pilot. Although

'Tony' LeVier (also famous for undertaking the maiden voyage of the U-2) made the first flight, it was Herbert 'Fish' Salmon who shouldered the burden for most of the early prototype flying. He was lucky to escape from the second aircraft in April 1955 when he successfully employed the strange downward-firing ejection seat.

Above: The first prototype XF-104 displays the simple hemispherical intakes of the prototypes, which featured a small splitter plate to stop the fuselage boundary layer from entering the engine.

Above: The rarely photographed second prototype shows the very clean lines of the basic Starfighter airframe before the appendage of tip tanks, weapon pylons and ventral fins. The aircraft's career was short, ending on 18 April 1955 after less than a year's development work.

The first XF-104 survived into 1957 before it, too, was lost in a crash. The prototypes were fitted with Vulcan cannon and APG-34 fire control radar.

extraordinary 227-14-1 of July 1952, with tip-mounted tail-booms and a tailwheel landing gear.

In the next month, the 227-13-1 scaled up April's 227-8-1 project into a conventional mid-wing design weighing no less than 50,000 lb (22680 kg), which would almost certainly have required two turbojet engines. At the same time, Johnson's team looked at the futuristic 227-15-3, resembling a stretched Bell X-1 and similarly rocket-propelled. Project 227 studies were effectively completed in October 1952 by the 227-20-1, which stretched the 13-1 concept even further in fuselage length, at somehow half its weight. Kelly Johnson then finalised his ideas on a substantially smaller fighter through the Project 242 series of design studies, starting with the 19-1 in November, which inaugurated the basic F-104 shape and layout, apart from its minuscule dimensions, 9,000-lb (4082-kg) empty weight, Vee-windshield and fuselage-mounted tailplane. Minor changes by the end of 1952 in the scaled-up 242-23-1 included a stabilator mounted low on the extended-chord vertical fin, which it finally surmounted on the slightly smaller 242-27-1 of February 1953. This tail

arrangement and the 27-1's unraked cheek intakes were then combined with the more elongated Project 246-1-1 which had evolved in the preceding few weeks. It was the finalised Lockheed L-246, or Model 83, with an empty weight of some 12,000 lb (5443 kg), which was eventually submitted for USAF approval in the spring of 1953. Although its initial design gross weight of 17,500 lb (7938 kg) was similar to that of the F-86, Lockheed's radical new combat aircraft emerged with a maximum take-off weight of only 15,700 lb (7121 kg), or less than half the amount of some of its contemporary 'Century Series' fighters. This provided the basis for Lockheed's claims for the F-104 as the USAF's first lightweight high-performance fighter.

Although swept wings were then *de rigueur* for supersonic aerodynamics, Kelly Johnson broke new ground in basing

Below: Not a glider variant but the second YF-104 with its then-secret intake centrebodies hidden by carefully constructed fairings. These pictures were released in April 1956 along with flying shots of the XF-104. As the latter had only simple intakes this posed no security risk.

55-2955 was the first of a batch of 17 YF-104As. It joined the test programme on 17 February 1956. There were many differences between the YFs and XFs, the most visibly obvious in this view being the forward-retracting nosewheel.

A later view of the first YF-104A shows the aircraft landing in clean configuration at Edwards AFB with only partial flap deployed (maximum deflection was 45°). In order to keep landing speeds to a barely acceptable (but nevertheless still very high) figure, Lockheed designed a powerful flap-blowing system to provide massive amounts of extra lift at full flap deflection.

his L-246 design on ultra-thin, low aspect-ratio, symmetrical-section mainplanes with only a moderate 26° sweep on the leading-edge alone. Earlier Lockheed experience with the X-7 ramjet test vehicle, wind tunnel evaluations and extensive study of various wing profiles propelled at high velocities in desert tests by over 400 5-in (13-cm) aircraft rockets confirmed the high lift potential of thin unswept aerofoils at low angles of attack and high speeds, although at the cost – especially with low aspect-ratio plan-forms – of very high induced drag at large angles of attack and in high-*g* conditions. With a mean thickness-chord ratio of only 3.36 per cent, compared with about 8.5 per cent for the contemporary Hawker Hunter, the low-wave-drag tapered wings, which had zero sweep at the 70 per cent chord line, were designed, like the high-set one-piece stabilator, with a leading-edge radius of only 0.016 in (0.41 mm). This was sharp enough to require felt covering strips during maintenance to protect ground personnel from possible injury. Potential flutter problems from possible aeroelasticity resulting from the thin wings were minimised by the short span, which gained some end-plate and damping effects from long jettisonable 170-US gal (644-litre) tip-tanks supplementing 908 US gal (3437 litres) of fuselage-stowed fuel. For short-range interception missions, the XF-104 had a claimed maximum range on internal fuel alone of some 800 nm (920 miles/1480 km).

Sidewinder rails

The XF-104's tip-tanks could be replaced by mounting rails for single early-model Philco Sidewinder AAMs. designated AAM-N-7 by the US Navy and GAR-8 by the Air Force, and redesignated AIM-9B in October 1962. The aircraft flown without either load. Because the vertical fin of Lockheed's new design was only slightly shorter than each mainplane, a marked roll tendency from rudder application had to be countered by incorporating 10° of anhedral in the mainplane attachment to the fuselage. Unlike most fighters of its time, the multiple wing spars of the new Lockheed design were not carried through the fuselage, being mounted instead on five heavy-duty precision-forged formers tied into the wing skins and intermediate channels.

Low-speed lift augmentation to help offset the very high wing loading was achieved by several means, including full-span leading-edge alloy flaps, attached by piano hinges along their lower edge and actuated initially for take-off

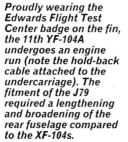

Proudly wearing the Edwards Flight Test Center badge on the fin, the 11th YF-104A undergoes an engine run (note the hold-back cable attached to the undercarriage). The fitment of the J79 required a lengthening and broadening of the rear fuselage compared to the XF-104s.

and landing by a rotary electro-mechanical actuator within the wing root fillet. The entire trailing edge was also similarly hinged, with the outer sections, fabricated from steel, comprising hydraulically servo-boosted ailerons, and the inner surfaces, built of alloy, acting as electrically-operated take-off, landing and eventually combat manoeuvering flaps. In addition to a degree of variable wing-camber from its leading- and trailing-edge flaps, the new Lockheed design obtained further increases in wing lift to improve its low-speed performance by the introduction, for the first time in a production combat aircraft (beating the Blackburn Buccaneer by about four years), of boundary-layer control.

This is applied by the ducting through 55 tiny nozzles of hot compressor bleed air at 1,600 ft/sec (488 m/sec) to the upper surfaces of each 47-in (120-cm) trailing-edge flap through a valve which opens progressively during extension between 15° and 45°. By minimising boundary layer turbulence, flap-blowing, after a prolonged development programme on early production Starfighters, eventually provided an increase in wing lift which reduces F-104 stalling or landing speeds by over 17 kt (20 mph; 32 km/h), resulting in reductions in required landing distances of almost 25 per cent. Large contoured slab-type airbrake surfaces open hydraulically from each side of the fuselage behind the wings for large drag increments without trim changes or aerodynamic buffet.

Prototype and pre-production orders

Submission to the US Defense Department of the preliminary Lockheed L-246 design with these features was followed by further engineering refinement from an official study contract. An order for two XF-104 prototypes then followed in March 1953, to meet the USAF's WS-303A weapon system requirement for a high-performance tactical day fighter. The first of these (53-37786) made its initial hop over the dry lake at Edwards AFB, CA, less than a year later on 28 February 1954, in the hands of A. W. (Tony) Le Vier, its first full flight following soon afterwards at the same base on 4 March. The chase aircraft was a two-seat Lockheed F-94C all-weather fighter flown by Herman 'Fish' Salmon, who was later to take over most of the XF-104 flight development programme. The Starfighter prototype was soon joined by the second XF-104, 53-7787, similarly powered, in the absence at that time of a more potent turbojet, by the Curtiss-Wright XJ65-W-6 version of Britain's Armstrong Siddeley Sapphire, initially developing 7,200 lb (32.03 kN) maximum dry thrust, or around 10,200 lb (45.4 kN) with afterburning.

Although down on power, the XF-104s had an empty weight of only 11,500 lb (5216 kg), and demonstrated a remarkable advance in performance compared with earlier

F-104 development

With 17 YF-104As (55-2955 to 2971) joining the test programme in quick succession, the task of bringing the Starfighter into operation speeded up considerably. Most of the development work took place at Edwards.

The YF-104As had many differences compared to the prototypes, the most obvious being the fitment of the intended J79 engine, necessitating a major redesign of the fuselage. The all-important supersonic intake centrebodies were finally revealed to the world in mid-1956, setting a trend for other fighter designs which persisted until the ramp-style intake.

Left: '956' was the second YF-104A. In this view the small dorsal spine added to the YF-104A is clearly visible, this addition being used to house control runs and free up room in the cramped fuselage.

Right: The second and fourth YF-104As fly in formation, the furthest aircraft displaying its recently fitted ventral fin. The F-104 had an ongoing directional stability problem which was not fully resolved until the adoption of the larger rudder of the two-seat variants.

Below: F-104A displays the fitment of the airfield arrester hook, used to snag cables stretched across runways in the event of a brake failure. Visible just above are the barely deployed airbrakes.

Climatic testing took place at Eglin AFB, Florida, where the systems of the YF-104 were tested at temperatures down to -65°F (-54° C).

US fighters, including the early 'Century Series' types, achieving a maximum speed of Mach 1.79 on 25 March 1955. Between them, the prototypes went on to complete over 300 test flights, although -787 crashed after 'Fish' Salmon was forced to eject during initial gun-firing trials on 18 April 1955, followed by -786 in 1957.

Standard internal armament of the F-104 was a single General Electric T-171-E3 Vulcan six-barrelled 20-mm Gatling-type rotary cannon (later designated M61A1) in the port lower fuselage below the cockpit, electrically powered to fire at selectable rates of either 3,000 or 6,000 rounds per minute. With an overall length of 72 in (183 cm), the Vulcan cannon weighs around 300 lb (136 kg) in the Starfighter installation, which features up to 725 rounds of belted ammunition in a container behind the pilot, this armament installation being replaceable by an additional 120-US gal (455-litre) fuel tank, if required. In the XF-104, the Vulcan cannon was integrated with a Type K-19 fire control system incorporating an AN/APG-34 radar and a computing gunsight. Apart from Sidewinder, the F-104 was also designed to carry the USAF's Douglas MB-1 Genie nuclear AAM, developed in the mid-1950s with a 1.5-kT atomic warhead, and successfully launched in later trials from the Starfighter at speeds up to Mach 2 by means of an underfuselage trapeze.

Pre-production aircraft

XF-104 flight development was expedited by follow-on deliveries, from 17 February 1956, of 17 pre-production YF-104A aircraft (55-2955 to 2971), which featured the definitive General Electric J79-GE-3A turbojet for which the Starfighter had been designed. As the first high-compression variable-stator turbojet to be built in the US, the J79 is of mainly steel construction and initially developed some 9,600 lb (42.7 kN) maximum dry thrust and over 14,800 lb (65.8 kN) with afterburning.

With the characteristic shapes of Joshua Trees in the background, the final YF-104A taxis out for a test hop, the canopy cranked open slightly to provide some ventilation. The aircraft wears the AFFTC badge on the fin and that of the Air Research and Development Command (forerunner of Air Force Systems Command) on the nose.

An F-104A pilot, wearing the partial pressure suit necessary for high-altitude operations, displays the General Electric T-171-E3 Vulcan cannon. Forty years on this is still the standard US fighter gun.

Rocket ships

Following their service with ADC, three F-104As (56-0756, 0760 and 0762) were transferred to the Edwards-based Aerospace Research Pilot School as astronaut/X-plane trainers. Fitted with a Rocketdyne booster rocket in the tail these NF-104As could achieve astonishing altitudes. Aerodynamic control was effectively lost in the outer reaches of their altitude envelope, so they employed small reaction nozzles strategically placed around the airframe. The larger G-style rudder was fitted, and the aircraft later featured an extended ventral fin to further increase directional stability.

Right: With its LR 121-NA-1/AR 2-3 rocket booster in full thrust, '760' heads for the upper atmosphere on a carefully controlled ballistic trajectory. The principal role of the NF-104A was to provide high-altitude and zero-g experience to astronauts and pilots of aircraft such as the X-15. The aircraft is seen with the lengthened ventral fin fitted part way through the programme.

Above and right: Quite apart from the thrust rocket and reaction control nozzles, the NF-104As differed in other significant areas. The wings were extended in span to provide extra lift and accommodation for the wingtip nozzles, while the engine intake cones were extended forward slightly. Combined with other modifications, the new cones gave the aircraft an increased maximum speed even without the rocket booster.

Right: 56-0737 was the eighth production F-104A, retained for a while at Edwards for ongoing flight tests.

Below: Factory-fresh F-104As gather at the Lockheed facility at Palmdale, with Navy TV-2s in the background.

Apart from the substantially longer and wider rear fuselage to accommodate the bigger engine, increasing the overall length from 49.17 ft (14.98 m) to 54.77 ft (16.7 m), the YF-104s incorporated a number of other changes, including a slightly taller fin, raising the overall aircraft height from 12.7 ft (3.87 m) to 13.49 ft (4.11 m); forward- instead of aft-retracting nosewheel; the addition of a narrow dorsal spine, removing the control runs from valuable fuselage space to allow more fuel; an AN/ASG-14T1 fire-control system, plus AN/ARN-56 TACAN.

With no wing stowage space available for fuel or landing gear, both were accommodated within the fuselage, the widely splayed mainwheel legs with their Dowty-licensed Cleveland Pneumatic liquid-spring oleos being mounted on skewed pivots to twist during retraction so that the thin high-pressure wheels then lay flat in the lower belly. With an empty weight increased only slightly to some 12,561 lb (5698 kg), the YF-104A maximum take-off weight in the clean configuration rose from the 15,700 lb (7121 kg) for which the XF-104s were cleared, to 18,881 lb (8564 kg). With provision for four underwing and one fuselage stores pylon, and the additional power available, the maximum allowable take-off weight was increased to no less than 24,584 lb (11151 kg).

The design of the F-104, and particularly the shape of its wings, were grist for considerable speculation before the first, doctored photos of the new aircraft were revealed. In the 1950s, it was customary to keep the external appearance of a new warplane secret at least until its first flight and sometimes afterward. When it was learned that Lockheed was developing the fighter, it was widely understood that this would be a revolutionary machine – and details were avidly sought. Pentagon officials were furious when the Japanese magazine *Koku-Joho* (*Aireview*) published an artist's rendering of the yet-unseen F-104 which proved surprisingly accurate.

Starfighter revelations

Though it was never a secret that the F-104 was being developed, unlike the situation with Lockheed's later F-117 – itself another quantum leap in technology – none of these details, or any other features of F-104 design, had been made public at that time, and it was not until just over two years after its first flight, in the spring of 1956, that the first Starfighter photographs were officially released. These were limited to air-to-air shots of the prototype, plus ground photos of the second YF-104A (55-2956, the second of 17 pre-production machines, which wore 'buzz number' FG-956) and, even then, the latter aircraft was fitted with specially-fabricated, polished metal fairing cones on the front of the intakes to conceal their details. The variable air intakes of the YF-104A and subsequent Starfighters, with their 'bullet' fairing astride the inlet were considered a military secret in 1956. With their limited engine thrust, the two XF-104s had required no more than simple fixed cheek intakes, similar to those on the subsonic Lockheed F-94C, mounted slightly proud of the fuselage with an inner splitter plate for the necessary boundary layer bleed.

It was not until mid-1956 that the J79-engined F-104 lateral intakes, again just clear of the fuselage sides to avoid the turbulent boundary layer, were finally revealed to have an additional large fixed-geometry central intake shock cone, with an internal bleed slot. The latter exhausts

A graphic illustration of just how far aviation technology had progressed since the war's end is provided by the relative attitudes of this tanker/receiver pair. Even with jet augmentation, the Boeing KB-50J is nose down and 'balls to the wall', while the F-104A with flaps deployed is struggling to stay in the air.

some intake air through the fuselage for afterburner cooling, and also helps reduce the aircraft's base drag. This inlet configuration, initially surrounded by a grid of guide-vanes, predated similar although more complex variable geometry features added to the first production Mirage IIIs to allow their level-flight performance to be extended up to and beyond Mach 2. This magic milestone was finally reached by a YF-104A flown by test pilot Joe Ozier on 27 April 1955, and was followed by an initial $100 million USAF production order for an eventual total of 146 F-104As (56-730 to 56-882, comprising seven F-104A Block-1s, 11 -5s, 16 -10s, 25 -15s, 37 -20s, 52 -25s and five -30s) on 14 October of the same year.

Production version flies

After the installation of a production J79-GE-3B engine, the planned addition of a long ventral fin under the rear fuselage to decrease a directional snaking problem, and provision for inflight-refuelling equipment, the first F-104A (56-730) made its initial flight on 17 February 1956, The first Starfighters completed their USAF acceptance trials – not without considerable technical problems – by December 1958. Long before then, on 15 October 1956, the USAF had placed further contracts worth $166 million for another batch of F-104As, increasing the overall total to 153 (56-730 to 56-882), and for the first two-seat F-104B trainer versions, with an extended tandem cockpit and full dual controls.

Although mainly intended for operational conversion, the F-104B was also designed to maintain some tactical combat capabilities. It retained the F-104A's AN/ASG-14T1 fire control system and provision for two wing-tip GAR-8 (later AIM-9B) Sidewinder AAMs. It dispensed

with the Vulcan cannon in favour of the 120-US gal (455-litre) additional fuel option in the gun bay to help offset some of the tank capacity lost from the fuselage by the second cockpit installation. This gave the F-104B a maximum range with tip-tanks of 1,091 nm (1,255 miles/2020 km), compared with 1,444 nm (1,660 miles/2672 km) for the F-104A. The first of an initial batch of six F-104Bs (56-3719 to -3724) made its flight debut on 7 February 1957. Twenty subsequent production versions (57-1294 to 57-1313) were given considerably greater fin area and a broad-chord, fully power-assisted rudder extending well beyond the J79 tailpipe, as well as the F-104A's ventral fin, to help improve directional stability. Because of the space demands of the second cockpit within an unchanged fuselage length, all two-seat Starfighters reverted to the rearward-retracting nosewheel arrangement of the original XF-104s.

In these forms, and after a total of more than 65,000 development hours, the first F-104As and Bs entered USAF service in early 1958 with the 83rd Fighter-Interception Sqn of Air Defense Command, which took delivery of its first Starfighters at Hamilton AFB, California, on 20 February of that year. The USAF lost no time in demonstrating the potency of its new fighter by establishing a series of international performance records, achieved by serving officers flying instrumented YF-104As from the Lockheed test facility at Edwards AFB, CA. In the first of these flights Major Howard C. Johnson, with the help of

A proud Captain Rayford of the 83rd Fighter Interceptor Squadron poses by 'his' F-104A Wailing Lady. The nickname was in reference to the unique resonance sound created by the F-104 when in the landing pattern. The pilot wears the T-1 high-altitude pressure suit which was standard attire for ADC interceptor crews of the period.

Into ADC service

Air Defense Command glowed warmly in the media attention as the first Starfighters were taken into service. In the internecine warfare of US military politics ADC had often lost out to the might of Strategic Air Command in budgetary and publicity battles, but from 20 February 1958 it became the first operator of a Mach 2 fighter anywhere in the world. The first F-104As were assigned to the 83rd

Fighter Interceptor Squadron at Hamilton AFB, California. Despite the huge number of flying hours already amassed by the test fleet, the 83rd was nevertheless heavily involved in further trials work. Deliveries of the F-104A were completed rapidly, allowing the conversion of other units to follow the 83rd, although a maximum of just seven squadrons flew the type.

Above: The 83rd FIS had flown the huge and sluggish Northrop F-89 Scorpion for most of the 1950s, so the arrival of the slender and swift F-104 provided an interesting lesson in state-of-the-art technology. It was also a painful one: ADC began losing F-104As at an alarming rate.

Right: Starfighter crews race to their mounts during a practice scramble. For US defence missions the F-104 was woefully short on range.

To speed the conversion process of the 83rd FIS, the unit received a handful of pre-production YF-104As (55-2969 shown here) along with its first true operational aircraft.

This quartet of F-104As from the 83rd FIS (minus the famous horseshoe and ace-of-spades badge) is a mixed bag of Block 5, Block 10 and Block 15 aircraft. The third aircraft has wingtip rails fitted for the carriage of the Sidewinder missile. The standard air-to-air load consisted of two of these weapons and the internal cannon.

the USAF's T-1 partial-pressure suit – essential for flights above 50,000 ft (15240 m) – exceeded the previous world altitude record by more than 10,000 ft (3281 m) on 7 May 1958, with a zoom climb to 91,243 ft (27811 m). Only 10 days later, on 18 May, the previous absolute speed record was exceeded by over 170 kt (195 mph; 315 km/h) by Captain Walter W. Irwin from the same base with a flight at altitude measured at 1,219.34 kt (1,399.79 mph; 2252.69 km/h).

For the first time in history, a single aircraft type simultaneously held both the world speed and altitude records. The F-104 soon went on to add a third jewel to its crown with a series of new record-breaking climbs to various heights, which emphasised its operational capabilities in its designed interception roles. Flown alternately by two young USAF pilots, Lieutenants William T. Smith and Einar K. Enevoldson, from NAS Point Mugu, California over a two-day period from 18 December 1958, these timed climbs-to-height from brake

release not only broke five previous records but also established two completely new marks never previously attempted. As eventually homologated by the FAI, they comprised the following:

Height	Previous time	F-104 record
3000 m (9,842.5 ft)	(44.39 secs)	41.85 secs
6000 m (19,685 ft)	(1min 06.13 secs)	51.41 secs
9000 m (29,527.5 ft)	(1min 29 secs)	1min 21.14 secs
12000 m (39,370 ft)	(1min 52 secs)	1min 39.90 secs
15000 m (49,212.5 ft)	(2min 36 secs)	2min 11.10 secs
20000 m (65,616.7 ft)	No previous record	3min 42.99 secs
25000 m (82,020.8 ft)	No previous record	4min 26.03 secs

Flying the F-104A

Despite the dazzling performance of its latest 'Century Series' fighter, the USAF was faced with some daunting problems accompanying F-104 service entry, including the loss of a distressing number of lives, many being those of experienced test pilots. Teething troubles with the new J79 engine were rendered even more hazardous by the pilot escape system of the early F-104s, which were uniquely fitted with a Lockheed-developed ejection seat which, for reasons apparently associated with the Starfighter's high tail, was propelled downwards through the bottom of the cockpit. A handle on the front of the seat pan sequentially depressurised the cockpit, pulled the control column forwards, tightened the pilot's parachute harness, applied leg restraints and ankle clamps, blew off the ventral hatch, and propelled the seat and occupant downwards before automatic separation.

This escape system was nominally cleared for use at heights down to 500 ft (152 m). When Canberra and Lightning chief test pilot Roland Beamont visited the US in June 1958 to fly several of the USAF's 'Century Series' fighters, including the F-104, as he recounted in his autobiography *Testing Years* (Ian Allan Ltd, 1980), he was briefed that in any emergency involving ejection below 2,000 ft (610 m) the F-104 should first be rolled, if possible, to the inverted position. This, of course, was often not feasible, and Beamont recalled that famed USAF Korean war ace and X-2 test pilot Iven C. Kincheloe was among 21 F-104 aircrew whom this escape system had failed to save after he experienced an engine problem just after take-off.

The F-104A and F-104C could be fitted with a refuelling probe on the port side for use with drogue-equipped tankers. Fuel tanks could be carried either on the wingtips or on underwing pylons.

Right: In the 1950s the United States took the defence of its homeland and its children seriously, and much of the publicity of the time highlighted this fact. The exact nature of the threat to the US and the ability of the F-104 to counter it is open to question.

After briefing Beamont and leaving him to kit out at Palmdale for his initial flight in the 33rd production F-104A (56-762), powered by a J79-7 engine slightly uprated to 10,000/15,800 lb (44.5/70.3 kN) thrust, Lockheed test pilot Dave Holloman went off first in another Starfighter and crashed fatally after engine failure and an attempted emergency return to the airfield. Thus encouraged, Beamont then got airborne, only to experience a total loss of engine oil pressure immediately after take-off. The fact that this was due to a poor electrical contact in the instrument only became apparent after he had scraped round a full-power emergency circuit in pre-stall buffet at about 220 kt (253 mph; 406 km/h) and had touched-down safely at about 165 kt (189 mph; 305 km/h).

Two extended flights of around 35 minutes each ensued on the following day, when Beamont took the F-104A to Mach 2 at 37,000 ft (11278 m), where the limiting speed factor was a maximum permissible compressor inlet temperature (CIT) from kinetic heating, of around 100°C (212°F). During his F-104A flights, the last of which was at a take-off weight of 18,886 lb (8567 kg), including 5,889 lb (2671 kg) of usable fuel, Beamont recorded CITs of up to 90°C (194°F) when approaching 700 kt (803 mph; 1293 km/h) IAS, resulting in a large flashing green 'SLOW' annunciator warning on the central panel.

Scathing report

In his subsequent report to his British Aircraft Corporation employers, this very experienced British test pilot concluded that "the relatively poor standard of development of this aircraft in respect of stability and control was unexpected." His major criticisms included inadequate directional damping, evidenced by a persistent low-amplitude short-period oscillation throughout much of the F-104's flight regime – the 'snaking' characteristic of

many early jet aircraft (perhaps because this early production F-104A may have still lacked the additional ventral fin) – and the 'severe effect' of its thin and highly-loaded wing on turning manoeuvrability. First fitted to the last YF-104A built, the ventral fin was not a universal feature of production Starfighters even by early 1961.

Beamont also noted excessive break-out forces of the power-controlled ailerons, as well as pre-stall buffet and stick-shaker actuation when attempting 'Lightning-style' manoeuvres at any speeds below 500 kt (574 mph; 924 km/h). From his briefing, it was apparent that the F-104A was even then provided with artificial stall warning because of the very poor pitch-up characteristics associated with the T-tail configuration, which had been designed to avoid transonic airflow complications from the wings at high angles of attack. AoAs of about 30° resulted in the high-set stabilator stalling in the wing downwash, and an invariable departure into a flat spin from which recovery was only possible, given sufficient height, by applying enough engine power to accelerate back into controlled flight. This unpleasant and inherent characteristic necessitated the

In the wake of the Cuban Missile Crisis, F-104As were taken out of ANG control and assigned to the active-duty 32nd Air Division (ADC) at Homestead AFB, Florida. From here the three squadrons provided a rapid-reaction capability to deter any aggression from the south.

Two-seaters

With the performance and handling characteristics of the Starfighter, the provision of a two-seat trainer was considered a priority. Fitting the extra seat caused a drop in fuel capacity, although this was partially offset by putting a new fuel tank into the cannon bay in place of the weapon.

Right: 56-3719 was the first two-seat Starfighter, designated F-104B. As originally designed, the two-seaters were not given any extra keel area, although this was soon rectified when they showed a snaking tendency. Indeed, only the first batch of F-104Bs was built without the extended rudder.

Left: The most produced two-seater was the TF-104G (and similar CF-104D), which featured the NASARR system of the single-seater. The autopilot was omitted.

Right: The later F-104Bs were fitted with the ventral fin and an extended rudder.

Below: Twenty-one F-104Ds were built, these being based on the F-104C but with cannon deleted. The nosewheels of all two-seaters retracted backwards.

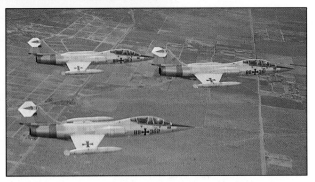

Above: A German special variant was the F-104F. Thirty were hastily procured for the Luftwaffe to allow training to begin. The Fs were equipped to G standards with upward-firing ejection seats but lacked the NASARR equipment.

Far right: Although not in quite the same class as today's 'drop-down' engine installations, that in the F-104 was considered advanced for its day, offering rapid access and quick changes. The entire rear section of the fuselage, including the empennage, was attached at just four positions. With these unfastened the rear end could be trolleyed away and the engine then extracted easily. The large dolly ring around the middle of the engine allowed it to be rotated easily for inspection and repair. Here are C models, seen in the engine maintenance shop at George AFB.

development of a two-stage automatic pitch control (APC) system, actuated through a rate gyro until disengaged with landing-flap selection. Initial stick-shaker actuation at high AoAs was followed by a 33 lb (15 kg) servo push force on the control column, forcing the nose down to stay within flight envelope limitations – an early, if imperative, example of current carefree handling philosophies.

In the circuit, Beamont again recorded intermittent stick-shaker actuation in turbulence at 220 kt (253 mph; 406 km/h), even with gear and landing flap extended. He also noted the necessity to maintain 88 per cent power on the approach at the required 180 kt (207 mph; 333 km/h) air speed and during the landing flare so as not to reduce flap blowing and cause a high rate of descent. While praising the F-104's cockpit layout, engineering and visibility as among the best he had encountered, Beamont summarised the early Starfighter's subsonic handling qualities as being "at no point pleasant, and in the take-off and landing configuration, critical, and not compatible with bad weather operation." He predicted that the F-104 was likely to continue to suffer a high accident rate in operation, and noted that even at its early stage of service, the USAF had decided to limit its procurement. This, he warned, would leave Lockheed with unplanned excess production capacity and a more than usually strong compulsion to seek major export orders.

ADC loses its F-104As

Starfighter handling was progressively improved during the flight development programme, in which the first 52 production Starfighters were eventually involved in over 8,000 sorties costing more than $30 million, but Roly Beamont's prescience regarding the type's future was soon to prove remarkably well founded.

Teething troubles with the USAF's first F-104As resulted in the early Starfighters being grounded in April 1958 after only a few months of service. These problems were mostly associated with actuator failures of the J79's new variable afterburner eyelid nozzle, leaving it fully open and therefore restricting available engine power to not much above idle thrust, which was insufficient to maintain level flight. This caused the loss of at least seven F-104s during early flight tests and development, and, according to Kelly Johnson, took about nine years to solve satisfactorily. The early F-104s also lacked modulated afterburning,

which meant that they could only be operated in combat at either maximum dry thrust or full reheat power – effectively offering a level speed choice of either Mach 1 or Mach 2.2.

By July 1958, when the F-104As were again cleared for flight, engine modifications to J79-GE-3B standard resulted in some improvements to Starfighter handling but, in 1959, the USAF decided to withdraw these early versions from front-line service with Air Defense Command. Officially, this was because of the F-104's lack of all-weather capability, inability to operate within the SAGE air defence system and relatively short range for North American operational requirements. But this decision may not have been unconnected with the loss of five F-104As, Bs and Cs in crashes between 29 October and 12 November 1959. Most of the surviving F-104A/Bs were then transferred to Air National Guard units in Arizona, South Carolina and Tennessee, where their misfortunes continued.

By April 1961, when a total of 100,000 flying hours had been accumulated by the F-104As and the additional F-104Cs funded in 1956, some 49 USAF Starfighters had been lost in accidents – the highest crash rate of any of the 'Century Series' fighters. Comparative loss rates in their first 5,000 hours of service flying comprised three for the General Dynamics F-111, six for the McDonnell Douglas F-4, seven for the North American F-100 and Convair F-106, eight for the Republic F-105, nine for the Convair F-102, 11 for the McDonnell Douglas F-101 and 14 for the F-104.

Drone conversion

After their withdrawal, about 24 early Starfighters were converted by Lockheed from 1960 onwards as remotely-controlled QF-104A drones for missile evaluation and firing practice. Painted pillar-box red overall, the QF-104As, including some with four underwing drop tanks for extended endurance, were operated by the USAF's 3205th Drone Squadron from Eglin AFB, Florida on both manned and pilotless test missions. In view of the F-104's demanding flight characteristics, and the relatively primitive remote radio control at that time, the latter must have proved particularly interesting.

At a much later stage, this experience was repeated in Japan when, after the retirement of the JASDF's Starfighters, trials were started in 1990 by Mitsubishi, in conjunction with Honeywell and Motorola in the US, to convert two F-104Js as prototype remotely-piloted drones for similar missile development trials. By late 1991, the two QF-104Js had successfully completed from the island of Iwo Jima 147 manned and unmanned flights, the latter being controlled by telemetry from a complete Starfighter cockpit section on the ground. An initial batch of six more QF-104Js was then similarly modified.

US dissatisfaction with the F-104 during its initial service was also reflected by the unexpected release of an initial batch of 24 F-104As and five F-104B trainers to the Republic of China air force in Taiwan (to where ADC's Starfighter-equipped 83rd and 337th Fighter Interceptor Squadrons had alternately been deployed, sharing the same aircraft on detachment during the Quemoy crisis from September 1958), followed by 10 F-104As and two F-104Bs to the air force of Pakistan. Taiwan also received

Below: Two views show 56-0741, one of the 24 retired interceptors modified with radio control equipment to act as target drones. Designated QF-104A, the drones were operated out of Eglin AFB and were of great use as supersonic targets for air-to-air missiles. In the lower photo the aircraft wears the red diamond fin-stripe associated with the Armament Development & Test Center to which the aircraft were assigned.

1962/63-funded MAP deliveries from Lockheed and Canadair of 46 F-104Gs, 21 RF-104Gs and eight TF-104Gs, apart from subsequent major transfers from several NATO air forces, to help counter aggressive Chinese tactics over the disputed islands of Quemoy. In one of the few air clashes at that time, Chinese Nationalist air force F-104Gs proved their combat capabilities in shooting down two AF/PLA MiG-19s from a formation of 12 over Quemoy in 1967.

Into battle

Pakistan's F-104A/Bs were supplied in response to proposed Indian Mach 2 fighter procurement, fulfilled by later Soviet MiG-21 deliveries, although the government in Delhi had approached the US after Chinese border attacks in 1962 attempting to buy up to 36 F-104s. Pakistan began receiving its first F-104As in September 1961, initially without their Vulcan cannon, to replace the piston-engined Hawker Furys of No. 9 Sqn. Its pilots, mostly then with 800-1,000 hours each on type, were still operating all 12 GAR-8 (AIM-9B) Sidewinder- and now Vulcan-armed Starfighters at the outbreak of the 1965 war with India on 1 September.

Above: Tensions between Nationalist and Communist China resulted in Taiwan becoming the first foreign recipient of the Starfighter in 1960 when the F-104A/B was supplied. In 1964 a batch of F/RF-104Gs (illustrated) was delivered, and it was these aircraft which were involved in air-to-air skirmishes that resulted in at least one MiG kill.

Left: Taxiing out from its shelter is one aircraft of the F-104A batch rushed to Taiwan to bolster the Nationalist's defence in 1960. The A model was no stranger to the island, USAF aircraft having been deployed during the 1958 Quemoy crisis.

By that time, the reputation of the F-104, referred to by Indians as the Badmash (Scoundrel), was such that an early encounter by a pair of PAF Starfighters with IAF Gnats resulted in the immediate surrender of one of these diminutive aircraft, which promptly lowered its wheels and landed at the nearest Pakistani forward airfield at Pasrur, without a shot being fired. In later combat, on 6 September, a PAF F-104A flying at about 600 kt (689

NASA test fleet

With its high speed, climb performance and high-altitude capability, the Starfighter became a natural for a variety of test purposes, including both acting as a vehicle for experiments and as a chase aircraft for other high-performance types. While the Air Force operated a fleet of JF-104s for various test uses, NASA's Dryden Flight Research facility at Edwards adopted the type as the mainstay of its high-performance test fleet,

employing a sizeable number on a wide variety of programmes. The Ames Research Facility at Moffett Field, California, also flew the type. Variants in use included the F-104A, JF-104A, F-104B, F-104G, TF-104G and F-104N, the latter being an astronaut training version similar to the NF-104A but without rocket booster. The Starfighter gave way to the F/A-18 as the main NASA fighter test platform.

This fine formation of NASA 'Stars' is led by an F-104B two-seater. On the left side of the formation are two F-104As, although one has been modified with an F-104G-style extended rudder. On the right side are two of the three F-104N astronaut trainers operated by NASA from Edwards.

Left: Seen in the twilight of its NASA career in 1993, this TF-104G is heavily modified for a test programme.

Right: NASA 812 was an F-104N, seen here in formation with a T-38, another type used for training astronauts.

Left: The F/A-18 adopted many of the F-104's tasks.

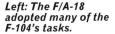

Right: This ex-Luftwaffe F-104G is fitted with the Flight Test Fixture which allowed rapid testing of small-scale experiments.

Indo-Pakistan Wars

A batch of 12 F-104A/Bs had been rushed to Pakistan as early as September 1961 to offset the impending delivery of MiG-21s to India. When war between the two nations broke out four years later the PAF F-104 pilots were well trained and experienced in their new mounts, and were a decisive factor in the air fighting. Although they only scored four kills (for two losses), they nevertheless posed a big threat to the Indians, and their deterrent value was considered enormous. The war with India forced the United States to impose an arms embargo on Pakistan, with the result that no further Starfighters could be obtained. When fresh fighting started in late 1971 the F-104 force had to be bolstered by aircraft from Jordan. Even so, the Pakistanis were hopelessly outnumbered by the Indian MiG-21s and up to seven F-104s from the combined force were lost. While the Pakistanis had the edge in 1965, in no small way thanks to the F-104, the Indians scored a resounding victory in 1971.

Above: Locals examine the wreckage of an F-104A downed in 1971. The aircraft was reported to have been shot down by an HF.24 Marut, but may have been hit by groundfire.

Below: Headed by two F-104Bs, this line-up shows some of the first batch of F-104s delivered to Jordan. These were initially flown by Pakistani pilots. They were not committed in the Six Day War.

Above: Illustrating the first three supersonic aircraft of the PAF, a Shenyang F-6 leads a Mirage IIIEP and an F-104A. All three types figured prominently in the 1971 war with India.

Right: During fighting with MiG-21s the F-104 showed superior speed but suffered if forced to manoeuvre with the nimble 'Fishbed'. One was lost to a Mystère in 1965.

mph; 1108 km/h) at virtually tree-top height shot down an IAF Mystère IVA with a Sidewinder, while another Mystère fell to the Vulcan cannon of a No. 9 Sqn Starfighter on the following day. Its PAF pilot then made the fundamental error of slowing down to dogfight with a second Mystère, which promptly out-turned him and scored cannon hits on the F-104, forcing the pilot to eject at very low level. Since the PAF F-104As had been modified to incorporate the later upward-firing Lockheed C-2 rocket ejection seat, he managed to survive.

Other changes to the PAF Starfighters had included the installation of the later stall-free 15,800-lb (70.3-kN) thrust J79-GE-11A turbojet, as well as of a retractable hook beneath the rear fuselage to engage emergency runway arrester wires. With cannon and AAM armament, they

made use of their AN/ASG-14T1 fire-control radar to operate as night-fighters in the 1965 war, in which at least one successful non-visual interception of a high-flying (33,000 ft/10060 m) IAF Canberra was achieved with a Sidewinder AAM on 21 September. A second F-104 had been lost on the previous night, when its pilot flew into the ground at about 200 kt (230 mph; 370 km/h) during the Starfighter's usual long flat approach when attempting to land at Peshawar during a severe dust storm. Remarkably, its pilot was thrown clear still strapped to his ejection seat and survived with minor injuries.

Mach 2 encounter

During PAF Starfighter daylight operations, what was probably the first encounter in history between opposing Mach 2 fighters took place on 11 September 1965. On encountering four MiG-21s from Halwara, a single PAF F-104A managed to escape by exiting at tree-top height and Mach 1.1, which the MiGs were unable to match, nearly running out of fuel in the process. In the course of the 1965 war, the PAF F-104s flew a total of 246 sorties, including 42 at night, and claimed four IAF aircraft destroyed for the loss of two Starfighters. These were later replaced by two F-104As transferred from the Republic of China air force, but when hostilities with India flared up again in December 1971 over East Pakistan, the PAF's Mach 2 fighter complement comprised only seven single-seat Starfighters in No. 9 Sqn and a single Mirage III unit, compared with no fewer than eight IAF squadrons with MiG-21s.

A US arms embargo imposed on both India and Pakistan after the 1965 war had prevented further PAF expansion, offers from Washington in 1970 for the limited release for cash of six F-104s, among other aircraft and equipment, having been unacceptable to Islamabad because of funding shortages. The large disparity between IAF and PAF

Another view of the Jordanian Starfighter line at Mafraq. Having been flown by PAF pilots in 1969, the RJAF F-104s returned the favour in 1971 by flying alongside their Pakistani brethren in the war against India. It is believed many of the Jordanian aircraft remained in Pakistan at the end of the war, while Jordan received the batch of F-104A/Bs originally supplied to Taiwan.

Below: An F-104C of the 479th TFW is displayed with some of the attack weapons it could carry. Conventional weapons included rocket pods, iron bombs and napalm (far right), but the main weapon envisaged for the aircraft was a single tactical nuclear weapon, represented here by the 'Special Weapon Practice Unit'. This was carried on the centreline pylon.

combat strengths in 1971 resulted in the transfer of No. 9 Sqn of the Royal Jordanian air force, with 'about 10' Lockheed F-104As, according to later US State Department reports, to Pakistan during the period of hostilities. A US spokesman said that he had no information on whether these aircraft were used in combat, or whether they were flown by Jordanian or PAF pilots, but indicated that only four of the RJAF Starfighters returned to Jordan after the 1971 war. Indian air historians, led by the well-known authority Pushpindar Singh, claim that two RJAF Starfighters were shot down on the last day (17 December) of the 1971 war over the southern sector of West Pakistan, increasing total Jordanian losses to four, plus five PAF Starfighters, although only two of the latter were admitted by Pakistan in combat with IAF MiG-21s, plus another from ground fire over Amritsar.

In theory, this left the PAF with only four of its original F-104As, but these may have been reinforced by retention of some of the RJAF Starfighters. Certainly the PAF continued operating F-104s with No. 9 Sqn until it re-equipped with Mirage 5PAs in 1975. The RJAF had only received its first 18 F-104As in mid-1969, when they were flown for a while in Jordan by PAF pilots, and went on to operate two squadrons (Nos 9 and 25) until these re-equipped with Mirage F1s from mid-1981.

USAF orders curtailed

Although planned orders for 18 RF-104A Starfighters (56-939 to -956) for USAF tactical reconnaissance roles for which funding had been allocated in 1956 were cancelled as early as 1957, a preceding contract for an initial batch of 56 F-104C-5-LO versions (56-883 to -938) for Tactical Air Command was allowed to continue. Powered by a J79-GE-7A turbojet with a 2-in (5-cm) increase in turbine diameter allowing a thrust output of 15,800 lb (70.28 kN) with decreased fuel consumption, the F-104C was designed mainly for delivery of Mk 12 and later US tactical nuclear weapons, and had a centre-line pylon attachment with a 2,000-lb (907-kg) capacity. This could also carry a 225-US gal (851-litre) drop-tank, and was supplemented by two underwing pylons with capacities of up to 1,500 lb (680 kg)

each, or a 195-US gal (738-litre) drop-tank, in addition to the wing-tip stations for two 170-US gal (773-litre) fuel tanks. The F-104C could also be equipped with a fixed inflight-refuelling probe on the port side of the cockpit, but retained the earlier Starfighter's fire-control radar. Its maximum take-off weight in clean configuration was increased from 17,350 lb (7870 kg) to 20,500 lb (9300 kg), or 23,590 lb (10700 kg) with external stores, at which the wing loading became 120.35 lb/sq ft (588 kg/m²).

The F-104C also retained the F-104A's 20-mm Vulcan cannon, but featured the upward-ejecting Lockheed C-2 rocket-boosted seat as standard. Orders for 21 additional F-104C-10-LOs (57-910 to -930) were included in 1957 USAF funding, together with a similar quantity of two-seat F-104D-5-LO (7), -10-LO (8) and -15-LO (6) trainer versions (57-1314 to -1334), with a new wide-chord rudder having full hydraulic boost. The planned orders for another 363 F-104Cs (57-0931 to -1293) and 83 F-104Ds (57-1335 to -1417) from 1957 funding were later cancelled when the USAF terminated all its Starfighter procurement plans. From original requirements for 676 aircraft, USAF total purchases were confined to 170 F-104As plus the two prototypes, 26 F-104Bs, 77 F-104Cs, and 21 F-104Ds, or 296 in all.

F-104C deliveries began on 16 October 1958 to the three squadrons of the 479th Tactical Fighter Wing at George AFB, where their training also included ground attack roles with conventional weapons, among which was the Martin GAM-83A/B Bullpup conventional/nuclear ASM. During the height of the Cold War in the

Above: 56-0883 was the first F-104C, these following on directly from the A model on the production line. Outwardly similar, the C had a more efficient engine and was fitted for more of an attack role, although it retained the same weapon system and air defence capability of its predecessor.

Lockheed test pilot Lou Schalk (famous for undertaking the first flight of the A-12) brings in the first F-104C to be delivered to Tactical Air Command on 16 October 1958. The location is Nellis AFB, Nevada, and the aircraft is marked in the flamboyant colours of the 479th TFW. The aircraft carries the legend 'Really George' under the cockpit, a reference to the 479th's home base at George AFB, California.

Above: A pair of bomb-laden F-104Cs heads into Vietnam from the base at Udorn during the second phase of detachments to the theatre. The weapons were M117 750-lb (340-kg) iron bombs, and two was the maximum load. General dissatisfaction with the Starfighter in this role led to its withdrawal from the theatre in June 1967.

Above: A pair of F-104As patrols from Da Nang in 1965. The consitutent squadrons of the 479th TFW rotated through the Southeast Asia deployment.

As USAF tactical aircraft faced an ever-growing threat from MiGs, the 479th TFW dispatched its 435th TFS to Da Nang in April 1965 to fly top cover for tactical operations. During the course of these the F-104 proved to be too short on range to be a useful escort fighter, a fact the North soon learned. All they had to do was wait for the F-104s to turn back before launching their own fighters in safety. In one rare occasion where the F-104 was engaged, one aircraft was shot down (by Chinese MiG-19s). The first detachment lasted until December, but resumed in May 1966 at Udorn in Thailand. During the second phase the ground attack mission prevailed, although with a full bomb load (of just two weapons) the F-104 had a very limited range. The Starfighter took part in Operation Bolo, a successful attempt to lure the MiGs into the air. Here the F-104s failed to engage, while F-4 Phantoms scored heavily. In addition to the MiG loss, two F-104s fell to SAMs, six to AAA and six to non-combat causes.

Above: 479th TFW F-104Cs share the Udorn ramp with T-28s and RF-101s. When the Starfighter first went to Southeast Asia it was expected to fly intercept missions against North Vietnamese Il-28 bombers, but such raids never materialised and the aircraft was left in the less-than-ideal escort and attack role.

Homestead AFB, Florida, as part of the 32nd Air Division.

The F-104As continued in regular USAF service until December 1969. Twenty-six aircraft from the 319th FIS were re-engined from late 1967 with the 17,900-lb (79.94-kN) J79-GE-19 turbojet, as used in the much later F-104S version developed for Italy.

With USAF bombers and attack aircraft facing a growing threat from Chinese-flown MiG-21s over North Vietnam, aircraft of the 479th TFW undertook top cover missions from April 1965. Flying from Da Nang, 25 F-104Cs in each of the wing's three squadrons were rotated in turn for tours of duty, flying sorties of four to seven hours over an eight-month period. The appearance of the USAF's F-104s over North Vietnam was enough to establish instant air superiority; encountering no air opposition during that time, they quickly reverted to ground attack roles. On 20 September 1965, Major Philip E. Smith was shot down by Chinese MiGs over Hainan Island to become the sole F-104 POW (prisoner of war); during unsuccessful attempts

Two photographs show F-104Cs of the 479th TFW flying a training mission (left) and shortly after arriving at a European base (below). Regular deployments were made to Europe during the 1960s at the height of the Cold War.

early 1960s, both the TAC F-104Cs and the ANG F-104As were periodically deployed to western Europe. In response to the Soviet build-up in Cuba, Air Defense Command reclaimed the earlier Starfighters from the Air National Guard in 1963 to equip two regular squadrons (the 319th and 331st Fighter-Interceptor Squadrons) at

Right: When the F-104C first went to Vietnam it retained its natural metal finish, but this was replaced by the standard T.O.114 tactical camouflage. The refuelling probe was a 'must' for combat operations.

to rescue Smith, two more F-104s were lost in a collision – making it a painful day for the Starfighter community. During their initial deployments until December 1965, the F-104Cs flew a total of 2,269 combat sorties totalling 8,820 hours, and their detachments to the 7th Air Force in Vietnam were resumed from May 1966 to June 1967.

At that time, the USAF was operating a total of 115 Starfighters, with an overall accident rate of 34 per 100,000 flying hours, compared with an average of only 4.4 for other US combat aircraft. Only one F-104C squadron was still in regular USAF service by January 1967, when Defense Secretary Robert McNamara announced that the last operational Starfighters would be retired from US first-line units in early 1968.

More height records sought

Not long after entering service, the F-104C continued its record-breaking tradition with a new zoom height achievement to 103,395 ft (31515 m) on 14 December 1959, at Edwards Flight Test Center in the hands of Captain Joe B. Jordan. In the process, it also reached an airspeed of Mach 2.36 and established a time-to-height record to 30000 m (98,425 ft) of 15 minutes 4.92 seconds from brake release.

Development of the US X-series aircraft tended to overtake these altitude achievements, although the Starfighter reached into space with three specially-modified F-104As transferred in 1963 to the USAF's Aerospace Research Pilot School at Edwards AFB, then commanded by Colonel (later Brigadier General) Charles E. 'Chuck' Yeager. Operating alongside 10 JF-104As and three JF-104Bs used at Edwards for chase and development roles, these NF-104As were modified in a $3,815,382

Left: A 479th TFW F-104C sits on the ramp of an English air base during one of the type's numerous deployments to Europe. The presence of the Starfighter, with its interception and nuclear capability, bolstered European defences at a time when the threat of a Central European war was at its highest.

contract by Lockheed from September 1962. Changes included the addition of a 6,000-lb (26.7-kN) Rocketdyne LR 121-NA-1/AR 2-3 variable-thrust HTP/JP-4 booster rocket at the base of the larger-area TF-104G-type fin, and the fitment of a powered rudder for ballistic flights above 100,000 ft (30480 m) for the purposes of space and zero *g* training.

A dozen small hydrogen peroxide jet reaction nozzles similar to those in the North American X-15 were mounted in pairs in the NF-104's nose and in the wingtips, which were each extended by 2 ft (0.6 m). The 43-lb (0.19-kN) thrust nozzles were used to take over from the aerodynamic control surfaces at extreme altitudes, where the rocket booster provided continued thrust after the J79-3B turbojet had to be reduced to idling through lack of oxygen. The nozzles in the nose comprised four 113-lb (0.50-kN) pitch and four yaw thrusters, mounted in opposing pairs. Other changes included lengthened air intake cones and redesigned engine air bypass doors for better ram recovery and improved compressor stall characteristics. Permissible maximum airspeed was increased from Mach 2.0 to 2.2, resulting from a higher compressor inlet temperature limit of 155°C (311°F).

F-104 Guardsmen

From February 1960 the F-104A/B began to transfer from active-duty ADC use to the ANG, although it remained an ADC asset under the gaining command system. ADC had disposed of the aircraft after less than two years' service owing to an appalling loss rate and inability to operate within the SAGE air defence network. The F-104A's career with the Guard lasted only three years, ADC taking back the aircraft for active duty in 1963 after the Cuban missile crisis. During their Guard tenure, the F-104A/B units were called to FAD (federal active duty) during the Berlin crisis of 1961. Detachments were made to Morón in Spain and

Ramstein in West Germany where they sat air defence alert. The Puerto Rico Air National Guard later flew surplus F-104C/Ds on fighter-bomber duties, retaining them until 1975.

Left: The 157th FIS/South Carolina ANG was the first Guard unit to get the F-104.

Below: F-104s of the 151st FIS line up at Knoxville prior to their 1961 deployment to Ramstein.

Left: Following the end of combat operations in Southeast Asia in 1967, the 479th TFW disposed of its F-104C/Ds, some being passed to the 198th TFS/Puerto Rico ANG, with whom they served until the summer of 1975 when the A-7D was taken on charge. This F-104D from the 198th TFS is seen at Davis-Monthan shortly after arrival at the 'boneyard'.

Canadair (Lockheed) CF-104 Starfighter
No. 1 Canadian Air Group
Canadian Armed Forces
Baden-Söllingen, West Germany

Markings
For the early part of their career, CF-104s flew in an unpainted natural metal finish. This changed in early 1972 when they gave up the nuclear strike role and gained tactical camouflage. As befitted an aircraft with a strategic mission, the nuclear CF-104s rarely carried any unit markings. National markings consisted of the standard maple leaf roundels on wings and fuselage, 'RCAF' titles and a national flag on the fin. The national flag changed to the current 'Band Aid' in the mid-1960s and, on 28 February 1968, the RCAF was absorbed into the unified Canadian Armed Forces, and the Starfighters began to carry 'CAF' on the nose. This was later dropped in favour of the word 'Canada'.

Attack ordnance
This CF-104 is depicted dropping Hunting BL755 cluster bombs, one of the principal weapons it would have used in the ground attack role. This was a secondary tasking during the 1960s, when the CF-104 force was assigned to nuclear strike (with a quick reaction alert maintained). When the force 'went tactical', it assumed a green and grey camouflage, had the internal cannon fitted, and began to carry a wide range of conventional stores. In addition to bombs the aircraft was often fitted with rocket pods.

Wing surfaces
The tiny wing bestowed true Mach 2 performance on the Starfighter, but provided very little lift at low speeds. To overcome this, and to prevent the aircraft becoming too much of a 'hot ship' on landing, the F-104 was fitted with an array of high-lift devices. The leading edge featured a full-span drooping flap, electrically actuated. The entire trailing edge was hinged, consisting of outboard ailerons which were hydraulically powered to provide enough control authority at high speeds. The inboard flaps were large and electrically powered. Above all, they were 'blown' with bleed air from the engine compressor, this providing a great deal of extra lift. The blown flaps were the mechanism which really allowed the F-104 to function as a practical warplane.

Canadair built a total of 200 CF-104 Starfighters (under the company designation CL-90), based on a single prototype F-104G supplied by Lockheed (itself produced as a conversion of an F-104A with new tail). The Starfighter was originally to have been identified as CF-111 under the Canadian numbering system, with CF-111D assigned to the two-seater.

The principal differences between Canadian CF-104 aircraft and the standard F-104G were the Orenda-built J79 engine and the fact that most CF-104s were intended only for the nuclear strike role, and had an extra 1,000 lb (454 kg) of fuel in place of the 20-mm cannon of the F-104G. The NASARR radar had only air-to-ground modes. In January 1972 the nuclear strike role was relinquished in favour of purely tactical operations, and the cannon was reinstated. Apart from an OCU (6 Strike/Recce OTU, later 417 Operational Training Sqn) in Canada, all CF-104s were assigned to the Canadian 1st Air Division in Europe, part of 4th Allied Tactical Air Force.

The CF-104 in Europe

In the early 1960s the RCAF's No. 1 Air Division (its Europe-based organisation) operated four wings, each consisting of one squadron of Avro Canada CF-100 Mk 4Bs and two of Canadair CL-13 Sabre Mk 6s. The arrival on 11 October 1962 of the first CF-104 heralded a considerable period of change. The four CF-100 squadrons (419, 423, 440 and 445) were disbanded, while the eight Sabre squadrons quickly converted on to the Starfighter. The order of conversion was 427, 434, 444, 422, 441, 430, 421 and 439, the process being completed by early 1964. Thus, the organisation consisted of No. 1 Fighter Wing (439 and 441 Sqns) at Marville, No. 2 (421 and 430 Sqns) at Gros Tenquin, No. 3 (427 and 434 Sqns) at Zweibrücken and No. 4 (422 and 444 Sqns) at Baden-Söllingen. In 1964, however, Gros Tenquin was closed, with 430 Sqn going to No. 3 Wing at Zweibrücken and 421 Sqn joining No. 4 Wing at Baden. When France decided to leave NATO in 1966, the remaining French base, Marville, also closed, the two recon-dedicated squadrons (439 and 441) of No. 1 Wing moving to Lahr. In 1967, 434 and 444 Sqns were disbanded to even out the number of squadrons (two) at each of the three German bases. Two years later the Canadians decided to remove No. 3 Wing from Zweibrücken, the base being reassigned to USAFE units. The two squadrons were relocated to No. 1 Wing at Lahr (430 Sqn) and the combined Nos 3/4 Wing at Baden (427 Sqn). This organisation lasted only a brief time, for in 1970 the Canadian government introduced a new defence policy which dictated a halving of the force in Europe and a total transition from nuclear to conventional missions by 1972. Baden-Söllingen was chosen as the base to survive (Lahr was retained for non-combat operations), although only 421 Sqn remained intact from its three existing units. 439 and 441 moved in from Lahr, while 422, 427 and 430 disbanded. Attack missions were assigned to 421 and 439, leaving 441 to continue its tactical reconnaissance duties. The Baden wing was retitled No. 1 Canadian Air Group, and the position remained unchanged until 1985, when the first CF-188s arrived to begin replacement of the CF-104. The last Starfighter left 439 Sqn two years later after 25 years' service in the defence of Western Europe.

Canadair production

When both West Germany and Canada chose the F-104 as their new tactical strike platform, the two nations agreed on a basic configuration to ease licence production in both Europe and Canada, although the RCAF's CF-104 differed from the European F-104G in small respects. Using the sole CF-104A (56-0770/12700) as a pattern aircraft, Canadair completed 200 CL-90/CF-104s (12701 to 12900, later 104701 to 104900) for the RCAF, to which were added 38 CF-104D two-seaters built by Lockheed. The first Canadair-built CF-104 (12701) was trucked to Palmdale for its first flight, which took place on 26 May 1961. In addition, the Canadian company received MAP contracts covering a further 140 aircraft, completed as F-104Gs with the Orenda-built J79-GE-11A engines. These received MAP serials 62-12302 to 62-12349, 62-12698 to 62-12707, 63-13638 to 63-13647 and 64-17752 to 64-17795, and were given construction numbers in the 6001 to 6140 range. F-104Gs from Canadair production were supplied to Denmark, Greece, Norway, Taiwan and Turkey. In addition to the 340 complete aircraft it built, Canadair also manufactured the wings, tail units and aft fuselages for the Lockheed production line, and fed many similar sets into the massive European production effort, most notably to the Italian Group.

CF-104 equipment

In addition to the NASARR radar (with most air-to-air modes deleted), the CF-104 was equipped with a General Electric TAB (Tactical Analogue Bombing) computer and missile launch computer. Central to the navigation system was the Litton LN-2 inertial system, which could fly the CF-104 to any one of 12 pre-programmed targets without recourse to ground-based systems. Further vital systems were a Garrett central air data computer and a Honeywell automatic flight control system. The position and homing indicator was made by Computing Devices of Canada. As built, the CF-104 lacked the internal cannon, featuring an auxiliary tank of 120 US gal (455 litres) in its place. Aircraft assigned to the tactical reconnaissance role had a ventral Vicon pod housing four 70-mm Vinten cameras.

Wings

The most remarkable feature of the Starfighter was its wings, which seemed far too small for the size of fuselage – each wing was only 7 ft 7 in (2.31 m) from root to tip. Of simple trapezoidal plan, the wings were built around two main spars, and featured extremely sharp leading edges. The wing itself was very thin, with a thickness:chord ratio of only 3.36 per cent. Anhedral was set at 10° to destabilise the aircraft in the rolling plane.

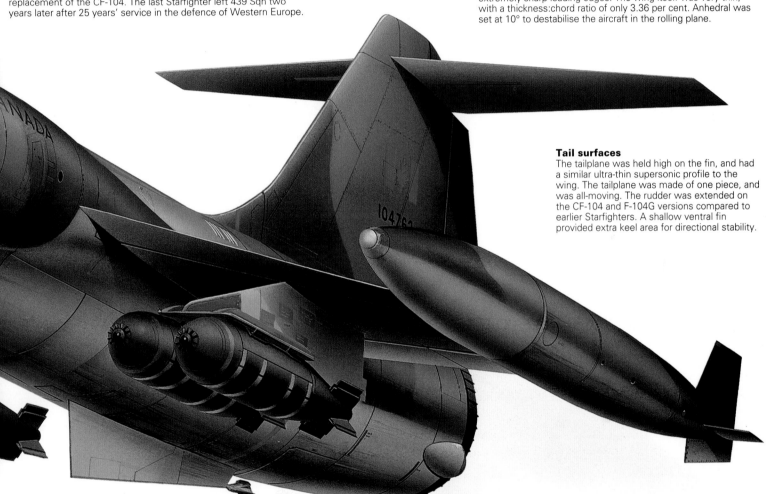

Tail surfaces

The tailplane was held high on the fin, and had a similar ultra-thin supersonic profile to the wing. The tailplane was made of one piece, and was all-moving. The rudder was extended on the CF-104 and F-104G versions compared to earlier Starfighters. A shallow ventral fin provided extra keel area for directional stability.

Powerplant

Powering the CF-104 was a version of the General Electric J79 built by Canadian manufacturer Orenda. Designated J79-OEL-7, the engine had a 17-stage compressor, the first six stator stages of which had variable incidence. In all the compressor featured no fewer than 1,260 stator vanes and 1,271 rotor blades. Downstream was the combustor, consisting of 10 combustion cans with dual igniters in each. Next came the three-stage turbine, leading to the three-ring, quadrant-burning afterburner and petal-type nozzle. Vital statistics for the J79-OEL-7 were: length 17 ft 4 in (5.28 m); diameter at compressor 30.34 in (771 mm); diameter at nozzle 3 ft 3.3 in (998 mm); and dry weight 3,385 lb (1535 kg). Standard non-afterburning military power rating was 10,000 lb (44.5 kN) thrust. With minimum afterburning this was increased to 12,300 lb (54.73 kN) and with full afterburning to 15,800 lb (70.31 kN). The OEL-7 engines differed in small respects from the J79-GE-11A engines for the F-104G. They were slightly lighter and had slightly wider nozzles. In operation they were notable for failing to produce the wailing noise characteristic of most Starfighters. In addition to the OEL-7s for the CF-104, Orenda also licence-produced the GE-11A for MAP F-104Gs.

Nuclear NATO

Between 1958 and 1961 West Germany, Canada, the Netherlands, Belgium and Italy all bought the Starfighter, chiefly as a means of delivering the B43 tactical nuclear weapon. These weapons were 'owned' by the United States, although kept on or near the Starfighter bases. A dual-key arrangement existed for their issue to the users. Norway subsequently joined the Starfighter club in the early 1960s, as did Turkey and Greece. Denmark and Spain were the final **NATO** recipients, leaving just France and the UK to maintain their commitments with indigenous designs.

Left: Greece flew the F-104 from 1964 to 1993, albeit with only two units. Many aircraft were held for spares.

Above: Dutch Starfighters were arranged into two wings handling air defence and tactical strike, with one squadron dedicated to reconnaissance.

Above: Belgium's nuclear strike wing operated from Kleine Brogel, later turning to conventional duties.

Above: Denmark was a late entrant in the Starfighter club, receiving its first aircraft in 1965. These were configured for the air defence mission.

Left: Spain was unique among F-104 users in never losing one of its aircraft. The type flew with specially-renumbered Esc 104 at Torrejon from 1965 to 1972.

Above: Norway's F-104Gs initially had both the reconnaissance and air defence missions, although maritime strike was added later. This example wears the rarely seen red/white/blue fin flash of 331 Skvadron.

Wearing a full pressure suit, project pilot Major Robert W. Smith set an unofficial world altitude record of 118,860 ft (36229 m) on 15 November 1963. In attempting to top this mark on 12 December 1963, Colonel Yeager encountered an uncontrollable pitch-up at 28° Alpha and 104,000 ft (31700 m), followed by the inevitable flat spin. This was accompanied by an engine flame-out and rpm run-down which prevented a relight and the mandatory powered recovery, but Yeager continued to fight the controls through 13 of the NF-104A's 14 spin rotations before finally ejecting at 12,000 ft (3660 m). The rocket-boosted ejection seat fouled his parachute, smashing into his helmeted head and breaking the face plate of his pressure suit and then igniting the oxygen supply being forced under pressure into his helmet from the seat's still red-hot rocket packs. Had Yeager not wrestled open the face plate, thereby automatically shutting off the suit's oxygen supply and the fierce blow-torch around his head, he would surely have lost the last of his nine test-flying lives. As it was, he endured months of painful surgery on his face and one hand.

The 'Sale of the Century'

In the mid-1950s, the NATO air forces in Europe, apart from Britain and France, began looking for a first-generation supersonic multi-role fighter capable of delivering the (US-supplied) 1-MT B-43 tactical nuclear weapon. Britain and France already had the highly promising Mach 2 Lightning and Mirage III in the final stages of development. These aircraft might have been

Seen after its first flight on 10 August 1962, c/n 4001 was the first Lockheed-built F-104G aircraft produced under the Mutual Assistance Program (MAP). It was subsequently delivered to Greece.

Above: FX-1 (c/n 9016) was the first F-104G for the Belgian air force, all of which were built by the Western Group, comprising SABCA and Avions Fairey. The first 15 from Belgian production (and a total of 88) went to West Germany. Belgium introduced tactical camouflage in 1967.

thought obvious choices for NATO, despite their initial optimisation for air defence. While both were offered for the new NATO requirement, they faced very strong opposition from the government-backed US industry.

With a potential market for more than 2,000 aircraft, the new requirement quickly became known in industry circles as 'the sale of the century', and it also became apparent that it was one the US would go to any length to attain. The US was offering the Vought F8U Crusader and the Republic F-105 Thunderchief, but its main contenders were the projected J79-engined Grumman G-98 Super Tiger and the planned Lockheed F-104G, and the loss of its lucrative USAF contracts drove Lockheed to new levels of salesmanship. Attempts by Rolls-Royce to promote an Avon-engined Grumman Tiger were eventually unsuccessful, and German interest in the projected and similarly-powered Saunders-Roe 177, with an additional de Havilland liquid-rocket motor, collapsed when that aircraft was cancelled by the British government after the 1957 Defence White Paper advocated missile development in place of further manned combat aircraft.

German decision

It has never been made clear how Lockheed managed to persuade the Germans to select a paper project derived from a design with a highly questionable accident record, which was in the process of being rejected by the US Air Force. In a dramatised account of the final fly-off, apparently against a Grumman F11F Tiger, Lockheed claimed that on the initial landing trials the Starfighter demonstrator – presumably an F-104C – stopped in a roll 455 ft (139 m) shorter than that of its rival, and in a simultaneous climb to 50,000 ft (16400 m), reached that height in 4 minutes 57 seconds after accelerating to 974 kt

(1,118 mph; 1800 km/h) at 35,000 ft (11480 m). There had been silence from the competing pilot until, when asked after 6 minutes to report his position, he answered, "Still at 35,000 ft (11480 m) trying to accelerate past Mach 1.3."

On 6 November 1958, preference for the proposed F-104G for the Luftwaffe's interceptor, fighter-bomber and reconnaissance requirements was announced by Federal Defence Minister Franz Josef Strauss in Bonn. This was followed by an initial contract on 18 March 1959 for the first batch of 66 (later 96) Lockheed-built single-seat Super Starfighters and 30 two-seat F-104F versions. Herr Strauss said that German industry would also build 210 F-104Gs, and buy 364 more from joint co-production in Europe, increasing overall FRG Super Starfighter procurement to 670.

Canada was the next NATO country to select the F-104G as its new fighter. On 2 July 1959 plans were announced for the co-production of 200 CL-90 or CF-104 (originally CF-111) versions by Canadair Ltd, plus 38 two-seat CF-104Ds (CF-111Ds, not CF-113 as widely

Canada was the second major foreign customer for the Starfighter. Powered by an Orenda-built J79, the CF-104s did not wail the way other F-104s did in the landing pattern.

Below: A Danish F-104G clutches a pair of AIM-9B Sidewinders to its belly. The twin ventral 'Winder rails were the best way of carrying this weapon, leaving the wingtips free for the fuel tanks. Not all F-104Gs were equipped to carry these launchers: for instance, Luftwaffe air defence Starfighters had to carry their missiles on the wingtips.

Below: KF+134 was the 34th Lockheed-built F-104G for West Germany, seen here on air test in company with an F-104A. The much larger rudder and taller fin of the 'Super Starfighter' are readily apparent. What cannot be seen is the much-strengthened airframe.

Marineflieger ship-killers

In the early 1960s the Bundesmarine (West German navy) was eagerly awaiting replacements for its two wings of Sea Hawks, which were rapidly approaching total obsolescence. The service had hoped to receive either the Phantom or the Buccaneer, and the latter was demonstrated widely between 1960 and 1962. However, the major Luftwaffe purchase of the Starfighter sealed the fate of the Marineflieger, which

began acquiring the Starfighter in 1963 in the interests of commonality. The F-104Gs assigned to anti-ship duties were operated by Marineflieger-geschwader 1 at Schleswig, armed with Nord AS30 line-of-sight TV-guided weapons. These were replaced by the far better MBB AS-34 Kormoran from 1977, a weapon which was also used by the Tornado when it began replacing the Bundesmarine Starfighters from 1982.

Right: Prior to the arrival of Kormoran, the Nord AS30 was the main anti-ship weapon for navy Starfighters. These missiles are on an RF-104G.

Below: A navy F-104 temporarily assigned to E-stelle 61 launches a test round of the Kormoran.

Right: This F-104G is from 2./MFG 2, the attack-dedicated Staffel of the second MFG Starfighter wing.

This gaggle of Luftwaffe RF-104G Starfighters contains aircraft from the two operational units, AKG 51 and AKG 52, and the training unit, Waffenschule 10. When the RF-4E replaced the RF-104G in 1971/72, many of the displaced Starfighters were modified to F-104G standards and joined strike units.

reported) to be bought directly from Lockheed, to re-equip its eight F-86 Sabre squadrons in the RCAF's European Air Division. J79 (OEL-7) production and assembly was undertaken in Canada by the Orenda Engine Ltd company, at Malton, Ontario.

Licence-production and associated technology transfers, to expand and modernise the newly established national aerospace industry, were key features of German F-104 procurement. When most of the other continental NATO countries, led by the Netherlands on 20 April 20 1960 and including Belgium (20 June 1960) and later Italy (2 March 1961), followed suit with additional Starfighter orders, licensing agreements were concluded with Lockheed by December 1960 for international co-production on a major scale. These included, in November of that year, an extension of Super Starfighter licence-production to a

third continent, with Japan's decision to purchase an initial batch of 180 F-104J air superiority versions of the F-104G and 20 F-104DJ two-seat trainers, to be built by an industrial consortium led by Mitsubishi Heavy Industries.

In Europe, F-104G production centred mainly on Germany, where four main companies – Messerschmitt in Augsburg and Manching for final assembly; Dornier in Munich; Heinkel at Speyer; and Siebel at Donauworth – plus BMW in Koblenz for J79 production, formed an Arbeitsgemeinschaft (ARGE), or working group, known as ARGE Süd to produce the initial batch of 210 F-104Gs for the German armed forces. A northern group (ARGE Nord) comprising other German companies, including Focke-Wulf in Bremen, Hamburger Flugzeugbau in Hamburg, and Weser Flugzeugbau at Einswarden, in conjunction with Fokker at Schiphol (where final assembly took place) and Dordrecht, and Aviolanda at Papendrecht, was formed to co-produce 350 F-104Gs. Of these, 255 would be for the German armed forces and 95 for the Royal Netherlands air force.

Italy joins production

As the third European F-104 production component, a Western Group was formed in Belgium by Avions Fairey and SABCA with the establishment of a joint production line and flight test facility at Gosselies, near Charleroi, in conjunction with Fabrique Nationale in Brussels for J79 components and assembly, for the eventual manufacture of 189 F-104Gs. Of these, 100 were for the Force Aérienne Belge and 89 for German service, although one of the Belgian aircraft crashed on test and was replaced from the German allocation (reducing their uptake to 88). When Italy joined the European F-104 programme and the Italian Group in the following year, Fiat in Turin as prime contractor was responsible for assembling F-104G components built by Alfa Romeo and Macchi, with an eventual programme target of 200 aircraft of which 125

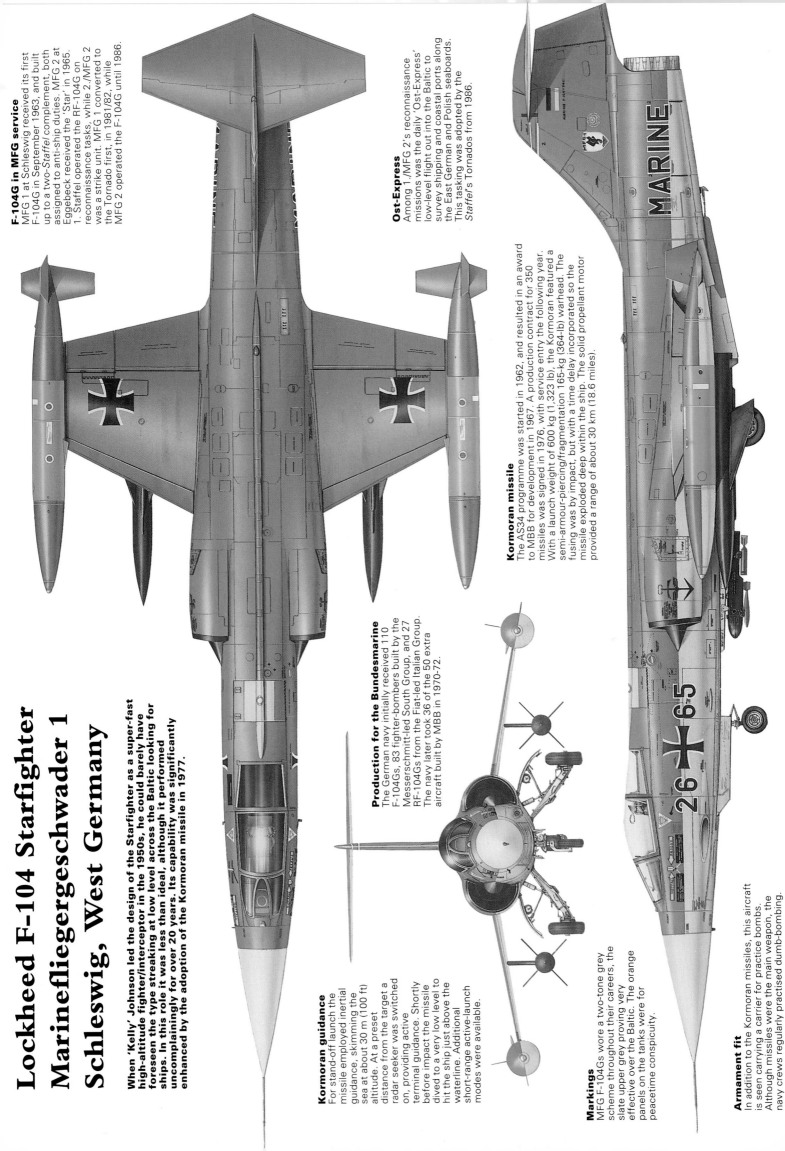

F-104G in MFG service

MFG 1 at Schleswig received its first F-104G in September 1963, and built up to a two-*Staffel* complement, both assigned to anti-ship duties. MFG 2 at Eggebeck received the 'Star' in 1965. 1. Staffel operated the RF-104G on reconnaissance tasks, while 2./MFG 2 was a strike unit. MFG 1 converted to the Tornado first, in 1981/82, while MFG 2 operated the F-104G until 1986.

Ost-Express

Among 1./MFG 2's reconnaissance missions was the daily 'Ost-Express' low-level flight out into the Baltic to survey shipping and coastal ports along the East German and Polish seaboards. This tasking was adopted by the *Staffel's* Tornados from 1986.

Lockheed F-104 Starfighter
Marinefliegergeschwader 1
Schleswig, West Germany

When 'Kelly' Johnson led the design of the Starfighter as a super-fast high-altitude fighter/interceptor in the 1950s, he could barely have foreseen the type streaking at low level across the Baltic looking for ships. In this role it was less than ideal, although it performed uncomplainingly for over 20 years. Its capability was significantly enhanced by the adoption of the Kormoran missile in 1977.

Kormoran missile

The AS34 programme was started in 1962, and resulted in an award to MBB for development in 1967. A production contract for 350 missiles was signed in 1976, with service entry the following year. With a launch weight of 600 kg (1,323 lb), the Kormoran featured a semi-armour-piercing/fragmentation 165-kg (364-lb) warhead. The fusing was by impact, but with a time delay incorporated so the missile exploded deep within the ship. The solid propellant motor provided a range of about 30 km (18.6 miles).

Kormoran guidance

For stand-off launch the missile employed inertial guidance, skimming the sea at about 30 m (100 ft) altitude. At a preset distance from the target a radar seeker was switched on, providing active terminal guidance. Shortly before impact the missile dived to a very low level to hit the ship just above the waterline. Additional short-range active-launch modes were available.

Production for the Bundesmarine

The German navy initially received 110 F-104Gs, 83 fighter-bombers built by the Messerschmitt-led South Group, and 27 RF-104Gs from the Fiat-led Italian Group. The navy later took 36 of the 50 extra aircraft built by MBB in 1970-72.

Markings

MFG F-104Gs wore a two-tone grey scheme throughout their careers, the slate upper grey proving very effective over the Baltic. The orange panels on the tanks were for peacetime conspicuity.

Armament fit

In addition to the Kormoran missiles, this aircraft is seen carrying a carrier for practice bombs. Although missiles were the main weapon, the navy crews regularly practised dumb-bombing.

European production

When West Germany ordered the F-104G in 1959, it opened the floodgates for massive production of the type. In order to satisfy the huge production requirement, and to satisfy European politicians eager to appease home voters, production lines were opened at four European locations. The first was at Messerschmitt (ARGE Süd), the production agreement being signed with Lockheed on 18 March 1959. The ARGE Nord was established in January 1960 with Fokker as the principal contractor, the ARGE West (SABCA in Belgium) in March 1960, and finally the Italian Group (led by Fiat) in November 1960. In mid-1960 NATO established a Starfighter management organisation, headquartered in Koblenz, to oversee and co-ordinate production at the four facilities. All four lines produced aircraft for Germany in addition to their respective home users, while the Italian Group also supplied 25 to the Netherlands. Both Lockheed and Canadair were also busy with building F-104s, many destined for Europe.

Right: The original ARGE Süd produced 210 F-104Gs, with final assembly undertaken at Manching. The aircraft wearing markings in the left-hand line were actually from the first Lockheed-built batch, the others being from the first 30 off the line.

Below: Freshly completed, the 10th ARGE Süd-built F-104G stands outside the shed at Manching, while two others roll out for engine fitment.

Above: Wearing delivery codes 'KG 101' and c/n 8001, this aircraft was the first to be produced by the ARGE Nord, led by Fokker at Schiphol. This group was the most prolific of the four, responsible for 255 for the Luftwaffe and 95 for the Dutch air force.

Above: Bearing the c/n 9998, this aircraft was the first F-104G for Italy. It was built and flown by Lockheed at Palmdale before dismantling and shipping to the Fiat group at Torino. It flew again at Caselle on 9 June 1962, with serial MM6501 assigned.

were for the Aeronautica Militare Italiano, 50 for West Germany, and 25 for the Dutch air force.

For the initial 1,045 Super Starfighters to be built for the four European air forces (Belgium, Germany, Holland and Italy), including 96 from Lockheed, 1,369 J79s were planned for manufacture, comprising 144 by General Electric in the US, 627 by BMW, 334 by Fabrique Nationale, and 264 by Fiat.

All the remaining countries in the Super Starfighter licence-production programme were interlinked so far as component and sub-assembly transfers were concerned. Canadair, for example, was contracted to supply 121 sets of wings, aft fuselage and tail assemblies to Belgium, the FRG and the Netherlands, 40 sets to Lockheed, and 40 to Japan.

The Canadian company also received later contracts from US MDAP funding between 1962-64 for 140 more F-104Gs, mainly for the Danish, Greek, Norwegian and Turkish air forces. Lockheed itself remained heavily involved in its licence-production programmes, from which it received at least $1 billion from royalties and the supply of small quantities of complete F-104Gs and knocked-down kits of parts to launch these individual programmes, and from larger orders such as the initial 66 for the FRG and 84 for USAF Mutual Aid contracts, and widespread component production.

Lockheed-built trainers

Lockheed's Burbank and Palmdale factories were initially responsible for producing all the two-seat trainer versions in the global procurement programmes, including 38 CF-104Ds for Canada, 30 F-104Fs and 137 TF-104Gs for the FRG, 20 F-104DJs for Japan, and 29 TFs for MAP contracts (Denmark, four; Greece, six; Norway, two; Spain, three; Turkey, six; Taiwan, eight). Lockheed built a total of 191 TF-104Gs for NATO use, including 12 for Belgium, 137 for the FRG, 12 for Italy and 18 for the Netherlands. Some of these were assembled in Europe from Lockheed-supplied kits, including 55 by the Messerschmitt group for the FRG, four from Avio Diepen for the KLu, and nine from SABCA for the FAB; Fiat delivered an extra 16 for the AMI.

The CF-104D and TF-104G (the latter with a 1961 fly-away unit cost of $1.068 million) incorporated all the F-104G's weapons system and associated avionics, including its radar, apart from the Vulcan cannon (replaced by fuel). For rapid delivery Germany's small batch of 30 specialised

The townsfolk of Bodø seem remarkably unconcerned as three Mach 2 fighters are towed along their main street in 1963. The Lockheed-built RF-104Gs had just arrived by ship at the harbour, and were being delivered to the nearby air base.

With special scheme for the KLu's 65th anniversary in 1978, this F-104G pulls some g during an air show routine. Experience showed that the Starfighter could manoeuvre well in the vertical plane, but that it could be out-turned by most contemporary fighters.

F-104Fs were basically F-104Ds with the G's J79-GE-11A turbojet plus simplified systems, and were used for type conversion rather than operational training. Without the G's strengthened airframe, the F-104Fs were limited to a maximum take-off weight of 24,383 lb (11060 kg). The first example (BB-360), costing only $650,000, was accepted at Palmdale in October 1959 for service with a detachment of Waffenschule 10 at Norvenich in early 1960. The surviving 21 F-104Fs were eventually withdrawn from operations with WS 10 in mid-1972.

F-104G features

While the F-104G retained all the basic design features and contours of the original Starfighter, extensive internal redesign was necessary to accommodate the completely new all-weather multi-role nav/attack systems developed from 1958 Lockheed studies for optimised individual tactical (F-104-7) and advanced air superiority (F-104-9/11) roles. German engineers had taken part in these studies, which had started in 1956 when Lockheed had begun seeking international partners, and helped to define the systems specifications for the F-104G (for Germany), the heart of which was the new F-15A NASARR search and range radar and fire-control computer, developed by North American Aviation's Autonetics Division.

The F15A-41B version selected for German F-104Gs, which initially had to use the earlier -31MC, was optimised in two basic air-to-ground and air-to-air modes, for bombing and navigation, and target interception, respectively, and was also capable of providing datalink information read-out. Similar multi-role NASARR versions in other NATO F-104Gs were designated F15AM-11, but Canadian CF-104s (with their initial nuclear role) used the R24A NASARR with only air-to-ground functions, while Japan's F-104Js were fitted with the air-to-air optimised F15J-31. For air-to-ground operation, NASARR provided ranging information for visual bombing computation, ground-mapping for all-weather bombing and navigation, contour mapping for navigation, and terrain-avoidance for low-level approaches to target areas.

In air-to-air modes, the F-15A provided radar search, acquisition and automatic tracking of air targets to achieve the capability for lead-collision attack with automatic missiles release; lead-pursuit interceptions using the 20-mm Vulcan cannon, in conjunction with the director-type gunsight which replaced the disturbed reticle computing sight fitted to earlier F-104s; and pursuit attack with missiles. The F-104G's weapons sight incorporated a basic infra-red facility with common optics developed by Lockheed at Burbank, to confer some night-sighting capabilities. The simple IR sight is capable of detecting targets over considerable distances, while also providing measurement of angular target movement after initial radar contact.

Inertial navigation

Apart from its IR sight, the F-104G was also one of the first combat aircraft to make use of an inertial navigation system – the new Litton LN-3 – which was to encounter major development problems in meeting its specified design goals of a 1 nm (1.15 miles/1.85 km) maximum deviation per flying hour, and a 200-hour mean time between failures (MTBF).

In the air defence role the F-104G was restricted to the use of AIM-9s. Its acceleration and climb rate made it an excellent interceptor over short ranges. This Fokker-built Dutch aircraft wears the parrot badge of 322 Sqn, one of two assigned an air defence mission within the KLu structure.

Far removed from its original role as a tactical nuclear bomber, this CF-104 (wearing the 'X' badge of the AETE) demonstrates the use of rocket pods. The provision of only two underwing pylons significantly hampered the Starfighter in conventional air-to-ground operations.

Left: Now preserved in the Canadian National Aviation Museum, 12700 was the F-104A (ex-56-0770) converted by Lockheed with some of the features of the F-104G. It was used to set a Canadian altitude record of 100,110 ft (30513.5 m) in 1967, this aircraft being chosen as it was considerably lighter than the standard CF-104. It was officially designated CF-104A.

Canada adopted the Starfighter to fulfil its tactical nuclear strike role in Europe, and apart from a training squadron all were based in either France or West Germany. The first Canadian aircraft was the aerodynamic prototype of the F-104G, converted by Lockheed. This went to Canadair as a CF-104A pattern aircraft for the Canadian production line, which produced 200 aircraft for the RCAF, in addition to others under MAP funding. With the Canadair company designation CL-90, they were initially given the military designation CF-111, but this was changed to CF-104 in line with other users. West German officials visited Ottawa in 1959 to establish a standardised variant for both customers, and the CF-104 was very similar in most respects to the F-104G. However, the designation CF-104G was never applied to Canadian aircraft.

Above: All of Canada's 38 CF-104D two-seaters were built by Lockheed. This example served with 417 Operational Training Squadron at Cold Lake, Alberta, the operational conversion unit. This was formed out of 6 Strike-Recce OTU. Canada received two standards of two-seater: the CF-104D Mk 1 was intended only for OTU use while the Mk 2s were dual-role operational aircraft for 1 CAG.

A CF-104 from 439 Sqn returns to Baden-Söllingen after a low-level training mission. The Starfighter pilot usually employed a long, flat approach.

During qualification trials involving some 1,500 one-hour F-104G flights in 1964, the LN-3 achieved its design performance in only 3 per cent of its sorties, with an MTBF of 18.3 hours, added to which it exceeded its 77-lb (35-kg) design weight by no less than 22 lb (11 kg).

Other new systems included an AiResearch air data computer, a lightweight Computing Devices of Canada automatic position and homing indicator (PHI) linked with the usual military TACAN installation, and a Minneapolis Honeywell MH-97G automatic flight-control system. All this equipment, together with the F-104G's new 8-ft (2.5-m) filament-wound glass-fibre radome produced by Lockheed in Burbank, and a full-scale Super Starfighter cockpit mock-up, was developed and tested in a company-operated Douglas DC-3, which made about 50 flights during an intensive 16-week programme. Most of the F-104G's electronics are located beneath the aft section of the cockpit extending for about 5 ft (1.52 m) along the fuselage, with upward-hinged semi-circular-section access doors, the various components being packaged in quickly-changeable modules known as 'jeep-cans'.

Strengthened airframe

These new avionics accounted for all but about 350 lb (159 kg) of the 1,000-lb (454-kg) increase in empty weight of the F-104G, which rose to 13,592 lb (6165 kg), the remainder comprising airframe reinforcements to meet fighter-bomber strength requirements with full external loads, and allow high-speed low-altitude ground attack and nuclear penetration/strike missions. For these, provision was made for installation of an inflight-refuelling

After 1972 1 CAG crews practised conventional interdiction missions, mostly at low level. The Canadian NASARR weapon system was optimised for the air-to-ground mission, with terrain avoidance and ground mapping functions. CF-104s received extra defensive avionics, resulting in prominent RWR fairings being added either side of the jetpipe and under the nose.

probe on the port side of the cockpit, but this was rarely fitted, if only because few of the NATO Starfighter operators then had the necessary tanker aircraft.

A total of 36 new forgings was required to reinforce such major structural items as fuselage mainframes, wing fittings and beams, fuselage longerons, joints and tail frames, empennage beams and ribs, plus some fuselage skins. Some reinforcement was also made of the trailing-edge flap fittings to allow partial deflection to 15° during combat, allowing reductions of up to 33 per cent in turn radius, according to Lockheed, at altitudes of around 5,000 ft (1525 m).

At 54 ft 9 in (16.69 m), the F-104G fuselage length was similar to that of earlier Starfighters, although the new design featured installation of the extended fin and powered rudder of the two-seat F-104B/D versions with some 25 per cent greater area than the vertical surfaces of the F-104A/C, for improved directional stability at high Mach numbers. With the extra area, the irreversible hydraulically-powered rudder of the F-104G provided both directional control and yaw damping, eliminating the separate yaw damper tab of earlier Starfighters, and gave it the characteristic rudder overhang, first seen on the F-104B/D, above the variable nozzle of the improved 15,800-lb (70.28-kN) thrust J79-GE-11A turbojet. The servo mechanism of the stabilator was also modified to achieve increased hinge moments, the hinge and operating controls then being contained within the empennage contours, thus avoiding external fairings normally used to cover these items.

An F-104A-15-LO (56-0770) was modified by

Above: In order to get the Starfighter into Luftwaffe service as quickly as possible, Lockheed built 96 F-104Gs before European production could start. Intended for service with JBG 31 (hence the 'DA' code), the majority remained in the US to form the core of the 4510th CCTW at Luke AFB.

Lockheed to have the new and bigger tail surfaces and other modifications to become the prototype L.683-10-19 Super Starfighter, although it lacked the internal airframe strengthening and many of the systems of the definitive F-104G. In its revised form, it made its first flight at Palmdale on 1 September 1960 in Royal Canadian Air Force colours as the prototype CF-104. The aircraft was retained for at least a year by Lockheed on Super Starfighter development trials, including the installation of a Vinten Vicom ventral reconnaissance pod. The first true Canadair-built CF-104 (12701) with the full 'G' systems and the RCAF's specified runway arrester hook came off the Cartierville assembly line for shipment to Palmdale to make its initial flight on 18 March 1961. The real and fully modified prototype F-104G (WkNr 2001), flown by Lockheed for the first time on 5 October 1960, was also the first of the initial German order for 66, costing DM5.2 million (about $1.3 million) each. Even before development testing had been completed at Palmdale in 1962, production deliveries had started in May 1961.

With the same five wingtip, underwing and central fuselage stores attachment points as the F-104C, the F-104G has a slightly higher maximum take-off weight of 28,580 lb (12965 kg). To cope with the extra landing weight and higher approach speeds, larger wheels were fitted, the brakes were made fully powered and incorporated a new anti-skid system, and the tail braking parachute diameter increased from 16 to 18 ft (4.87 to 5.48 m). Standard escape installation in the F-104G was the Lockheed C-2 rocket-boosted ejection-seat, cleared for use at all altitudes down to ground level at speeds between 90 and 550 kt (103 and 631 mph; 165 and 1015 km/h), although when Denmark ordered F-104Gs in 1962 it specified installation of the Martin-Baker Mk Q7 ejection-seat with full zero-height zero-speed capabilities. Oddly enough, the first 15 German F-104Gs started life with an earlier and less capable Martin-Baker Mk Q5 seat, but were then changed back to the Lockheed C-2 after a government decision in Bonn.

In 1964, when Saudi Arabia was looking for a Mach 2 fighter, Lockheed proposed a stripped version of the F-104G, without the NASARR fire-control system, designated the F-104H. A two-seat TF-104H was also offered to the RSAF, which finally selected the twin Avon- and radar-equipped BAC Lightning.

F-104G airfield concern

Although the F-104 was seen by some German politicians as a convenient entry into NATO's nuclear club, only 560 or so of Germany's first 700 Starfighters (the 'Super' appellation was soon dropped) were equipped to carry the 1-MT nuclear store. A maximum of 250 Luftwaffe Starfighters was actually committed to NATO's nuclear forces, which would therefore have involved all six F-104G fighter-bomber wings, each of which was allocated 50 B-43 tactical nuclear weapons. At the peak of the Cold War in the mid-1960s, each of the fighter-bomber wings maintained a 24-hour force of six nuclear-armed Starfighters on Quick Reaction Alert, fuelled and ready to take off to attack previously designated targets within 17 minutes of authorisation. On each of the German F-104 bases concerned, including Büchel, Lechfeld, Memmingen, Nörvenich and Rheine, were also four USAF officers with the necessary dual keys to arm the American-owned nuclear weapons before the QRA aircraft could be scrambled.

F-104G service clearance was completed by JBG 31 by early 1963, and the main production batches in Europe and the US had been almost completed by late 1965. As early as mid-1966, however, the NATO Council meeting in Paris urged Bonn to abandon the Starfighter's nuclear role, and use the aircraft instead for conventional ground support. The nuclear tasks then performed by the Luftwaffe's F-104s would be taken over by a German-manned force of 72 Pershing 1A SSM launchers with a 435-nm (500-mile/805-km) range, and also equipped with US nuclear warheads,

Another expedient measure was the supply of 30 Lockheed-built F-104F two-seaters to the Luftwaffe to allow conversion training to begin prior to the delivery of the full-standard TF-104G. The F model had the J79-GE-11A engine and some G systems, but not the strengthened airframe. The F-104F was used initially to form a Lockheed-manned training detachment at Palmdale, the first pilot to solo being Lt Col Günther Rall, the third-highest scoring World War II ace with 275 victories. The F-104Fs then went to Waffenschule 10 at Nörvenich ('BB' code) to continue conversion of Luftwaffe pilots.

Canadian special schemes

417 Operational Training Squadron – CFB Cold Lake

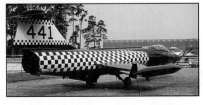

421 'Red Indians' Sqn – 30 years, 1983   *441 'Silver Fox' Sqn – Baden-Söllingen*

One example was produced of the Canadair CL-41R, converted from the second CL-41 trainer prototype. First flying as such on 13 July 1962, the CL-41R was intended to operate as a low-cost trainer for the CF-104/F-104G. A full NASARR system could be accommodated in the nose.

Flying over the unfamiliar terrain of Greece, one of 1./MFG 2's RF-104Gs displays the four-tank ferry fit. The German navy reconnaissance aircraft were among the most capable, being fitted with a variety of sensors, including side-looking cameras.

although this changeover was not implemented until 1971 to meet the new NATO concept of flexible response.

Of the initial 700 F-104Gs ordered by Bonn, 605 were allocated to the Luftwaffe, comprising 395 fighter-bomber versions, 107 as interceptors and 103 RF-104Gs for tactical reconnaissance. The remaining 95 F-104Gs went to the Marineflieger, which also had seven of the 137 TF-104G trainers eventually ordered from Lockheed, with German industrial participation, as a follow-on to the first 30 F-104Fs. Fly-away unit cost of the last batch of 33 TF-104Gs was $2.1 million. The unexpectedly heavy accident rate (then totalling 91 aircraft) necessitated a resumption of German production by MBB, to meet a late 1968 Federal Defence Ministry order for another 50 F-104Gs as attrition replacements, at a cost of DM350

million ($87.5 million). These were delivered between November 1970 and March 1973, most (36, serialled 7401-36) going to the Marinefliegergeschwadern. They increased overall German Starfighter procurement to 917, costing $1.488 billion, of which almost exactly half was spent in the US.

The German Defence Ministry was much concerned in the 1960s with the vulnerability of its airfields to WarPac air and missile attacks, and had studied several techniques to operate its combat aircraft from short and semi-prepared airstrips. Inputs to these studies included several Lockheed proposals for V/STOL adaptations of the F-104 to meet NATO's ambitious 1961 NMBR-3 requirement for a supersonic vertical take-off fighter with a 250-nm (287-mile/463-km) radius of action with a 2,000-lb (907-kg)

NATO photo-birds

Although the USAF cancelled its batch of RF-104A aircraft, the Starfighter found favour among other users as a natural tactical short-range reconnaissance platform. Its steadiness, speed and low-level flying qualities were appreciated by most of the European operators. Sensors could be carried in a variety of ways: downward-looking cameras or infra-red linescan could be mounted on a pallet in the lower forward fuselage, necessitating the removal of the cannon. Alternatively, sensors could be externally mounted in pods, this providing greater flexibility and the ability to fit forward oblique cameras. The German navy RF-104G aircraft added the capability to carry side-looking cameras in a bay behind the cockpit.

Above: The side window of this 116 Pterix RF-104G reveals it to be an ex-MFG 2 aircraft. The 'RF' buzz-code was rarely seen.

Above left and left: Canadian CF-104s used for reconnaissance were fitted with a conformal Vicon pod. This housed up to four Vinten 70-mm cameras, including a forward-oblique unit. In 1 CAG the RCAF had two squadrons assigned to reconnaissance – Nos 439 and 441.

Below: An RF-104G of 1. Staffel/MFG 2.

306 Sqn shouldered the KLu's reconnaissance effort. In addition to dedicated RF-104Gs (above), the squadron also used F-104Gs wired to carry the Orpheus sensor pod, seen below on an Italian RF-104G.

(nuclear) warload. These included projects with GE J85 lift engines in swivelling pods at the wingtips, both with and without the normal propulsion powerplant. Another V/STOL project, undertaken jointly with Short Brothers in Belfast and based on the latter's SC.1 research aircraft experience, was known as the CL-704. This involved the installation of no fewer than seven of the proposed 2,600-lb (11.57-kN) Rolls-Royce RB.181 lift engines with variable inlet shutters and vectoring nozzles, plus fore and aft fuel tanks in large wingtip pods. Perhaps optimistically, as Dassault could later confirm from its V/STOL Mirage programmes, Lockheed claimed that the CL-704 would require few other F-104 modifications, apart from a strengthened wing structure and associated engine and reaction controls. A more powerful and economical Rolls-Royce RB.168R or scaled-down Spey turbofan would have replaced the J79 for propulsion, but the V/STOL F-104s were destined to remain strictly paper projects.

SATS and ZELL

More technically attainable short-field techniques, in the Luftwaffe's projected Short Airfield for Tactical Support (SATS) programme, involved fitting three F-104Gs, including the renumbered DB+257 (13271), with catapult spools and underfuselage arrester hooks for accelerated take-off and wire-decelerated landing trials on Lechfeld airfield. Major components of the SATS system comprised the All-American Engineering CE1-3 catapult, powered by two converted GE J79-2 turbojets, and the Vortec Products Co M21 airfield arrester gear, in association with rocket-boosted zero-length launching (ZELL) from special 45° ramps, as the next best thing to VTO. Martin-Baker Mk GQ7(F) ejection seats with zero-zero capability had already been ordered in 1963 for nine West German F-104Gs for ZELL trials, which involved fitting an enormous jettisonable NAA Rocketdyne solid rocket developing no less than 120,000 lb (533.81 kN) of thrust under the rear fuselage. Originally developed for the aircraft-configured Martin TM-61 Matador nuclear cruise missile of the 1950s, this technique was later applied with M-34 rocket-boosters for zero-length launches of the Chance Vought KD2U-1 and NAA F-100.

For the first few seconds of the launch, the ZELL 104s flew purely ballistically, since their flight controls would not become effective until their stalling speed of about 150 kt (172 mph; 278 km/h) had been exceeded. The first zero-length take-off for the German programme was successfully achieved by this means at Edwards AFB by Ed Brown, a particularly intrepid Lockheed test pilot, in June 1963. US and German pilots (from JBG 32) undertook further ZELL tests at Lechfeld from 4 May 1966, remarkably without undue incidents, but both the SATS and ZELL programmes were later abandoned after German expenditure of more than $25 million.

A chapter of accidents

As by far the largest operator, Federal Germany ordered a total of 917 F-104s for the Luftwaffe (766) and Marineflieger (151) in the decade since the first F-104F was handed over at Palmdale to Major Fritz Paulo in October 1959, the last 50 attrition replacements being delivered from 1971 with uprated J79-MTU-J1K turbojets. Developing 15,950 lb (70.95 kN) maximum thrust, this engine had been developed by MAN Turbo (later MTU), which had taken over J79 licence rights from BMW. Afterburner improvements doubled the overhaul period from 400 to 800 hours, and the engine was scheduled for retrofitting to all West German F-104s.

The Tiger club

439 'Sabre-toothed Tiger' Sqn, CAF, early 1970s – with recon pod

No. 31 'Tiger' Sqn, 10 Wing, Belgian air force

335 'Tiger' Mira – Greek air force

21º Gruppo/53º Stormo – Italian air force

439 'Sabre-toothed Tiger' Sqn, CAF, 1980

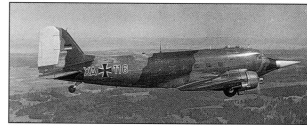

West Germany (above) used the C-47 as a trials aircraft for the NASARR radar system, the aircraft serving with the FVSt (Fernmelde Vermessungsstaffel). Canada had a similar aircraft (below), inevitably called Pinocchio.

Three F-104Gs from the Luke-based Luftwaffe training unit overfly the Arizona countryside. The unit had something of a split personality: to the US Air Force it was known as the 4510th Combat Crew Training Wing (later 58th TTW), to the Luftwaffe it was the 2 Dt.Lw. Aus.St.

Intensive flying operations with the F-104 did not start in Germany until 1961, when only two Starfighter crashes were reported. This total increased to seven in 1962, when only handful of the new aircraft were in service, increasing to 12 in 1964 and reaching a peak in the following year with around 28, or more than two per month. Engine problems, including continuation of the early difficulties with the J79's variable afterburner nozzle (which had resulted in an early 1967 decision to ensure the automatic closure of the afterburner eyelids in an emergency to avoid power loss) and contamination of the F-104's liquid oxygen system causing loss of consciousness, were listed among the main technical snags which contributed to 28.5 per cent of the accidents. These also included problems encountered with the automatic pitch-up limiter during low-altitude flying and in tight turns which resulted in its temporary removal, with accompanying restrictions on Starfighter manoeuvrability. Human error, however, was quoted as the cause of some 43 per cent of the accidents, casting suspicion on German Starfighter training of mainly conscripted ground technicians and aircrew (38-45 hours of maintenance being required for each flying hour), and the fact that Germany's F-104 pilots were only flying about 13-15 hours per month, compared with the monthly NATO average of around 20 hours.

German trainee pilots at that time graduated in the US to the Starfighter from Northrop T-38s in 125 hours flown on Luftwaffe TF-104Gs operated by the 4510th Combat Crew Training Wing at Luke AFB, AZ. German-built F-104Gs were also operated here, together with several supplied from MAP funding. Final F-104G training in European environment was given at Waffenschule 10 at Jever, but the sudden transition from the virtually cloudless desert skies of Arizona to typical Northern Europe weather, especially in the winter, was considered to be another major contributory factor to the FRG's Starfighter accident rate. In 1965, this reached the extraordinary figure of 83.6 per 100,000 flying hours, accompanied by pilot fatality rate of about 55 per cent. This was reflected in the total reached in mid-1966 of 61 German Starfighter crashes with the loss of 35 pilots, apart from about 20 F-104s

Luftwaffe training

European weather and operational restrictions posed a serious problem for the young Luftwaffe Starfighter force: with new aircraft being delivered daily, a massive pilot training programme was required to get them into service quickly. The sunny skies and large areas of clear airspace in Arizona provided the answer, so with US help the 4510th CCTW was established with 52 F-104Gs and 27 TF-104Gs. The first class started in 1964, and the training programme was further enhanced by the creation of the 3525th PTW at nearby Williams AFB with T-37s and T-38s. Following completion of the Luke course, F-104 pilots then went to WS 10 at Nörvenich (later Jever), for an introduction to the realities of European operations.

Above: The Luftwaffe training establishment underwent several unit numbering changes, having started as the 4512th, 4518th and 4443rd CCTS of the 4510th CTW. It subsequently became the 69th and 518th TFTS of the 58th TFTW, the wing then redesignating as the 58th TTW in 1977. Administration later passed to the 405th TTW. This aircraft above proudly proclaims its heritage of the 'Fighting 69th'.

Above: Aircraft 61-3076 was an obvious candidate for special markings during the United States' bicentennial celebrations in 1976.

Right: Despite their USAF titles and serials, the Luke Starfighters were paid for in Deutschmarks. The aircraft were retired in 1983.

Lockheed F-104G Starfighter

Jagdbombergeschwader 33
Büchel, West Germany

The most important role of the F-104G within Luftwaffe service was as a tactical nuclear bomber, serving with five heavy fighter-bomber wings. For much of its career, the Starfighter sat nuclear alert. Each wing kept six aircraft on a 17-minute readiness, armed with a 1-MT B43 bomb. The weapons were US-owned, and would require authority from both US and German governments for their use.

Jagdbombergeschwader 33

JBG 33 was formed in 1958 at Büchel, a base in the Eifel region near the Luxembourg border. The wing transitioned from F-84F to F-104G in 1962, and in addition to its mission aircraft operated four F-104Fs, eight F-104Gs and five Lockheed T-33As in support. The wing's badge depicted a diving eagle with a Starfighter silhouette superimposed (today replaced by a Tornado).

Production for the Luftwaffe

Luftwaffe F-104Gs came from all five production lines. Lockheed supplied 96 fighter-bomber F-104Gs, Messerschmitt built 127 fighter-bombers (and 14 from the follow-on MBB batch), Fokker built 100 fighter-bombers, 63 interceptors and 92 RF-104Gs, SABCA produced 32 interceptors and 56 fighter-bombers, while Fiat was responsible for 15 interceptors and eight RF-104Gs. These figures do not include those delivered to the navy, or the 30 F-104Fs and 130 TF-104Gs delivered to the Luftwaffe, all of which were built by Lockheed.

Configuration

This aircraft is shown in maximum range loadout with four external tanks. The single 1-MT B43 nuclear bomb would have been carried on the centreline.

Sub-system production

As part of the massive European production effort, many of the F-104G sub-systems were also built or assembled in Europe. The key components were, with original US manufacturer and European licensee in parentheses: air data computer (AiResearch/Interaero), autopilot (Minneapolis Honeywell/Honeywell GmbH), bomb timer (Lear/Lear GmbH), engine (General Electric/BMW, FN, Fiat), IFF (Hazeltine/Siemens and Halske), INS (Litton/Litton GmbH), IR sight (Lockheed/Eltro, Oude Delft), launch distance computer (General Electric/Allgemeine Elektricitats), NASARR (Autonetics/Telefunken, MBLE, HSA, Fiat), nav computer (Computing Devices Canada/Teldix-Luftfahrt-Ausrustungs), optical sight (General Electric/Allgemeine Elektricitats), TACAN (IT&T/Standard Elektrik Lorenz) and UHF (Collins of Canada/Van der Heem). West German companies took the bulk of the sub-system work. Roughly 18 per cent of all the components were supplied direct by the US manufacturers, 10 per cent were assembled in Europe from US-supplied kits, and the remaining 72 per cent was wholly European-built.

Arrester hook

The field arrester hook was for use with runway arrester wires in the event of an emergency, the hook being stowed on the starboard side of the ventral fin.

Conventional attack

In addition to the nuclear role, the F-104G could drop conventional weapons and fire unguided rockets. The Vulcan cannon was a useful strafing weapon.

ZELL

Worried by the vulnerability of its airfields, the Luftwaffe investigated the Zero Length Launch system as a means of dispersing its Starfighters around the country. In time of tension, the concept envisaged fleets of nuclear-armed F-104Gs being trucked out into the countryside, to be mounted on pre-positioned ramps. The aircraft would launch under the power of a huge Rocketdyne motor, which would take the F-104G safely to flying speed before dropping away. Recovery was to be made at hastily-prepared landing strips (perhaps using the *autobahnen*) fitted with runway arrester gear for short landing (SATS). The ZELL system was comprehensively tested following work in the US with F-100 Super Sabres, but was eventually cancelled along with SATS.

From 1966, ZELL testing was accomplished at Lechfeld, home of JBG 32. Two of the wing's aircraft were assigned to the project (DB+127 and DB+128).

Lockheed pilot Ed Brown demonstrates a ZELL launch from Lechfeld. The launch and rocket angle were critical to avoid the F-104 pitching forward or too far back.

VFW built the ZELL ramp at Lechfeld for the German tests, which involved both Lockheed and JBG 32 pilots. The steps were needed for access to the cockpit.

DA+102 was the third Lockheed-built Starfighter for the Luftwaffe, assigned to JBG 31. It was used for the initial F-104G ZELL trials which were undertaken at Edwards AFB from June 1963.

written off in ground accidents. This resulted in the eventual resignation at that time of the Luftwaffe chief, General Werner Panitzki, after he had criticised the FRG's Starfighter procurement programme as 'a political decision'.

His successor, Lieutenant General Johannes Steinhoff, who had flown Me 262 jets in combat during World War II, had earlier complained about the Bonn Defence Ministry's failure to implement the recommendations of his 1964 report on F-104G survival measures, and was on record as having opposed Starfighter procurement in such large quantities in the late 1950s. He considered at that time that the Luftwaffe could cope with only about 250 Starfighters, and subsequently became one of only four German senior officers above the rank of colonel to have flown the F-104G.

One of his first moves was to review its escape system to improve the survivability rate from the Starfighter's predominantly ultra-low-level operations. The Lockheed C-2 ejection seat initially fitted to Belgian, Canadian, Dutch and Italian, as well as the German Super Starfighters, had been developed by November 1966, to have zero-zero

capability by the installation of the more powerful Talley Corp 10100 rocket booster, Weber gun-deployed drogue parachute and improved seat/man separation. Despite rocket-sled tests up from 200 to over 500 kt (230 mph to 575 mph; 370 to 926 km/h) and the installation of these modifications in the C-2 seats of all the F-104Gs in Europe, the Talley rockets were found to have destabilising effect after ejection, and had to be removed.

Martin-Baker seats

After the German Starfighter had been grounded once again for modifications to the C-2 seats in December 1966, when the 16th crash in that year brought overall accident losses to 65, acrimonious arguments between the rival Lockheed and Martin-Baker factions in the Bonn Defence Ministry and the Luftwaffe finally culminated in a $2.387 million contract being placed on 8 March 1967, to re-equip the entire 770-strong German F-104G force with British Mk GQ7A zero-zero ejection seats. This took little more than year from the programme start in October 1967, as evidenced by the fact that when the first recorded

A Starfighter seen in its most natural element: over the forests and farmland of West Germany. On 1 January 1968 the Luftwaffe introduced a new tri-service serial system, dispensing with the old unit codes. F-104Gs were recoded in serials according to manufacturer as follows: 20+01 to 20+84 (Lockheed); 20+85 to 21+32 (Fiat); 21+33 to 23+26 (Messerschmitt); 23+27 to 25+55 (Fokker) and 25+56 to 26+37 (SABCA), while the two-seaters became 27+01 to 28+35 (Lockheed TF-104G) and 29+01 to 29+21 (Lockheed F-104F).

use of a GQ7 seat from German F-104G took place in ground-level runway overshoot at Ramstein on 24 September 1968, about 70 per cent of Germany's Starfighters had been so modified. This was reported at the time to be the 90th German F-104G crash, involving the loss of 44 pilots, and was followed by another successful GQ7 ejection on the same day from 6,000 ft (1830 m). Apart from Denmark and Germany, only Greece and Italy, among NATO's F-104 operators, specified for their Starfighters Martin-Baker ejection seats, in the form of HQ7As and IQ7As respectively, which then cost little more than $3,000 each. Turkey accepted whatever seats were in the F-104s it was given, and so operates a mixture of Martin-Baker Mk 7As and Lockheed C-2s, as does Taiwan.

Coincidentally with the new training techniques and procedures introduced by General Steinhoff, the German Starfighter accident rate dropped by about 50 per cent to only eight or so aircraft in 1967, or a more modest 12.6 per 100,000 hours. This reduction proved only temporary, and from 1968 to 1972 varied between 15 to 20 per year. The latter figure, in 1971, included no fewer than seven crashes in less than a month, increasing to 11 in 12 weeks.

In September 1969, General Steinhoff quoted the German Starfighter inventory as comprising 607 F-104Gs, 130 TF-104Gs and 21 F-104Fs, indicating apparent losses of some 93 single-seat versions, seven TFs and nine F-104Fs, up to that time, or 109 aircraft in all. Thereafter, progressive rundown of Starfighter operations as a result of re-equipment with McDonnell Douglas F-4F and RF-4E Phantoms resulted in annual crash rates averaging nine to 11 aircraft until the early 1980s, when all German F-104Gs began to be replaced by Tornados.

Disparate figures

Some confusion was caused at about this time by a change in the official totals quoted from Bonn for German F-104 accidents. Although records existed of at least 220 crashes to the end of 1980, when total losses (including about 21 on the ground from fire and other causes) reached the figure of 200 on 21 June 1978, official announcements then began quoting only the number of aircraft destroyed in flying mishaps. In the early 1980s this total also exceeded 200, so separate German figures were quoted for F-104s written off in Europe and with the training unit at Luke AFB in the US until its closure at the end of 1982. By late

From their two bases in northern Germany (Schleswig and Eggebeck), the Starfighters of the German navy were in the front line of the Cold War in the Baltic Sea. Here examples from 1./MFG 2 (RF-104G, background) and 2./MFG 2 (F-104G) illustrate the two major roles which concerned the force: maritime strike and maritime/littoral reconnaissance.

German special schemes

JBG 34 at Memmingen

Above and right: MFG 2 'Vikings' display team

JBG 32 at Lechfeld – 1983

JBG 31 F-104G painted to resemble 'Red Baron'

JBG 34 at Memmingen

JBG 33 at Büchel – retirement ceremony 1985

JBG 31 at Nörvenich – retirement ceremony

25th anniversary of LWS 11 – MFG 2 aircraft, last LVR 1 aircraft (silver) and LWS 11 special

Designed with high-altitude operations in mind, the Starfighter made the transition to low-level work easily. Thanks to its low wing loading the ride close to the ground was very smooth, while the NASARR radar of the F-104G introduced a terrain avoidance function. Demonstrating the aircraft's speed at low level is an aircraft from WTD 61, the German test centre.

November 1981, overall German Starfighter losses, including those on the ground, therefore actually totalled 244, of which 203 were in Europe and 41 in the US, together with 105 downed pilots. By 26 August 1982, overall German Starfighter losses had grown to 252 aircraft, although the rate per 100,000 flying hours had dropped from 14.7 in the 1970s to around 10. This was still about twice the 1981 average for USAF combat aircraft, but was well below the percentages of many other NATO F-104 operators. Between 1962 and 1985, Canada gained the unenviable record of losing just over 50 per cent of its 200 single-seat CF-104s in flying accidents, while Italy's overall losses for its Starfighter fleet have so far amounted to 37.5 per cent. The Luftwaffe had suffered 36 per cent attrition with the Republic F-84F, as the Starfighter's predecessor, in nine years of operation; Belgium had lost over 53 per cent of its similar aircraft.

Although the last Starfighter retired from German front-line service with JBG 34's 342 Staffel at Memmingen on 16 October 1987, some half a dozen F-104Gs and four TF-104Gs, gradually reducing to three Gs and one TF, continued flying with WTD 61 at Manching for another three years or more on various avionics trials and systems development programmes. By the time Lieutenant Colonel Armin Ewert made the final flight of a German Starfighter (26+60) from Manching on 22 May 1991, overall losses, including about 30 on the ground, totalled no fewer than

270, or 29.44 per cent of the original total, killing 110 pilots. The last German Starfighter loss appeared to be that of TF-104G in the circuit at Manching on 16 April 1989, from which both pilots ejected safely.

A record interlude

Starfighters were used from time to time by one or two civilian pilots to set new world speed records, notably by the renowned US aviatrix Jacqueline Cochrane. She alternated with her equally famous French counterpart, Jacqueline Auriol in a Mirage III, in setting new standards for women pilots over a 54-nm (100-km; 62-mile) closed-circuit in borrowed USAF Starfighters, including 1,203.68 mph (1937.08 km/h) in a TF-104G on 1 May 1963, and 1,303.24 mph (2097.30 km/h) in an F-104G on 1 June 1964. Her fastest speed in 1964 was 1,429.3 mph (2300.17 km/h) over 15/25 km (8/13.5 nm; 9.3/15.5 mile) course in a TF-104G. Another Starfighter speed record, this time a strictly private venture, resulted from the remarkable achievement of sometime Lockheed test pilot Darryl Greenamyer in building his own F-104 from surplus parts to attack the FAI absolute low-altitude speed record. Greenamyer had already succeeded in finally shattering Fritz Wendel's straight line world speed record of 469.22 mph (755.12 km/h) (established on 26 April 1939 in the much-modified Me 209V-1 prototype at Augsburg) when he flew a souped-up Grumman F8F-2 Bearcat to 482.462 mph (776.426 km/h) at Edwards AFB on 16 August 1969. He then sought to achieve the double speed crown with a jet, and began collecting F-104 components in 1964.

It took him over 12 years and $200,000 to complete the civilianised F-104RB *Red Baron*, which he powered with a borrowed GE J79-17/1 turbojet from a McDonnell Douglas Phantom, developing over 2,000 lb (8.9 kN) more thrust than the then-standard Starfighter engine. After many vicissitudes, he finally made four consecutive

Backbone of the Luftwaffe

With the introduction of the F-104G, the Luftwaffe became virtually a 'one-aircraft air force', and the Starfighter can lay claim to being the first truly multi-role warplane. The bulk of the Luftwaffe's force was tasked with nuclear strike (with secondary conventional attack roles), these duties embracing the activities of five wings (JBG 31, 32, 33, 34 and 36). Two wings each were assigned to the vastly different roles of air defence (JG 71 and 74) and tactical reconnaissance (AKG 51 and 52) with no airframe changes and only minor system differences. In addition, the type provided type training in its two-seat form (WS 10). The extent of its versatility can be realised when compared with the vaunted follow-on 'Multi-Role Combat Aircraft' (Tornado), which in the event was not a satisfactory replacement for the F-104 in the air defence role. Phantoms were purchased to fill this particular gap.

Above: Waffenschule 10 handled the operational portion of the F-104 training programme.

Above: This TF-104G served with JG 71 'Richthofen', one of two air defence wings.

Right: The black panther badge identified AKG 52, one of two Luftwaffe recon outfits.

Below: Streaming a brake chute, an F-104G of JBG 34 comes to a halt. This was the last fighter-bomber unit to operate the F-104G.

runs at about 100 ft (30.5 m) above the 3-km (1.8-mile) course at Mud Lake, near Tonopah, Nevada. On 24 October 1977, only about five weeks after his first flight in the F-104RB, he set a new FAI record of 988.26 mph (1590.41 km/h). He remained well supersonic and not above 100 m (327 ft) for most of the 20-minute flight, which consumed 850 US gal (3218 litres) of fuel. In the following year, Greenamyer planned to attack the 123,523 ft (37650 m) world altitude record then held by the USSR with an E-266M (MiG-25). During a preliminary flight on 26 February 1978 one undercarriage leg failed to extend, and he was forced to eject. That was the end of the F-104RB, of which only its Lockheed C-2 ejection seat then remained. This had been bought by Greenamyer from surplus stores for the princely sum of $50, undoubtedly the most rewarding investment he would ever make.

F-104S: The last of the breed

On 13 December 1965, Lockheed announced the completion of 2,200 Starfighters of all types for the air forces of 14 countries since the start of the programme. This was soon to move into a further phase with the production of the new F-104S, developed by Lockheed as one of its CL-980 design studies to meet the AWX (all-weather interceptor) requirements of the Italian air force. The F-104S (S for Sparrow) was selected by the AMI for this requirement after extensive evaluation of contemporary designs, including the Dassault Mirage III, McDonnell Douglas F-4, Northrop F-5 and North American F-100, to achieve BVR interception capability using Raytheon AIM-7E Sparrow III-6B semi-active radar guided air-to-air missiles. For this it required a more powerful and versatile multi-mode radar and fire-control system, in the form of NAA's new NASARR R21G/F15 installation, while retaining most of the F-104G's avionics, including an upgraded Litton LN-3-13 inertial platform but not its 20-mm Vulcan cannon for interception roles, the space being required for Sparrow guidance systems.

Other changes were otherwise small, apart from installation of the J79-GE-19 (redesignated J79-J1Q in NATO use) turbojet requiring auxiliary inlet doors and developing 13 per cent more power, or 17,900 lb (79.63 kN) for take-off, combined with 11 per cent lower cruise specific fuel consumption than the J79-GE-11A. Provision was also made for the new Lockheed SR-2 ejection seat with full zero-zero capability, although the AMI refused to change from the Martin-Baker IQ7A it had originally specified for its F-104Gs.

The F-104S had more underwing and fuselage stores attachments, including two extra fuselage pylons beneath the intakes, increasing total strong-point provisions, with the wing-tip stations, to nine; more fin and rudder area; new automatic pitch control (APC) system; and two additional anhedralled rear stabilising surfaces supplementing the original single under fin. From an empty equipped weight of 14,900 lb (6760 kg), the F-104S can carry up to 5,850 lb (2653.5 kg) of internal fuel, and with 7,000 lb (3175 kg) of external stores, the max take-off weight becomes 31,000 lb (14060 kg), resulting in wing-loading of 158 lb/sq ft (770 kg/m²). Tests were made by the RSV of an F-104C-type refuelling probe, but this has yet to be used by the AMI on the F-104S.

Most of the Italian aerospace industry participated in the F-104S programme, after the engineering and production design, prototype development and flight-testing had been completed by Lockheed at its Burbank and Palmdale factories. The first of two F-104S prototypes, converted

Although it served first, saw action and served longer with other users, the Starfighter is best remembered as a German aircraft. This 'lizard' camouflaged example was one of the last, flying with WTD 61 at Manching.

Lockheed F-104 Starfighter

A T-171E3 Vulcan is shown with its Gatling gun ancestor. The original caption described the scene as: 'Something old, something new, something borrowed ... and something capable of blasting hostile aircraft right out of the blue'.

The Vulcan cannon was redesignated M61, and was fitted to all Starfighters apart from the RF-104G, CF-104 and F-104S, although both the latter two acquired the gun later in their careers.

The wingtip was stressed for the carriage of either a fuel tank or for launching Sidewinder missiles. The latter required dedicated launch rails.

Aeritalia/Lockheed F-104S Starfighter

1 Pitot tube
2 Radome
3 Radar scanner dish
4 R21G/H multi-mode radar equipment
5 Radome withdrawal rails
6 Communications aerial
7 Cockpit front bulkhead
8 Infra-red sight
9 Windscreen panels
10 Reflector gunsight
11 Instrument panel shroud
12 Rudder pedals
13 Control column
14 Nose section frame construction
15 Control cable runs
16 Pilot's side console panel
17 Throttle control
18 Safety harness
19 Martin-Baker IQ-7A ejection seat
20 Face blind seat firing handle
21 Cockpit canopy cover
22 Canopy bracing struts
23 Seat rail support box
24 Angle of attack probe
25 Cockpit rear bulkhead
26 Temperature probe
27 Nosewheel doors
28 Taxiing lamp
29 Nosewheel leg strut
30 Nosewheel
31 Steering linkage
32 AIM-7 Sparrow avionics (replacing M61 gun installation of strike model)
33 Inertial platform
34 Avionics compartment
35 Avionics compartment shroud cover
36 Cockpit aft glazing
37 Ram air turbine
38 Emergency generator
39 Avionics compartment access cover
40 Fuselage frame construction
41 Pressure bulkhead
42 Ammunition compartment auxiliary fuel tank (101.5-Imp gal/462-litre capacity)

43 Fuel feed pipes
44 Flush-fitting UHF aerial panel
45 Anti-collision light
46 Starboard intake
47 Engine bleed air supply to air conditioning
48 Gravity fuel fillers
49 Fuselage main fuel tanks (total internal capacity 746 Imp gal/3391 litres)
50 Pressure refuelling adaptor
51 Intake shock cone centre body
52 De-iced intake lip
53 Port intake
54 Shock cone boundary layer bleed
55 Boundary layer bleed air duct
56 Auxiliary intake
57 Hinged auxiliary intake door
58 Navigation light
59 Leading-edge flap jack
60 Intake trunking
61 Fuselage main longeron
62 Wingroot attaching members
63 Intake flank fuel tanks
64 Wing-mounting fuselage mainframes
65 Control cable runs
66 Electrical junction box
67 Dorsal spine fairing
68 Starboard inboard pylon
69 Leading-edge flap (lowered)
70 AIM-7 Sparrow AAM
71 Missile launch rail
72 Starboard outer pylon
73 Tip tank vane
74 Tip tank latching unit

75 Starboard wingtip tank
76 Fuel filler caps
77 Starboard aileron
78 Aileron power control jacks
79 Power control servo valves
80 Fuel lines to auxiliary tanks
81 Flap blowing duct
82 Starboard blown flap (lowered)
83 Engine intake compressor face
84 Intake spill flaps
85 Aileron torque shaft
86 Hydraulic reservoir
87 Air conditioning bleed air supply pipe
88 General Electric J79-GE-19 turbojet
89 Engine withdrawal rail
90 Starboard airbrake (open)
91 Fin root fillet

92 Elevator servo controls
93 Elevator/all-moving tailplane hydraulic jacks
94 Push-pull control rods
95 Tailfin construction
96 Fin tip fairing
97 Tailplane rocking control arm
98 Starboard tailplane
99 One-piece tailplane construction
100 Tailplane spar
101 Tailplane spar central pivot
102 Fin trailing-edge construction
103 Rudder construction
104 Rudder power control jacks
105 Rudder servo valves
106 Exhaust shroud

107 Fully-variable afterburner exhaust nozzle
108 Fin attachment joints
109 Fin-carrying mainframes
110 Afterburner duct
111 Nozzle control jacks
112 Steel and titanium aft fuselage construction
113 Rear navigation lights
114 Aft fuselage attachment joint
115 Brake parachute housing
116 Port airbrake (open)
117 Airbrake scissor links
118 Fuselage strake (both sides)

119 Emergency runway arrester hook
120 Airbrake jack
121 Air exit louvres
122 Primary heat exchanger
123 Wingroot trailing-edge fillet
124 Flap hydraulic jack
125 Flap blowing slot
126 Port blown flap (lowered)
127 Aileron servo valves
128 Aileron power control jacks

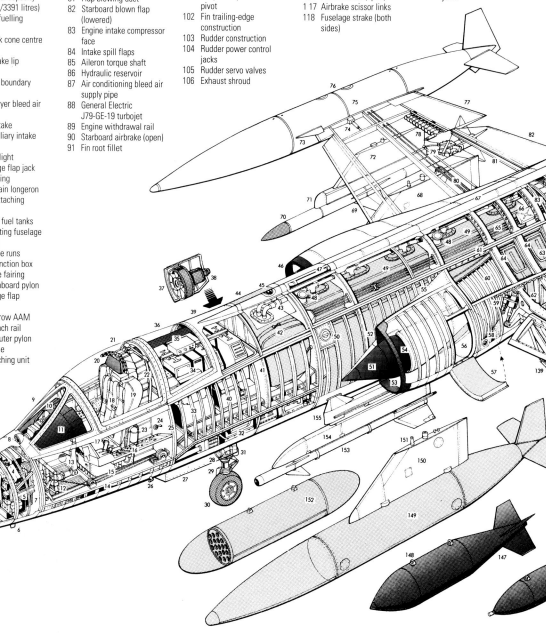

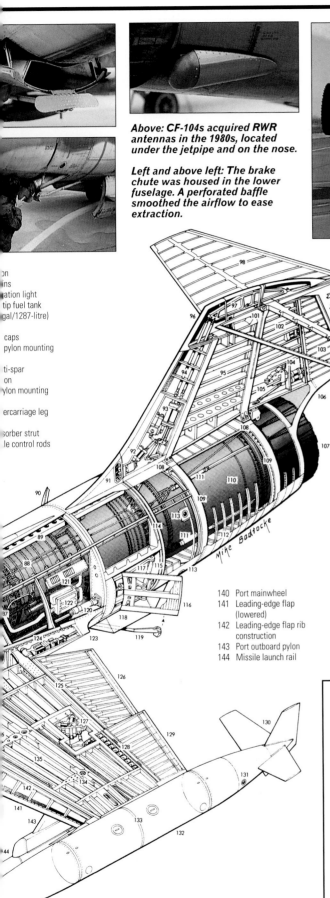

Above: CF-104s acquired RWR antennas in the 1980s, located under the jetpipe and on the nose.

Left and above left: The brake chute was housed in the lower fuselage. A perforated baffle smoothed the airflow to ease extraction.

For engine maintenance or exchange, the entire rear fuselage/fin assembly was removed on a trolley. This aircraft is being prepared for an engine run, the field arrester hook being used as an attachment point for a hold-back cable.

The original two-seater canopy (seen here on an F-104D) consisted of two halves with no centre section. Note the optional fixed refuelling probe.

The second-generation two-seaters (TF-104G and CF-104D) had a strengthened canopy offering far greater protection for low level birdstrikes. The main difference was the fixed centre section.

on
ins
ation light
tip fuel tank
gal/1287-litre)

caps
pylon mounting

ti-spar
on
ylon mounting

ercarriage leg

sorber strut
le control rods

Mike Badtocke

140 Port mainwheel
141 Leading-edge flap (lowered)
142 Leading-edge flap rib construction
143 Port outboard pylon
144 Missile launch rail

145 Port AIM-7 Sparrow AAM
146 Mk 82 500-lb (227-kg) bomb
147 Mk 83 1,000-lb (454-kg) bomb
148 Bomb mounting shackles
149 Auxiliary fuel tank (163-Imp gal/740-litre) capacity
150 Port inboard wing pylon
151 Pylon attachments
152 LAU-3A 2.75-in (70-mm) FFAR pod (19 rockets)
153 AIM-9 Sidewinder AAM
154 Missile launch rail
155 Fuselage stores pylon adaptor

Experimental variants

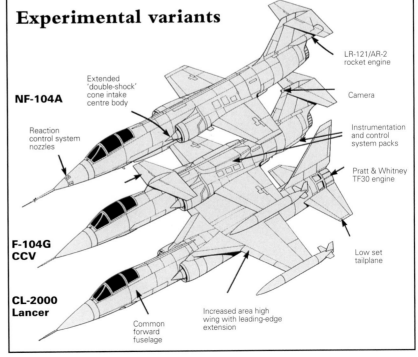

NF-104A

Extended 'double-shock' cone intake centre body

Reaction control system nozzles

LR-121/AR-2 rocket engine

Camera

Instrumentation and control system packs

Pratt & Whitney TF30 engine

Low set tailplane

F-104G CCV

CL-2000 Lancer

Common forward fuselage

Increased area high wing with leading-edge extension

Red Baron record breaker

The remarkable Darryl Greenamyer built the one-off F-104RB from spare parts, making the aircraft the world's fastest 'homebuilt'. It was produced with the principal aim of capturing the world low-level speed record, which was easily achieved in October 1977 at a staggering speed of nearly 1,000 mph. With this primary goal safely netted, Greenamyer went in search of the absolute altitude record, attainable by zoom climbing. This record was to remain in Soviet hands after he was forced to eject from the *Red Baron* during a practice flight prior to the record attempt.

Right: A close-up of the Red Baron reveals the flamboyant paint scheme applied to the aircraft. The artwork depicted Greenamyer in 'Kaiser'-style helmet riding an F-104.

Left: The F-104RB streaks across Mud Lake during the record attempt. This dry lake was just to the southeast of Tonopah, Nevada, and had earlier been the site of a much publicised crash landing by the North American X-15.

Below: The Red Baron was stripped of any non-essential equipment, and had an uprated Phantom engine installed.

from AMI F-104Gs (MM 6648/6660) with the new J79-GE-19 powerplant, although lacking the full systems installation, and intended only for aerodynamic evaluation, made its initial 75-minute flight from Palmdale on 22 December 1966, reaching a speed of Mach 1.4. The second prototype, which followed in March 1967, retained the F-104G's J79-GE-11A engine but had the full mission system avionics. Even before its development trials had started, however, a letter of intent was received by the Fiat group from the Italian Defence Ministry in January 1966, for the production of an initial batch of 82 F-104S Starfighters, with options for 83 more.

The full programme for the initial 165 F-104S aircraft, which subsequently materialised, was costed at L=225 billion (then $360 million), representing an overall unit cost of L=1.366 billion ($2.18 million), including spares and technical support. While contributing only 60 per cent of the programme costs, with the US providing the rest, Italian industry was responsible for 65 per cent by value of F-104S production, mostly involving the airframe, compared with its 65 per cent funding of the AMI's F-104G programme, with 35 per cent from the US. Fiat also signed a contract in early 1966 with GE International to produce 43 per cent of 250 J1Q engines for the

F-104S programme, while Selenia undertook licensed production of the Sparrow III AAM, for which BPD was commissioned to deliver 1,000 Mk 38 solid rocket motors. FIAR of Milan signed an agreement with NAA's Autonetics Division to co-produce over 200 NASARR R21-G radars for an overall cost of $8.2 million, with the US company providing only the first 12 systems from November 1967.

While prototype development continued, the Fiat group flew its first production F-104S in the four-year programme on 30 December 1968, with deliveries starting in the spring of 1969 to equip eight multi-role squadrons, although the first 40 aircraft were completed as fighter-bombers, apparently without their full air defence systems and equipment. In the early 1970s, AMI orders for the F-104S were increased by another 40 to 206, extending production to 1979, (plus 40 ordered by Turkey from October 1974) and these eventually equipped seven interception and three AMI fighter-bomber squadrons.

Budget economies which stretched the development programmes for new aircraft resulted in 1981 approval for a major weapons system upgrade (Aggiornamento Sistema d'Arma/ASA) programme for 153 of the AMI's remaining F-104S aircraft to extend their operating lives to

The F-104S was fitted with the uprated J79-GE-J1Q engine, with a significant increase in thrust to offset the extra weight of the variant and to increase warload.

While radically upgrading its front-line Starfighters with the introduction of the F-104S, Italy initially made no attempt to improve the TF-104G. However, 15 were upgraded to TF-104G-M standard with the avionics of the F-104S/ASA-M upgrade. These veterans are still in demand to provide training for new crews, serving with 20° Gruppo/4° Stormo at Grosseto as the type OCU.

Right: F-104S/ASA aircraft from 9° Stormo line the ramp at Bitburg during a NATO exercise.

Below: The Aspide 1A missile was tested on the first F-104S by the RSV (Reparto Sperimentale en Volo) prior to issue to ASA units.

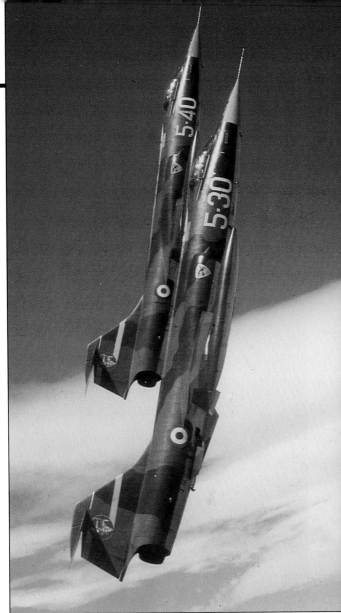

at least the turn of the century. Main changes progressively undertaken by Aeritalia, which completed its 100th upgrade to F-104S/ASA standard only in early 1990, include FIAR modifications of the original NASARR radar to the R–21G/M1 Setter system, from the addition of moving target indicator (MTI) conferring look-down/shoot-down capabilities, and automatic frequency changing. New avionics also include four-digit NATO IFF and improved weapons computer, plus provision for the use of all-aspect IR-homing AIM-9L Sidewinder and longer-range radar-guided Selenia Aspide 1A AAMs, in place of the original rear-attack AIM-9Bs and AIM-7E

Civilian Starfighters

Left: Some Starfighters are civilian-owned, but are stored for future use or as spares sources for other flying aircraft. This F-104A has languished at Mojave for some years.

In addition to the well-known Red Baron racer of Darryl Greenamyer, several Starfighters have found their way into civilian hands, although used for quasi-military purposes rather than as supersonic playthings. The aircraft work chiefly as testbeds for government/military contracts, or as chase/photo ships for other test programmes.

Above: A key feature of the F-104S is the addition of two extra ventral fins either side of the original. This pair displays the 'Diana the Hunter' badge of 5° Stormo on the tail, and the black greyhound badge of 23° Gruppo on the intake.

Left: Northern Lights Aircraft Inc. operated this suitably registered CF-104D on government tasks but is no longer trading. The company was based at Eden Prairie, Minnesota.

Below: The ex-Northern Lights F-104 was re-registered N166TB when it passed to Thunderbird. The company runs a sizeable fleet of ex-military types, providing a useful test facility for military programmes.

Left: Four extra pylons were added to the F-104S, two underwing for Sparrow carriage and two on the fuselage for AIM-9s.

Below: Further improvement came with the ASA upgrade, which added Aspide capability and the ability, as demonstrated here, to carry the all-aspect AIM-9L version of the Sidewinder.

Faced with a need to update its air defence forces, and provide them with a medium-range radar-guided missile, the AMI selected an upgrade of the Starfighter as the most cost-effective solution. Lockheed developed the upgrade, and converted the first two prototypes from Italian air force F-104Gs undergoing overhaul with 3° Gruppo Efficienzi Velivoli at Cameri. All subsequent production was undertaken by Aeritalia (and associated Italian Group companies), with final assembly at Caselle. The

F-104S was a major update to the original aircraft, and was optimised for air defence, using a NASARR that could provide continuous-wave illumination for the AIM-7E Sparrow missile. Extra pylons were added underwing to mount these weapons, but in order to accommodate the associated 'black boxes' the cannon had to be omitted. Extra keel area was added by the fitment of a slightly larger fin and two small ventral strakes to augment the existing unit.

Above: This aircraft, MM6658, was the first of two AMI F-104Gs converted to S standard by Lockheed, seen on the occasion of its first flight from Palmdale on 22 December 1966. The '5-41' codes were from its previous operational career.

A trio of F-104S Starfighters holds immaculate formation on a TF-104G of the Luftwaffe's JBG 34. In AMI tradition the aircraft wear the Stormo badge (51° – black cat chasing three mice) on the fin and the Gruppo badge (22° – pipe-smoking scarecrow) on the intake. The unit has flown the Starfighter at Treviso since 1969, and has notched up over 20 years's service on the F-104S alone.

Sparrow IIIs. Other armament changes in the F-104S/ASA include restoration of the 20-mm Vulcan cannon, and provision for the possible launch of AS 34 Kormoran anti-ship missiles. The 147th and final ASA was redelivered in 1993.

Studies continued for still further F-104S improvements through Operational Capacity Extension (ECE) proposals, to include new radar, head-up display and flight-refuelling probe, to extend Italian Starfighter service lives beyond even the then planned 2005, as back-up in the event of further delays or cancellation of the EFA programme. Following the early 1992 criticisms by AMI C-in-C General Stelio Nardini of Italian air defence shortcomings from reliance on only the present F-104S and Nike Hercules SAMs, further upgrading seemed likely. The result was the F-104ASA-M programme, which builds upon the ASA update with further enhanced air defence capability. This entails the replacement of radio and

navigation systems with those from the AMX. New equipment includes LN-39A2 INS, GPS and TACAN, although the latter two items are not integrated with the INS. Wiring, cabling and hydraulic systems were renewed as a safety measure, and the ALQ-70 self-defence system was removed. Forty-nine F-104S/ASAs were upgraded, together with 15 TF-104Gs (to be known as TF-104G-M) to provide sufficient aircraft for four squadrons and an OCU. The first F-104S/ASA-M flew at Torino-Caselle on 31 July 1995 and deliveries began in December 1997.

Projects cancelled

The increases in performance offered by the J79-J1Q in the F-104S, including a claimed reduction of 16 per cent in take-off run; 40 per cent less in the time to zoom to 82,000 ft (24993.6 m); 100 per cent increase in supersonic climb rate; and 12 per cent more ferry range compared with the F-104G, impelled Lockheed to offer the new design for wider sales as the CL-901. Further stimulus for this project resulted from the 1966 Soviet announcement of its plans to supply 100 more MiG-21s to North Vietnam to help counter USAF B-52 and F-105 attacks.

Lockheed therefore co-operated with Tactical Air Command to modify an F-104C (tail number 12624) with a J79-GE-19 turbojet, the new tail assembly and extra lateral rear-fuselage fins of the F-104S, plus modified NASARR F-15J radar similar to that in Japan's F-104J interceptors, to produce a prototype CL-901 as 'an unsolicited contractor proposal' for an interim air superiority fighter pending planned deliveries of the MDC F-4E Phantom. The CL-901 actually made its first flight a couple of months before the first F-104S, in September 1966, and Lockheed and the USAF completed their evaluation after 59 flights, mostly from Palmdale but including two from Edwards AFB, in the three months by the end of that year.

Although the USAF requested quotations for blocks of

Lockheed F-104S Starfighter 22° Gruppo, 51° Stormo Treviso/Istrana

The F-104S entered service in 1970, and thanks to two upgrade programmes (ASA and ASA-M) has served in the air defence role into the 21st century with four squadrons (9°, 10°, 18°, 23° Gruppi) plus the OCU (20° Gruppo). The AMI also operated the F-104G and RF-104G in the fighter-bomber and reconnaissance roles, although these were fully replaced by the Tornado and AMX by 1993.

Fuel

Internal fuel consists of 746 Imp gal (3391 litres) in the main fuselage tanks and 101.5 Imp gal (462 litres) in an auxiliary ammunition bay tank. Standard tip tanks each hold 283 Imp gal (1287 litres), while the underwing drop tanks hold 163 Imp gal (740 litres) each.

Markings

The black cat chasing three mice is the badge of 51° Stormo, applied on a grand scale to this Starfighter although it was only featured on one side of the aircraft. The starboard side has the standard AMI dark green/dark grey disruptive camouflage, with neutral grey undersurfaces. Worn on the starboard intake is the scarecrow badge of 22° Gruppo.

Radar

The F-104S initially featured the FIAR-built NAA Autonetics R-21G/F15 NASARR, this providing the ability to launch the semi-active Sparrow missile. In the ASA programme the radar was updated by FIAR to R-21G/M1 Setter standard, this adding automatic frequency-hopping and a moving target indicator, conferring look-down/shoot-down capability.

Italian Starfighter production

The Italian Group was the fourth and last of the European production lines to be established, with Fiat (later retitled Aeritalia) as the lead contractor. Alfa Romeo and Macchi were key sub-contractors, while Fiat built the J79 engine and provided final assembly and flight test facilities at Torino-Caselle. This group built 200 F/RF-104Gs during the initial production run, of which 50 went to West Germany and 25 to the Netherlands. The AMI also received 24 Fiat-assembled TF-104Gs (and later some ex-German aircraft). With F-104G production complete, Aeritalia proceeded with the F-104S, of which 246 were built. The first 40 were not fully equipped for air defence duties and were used as fighter-bombers. Turkey's 40 F-104S interceptors were interspersed through the production run.

Pylons

The F-104S has a total of nine hardpoints. Two under each wing are for fuel/bombs (inner) and Aspide/AIM-9 (outer). The wingtips usually mount tanks, as does the centreline. Two AIM-9 rails are located below the intakes.

F-104S weapons

Although it could carry the same range of free-fall weapons as the F-104G, the F-104S was primarily a fighter. The basic air defence configuration consisted of two AIM-9Bs and two AIM-7Es, the latter built under licence by Selenia. The ASA upgrade introduced the AIM-9L and Aspide 1, the latter being a developed version of the AIM-7E with a new CW monopulse seeker head with home-on-jam capability, improved ECCM, active radar fuse, longer range (35 km/22 miles) and new wing control actuators. Aspide entered service on the F-104S/ASA in 1988.

Cannon

In order to accommodate extra fuel and avionics, the F-104S dispensed with the cannon, the port being faired over (as on this aircraft). The effect of miniaturisation on avionics allowed the ASA programme to reinstate the gun.

Above: A pair of 203 Hikotai F-104Js launches from Chitose. The Japanese Starfighters were never intended for anything other than air defence, and consequently their NASARR radar (F15J-31) had virtually no air-to-ground capability.

Above: The F-104G enjoyed a long career with the Italian air force, mainly on fighter-bomber duties once the F-104S had been brought into service. 132° Gruppo/3° Stormo flew the variant until 1990.

After Lockheed had built three pattern F-104Js for the JASDF interceptor requirement, assembly switched to Mitsubishi, which produced 29 further aircraft from Lockheed-supplied kits before full licence production got under way. A total of 210 single-seaters was produced, augmented by 20 Lockheed-built but Mitsubishi-assembled F-104DJ two-seaters.

up to 1,000 CL-901s from Lockheed, which promised production within 13 months from go-ahead if air-to-air combat losses proved excessive in Vietnam, cost studies apparently showed that an all-Phantom force rather than a mix would be preferable. The CL-901 preceded 10 or more J79-19/J1Q-powered design studies at this time, however, as Lockheed sought to stretch the Starfighter concept still further, and capitalise on the F-104 licensed production organisations in three continents.

F-104J replacement plans

The CL-934 project was effectively an air defence-optimised version of the CL-901, with J79-J1F turbojet developing the same 17,900 lb (79.65 kN) of thrust for take-off as the J1Q, which was offered to Japan as an F-104J follow-up in mid-1966. A ground-attack variant of this project, the CL-984, was proposed to NATO at this time with a claimed maximum speed of Mach 2.4, although apart from its NASARR F-15A radar, it seemed to differ little from the F-104S. Some sources, however, claimed that its wing area would have been substantially

A wind tunnel model (right) and full-scale mock-up (below) of the proposed CL-1200 Lancer (note the 'Skunk Works' figure on the intake). Apart from the Mach 2.7 X-27 design, the Lancer represented the ultimate development of the F-104 airframe. After losing a 1974 fighter competition to the Northrop F-5E the project was shelved.

increased to around 275.5 sq ft (25.5 m²), remarkably without an apparent increase in span. A single photograph issued by Lockheed in early 1966 purporting to show CL-984 appeared to be an unmodified F-104G in German military markings with two F-104S-type additional weapons pylons beneath the intakes, supplementing four underwing and the centre-fuselage pylon points for over 7,000 lb (3175 kg) of external stores. According to Lockheed, European interest in the CL-984 resulted in the despatch by Belgium and the Netherlands of evaluation teams to Burbank for technical briefings.

This interest resulted in a tailored variation of this project in the form of the CL-985B (for Belgium), which Lockheed proposed to the FAB in mid-1967 as a co-production programme in conjunction with the similar F-104S in Italy to share lower units costs. It was to have involved 104 aircraft to replace the Belgian Republic F-84 fleet. Differing from the F-104S only in the elimination of the all-weather avionics for the Sparrow AAMs, plus the specified increase in wing area; nine weapons pylons for extra strike capacity; and replacement of the Litton INS by a Doppler nav system, the CL-985B was claimed to have an 84 per cent commonality with the F-104G, but

Turkey received over 400 Starfighters, although only a proportion were in use at any given time, the others being held in storage or as spares sources. Apart from 40 F-104S and 52 F/RF/TF-104Gs, all were second-hand transfers from a variety of NATO members.

Right: Not all of Turkey's Starfighters came from other countries. This unpainted example was from the THK's first batch, supplied direct from the manufacturers (Canadair and Lockheed) with MAP funding. 4 AJU was the first recipient, equipping 141 and 142 Filo.

Left: Some 60 two-seaters were eventually received by Turkey, including some CF-104Ds.

Right: These RF-104Gs wear the anti-corrosion grey scheme applied by their original operator, Norway.

Above: Ex-CAF CF-104s line up for stream take-off, each carring practice bombs. The CF-104 was the last variant in THK service, the aircraft having been upgraded by their former operator with defensive systems.

Left: Six of the 40 F-104S fighters purchased by Turkey await delivery outside the Caselle factory. Although both 142 and 192 Filo also operated this model, it was 191 Filo at Balikesir that was the principal operator. As part of the F-104S deal, Turkey purchased Selenia-built AIM-7E Sparrows to arm its Starfighters.

eventually lost out in the US and NATO to the simpler Northrop F-5.

The proposed CL-958 version broke new ground in extending the fuselage length by some 6 ft (1.82 m) to 60.94 ft (18.57 m), increasing the empty weight to 15,775 lb (7155 kg) and the clean take-off weight by some 4,000 lb (1814 kg), which would have been mainly fuel, to 25,345 lb (11496 kg). This would have resulted in a maximum range of 1,861 nm (3448 km) with drop tanks, although external stores capacity would have been reduced to 5,593 lb (2537 kg). More fundamental changes were proposed for the CL-981 studies, which specified an F-22B fire-control radar, but represented the first real attempt to redress the F-104's critical lack of wing area. Apart from a 5-ft 6-in (1.67-m) increase in span from previous F-104s to 27 ft 6 in (8.38 m), the CL-981 wings would have had much wider chord, with substantially bigger leading- and trailing-edge flaps. Wing area would have been increased by some 27 per cent to 250 sq ft (23.226 m²), with an aspect ratio of 3.0 instead of 2.5, and corresponding gains in low-speed and short-field performance, plus claimed maximum speed of Mach 2.4 and range increase to 1,939 nm (3593 km) with drop tanks. Airframe weight would have been only slightly heavier than the F-104S at 22,000 lb (9979 kg), but several alternative powerplants were considered for the CL-981, including the Rolls-Royce RB.168 Military Spey.

Supersonic canards

Apart from F-104S-type rear-fuselage strakes, another feature of the 1965 CL-981 projects was the provision of folding swept canard surfaces immediately behind the cockpit, for extension at supersonic speeds. According to Lockheed, these were provided 'to boost the aircraft's acceleration, climb and manoeuverability'. This early example of jet fighter canard technology was aimed at

joint Canadian/US proposals for an advanced FX close-support aircraft, as well as German requirement expressed by Luftwaffe chief General Werner Panitzki, before his 1966 resignation, for 150 more F-104S-type Starfighters for air defence roles, and converting 400 F-104Gs to similar standards.

Coming at the height of Germany's F-104 crash crisis, these proposals were received less than rapturously in Bonn's official circles, which have since rejected out of hand any single-engined combat aircraft. The Luftwaffe's interceptor requirement were then fulfilled within couple of years by orders for F-4F Phantoms, after Lockheed had

The book on the Starfighter's long German career was eventually closed on 22 May 1991 when this aircraft flew for the last time. The final handful served with WTD 61 (previously E-Stelle 61), the central German trials unit at Manching.

Above: A weapon rarely seen on Starfighters was the AGM-12 Bullpup, seen here in its live version on a 116 Ptérix F-104G. The aircraft was one of nine transferred from the Spanish air force.

Greece was another nation eager to gain cast-off Starfighters, although not in the numbers of neighbour and rival Turkey. In the foreground here is an ex-German navy RF-104G.

also made unsuccessful offers for the licensed production of up to 165 new Goodyear AN/APQ-102 SLAR and camera-equipped RF-104G-1s, powered by J79-GE-19 engines and also with terrain-following radar. The MBB group also submitted proposals to modify the 120 or so TF-104Gs then in German service as RTF-104G-1s, with similar sensors and powerplants. Some reports claimed that several TF-104Gs were so equipped for the covert radar mapping of Eastern Germany. Lockheed certainly confirmed that "side-looking radars had been tested in German air force Starfighters, which had shown the capability of skirting the borders of an unfriendly country,

mapping the terrain and transmitting the electronic data to strategically-positioned ground stations."

Canards were later fitted to the Starfighter under rather different circumstances, when an F-104G (98+36, formerly 23+91) was modified by MBB as part of a five-year research programme into control-configured vehicle (CCV) and fly-by-wire technologies involving electronic stabilisation, in preparation for the EFA project. Work

Italian special schemes

37º Stormo – 50th anniversary

4º Stormo – 60th anniversary

51º Stormo – 50th anniversary

3º Stormo – 30,000 hours

23º Gruppo, 5º Stormo – 75th anniversary

102º Gruppo, 5º Stormo – 25 years of F-104

5º Stormo – 100th ASA upgrade, 200th ASA hour

51º Stormo special 1995 (22º Gruppo special colours on other side)

12º Gruppo, 36º Stormo – 50,000 hours

28º Gruppo, 3º Stormo – Villafranca

22º Gruppo, 51º Stormo – Treviso/Istrana

4º Stormo – Grosseto. Ferrari 'twin' 1989

102º Gruppo, 5º Stormo – 100,000 hours, 50th anniversary, 26 years of F-104

20º Gruppo, 4º Stormo – 75,000 hours

CCV – forerunner of EFA and X-31

MBB was interested from an early date in high agility in fighter design. Replacing natural stability with computer-controlled fly-by-wire systems allowed the aircraft itself to be made unstable. This natural instability could then be controlled to provide considerable extra agility. The F-104CCV was a proving vehicle for MBB's fly-by-wire control system, intended for forthcoming highly-agile fighters such as the Eurofighter. The transition from the naturally stable Starfighter aerodynamics to those of a very unstable machine were made gradually, using increasing amounts of ballast to alter the centre of gravity. A complete F-104 tailplane section was then grafted to the spine forward of the wing to further destabilise the aircraft. The data gathered proved of great assistance in the design of the EFA, and was also employed during the development of the Rockwell/MBB X-31 super-manoeuvrable testbed.

Right: The CCV featured a long instrumented nose probe with vaned accelerometers to provide highly accurate measurements in all three axes. Calibration marks allowed precise observation from the ground and chase aircraft.

Above: The CCV aircraft was a Fokker-built F-104G which had previously served with JG 71 as an interceptor. It first flew with the triple-redundant fly-by-wire system in 1977, adding the destabilising tailplane section on the spine in 1980. Fairings were added over the wings and the aircraft was marked with extra Dayglo panels for high conspicuity.

on installing digital triple-redundant electrically-signalled controls and quadruplexed flight computers started in December 1974, and the F-104CCV made its initial take-off with these systems in conventional configuration exactly three years later. From its original 20 per cent positive stability, the F-104CCV was then flown at progressively increasing rearward CG positions, initially by means of ballast under the rear fuselage, to decrease its longitudinal stability. This became virtually neutral by late 1979, with the installation of canard surfaces (actually an F-104G stabilator), on a fin mounting behind the cockpit, being flown for the first time on 20 November 1980, in this configuration. Further aft ballast was then added until 20 per cent negative stability was finally achieved within the specified limits of Mach 1.3 and 650 kt (1204.58 km/hr) by the time the trials were successfully concluded after some 120 flights. The F-104CCV was then transferred to the Wehrtechnisches Museum in Koblenz.

The Lancer

Continuing the apparently endless J79-GE-19-engined projects of the mid-1960s, there appeared to be few differences from the F-104S, apart from internal systems and the installation of NASARR F-15J radar instead of the R-21G in the CL-1007, and the 1,000 lb (454 kg) lighter CL-1010, both of which were offered for follow-on orders to Japan. Also proposed was the CL-1010-II, with the big wings and F-22J radar. The CL-1195 offered to NATO (and particularly the Netherlands) in late 1969 also featured the CL-981's bigger wings, for which Lockheed had then completed wind-tunnel tests, but Kelly Johnson then undertook the first major redesign of the Starfighter with the CL-1200, or Lancer. In the CL-1200-1, this still retained the now well-developed J79-GE-19 in an F-104-type fuselage extended by 30 in (76 cm) to almost 57 ft (17.37 m). The much bigger wing, still with leading- and trailing-edge flaps, plus inner strakes and spanning some 29 ft (8.84 m), now surmounted the fuselage well to the rear. Stabilator surfaces on the engine thrust line were designed to avoid the downwash effects from the high-set wings at 'extreme attitudes', and eliminate the Starfighter's inherent pitch-up problems.

Although outwardly and in performance an entirely new aircraft, the CL-1200, according to Kelly Johnson, was designed to save costs and make maximum use of systems and components already developed and in wide-scale production for the F-104, with at least 75 per cent commonality. While optimised as 'a dogfighter' for air-to-air combat, for which Johnson claimed that it would be superior to any known fighter, including the MiG-21, the CL-1200 could undertake close air support or interdiction missions or other roles, with extreme flexibility. The CL-1200-2 was proposed with the F-111's considerably more powerful Pratt & Whitney TF30-P-1 or JTF22 turbofans, conferring 30-50 per cent performance improvements within the same max take-off weight of 35,000 lb (15876 kg), of which 6,500 lb (2948 kg) would have been internal fuel. Initial deliveries were promised for 1974, but having lost out to the Northrop F-5-21 in the USAF's 1970 International Fighter Aircraft Competition, and finding no takers in NATO, the CL-1200 was never built. A Mach 2.6 version known as the X-27 was also

Below left: As the Starfighter entered the 1990s, just Italy, Taiwan and Turkey were left operating the type. Turkey was the first to go, its last 'Stars' giving way to F-16s in 1995.

Below: Japan's last operational F-104Js were retired in 1986, leaving a few flying with the Air Proving Wing, the Self Defence Force's central trials unit. Here one of the APW survivors is seen at the unit's Gifu base.

Above: Taxiing at its base at Taoyuan, this is one of the RF-104G 'Stargazers' assigned to the 12th Special Missions Squadron. Some of these aircraft were modified to house LOROP cameras.

Below: The RoCAF's aircraft, like this TF-104G, were housed in well-camouflaged shelters.

Taiwanese '104s

Taiwan was the first location for the Starfighter in a combat scenario (1958 Quemoy Crisis), and more than 200 were supplied from various sources, including Japan. In the mid-1990s the island was still home to a sizeable force. Most were used in the air defence role, more recently with the locally-developed Sky Sword family of missiles. A handful of RF-104G 'Stargazers' handled Taiwan's reconnaissance effort. Deliveries of Ching-Kuos, F-16s, RF-5E 'TigerGazers' and Mirage 2000s allowed the retirement of the Starfighter, the final in-service aircraft being the RF-104Gs.

For all of their career the Taiwanese Starfighters served in variations of an all-over light grey scheme. This offered low conspicuity against a sky background, while the paint had anti-corrosion properties, necessary for continued operations in a maritime environment. Mirage 2000s replaced the last of the air defence F-104Gs with the Hsinchu-based 2nd/499th TFW from May 1997, while the RF-104Gs were finally retired in December 1998, after replacement by the Northrop RF-5E 'TigerGazer'.

projected, but this effectively and finally marked the end of further Starfighter development, as well as of an epoch-making programme involving over 2,500 aircraft, of which some 765 were built by Lockheed as design authority.

These comprised 296 of the original F-104As, Bs, Cs and Ds, as well as 469 F-104Fs (30), F/RF-104Gs (181), TF-104Gs (220) and CF-104Ds (38) for MAP and some European deliveries, the former including 46 F-104Gs and eight TFs for Taiwan. The latter country also received 21 RF-104Gs from the 140 single-seat Starfighters built by Canadair for US-funded MAP deliveries, in addition to the company's completion of 200 CF-104s for the RCAF. European Starfighter production eventually comprised 200 F-104Gs and 246 F-104S interceptors from the

Today, the Starfighter is a rare sight in the skies even singly or in pairs, so the sight (and sound) of a nine-ship is one to be savoured. Italy aims to keep its old soldiers flying into the next century, pending potential replacement by the EFA.

Above: When Taiwan retired its Starfighters, the F-104G's career was ended. Italy retired the last of its Gs (like this 3° Stormo machine) in 1993.

A fate which befell many F-104s was to be used as an airfield decoy. The strange machine at left is a 'Mirage F1', produced by rearranging the F-104A's tail-feathers and adding extra crude panels to the wings. It protects the Mirages of the RJAF based at Al Salti AB. The F-104G, below left, is seen being towed out on to Leeuwarden AB for decoy duties.

Fiat/Aeritalia-led Italian group; 350 from Fokker's Northern Group; 260 from Messerschmitt/MBB's southern German consortium; and 189 from the SABCA-led Western Group. To this total of some 2,350 complete aircraft, including new-built prototypes, must be added the licensed production in Japan of 210 F-104Js and 20 two-seat F-104DJ trainers, resulting in an overall total for the entire Starfighter programme of some 2,580 F-104s of all variants, including 359 two-seat trainers.

John Fricker

Below: 4° Gruppo F-104s fly formation with an RAF Tornado F.Mk 3. In a surprise move the AMI leased 24 RAF Tornados to allow two of its F-104S gruppi to convert, one in 1995 and one by 1997. This covered an air defence shortfall pending the delivery of Eurofighter.

Starfighter Colour Schemes

Belgium

Three-tone tactical camouflage (right)
This scheme was unique to Belgium, and was unusual in that the camouflage extended over the radome, which on most other Starfighters was painted dielectric grey or black. Serial presentation was in white. Aircraft often wore the wing badge on the fin, just forward of the fin-flash.

Initial deliveries (below)
When first delivered in 1963, Belgian F-104s were left unpainted, apart from the nose cone and anti-glare panel. Illustrated is the first Belgian aircraft, with outsize fin-flash (reduced in size on subsequent aircraft).

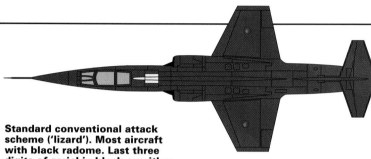

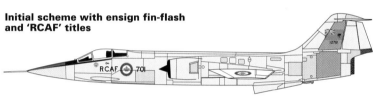

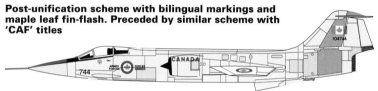

Canada

Owing to both political and tactical changes, the Canadian Starfighter fleet underwent several major paint scheme alterations during its operational career. Until 1972, most aircraft were flown unpainted and were originally delivered wearing 'RCAF' titles and the ensign fin flag. The latter subsequently changed to the current maple leaf insignia. On 28 February 1968, the RCAF was absorbed into the new Canadian Armed Forces organisation, reflected by a change to 'CAF' titles. In 1972 camouflage was adopted as the CF-104s switched from a nuclear to a conventional tasking. As the CF-104s were flown almost exclusively in an operational environment, squadron badges were rarely seen, usually only being applied for special occasions. Even after the nuclear role was relinquished, distinguishing unit markings remained a rarity.

Standard conventional attack scheme ('lizard'). Most aircraft with black radome. Last three digits of serial in black on either side of nose

Initial scheme with ensign fin-flash and 'RCAF' titles

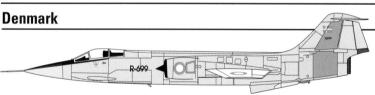

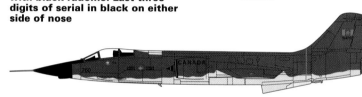

Post-unification scheme with bilingual markings and maple leaf fin-flash. Preceded by similar scheme with 'CAF' titles

Single-tone green wrap-round scheme introduced in 1972

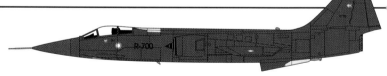

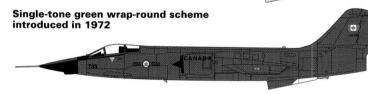

Denmark

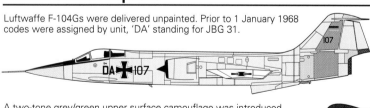

Danish aircraft were initially delivered in anti-corrosion grey and featured large national insignia.

Denmark received Canadian CF-104s in 1971, painted in wrap-round green. The rest of the fleet was painted likewise, all with small national insignia.

Federal German Republic

Luftwaffe F-104Gs were delivered unpainted. Prior to 1 January 1968 codes were assigned by unit, 'DA' standing for JBG 31.

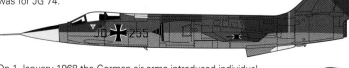

A two-tone grey/green upper surface camouflage was introduced in the mid-1960s, with a neutral grey underside. The 'JD' code was for JG 74.

Although the fuselage was largely unpainted, the wings of German Starfighters were initially painted white.

The grey/green tactical camouflage was highly effective in the Central European theatre. A feature of many Starfighters was the black anti-glare panel.

On 1 January 1968 the German air arms introduced individual aircraft codes. Starfighters were numbered in the sequence 20+01 to 29+21.

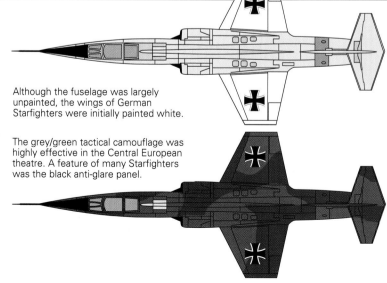

In the 1980s the Luftwaffe adopted a Tornado-style 'lizard' camouflage for its F-104Gs.

German navy Starfighters received a slate-grey upper surface for camouflage against the waters of the Baltic.

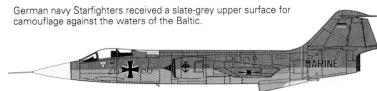

Greece

Greece acquired its Starfighters from several sources, the first being MAP-supplied aircraft delivered in natural metal. Later deliveries (from Germany, Spain and the Netherlands) arrived in their original schemes before being repainted in this tactical camouflage with light grey undersides and wavy demarcation.

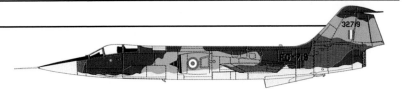

Italy

Although delivered in a natural metal finish, Italian Starfighters soon acquired a grey/green tactical camouflage which has been worn ever since. Large unit codes and national insignia were a feature for many years.

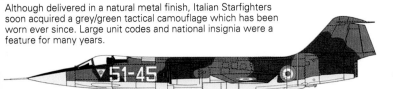

In the 1980s more restrained unit codes (in outlined light blue or black) and national insignia were introduced. Most aircraft wear the *Gruppo* badge on the intake and *Stormo* badge on the fin.

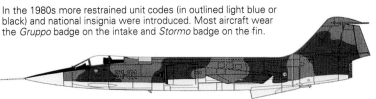

Japan

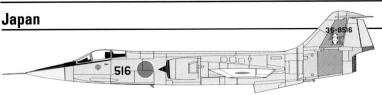

Initial deliveries were made in natural metal with white-painted wings. Colourful *Hikotai* markings were applied on the vertical fin.

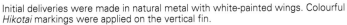

Natural metal later gave way to anti-corrosion grey for extended overwater operations. Some aircraft also picked up a black radome.

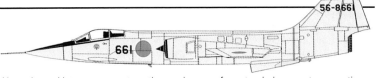

Jordan

Jordan's Starfighters were delivered in anti-corrosion grey. Unit insignia was not applied.

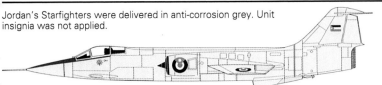

A three-tone camouflage was applied toward the end of the F-104's career, also wortn by airfield decoys still in use.

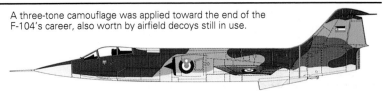

Netherlands

The first few F-104Gs appeared in grey, but the tactical camouflage (as introduced on the F-84 from 1959/60) was soon applied fleetwide. The scheme remained essentially the same throughout the Starfighter's career. Aircraft of the fighter-bomber and interceptor wings were maintained on a pool basis within each wing, and tended to wear the two consitutuent squadron badges, one on each side of the fin.

Standard NATO green/grey disruptive pattern upper surfaces

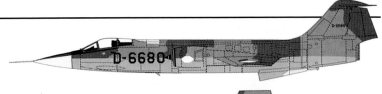

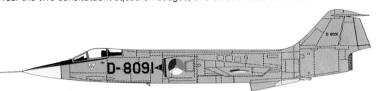

Original anti-corrosion grey scheme

Norway

Norway acquired a batch of RF-104Gs, and these first appeared in natural metal with high-visibility markings. The aircraft were painted grey soon after, and the colourful markings were withdrawn. Ex-Canadian CF-104s, which arrived in 1973, retained their CAF wrap-round green scheme.

Anti-corrosion grey

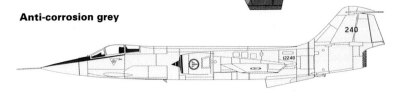

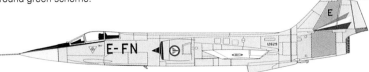

Original metal finish with wartime RAF-style squadron codes and fin-flash

CAF-style wrap-round camouflage

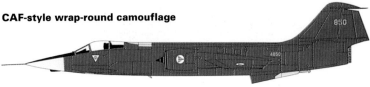

Starfighter Colour Schemes

Pakistan

Pakistan's Starfighters served in natural metal throughout their careers. They initially featured dielectric grey radomes with black anti-glare panel, but some later adopted black radomes with a dark green panel aft of the radome and along the cockpit rails.

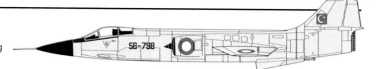

Spain

Anti-corrosion grey, retaining USAF buzz-number.

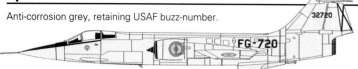

Natural metal, full Escadrón 104 codes

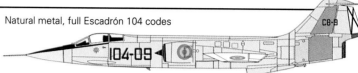

Taiwan

Taiwan's first aircraft were F-104A/Bs, and featured anti-corrosion grey in keeping with their overwater air defence role. The scheme included large national insignia and rudder stripes. The F-104Gs which followed were initially painted in a similar fashion, but the insignia was later made smaller and the rudder stripes dispensed with. Current survivors are painted in various disruptive patterns of two shades of light grey.

F-104A, initial delivery

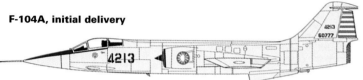

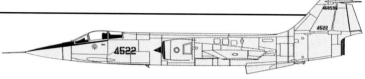

F-104G, after reduction in size of insignia

F-104G in current low-visibility two-tone scheme

Turkey

Coming as they have from a wide variety of sources, Turkey's aircraft show an even wider variation in schemes. Many reflect their former ownership, although some have been repainted. Some ex-Luftwaffe RF-104Gs were given an overall light grey scheme.

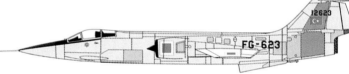

Initial batch, metal finish, square national insgnia

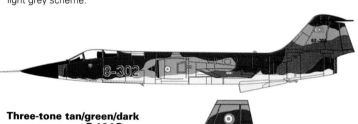

Three-tone tan/green/dark green on many F-104Gs, white outlined codes

Initial batch after national insignia changed to current roundel

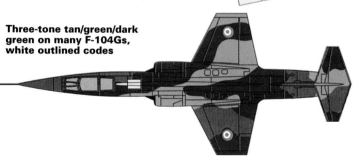

Standard NATO camouflage on many aircraft, white outlined codes

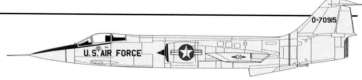

United States

For the early part of their careers, USAF Starfighters were unpainted, apart from the unit insignia. In the case of the 479th TFW these were very prominent. The first aircraft in Souitheast Asia served in the anti-corrosion grey scheme, but subsequent deployments featured aircraft painted in the standard three-tone tactical camouflage. The F-104Gs operated by the USAF on behalf of the Luftwaffe were unpainted with white wings. NASA aircraft wore variations on the Administration's house style.

Anti-corrosion grey applied to some aircraft

Most F-104A/Cs delivered and operated in natural metal (prototype illustrated)

Air National Guard aircraft mostly in natural metal

T.O. 114 tactical camouflage for service in Southeast Asia

NASA house colours

Early F-104 variants

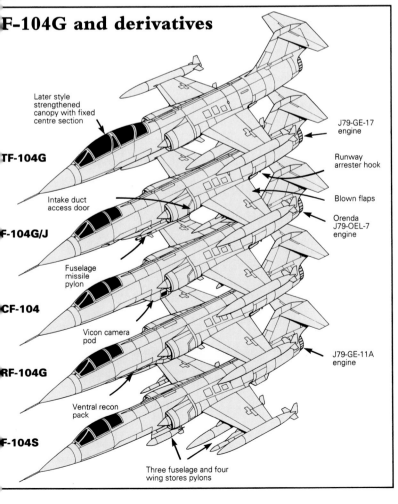

Wright J65 engine

Fixed geometry pitot-type intake

Original fuselage length 49.17 ft

XF-104

Intake half-cone centrebody

General Electric YJ79 engine

YF-104

J79-GE-3A engine

Longer fuselage

Further lengthened

Added ventral fin

F-104A

M61 Vulcan

Wingtip mounted Sidewinder

Original two-seat cockpit

J79-GE-7 engine

F-104B

Stabilising fins added to tip tanks

F-104C

Fixed refuelling probe

Added wing and centreline stores pylons

Additional vertical fin on tip tanks

F-104G and derivatives

Later style strengthened canopy with fixed centre section

TF-104G

J79-GE-17 engine

Intake duct access door

Runway arrester hook

F-104G/J

Blown flaps

Orenda J79-OEL-7 engine

Fuselage missile pylon

CF-104

Vicon camera pod

J79-GE-11A engine

RF-104G

Ventral recon pack

F-104S

Three fuselage and four wing stores pylons

Starfighter weapons

An F-104S of 51° Stormo is displayed with a representative group of weapons, including AIM-7 and AIM-9 AAMs, M117 bombs, various rocket pods and (far right) a B43 tactical nuclear weapon.

An armourer loads a JBG 34 F-104G with practice bombs and rockets. The 'blue bombs' simulated the ballistics of full-size weapons, usually containing a smoke charge for marking the impact point.

A variety of rocket pods was used by the Starfighter, this being the LAU-51 launcher, carried either singly or in pairs on the wing pylons. Each pod contained 19 2.75-in (70-mm) rockets.

In the anti-ship role German navy F-104Gs used the AS 34 Kormoran missile from 1977. Other guided missiles for the F-104 included the Bullpup and Nord AS.30.

Sidewinders could be carried on the wingtip launchers or on fuselage rails. Shown on this Marineflieger aircraft are AIM-9D IR-guided missiles.

Two weapons unique to the F-104S are the AIM-9L all-aspect Sidewinder and the AIM-7 Sparrow. The ASA upgrade allowed the F-104S to also carry the Aspide development of the Sparrow.

F-104 Operators

Belgium

RECEIPTS: SABCA's share in the European Starfighter production programme involved the licensed construction from 1963 of 101 F-104Gs, including 25 from MAP funding, for four FAB/BLu squadrons in two wings, plus 12 Lockheed-built TF-104G two-seat trainers (three MAP-funded), although the original Belgian requirement had been for 170 single-seat versions and 70 trainers. Their total cost was about BFr7.8 billion (then worth about $155 million), but Belgian industry received some BFr12.5 billion ($248 million) back in offset contracts, including producing 89 F-104Gs for Germany. Delivery of the first SABCA-built FAB/BLu aircraft took place on 14 February 1963, Belgian production being completed in mid-1965. An extra F-104G was built to replace FX27 (which crashed before delivery), but was given the same serial number. With replacement from early 1979 by F-16s, some of the F-104s of 349 and 350 Sqns of 1 Wing – the first NATO unit to re-equip from Starfighters – were transferred to 10 Wing at Kleine Brogel pending their planned similar re-equipment in 1982-83. An F-104G and a TF-104G made the FAB/BLu's last formal Starfighter flights on 19 September 1983. A total of 41 Belgian Starfighters, including three TF-104Gs, was lost in air and ground accidents, or nearly 37 per cent. Eighteen Belgian F-104Gs were later transferred to Turkey.

SERIALS:
F-104G: 9016/FX01 to 9023/FX08, 9025/FX09, 9026/FX10 to 9029/FX12, 9032/ FX13 to 9034/FX15, 9038/FX16 to 9040/FX18, 9044/FX19 to 9046/FX21, 9050/FX22 to 9052/FX24, 9056/FX25, 9057/FX26, 9082/FX-27, 9062/FX27 to 9064/FX30, 9068/FX31 to 9073/FX36, 9077/FX37 to 9079/FX39, 9083/FX40 to 9109/FX66, 9113/FX67 to 9115/FX69, 9119/FX70 to 9121/FX72, 9125/FX73 to 9127/FX75, 9131/FX76 to 9133/FX78, 9137/FX79 to 9142/FX84, 9146/FX85 to 9148/FX87, 9152/FX88 to 9154/FX90, 9158/FX91 to 9160/ FX93, 9164/FX94 to 9166/FX96, 9170/FX97 to 9172/FX99, 9176/FX100 (100)
TF-104G: 583D-5786/FC01 to 5788/FC03, 583G-5101/FC04 to 5109/FC12 (12)

UNITS:
All-weather air defence: 1 Wing, Beauvechain; 349 Sqn (mid-1963 to July 1979); 350 Sqn (April 1963 to 10 April 1981)
Tactical strike/fighter-bomber: 10 Wing, Kleine Brogel; 23 Sqn (6 April 1964 to mid-1982); 31 (Tiger) Sqn (mid-1964 to early 1983)
Starfighter Conversion Flight: F/TF-104G, Beauvechain/Kleine Brogel

Above: 1 Wing (with two squadrons) was the air defence unit. The gold falcon replaced a winged wolf's head as the wing badge in 1965.

Left: In common with most other customers, Belgium did not paint its Starfighters during the early years. This F-104G is seen in 1964. Tactical considerations dictated a change to camouflage.

Above: Belgium operated two wings of F-104s; this aircraft wears the badge of the Kleine Brogel-based 10 Wing. The two squadrons of this wing were assigned the strike mission.

Canada

RECEIPTS: Canadair Ltd built 200 CL-90/CF-104 versions of the F-104G for the RCAF after Lockheed's prototype conversion. The first (12701) was rolled-out from Cartierville in Montreal on 18 March 1961, before making its initial flight at Palmdale 10 days later. Powered by the Orenda-built J79-OEL-7 turbojet developing 10,000 lb (44.58 kN) military thrust, or 15,800 lb (70.31 kN) with afterburning, the CF-104 was virtually identical to the F-104G. However, all but the two tactical recce squadrons of No. 1 Wing were intended for nuclear roles, so the Canadian Starfighters had 1,000 lb (454 kg) of additional fuel in place of the normal 20-mm Vulcan cannon. These were later installed when the CF-104s relinquished their nuclear role in January 1972 in favour of conventional ground attack, for which they also received twin bomb ejector rack carriers and multi-tube rocket-launchers. RCAF Starfighter orders, costing an overall total of $463.762 million, also included 38 Lockheed-built two-seat CF-104D trainers, the first of which (12631) made its initial flight at Palmdale on 14 June 1961. Canadair further received US-funded Mutual Aid orders for another 140 Starfighters to F-104G standard, mainly for Greece (35), Taiwan (25?) and Turkey (34), as well as Denmark (25), Norway (three) and Spain (18). These comprised batches 62-12302 to '349; 63-12697 to '734; 63-13638 to '647 and 64-17752 to '795, the first of which (c/n 6001) made its initial flight on 30 July 1963, the last (6140) being delivered in September 1966.

Apart from one operational conversion unit established at Cold Lake, Alberta in late 1961, eventually redesignated No. 417 Sqn, RCAF Starfighters were all committed to NATO support operations through the Canadian Air Division in Europe, which formed part of 4th Allied Tactical Air Forces. Air Division organisation originally comprised four Starfighter wings, with eight squadrons each with 25 aircraft; No. 427 was the first to form, with initial CF-104 deliveries to Zweibrücken in December 1962. In February 1964, even before France withdrew from NATO in 1966, 2 Wing at Gros Tenquin was disbanded and its two CF-104 squadrons transferred elsewhere within the Air Division, No. 421 moving to 4 Wing at Baden-Söllingen and No. 430 to 3 Wing at Zweibrücken. As the RCAF's other French base, Marville, was also closed by 31 March 1967, its two CF-104 recce squadrons (439 and 441) then moved to Lahr, in Germany. Air Division strength was reduced by 25 per cent with the disbandment in 1967-1968 of Nos 434 and 444 Sqns, the remaining six CF-104 squadrons

comprising four with a nuclear strike role and two for tactical reconnaissance with VICON pods containing four 70-mm (2.75-in) Vinten cameras, with a total of some 108 Starfighters.

In May 1969, Canadian defence economies further reduced NATO commitments in Europe, including the closure of 3 Wing at Zweibrücken, which was transferred to USAFE, and the relocation of its squadrons to Baden (427) and Lahr (430). Air Division organisation in late 1969 then comprised Nos 430, 439 and 441 Sqns in 1 Wing at Lahr and 421, 422 and 427 Sqns at Baden. In the following year, however, the Canadian government decided to halve the strength of the Air Division to only three squadrons, and relinquish its nuclear strike role in favour of conventional ground attack by 1972. 1 AirDiv was redesignated 1 Canadian Air Group, with HQ at Baden-Söllingen which, with the closure of Lahr, the disbandment of 1 Wing and of Nos 422, 427 and 430 Sqns, became the sole CF-104 base in Europe. Nos 439 and 441 Sqns replaced all but 421 Sqn in Nos 3 and 4 Wings at Baden. Of

Above: Canada purchased 200 CF-104s to fulfil its sizeable commitment to NATO's 4 ATAF. As originally delivered these sported the ensign fin marking and 'RCAF' titles.

Left: Seen in 1972, this CF-104 wears the 'Red Indian' badge of 421 Sqn. Until that year, the CF-104s had a nuclear commitment, and had the cannon removed in favour of additional internal fuel. The cannon port was simply faired over.

Above: From 1972 the CF-104s had the gun reinstated in line with the transition to a tactical tasking.

Above right: AETE at Cold Lake operated a large number of aircraft on trials duties.

the remaining three squadrons, 421 was committed to converting to ground attack roles, together with No. 439 Sqn, leaving only No. 441 to continue tactical recce tasks using the Vinten VICON underfuselage camera pod. With deliveries to the CAF of CF-18 Hornets, the last CF-104s were retired from service with 441 Sqn on 28 February 1986. Many CAF Starfighters were transferred to Turkey, which in early 1986 was allocated 20 for active operations, plus a further 30 for spares. Around 110 CF-104/104Ds were lost (from 239 received) in accidents to June 1983, or no less than 46 per cent.

SERIALS:
Canadair CF-104 (CL-90): prototype (ex-F-104A), 56-0770/12700, 12701 to 12900, becoming 104701 to 104900 (200)
CF-104D: 12631 to 12668 (becoming 104631 to 104668), 12635 first to be delivered to RCAF, 16 January 1962 (38 Lockheed-built)

UNITS:
Central Experimental & Proving Establishment/Aerospace Engineering & Test Establishment: Cold Lake (16 January 1962), to 6 Strike-Recce OTU, reformed as 417 Operational Training Sqn, mostly with CF-104Ds, Cold Lake (March 1962 to June 1983)
421 (Red Indian) Sqn: 2 Wing, Gros Tenquin/Baden-Söllingen (December 1963 to December 1985)
422 (Tomahawk) Sqn: 4 Wing, Baden-Söllingen (July 1963 to 1972)
427 (Lion) Sqn: 3 Wing, Zweibrücken/Baden Söllingen (first 1 CAG F-104s) (11 October 1962 to 1972)
430 (Silver Falcon) Sqn: 2 Wing, Gros Tenquin/Lahr (September 1963 to 1972)
434 (Bluenose) Sqn: 3 Wing, Zweibrücken (April 1963 to March 1967)
439 (Sabre-Toothed Tiger) Sqn: 1 Wing, Marville/Baden-Söllingen (March 1964 to April 1987)
441 (Silver Fox) Sqn: 1 Wing, Marville/Baden-Söllingen (September 1963 to 28 February 1986)
444 (Cobra) Sqn: 4 Wing, Baden Söllingen (May 1963 to 1967)

Above: In wrap-round camouflage, this CF-104 is from 439 Sqn.

Below: All of Canada's 38 CF-104D two-seaters were built by Lockheed.

Denmark

RECEIPTS: The RDAF received a total of some 40 F-104G Starfighters and 11 two-seat TF-104G/CF-104D trainers, mostly from Canada. An initial batch of 25 Canadair-built single-seat F-104Gs and four Lockheed TF-104Gs were supplied through the US Mutual Aid Program from FY1962-64 funding, the first being formally accepted at Aalborg on 29 June 1965. A second batch of 15 ex-RCAF CF-104s and seven CF-104Ds was bought from Canada in September 1971 to expand unit establishments. After a prototype conversion by Lockheed, the single-seaters were overhauled and modified to F-104G standard with factory-supplied kits by the RDAF at Aalborg, including replacing Lockheed C-2 ejection-seats with higher-performance Martin-Baker Mk DQ7 units. Of the 51 Starfighters received between 1965-1986 (the last 14 being retired on 30 April of the latter year), the RDAF lost 11 single-seat versions and one two-seater in accidents (23.5 per cent). The surviving 15 Lockheed-built MAP-funded F-104Gs and three TF-104Gs were transferred to Taiwan between February and April 1987.

SERIALS:
F-104G: 6039/62-12340/R-340 to 6042/62-12343/R-343, 6044/62-12345/R-345 to 6048/62-12349/R-349, 6050/63-12698/R-698 to 6055/63-12703/R-703, 6059/63-12707/R-707, 6094/63-13645/R-645 to 6096/63-13647/R-647, 6097/64-17752/R-752 to 6101/63-17756/R-756, 6104/64-17759/R-759 (25, 1965-66)
(C)F-104G: 1003/12703/R-704, 1057/12757/R-757, 1058/12758/R-758, 1071/12771/R-771, 1112/12812/R-812, 1114/12814/R-814, 1119/12819/R-819, 1125/12825/R-825, 1132/12832/R-832, 1146/12846/R-846, 1151/12851/R-851, 1155/12855/R-855, 1187/12887/R-887, 1188/12888/R-888, 1196/12896/R-896 (15, 1971-73)
(C)F-104D: 12654/RT-654, 12655/RT-655, 12657/RT-657, 12660/RT-660, 12662/RT-662, 12664/RT-664, 12667/RT-667 (7, 1971-73)
TF-104G: 63-12681/RT-681 to 63-12684/RT-684 (4, 1965-67)

UNITS:
Esk 723: Aalborg (1965 to 1 January 1983)
Esk 726: Aalborg (1965 to 30 April 1986)

Above: Serialled in the 'R-3xx' range, the first batch of Danish Starfighters was built as F-104Gs by Canadair through MAP funds. The aircraft were delivered in an anti-corrosion grey scheme.

Below: Wearing the blue and white eagle badge of Eskadrille 723, this two-seater was one of seven ex-Canadian CF-104Ds supplied to bolster the fleet in the early 1970s.

Left: A pair of Esk 726 Starfighters takes off, displaying the all-over dark green scheme which adorned RDAF F-104s for most of their career.

Federal German Republic

RECEIPTS: Federal Germany took delivery of its first Starfighter, a Lockheed-built two-seat F-104F, at Nörvenich to begin converting pilots for JBG 31 in July 1960, and went on to order a total of 750 F/RF-104Gs (including the prototype and first 96 production aircraft), 30 F-104Fs and 137 two-seat TF-104Gs from Lockheed, or 917 F-104s in all. At their peak, in the mid-1970s, these equipped five 'heavy' Luftwaffe nuclear-armed (with standard NATO 1-MT store) fighter-bomber wings or *Jagdbombergeschwader*, each comprising two squadrons or *Staffel*, with individual complements of 18 combat-ready aircraft, plus six in reserve and 10 on maintenance, or 52 Starfighters per wing. Completing this force were two interceptor or *Jagdgeschwader* wings, with another four F-104G squadrons, plus two tactical reconnaissance wings, or *Aufklärungsgeschwader* with four RF-104G squadrons. From 1964 onwards, two naval attack wings, Marinefliegergeschwader (MFG) 1 and 2, replaced their Hawker Sea Hawks with 100 F-104Gs in four squadrons, each of 18 aircraft armed with AS-34 Kormoran anti-ship missiles, plus reserves. To restore crash attrition, the Marineflieger received 36 of 50 F-104Gs later ordered by the FRG, plus a similar quantity of RF-104Gs transferred from the Luftwaffe as these were replaced by RF-4Es from 1971 onwards. German forces lost about 270 Starfighters and 110 pilots in air and ground accidents, or just under 30 per cent of their total force.

SERIALS:
F-104G: c/n 2001 to 2050, 2052 to 2097, 6600, 6602, 6604 to 6607, 6612 to 6620, 7001 to 7191, 7193, 7195 to 7199, 7203 to 7205, 7208 to 7210, 8001 to 8044, 8046, 8054 to 8056, 8064, 8067 to 8081, 8088, 8092, 8096/7, 8100, 8162, 8166, 8168/69, 8172, 8182 to 8188, 8190 to 8204, 8207, 8212, 8216, 8220, 8224, 8228, 8231, 8234, 8237, 8250, 8263, 8275, 8277, 8284/85, 8287, 8289 to 8292, 8295/96, 8298/99, 8301 to 8303, 8305 to 8307, 8309/10, 8313 to 8317, 8321 to 8323, 8327 to 8330, 8333 to 8335, 8339/40, 8344 to 8350, 9001 to 9015, 9025/26, 9030/31, 9035 to 9037, 9041 to 9043, 9047 to 9049, 9053 to 9055, 9059 to 9061, 9065 to 9067, 9074 to 9076, 9080/81, 9110 to 9112, 9116 to 9118, 9122 to 9124, 9128 to 9130, 9134 to 9136, 9143 to 9145, 9149 to 9151, 9155 to 9157, 9161 to 9163, 9167 to 9169, 9173 to 9175, 9177 to 9189, 7301 to 7314, 7401 to 7436 (604)
RF-104G: c/n 6621 to 6630, 6639 to 6642, 6661 to 6665, 6672 to 6679, 6686 to 6693, 7192, 7194, 7200 to 7202, 7206/7, 8085 to 8087, 8094/95, 8102, 8106, 8108, 8111, 8113, 8116, 8118, 8122, 8124, 8126, 8128, 8130, 8132, 8134, 8136, 8137, 8139/40, 8142, 8144, 8146, 8148 to 8161, 8163 to 8165, 8167, 8170/71, 8173 to 8181, 8189, 8205/6, 8208 to 8211, 8213 to 8215, 8217 to 8219, 8221 to 8223, 8225 to 8227, 8229/30, 8232/33, 8235/36, 8238 to 8242, 8246 to 8249, 8251 to 8255, 8261/62, 8264/65, 8269 to 8271, 8274, 8276, 8278, (145)
Lockheed F-104F: c/n 5047 to 5076 (30)
Lockheed TF-104G: 5701, 5703 to 5766, 5768, 5770/71, 5773, 5775, 5777, 5779, 5901 to 5965 (137)

In early 1968, the remaining German Starfighters were reserialled in batches of 100, becoming 20+01 to 29+21. The surviving 135 TF-104Gs became 27+01 to 28+35, the remaining 21 of 30 F-104Fs becoming 29+01 to 29+21.

UNITS:
AKG 51 'Immelman': RF-104G, Ingolstadt/Manching (November 1963 to January 1971)
AKG 52: Leck, RF-104G/TF-104 (October 1964 to September 1971)
JBG 31 'Boelcke': Nörvenich (spring 1961 to 30 April 1983)
JBG 32: Lechfeld (December 1964 to 18 April 1984)
JBG 33: Büchel (August 1962 to 30 May 1985)
JBG 34: Memmingen (July 1964 to 16 October 1987)
JBG 36: Rheine-Hopsten (February 1965 to 1975)
JG 71 'Richtofen': Wittmundhaven (May 1963 to May 1973)
JG 74 'Mölders': Neuberg (May 1964 to June 1974)
2 Dt.Lw.Ausb.Stff.: (4512th, 4518th, 4443rd USAF Combat Crew Training Sqns of the 4510th CCT Wing), becoming the 69th Tactical Fighter Training Squadron and 418th TFTS, 58th USAF Tactical Training Wing, Luke AFB (65 F-104G/36 TF-104Gs, 112 establishment in all). Forty-five remaining Starfighters, plus 21 in storage withdrawn from surviving 69th TFTS on 16 March 1983, and last US-based unit then disbanded
Waffenschule 10: F/TF-104G, Norvenich (early 1961 to 1963) moving to Jever (1963 to 1983)
Erprobungsstelle 61: Manching, established 1960 with six F-104G/TF-104. Later redesignated WTD (Wehrtechnische Dienstelle) 61 and operated last three F-104Gs and one two-seat TF-104G on avionics and systems development until last German Starfighter sortie on 22 May 1991
Luftwaffenversorgungsregiment 1: Erding, incorporating Technical Group (LwSchleuse) 11 (LVR-1/LW11) for F-104G/TF-104G maintenance, overhauls and technical support (1962 to September 1988)
MFG 1: Schleswig-Jagel, two squadrons with 18-aircraft establishments plus reserves (September 1963 to 1982). Last F-104 sortie was 29 October 1981
MFG 2: Eggebeck, two squadrons with 18 aircraft establishments plus reserves, of F-104G/ RF-104G/TF-104Gs (early 1965 to late 1986)

Above: Luftwaffe F-104 pilots trained at Luke AFB with the 4510th CCTW, which operated mainly Lockheed-built F-104Gs and TF-104Gs. Successful students then joined WS-10 for a Europeanisation course.

Above: JBG 31 was the first operational Luftwaffe unit to receive the Starfighter, declaring IOC on 20 February 1961. It flew the type for 22 years before conversion to the Tornado.

Above: LVR 1 was the last major Luftwaffe F-104 operator.

Right: Several Starfighters were operated by E-Stelle (now WTD) 61, the main trials unit.

Below: The navy operated two wings of F-104Gs, this being MFG 2.

Greece

RECEIPTS: Originally allocated 35 Canadair-built F-104Gs from 1961 MAP funding, the HAF also received four TF-104Gs from Lockheed initial deliveries, plus another 10 MAP-funded Lockheed-built F-104Gs and two TF-104Gs from USAF stocks, to equip two squadrons each with 18 Starfighters for nuclear strike roles in the 1st Tactical Air Force. The first HAF Starfighter unit was 335 Mira or 'Tiger' Squadron in the 114th Wing (Pterix) at Tanagra which began replacing its Republic F-84Fs in April 1964, soon followed by 336 'Olympus' Mira in the 116th Wing at Araxos. Although these remained the HAF's only two F-104 squadrons, reverting to ground-attack with conventional weapons in the early 1970s, Greece eventually received at least 170 Starfighters through US and NATO aid programmes, including nine F-104Gs and one TF-104G from Spain in 1972, and two TF-104Gs from the FRG in 1977. These were reportedly reduced by accident attrition to 29 F-104Gs and three TF-104Gs by early 1981, but 10 Fiat-built Gs were then transferred from the Netherlands in mid-1982, in addition to continuous supplies from West Germany between 1981-1988 as part of Bonn's 'Minerva' military aid programmes to Greece. This eventually involved the supply of a total of 79 German Starfighters, including 38 F-104Gs and 22 RF-104Gs, mostly ex-Marineflieger, plus 20 TF-104Gs. Not all these aircraft were put into HAF service, some remaining in storage or used for spares.

KNOWN SERIALS:
F/RF-104G (MAP): 4001/12601 to 4009/12609, 6001/22302 to 6010/22311, 6013/22314, 6014/22315, 6016/22317, 6019/22320 to 6021/22322, 6049/32697, 6056/32704, 6058/32706, 6060/32708 to 6065/32713, 6071/32719, 6073/32721 to 6075/32723, 6077/32725, 6078/32726, 6125/47780 to 6127/47782, 6132/47787, 6133/47788 (45)
RF-104G, ex-GAF (1984-87): 6629/21+07, 6639/21+09, 6642/21+11, 6662/21+13, 6664/21+15, 6665/21+16, 6672/21+17, 6674/21+19, 6676/21+21 to 6679/21+24, 6690/21+29 to 6693/21+32, 7201/23+17, 7206/23+22, 7207/23+23, 8170/24+28, 8176/24+33, 8229/24+79 (22)
F-104G, ex-EdA: 6067/32715 (ex-EdA C.8-1), 6068/32716 (ex-C.8-2), 6069/32717 (ex-C.8-3), 6072/32720 (ex-C.8-5), 6079/32727 (ex-C.8-6), 6082/32730 (ex-C.8-7), 6086/32734 (ex-C.8-11), 6087/33638 (ex-C.8-12), 6088/33639 (ex-C.8-18) (9)
F-104G, ex-GAF (1980-88): 7057/21+88, 7073/22+03, 7080/22+10, 7082/22+12, 7087/22+ 16, 7088/22+17, 7090/22+19, 7094/22+21, 7097/22+22, 7106/22+29, 7151/22+70 to 7153/ 22+72, 7155/22+74, 7163/22+81, 7167/22+85, 7168/22+86, 7172/22+89, 7176/22+93, 7180/22 +97, 7183/23+00, 7195/23+12, 7203/23+19, 7205/23+21, 7409/26+63, 7415/26+69, 7420/26+74 to 7422/ 26+76, 7424/26+78 to 7429/26+83, 7433/26+87 to 7435/26+89 (38)
F-104G, ex-RNAF: D-6666, 6668, 6670, 6680, 6681, 6684, 6695, 6697, 6699, 6700 (10). TF-104G: 5512/62-12267, 5517/12272 to 5520/12275, 5523/12278 (ex-EdA CE.8-1), 63-13025 (7)
TF-104G, ex-GAF: 5708/27+07, 5712/27+11, 5715/27+14, 5717/27+16, 5719/27+18, 5733/27 +31, 5736/27+34, 5777/27+70, 5901/27+72, 5906/27+77, 5908/27+79 to 5910/27+81, 5912/ 27+83, 5916/27+86, 5917/27+87, 5953/28+23, 5954/28+24, 5958/28+28, 5959/28+29 (20)

UNITS:
335 'Tiger' Mira: 114 and then 116 Pterix, Tanagra/Araxos (April 1964 to March 1993)
336 'Olympus' Mira: 114 Pterix, Araxos, January, 1965; 116 Pterix (December 1966 to March 1993)

Below: Greece acquired its Starfighters from a variety of sources. This RF-104G was one of 22 ex-Luftwaffe aircraft transferred in the 1980s.

Greece's first Starfighters were F-104Gs built by Canadair, delivered in natural metal finish. The tail number and USAF-style buzz-code were based on the USAF/MAP serial (in this case 62-12309).

Italy

RECEIPTS: Fiat produced 200 F-104Gs for the AMI, Luftwaffe and KLu, including 125 (50 MAP-funded) for the Italian air force, which received a prototype from the US in March 1962, followed by the initial flight of the first F-104G from Turin on 9 June 1962. Apart from 51 F-104G interceptor versions and 54 equipped as fighter-bombers, the AMI also received 12 TF-104G trainers from Lockheed and 16 from Aeritalia, to re-equip three F-86K Sabre all-weather interceptor, two strike-fighter and a tactical-recce squadrons. The 20 RF-104Gs were equipped with the Orpheus reconnaissance pod. F-104Gs and TF-104Gs first entered service at Grosseto with 4° Stormo in 1963. Seven Lockheed TF-104G trainers were transferred from the Luftwaffe to the AMI in 1984-85, and at least two were refurbished by Aeritalia, but there are doubts that the others entered Italian service, probably being cannibalised for spares. The AMI's last F-104G fighter-bomber unit (154° Gruppo/6° Stormo) replaced its Starfighters with Tornados from early 1983, leaving 28° Gruppo/3° Stormo as the last combat operator of earlier-generation Starfighters with Orpheus sensor pod-equipped RF-104Gs. The two-seaters remained in service in limited numbers in 1995.

The first two F-104S, MM6658/660, armed with two AIM-7 Sparrow 3 and four AIM-9 Sidewinder AAMs, were converted by Lockheed from AMI F-104Gs at Palmdale, their flight trials starting in December 1966. The first production F-104S was delivered to 22° (interceptor) Gruppo from Turin on 9 June 1969. Planned production for the AMI was 205, eventually to equip 10 *Gruppi*, but a further 20 were laid down for a subsequently-cancelled Turkish order. Only one of these – MM6946/5-06 – was completed as a replacement for

Two F-104Gs from early in the Fiat production run wear the prancing horse badge which was shared by 9° Gruppo and 4° Stormo. The unit was the first Italian F-104 operator.

9° Stormo operated the F-104S from 1972/73. The name 'F. Baracca' was worn on the fin to commemorate the World War I Italian ace.

MM6766, which crashed before delivery. Some 73 Italian Starfighters, including 49 F/RF-104Gs, 21 F-104S and three TF-104Gs, were officially admitted to have been lost in accidents between January 1964 and 31 March 1976. By July 1980, this total had increased to at least 106, and by early 1992 to around 138, representing 37.5 per cent of the 368 eventual AMI deliveries.

SERIALS (as constructors' numbers):
F-104G: MM6501 to 6599; 6601, 6603, 6608 to 6611, 6631 to 6638, 6643 to 6651, 6658 to 6660 (125, including 11 RF-104Gs and 104S prototype conversion)
TF-104G (Lockheed): MM54226 to 54237 (12); (Aeritalia), MM54250 to 54265 (16) ex-Luftwaffe, 5738/27+36, 5739/27+37, 5743/27+41, 5902/27+73, 5919/27+89, 5946/28+16, 5949/28+19 (7)
F-104S: MM6701 to 6850, 6869 to 6883, 6890, 6901, 6905 to 6946 (208)

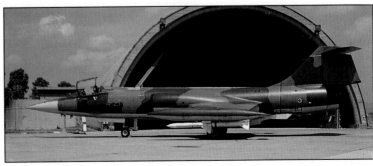

4° Stormo went on to operate the uprated F-104S version at Grosseto with two Gruppi assigned.

UNITS:
9° Gruppo/4° Stormo: Grosetto, F-104G (March 1963); F-104S (1970 to date)
10° Gruppo/9° Stormo: Grazzanise, F-104G (27 January 1967); F-104S (1973 to date)
12° Gruppo/36° Stormo: Gioia del Colle, F-104G (1965); F-104S (1970 to 1995)
18° Gruppo/37° Stormo: Trapani/Birgi, F-104S (October 1984 to date)
20° Gruppo/4° Stormo: Grosseto, F/TF-104G (from late 1963), F-104G retired June 1994, F-104S/TF-104G (1980 to date), Starfighter OCU
21° Gruppo/53° Stormo: Cameri/Novara, F-104G (1 April 1967); F-104S (1970 to date)
22° Gruppo/51° Stormo: Treviso/Istrana, F-104G (June 1969); F-104S (1974 to date)
23° Gruppo/5° Stormo: Rimini/Miramare (formed as 101° Gruppo/5° Aerobrigata) F-104G (September 1967); F-104S (March 1973 to date). To Cervia 1995
28° Gruppo/3° Stormo: Villafranca, RF-104G (1964 to June 1993)

Partnered by the 132° Gruppo within 3° Stormo at Verona-Villafrance, the 28° Gruppo flew the RF-104G, equipped from 1977 with the Orpheus pod. The badge consisted of a witch on a camera-equipped broomstick.

102° Gruppo/5° Stormo: Rimini, F-104G (May 1964); F-104S (March 1973 to July 1993)
132° Gruppo/3° Stormo: Villafranca, F-104G/RF-104G (1965 to October 1990)
154° Gruppo/6° Stormo: Ghedi, F-104G (1964 to early 1993)
155° Gruppo/51° Stormo: formerly in 50° Stormo, Piacenza, F-104G (until 1974); then Istrana, F-104S (to 1 January 1985)
156° Gruppo/36° Stormo: Gioia del Colle, F-104G (1966); to F-104S (1970 to late 1982)
Reparto Sperimentale di Volo (RSV): Pratica di Mare. Various F-104s, including F-104S prototype MM6848/RS-04

Japan

RECEIPTS: The F-104J was selected in 1960 to replace the JASDF's F-86F Sabres in a $207 million joint US/Japanese programme with local manufacture by Mitsubishi and Ishikawajima/Harima, the latter group producing the J79-IHI-11A powerplants. Initial orders comprised 180 F-104J fighter-bombers plus 20 locally-assembled two-seat F-104DJ trainers, with deliveries starting from Lockheed in early 1962. A further 30 F-104Js were then ordered for local production, with deliveries by 1967. Programme completion was scheduled by January 1965, with seven squadrons re-equipped. Mitsubishi assembled or built a total of 210 Model 683B-F-104J Starfighters at Komaki between 1 April 1962 and 2 December 1967. The first example (26-8501) was built by Lockheed Burbank, and first flown on July 1961, before being shipped to Japan and reassembled to fly at Komaki on 8 March 1962. The second and third examples followed a similar pattern, with 17 more F-104Js then assembled by Mitsubishi from knocked-down kits before Japanese production began, to equip seven all-weather interceptor squadrons between October 1962 and December 1967. Assembly was also undertaken by Mitsubishi from Lockheed-built kits of another 20 two-seat Model 583B F-104DJ trainers between 1962-64. At least 34 F-104Js and two F-104DJs (just over 15 per cent) had been written-off in accidents when the last JASDF unit (207th Sqn) began re-equipping with MDC F-15Js in 1984-85.

SERIALS:
F-104J: 26-8501 to 26-8507, 36-8508 to 36-8538, 46-8539, 36-8540 to 36-8552, 46-8553, 36-8554 to 36-8559, 46-8560/61, 36-8562/63, 46-8564, 36-8565/66, 46-8567 to 468652, 56-8653, 46-8654 to 8658, 56-8659, 46-8660, 56-8661 to 8664, 46-8665, 56-8666 to 56-8680, 76-8681 to 76-8710 (210, c/n 3001-3210)
F-104DJ: 26-5001 to 5007, 46-5008/09, 26-5010, 36-5011 to 5019, 46-5020 (20, c/n 5401-5420)

UNITS:
201st Hikotai: 2nd Kokudan, Chitose Air Base (1 October 1962 to 1 October 1974)
202nd Hikotai: 5th Kokudan, Nyutabaru (1964 to late 1981)
203rd Hikotai: 2nd Kokudan, Komatsu (1965 to 1983)
204th Hikotai: 5th Kokudan, Tsuiki (1964 to 1984)
205th Hikotai: 6th Kokudan, Komatsu (1965 to 1981)
206th Hikotai: 7th Kokudan, Hyakuri (1966 to 1 December 1978)
207th Hikotai: 7th Kokudan, Hyakuri (3 March 1966); to Naha (1972 to 1985-86)
Air Proving Group/Wing: Gifu, F-104J/F-104DJ/QF-104J (1964 to 1986)

Above: This was the first Japanese F-104J, built entirely by Lockheed. The J version was tailored to the JASDF's air defence mission, being able to carry four AIM-9s and featuring many Japanese-built components. Mitsubishi assembly/production accounted for 210 aircraft.

Left: 207 Hikotai served on the mainland at Hyakuri until moving to Naha in 1972. While mainland units re-equipped with F-4EJs, 207 Hikotai was left defending Okinawa until 1986, making it the last JASDF front-line user of the Starfighter.

Above: Twenty Mitsubishi-built F-104DJs were procured for conversion training, which was undertaken by 202 Hikotai at Nyutabaru. The white wings were adopted for greater conspicuity in the training role.

Jordan

RECEIPTS: A total of 36 early ex-USAF Starfighters were promised to Jordan by the US government in April 1966, for a nominal $1 million each, and an initial batch of three F-104As and three two-seat F-104Bs were airlifted to the RJAF in early 1967. Apart from one F-104A which had already crashed, these were almost immediately withdrawn to Turkey at the outbreak of the six-day Middle East war between 5-10 June 1967, in which a large part of the Arab air forces, including most of the RJAF's operational strength, was destroyed on the ground by initial Israeli air attacks. It was not until late 1968 that RJAF pilots and ground crews resumed Starfighter training in the US, prior to the receipt in mid-1969 of the first six of 18 ex-USAF F-104As and four F-104Bs, and these were initially flown by Pakistan air force pilots. A visit to Washington by King Hussein earlier in 1969 had resulted in President Nixon agreeing to supply Jordan with a second squadron of 18 F-104As, to be transferred from Taiwan's Nationalist Chinese air force storage following their replacement by F-104Gs, after the Jordanian monarch had pointed out that he had been offered MiG-21s by the USSR for about one-third the price of comparable Western equipment. No. 9 Sqn was sent with its F-104As to Pakistan to help out in the 1971 war with India, in which it is believed to have suffered several losses. The RJAF was reported to have operated about 20 F-104As and four Bs in two squadrons by July 1979, to be replaced by 34 Mirage F1s.

Above: Jordan's F-104s were ex-USAF A models, supplied after their with Air Defense Command were finished.

KNOWN SERIALS:
F-104A (ex-USAF): 56-750, 752, 754, 759, 766, 771, 779, 782, 784, 791, 793, 795, 811, 824, 826, 839, 849, 872 (18); ex-RoCAF F-104A, 56-908, 916, etc. (18)
F-104B: 57-901 to 906 (6)

UNITS:
No. 9 Sqn: Prince Hassan Air Base/Mafraq (1969-1981)
No. 25 Sqn: Mwaffaq Salti (Azraq), (1969-1980)

Right: Six two-seaters were supplied to Jordan, these being late-model F-104Bs with the extended rudder. This example has been restored for display/decoy use at Mafraq.

Netherlands

RECEIPTS: Most Dutch tactical units committed to NATO's 2nd ATAF planned to re-equip from Republic F-84F/RF-84s and Lockheed RT-33As with 120 F/RF-104Gs ordered for the RNAF. Fokker built 95 F-104Gs, including 25 as RF-104Gs, for the KLu, financed by the Dutch government and delivered between 11 December 1962 and 20 May 1965, as well as 255 F-104Gs for the FRG. A further 25 F-104Gs were funded through MAP for the KLu from Fiat production, with deliveries starting in early 1963. The US also supplied 10 Lockheed-built TF-104G two-seat trainers, with deliveries from mid-1963, while eight more were supplied from Fokker assembly. Five first-line F-104 squadrons were eventually equipped, the first from late 1962 being No. 306 Sqn, which later received (from 13 September 1963) all RF-104Gs, equipped with 20 NVOI Orpheus sensor pods containing five TA-8M cameras and an infra-red linescan, for tactical recce. Dutch squadron establishment comprised 18 F-104Gs and two TF-104Gs per unit, apart from two OCUs. When 312 Sqn disbanded in mid-1984 as the last KLu Starfighter unit, its 18 F-104Gs and four TF-104Gs were transferred to the CAV at Volkel until their last formal fly-past on 21 November of that year. By then, 43 KLu F-104Gs and 10 TF-104Gs had been transferred to the Turkish air force, and 10 F-104Gs to Greece. Some 43 KLu F/RF-104Gs were lost in accidents (35.8 per cent), including three TF-104G trainers.

SERIALS:
F/RF-104G: D-6652 to 6657; 6666 to 6671; 6680 to 6685; 6694 to 6700 (25); D-8013, 8022, 8045*, 8047*, 8048, 8049* to 8053*, 8057*, 8058 to 8063, 8065*, 8066, 8082 to 8084, 8089 to 8091, 8093, 8098, 8099, 8101*, 8103*, 8104*, 8105, 8107*, 8109, 8110, 8112*, 8114, 8115, 8117*, 8119*, 8120, 8121, 8123*, 8125*, 8127*, 8129*, 8131*, 8133*, 8135, 8138*, 8141*, 8143*, 8145, 8147, 8243 to 8245, 8256 to 8260, 8266 to 8268, 8272, 8273, 8279 to 8283, 8286, 8288, 8293, 8294, 8297, 8300, 8304, 8308, 8311, 8312, 8318, 8319, 8324 to 8326, 8331, 8332, 8336 to 8338, 8341 to 8343 (95, including 25 RF-104Gs)
Lockheed TF-104G: D-5702 (formerly N-104L), D-5801 to 5817 (18)

6000 series built by Fiat, 8000 series built by Fokker. Serials coincide with constructors' numbers with D-prefix. *indicates RF-104Gs

UNITS:
OCU/306 Sqn: RF-104G with Orpheus pod, Twenthe, 19 December 1962 (as OCU until January 1964; then to tactical-recce roles, and moved to Volkel on 3 September 1969) to late 1983
Tactical strike: F-104G/TF-104: 311 Sqn, Volkel (June 1964 to August 1982); 312 Sqn, Volkel (April 1965 to 14 June 1984)

A quartet of F-104Gs represents the Volkel strike wing. The leading three aircraft show the 311 Sqn badge, while the aircraft in the slot has that of 312 Sqn. In practice, central servicing resulted in most aircraft wearing the two squadron badges on either side of the fin.

All-weather interceptor: F-104G/TF-104: 322 Sqn, Leeuwarden (1 August 1963 to mid-1979); 323 Sqn, Leeuwarden (17 March 1964 to 1 August 1980)
Training & Conversion Unit A: Leeuwarden, TF-104G (initially 8) (January 1964 to March 1978)
CAV (Conversie Afdeling Volkel): Volkel, F-104G/TF-104G (18/4) (January 1969 to November 1984)

An aircraft marked with the 312 Sqn badge sets out for the 1,000th towed gunnery target flight, the dart itself being adorned with flag of the Frisian region. The '8' in the serial denoted a Fokker-built machine.

306 Sqn has always been the KLu's tactical reconnaissance unit, and in the Starfighter era it operated RF-104Gs equipped with the Orpheus pod. This example has been 'zapped' by the German navy.

Norway

RECEIPTS: RNoAF Starfighter procurement was originally restricted to MAP deliveries of 21 examples, comprising 16 Lockheed-built RF-104Gs for tactical recce, three Canadair-built F-104Gs and two Lockheed TF-104G trainers, delivered from late 1963 onwards. These were later supplemented by two ex-Luftwaffe TF-104Gs from Luke AFB in the US. In May 1973, 18 surplus CAF CF-104s and two CF-104Ds from storage at Prestwick were further acquired at a cost of NKr136 million ($20.4 million), including overhaul and modification, to equip a second squadron (Skv 334), for anti-ship roles with Martin Bullpup ASMs between April 1973 and February 1974. At least 12 RNoAF MAP-funded Starfighters, including 232, 233, 239, 240, 626, 630, 631, 633, 757, 758, 785 and one TF-104G (62-12263, written-off on 4 April 1985), were transferred to Turkey in June and July 1981. Only six of a total of 44 Starfighters (13.6 per cent) were lost in Norwegian service, including one two-seat TF-104G, in over 56,000 flying hours.

SERIALS:
Lockheed F/RF-104G: 64-17757, 64-17758, 64-17785, 4034/62-12232 to 4036/ 62-12234, 4039/62-12237 to 4042/62-12240, 4025/61-2625 to 4033/61-2633 (19)
(C)F-104G: 1017/12717, 1030/12730, 1055/12755, 1059/12759, 1066/12766, 1097/12797, 1100/12800, 1101/12801, 1118/12818, 1133/12833, 1136/12836, 1150/12850, 1170/12870, 1182/12882, 1186/12886, 1189/12889, 1190/12890, 1200/12900 (18)
TF-104G/CF-104D: 5508/62-12263, 5509/12264, 5779/63-8469, 5938/66-13627, 5302/ 104632, 5303/104633, (4/2, 1971-73)

UNITS:
331 Skvadron: Bodø (late 1963 to June 1981)
334 Skvadron: Rygge (April 1973)

Above: 331 Skvadron at Bodø was primarily equipped with the RF-104G for reconnaissance purposes, but it also maintained a secondary air defence tasking. The finish was anti-corrosion grey.

Only six two-seat aircraft were delivered to Norway, this aircraft being one of the four Lockheed-built TF-104Gs. The serial was the MAP/USAF serial (62-12263), contracted to the last three on the fin.

The reduction of the Canadian Starfighter force in 1970 allowed both Denmark and Norway to boost their fleets. Distinguished by its RCAF wrap-round scheme, this is one of the two CF-104Ds gained by the KNL.

Pakistan

RECEIPTS: Ten F-104As and two F-104Bs were initially delivered through MAP from the US from 15 September 1961 onwards as the first Starfighter exports, some reports claiming that they were re-engined with J79-GE-11A turbojets, developing another 1,000 lb (4.45 kN) of thrust with a maximum afterburner rating of 15,800 lb (70.31 kN). Two F-104As were later delivered from Taiwan as combat attrition replacements for 1965 losses during the war with India. Others were reported to have been donated to Pakistan following Jordanian assistance by the provision of the F-104As of No. 9 Sqn, RJAF, to help the PAF in the 1971 war with India, in which the Pakistanis admitted the loss of three more Starfighters. Pakistan has also been officially listed as receiving a single tactical-recce RF-104G from Lockheed production at a relatively early date, but no further details have ever become available.

KNOWN SERIALS:
F-104A: 56-773, 56-0798/4219 (ex-RoCAF), 56-0799/4221 (ex-RoCAF), 56-800 to 56-805, 56-807/08, 56-868, 56-875, 56-877, 56-879 (14)
F-104B-10-LO: 57-1309, 57-1312 (2)

UNITS:
No. 9 Sqn: Sargodha (early 1962 to 1975)

Above: Resplendent in its natural metal finish, a No. 9 Sqn F-104 flies over the Karakorum mountain region close to the border with India. Starfighters flew in both major wars, augmented in 1971 by Jordanian aircraft.

Below: No. 9 Sqn today flies the F-16 from Sargodha, but this F-104A is retained for display purposes.

Spain

RECEIPTS: Eighteen Lockheed-built F-104Gs were delivered through MAP to the EdA with the Spanish designation C (=fighter).8, the first arriving on 5 March 1965. These replaced the North American F-86F Sabres of 61 Esc in Ala 6 at Torrejon, and were accompanied by two (later three) Lockheed TF-104G (CE.8) two-seat trainers. The wing was later renumbered Ala 16, the squadron becoming 161 Esc. Spain was unique in operating its small number of Starfighters without a single accident during their seven years of service and 17,500 flying hours, the entire fleet being returned to the USAF following formal retirement on 31 May 1972. All 21 of the former Spanish Starfighters were later transferred to the air forces of Greece (nine F-104Gs, one TF) and Turkey (nine Gs, two Fs).

SERIALS:
F-104G: 63-12715 to 12718 (C.8-1 to C.8-4), 63-12720 (C.8-5), 63-12727 (C.8-6), 63-12730 (C.8-7), 63-12731 to 12734 (C.8-8 to C.8-11), 63-13638 (C.8-12), 63-13644 (C.8-13), 63-13640 to 13643 (C.8-14 to C.8-17), 63-13639 (C.8-18) (18)
TF-104G: 62-12278/79 (CE.8-1/2), 65-9415 (CE.8-3) (3)

UNITS:
Escadrón 61 (161 then 104): Ala 6/16, Torrejon (5 March 1965 to 31 May 1972)

Spain's Starfighters served with the appropriately numbered 104 Escadrón only until 1972, when the type was replaced by the F-4C Phantom. Only three CE.8/TF-104G two-seaters were delivered.

Escadrón 61 renumbered to the more appropriate Escadrón 104 soon after the Starfighter's delivery to Spain. The wildcat badge was transferred from Ala 6/16 (F-104) to newly-established Ala 12 (F-4C) when the Phantom arrived to replace the Starfighters.

Taiwan

RECEIPTS: Reliable reports of Taiwanese Starfighter deliveries have not so far become available, but most sources agree that an initial batch of 24 ex-USAF Lockheed F-104As and five two-seat F-104B trainers delivered in 1960-61 were followed in 1964-1969 by 46 Lockheed-built F-104Gs and eight two-seat TF-104Gs, plus 21 tactical-recce RF-104Gs from Canadair (RoCAF serials 4301 to 4362 identified). Another six two-seat Lockheed F-104Ds were received in 1975 from former USAF Air National Guard squadrons to supplement RoCAF Starfighter units in the sole wing at Ching Chuan Kang air base. Further batches of 64 Canadair/ Lockheed F-104Gs and TF-104s, comprising 38 Gs (4363 to 4400?) and 26 TFs (4171 to 4196?), were transferred from the inventory in 1983 with the closure of the German training centre (69 TFTS) at Luke AFB. By 1987, the RoCAF had received at least 22 F-104Js and five F-104DJs, both airworthy and unairworthy, from Japan through the 'ALISAN 9' project, together with 15 F-104Gs and three TF-104Gs from the Royal Danish Air Force from the 'ALISAN 10' programme between February and April of the same year. Deliveries to Taiwan of at least 24 + 67 + 38 + 22 + 15, or 166 single-seat Starfighters and about 53 two-seaters in all, are therefore reasonably well-documented, plus possible additional and unknown quantities from Japan. All the early series F-104As, F-104Bs and F-104Ds were withdrawn from service in the early 1980s, some being transferred to Pakistan and Jordan. Others were used as drones or decoys. In 1990, the RoCAF's remaining Starfighters equipped six tactical fighter and one recce squadrons. Their armament package included AIM-9J Sidewinder AAMs and locally developed Sky Sword I and II IR and semi-active radar homing AAMs. Earlier plans to upgrade RoCAF F-104s to F-104ASA standard by the installation of FIAR Grifo fire-control radar and beyond-visual-range radar-guided AAMs were abandoned.

KNOWN SERIALS:
F-104A: 4202/56-828, 4204/56-845, 4208/56-775, 4211/56-775, 4213/56-777, 4221/56-799, etc. (24)
F-104G: 4313/62-12216 to 4328/12231, 4333/63-12738, 4336/417762, 4337/417763, 4338/64-17765 to 4341/64-17768, 4342/64-17764, 4343/64-17769, 4347/64-17773 to 4351/64-17777, ??(6131)/64-17786, etc. (46)
RF-104G: 4301/62-12250, 4302/62-12251, 4303/62-12252, 4304/12254, 4306/12247, 4308/212256, 4309/21258, 4311/212214, 4312/212215 etc. (21)
F/RF-104G: 2015/20+13/13234, 2016/20+14/13235, 2021/20+17/13238, 2023/20+18/13240, 2025/20+23/13242 to 2028/20+23/13245, 2033/20+26/13249, 2035/20+28/13251 to 2039/20+32/13255, 2041/20+34/13257, 2069/20+60/14887, 2076/20+65/13260, 2086/20+73/13262, 2092/20+79/13264, 2093/20+80/13265, 2095/20+82/13266, 7001/21+33/12745, 7015/21+47/14889, 7039/21+70/12748, 7098/22+23/12747, 7133/22+53/14885, 7177/22+94/13526, 8002/23+28/13269, 8008/23+33/13272, 8009/23+34/13273, 8056/23+66/13229, 8067/23+68/12750, 8068/23+69/12752, 8071/23+72/12753, 8183/24+40/13690, 8188/24+45/13691, 8204/24+56/14890, 8230/24+80/22517 (38)
F-104G (ex-RDAF): (Feb-April 1987) 4411/62-12340/R-340, 4412/62-12342/R-342, 4413/62-12345/R-345, 62-12347/R-347 to 62-12349/R-349, 63-12645/R-645 to 63-12647/ R-647, 63-12699/R-699, 63-12702/R-702, 4422/63-12703/R-703, 63-12707/R-707, 64-17754/ R-754, 64-17755/R-755 (15)

This mixed quartet of F-104Gs and RF-104Gs is from the second major batch delivered to Taiwan, the first having comprised F-104A/Bs. As displayed by their Sidewinder armament, air defence was the Starfighter's primary responsibility. They were replaced by the Mirage 2000-5 (2nd TFW) and Ching-kuo (3rd TFW).

F-104J (ex-JASDF): 4501/46-8612, 4503/36-8531, 4504/36-8554, 4506/36-8555, 4509/36-8508, 4510/46-8577, 4511/46-8582, 4515/46-8616, 4516/46-8619, 4517/??, 4521/36-8514, 4522/46-8596, etc. (22+)
F-104B: 4101/57-1294, 4102/57-1300, etc. (5)
F-104D (MAP): 57-1315, 57-1316, 57-1318 to 1320 (6)
F-104DJ (ex-JASDF): 4593/26-5006, 4595/36-5017, etc. (5+)
TF-104G (MAP): 4147/61-3030, 4149/61-3026, etc. (8)
TF-104G (ex-GAF): 5744/27+42/13073 to 5747/27+45/13076, 5749/27+47/13078 to 5751/27+49/13080, 5753/27+51/13082 to 5755/27+53/13084, 5756/27+54/38452, 5758/27+ 56/38454 to 5762/27+60/38458, 5764/27+62/38460 to 5766/27+64/38462, 5768/27+65/ 38463, 5770/27+66/38464, 5771/27+67/38465, 5775/27+69/38467, 5933/28+03/613622, 5936/28+06/613625, 5942/28+12/613631 (26)
TF-104G (ex-RDAF): 63-12682/RT-682, 4152/63-12683/RT-683, 63-12684/RT-684 (3)

UNITS:
2nd/499th Tactical Fighter Wing: 41st, 42nd and 48th Tactical Fighter Squadrons, Hsinchu, 25 each F/TF-104Gs (1984 to 1997)
3rd/427th Tactical Fighter Wing: 7th, 8th, 28th and 35th Tactical Fighter Squadrons, Ching Chuan Kang Air Base, 25 each F/TF-104Gs (1965 to 1995)
5th/401st Tactical Combined Wing: 12th Special Mission Sqn, Taoyuan, six RF-104G Stargazers, a few F-104/TF-104Gs (to December 1998)

Left: Seen with a towed dart gunnery target, this F-104G is from the first Lockheed-built batch.

Above: The 12th SMS RF-104G 'Stargazers' could be identified by the faired-over gun port.

Turkey

RECEIPTS: The THK was one of the first NATO air forces to receive Starfighters through Mutual Aid Program funding, and the first of an initial batch of 34 Lockheed- and Canadair-built F-104Gs, plus 12 more (including two RF versions) and six TF-104G trainers from Lockheed production, reached Turkey from May 1963, to equip 141 and 142 Filo, plus an OCU, in AJU 4 at Murted. The first of many NATO transfers then followed with deliveries from Spain in 1972 of nine F-104Gs and two TF-104Gs to reinforce two squadrons in 9 Wing at Murted. In late December 1974, the first six of an initial batch of 18 F-104S interceptors bought new from Italy at a fly-away unit cost of $3.8 million (reputedly funded by Libya in return for Turkish assistance with building up the LARAF) were delivered to 9 Wing. The remainder followed at three per month, the THK F-104S order being doubled in May 1975, plus 200 Selenia-built Sparrow AAMs, and finally increased to 40, initially equipping Filos 142 and 182.

Most THK Starfighter procurement, however, resulted from continuing large-scale NATO transfers, including 18 F-104Gs from Belgium in 1981-83 (withdrawn by 1987); 43 F-104Gs (including 22 RFs) and 10 TF-104Gs from the Netherlands from August 1980 to March 1984; nine RF-104Gs, three CF-104s and a single TF-104G ex-Norway in June and July 1981; and from October 1980 170 ex-FRG Starfighters, including 33 TF-104Gs, of which the 100th was supplied in early 1985 and the final 28 in 1988. Following their replacement in 1 Canadian Air Group by CF-18s, Canada offered Turkey an initial batch of 20 CF-104s, later increased to 52, including six CF-104Ds. Thirty of these were sent to MBB at Manching in March 1986, for overhaul through a $17.5 million contract funded by the German government through a NATO military aid programme before despatch to AJU 8, the remaining 20 being broken-down for spares. In all, the THK therefore appears to have received just over 400 Starfighters, including 276 F-104Gs and CF-104s, 33 RF-104Gs, 60 TF-104Gs and CF-104Ds, and 40 F-104S, although many of these have been withdrawn from service or cannibalised for spares. Large numbers have also been lost in crashes, and although no overall accident statistics have become available, it was known, for example, that only 21 of the original 40 F-104S interceptors bought from Italy were still in service by late 1987.

KNOWN SERIALS:
F/CF/RF-104G (MAP): 4010/61-2610 to 4023/61-2623 (14); 6012/62-12313, 6015/62-12316, 6018/62-12319, 6022/62-12323 to 6038/62-12339, 6043/62-12344, 6128/64-17783, etc. (8)
F-104G (ex-EdA): 6070/63-12718 (C.8-4), 6083/63-12731 (C.8-8), 6084/63-12732 (C.8-14), 6085/63-12733 (C.8-15), 6089/63-13640 (C.8-9), 6090/63-13641 (C.8-10), 6091/63-13642 (C.8-16), 6093/63-13644 (C.8-13), etc. (9)
F-104G (ex-FAB): 9034/FX-15, 9039/FX-17, 9044/FX-19, 9045/FX-20, 9050/FX-22, 9051/FX-23, 9052/FX-24, 9057/FX-26, 9082/FX-27, 9062/FX-28, 9063/FX-29, 9064/FX-30, FX-31/9068, FX-32/9069, FX-33/9070, FX-34/9071, FX-38/9078, FX-40/9083 (18)
F/RF-104G (ex-KLu): D-6652 to 6656, 6667, 8013*, 8049, 8052*, 8058* to 8060, 8065*, 8066*, 8082/83, 8089/90, 8093, 8105*, 8107*, 8109*/10*, 8112*, 8115*, 8119*/20*, 8125*, 8127*, 8129*, 8138*, 8143*, 8145*, 8272, 8273*, 8286, 8288, 8293, 8304, 8311*, 8319, 8324, 8342 (43)
CF-104 (ex-CAF): 1011/104711, 1013/104713, 1016/104716, 1033/104733, 1035/104735, 1037/104737, 1039/104739, 1043/104743, 1047/104747, 1051/104751, 1053/104753, 1056/104756, 1060/104760, 1061/104761, 1070/104770, 1073/104773, 1076/104776, 1080/104780, 1086/104786 to 1088/104788, 1095/104795, 1096/104796, 1106/104806, 1108/104808, 1110/104810, 1115/104815, 1124/104824, 1126/104826, 1137/104837, 1139/104839, 1141/104841, 1142/104842, 1145/104845, 1147/104847, 1148/104848, 1162/104862, 1165/104865, 1166/104866, 1169/104869, 1173/104873, 1183/104883, 1191/104891, 1193/104893, 1199/104899 (46)
RF-104G (ex-RNoAF): 4026/61-2626, 4029/61-2629 (w/o on delivery, 29/6/81), 4030/61-2630, 4031/61-2631, 4033/61-2633, 4034/62-12232, 4035/62-12233, 4041/62-12239, 4042/62-12240 (9)
(C)F-104G (ex-RNoAF): 6102/64-17757, 6103/64-17758, 6130/64-17785 (3)
F/RF-104G (ex-GAF): (1980-88) 2001/20+01, 2005/20+05, 2045/20+38, 2046/20+39, 2056/20+48, 2057/20+49, 2065/20+56, 2066/20+58, 2070/20+61, 2072/20+62, 2079/20+67, 2080/20+68 to 2083/20+71, 2087/20+74, 2089/20+76, 6622/21+01* to 6624/21+03*, 7003/21+35, 7005/21+37, 7008/21+40?, 7012/21+44, 7013/21+45, 7017/21+49, 7019/21+50, 7027/21+58, 7032/21+63, 7034/21+65, 7037/21+68, 7041/21+72, 7047/21+78, 7050/21+81, 7051/21+82, 7059/21+90, 7061/21+92,

Above: The first of many batches of Starfighters for Turkey came from Lockheed MAP production. These were initially flown in natural metal finish, with the early-style square national insignia.

Turkey's Starfighters displayed a bewildering array of schemes, recipients from other air arms rarely receiving a respray. This pair continued to wear the MFG grey scheme long after joining the THK.

7067/21+98, 7068/21+99, 7081/22+11, 7083/22+13, 7085/22+ 14, 7089/22+18, 7093/22+20, 7101/22+26, 7108/22+30, 7119/22+41, 7122/22+44, 7125/22+ 47, 7130/22+50, 7144/22+63, 7150/22+69, 7154/22+73, 7161/22+79, 7162/22+80, 7164/22+82, 7170/22+87, 7171/22+88, 7178/22+95, 7179/22+96, 7182/22+99, 7185/23+02, 7186/23+ 03, 7188/23+05 to 7190/23+07, 7209/23+25, 7210/23+26, 8004/23+29, 8027/23+48, 8029/23 +50, 8055/23+65, 8073/23+74, 8087/23+84*, 8102/23+92*, 8128/23+99*, 8130/24+00*, 8134/ 24+02*, 8137/24+03*, 8144/24+06*, 8152/24+12*, 8163/24+21*, 8164/24+22*, 8168/24+26, 8175/24+33*, 8185/24+42, 8195/24+51, 8200/24+53, 8205/24+57*, 8218/24+69*, 8223/24+ 74*, 8248/24+95*, 8262/25+04*, 8277/25+13, 8284/25+15, 8287/25+17, 8290/25+19, 8296/25+24, 8299/25+24, 8302/25+26, 8303/25+27, 8310/25+32, 8316/25+35, 8333/25+44 to 8335/25+46, 8339/25+47, 8340/25+48, 8346/25+51, 8347/25+52, 9035/25+74, 9075/25+90, 9128/26+03 to 9130/26+05, 9136/26+08, 9145/26+11, 9150/26+12, 9151/26+13, 9156/26+ 15, 9163/26+18, 9164/26+19, 9181/26+29, 9182/26+30, 9185/26+33, 9186/26+34, 9188/26+ 36, 7301/26+41, 7302/26+42, 7402/26+56, 7404/26+58, 7431/26+85, 7432/26+86, 7436/26+90 (137)
TF-104D (ex-CAF): 5306/104636, 5308/104638, 5312/104642, 5320/104650, 5328/104658, 5331/104661 (6)
TF-104G (MAP): 5503/61-3027 to 5505/61-3029, 5520/62-12275 to 5522/62-12277 (6)
TF-104G (ex-GAF): (1981-89) 5701/27+01, 5703/27+02, 5704/27+03, 5707/27+06, 5710/27 +09, 5711/27+10, 5713/27+12, 5716/27+15, 5720/27+19 to 5723/27+22, 5725/27+24, 5728/ 27+27, 5731/27+29, 5737/27+35, 5740/27+38, 5741/27+39, 5905/27+76, 5911/27+82, 5913/ 27+84, 5914/27+85, 5918/27+88, 5919/27+89, 5920/27+90, 5923/27+93, 5924/27+94, 5926/ 27+96, 5927/27+97, 5932/28+02, 5945/28+15, 5950/28+20, 5960/28+30, 5962/28+32, 5964/28+34 (35)

Above: Turkey applied a new three-tone camouflage to several of its aircraft in the early 1970s.

Right: The Turkish F-104s fulfilled both air defence and ground attack roles, and have now been totally replaced by the F-16. Surprisingly it was the CF-104s of 8 AJU (rather than the much younger F-104S fleet) which were the longest survivors.

Above: Turkish RF-104Gs have come from the KLu, KNL and Luftwaffe (illustrated). Some aircraft have received an all-over grey scheme.

TF-104G (ex-EdA): 5524/62-12279 (CE.8-2), 5529/65-9415 (CE.8-3) (2)
TF-104G (ex-KLu): D-5702, 5801, 5807 to 5809, 5812 to 5814, 5816/17 (10)
TF-104G (ex-RNoAF): 5508/62-12263 (1)
Aeritalia F-104S: 6851 to 6868, 6882 to 6885, 6888/89, 6891 to 6906 (40)
*indicates RF-104Gs

UNITS:
4 Ana Jet Us: Mürted, 141 Filo, F-104G/TF-104G (late 1963 to 1988); 142 Filo, F-104G/
F-104S/TF-104G (late 1963 to early 1989); Oncel Flight (OCU) (1963 to 1987)
6 Ana Jet Us: Bandirma, 161 Filo, F/TF-104G to 1989; 162 Filo, RF-104G/TF-104G (1982
to 1990)
8 Ana Jet Us: Diyarbakir, 181 Filo, CF-104/TF-104G (1985 to 1995); 182 Filo, CF-104/
CF-104D (1985 to 1995)
9 Ana Jet Us: Balikesir, 191 Filo, F-104S/TF-104G (1975 to 1993); 192 Filo (F-104S until
1987, then F-104G/TF-104G to 1992); 193 Filo (OCU), F-104G/TF-104G (1987 to 1993)

*TF-104Gs were assigned in small numbers to all of the front-line squadrons,
and in larger numbers to 4 AJU's Oncel Flight which undertook type
conversion.*

United States

The first XF-104 was trucked to the Air Force Flight Test Center (AFFTC), Edwards AFB,
California on 25 February 1954 and flew on 5 March. The YF-104A was tested at Edwards
beginning 17 February 1956. The first operational F-104A in USAF service reached the 83rd
FIS at Hamilton AFB, California on 29 January 1958. Initially slated for Tactical Air Command
(TAC) where it had been viewed as an F-100 Super Sabre replacement, the F-104A went to
Air Defense Command (ADC) instead due to ADC's urgent need for an interceptor to fill in
between the F-102 and F-106. The 83rd FIS received its first F-104B in 1958.
  The first F-104C for the USAF was accepted by the 476th TFS/479th TFW at George AFB,
California on 15 October 1958. The first operational F-104D was accepted by the same
squadron the following month.
  USAF F-104A Starfighters from two squadrons from Hamilton AFB went into action for
the first time from Nationalist Chinese and American bases on Formosa (it was not referred
to in English at the time as Taiwan) in late 1958, following Chinese Communist aggression
against the Republic of China island of Quemoy in the Straits of Formosa. The display of
their Mach 2 capabilities recorded by PRC ground radars proved a sufficient deterrent,
although in reality most of the action was over by the time the Starfighters arrived and their
impact on Peking's leadership was negligible. In October 1961, when the USSR cut West
German access links to Berlin, three ANG F-104A squadrons assigned to Air Defense
Command were transferred to Tactical Air Command and rushed to Europe to reinforce
NATO's air defences. During the 1962 Cuban missile crisis, USAF F-104Cs were deployed to
bases in the southeastern US as the most effective available counter to the threat of Soviet-
supplied MiG fighters operating from that island. They remained in that area until the late
1960s. Fifteen F-104Cs of the 479th TFW were also sent to South Vietnam in March 1965 to
counter North Vietnamese interference with USAF strike aircraft, after the shooting-down of
two Republic F-105s by MiG-17s of the NVAF. Each of the 479th's three F-104 squadrons
served rotation tours, which were repeated in mid-1966, when the USAF still operated some
115 Starfighters, including 40 F-104As at Homestead and Webb AFBs, and about 75
F-104Cs at George AFB. By early 1967, however, only one Starfighter squadron remained in
the regular USAF inventory, and this was finally disbanded a year later. F-104B/Cs continued
operating with the Air National Guard until July 1975.

SERIALS:
XF-104 prototypes: 53-7786, 53-7787 (2)
YF-104 pre-production aircraft: 55-2955 to 55-2971 (17)
F-104A: F-104A-1-LO, 56-730 to 56-736 (7); F-104A-5-LO, 56-737 to 56-747 (11); F-104A-10-

*The first operational unit to receive any Starfighter was the 83rd Fighter
Interceptor Squadron at Hamilton AFB, California.*

LO, 56-748 to 56-763 (16); F-104A-15-LO: 56-764 to 788 (25); F-104A-20-LO, 56-789 to 56-
825 (37); F-104A-25-LO, 56-826 to 56-877; F-104A-30-LO, 56-878 to 56-882 (5); RF-104A-LO,
56-939 to 56-956 (18 RF-104A cancelled); total 153
F-104B: F-104B-1-LO, 56-3719 to 56-3724 (6); F-104B-5-LO, 57-1294 to 57-1302 (9);
F-104B-10-LO, 57-1303 to 57-1311 (9); F-104B-15-LO, 57-1312, 57-1313 (2); total 26
F-104C: F-104C-5-LO, 56-883 to 938 (56); F-104C-10-LO, 57-910 to 57-930 (21); F-104C-15-
LO, 57-931 to 57-1293 (363 cancelled); total 77.
F-104D: F-104D-5-LO, 57-1314 to 57-1320 (7); F-104D-10-LO, 57-1321 to 57-1328 (8);
F-104D-15-LO, 57-1329 to 57-1334 (6); F-104?-LO, 57-1335 to 1417 (83 cancelled); total 21

UNITS:
USAF Air Defense Command: F-104A/B, 83rd Fighter-Interceptor Sqn; 337th FIS,
Hamilton AFB, California, February 1958, and Patrick AFB, Florida, (1961); 56th FIS, Wright-
Patterson AFB, Ohio (1957); 319th FIS; 331st FIS; 337th FIS, Westover AFB,
Massachusetts, to 1959/60; 319th, 331st and 482nd FIS, 32nd Air Division, Homestead
AFB, Florida, March 1963 to December 1969; 538th FIS, Larson AFB, Washington (1958)
Tactical Air Command: F-104C/D, 434th, 435th, 436th, and 476th Tactical Fighter
Squadrons (479th Tactical Fighter Wing), 831st Air Division, George AFB, California (16
October 1958 to 1965). 435th TFS to Torrejon (Spain), November 1959; 4512th, 4518th,
4443rd USAF Combat Crew Training Sqns, 4510th Combat Crew Training Wing; 4512th,
4518th, 4443rd Combat Crew Training Squadrons, 58th Tactical Fighter Training Wing, 405th
Tactical Training Wing, Luke AFB, Arizona (training of German pilots)
Air National Guard: F-104A/B, 151st Fighter-Interceptor Sqn, Tennessee ANG (June
1960 to March 1963), Knoxville; 157th FIS, South Carolina ANG (February 1960 to June
1963), McEntire ANGB; 197th FIS, Arizona ANG (July 1960 to September 1962), Phoenix
Sky Harbor; F-104C/D, 198th Tactical Fighter Sqn (15th Tactical Fighter Group), Puerto Rico
ANG, Muniz ANGB/San Juan (summer 1967 to July 1975)
Air Research and Development Command: Air Force Flight Test Center and Air Force
Test Pilots School, Edwards AFB, California: F-104A/B/C/D/G, NF-104A (three assigned
September 1963, including 56-0756/60)
Air Proving Ground Command: Armament Development & Test Center, Eglin AFB,
Florida; 3205th Drone Squadron: QF-104A-5-LO (11)
National Aeronautics and Space Administration (NASA): Dryden Flight Research
Facility, Edwards AFB, California, YF-104A (55-2961/NASA 818), F-104A (56-0749; 56-1734),
F-104A/G (56-0790/NASA 820), F-104B (57-1303/NASA 819), TF-104G (61-3065/27 and
37/NASA 824, 66-13628/28 and 09/NASA 825, 24+64/NASA 826), F-104N (NASA 011/811;
NASA 012/812; NASA 013/813); Ames Flight Research Facility, NAS Moffett Field,
California, JF-104A (56-0745), F-104B (57-1303/NASA 819)

*Left: In their early service with the 479th Tactical Fighter Wing, the USAF
F-104Cs wore flamboyant markings. These disappeared as the F-104 adopted
serious tasks during the Berlin and Cuba crises. The 479th had four
squadrons assigned throughout the Starfighter period.*

*Right: During 1960-63 squadrons of
the Arizona, South Carolina and
Tennessee (illustrated) Air National
Guards operated the F-104A/B on air
defence duties. In November 1961
all three were called to active duty
during the Berlin Wall crisis to
bolster NATO's defences. Arizona
aircraft went to Ramstein in
Germany while South Carolina
went to Moron in Spain. The 151st
FIS/TN ANG joined the 197th at
Ramstein, assuming alert duties on
19th December. It returned to state
control in August 1962.*

Republic's legendary 'Lead Sled'

F-105
Thunderchief

The final member of Republic's 'Thunder' family, the F-105 Thunderchief was conceived to deliver a nuclear weapon against a point target while flying at supersonic speed at low level. Powered by the largest jet engine then available, the 'Thud', as it was mockingly known, was plagued with early problems, but as the 'bugs' were ironed out and the largest single-engined fighter yet built became embroiled in an entirely different sort of conflict, its reputation was transformed. Flying more missions than any other type over the jungles of Indo-China, the F-105 formed the backbone of the Rolling Thunder bombing campaign against North Vietnam between 1965 and 1968 and later helped pioneer USAF defence suppression techniques in the ground-breaking Wild Weasel III programme. To those that flew it the 'Thud' nickname had become a term of endearment.

F-105F 63-8326 of the 49th Tactical Fighter Wing at Spangdahlem AB was photographed over the Atlantic from a KC-135 tanker during December 1965. Like the vast majority of the Thunderchief fleet, 'FH-326' was destined to see service in Vietnam and eventually joined the F-105G Wild Weasel III programme.

The aircraft was known by various names, most of which were derogatory in nature. Its official name was Thunderchief, but Air Force air and ground crews referred to it as 'Hog', 'Ultra Hog', 'Squash Bomber' and 'Lead Sled', because of its size and the amount of runway it consumed on take-off. It was said that if you built a runway that ran completely around the earth, Republic would build an aircraft that would use all of it. 'Thud' was the preferred name. It was said to be the sound an F-105 made when crashing into the jungle! However, 'Thud' was later to become a term of reverence; if you flew the F-105, you didn't want to fly anything else. Down 'in the weeds', where the Thunderchief operated, no other aircraft could catch it.

Initially, it was known simply as Advanced Project 63 Fighter Bomber Experimental, or AP-63FBX, a company-funded project begun in 1951 that had as its aim the construction of a Mach 1.5 fighter-bomber with a nuclear strike capability. A formal proposal was made to the US Air Force in April 1952, resulting in a verbal 'go-ahead' commitment in May of that year. A formal contract was issued to Republic in September 1952, calling for initial production of 199 aircraft that would be operational in 1955.

However, in March 1953, the Air Force cut that contract down to 37 fighter-bomber and nine reconnaissance aircraft. This was followed in December by a complete shut-down of F-105 project development; it was reinstated in February 1954, but only for 15 development aircraft. By September 1954 even that contract had been cut, from 15 down to three, a figure quickly amended one month later to six and then back to 15 in February 1955.

GOR amendments

The original General Operational Requirement, GOR-49, issued by the Air Force in December 1954, called for three amendments: the F-105 was to have in-flight refuelling capabilities, a new, highly complex fire control system and enhanced performance compared to the aircraft envisaged in the original proposal. The latter would be accomplished by replacing the proposed Allison J71 engine with the new Pratt & Whitney J75 engine, then still under development.

The initial AP-63FBX proposal issued in December 1953 was intended to be powered by a pair of Allison J71s, later changed to a single J71-A-7 axial-flow turbojet engine rated at 14,500 lb (64.49 kN) of thrust with afterburner. The AP-63FBX was a single-seat aircraft with a 36.7-ft (11.19-m) wing span and a length of 52.3 ft (15.94 m). Combat weight was set at 27,500 lb (12474 kg), with a maximum take-off weight estimated to be 37,000 lb (16783 kg) with 6,000 lb (2722 kg) of ordnance. Defensive armament was to be four T-130 0.60-in machine-guns with 300 rounds per gun.

"A decade of Thundercraft" reads the caption to this company publicity photograph. Republic's pedigree as a builder of fighter aircraft was beyond question. The F-105, represented here by F-105B 54-0102, was preceded by the widely-produced F-84 family (from right) – F-84E Thunderjet, RF-84F Thunderflash and F-84F Thunderstreak. The aircraft are pictured outside the company's Farmingdale, Long Island, factory on what would appear to have been a chilly winter's day.

On 22 October 1955 the YF-105A prototype 54-0098 (below) made its first flight, from Edwards AFB, California. The two prototypes had RF-84 type wing root intakes, also seen on 54-0099 (below right).

The second YF-105A demonstrates Republic's buddy refuelling system with the third F-105B. There were few outward differences between the first two prototypes, though 54-0099 had a one-piece, unpetalled exhaust, unlike the first aircraft. The differences between the YF-105As and the redesigned F-105Bs were more apparent, including the 'Coke bottle' area-ruled fuselage, taller fin and distinctive 'nostril'-type intakes of the latter.

The bomb load was estimated to be 2,000 lb (907 kg) of conventional weapons or a single 'special store' – i.e., nuclear weapon – weighing up to 3,400 lb (1542 kg), in an internal rotary weapons bay. Externally, the AP-63FBX would be capable of carrying up to six 1,000-lb (454-kg) bombs on underwing pylons, or another 'special store'. The weapons were to be delivered using the new MA-8 fire control system, using a 'toss-bombing' technique in the case of nuclear weapons. Initially, the AP-63FBX design looked very similar to the RF-84F Thunderflash reconnaissance aircraft – though much bigger.

By 1 January 1954, the design had evolved into the basic shape of the F-105 production aircraft. The nose was much more pointed and the horizontal stabilisers had been moved from the middle of the vertical stabiliser to low on the fuselage. Wing sweep remained at 45° at 25 per cent of the wing chord, but the span had been reduced from

36.7 to 35 ft (16.65 to 15.88 m). The aircraft's length was drastically increased from 52.3 to 62 ft (15.94 to 18.90 m).

The proposed engine remained the Allison J71-A-7, but it was modified with a variable-area tail pipe that increased maximum thrust from 14,500 lb (64.49 kN) to 15,500 lb (68.93 kN) in afterburner. The maximum weapons load was set at 6,000 lb (2722 kg), more external hardpoints allowing loading variations. The four T-130 0.60-in guns were replaced by a single General Electric T-171D six-barrelled, 20-mm rotary cannon that had a rate of fire of up to 6,000 rounds per minute and an ammunition drum that held up to 1,028 20-mm shells.

Designated the F-105A, an official mock-up was inspected and approved in October 1953. The MA-8 fire control system comprised an AN/APG-31 ranging radar, K-19 sight, a toss bomb and time-of-flight computer, and the T-145 special stores release system. Combat weight was increased to

Far left: Republic's chief engineer, Alexander Kartveli took some convincing as to the necessity of the area-ruled fuselage and, in the event, the bulged rear fuselage of the F-105B was, at his insistence, only 80 per cent of the size recommended by NACA.

Below: Four F-105Bs were constructed for service test, the first taking to the air on 26 May 1956. The following month Republic applied to the Air Force for approval of the name 'Thunderchief'; this was granted in July, an official naming ceremony taking place in August.

Back to the drawing board – F-105B

It became apparent after the type's first flight that, as originally designed, the Thunderchief was not going to achieve supersonic flight because it was underpowered and was held back by transonic drag produced by its fuselage. The assistance of aerodynamicists from NACA (NASA after October 1958) was requested and their solution was Richard T. Whitcomb's area-ruled, so-called 'Coke bottle' or 'wasp-waisted' fuselage, as already applied to Convair's similarly-handicapped F-102. Other changes included the new Pratt & Whitney J75 engine, revised air intakes to assist the increased airflow and shock waves produced during supersonic flight and a taller tail fin to improve directional stability at high angles of attack.

The third of the F-105B-1-RE aircraft, 54-0102 (top), was used extensively for publicity photographs, usually with the designation painted on its nose in place of the more usual 'FH-102' buzz number (above). In the latter view the aircraft carries a dummy bomb load, including 3,000-lb weapons on the inboard pylons.

28,530 lb (12941 kg) and maximum take-off weight with a single 3,400-lb (1542-kg) 'special store' rose more than 4,000 lb (1814 kg), to 41,248 lb (18710 kg). However, a normal nuclear strike would have been accomplished with one of the smaller 1,700-lb (771-kg) 'special stores'.

Maximum speed of the F-105A was estimated to be 765 kt (1417 km/h) at 35,000 ft (10668 m) with a single 1,700-lb (771-kg) 'special store' and external drop tanks. Combat radius was estimated to be 959 miles (1543 km) on internal fuel but, with its in-flight refuelling capability, the F-105A's combat radius was virtually unlimited.

By April 1955, the GOR-49 had been amended to include installation of the new Pratt & Whitney YJ75-P-3 engine in place of the Allison J71. The YJ75 engine was a twin-spool, axial-flow turbojet with a two-position convergent tail pipe with a Republic-designed ram air ejector. The YJ75-P-3 was rated at 23,500 lb (104.51 kN) of thrust in afterburner, an 8,000-lb (35.58-kN) increase over the J71. However, development of the powerplant at Pratt & Whitney lagged behind schedule, which in turn caused several setbacks to the F-105A programme. The end result of these setbacks was that both YF-105As were built with P&W J57-P-25 powerplants.

Through the sound barrier

The first prototype, YF-105A 54-0098, was rolled out from the Republic factory in early October 1955. Ground testing and taxi tests began shortly after it had been shipped to Edwards AFB, California. On 22 October 1955, Republic's chief test pilot, 'Rusty' Roth, lifted the YF-105A off the dry lake runway at Edwards for its first flight. During this initial flight, which lasted some 45 minutes, Roth took the new aircraft through the sound barrier for the first time. However, ensuing high-speed testing revealed that the design would not come close to the requirements laid out in GOR-49. The problem was not simply the lack of power available with the substitute J57 powerplant; drag along the fuselage contours during transonic flight also played a part.

The second YF-105A made its first flight on 28 January 1956. The programme suffered a variety of problems that ultimately led to the crash of both YF-105A prototypes. In March, Roth had almost completed a series of flight tests when the aircraft suddenly lost power: the right main land-

Right: Officers inspect 54-0105, the first of the former RF-105B prototypes. The flat nose panels for camera ports are evident; five cameras were envisaged for the aircraft.

Reconnaissance variant – RF-105B

Known to Republic as AP-71, the specification for the RF-105B was issued in August 1955 and described a day photo-reconnaissance fighter based on the F-105B. Two months prior to the maiden flight of the first F-105B $10 million was set aside from FY1957 funds for 65 F-105Bs and 17 RF-105Bs; in the event only three aircraft were completed with camera noses – 54-0105, -0108 and -0112. When the RF programme was cancelled in July 1956 all were completed, less camera equipment, as JF-105B test airframes and joined the other F-105B aircraft in the ongoing test programme.

The RF-105 was revisited in late 1960, when an F-105D variant was proposed with a pod-mounted SLAR, IR sensors, various cameras and in-flight film development and ejection capability. The project was finally abandoned in December 1961, in favour of the RF-110A (later RF-4C) Phantom.

The last of the RF-105Bs and the only RF-105B-2-RE, 54-0112 sits on the ramp at Farmingdale. The 'JF-3' legend on the tail indicates the aircraft's new role as the third of the JF-105Bs.

By early 1958 there were 11 F-105Bs involved in various test programmes, namely the two YF-105As, the four pre-production F-105Bs, three F-105B-5-REs and a pair of JF-105B-1-REs (the former RF-105B prototypes). Here F-105B-5-RE 54-0106 is seen in typically garish test colours at Farmingdale.

ing gear had extended at over 500 kt (926 km/h) in a 5.5-*g* turn, shearing off the landing gear and wheel. Roth was forced to make a belly landing on the lakebed, breaking the back of the first prototype.

Republic test pilot Hank Beaird also suffered an in-flight emergency, in the second aircraft. After a normal take-off the nose gear had retracted exceptionally quickly, breaking the 'unlock' that held it in place in the nose gear bay. The gear would neither stay retracted nor extend and lock in the down position. Beaird had no choice but to crash land on the lakebed, also breaking the YF-105A's back. Both pilots were able to walk away with only injured pride.

F-105B debuts new engine

In mid-May 1956, the third prototype arrived at Edwards AFB. It was the first F-105B service test aircraft, 54-0100, and was quite different from both YF-105A prototypes. In addition to installation of the new YJ75-P-3 engine, the design of the air intakes and fuselage was completely changed. The fuselage was redesigned to incorporate Richard Whitcomb's area-ruled 'Coke bottle' or 'wasp waist' design, developed by the National Advisory Committee for Aeronautics (NACA). Area ruling the fuselage reduced drag caused by shock waves that occurred along the straight fuselage contours of conventional designs. Republic engineers bulged the fuselage at a point 1 ft (0.3 m) in front of the spot where wind tunnel tests indicated that increased drag first took effect. On the F-105, this was near the trailing edge of the wing-fuselage joint.

Concurrently, Antonio Ferri completely redesigned the air intake system. His new intake design was swept forward and had a variable air inlet (VAI) control system that used a set of intake 'ramps' to increase or decrease airflow. These were controlled by a Bendix central air data computer (CADC) that measured the amount of air needed

for maximum power at any speed, and moved the ramps in or out accordingly. For low-speed operation, the ramps retracted, allowing maximum air ingestion; at high Mach numbers, the ramps were extended to decrease air flow. These two changes – area ruling and the controllable air intakes – were all that was needed to put the F-105 design into the Mach 2 speed range.

However, this additional speed exacerbated another problem with the original design – vertical tail flutter. It had been discovered on both the earlier F-100A Super Sabre and the YF-105A that their vertical tails were much too short, causing flutter and a loss of lateral control. Republic engineers thus increased the height and chord of the vertical tail and rudder. In addition, on production aircraft rear vision windows behind the canopy were deleted; these had been carried over from the F/RF-84F.

The first production F-105B-10-REs were accepted by the Air Force on 27 May 1958, some three years late. This view of the crowded Farmingdale production line show F-105B-15-REs in final assembly with fuselages for later aircraft in the foreground. A number of the aircraft in this view would later equip the USAF's 'Thunderbirds' display team.

The final pair of F-105B test airframes (B-5-REs 54-0109 and -0110), plus the sole B-6-RE, 54-0111 (pictured) were employed to test the type in simulated combat conditions in a programme run jointly by Republic, TAC, Air Research and Development Command and Air Proving Ground Command. 54-0111 was later among the first F-105Bs accepted for service with the Air Force and was issued to the 4th Tactical Fighter Wing.

Project Fast Wind

As the first unit in the world equipped with a Mach-2 strike capability, the 4th TFW was keen to demonstrate the performance of its new aircraft, especially in view of the problems plaguing the F-105 programme. Project Fast Wind saw a new world closed-circuit speed record set by the wing's commanding officer, Brigadier General Joseph H. Moore, on 11 December 1959. Moore flew F-105B 57-5812 over a 100-km (62.14-mile) course at Edwards AFB at 36,000 ft (10973 m) and at an average speed of 1216.48 mph (1957.73 km/h), breaking an earlier record set by the French Nord Griffon II by a substantial margin.

Six newly delivered F-105B-10-REs, complete with 4th TFW markings, make an impressive sight on the ramp at Eglin AFB. The 335th TFS was soon moved to Seymour-Johnson AFB, North Carolina, where it would conduct operational testing of its new mount.

Above right: This echelon formation of unmarked F-105Bs belonged to the 334th TFS, the second unit to receive Thunderchiefs. All are examples of the F-105B-20-RE, which introduced the uprated J75-P-19W engine.

Production delays and modifications meant that it would be mid-1959 before the 335th TFS was fully equipped with F-105Bs and another year before the other two squadrons in the 4th TFW had received their aircraft. Despite this the Thunderchief had been declared operational in January 1959. Among the modifications were the retrofitting of J75-P-19W engines and a Goodyear anti-skid braking system to earlier B-10 and B-15 aircraft. Additionally, toward the end of 1959, problems with the air data computer, GE MA-8 fire control system and the F-105's autopilot prompted Project Optimise, a 26-point modification programme. It was little wonder that at this time fewer than one quarter of the F-105 fleet was flyable.

It was on the F-105B that the four-petal, clover-leaf air brakes were first installed. Designed to fit around the exhaust jet orifice, the four segments could be deployed in several different configurations, depending on requirements. During landing, only the two side segments were deployed (as the bottom segment had insufficient ground clearance and brake 'chute deployment negated the use of the top segment), while all four segments could be deployed simultaneously in flight.

First F-105B's first flight mishap

On 26 May 1956, the first F-105B, 54-0100, took to the air for the first time. Republic test pilot Lin Hendrix put the aircraft through the required flight tests, including operation of the new air brakes, and came around for a landing. Checking his instrument display, Hendrix found he did not have a green 'down and locked' light on the main landing gear. Chase pilots confirmed that the main landing gear had not extended.

Hendrix had forgotten to retract the air brakes, causing him to apply more power to keep the aircraft in the air.

With the VAI intakes fully opened, the central air data computer had determined that still more air was needed, and opened the auxiliary air intake doors (normally used only during ground operations), which were located inside the main wheel bays. Operation of the auxiliary air intakes, combined with a set of brand new seals on the main landing gear doors, caused a suction effect in the wheel bay that kept the doors closed.

Nothing Hendrix tried seemed to work and the main gear remained firmly in the 'up' position. Hendrix followed his F-105 predecessors and put the F-105B prototype down on its belly on the dry lakebed at Edwards. Following a controlled crash, Hendrix started to walk away from the aircraft when he heard a noise – a 'whoosh'. Turning to look at the aircraft, he watched as the main landing gear slowly lowered on to the lakebed. The suction seal on the main gear doors had broken after engine shutdown, allowing the gear to cycle into the down position. Unlike the previous crashes, the F-105B was back on flight status six weeks later.

F-105B testing continued into 1957. On 28 July the public got its first look at the huge new fighter, which had been named Thunderchief in 1956, at the Andrews AFB Open House and Air Show celebrating the 50th anniversary of military aviation. Two sub-types were also under development – the RF-105B and the F-105C. The production contract called for development of three reconnaissance aircraft using the F-105 airframe, to be designated RF-105B. Five cameras in its nose would replace the T171E-3 Vulcan

'Thunderbirds'

Nine F-105Bs (seven B-15s, plus single examples from the B-10 and B-20 blocks) were allocated to the 4520th Air Demonstration Squadron 'Thunderbirds' in May 1963, as follows: 57-5782, 57-5787, 57-5790, 57-5793, 57-5797, 57-5798, 57-5801, 57-5802 and 57-5814. Despite misgivings expressed by some that the aircraft was too big and heavy to be flown in close formation, the team had few problems adapting to the F-105.

Left: Ground crews look on during a photo shoot involving 'Thunderbirds' pilots and an immaculately presented Thunderchief.

Below: A pair of the 'Thunderbirds' F-105B-15s demonstrates the team's 'Calypso' routine over Nellis during early 1964. The sooty marks on the tail of the trailing aircraft suggest that it normally flew the 'slot' position below and behind the lead aircraft. Four of the 'Thunderbirds' F-105s were fitted with stainless steel tail fins so that they could fly the slot without risking damage from the exhaust of the lead aircraft.

cannon and E-34 ranging radar. Defensive armament would consist of a pair of M39A1 high-speed 20-mm cannon, mounted inside bulges on the fuselage sides under the air intakes, while a 340-US gal (1287-litre) fuel tank would be installed in the area originally designed as the bomb bay. However, the USAF cancelled the RF-105B project in July 1956, and these three airframes were completed as JF-105B service test aircraft.

An amendment to the contract also called for development of five airframes as F-105C two-seat fighter-bomber or trainer aircraft. The F-105C would utilise the same fuselage as the F-105B, with the second cockpit in a tandem position behind the original cockpit and taking the place of one of the fuselage fuel cells. Otherwise, the F-105C would be identical to the B model, with all its combat capabilities, weapons, electronics, and ordnance carriage. However, the Air Force cancelled the F-105C in 1957 as the aircraft entered the mock-up stage. Republic completed 15 pre-production F-105s: two YF-105As, four F-105Bs, three JF-105Bs, and five F-105B-5s.

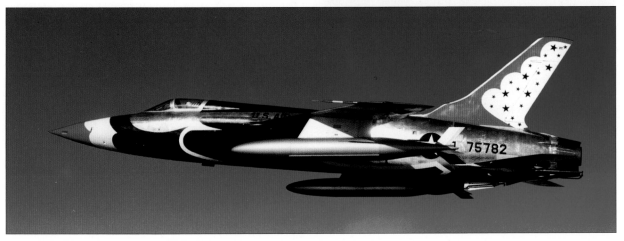

Left: Most of the modifications made to the F-105 for the 'Thunderbirds' and carried out by Republic between October 1962 and April 1964, were prompted by the need to reduce its weight. The M61A1 cannon, Doppler equipment and other items were removed and ballast added to maintain the aircraft's centre-of-gravity. The twin pipes directing smoke oil into the aircraft's exhaust are visible in this view of F-105B-10-RE 57-5782.

The 141st TFS, 108th TFG had been operating F-105Bs for just over a year when a smartly turned out 57-5784 was photographed at the New Jersey ANG unit's station – McGuire AFB – in 1965. The 141st acquired most of the ex-'Thunderbird' aircraft when the team abandoned the Thunderchief in 1964.

The first true production version of the F-105B came off the Republic assembly line in mid-May 1958 and was accepted by the Air Force on 27 May. It was designated F-105B-6, 54-0111, and was the only B-6 built. Delivered to Eglin AFB test facility in August 1958, the F-105B-6 was handed over to pilots and crews of the 335th Tactical Fighter Squadron, who conducted the Category I and II flight tests in addition to bringing the type into operational service. The 335th Squadron was a unit within the veteran 4th Tactical Fighter Wing, which was slated to be the first combat unit to operate the F-105B.

However, the many problems within the F-105B development programme, including all the modifications needed to meet the often-revised GOR-49 requirements, set back the production schedule by several months. The 335th Squadron would not be at full strength until summer 1959. By late spring 1960, three of the four squadrons within the 4th TFW had been equipped with F-105Bs – or should have been; in early 1960, all 56 F-105B aircraft in the 4th TFW were grounded for various reasons, including spare parts availability problems. The fourth squadron, the 333rd TFS, would not be equipped until 1961 when the first F-105Ds became available.

In December 1959, the last six F-105B-20 aircraft, featuring the J75-P-19W engine with 24,500 lb (108.95 kN) of thrust in afterburner, came off the Republic assembly line. This brought total production of the B model to 75 examples, including the 15 pre-production service test aircraft.

Four units operated the F-105B in first-line service with the US Air Force. The 4th TFW had three squadrons equipped with the type – the 334th, 335th, and 336th Squadrons – and the 4520th CCTW had one squadron of F-105Bs at Nellis AFB, the 4537th CCTS. The 23rd TFW at McConnell AFB, Kansas, converted to F-105D Thunderchiefs in 1964, and flew many ex-4th TFW F-105Bs during its initial transition to the Thunderchief. The other Thunderchief unit was the 4520th Air Demonstration Squadron, otherwise known as the 'Thunderbirds'.

'Thuds' for the 'Thunderbirds'

In May 1963, the Air Force decided to re-equip the 'Thunderbirds' with the F-105 Thunderchief. The first of nine F-105B aircraft were withdrawn from service with the 4th TFW, then flown to Republic for modification to 'Thunderbird' demonstration aircraft standard. The weapons and fire control system were removed and replaced by ballast. Two 50-US gal (189-litre) smoke oil tanks (one for red and the other for blue smoke) were installed in the ammunition bay in lieu of one of the fuel cells, operated by buttons on the control stick. The flaps were modified for employment at speeds up to 500 kt (926 km/h) and the fuel system was changed to allow for extended periods of time in inverted flight. To the onlooker, however, the most obvious external change was the application of the team's spectacular red, white and blue paint scheme.

All nine aircraft had been delivered to Nellis AFB, home of the 'Thunderbirds', by 16 April 1964. Less than a month later, the team flew its first air show with the 'Chief. However, it was at one of these early public shows that a disastrous crash occurred: on 9 May 1964 at Hamilton AFB, California, F-105B 57-5801 disintegrated during landing and

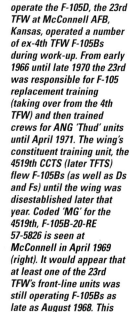

Reactivated in 1964 to operate the F-105D, the 23rd TFW at McConnell AFB, Kansas, operated a number of ex-4th TFW F-105Bs during work-up. From early 1966 until late 1970 the 23rd was responsible for F-105 replacement training (taking over from the 4th TFW) and then trained crews for ANG 'Thud' units until April 1971. The wing's constituent training unit, the 4519th CCTS (later TFTS) flew F-105Bs (as well as Ds and Fs) until the wing was disestablished later that year. Coded 'MG' for the 4519th, F-105B-20-RE 57-5826 is seen at McConnell in April 1969 (right). It would appear that at least one of the 23rd TFW's front-line units was still operating F-105Bs as late as August 1968. This F-105B-20-RE (above right), taking off from NAS Miramar, carries the 'MD' tail code of the 561st TFS.

Cancelled two-seaters – F-105C and F-105E

Republic's first attempt at generating Air Force interest in a fully operational two-seat Thunderchief came in early 1956, when the F-105C was proposed. Based on the F-105B, the new variant was designed around a specification issued by Training Command. A mock-up was completed and Air Force approval gained in April; five examples were to be built for evaluation. However, before any were built the Air Force had a change of heart and the two-seat Thunderchief was cancelled the following year.

The F-105E – similar to the F-105C, but based on the F-105D – fared better than had its predecessor; no fewer than eight forward fuselages were 45 per cent complete when it, too, was cancelled, on 18 March 1959. The USAF felt that Republic should concentrate on the F-105D in order to make up lost time and reduce costs.

The F-105C mock-up (right) had tandem seats under a large double canopy with bulged sides to improve visibility. The F-105E (below) was essentially similar, but based on the F-105D.

pilot Captain Gene Devlin was killed. The F-105B had suffered a structural break along its upper fuselage spine. The 'Thunderbirds' transitioned back to F-100 Super Sabres for the remainder of the 1964 season, with the intention that the Thunderchief would be re-introduced in 1965. The Air Force grounded all F-105s and introduced Project Backbone, under which the structural brace in the upper fuselage was replaced by a much stronger design in all F-105Bs and a handful of early F-105Ds.

The 'Thud' never rejoined the 'Thunderbirds'. All remaining front-line F-105Bs, including the display aircraft, were transferred to reserve status with the 141st Tactical Fighter Squadron, New Jersey Air National Guard, beginning on 16 April 1964. The 141st TFS operated the F-105B until 1981. F-105Bs were also later operated by the 119th TFS, New Jersey ANG, and the 466th TFS, Air Force Reserve, at Hill AFB, Utah until 1981.

F-105D – the ultimate Thunderchief

With the B-model service test aircraft in the initial stages of development, the Air Force and Republic began a design proposal for the follow-on aircraft, the F-105D. It was drastically different from the F-105B and showed so much more promise that the Air Force verbally committed to no fewer than 1,500 aircraft to equip 14 tactical fighter wings, though subsequently production of the Air Force version of the renowned McDonnell F-4 Phantom led to reductions in the F-105D contract of almost 50 per cent.

The revision to the original General Operating Requirement on the F-105, i.e., GOR 49-1, called for three major differences between the F-105B and the F-105D: a far more sophisticated fire control system, a more powerful engine, and a completely revised instrument display in the cockpit. These, in turn, required several minor changes throughout the design. All the changes mandated in GOR 49-1, plus those called for when newer advanced offensive and defensive weapons systems became available, made the F-105D into the ultimate Thunderchief.

A completely new fire control system was installed in the D-model – the AN/ASG-19 Thunderstick system. The ASG-19 could be used in both a visual or limited blind-bombing mode; with both air-to-air and air-to-ground capa-

bility; and was capable of handling the latest in conventional or nuclear weapons.

The new NASAAR R-14A (North American Search and Range Radar) had a ground and contour mapping feature. It also featured the APN-131 Doppler radar for terrain avoidance, plus an X-band beacon. The R-14A ranging radar had a much larger antenna dish, which required a complete redesign of the forward fuselage contours of the F-105D. Installation of the R-14A also required a 15-in (38.1-cm) increase in the overall length of the fuselage through an extension of the nose. The pitot tube was moved from the left wingtip on the B-model to the tip of the nose on the F-105D.

Power for the D-model would come from the J75-P-19W engine that had been introduced on the F-105B-20. With water injection, the -19W engine offered a maximum thrust of 26,500 lb (117.85 kN) in afterburner. The additional thrust required more air, so Republic engineers redesigned the interior contours of the air intakes and ramps, and

Demonstrated at Fort Bragg, North Carolina in 1961, F-105D 58-1173 set a weight-lifting record for a single-engined aircraft with this load of 16 750-lb M117 bombs. Given that an M117 actually weighed around 820 lb (372 kg), the total load was 13,120 lb (5951 kg). In combat bomb loads like this were rarely realistic; certainly in Southeast Asia loads of 4,000-6,000 lb (1814-2722 kg) were more typical.

Enter the 'D'

Left: In time-honoured fashion the first F-105D (58-1146) poses for the company photographer on the ramp at Farmingdale around the time of its first flight on 9 June 1959. There was no prototype, the first production examples going to the 4th TFW and the 4520th CCTW at Nellis AFB.

The F-105F and F-105G (right) shared essentially the same cockpit instrumentation as the F-105D, simplified tape instrumentation for the Airspeed Mach Indicator (AMI) and the Altitude-Vertical Velocity Indicator (AVVI) replacing the conventional dials of the F-105B (above). Between the tape instruments were an enlarged Attitude Director Indicator (ADI) and Horizontal Situation Indicator (HSI) and, below these, a radar scope – a feature new to the F-105D and subsequent variants.

Above: During conversion from F-105F to F-105G standard (pictured), the aircraft's rear cockpit instrumentation was extensively remodelled to make room for mission equipment, most of which was installed above the radar scope. A full set of flight controls and basic flight instrumentation was retained, though tape-type instruments were deleted.

F-105D Thunderchief cutaway

1 Pitot tube
2 Radome
3 Radar scanner dish
4 Radar mounting and tracking mechanism
5 Forward electronic countermeasures (ECM) antenna
6 Aft-facing strike camera
7 Radome hinge
8 ADF sense aerial
9 Fire-control radar transmitter/receiver
10 Cannon muzzle
11 Instrument electronics
12 In-flight refuelling position light
13 Air refuelling receptacle
14 Cannon ammunition drum, 1,028 rounds
15 Liquid oxygen converter
16 Angle of attack transmitter
17 Cannon barrels
18 Nosewheel doors
19 M61, 20-mm, six-barrelled rotary cannon
20 Ammunition feed chute
21 Gun gas venting pipe
22 Air refuelling probe housing
23 Alternator and electrical bay
24 Air-driven turbine
25 Air refuelling probe
26 Windshield rain dispersal duct
27 Bulletproof windscreen panels

30 Navigation radar display
31 Rudder pedals
32 Cockpit front pressure bulkhead
33 Cannon mounting
34 Nosewheel leg strut
35 ILS system radar reflector
36 Taxiing lamps
37 Nosewheel
38 Torque scissor links
39 Hydraulic steering controls
40 Flight control system hydraulics bay
41 Electronics cooling air outlet
42 IFF aerial
43 UHF aerial
44 Underfloor radio and electronics bay
45 Cockpit pressure floor level
46 Pilot's side console panel
47 Engine throttle
48 Control column
49 Pilot's ejection seat
50 Seat back parachute pack
51 Headrest
52 Cockpit canopy cover
53 M118 3,000-lb (1360-kg) HE bomb (inboard pylon)
54 Starboard air intake
55 Cockpit canopy jack

59 Secondary electronics bay
60 Air data computer
61 Port air intake
62 Bomb bay fuel tank, 390-US gal (1476-litre)
63 Boundary layer splitter plate
64 Intake duct variable-area sliding ramp
65 Forward group of fuselage fuel tanks; total internal fuel capacity 1,160 US gal (4391 litres)

66 Gyro compass platform
67 Bomb bay fuel tank fuel transfer lines
68 Fuselage/front spar main frame
69 Dorsal spine fairing
70 Starboard mainwheel, stowed position

28 Radar attack sight
29 Instrument panel shroud

56 Canopy hinge
57 Air-conditioning pack
58 Cockpit rear pressure bulkhead

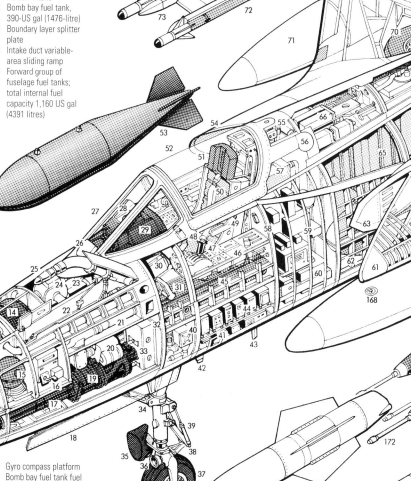

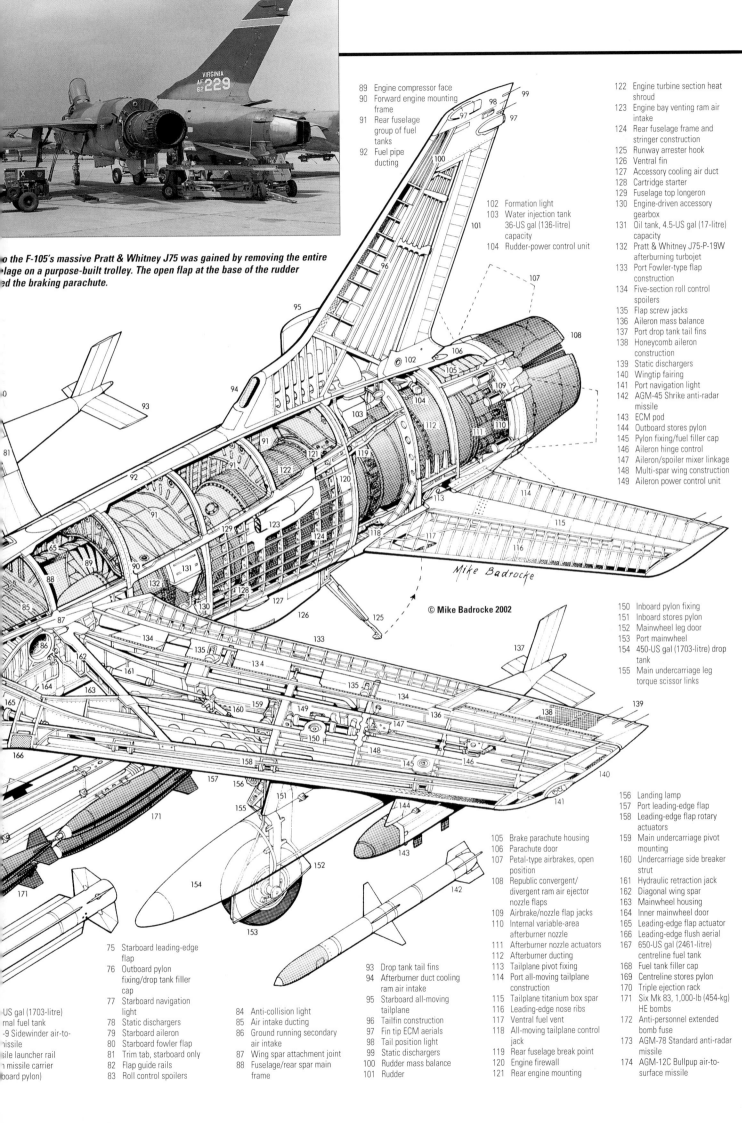

Access to the F-105's massive Pratt & Whitney J75 was gained by removing the entire rear fuselage on a purpose-built trolley. The open flap at the base of the rudder covered the braking parachute.

89 Engine compressor face
90 Forward engine mounting frame
91 Rear fuselage group of fuel tanks
92 Fuel pipe ducting

102 Formation light
103 Water injection tank 36-US gal (136-litre) capacity
104 Rudder-power control unit

105 Brake parachute housing
106 Parachute door
107 Petal-type airbrakes, open position
108 Republic convergent/divergent ram air ejector nozzle flaps
109 Airbrake/nozzle flap jacks
110 Internal variable-area afterburner nozzle
111 Afterburner nozzle actuators
112 Afterburner ducting
113 Tailplane pivot fixing
114 Port all-moving tailplane construction
115 Tailplane titanium box spar
116 Leading-edge nose ribs
117 Ventral fuel vent
118 All-moving tailplane control jack
119 Rear fuselage break point
120 Engine firewall
121 Rear engine mounting

122 Engine turbine section heat shroud
123 Engine bay venting ram air intake
124 Rear fuselage frame and stringer construction
125 Runway arrester hook
126 Ventral fin
127 Accessory cooling air duct
128 Cartridge starter
129 Fuselage top longeron
130 Engine-driven accessory gearbox
131 Oil tank, 4.5-US gal (17-litre) capacity
132 Pratt & Whitney J75-P-19W afterburning turbojet
133 Port Fowler-type flap construction
134 Five-section roll control spoilers
135 Flap screw jacks
136 Aileron mass balance
137 Port drop tank tail fins
138 Honeycomb aileron construction
139 Static dischargers
140 Wingtip fairing
141 Port navigation light
142 AGM-45 Shrike anti-radar missile
143 ECM pod
144 Outboard stores pylon
145 Pylon fixing/fuel filler cap
146 Aileron hinge control
147 Aileron/spoiler mixer linkage
148 Multi-spar wing construction
149 Aileron power control unit

150 Inboard pylon fixing
151 Inboard stores pylon
152 Mainwheel leg door
153 Port mainwheel
154 450-US gal (1703-litre) drop tank
155 Main undercarriage leg torque scissor links

156 Landing lamp
157 Port leading-edge flap
158 Leading-edge flap rotary actuators
159 Main undercarriage pivot mounting
160 Undercarriage side breaker strut
161 Hydraulic retraction jack
162 Diagonal wing spar
163 Mainwheel housing
164 Inner mainwheel door
165 Leading-edge flap actuator
166 Leading-edge flush aerial
167 650-US gal (2461-litre) centreline fuel tank
168 Fuel tank filler cap
169 Centreline stores pylon
170 Triple ejection rack
171 Six Mk 83, 1,000-lb (454-kg) HE bombs
172 Anti-personnel extended bomb fuse
173 AGM-78 Standard anti-radar missile
174 AGM-12C Bullpup air-to-surface missile

75 Starboard leading-edge flap
76 Outboard pylon fixing/drop tank filler cap
77 Starboard navigation light
78 Static dischargers
79 Starboard aileron
80 Starboard fowler flap
81 Trim tab, starboard only
82 Flap guide rails
83 Roll control spoilers
84 Anti-collision light
85 Air intake ducting
86 Ground running secondary air intake
87 Wing spar attachment joint
88 Fuselage/rear spar main frame

93 Drop tank tail fins
94 Afterburner duct cooling ram air intake
95 Starboard all-moving tailplane
96 Tailfin construction
97 Fin tip ECM aerials
98 Tail position light
99 Static dischargers
100 Rudder mass balance
101 Rudder

US gal (1703-litre) internal fuel tank
-9 Sidewinder air-to-missile
missile launcher rail
missile carrier
board pylon)

reconfigured the central air data computer that controlled the amount of air going to the engine. The installation of the water injection plumbing inside the rear fuselage also necessitated some redesign work.

In the cockpit, the entire instrument panel was changed. Gone were many of the old circular design dials, replaced by new vertical 'tape' instruments, which were far more accurate and easier to read in a combat situation. Four major instruments were changed – the attitude direction indicator, horizontal situation indicator, Mach meter, and altitude vertical velocity indicator, which measured rate of climb.

Other new systems included an ASQ-37 radio, ARA-48 direction-finder, ARN-61 instrument landing system, ARN-62 TACAN system, APX-27 IFF beacon, and an APN-131 Doppler radar. With all this new equipment, plus the additional length of the redesigned fuselage, the D-model weighed over 1,000 lb (454 kg) more than the B, requiring that its landing gear be strengthened accordingly.

The first F-105D (58-1146) came off the Republic production line in May 1959. Lin Hendrix made the maiden flight on 9 June 1959, and this time the first flight went off without a hitch. Less than a year later, in May 1960, the first F-105Ds were delivered to the 335th TFS, which again was to bring the type into operational service as well as conduct the Category II flight test programme at Eglin AFB, Florida.

Engine problems delayed the Category II testing until late December 1960. Once again, the F-105 programme was in jeopardy, and once again, the Air Force needed 'something' to save the F-105. This time it was a head-to-head fly-off competition between the two best fighter-bomber types in the US Air Force – the McDonnell F-101C Voodoo and the F-105D. The Thunderchief won the competition easily and the Air Force gave Republic a commitment that it would take 1,500 Thunderchiefs. However, Secretary of Defense Robert McNamara's so-called 'all-service' fighter, the F-4 Phantom, was coming off assembly lines. McNamara ordered that no more than seven Air Force wings would be equipped with the F-105D, accounting for roughly half of the production order.

Pilot training for the F-105D began when the 4520th Combat Crew Training Wing at Nellis AFB received its first aircraft on 28 September 1960. Both the aircraft delivered to the 335th TFS at Eglin and those delivered to the 4520th at Nellis were basically flight test machines and were not equipped with many of the weapons systems required under GOR49-1. The first true combat-operational aircraft were delivered to the 4th TFW at Seymour Johnson AFB in early 1961. The second unit to convert to the F-105 was the 36th TFW at Bitburg AB, Germany, in May 1961, followed by the 49th TFW at Spangdahlem AB in October 1961. Both of these units had a nuclear strike mission and were based within minutes of the 'Iron Curtain'.

Project Look Alike

Problems encountered by these units brought about the next major external change. The Europe-based Thunderchiefs were subject to different weather conditions on the Continent. Although the F-105D was considered an 'all-weather' aircraft, that reference was to its combat capabilities. USAFE discovered that moisture was getting through seals and penetrating avionics and electronics compartments.

The Air Force countered this with Project Look Alike, which corrected the moisture problems by applying silver acrylic paint to the entire surface of the aircraft. The 'down time' was also used to correct and enhance the Thunderchief's effectiveness with the newest weapons. All the aircraft were brought up to the latest factory standard, F-105D-25, to correct flight control problems and hydraulic line chafing. The necessary wiring to launch and guide the Martin AGM-12 Bullpup air-to-ground tactical missile was installed. A tail hook was installed under the fuselage for short or rough field operations. The Look Alike modifications, which included remaining F-105Bs, were carried out at Brookly AFB, Alabama.

First combat and new problems

In August 1964, North Vietnamese gunboats attacked US Navy destroyers in the international waters of the Gulf of Tonkin. It marked the beginning of 11 long years of war in Southeast Asia (SEA), nine of which saw heavy participation by US forces. Several of the first squadrons involved were Air Force F-105D units. Combat in SEA soon created new problems for the F-105D. The first was excessive heat

Left: The first F-105Ds went abroad in May 1961 as the 36th TFW at Bitburg AB, West Germany, re-equipped with F-105Ds. Here a pair of 23rd TFS F-105D-10-REs takes fuel from a KB-50J tanker during 1965.

Below left: Operational flying in Europe included not only regular exercises with other NATO air forces, but also armament training courses. This 49th TFW is pictured during a practice bombing run during a mission from Wheelus AB, near Tripoli, Libya. Both of the USAFE F-105 wings had a small detachment permanently based at Wheelus and crews undertook 50 per cent of their flying from the North African base. Weapons courses were run by the 7272nd Flying Training Wing and included live firing at the nearby El Uota range.

Worldwide deployment

The USAF had hoped to equip a total of 16 wings with Thunderchiefs – 14 in Tactical Air Command and two in US Air Forces Europe. However, the changes brought by the Kennedy Administration in 1961, under the guiding hand of Secretary of Defense Robert S. McNamara, saw to it that only eight wings would operate F-105s; the remaining six would receive F-4 Phantoms. The eight original Thunderchief wings were: 36th and 49th TFWs (Seventeenth Air Force, USAFE); 23rd, 355th and 388th TFWs (Twelfth Air Force, TAC); 4th TFW (Ninth Air Force, TAC) and the 8th and 18th TFWs (Fifth Air Force, PACAF).

build-up in the aft fuselage around the afterburner, for which Republic designed a pair of small air scoops that attached to the rear fuselage over the auxiliary air intakes. The scoops pulled in cooling air for the affected area around the afterburner.

When the first flights began flying combat over North Vietnam, they encountered a very formidable air defence system, which only increased in intensity and effectiveness as the war dragged on. The flight crews discovered a potentially deadly problem with the stabiliser unit on the Thunderchief. It was controlled by a single hydraulic system, and one hit in a vital area could take out the entire flight control system, locking the horizontal stabiliser in full 'up' position, which forced the Thunderchief into a nose-down attitude. Several aircraft were hit and ended up in the jungle.

Initially, Republic came up with a 'quick fix' before modifying the aircraft permanently to eliminate the problem. A mechanical lock was installed on the stabiliser, which the pilot could engage manually from the cockpit as soon as he realised the hydraulic system had been damaged. Later, Republic engineers designed and installed a third, redundant hydraulic system in a small tunnel on top of the rear fuselage.

Another change was made to the appearance of the aircraft when, from 1965, the Air Force ordered all tactical aircraft to be camouflaged to hide them from high-flying interceptors. The entire F-105 fleet and all other tactical aircraft in the Air Force, both in the combat zone and at

bases in Europe and the United States, was painted in what was dubbed the 'Southeast Asia scheme': dark green (FS 34079), olive green (FS 34102), and tan (FS 30219) over the upper surfaces, with light grey (FS 36622) on the underside. Not only were the aircraft camouflaged against the jungle, but the paint added still another moisture barrier over the Look Alike silver. Finally, the internal weapons bay would not be used during combat in SEA, so an addi-

PACAF Thunderchief assets were assigned to the 8th and 18th Tactical Fighter Wings, which had received F-105Ds in 1962 and 1963, respectively. Pictured are aircraft from the 12th TFS/18th TFW (left) and the 80th TFS/8th TFW (above).

Project Look Alike

Prompted by the conclusions of investigations into the cause of two crashes at Nellis AFB during June 1962, the entire F-105B/D fleet was grounded on 20 June and Project Look Alike implemented. Expected to take a matter of weeks to complete, Look Alike ran for two years and cost $50 million, the work being carried out by the Mobile Air Material Area (MOAMA) from October 1962. As well as involving the re-rigging of flight controls and replacement of chaffed hydraulic lines and wiring looms, Look Alike saw (in the case of the earliest production aircraft) over 300 technical orders issued to bring all existing F-105Ds up to the latest F-105D-25-RE standard, allowing all aircraft to, among other things, carry maximum 12,000-lb (5443-kg) bomb loads and fire AGM-12 Bullpup missiles. Among other changes was the fitting of arrester hooks to all aircraft and introduction of better sealing of avionics and instrument bays and cockpits to reduce the effects of damp and condensation. The latter changes had been suggested by the Europe-based wings and resulted in aircraft being finished in a new silver acrylic lacquer to seal them against the elements. Many of these modifications were also applied to the remaining F-105Bs.

This F-105D-6-RE is finished in the overall silver lacquer applied during the Look Alike modification programme. The air scoop above and to the rear of the national insignia on the fuselage was a later modification made in 1964 after a spate of crashes attributed to in-flight fires and explosions. Found on both sides of the rear fuselage, the scoops reduced temperatures in the engine bay. Fuel system piping was replaced at around the same time.

A handful of F-105Fs were issued to each F-105D-equipped squadron; this 22nd TFS, 36th TFW example is seen at a foggy Bitburg Air Base during 1964.

tional 390-US gal (1476-litre) bomb bay fuel tank was installed.

One of the biggest changes was one of the smallest to the naked eye. It was a modification directly linked to the North Vietnamese radar-directed anti-aircraft and surface-to-air missile (SAM) defence net. Applied Technologies Inc., a small computer company in California, had studied the Soviet air defence radars and created a 'black box' that monitored all Soviet radar signals. The box could advise the pilot of when he was being tracked and of the location of the radar emitter and its type. They even discovered a characteristic in the signal that told the pilot when a SAM had been launched toward him.

This box was the APR-25/26 radar homing and warning system, or RHAWS. Externally, the APR-25(V) had four antennas – two on the trailing edge of the vertical fin (with small plates covering the pre-amp located forward of the actual antenna) and two more in a small fairing under the nose just behind the radome – plus three small 'tit' antennas for the ER-142 OMNI radar under the nose. A small strike camera was installed immediately aft of the APR-25 fairing on most aircraft. The APR-26 launch warning receiver antenna was a short blade type under the fuselage. In the cockpit, a small strobe scope was mounted atop the right side of the instrument shroud. A threat display unit,

responsible for identifying the threat and indicating whether a SAM had been launched, was attached to the underside of the upper part of the windscreen. The APR-25/26 RHAWS equipment was installed on all aircraft flying into North Vietnamese airspace, both Air Force and Navy/Marine.

All of these modifications took a while to install, and by the time the Thunderchiefs were ready to take the war to the heart of North Vietnam, that country's defences had already downed over 100 of the big fighters. North Vietnamese anti-aircraft gunners exacted a terrible toll, shooting down over 90 F-105s. The North Vietnamese SAM threat, which had been greatly feared by the Western press, had not materialised, due in great part to a bunch of daring F-105 crews known as the 'Wild Weasels'. They flew the two-seat Thunderchief, the F-105F/G. However, the F-105F did not begin its combat career as the devastating specialised weapons platform it became.

A two-seat Thunderchief, at last

The F-105F was the third-generation two-seat design based on the F-105 airframe. The first was the previously discussed F-105C based on the B-model Thunderchief. Next was a similar effort based on the F-105D, designated the F-105E: it used a D-model airframe with the rear cockpit in tandem behind the front one, taking the place of one of the fuselage fuel cells. As with the F-105C, the E was proposed with a single, rear-hinged bubble canopy covering both cockpits. The F-105E would have had all the combat capability of the D, with a slight reduction in unrefuelled range. Also like the F-105C, the F-105E was cancelled (in 1959) before a prototype could be built.

However, as the Thunderchief went into full operation, the Air Force quickly discovered that it needed a trainer version of the Thunderchief, and needed it badly. The 'Thud' was a handful of an aircraft to fly, and available trainers such as the T-33A and the F-100F simply could not duplicate its flight characteristics. Initially, thought was

F-105F

The primary mission of the F-105F was that of tactical bomber; after all, the last 143 F-105D-31-RE single-seaters had been sacrificed to make way for the F-105F and the two-seat variant was fully equipped to D standard. However, the primary reason for the F-105F's development lay in the fact that the USAF urgently needed a two-seat derivative to smooth the hitherto protracted type conversion process. The first of 143 F-105Fs (62-4412, right) flew on 11 June 1963.

'Thud' at war, 1965-68

War service in Southeast Asia began for the F-105 in August 1964, as the last F-105Ds rolled off the Farmingdale production line. Among the USAF aircraft despatched to the region after the Gulf of Tonkin Incident were eight 36th TFS F-105Ds sent to Korat RTAFB on TDY from Yokota AB, Japan. Initially these Thunderchiefs were confined to operations in support of the CIA's secret war in Laos and their presence in Thailand was officially denied, though from 1965 until the bombing halt in 1968 the F-105 was to bear the brunt of operations against North Vietnam. Thunderchiefs flew more missions than any other type over the three years of Rolling Thunder raids 'up north' – and more were lost than any other type, with the exception of the F-4.

Below: 2 March 1965 saw the commencement of Rolling Thunder strikes against targets in North Vietnam, 25 18th TFW Thunderchiefs joined Martin B-57s in bombing an ammunition depot at Xom Bong; for the next three years the campaign was to become the almost exclusive province of the F-105s. Here an F-105D of the 354th TFS, 355th TFW hauls a load of eight 750-lb M117s on an early Rolling Thunder mission during April 1965.

Above: Pictured carrying the red markings of the 36th TFS, F-105D 62-4371 was one of the quartet of aircraft that undertook the type's first combat mission on 14 August 1964 – a ResCAP for an Air America T-28 over the Plain of Jars, Laos. Flown by Lt David Graben the aircraft was making a strafing pass over an anti-aircraft gun position when it was hit by 37-mm shells and caught fire. Graben nursed the aircraft back to Korat and made a successful emergency landing, though the F-105 was deemed beyond repair and scrapped – the first of close to 400 Thunderchiefs lost in the conflict.

given to equipping Thunderchief squadrons with F-100Fs to fill the need for a transition aircraft between the T-33A and the F-105D. However, a lack of F-100Fs, combined with the great difference in performance between the Super Sabre and the Thunderchief, created a need for a two-seat version of the F-105. In May 1962, Secretary of Defense Robert McNamara authorised the Air Force to contract with Republic to build a number of two-seat Thunderchiefs. These aircraft would not be just a trainer: they would be the first dual-mission aircraft with the Air Force – a transitional trainer and an attack aircraft, complete with a nuclear strike capability.

The two-seat Thunderchief, designated the F-105F, was a straightforward conversion based on the latest D airframe. An F-105D-31 fuselage was used for the conversion, but rather than try to put a second cockpit inside the already crammed fuselage contours of the F-105D at the expense of internal fuel, Republic engineers added 31 in (79 cm) to the forward fuselage just behind the rear bulkhead of the front cockpit. The rear cockpit was a virtual duplicate of the front cockpit, with flight controls, throttles, weapons control panels, and a second R-14A radar scope. Thus, the rear pilot could fly the mission even if the front pilot became incapacitated in some way.

Another change from previous two-seat proposals was in the canopy design. Rather than use a single canopy over both cockpits, as proposed on the C and E, the F model had two smaller individual canopies and ejection systems. The aircraft's overall length increased from 64 ft 4 in (19.58 m) in the F-105D to 66 ft 11 in (20.38 m), and Republic felt the aircraft would need more lateral stability, so increased the height and chord of the vertical tail assembly. The vertical tail was 6 in (15 cm) taller, standing 20 ft 1 in (6.12 m). Neither the wings nor the stabilisers were increased in size. The engine, air intakes, and CADC were the same as their counterparts on the D-31 model.

The weapons capabilities of the F-105F were identical to those of the F-105D-31, including the ability to carry out a nuclear strike mission. Defensive armament was the General Electric M61A1 Vulcan rotary cannon, with an ammunition drum that held a total of 1,000 rounds. The internal weapons bay was the same size as in the D, and could hold up to 2,000 lb (907 kg) of conventional weapons, up to 3,400 lb (1542 kg) of 'special stores', or a 390-US gal (1476-litre) bomb bay fuel tank.

F-105D-25-RE 61-0169 Hazel was flown by Captain Bill Sparks of the 563rd TFS 'Ace of Spades', 23rd TFW from Da Nang during May 1965. The squadron was about a third of the way through a three-month TDY deployment during which it lost 11 aircraft.

Thunderchiefs were among the first Air Force aircraft to be repainted in what became known as 'Southeast Asia' camouflage, as set out in Technical Order 1-1-4 and introduced during 1964. Here F-105Ds of the 334th TFS are pictured during 1965. Both photographs feature F-105D 61-0105 which fell to 37-mm AAA on 8 May 1967, at the height of the Rolling Thunder campaign.

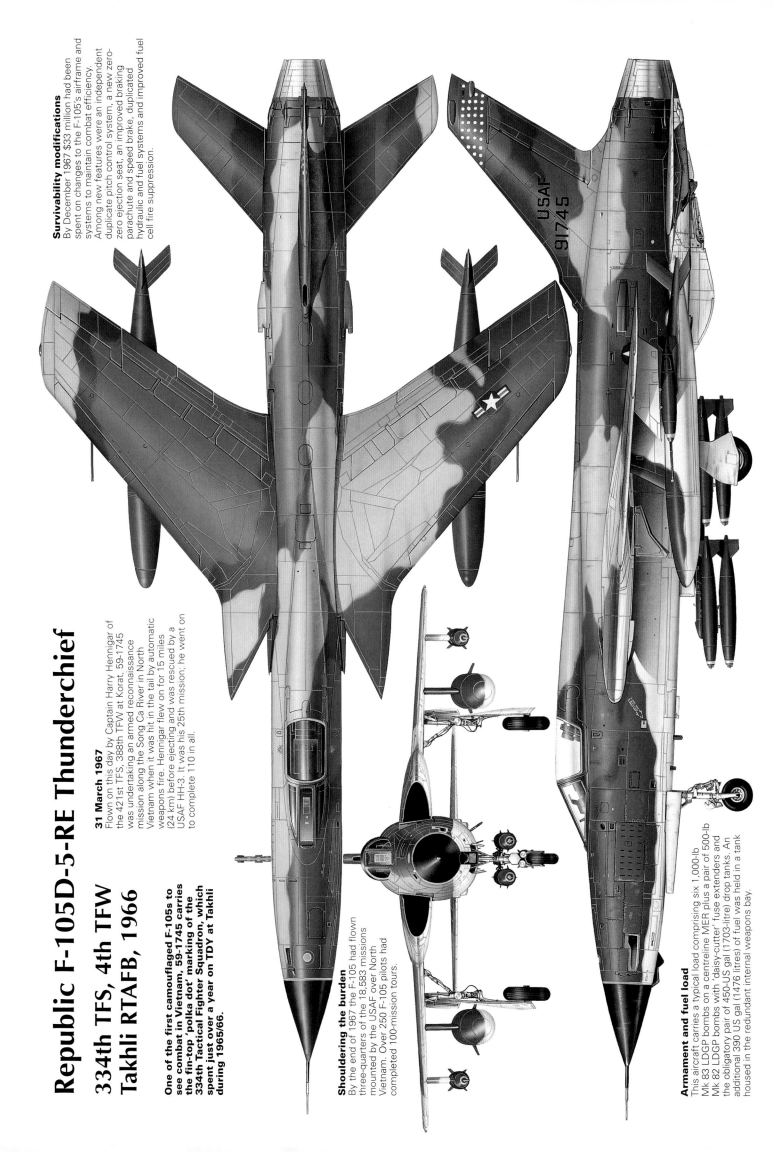

Republic F-105D-5-RE Thunderchief

334th TFS, 4th TFW Takhli RTAFB, 1966

One of the first camouflaged F-105s to see combat in Vietnam, 59-1745 carries the fin-top 'polka dot' marking of the 334th Tactical Fighter Squadron, which spent just over a year on TDY at Takhli during 1965/66.

Survivability modifications
By December 1967 $33 million had been spent on changes to the F-105's airframe and systems to maintain combat efficiency.
Among new features were an independent duplicate pitch control system, a new zero-zero ejection seat, an improved braking parachute and speed brake, duplicated hydraulic and fuel systems and improved fuel cell fire suppression.

31 March 1967
Flown on this day by Captain Harry Hennigar of the 421st TFS, 388th TFW at Korat, 59-1745 was undertaking an armed reconnaissance mission along the Song Ca River in North Vietnam when it was hit in the tail by automatic weapons fire. Hennigar flew on for 15 miles (24 km) before ejecting and was rescued by a USAF HH-3. It was his 25th mission; he went on to complete 110 in all.

Shouldering the burden
By the end of 1967 the F-105 had flown three-quarters of the 18,583 missions mounted by the USAF over North Vietnam. Over 250 F-105 pilots had completed 100-mission tours.

Armament and fuel load
This aircraft carries a typical load comprising six 1,000-lb Mk 83 LDGP bombs on a centreline MER plus a pair of 500-lb Mk 82 LDGP bombs with 'daisy-cutter' fuse extenders and the obligatory pair of 450-US gal (1703-litre) drop tanks. An additional 390 US gal (1476 litres) of fuel was held in a tank housed in the redundant internal weapons bay.

Above: The F-105D carried its General Electric AN/ASG-19 Thunderstick fire control system (which could be more accurately described as a bombing and navigation computer) in a modified nose that added 15 in (38.1 cm) to the length of the aircraft. Thunderstick did not have a truly all-weather capability until modified to T-Stick II standard – a change only applied to 30 F-105Ds.

Production

Thunderchief production ran to 833 examples (of 926 ordered), the bulk of which were F-105Ds and F-105Fs (610 and 143, respectively). All were built at Republic's Farmingdale, New York, factory.

variant	serial range	number
YF-105A-1-RE	54-0098/0099	2
F-105B-1-RE	54-0100/0103	4
F-105B-5-RE	54-0104	
	54-0106, 0107	
	54-0109, 0110	5
JF-105B-1-RE	54-0105, 0108	2
F-105B-6-RE	54-0111	1
JF-105B-2-RE	54-0112	1
F-105B-10-RE	57-5776/5784	9
F-105B-15-RE	57-5785/5802	18
F-105B-20-RE	57-5803/5840	38
F-105D-1-RE	58-1146/1148	3
F-105D-5-RE	58-1149/1165	
	58-1166/1173	
	59-1717/1757	
	(59-1775/1816, cancelled)	66
F-105D-6-RE	59-1758/1774	
	58-1817/1826	
	60-0409/0426	45
F-105D-10-RE	60-0427/0535	
	(60-0536/0546, cancelled)	
	60-5374/5385	121
F-105D-15-RE	61-0041/0106	66
F-105D-20-RE	61-0107/0161	55
F-105D-25-RE	61-0162/0220	
	(61-0221/0260, cancelled)	
	62-4217/4237	80
F-105D-30-RE	62-4238/4276	39
F-105D-31-RE	62-4277/4411	135
F-105F-1-RE	62-4412/4447	36
	63-8260/8366	107

F-105 weapons

Right: Among the weapons arrayed before this F-105B are two types of 'secret' nuclear weapon, iron bombs of various types and weights, napalm tanks, an M61 rotary cannon (with 1,029 rounds of 20-mm ammunition), AIM-9B Sidewinder AAMs, weapons bay, centreline and underwing drop tanks, 2.75-in FFAR pods and the Republic 'buddy' refuelling tank. The 'Bravo Chief' had a maximum ordnance load of 7,500 lb (3402 kg).

Left: The third JF-105B was used to trial the F-105's GAR-8 (AIM-9 from 1962) Sidewinder armament; a pair of AIM-9Bs could be carried on each outboard pylon.

Specifications and performance

	YF-105A	F-105D	F-105F	F-105G
powerplant:	one P&W J57-P-25	one P&W J75-P-19W	one P&W J75-P-19W	one P&W J75-P-19W
rating, dry	10,200 lb st (45.37 kN)	17,200 lb st (76.51 kN)	17,200 lb st (76.51 kN)	17,200 lb st (76.51 kN)
rating, afterburner	15,000 lb st (66.73 kN)	26,500 lb st (117.88 kN)	26,500 lb st (117.88 kN)	26,500 lb st (117.88 kN)
span:	34 ft 11 in (10.64 m)	34 ft 11 in (10.64 m)	34 ft 11¼ in (10.65 m)	34 ft 11¼ in (10.65 m)
length:	61 ft 5 in (18.72 m)	64 ft 3 in (19.58 m)	69 ft 7⅛ in (21.22 m)	69 ft 7⅛ in (21.22 m)
height:	17 ft 6 in (5.33 m)	19 ft 8 in (5.99 m)	20 ft 2 in (6.15 m)	20 ft 2 in (6.15 m)
wing area:	385 sq ft (35.77 m²)	385 sq ft (35.77 m²)	385 sq ft (35.77 m²)	385 sq ft (35.77 m²)
weight, empty:	21,010 lb (9530 kg)	27,500 lb (12473 kg)	–	–
weight, combat:	28,966 lb (13139 kg)	35,637 lb (16165 m)	–	41,091 lb (18638 kg)
weight, mto:	40,561 lb (18398 kg)	52,546 lb (23834 kg)	54,027 lb (24506 kg)	54,580 lb (24757 kg)
maximum load:	8,000 lb (3629 kg)	14,000 lb (6350 kg)	14,000 lb (6350 kg)	–
internal fuel:	850 US gal (3217 litres)	1,550 US gal (5867 litres)	1,160 US gal (4391 litres)	1,051 US gal (3978 litres)
maximum fuel:	2,500 US gal (9463 litres)	3,100 US gal (11734 litres)	3,100 US gal (11734 litres)	2,991 US gal (11321 litres)
maximum speed:	857 mph (1379 km/h) at 36,000 ft (10973 m); 778 mph (1252 km/h) at sea level	1,420 mph (2285 km/h) at 38,000 ft (11582 m); 836 mph (1345 km/h) at sea level	1,386 mph (2231 km/h) at 38,000 ft (11582 m); 876 mph (1410 km/h) at sea level	– 784 mph (1262 km/h) at sea level
stalling speed:	185 mph (298 km/h)	208 mph (335 km/h)	–	216 mph (348 km/h)
time-to-height:	30,000 ft (9144 m) in 17.6 mins	–	–	30,000 ft (9144 m) in 28 mins (combat speed)
climb rate, clean:	–	34,500 ft (10516 m)/min	34,500 ft (10516 m)/min	–
service ceiling	–	32,100 ft (9784 m)	–	–
combat ceiling	49,950 ft (15225 m)	48,500 ft (14783 m)	–	43,900 ft (13381 m)
combat radius:	–	778 miles (1252 km)	740 miles (1191 km)	450 miles (724 km)
normal range:	1,100 miles (1770 km)	–	–	–
maximum range:	2,720 miles	2,208 miles (3553 km)	–	1,866 miles (3004 km)

Above: A new weapon introduced with the F-105D was the Martin Marietta AGM-12 Bullpup air-to-surface missile, two of which could be carried. Under the Look Alike modification programme, surviving F-105Bs were also given a Bullpup capability. Bullpup development was initiated by the US Navy in 1953, under the designation ASM-N-7. Two years later the USAF contracted Martin to develop an advanced derivative of Bullpup, known as GAM-79 White Lance, which introduced a nuclear warhead option and a much improved radio command guidance system, the latter allowing guidance from an offset position. In the interim the USAF procured ASM-N-7 (as GAM-83) and later elected to cancel GAM-79 in favour of a Bullpup variant fitted with the new guidance system – GAM-83A (later AGM-12B) Bullpup A. F-105s carried both AGM-12B and the larger AGM-12C Bullpup B.

During 1966 a typical F-105 strike mission included a lead element of F-4Cs and Iron Hand Thunderchiefs, the F-105 bombers in flights of four aircraft, 'College Eye' EC-121s to warn of MiG launches and 'Brown Cradle' EB-66s providing high-altitude radar jamming support. Equipped with radar, the latter were also employed as pathfinders for F-105 formations bombing obscured targets. Often attached to Thunderchief wings, Brown Cradle aircraft remained an important part of F-105 operations, even after the 'Thuds' were equipped with their own ECM equipment.

Below: This well-known view of an F-105 being pursued by a VNAF MiG-17 was captured by the gun camera of second Thunderchief. The incident took place north of Hanoi on 19 December 1967, after an attack on the Paul Doumer Bridge.

Externally, the F model had the same five hardpoints under the wings and fuselage to carry up to an additional 6,000 lb (2722 kg) of ordnance or additional droppable fuel tanks. Electronically, the F-model had the complete AN/ASG-19 Thunderstick fire control system. It was wired at the factory to carry and launch the latest in both air-to-air and air-to-ground missiles, such as the AIM-9 Sidewinder and the AGM-12 Bullpup.

The first F-105F, 62-4412, came off the Republic assembly line on 23 May 1963. There was no prototype or service test model. The aircraft were delivered to the Air Force with all the Look Alike modifications, including the silver acrylic paint finish, and the installation of a tail hook. Republic test pilot Carlton Ardery made the first flight of the F on 11 June 1963, and pushed the aircraft through the speed of sound to Mach 1.15 without any problems.

Less than six months later, on 7 December 1963, the Air Force took delivery of the first F-105Fs for operational duties. They were assigned to the 4520th Combat Crew Training Wing at Nellis AFB, home of the Air Force's Fighter School. On 23 December, the first F-105Fs were delivered to the first combat unit, the 4th TFW at Seymour Johnson AFB. All F-105 units within the Air Force, and later the Air Guard and Air Force Reserve, had at least one F-105F in the inventory, serving as both a transitional trainer and an additional attack aircraft.

F-105 versus MiG

April 1966 saw an upsurge in the activities of the VNAF's fighters in the point defence role and, although F-4 Phantoms were tasked with MiGCAP duties, F-105s inevitably came into contact with MiG-17s, -19s and -21s. Between June 1966 and December 1967 F-105s were officially credited with 27½ MiG-17 kills (25 by F-105Ds; 2½ by F-105Fs); in a handful of incidents AIM-9B AAMs were employed, though most kills were scored using the 'Thud's M61 cannon, demonstrating to the USAF the continuing value of gun armament. On the other side of the coin, the first air-to-air encounter of the war saw a pair of F-105Ds fall to MiG-17s on 4 April 1965 – the USAF's first air-to-air losses of the conflict. Seventeen F-105 kills by MiG-17s and -21s have been matched with known USAF air-to-air losses. In addition, the Vietnamese claim that another 10 F-105s acknowledged as lost by the USAF to other causes (usually ground fire) were actually shot down by MiG crews, plus a further 13 where no corresponding USAF loss is acknowledged. Conversely, seven F-105 losses believed by the USAF to have been caused by air-to-air action cannot be traced in VNAF records.

Right: The loss of an F-105D on 14 December 1966 was the first kill acknowledged by the USAF as caused by an AAM (an RS-3/AA-2 'Atoll' fired by a MiG-21), though the VNAF claim that there had been a number of other such victories scored by this stage of the conflict. Here North Vietnamese personnel inspect the wreckage of the F-105, flown by Captain Robert Cooley, who ejected safely.

Republic built a total of 143 F-105Fs, funded with monies originally set aside for additional F-105Ds. The final F-105F, 63-8566, was the last Thunderchief to come off the Republic assembly line; it was finished and accepted by the Air Force in January 1965, bringing total Thunderchief production to 833 aircraft of all variants, including prototypes.

The F-model was not the final Thunderchief variant, however. There were two more, with very specialised missions brought about by the Vietnam War.

Wild Weasel 'Thuds'

As the war in Southeast Asia heated up, President Johnson attempted to halt North Vietnamese aggression by bombing targets in North Vietnam, using F-105s and Navy fighter-bomber aircraft. With every incursion into North Vietnamese airspace, American pilots encountered more and better anti-aircraft defences, culminating with the introduction of the Soviet SA-2 surface-to-air missile.

Soviet engineers began building the launch sites for the SA-2 'Guideline' missile in and around Hanoi in spring 1965. For unknown reasons, Secretary McNamara put all such sites 'off limits' to attack until after they became operational. The first site went on the air in late June 1965. The first launch took place on 24 July 1965 and was a complete success, destroying one 44th TFS F-4C and damaging two of the other three F-4Cs in the flight.

It was an entirely new air war. The Air Force responded to the threat with various types of new equipment and tactics, such as underwing jamming pods. The answer, though, was the development of an entirely new mission and aircraft type. It was to be known as the 'Wild Weasel'.

Applied Technologies Inc. had developed the VECTOR IV radar homing and warning system soon after encountering Soviet air defences over Cuba. The RHAWS consisted of the IR-133 panoramic scan receiver, which had four antennas – two under the nose and two more on the trailing edge of the vertical fin. The IR-133C monitored Soviet radar signals in the S-, C-, and X-band frequencies, displaying their presence to the pilot on a small cathode ray scope in the cockpit. The IR-133C was standardised as the AN/APR-25(V).

Another 'black box' developed by ATI was the WR-300 launch warning receiver. ATI engineers had noted that the SA-2's Fan Song radar signal increased in intensity immediately prior to launch of the missile. The WR-300 monitored this specific frequency and noted any changes on a threat display unit (TDU) in the cockpit. The TDU had a small field of lights that indicated the threat – AAA or SAM – and lit up according to what it identified. It was also able to detect a launch. The WR-300 launch warning receiver was standardised as the AN/APR-26.

Now that the Air Force had the equipment, it launched a crash programme to develop an aircraft to counter the SAM

threat. The aircraft chosen was the two-seat F-100F Super Sabre. The USAF dubbed the programme Project Wild Weasel and its mission was to ferret out North Vietnamese radar signals, locate them, and put them out of action by using ordnance such as bombs and HVAR rockets, or by simply scaring the radar operator into shutting down the radar. The first Wild Weasel F-100Fs arrived at Korat AB, Thailand, in late November 1965, less than five months after the SAM threat had materialised. 7th Air Force code-named the defence suppression mission Operation Iron Hand. The aircraft were an instant success, finding both SAM and AAA radars, then directing F-105 fighter-bombers to destroy the site.

EF-105F makes its debut

However, the F-100F was not the right aircraft for the job. It was too slow and the strike force it was protecting was forced to slow down to its speed, making it even more vulnerable. Moreover, the numbers of F-100Fs were dwindling. The strike force was made up primarily of F-105 Thunderchiefs, so the natural solution was to build a follow-on 'Wild Weasel' aircraft using the F-105, specifically the F-105F. On 8 January 1966, the Air Force accepted the recommendation of Brigadier General K.C. Dempster's defence suppression task group that the next generation Wild Weasel aircraft be based on the F-105F. Eight days later the first Wild Weasel III prototype, F-105F 62-4412, made its first flight. It was known within the Air Force as the EF-105F, for 'electronic fighter', although the official designation remained F-105F and it carried the same electronics package as the F-100F, comprising the APR-25(V) and the APR-26 as an integrated radar homing and warning system.

The first four EF-105Fs deployed to Thailand in late May 1966, arriving at Korat on 28 May. They flew their first mission on 3 June, working with veteran F-100F aircrews. The EF-105Fs led their first mission on 6 June, scoring their

Main picture: These 354th TFS, 355th TFW F-105Ds are pictured topping up their tanks from a KC-135 en route to a target during 1966. Each carries a pair of the largest bombs able to be carried by the 'Thud' – the M118 3,000-pounder.

Inset above: Sortie rates in the early months of the Rolling Thunder campaign were so high that a bomb shortage resulted in mid-1966. This pair of F-105Ds (F-105D-10-RE 60-0469 and, nearest the camera, F-105D-31-RE 62-4287), led by an F-100D flak suppression aircraft, appear to carry incomplete loads of Mk 83 750-lb bombs.

Below: This busy scene on the ramp at Takhli AB, Thailand, during 1968 shows F-105s being prepared for another mission. During October F-105D 62-4364, nearest the camera, was among the first four 'Thuds' to complete 3,000 combat flying hours.

first 'kill' on the next day. The aircraft carried a new weapon for the defence suppression mission – the Texas Instruments AGM-45 Shrike anti-radar missile (ARM). With a top speed of Mach 1.5, Shrike homed on enemy radar signals, destroying the radar with a 145-lb (66-kg) warhead. If the enemy radar was destroyed, the SAM missile was blind.

A 'Weasel' mission was considered a success if the enemy radar was either destroyed or forced off the air through fear of destruction. The EF-105Fs had a large variety of weapons other than the Shrike, including gravity

As the North Vietnamese strengthened their defences with additional radar-controlled AAA and, from April 1965, SA-2 'Guideline' SAMs, the carriage of ECM pods became a necessity. In this October 1968 view, all three 355th TFW F-105Ds carry at least one AN/ALQ-71 or -87 jamming pod on their outer wing pylons. Also evident is the comparatively low altitude at which refuelling often took place, due to the 'Thud's limited ceiling when loaded.

Inset: An F-105 banks sharply to port to avoid a SA-2 launched at its strike package.

Below: Although Bullpup missile performance against hardened targets had proved disappointing, Thunderchief units continued to use the weapon until the F-105Ds were withdrawn. This 44th TFS aircraft carries an AGM-12C missile during operations in February 1970. The naval AGM-12C Bullpup B, with its 1,000-lb (454-kg) warhead, was preferred over the AGM-12B which, though it had been developed for USAF service, was equipped only with a 250-lb (113-kg) warhead and clearly lacked sufficient punch. Bullpup other disadvantage was its radio command guidance system, which required the pilot of the launch aircraft to maintain line-of-sight with the missile until impact, placing him and his aircraft at considerable risk from ground fire.

Right: Radar installations and bridges located in the DMZ between the 17th and 19th Parallels were targets during the first months of Rolling Thunder. This 1965 photograph shows a Bullpup launch against a rail bridge 110 miles (177 km) northwest of Hanoi during 1965.

bombs, napalm, cluster bombs, and rocket pods. The 'fear factor' was one of the best weapons. The North Vietnamese gunners knew if a Weasel aircraft turned in their direction, it was probably going to launch a missile at them; they would turn off the radar, blinding the SAM and leaving the strike force relatively free to perform its task.

The 'Weasel' mission was easily the most dangerous of the entire war. The EF-105Fs preceded the strike force to the target area and 'trolled for SAMs', i.e. they flew around the hostile North Vietnamese skies making a target of themselves in the hope an enemy radar would try to pinpoint the aircraft, thereby becoming a target itself for the Shrike-equipped Weasel. It was this description of the Wild Weasel mission that led to their motto – "You Gotta Be Shittin' Me!", or "YGBSM".

On 11 July 1966, the last F-100F Wild Weasel aircraft departed Korat. The Iron Hand mission was now entirely in the hands of the Wild Weasel III aircrews. Slowly but surely, the number of Wild Weasel EF-105Fs and crews increased until both F-105 combat wings had the equivalent of a squadron of EF-105Fs available for the defence suppression mission. The two wings utilised the Weasel assets in different ways. The 388th Wing at Korat had an entire squadron, the 13th TFS, dedicated to the suppression mission; at the 355th Wing at Takhli, though, Weasels were split into flights of four within the three squadrons.

As the missions mounted, engineers in the US began to look at ways to improve the capabilities of the 'Weasel' aircraft. The IR-133C launch warning receiver was replaced by the improved ER-142 unit. Many aircraft were equipped with the AZ-EL (azimuth-elevation) antennas to improve the capabilities of the APR-25(V). A new weapon was introduced, the General Dynamics AGM-78 Standard ARM. The AGM-78A was the combination of a US Navy Standard missile, originally developed as a shipboard surface-to-air missile, with the seeker head from an AGM-45 Shrike. The Standard ARM weighed over 1,350 lb (612 kg) and an F-105 needed a special heavy-duty underwing launch pylon, the LAU-80A/80B, to carry the big missile. Later variants of the Standard ARM had internal memories that 'remembered' where a radar site was located even if the operator turned off his equipment. The first EF-105Fs with Standard ARM capability arrived at Takhli in late summer 1968.

SEESAMS and the F-105G

Many people equate the F-105G with the large ECM fairings on the sides of the fuselage, but it was the installation of something called SEESAMS that created the G-model. Air Proving Ground Command and North American had developed the SEESAMS (Search, Exploit, and Evade Surface to Air Missile Systems) as an improvement to the AN/APR-25. SEESAMS scanned the frequencies used by the 'Fan Song' radar that was searching for the strike aircraft, and monitored the tracking frequency of the SA-2 guidance radar, indicating to the EF-105F electronic warfare officer what the threat was, where it was, and how imminent the threat might be, i.e. 'search activity' or 'launch'.

It was developed under Quick Reaction Contract 317. Loral Industries improved the SEESAMS system as part of QRC-317A, which was designated AN/ALR-31. Installation of the ALR-31 required a redesign of the wingtip configuration, in which a pair of antennas took the place of the navigational lights, which were moved to the leading edge of the wingtip. At least 14 aircraft were modified with the ALR-31 SEESAMS equipment, and were known as the first-generation F-105G.

Installation of the fuselage ECM fairings was prompted by a 7th Air Force requirement that all F-105 aircraft flying into North Vietnamese airspace be equipped with underwing ECM or jamming pods, including the 'Wild Weasel' EF-105Fs. Installation of such a pod on one of the limited

number of underwing stores pylons meant the loss of an offensive weapon to the Wild Weasel crews. Republic and Westinghouse, prime contractor for the underwing ECM pods, worked together to develop an internal ECM system to free up the vital weapons pylon on the EF-105F. Under QRC-380, the engineers took an AN/ALQ-101 ECM pod, split it in two, and installed the pods on the sides of the fuselage above the bomb bay doors. Inside each pod was a modified version of the ALQ-101 ECM system. Standardised as ALQ-105, these ECM fairings were the second part of the complete F-105G modifications.

An upgrade of the APR-25/26 RHAW systems to APR-35/36, which improved the ER-142 panoramic scan receiver, became the third aspect of the F-105G. Finally, the next-generation Standard ARM, the AGM-78B – which had a dual seeker head that monitored the E- and G-bands with one seeker, and the I-band with the second seeker – was made available to the Wild Weasel III crews. The AGM-78B-2 had a single all-band head.

The first ALR-31-equipped F-105Gs began arriving in Thailand in April 1968, and in late 1970 the first F-105Gs with the QRC-380 internal ECM systems began to appear in Southeast Asia. With the exception of constant upgrades in the RHAWS and further development of the AGM-78, the F-105G was now complete. Republic and Sacramento Air Material Area modified a total of 61 F-105F aircraft, including veteran EF-105Fs and some F-105F trainer/attack aircraft, to F-105G specification.

Refining the F-105D – Thunderstick II

Information received from the crews flying the Project Northscope F-105F missions in the night skies over North Vietnam was the basis for an upgrade of the capabilities of the F-105D strike aircraft that offered much greater accuracy during any weather condition, including night bombing.

The programme, called Thunderstick II, applied to both F-105Ds and F-105Fs and involved installation of the AN/ARN-92 Long Range Navigation (LORAN) radar. The NASARR radar system was also improved by installation of solid-state components, now designated R-14K. Basically, the North American Aviation engineers who had created the NASAAR R-14 radar performed the 'fine tuning' that had been done to the Northscope F-105Fs operating in SEA – only they did it better, and permanently.

With the Thunderstick II, the F-105 pilot now had a circular error probability of +/- 50 ft (15 m) from a bombing altitude of 15,000 ft (4572 m). Republic Aviation modified at least 30 F-105Ds with the Thunderstick II between early 1969 and July 1971. All could easily be identified, as the installation of the new Doppler and ARN-92 LORAN systems required a large spinal fairing between the cockpit and the base of the vertical tail.

Although designed to help the F-105 crews who were flying combat over North Vietnam, none of the Thunderstick II aircraft left the US. All were initially assigned to the 563rd TFS, 23rd TFW at McConnell AFB, Kansas. When the F-105 was phased into Air Guard/Air Force Reserve squadrons, the Thunderstick II F-105Ds were all transferred to the 457th TFS, Air Force Reserve, at Carswell AFB, Texas, where they remained until January 1980 when the 457th TFS transitioned to F-4Ds.

Thunderchief at war

The first Thunderchief units into combat were those based in the Far East. The 36th TFS at Yokota had been on a rotational Zulu Alert deployment to Osan AB, Korea, when President Johnson called for retaliatory strikes in response to the Gulf of Tonkin incidents. It was easy for the squadron to deploy in early August 1964 to Korat AB,

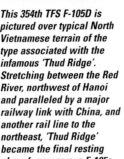

This 354th TFS F-105D is pictured over typical North Vietnamese terrain of the type associated with the infamous 'Thud Ridge'. Stretching between the Red River, northwest of Hanoi and paralleled by a major railway link with China, and another rail line to the northeast, 'Thud Ridge' became the final resting place for numerous F-105s.

During 1968, with the Tet Offensive at an end, missions against targets in North Vietnam were scaled back. From 1 April all bombing north of the 20th Parallel ceased; from 3 April this was extended to all offensive missions north of the 19th Parallel. Operations south of this latitude continued however, especially around the DMZ and the border with southern Laos. Ceasefire negotiations and mounting pressure from public opinion at home forced President Johnson to end all offensive missions against targets in North Vietnam on 1 November 1968, though reconnaissance missions (permitted by the Paris ceasefire accord) continued, often with an F-4 or F-105 escort. If hostile intent on the part of North Vietnamese AAA or SAM defences was shown, so-called 'protective reaction' retaliatory strikes were launched. By early 1970 10 F-105Ds had reached 3,500 flying hours, nine of them with the 355th TFW; in February the first F-105D (61-0169 of the 354th TFS) had reached 4,000 hours – the type's theoretical maximum fatigue life. By the end of 1970 the last of the surviving F-105Ds had been withdrawn to the US, replaced in the 355th and 388th TFWs by F-4s, including new F-4Es, the first of which had entered service in November 1968.

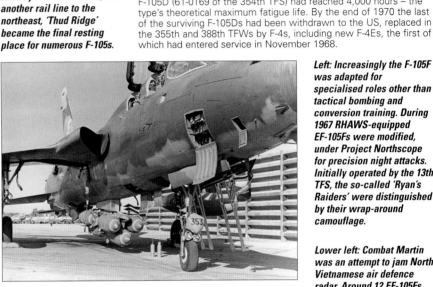

Left: Increasingly the F-105F was adapted for specialised roles other than tactical bombing and conversion training. During 1967 RHAWS-equipped EF-105Fs were modified, under Project Northscope for precision night attacks. Initially operated by the 13th TFS, the so-called 'Ryan's Raiders' were distinguished by their wrap-around camouflage.

Lower left: Combat Martin was an attempt to jam North Vietnamese air defence radar. Around 12 EF-105Fs were fitted with a large QRC-128 communications jamming set (variously known as 'Colonel Computer' and 'Fartin' Martin') in the rear cockpit, replacing both the EWO and his ejection seat, and a large blade aerial behind the rear cockpit canopy. This example is pictured in 561st TFS markings at McConnell AFB during 1971.

Below: Det. 1, 561st TFS F-105Gs refuel during a mission from Korat during 1972. Heavily utilised during the Linebacker raids, the F-105Gs of the 561st were among the last to operate over North Vietnam.

Thailand, where – officially – it was to supply ResCAP support for any airman downed over Laos or Cambodia. Its actual mission was combat air support of CIA and other friendly units fighting in Laos, Cambodia, and South Vietnam. On 9 August, the 36th TFS set up at Korat, putting eight F-105Ds on strip alert.

The Department of Defense began rotating squadrons in and out of Korat on a regular basis, initially from the 6441st TFW at Yokota and the 18th TFW at Kadena. In February 1965, the 36th Squadron redeployed back to the war. This

Republic F-105G Thunderchief
17th Wild Weasel Squadron
388th Tactical Fighter Wing
Korat RTAFB, Thailand, 1972

The sole remaining SAM-suppression unit in Southeast Asia, the 17th WWS was activated on 1 December 1971 from the assets of the 6010th WWS, itself a redesignation of Detachment 1, 12th TFS (comprising the surviving Wild Weasel assets from the deactivating Takhli RTAFB), equipped with 'ZB'-coded F-105Gs. Reinforced by Detachment 1, 561st TFS (deployed from the F-105 training base at McConnell AFB, Kansas) between April 1972 and September 1973, the 17th was operational until 29 October 1974 (when the last F-105 left the region), the squadron inactivating on 15 November, having turned its assets over to the 562nd TFS, 35th TFW at George AFB.

What made an F-105G an F-105G?

The 'EF-105F' became an F-105G once it had been fitted with the AN/ALR-31 RHAW set, the first part of a four-phase modification exercise. An aircraft equipped with ALR-31 could be distinguished by changes to its wingtips; the ALR-31's antennas displaced the aircraft's navigation lights; these, in turn, were moved to a position further forward to the leading edge of the wingtip. The most distinctive external features of the F-105Gs were their external AN/ALQ-105 ECM blisters. Though these are often quoted as being the definitive identifying feature of the variant, around 14 early F-105Gs operated without them until such a time as modifications could be completed. The upgrading of AN/APR-26 RHAW and -27 LWR systems to Standard-compatible APR-36/-37 and the introduction of AGM-78B Mod 1 and Mod 2 missiles completed the package (though RHAW sets were constantly subject to modification as the nature of the SAM threat changed; later versions of the Standard ARM were also introduced).

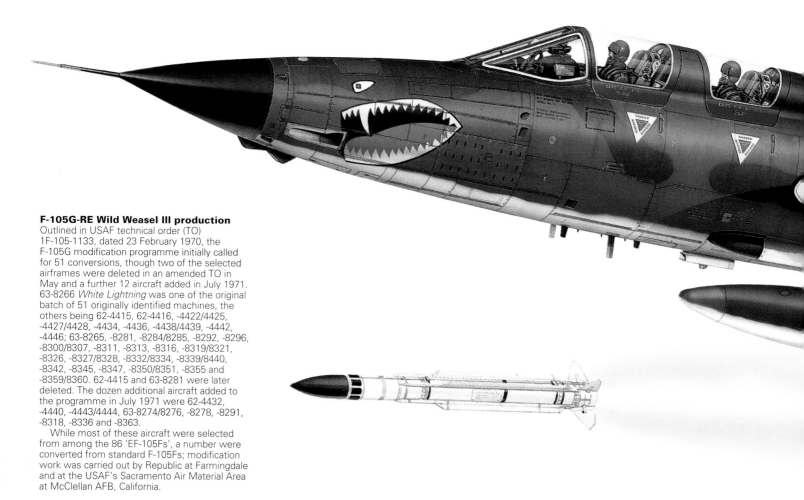

F-105G-RE Wild Weasel III production

Outlined in USAF technical order (TO) 1F-105-1133, dated 23 February 1970, the F-105G modification programme initially called for 51 conversions, though two of the selected airframes were deleted in an amended TO in May and a further 12 aircraft added in July 1971. 63-8266 *White Lightning* was one of the original batch of 51 originally identified machines, the others being 62-4415, 62-4416, -4422/4425, -4427/4428, -4434, -4436, -4438/4439, -4442, -4446; 63-8265, -8281, -8284/8285, -8292, -8296, -8300/8307, -8311, -8313, -8316, -8319/8321, -8326, -8327/8328, -8332/8334, -8339/8440, -8342, -8345, -8347, -8350/8351, -8355 and -8359/8360. 62-4415 and 63-8281 were later deleted. The dozen additional aircraft added to the programme in July 1971 were 62-4432, -4440, -4443/4444, 63-8274/8276, -8278, -8291, -8318, -8336 and -8363.

While most of these aircraft were selected from among the 86 'EF-105Fs', a number were converted from standard F-105Fs; modification work was carried out by Republic at Farmingdale and at the USAF's Sacramento Air Material Area at McClellan AFB, California.

AGM-78 Standard ARM

An attempt to address the performance weaknesses of Shrike, the General Dynamics AGM-78 Standard ARM was developed from an existing US Navy shipborne SAM, by simply combining the RIM-66 Standard missile with the seeker head of the AGM-45A-3A Shrike. The AGM-78A Standard ARM Mod 0 was introduced in 1968 and equipped a handful of US Navy A-6B and E Intruder aircraft, as well as being produced in larger numbers for the USAF's Wild Weasel force. AGM-78A was soon superseded by the AGM-78B Mod 1 variant, with a new Maxson broad-band seeker. This allowed the missile to be used against targets with differing guidance frequencies and incorporated a memory capability so that the missile would remain locked-on to a target if the latter's emitter was switched off.

A considerably larger weapon than Shrike, Standard ARM was 15 ft (4.57 m) in length, weighed 1,370 lb (621 kg) and carried a 215-lb (97-kg) blast-fragmentation warhead. Travelling at speeds of up to Mach 2.5, the missile had a range of around 35 miles (56 km).

Because of its expense, Standard ARM was not procured in sufficient numbers to completely replace Shrike; both missiles remained in use into the 1980s, latterly equipping the F-4G Phantom Wild Weasel V.

Defensive armament

The F-105's primary defensive weapon was its General Electric T-171E3 (later M61) Vulcan 20-mm rotary cannon, carried by all F-105s on the left side of the nose. Hydraulically driven, the M61 weighed 275 lb (125 kg) and was fed with 1,029 rounds of 20-mm electrically-primed ammunition, which it was able to deliver at a rate of 6,000 rpm, at a muzzle velocity of 3,380 ft/sec (1030 m/sec). The entire ammunition supply could be exhausted by an 11-second burst.

In order to maintain the aircraft's centre-of-gravity during firing (during which up to 500 lb/227 kg of ammunition would be expended) Republic's engineers devised a dual-feed ammunition system for the F-105B, which collected links and empty shells, storing them in separate compartments. In the F-105D, which required a redesign to accommodate radar, the feed system was altered so that the separate shell and link compartments could be eliminated; linkless ammunition was used and empty shells stored in the ammunition drum, saving 16 cu ft (0.45 m³) of space.

Though seldom carried, up to four AIM-9B/E Sidewinder AAMs could be mounted on a double launcher hung from the aircraft's outer wing pylon.

F-105 Wild Weasel development

The Wild Weasel I programme, which had seen the modification of a limited number of the F-100F Super Sabres for the defence suppression role, was limited in its scope to the installation of radar-homing and warning (RHAW) and launch warning receiver (LWR) equipment (installed in a wide range of USAF and USN aircraft of all types from late 1965) and the addition of an AGM-45A Shrike ARM launch capability. Having proved too slow to keep up with strike packages equipped with more powerful aircraft and unable to carry a sufficient bomb load for an effective lone attack, the F-100Fs were sidelined, early the following year, in favour of a modified F-105F variant. In all, 86 F-105Fs were already equipped with the aforementioned RHAW/LWR gear, comprising the Itek AN/APR-25 (VECTOR IV) radar-homing and warning set (detecting S-band emissions from SA-2 'Guideline' SAM, EW and GCI radars, C-band emissions from improved SA-2 radars and X-band radiation from AI radar) and the Itek AN/APR-26 (WR-300) SAM launch warning set (which sensed a power-level change in the SA-2's L-band command guidance radar). As part of what was dubbed Wild Weasel III, the F-105Fs (thereafter known in some quarters, unofficially, as 'EF-105F's) also received an IR-133 receiver (for the detection of S-band emissions at long range), a KA-60 panoramic strike camera and a two-track combat event tape recorder, plus the ability to carry a pair of Shrike ARMs.

By February 1968 14 of the 86 F-105F(WW)s had been further modified to carry AGM-78 Standard Mod 0 ARMs. To locate, identify and acquire targets for the

Standard guidance system, a Bendix AN/APS-107 RHAW system was also installed, along with a new AN/APR-35 RHAW set, and two sets of active ECM equipment – a Hallicrafters AN/ALQ-59 VHF communications jammer and a GE AN/ALQ-71 noise jammer. Towards the end of 1968 a further batch of 16 F-105F(WW)s was reworked so that they could fire the latest version of the Standard ARM – AGM-78B Mod 1. Concurrently, a package of equipment changes, many of them destined for the later F-105G, was also introduced.

The F-105G was an attempt to standardise the Wild Weasel III fit as well as introducing a number of new capabilities. Enshrined in a USAF technical order (TO) dated 23 February 1970, the F-105G modification programme eventually covered 61 aircraft. The variant's expanded array of systems comprised AN/APR-35, -36 and -37 RHAW systems (the latter to operate with Standard ARM), a Loral AN/ALR-31 (SEESAM) RHAW set (which scanned frequencies for 'Fan Song' radar activity, providing the location and status of any threat detected), an Itek ER-142 high-sensitivity video receiver (giving automated direction-finding and homing on a threat), a 14-channel combat event tape recorder, a QRC-373 noise jammer and fuselage-mounted Westinghouse AN/ALQ-105 ECM blisters. The latter system was effectively a repackaged ALQ-101 ECM pod, half of which was mounted on either side of the aircraft's lower fuselage in order to keep another wing station free for weapons carriage.

Vulnerability

Designed as a fast, stable, low-level platform for the delivery of nuclear weapons, the F-105 was a sturdy aircraft (in typical Republic fashion, thanks to the use of large forgings at points of high stress and machine-milled skins both of which saved weight without sacrificing strength) but had not been designed with an adequate degree of survivability in mind. There was very little in-built redundancy for its flight controls and fuel and hydraulic systems, and the fact that it was single-engined put it at a disadvantage compared to other types like the F-4 Phantom. Though there were numerous examples of aircraft returning to base with major damage to control surfaces and the like, the Thunderchief proved particularly vulnerable to fires caused by AAA and small arms damage.

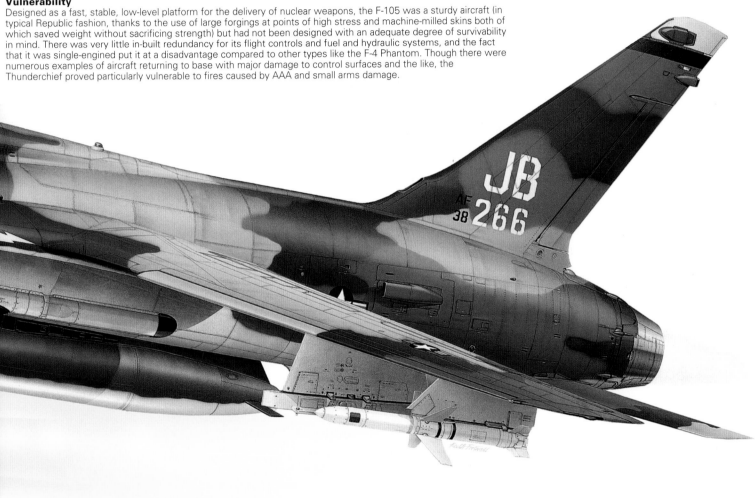

Fuel and weapons loads

Though used simply to accommodate an extra fuel cell for much of its service, the Thunderchief's internal weapons bay was among its key features. Measuring 15 ft 10 in (4.83 m) in length, with a 32 x 32-in (81 x 81-cm) cross-section, the weapons bay was positioned directly below the wing centre-section and enclosed by a pair of doors, which retracted into the fuselage to minimise drag. The bay's dimensions were determined by the size and shape of the nuclear weapons of the period; those identified with the F-105 include Mk 28, Mk 43, Mk 57 and Mk 61 devices, single examples of which could be accommodated internally. Other than an MN-1A practice bomb dispenser, the only other store available for internal carriage by the Thunderchief was a 390-US gal (1476-litre) fuel tank; this became a routine fitting for most of the type's career.

The F-105 had five external stores stations for nuclear and conventional weapons. Using multiple ejector racks (MERs) on all five pylons allowed a maximum of 16 750-lb M117 iron bombs to be carried; maximum loads of the order of six tons were routinely flown in Vietnam by F-105Ds and Fs. External fuel could be carried on the inner wing pylons and on the centreline station. The latter, as illustrated by 63-8266, was usually used for a 650-US gal (2460-litre) tank, while 450-US gal (1703-litre) tanks of Republic or Fletcher manufacture were carried beneath the wings.

AGM-45A Shrike

Developed directly in response to the threat posed by the Soviet S-75 (SA-2 'Guideline') SAM and its 'Fan Song' guidance radar, Shrike (normally carried on the outer wing stations) was an ARM derivative of the AIM-7C air-to-air missile with a larger warhead, a smaller motor and smaller tailfins. Entering service with the US Navy in 1965 and adopted for use aboard USAF F-100F Wild Weasel I aircraft in April 1966, Shrike was used with some success, though it suffered from a number of weaknesses that limited its effectiveness: its seeker had only a fixed frequency range (necessitating the time-consuming development of a raft of sub-variants); the seeker head was not gimballed and had only a limited field-of-view (and therefore needed to be aligned with a target in order to detect it) and it lacked a target 'memory', which meant that if an SA-2 site switched off its 'Fan Song' radar the missile lost lock and went ballistic. Measuring 10 ft (3.05 m) in length and weighing 400 lb (181 kg), Shrike had a range of 19-25 miles (30-40 km), had a Mach 2 top speed and carried a 145-lb (66-kg) proximity-fused, fragmentation warhead.

Though the missile is most often associated with the F-105F/G Wild Weasel aircraft, all Thunderchiefs from F-105D-5-RE onwards (as well as earlier aircraft modified to Look Alike standard) were able to carry Shrike, on the same pylon adapter developed to carry AGM-12 Bullpup.

T-Stick II

The high level of maintenance skill required to keep the more complex T-Stick II aircraft serviceable ultimately precluded their deployment to Southeast Asia. All 30 were issued to the 563rd TFS, 23rd TFW at Carswell instead and eventually finished up with the 457th TFS, Texas ANG before retirement in 1982. Known T-Stick II conversions, which are believed to have numbered 30, include 60-0458, -0464, -0465, -0471, -0485, -0490, -0493, -0500, -0513, -0527, -0533, -5375, 61-0044, -0047, -0063, -0075, -0080 (prototype), -0100 and -0110. The T-Stick II's AN/ARN-92 LORAN receiver was housed in a 'saddleback' fairing fitted along the spine of the aircraft, as seen in this view of 60-0464 of the 563rd TFS.

time, it was sent to Takhli AB, Thailand, about 100 miles (161 km) northwest of Korat. These were the two bases from which most of the F-105 sorties were launched.

Initially, all the squadrons operated under control of two provisional fighter wings – the 6234th TFW (Provisional) at Korat, and the 6235th TFW (Provisional) at Takhli. The first missions and losses took place within a week after arrival at Korat. On 14 August, the 36th TFS was assigned a ResCAP mission regarding a downed CIA T-28 pilot in Laos. Lieutenant Dave Graben's F-105D, 62-4371, was struck by 37-mm anti-aircraft fire. Graben brought the badly damaged 'Thud' back to Korat, but it never flew again.

On 10 December 1964, 13th AF began Operation Barrel Roll, an open air support campaign of Royal Laotian troops who were fighting both North Vietnamese and Communist Pathet Lao troops.

Flaming Dart

The first mission into North Vietnam was conducted under Operation Flaming Dart. F-105s with F-100 MiGCAPs attacked the Donghoi military barracks and Vinh Linh communications centre about 100 miles (161 km) north of the DMZ that separated North and South Vietnam. The Viet Cong answered with an attack against US personnel at bases in South Vietnam. Flaming Dart II was the 13th AF's answer to those attacks. And so it went, punch and counter-punch. More and more F-105 squadrons were deployed to the combat zone, with units from Japan and the US arriving in Thailand in early 1965.

By late February 1965, enough Thunderchief squadrons were in place to begin a systematic destruction of all the military targets throughout North Vietnam. This was known as Operation Rolling Thunder. The first Rolling Thunder missions included an attack by F-105s against the Xom Biang military depot, just north of the DMZ. Although the target was destroyed, so were three F-105s from the 67th Squadron, with one pilot killed.

Thirteenth Air Force had divided North Vietnam into six military 'regions' for targeting purposes and called them Route Packages, Route Packs or simply RPs. The higher the RP number, the heavier the concentration of its defences. The first Rolling Thunder missions against Xom Biang were in RP-1, just north of the DMZ. The most dangerous was any mission to Route Pack 6, and later to -6A, the immediate area around the North Vietnamese capital city of Hanoi.

The target list was chosen by military and political leaders in Washington, D.C. Just prior to the start of Rolling Thunder, the Joint Chiefs of Staff (JCS) drew up an initial list of 94 targets inside the borders of North Vietnam. Pilots were not free to deviate from the assigned target for any reason other than being attacked themselves; in other words, if the first F-105 pilot completely destroyed the target on his bomb run, the other flights had to bomb the rubble! If a Thunderchief flight passed over a column of North Vietnamese tanks and troops heading directly into South Vietnam, they could not attack them. They could report them to 13th AF and possibly attack them the following day – by which time, the column would be long gone. The same rules applied to anti-aircraft artillery (AAA) sites, SAM sites, and MiGs.

The SAM and MiG threats were heaviest in and around Hanoi. The North Vietnamese Air Force was made up of Soviet-supplied MiG-17, MiG-19, and MiG-21 interceptors. Some of their pilots were very good, especially in a MiG-17, which was much more manoeuvrable than the

Above: A number of Thunderchiefs were assigned to test units throughout the type's career, including this unusual silver USAF Systems Command F-105G, pictured at Eglin AFB during August 1970.

Right: The second production F-105F, 62-4413, was with the 3246th Test Wing, Armament Development Test Center at Eglin AFB during 1977.

Post-war 'Gs'

While F-105Ds returning from Southeast Asia were passed to ANG and Air Force Reserve units, the F-105Gs joined the 35th TFW at George AFB. Eventually including three squadrons from the 23rd TFW, the 35th was the USAF's last front-line F-105 unit, training crews in the Wild Weasel mission in preparation for the arrival of F-4Gs in the late 1970s. Some systems upgrading took place post-war, AN/ALR-46 RHAWS equipment, with improved digital displays for the EWO, replacing the earlier ALR-36/37 set. The 'Thud' finally bowed out of front-line service beginning in April 1978, the 25 best airframes going to the 128th TFS, Georgia ANG. The last 'G' left George on 12 July 1980, bring the 22 years of eventful front-line service to an end.

F-105. The MiGs were armed with 'Atoll' air-to-air missiles in addition to the 23-mm and 37-mm cannon. Although the MiGs did relatively minor damage to the F-105 forces striking North Vietnam, they could force the 'Thud' pilots to jettison their bomb loads in order to evade the MiGs. F-105 pilots shot down 27½ MiG interceptors during the war.

The North Vietnamese SAM threat was not as effective as the Western press would have led people to believe. The SA-2 could be defeated a number of ways, such as forcing it out of its flight envelope or forcing the guidance radar off the air. If the pilot saw it coming, he could perform a 'split S' manoeuvre and fly directly at the missile, something its limited flight controls could not follow. Or he could close the gap before the SAM could arm itself. The addition of Wild Weasel flights was very effective at shutting down the 'Fan Song' radars that controlled the SAMs. Losses to SAMs totalled 32 by the end of the war.

By far the deadliest North Vietnamese defensive weapons were the radar-directed anti-aircraft artillery that ranged from the mobile ZSU-23/4 23-mm automatic cannon to fixed 37-mm, 57-mm, and 85-mm artillery guns. The 'Weasels' could monitor and shut down the AAA radars in the same manner as with the SAM, but there were simply too many radar-directed guns for the 'Weasels' to be effective. Anti-aircraft artillery accounted for 280 F-105 losses during the war.

Despite the fierce defences – often referred to as "the heaviest air defences in the history of air warfare" – the Rolling Thunder missions continued successfully. Every major target on the JCS list was struck, some several times. The Thai Nguyen Steel Works, Thanh Hoa Bridge, the Northeast Railway that brought war supplies in from China; all were struck. The only viable target that steadfastly remained standing was the Paul Doumer Bridge in Hanoi, which refused to go down despite repeated attacks by the F-105s using bombs that weighed up to 3,000 lb (1360 kg). (F-4s with 2,000-lb/907-kg laser-guided bombs eventually dropped the Doumer Bridge.)

Of course, facing this formidable array of defences on a daily basis took a deadly toll on the Thunderchief aircraft and crews. In 1965, F-105 forces in Thailand lost 60 aircraft. In 1966, the 355th and 388th Wings lost an incredible 111 aircraft, 103 to AAA; another 97 were shot down in 1967. On 31 October 1968, President Johnson ordered a complete cessation of offensive air strikes against targets inside North Vietnam – an action that probably prevented the eventual loss of the entire F-105D/F inventory. The following month, the 388th Wing at Korat traded in its veteran F-105 Thunderchiefs for new F-4E Phantoms.

Project Northscope and Combat Martin

In January 1967, General John Ryan perceived a need for an all-weather, night capability over North Vietnam. By March of that year, training had begun at Yokota AB, Japan. All the aircraft modified for Northscope were EF-105Fs. The main modification was to adjust the R-14A radar to allow an expanded radar picture with a faster sector sweep. This gave the rear pilot a better target definition and much greater accuracy during night attacks.

Northscope crews, known as 'Ryan's Raiders', arrived at Korat on 24 April 1967 and were assigned to the 13th TFS, which also had the Wild Weasel mission in the 388th Wing. Its first night mission came on 26 April, striking the Ron Ferry. By 22 May, there were 12 Northscope crews at Korat. Between 26 April and 4 October 1967, 'Ryan's Raiders' flew 415 'one-plane, one target' sorties to RP-1, -5 and -6A. In July, the 'Raider' aircraft were used as pathfinders on daylight missions. Three 'Raider' Thunderchiefs were shot down before the programme came to a close in late 1967.

With the success of the Wild Weasel programme, Air Force engineers reasoned that if they could develop a system to counter the ground air defences of North Vietnam, they could perhaps find one to restrict the MiG threat. It was known as Project Combat Martin. At least 12 Wild Weasel EF-105Fs were modified with the Hallicrafters QRC-128 airborne jamming system to jam communications between North Vietnamese ground controllers and the MiGs.

The QRC-128, which pilots called 'Colonel Computer', was installed in the rear cockpit in place of the rear ejection seat. The large blade antenna on top of the fuselage easily distinguished the Martin aircraft, which were assigned to both combat wings of F-105s. In December 1970, all remaining Martin aircraft were demodified, brought up to F-105G 'Weasel' standard and returned to combat in Southeast Asia.

Top: A trio of 'GA'-coded 561st TFS F-105Gs, each carrying a practice bomb dispenser, returns from a training mission. Towards the end of its time operating F-105s, the 561st was averaging 10 1½-hour sorties per day, these including a high proportion of simulated and live weapons firing at a number of ranges.

Above left: 63-8300 of the 563rd TFS undergoes maintenance at George AFB in the late 1970s. 'WW' tail codes replaced 'GA' during 1978/79.

The US bicentennial celebrations were marked by the 141st TFS, New Jersey ANG, which applied appropriate markings to one of its veteran F-105Bs.

The first F-105Ds to join an ANG unit were those handed to Virginia's 149th TFS in 1971. F-105D-5-RE 59-1743 Hanoi Express sported artistic reminders of its service in Southeast Asia when pictured in 1978. Visible beneath the aircraft is the weapons bay fuel tank, lowered for inspection.

Below: Upon its conversion to the F-105 shortly after the 149th, the 127th TFTS, Kansas ANG, took over the RTU role from the 23rd TFW. This F-105D-10-RE, returning after a training sortie, is pictured at McConnell AFB during 1976.

Georgia's 128th TFS transitioned from the F-100D/F to the F-105F/G over a 270-day period during the summer of 1979. Aircraft serviceability was a problem from the outset, the 'Thuds' suffering from the rigours of war service, several years with a training unit and plain old age. The situation came to a head in 1980/81 when fuel cell and engine combustion chamber problems required attention; the latter problem reduced the squadron to just three flyable aircraft in July 1981 as 31 of the unit's 34 J75 engines awaited repairs. Landing gear and wing cracks were also discovered, but perseverance on the part of the 128th eventually saw 12 of the unit's establishment of 24 aircraft in service. Despite its problems the 128th managed to take part in 17 exercises during the year ending 30 June 1982, including eight that required deployments. Pictured is F-105F 63-8299, callsign PEACH 91, which made the last official flight by an ANG Thunderchief, on 25 May 1983.

the 12th TFS and transferred back to Korat. Det. 1, which evolved into the 6010th Wild Weasel Squadron and later the 17th WWS, flew 'protective reaction' support of RF-4C reconnaissance flights until Easter 1972.

When North Vietnam launched its Easter Offensive on 30 March 1972, 13th AF had insufficient in-theatre assets to counter the initial attack. The bombing halt imposed by President Johnson on 31 October 1968 remained in effect until President Nixon cancelled it in early April 1972. Of the F-105 units that could have been redeployed to SEA, only the F-105F/G 'Weasels' returned to full combat, supporting 13th AF F-4 and B-52 strikes throughout North and South Vietnam. The small force of F-105Gs, i.e., the under-strength 17th WWS at Korat, was quickly overwhelmed with the mission requirements of Operation Linebacker.

Initially, PACAF decided that the best way to increase the effectiveness of the defence suppression units was to have 'hunter-killer' teams of F-105Gs paired with F-4E Phantoms. This virtually doubled the size of the 'Weasel' force overnight, but more aircraft were needed to stem the North Vietnamese offensive. Operation Constant Guard sent many different squadrons to the combat arena of Vietnam, one being the F-105G-equipped 561st TFS from McConnell AFB. The 561st combined with the 17th WWS at Korat and acted as 'hunter-killer' teams with 388th Wing F-4Es, becoming a very credible presence in the skies over North Vietnam.

The crews of the 17th and 561st Squadrons flew up to four sorties per day, supporting the Linebacker and Linebacker II missions that inflicted heavy losses on North Vietnamese military capabilities. The decisive raids during the 18-day Christmas air offensive proved to be enough to bring the North Vietnamese back to the peace talks in earnest. The last F-105G mission into North Vietnam returned to Korat in the early morning hours of 29 December 1972.

However, this was not the final mission to be flown by 'Thuds' in the region. For the next two years, F-105G

After 1968, only the 355th Wing at Takhli continued to fly missions with the F-105. These included 'protective reaction' strikes against air defences inside North Vietnam that were attempting to restrict RF-4 reconnaissance flights, which were trying to monitor North Vietnamese activity. The 355th was also very active against the North Vietnamese supplies flowing down the Ho Chi Minh Trail through Laos and Cambodia into South Vietnam.

Last F-105D missions flown

The days of the Thunderchief were numbered through both attrition and advances in aircraft design. One of the first things accomplished by President Nixon's 'Vietnamisation' plans was to end operations with the 355th Wing at Takhli. On 9 October 1970, the last F-105D mission was flown, and the 355th Wing was shut down and rotated back to the United States on 9 December. Most of the F-105D assets were transferred to the 18th Wing at Kadena, or returned to the US and the 23rd Wing at McConnell AFB, Kansas. The remaining Wild Weasel F-105F/G assets, about a dozen aircraft, were combined with Det. 1 F-105Gs from

Like the Air National Guard, the Air Force Reserve picked up Thunderchiefs returning from the war in Vietnam. The first examples were issued to the 305th TFS at Tinker AFB, Oklahoma, in May 1972.

Below: The unique F-105D T-Stick II aircraft, which had seen service with the 563rd TFS, were passed to the Carswell AFB, Texas-based 457th TFS. During May 1981 60-0471 was the commanding officer's aircraft.

Weasels escorted B-52 Arc Light strikes into Laos and Cambodia, or RF-4C flights into North Vietnam that were monitoring the effectiveness of the 1973 Paris Peace Accords which supposedly ended North Vietnamese aggression against South Vietnam.

On 15 August 1973, all US involvement in the wars in Southeast Asia, apart from reconnaissance flights, was halted. In September, the 561st TFS returned to the US, assigned to the 35th TFW at George AFB. On 29 October 1974, the last 17th WWS F-105Gs left Korat and also flew to George AFB, where the unit was redesignated the 562nd TFS. The war in Southeast Asia had decimated F-105 forces. A total of 395 F-105D/F/G Thunderchiefs was lost during the war – 296 F-105Ds and 38 F-105F/Gs to enemy action, and 61 more to operational causes such as engine problems, mid-air collisions or hydraulic failures.

Post-war Thunderchiefs

In 1974, the only F-105s remaining on operational status with the US Air Force were the Wild Weasel squadrons, the 561st and 562nd Squadrons at George AFB, California. They continued to perform the defence suppression mission for Air Force units throughout the world until next-generation 'Weasel' aircraft became operational. A third squadron, the 563rd TFS, was added to the wing at George AFB in 1975. Along with carrying out the defence suppression mission, the F-105G crews taught the new F-4G Wild Weasel IV crews the tactics that had been learned the hard way and had proved effective in the skies over Vietnam.

On 28 April 1978 the first F-4Gs became available and the phase-out of the F-105Gs began, though it was 12 July 1980 before the last F-105G left the 35th, that day being marked with a ceremony at George which brought together a 'reunion' of F-105Ds from AFRES and ANG units. Twenty-five of the remaining F-105Gs were transferred to the 128th TFS, Georgia Air National Guard at Dobbins AFB; the remainder either went directly to the scrapyard at Davis-Monthan AFB or were used as targets on the gunnery ranges in Nevada. In October 1982, the F-105Gs of the Georgia ANG were replaced by the F-4D Phantom. The last F-105G flight took place on 25 May 1983.

When PACAF closed down the 355th Wing at Takhli in December 1970, the remaining D-models were distributed to units that still had F-105Ds on the inventory, including the 347th Wing at Yokota, the 23rd Wing at McConnell AFB, Kansas, and the 57th Fighter Weapons Wing at Nellis AFB. Their time in active Air Force service was brief, and the D-models were rapidly transferred to Air Guard squadrons, including the 121st TFS, District of Columbia ANG at Andrews AFB; the 127th TFS, Kansas ANG at McConnell AFB; and the 149th TFS, Virginia ANG at Byrd Field ANGB.

In addition, three Air Force Reserve squadrons flew F-105Ds – the 466th TFS at Hill AFB, Utah; the 457th TFS at Carswell AFB, Texas; and the 465th TFS at Tinker AFB, Oklahoma. On 25 February 1984, the last official F-105 flight took place when a 466th TFS Thunderchief landed at Hill AFB, where the type was replaced by F-4D Phantoms.

It was the end of an era. F-105 Thunderchiefs remain on static display as gate guards or museum aircraft at many Air Force installations in the United States. One of the best places to view the huge fighter that symbolised the air war in Vietnam is the US Air Force Museum in Dayton, Ohio, where F-105D 60-0504 *Memphis Belle II* and F-105G 63-8320 *Wham Bam*, both veterans of the conflict in Southeast Asia, sit proudly as visitors still marvel at the immense size of the 'Chief.

Larry Davis

The 'Thud' finally bowed out of service on 25 February 1984 when an 466th TFS F-105D made the final flight (the last of the unit's F-105Bs had left during 1981). During the latter years of their service the unit's 'HI'-coded aircraft became well known for their non-standard camouflage schemes, as illustrated in this 1983 view of three of the squadron's aircraft over Salt Lake City with an example of the squadron's new equipment – a recently acquired F-16A.

Thunderchiefs were first assigned to the 335th TFS, 4th TFW in May 1958 and remained in front-line USAF service until 1979, when the 35th TFW finally relinquished its last F-105Gs to the Georgia Air National Guard. Here active-duty wings are listed in the order in which they were equipped with F-105s.

UNITED STATES AIR FORCE

4TH TACTICAL FIGHTER WING

333rd Tactical Fighter Squadron
334th Tactical Fighter Squadron
335th Tactical Fighter Squadron
336th Tactical Fighter Squadron

The 4th Fighter-Day Wing returned from its Far East deployment (which had commenced in 1950 at the outbreak of the Korean War) on 8 December 1957, taking over the few F-86H and F-100C assets of the 83rd FDW at Seymour Johnson AFB, North Carolina. On 1 July 1958 the unit was redesignated the 4th Tactical Fighter Wing, with four squadrons assigned.

On 1 May 1958, the first F-105Bs arrived and were assigned to the 335th Squadron which was TDY at Eglin AFB, Florida, and would conduct the Category II Operational Flight Testing on the new Thunderchief. Operational tests continued as the F-105B was brought into active service with the 4th Wing. By mid-1960, three squadrons – the 334th, 335th, and 336th – were operational with F-105Bs.

On 18 October 1962, at the height of the Cuban Missile Crisis, the 4th TFW deployed to McCoy AFB, Florida, for possible combat over Cuba.

In the spring of 1964, the 4th Wing began the transition from F-105Bs to F-105D/Fs, a process that was completed on 23 June.

As the war in Southeast Asia heated up in the late summer of 1964, the 4th Wing was alerted for deployment to the Far East. On 3 July 1965, as part of Operation Two Buck 13, the 335th TFS deployed to Yokota AB to take the place of units assigned there but which were on TDY to Thailand, standing the normal VICTOR nuclear alert rotations at Osan AB, Korea.

On 8 November 1965, the 335th TFS moved TDY to Takhli RTAFB, Thailand, for combat operations against North

Vietnam. At Takhli, the squadron was under the control of the newly-activated 355th TFW. The 335th TFS returned to Seymour Johnson AFB on 15 December 1965.

On 28 August 1965, also under Operation Two Buck 13, the 334th TFS deployed TDY direct to Takhli RTAFB for combat operations against North Vietnamese targets, coming under the control of the 6235th TFW(P) at Takhli. The 334th TFS returned to Seymour Johnson AFB on 10 October 1966, leaving its aircraft at Takhli.

On 4 December 1965, the 333rd TFS deployed to Korat RTAFB for combat operations. However, the 333rd then transferred to Takhli to relieve the 335th TFS. On 8 December 1965, the 333rd TFS deployment was changed from TDY to PCS (Permanent Change of Station), and the squadron was permanently assigned to the 355th TFW at Takhli. Aircraft and pilots of the 336th TFS rotated between Seymour Johnson and Takhli in 1965/66 but the squadron did not deploy to the war in Southeast Asia.

Aircraft markings on the F-105B included a natural metal finish; silver lacquer after Operation Look Alike, with a green band with white trim around the nose and across the vertical fin. A 'native American' logo was painted either on the side of the fuselage under the cockpit, or on the tail band. These markings were retained on F-105D/F aircraft as delivered, though in SEA coloured tail bands were used for squadron identification, as follows: 333rd TFS – red tail stripe with white borders; 334th TFS – blue band with white 'polka dots'; 335th TFS – green band with white borders or green band with a white 'V' superimposed. Camouflaged aircraft retained coloured tail bands.

The first Air National Guard unit to operate the F-105D variant, Virginia's 149th TFS, converted to the Thunderchief in early 1971. Its F-105D/F complement was replaced by Vought A-7D/Ks in 1982.

4520TH COMBAT CREW TRAINING WING (4525TH FIGHTER WEAPONS WING)

4537th Combat Crew Training Squadron
(4537th Fighter Weapons Squadron)
4520th Air Demonstration Squadron

The 4520th Combat Crew Training Wing was established at Nellis AFB, Nevada, on 1 July 1958, taking over the role of the Air Force Fighter School. Two squadrons with F-105B assets were assigned to the 4520th CCTW – the 4537th CCTS and the 4520th Air Demonstration Squadron, 'Thunderbirds'.

The 4520th ADS had nine F-105B aircraft assigned between May 1963 and May 1964. Following a fatal crash, the 'Thunderbirds' converted to F-100D

Super Sabres for the remainder of the 1964 season. The remaining F-105Bs were transferred to the 141st TFS, New Jersey ANG, following the implementation of Operation Backbone.

On 1 September 1966, the 4520th CCTW was redesignated the 4525th Fighter Weapons Wing, with one F-105D/F squadron assigned – the 4537th FWS.

Unit markings for the 4537th included a black/yellow checkerboard band across the vertical fin on silver aircraft. Aircraft were camouflaged beginning in 1965, the tail code 'WC' being assigned from 1967.

Below: The 4537th FWS operated a number of F-105Ds and Fs in the training role. This F-105D-10-RE was pictured at George AFB in June 1962.

57TH FIGHTER WEAPONS WING

4537th Fighter Weapons Squadron
66 Fighter Weapons Squadron

Activated at Nellis AFB, Nevada on 15 October 1969, the 57th FWW took over the assets of the 4525th FWW. F-105D/F/G assets within the 57th FWW were assigned to the 66th FWS and the 4537th FWS which conducted combat crew training, test and

evaluation, and flew weapons systems demonstrations until 1975.

Aircraft of the 57th FWW continued to carry the black/yellow tail band; when tail codes were adopted 66th FWS aircraft carried 'WA' and 4537th FWS aircraft 'WC'. The left side of 66th FWS aircraft carried a unit badge, with the badge of the 57th FWW appearing on right side of all aircraft.

Above: The 4th TFW's colourful markings are clearly displayed on this pair of F-105Bs. The 'native American' logo is situated next to the aircraft's buzz number below the cockpit; a TAC badge and lightning bolt were applied over the green tail band.

Right: From late 1969 the F-105 Wild Weasel community learnt its trade with the 66th FWS at Nellis AFB. F-105G 63-8318 was typical of aircraft assigned to the unit; its markings include a 57th FWW badge and black/yellow checkerboard tail band.

36TH TACTICAL FIGHTER WING

22nd Tactical Fighter Squadron
23rd Tactical Fighter Squadron
53rd Tactical Fighter Squadron

Based at Bitburg AB, West Germany, the 36th Wing had three squadrons attached – the 22nd, 23rd, and 53rd TFSs. The 36th Wing was the second unit to re-equip with the F-105D Thunderchief, beginning in May 1961.

In 1966, the 36th Wing began to transition to the F-4D Phantom, its F-105D/F assets passing to combat units in SEA.

Aircraft markings on natural metal/silver aircraft included diagonal stripes on the vertical tail in squadron colours, as follows: 22nd TFS – red bands with white trim; 23rd – blue bands with white trim; 53rd – yellow bands with black trim. In late 1964, all aircraft had tri-colour tail bands in red/blue/yellow. In 1965, F-105D/Fs of the 36th Wing were among the first aircraft to receive the new dark green/olive green/tan tactical camouflage scheme, with light grey undersides.

The medium blue canopy of this F-105D (above) indicates service with the 44th TFS; the 44th was absorbed by the 13th TFS before tail codes were introduced in 1967; the 12th TFS was allocated 'ZA' (below).

These views of 36th TFW F-105Ds show the initial use of individual squadron tail striping (above, red representing the 22nd TFS) and the later adoption of a generic wing marking with all three squadrons represented (below).

49TH TACTICAL FIGHTER WING

7th Tactical Fighter Squadron
8th Tactical Fighter Squadron
9th Tactical Fighter Squadron

The 49th Tactical Fighter Wing was the third unit to transition into the F-105D/F, beginning in October 1961. The 49th Wing was based at Spangdahlem AB, West Germany. Three squadrons were attached – the 7th, 8th, and 9th Tactical Fighter Squadrons.

The 49th received two Air Force Outstanding Unit Award for F-105 operations during the periods 1 March 1964 to 28 February 1966, and 1 March 1966 to 30 June 1967.

In 1967, the 49th Wing transitioned from the F-105D/F to the F-4D Phantom, its remaining F-105 assets being transferred to other combat units.

Aircraft markings on natural metal/silver aircraft included the 49th Wing badge on both sides of the vertical tail; above this was a red/yellow/blue flash. Around the rear of the radome was a band in the squadron colour: 7th TFS – blue; 8th TFS – yellow; 9th TFS – red. Later, the three-colour lightning bolt was added behind the radome and nose gear doors were painted in squadron colours.

18TH TACTICAL FIGHTER WING

12th Tactical Fighter Squadron
44th Tactical Fighter Squadron
67th Tactical Fighter Squadron

The 18th TFW began operations with F-105D/F aircraft at Kadena AB, Okinawa, in 1962. Three squadrons were attached – the 12th, 44th, and 67th TFS – deployments to Southeast Asia beginning in 1964, as follows: 67th TFS deployed TDY to Korat RTAFB, Thailand, in August 1964, returning to Kadena in May 1965. Det. 2, 18th TFW deployed from Korat to Da Nang AB, RVN, on 25 December 1964 with aircraft and crews from the 67th and 44th Squadrons.

The 44th TFS deployed TDY to Korat RTAFB with the 67th TFS in August 1964, returning to Kadena in May 1965. Det. Two, 18th TFW, deployed to Da Nang AB, RVN, on 25 December 1964 with aircraft and crews from the 67th and 44th TFS. Aircraft of Det. 2, 18th TFW, returned to Korat in January 1965. F-105D/F assets of the 44th TFS were absorbed by the 13th TFS at Korat when the 13th was activated in May 1966.

The 12th TFS deployed six F-105D aircraft to Da Nang as part of Det. Two, 18th TFW, which began operation on 25 December 1964. With deactivation of Det. Two, 18th TFW, the aircraft and crews of the 12th TFS deployed TDY to Korat beginning on 1 February 1965, remaining at Korat until 15 March 1965. The 12th re-deployed to Korat on 15 June 1965, returning to Kadena on 25 August 1965.

During the TDY deployments, the 12th TFS lost four aircraft, the 44th TFS lost one F-105D, and the 67th TFS lost nine aircraft, including three on the first day of the Rolling Thunder operations.

F-105F/G Wild Weasel aircraft from the 12th TFS deployed to Korat AB as Det. 1, 12th TFS, beginning on 24 September 1970. Det. 1 aircraft were integrated with the remaining F-105D/F/G assets transferred from the 355th Wing at Takhli. Under the control of the 388th TFW at Korat, Det. 1 was operational for one month before being redesignated the 6010th WWS on 1 November 1970.

Aircraft markings on natural metal/silver F-105D/F aircraft included a PACAF badge on both sides of the vertical fin, and a coloured band around the nose directly behind the radome, as follows: 12th TFS – yellow; 44th TFS – medium blue; 67th TFS – red. On camouflaged aircraft, the radar reflector, canopy sills or fin cap was painted in the appropriate squadron colour. 12th TFS aircraft are known to have carried 'ZA' tail codes; Det. 1, 12th TFS machines are known to have had 'ZB' codes during 1970.

This view shows both the 49th Wing's tail marking and the three-colour lightning bolt applied to the nose. Camouflage was applied to Europe-based F-105s from 1965.

8TH TACTICAL FIGHTER WING

35th Tactical Fighter Squadron
36th Tactical Fighter Squadron
80th Tactical Fighter Squadron

The 8th Tactical Fighter Wing with three squadrons – the 35th, 36th, and 80th TFS – was based at Itazuke AB, Japan with F-105D/F aircraft from 1963 to 10 July 1964, at which time the Wing HQ moved to George AFB, California. All squadrons and F-105 assets remained in Japan, but were now attached to the 6441st TFW(P) based at Yokota AB, Japan.

Unit markings included coloured engine air intakes, canopy rails and ailerons. Squadron colours were: 35th TFS – blue; 36th TFS – red, and 80th TFS – yellow.

6441ST TACTICAL FIGHTER WING (P)

35th Tactical Fighter Squadron
36th Tactical Fighter Squadron
80th Tactical Fighter Squadron

The 6441st TFW (Provisional) took over the squadrons and F-105D/F assets of the 8th TFW in July 1964.

At regular intervals, the squadrons of the 6441st TFW(P) deployed first to Korat RTAFB, then to Takhli RTAFB. In May 1965, the entire 6441st TFW(P), moved TDY from Yokota AB, Japan to Takhli RTAFB, Thailand, returning to Yokota in July 1965 when the 6235th TFW(P) was established at Takhli.

On 9 August 1964, following the Gulf of Tonkin Incident, the 36th TFS deployed TDY to Korat RTAFB, Thailand, for combat operations against North Vietnam. TDY ended in November and was followed by further TDYs in February 1965 (to Takhli RTAFB, returning to Yokota in May 1965) and August 1965 (to Takhli, returning to Yokota in October).

The 80th TFS deployed TDY to Takhli from February 1965 to 26 August, when it returned to Yokota AB.

The 35th TFS deployed TDY to Takhli in May 1965, replacing the 36th TFS. The 35th TFS was relieved in June 1965, then returned to Takhli in October before returning to Yokota once again on 9 November 1965. The 35th TFS, although not officially assigned to the 355th TFW or 388th TFW, rotated aircraft and crews to augment both combat wings because of attrition.

Aircraft markings remained as they had been when the squadrons were under the control of the 8th TFW.

347TH TACTICAL FIGHTER WING

35th Tactical Fighter Squadron
36th Tactical Fighter Squadron
80th Tactical Fighter Squadron

The 347th Tactical Fighter Wing, under control of Fifth Air Force, took over the F-105D/F assets of the 6441st TFW at Yokota AB, Japan, on 15 January 1968. As F-105Ds were phased out with the 388th TFW at Korat, these Thunderchiefs were assigned to the 347th TFW at Yokota. The 347th's

mission was the air defence of Japan, with a tactical and Zulu Alert mission in support of the Republic of Korea. The 347th TFW had F-105Ds for a matter of months during early 1968; when the wing re-equipped with F-4Cs, all were transferred to stateside units.

Aircraft were finished in standard T.O.1-1-4 camouflage; tail codes were as follows: 35th TFS – 'GG'; 36th TFS – 'GL'; 80th TFS – 'GR'

Thunderchiefs were seen with 'Gx' codes for only a brief period, during early 1968, flown by the Yokota-based 347th TFW.

388TH TACTICAL FIGHTER WING

560th Tactical Fighter Squadron
561st Tactical Fighter Squadron
562rd Tactical Fighter Squadron
563rd Tactical Fighter Squadron

On 1 October 1962, the 388th Tactical Fighter Wing was activated at McConnell AFB, Kansas, with four squadrons assigned – the 560th, 561st, 562nd and 563rd Tactical Fighter Squadrons, all equipped with F-105D/F aircraft. Once conversion to the Thunderchief had been completed, in the spring of 1963, the 388th TFW was inactivated and replaced at McConnell by the 23rd TFW, on 28 January 1964.

13th Tactical Fighter Squadron
34th Tactical Fighter Squadron
44th Tactical Fighter Squadron
421st Tactical Fighter Squadron
469th Tactical Fighter Squadron
Det. 1, 12th Tactical Fighter Sqn (TDY)
6010th Wild Weasel squadron
17th Wild Weasel Squadron
561st Tactical Fighter Squadron (TDY)

The 388th Tactical Fighter Wing was reactivated PCS at Korat RTAFB, Thailand, on 8 April 1966, taking over the F-105 assets of the 6234th TFW(P),

which included the 421st and 469th Tactical Fighter Squadrons.

The 469th TFS originally deployed to Kadena on 30 November 1964 from McConnell AFB, assuming the mission assignment of squadrons under the control of the 18th TFW. In January 1965, the 469th TFS moved from Kadena to Korat AB, Thailand, where it was under the control of 2nd AD. On 13 March 1965, the 469th TFS returned to McConnell AFB. The 469th returned to Korat PCS in early November 1965, and was assigned to the 6234th TFW(P). On 8 April 1966, the 469th TFS was assigned to the newly activated 388th TFW, remaining with the 388th Wing until the F-105D was replaced with F-4Es.

The 421st TFS originally deployed TDY from McConnell AFB, Kansas, to Korat RTAFB on 15 September 1964, the deployment lasting until 23 November 1964. The squadron returned to Korat TDY on 7 April 1965 (and back to McConnell AFB on 20 August 1965). The 421st TFS lost three F-105D aircraft during the two TDY deployments.

On 8 April 1966, the 421st TFS moved PCS to Korat RTAFB, where it

F-105D 59-1743 Arkansas Traveler of the 34th TFS was the mount of Colonel Paul P. Douglas Jr, commander of the 388th TFW between January and July 1968. Douglas achieved ace status flying P-47s in the ETO during World War II (note the German kill markings below the cockpit); the same name also appeared on his P-47s as well as an F-4E Phantom he flew after the 388th re-equipped in 1969.

was assigned to the 388th TFW. The 421st TFS returned to the US on 25 April 1967, and was assigned to the 15th TFW at McDill AFB, Florida. The 421st lost 21 F-105Ds during the PCS tour at Korat. Aircraft markings on camouflaged aircraft included red canopy sills and radar reflector; and red trim with white stars on the bottom of the main landing gear doors. No tail codes were applied to 469th TFS aircraft.

The 13th TFS was activated at Korat RTAFB, under the control of the 388th TFW, on 15 May 1966 as a PCS assignment, taking over the F-105 assets from the 44th TFS. On 11 July 1966, the 13th TFS absorbed the EF-105F Wild Weasel assets from the Project Wild Weasel Detachment, which had been at Korat under control of the 6234th TFW(P).

The mission of the 13th TFS became defence suppression – the entire squadron being equipped with EF-105F aircraft. Aircraft and crews from the 13th TFS also carried out the all-weather, night attack mission of Project Northscope. On 20 October, the EF-105F assets of the 13th TFS were given to the 44th TFS, and the 13th TFS was then assigned to the 432nd TFW at Udorn. The 13th TFS lost 13 F-105D/F aircraft to enemy action.

The 34th TFS was activated PCS at Korat on 15 May 1966 under the control of the 388th TFW, and was equipped with F-105D aircraft until November 1968 when F-4E Phantoms replaced the type in service at Korat. During the period of time that the 34th TFS was equipped with F-105Ds, a total of 28 aircraft was lost to enemy action. Pilots of the 34th TFS shot down a total of 5½ NVAF MiGs.

The 12th TFS at Kadena sent a detachment of 12 EF-105Fs TDY to Korat on 24 September 1970. Detachment 1, 12th TFS augmented the F-105F/G assets that were transferred from the 355th TFW at Takhli. Det. 1 was the only unit assigned to the defence suppression mission. On 1 November 1970, Det. 1

was redesignated the 6010th WWS.

The 6010th Wild Weasel Squadron was activated on 1 November 1970, taking over the F-105G assets of Det. 1, 12th TFS at Korat. The 6010th WWS remained at Korat until 1 December 1971, when the unit was redesignated the 17th WWS.

The 17th Wild Weasel Squadron was activated at Korat on 1 December 1971, taking over the F-105F/G assets of the 6010th WWS. The 17th WWS performed valiantly during the Linebacker I and II campaigns against North Vietnam between April 1972 and January 1973. Six Wild Weasel F-105Gs were shot down during the Linebacker operations. The 17th WWS remained at Korat until 15 November 1974 when the unit was transferred to George AFB, California. The 17th was then inactivated and the F-105G assets were absorbed into the 562nd TFS at George AFB.

Detachment 1, 561st TFS deployed TDY to southeast Asia as part of Operation Constant Guard I on 7 April 1972. Under the operational control of the 388th TFW at Korat, the F-105G assets of Det. 1 were integrated with those of the 17th WWS, and flew defence suppression mission in support of 13th AF aircraft during Operations Linebacker I and II. One Det 1 F-105G was shot down. On 5 September 1972, Det 1 was relieved and returned to George AFB, California, to begin the training of F-105G air and ground crews.

Markings on the 469th's silver-lacquered aircraft consisted of 4-in (10-cm) green/white/green stripes with the TAC badge and lightning bolt on both sides of the vertical tail. Camouflaged 469th TFS aircraft had a green tail band, canopy rails and radar reflector, with 'JV' tail codes from 1968. Camouflaged 13th TFS aircraft sported a yellow canopy rail and radar reflector. No tail codes were applied. Aircraft involved in Project Northscope had a distinctive 'wrap-around' camouflage of olive green/dark green/tan on the upper surfaces; with tan and blue-green on the undersides.

'ZB' codes were first assigned to Det. 1, 12th TFS – then the USAF's only dedicated defence suppression unit. On 1 November 1970 Det. 1 became the 6010th WWS, retaining 'ZB' codes. A year later it became the 17th WWS ('JB' codes).

Having taken over the assets of the 6010th WWS, the 17th WWS recoded its aircraft 'JB'. The last Thunderchief unit in the region, the 17th finally withdrew in October 1974, its aircraft passing to the 562nd TFS, 35th TFW at George AFB. This F-105G is at Korat in September 1973.

23RD TACTICAL FIGHTER WING

560th Tactical Fighter Squadron
561st Tactical Fighter Squadron
562rd Tactical Fighter Squadron
563rd Tactical Fighter Squadron
4519th Combat Crew Training Squadron
(4519th Tactical Fighter Training Squadron)

Activated at McConnell AFB, Kansas on 28 January 1964, the 23rd TFW took over the F-105D/F assets of the 388th TFW and its four squadrons – the 560th, 561st, 562nd and 563rd TFSs.

The mission of the 23rd TFW changed to that of the F-105 Replacement Training Unit in 1966, the 4519th Combat Crew Training Squadron being added on 1 August 1967. The 560th TFS was inactivated on 25 September 1968.

The 23rd Wing deployed three squadrons on a TDY basis to combat in Southeast Asia, beginning in February 1965. These units were initially under the control of 2nd AD until the 6441st TFW(P) was activated at Takhli. The TDY squadrons then came under the control of the 6235th TFW(P), beginning in July 1965.

The 561st Squadron deployed to Takhli on 6 February 1965, returning to McConnell on 10 July 1965. The 563rd TFS deployed to Takhli on 8 April 1965, returning to McConnell AFB on 10 July

1965. The 562nd TFS deployed to Takhli and relieved the 563rd Squadron, returning to McConnell on 8 December 1965. Detachments of the 561st TFS were also deployed to Da Nang AB, RVN, for operations within the borders of the Republic of Vietnam.

During combat operations in Southeast Asia, the 562nd TFS lost three aircraft; while the 563rd TFS lost 11 aircraft. On 1 July 1972, the 23rd TFW moved to England AFB, Louisiana, to begin operations with the LTV A-7D. The 561st, 562nd and 563rd Squadrons were assigned to the 35th TFW at George AFB, California, and equipped with F-105G Wild Weasel aircraft.

Squadron markings on the natural metal/silver lacquered aircraft included the following: 561st TFS – black/yellow checkerboard on rudder; 562nd TFS – a red, white and black 'sharkmouth' on the nose of the aircraft; 563rd TFS – red and white stripes on the rudder, wing tips, and stabilisers, with a white band on the top of the vertical fin, on which was painted a black 'Ace of Spades' decoration. All aircraft had the TAC badge on both sides of the vertical fin. Camouflaged aircraft carried the following tail codes: 561st TFS – 'MD'; 562nd TFS – 'ME'; 563rd TFS – 'MF'; 4519th TFTS – 'MG'.

Above: 562nd TFS F-105Ds pause on Guam, en route to Takhli during August 1965. Each of the 23rd TFW's squadrons adopted distinctive markings; the 562nd's aircraft were adorned with a 'sharkmouth'.

Below: Pictured a short time before the wing inactivated, this 563rd TFS F-105F carries the squadron's 'MF' code with a red canopy rail and tail band.

2ND AIR DIVISION

Korat-based units
36th Tactical Fighter Squadron
67th Tactical Fighter Squadron
44th Tactical Fighter Squadron
357th Tactical Fighter Squadron
35th Tactical Fighter Squadron
469th Tactical Fighter Squadron
12th Tactical Fighter Squadron
354th Tactical Fighter Squadron
421st Tactical Fighter Squadron

Takhli-based units
36th Tactical Fighter Squadron
80th Tactical Fighter Squadron
561st Tactical Fighter Squadron

The 2nd Air Division had control over all TDY squadrons deployed for combat in SEA from August 1964 until the activation of the 6234th TFW(P) at Korat on 5 April 1965, and the transfer of the 6441st TFW(P) from Yokota AB to Takhli in May 1965.

6234TH TACTICAL FIGHTER WING (P)

67th Tactical Fighter Squadron
44th Tactical Fighter Squadron
469th Tactical Fighter Squadron
12th Tactical Fighter Squadron
354th Tactical Fighter Squadron
421st Tactical Fighter Squadron

The 6234th Tactical Fighter Wing (Provisional) was activated at Korat

RTAFB on 5 April 1965 to assume command of the TDY squadrons that were operating from Korat under the temporary control of 2nd Air Division. The status of the 6234th TFW(P) was changed from TDY to PCS on 8 July 1965, remaining in control of all TDY squadron assignments until activation of the 388th TFW on 8 April 1966.

6235TH TACTICAL FIGHTER WING (P)

35th Tactical Fighter Squadron
36th Tactical Fighter Squadron
80th Tactical Fighter Squadron
334th Tactical Fighter Squadron
335th Tactical Fighter Squadron
354th Tactical Fighter Squadron
357th Tactical Fighter Squadron
561st Tactical Fighter Squadron
562nd Tactical Fighter Squadron
563rd Tactical Fighter Squadron

The 6235th Tactical Fighter Wing (Provisional) was activated at Takhli RTAFB, Thailand, on 8 July 1965, taking over control of the 6441st TFW(P) squadron assets at Takhli. The 6235th TFW(P) remained in control of TDY squadrons operating from Takhli until the 355th TFW was activated on 8 November 1965.

The 36th TFS was TDY to Takhli, and assigned initially to the 2nd AD, from February 1965 until the 6441st TFW(P)

was activated at Takhli in May 1965, when it passed to the 6235th TFW(P), on 8 July 1965. In October 1965, the 36th TFS returned to Yokota AB, Japan. During the TDY assignment, the 36th TFS lost seven aircraft to enemy action.

The 80th TFS made a TDY deployment to Takhli in February 1965, initially under the control of 2nd AD, then the 6441st TFW(P), and finally the 6235th TFW(P) beginning July 1965. On 26 August 1965, the 80th TFS returned to Yokota AB and resumed the Zulu Alert mission. Two 80th TFS F-105Ds were shot down over North Vietnam.

The 561st TFS deployed TDY to Takhli from McConnell AFB on 6 February 1965, under control of the 2nd AD initially, then the 6441st TFW(P) and the 6235th TFW(P) in July 1965. The 561st TFS returned to McConnell AFB, Kansas on 10 July 1965.

355TH TACTICAL FIGHTER WING

44th Tactical Fighter Squadron
333rd Tactical Fighter Squadron
354th Tactical Fighter Squadron
357th Tactical Fighter Squadron

The 355th Tactical Fighter Wing was activated at George AFB, California, on 8 July 1962, with four squadrons assigned – the 354th, 357th, 421st, and 469th TFS. On 21 July 1964, the 355th TFW, now equipped with F-105D/F aircraft, made a PCS move from George AFB to McConnell AFB, Kansas. All four squadrons assigned to the 355th TFW deployed on a TDY basis to either Korat or Takhli following the 4 August 1964 Gulf of Tonkin

Incident. On 8 November 1965, the 355th TFW moved PCS from McConnell AFB to Takhli RTAFB, Thailand, taking over the assets of the 6235th TFW(P). The 355th TFW was inactivated at Takhli on 10 December 1970, and all remaining F-105D/F assets were transferred to units in Southeast Asia, the Far East, and in the United States that were still operating the type.

When the 355th TFW was activated at Takhli, there were two squadrons assigned PCS – the 354th and 333rd TFS. The 354th TFS was transferred PCS on 27 November 1965, and remained assigned until deactivation of

The 355th TFW operated F-105Ds and Fs until December 1970. Here 44th TFS ('RE' tail code) and 357th TFS ('RU') F-105Ds are seen during combat operations from Thailand.

Most Thunderchiefs units flew a mixture of F-105Ds and Fs; this heavily-loaded F-105F is a 44th TFS machine.

the Wing on 10 December 1970. Aircraft losses totalled 46 aircraft to enemy action.

The 333rd TFS was transferred PCS from the 4th TFW at Seymour Johnson on 8 December 1965 to the 355th TFW at Takhli, remaining with the 355th Wing until inactivation on 10 December 1970. F-105D/F losses totalled 37, with 333rd TFS pilots accounting for 7½ NVAF MiG interceptors.

The 357th TFS was the third squadron assigned PCS to the 355th TFW at Takhli. After a TDY assignment between 12 June 1965 and 29 January 1966, the status of the 357th was changed to PCS and assigned to the 355th Wing. The squadron remained assigned to the 355th Wing until deactivation on 10 December 1970.

The 354th TFS lost 40 aircraft to enemy action, while shooting down four MiGs.

On 15 October 1969, the 44th TFS was transferred PCS from the 388th TFW at Korat to the 355th TFW at Takhli. The 44th TFS remained with the 355th TFW until deactivation on 10 December 1970. Following deactivation of the 355th TFW, all remaining F-105F/G Wild Weasel assets were transferred to the 388th TFW at Korat.

Aircraft markings included coloured canopy sills and radar reflectors, with an 'arrow device' in the intake, also in the squadron colour, with tail codes applied in 1967: 354th TFS – medium blue/'RM'; 333rd TFS – red/'RK'; 357th TFS – yellow/'RU'; 44th TFS – silver with black trim/'RE'.

35TH TACTICAL FIGHTER WING

561st Tactical Fighter Squadron
562nd Tactical Fighter Squadron
563rd Tactical Fighter Squadron

The 35th Tactical Fighter Wing was re-activated at George AFB, California on 1 October 1971, replacing the 479th TFW. Three F-105G squadrons were transferred from the 23rd TFW at McConnell AFB – 561st, 562nd, and 563rd TFS, beginning on 1 July 1973, when the 561st TFS returned from duty with the 388th TFW at Korat. The 562nd TFS was activated on 31 October 1974; with the 563rd TFTS being activated as a tactical training squadron on 31 July 1975.

Initially, the mission of the F-105G units in the 35th TFW was that of defence suppression; in 1975, the F-105G squadrons were given the mission of training new Wild Weasel pilots in missions and tactics for use with the newly developed F-4G Wild Weasel aircraft. F-105G operations phased out, beginning in 1978, and all F-105G assets were transferred to the 128th TFS, Georgia ANG.

Aircraft markings included 'GA' tail codes on 561st TFS F-105Gs returning from combat, and 'WW' on 17th WWS F-105Gs returning from combat. Tail codes for all 35th TFW F-105G, F-4E and F-4G aircraft were changed in 1978/79 to 'WW' to reflect the Wild Weasel mission of the 35th TFW.

Reflecting their Wild Weasel role, the 35th TFW soon adopted 'WW' tail codes, as previously used by the 561st TFS at Korat during 1973. F-105G 63-8332, pictured at Nellis AFB, retains T.O.1-1-4 camouflage, but has black codes as introduced in the late 1970s.

AIR NATIONAL GUARD

Thunderchiefs joined the Air National Guard in 1964, when F-105Bs from the 4th TFW were transferred to the 141st TFS. This was the only Guard F-105 unit until 1970/71, when a further four squadrons received aircraft made available as front-line units re-equipped with F-4 Phantoms. Here the six squadrons that operated Thunderchiefs are listed in the order in which they were equipped.

141ST TFS/108TH TFG, NEW JERSEY ANG

Based at McGuire AFB, New Jersey, the 141st Tactical Fighter Squadron, New Jersey ANG converted from F-86H Sabres to F-105Bs transferred direct from the 4th TFW in April 1964 when the 4th Wing had completed the transition to the F-105D. In May 1981, the 141st TFS converted from F-105Bs to F-4D Phantoms.

Markings on 141st TFS F-105Bs, whether in silver lacquer or SEA camouflage, was the Air Guard badge on the vertical fin with the logo 'New Jersey' in black or white. Most aircraft also had the Air Force OUA ribbon painted on the top of the vertical fin. On the fuselage below the intakes was a miniature 141st TFS emblem.

The sign on the hangar in the background, proclaiming McGuire AFB as the 'Home of the Air Guard Thunderchiefs', seems appropriate given that New Jersey's F-105Bs operated from the base for some 17 years before their retirement in 1981. Like their front-line counterparts, all received T.O.1-1-4 camouflage during the 1960s.

119TH TFS/177TH TFG, NEW JERSEY ANG

In June 1970, the 119th Tactical Fighter Squadron, New Jersey ANG, converted from F-100C Super Sabres to F-105Bs at Atlantic City ANGB, New Jersey. The 119th TFS was the second and only other Air Guard squadron to operate the F-105B. In January 1973, the mission of the 119th Squadron was changed to air defence, and the unit, now designated the 119th FIS, converted from F-105Bs to Convair F-106A Delta Daggers.

Differing slightly from those of the 141st TFS, the markings applied to 119th TFS F-105Bs incorporated a thin red band on the top of the tail fin and the 119th TFS emblem on the fuselage. Other markings were similar to those of the 141st TFS.

The red fin stripe on this NJ ANG F-105B marks it out as a 119th TFS aircraft. An Air Force OUA ribbon is also visible on the tail, immediately above the ANG emblem.

121ST TFS/113TH TFG, DISTRICT OF COLUMBIA ANG

Based at Andrews AFB, Maryland, the 121st Tactical Fighter Squadron, District of Columbia ANG, converted from F-100C Super Sabres to F-105D/Fs in July 1971. In July 1981, the 121st TFS began conversion to the F-4D Phantom, completing the transition in March 1982.

Markings on 121st TFS F-105s included the legend 'District of Columbia' on a thin blue stripe with white borders on the vertical tail, a yellow radar reflector, the ANG badge on the middle of the vertical fin, and the 121st TFS squadron emblem on the fuselage below the cockpit.

Other than the ANG emblem and a 'District of Colombia' legend, this F-105F is comparatively free of markings. Like the other two ANG squadrons equipped with F-105Ds and Fs, the 121st TFS was equipped with 'Thuds' for much of the 1970s.

As the Thunderchief was being retired from the front-line USAF, the Kansas ANG was given the important role of F-105 RTU, tasked with training new crews on the type. A 127th TFTS F-105F is pictured.

149TH TFS/192ND TFG, VIRGINIA ANG

The 149th Tactical Fighter Squadron, Virginia ANG, converted from Republic F-84F Thunderstreaks to F-105D/Fs at Byrd Field ANGB in February 1971. The 149th TFS was the first F-105D unit in Air Guard service, flying the type until 1982 when the squadron converted to LTV A-7Ds.

Markings on 149th TFS Thunderchiefs included a yellow tail stripe with white trim and a black

lightning bolt superimposed. The ANG badge was displayed in the middle of the fin, and the legend 'Virginia' was painted above the serial number. Some aircraft had the canopy rail painted yellow. Many of the 149th TFS Thunderchiefs had 'nose art' painted under the intakes, very similar to that which adorned the combat Thunderchiefs in SEA.

128TH TFS/116TH TFG, GEORGIA ANG

The 128th Tactical Fighter Squadron, Georgia ANG converted from F-100D Super Sabres to F-105Gs transferred from the 35th TFW, beginning in early 1979, the transition being completed in the summer. Based at Dobbins ANGB, Georgia, the 128th TFS was the only ANG unit to operate the F-105G Wild Weasel. In August 1983, the 128th TFS completed conversion into the F-4D.

Some aircraft had yellow canopy rails and a yellow band with white borders on the tail fin. Many aircraft also had a 'sharkmouth' nose marking and wrap-around camouflage.

This 128th TFS F-105G, while devoid of squadron colours, sports a 'sharkmouth' and wrap-around camouflage. An AGM-45 acquisition round is also carried.

127TH TFTS/184TH TFTG, KANSAS ANG

The McConnell AFB-based 127th Tactical Fighter Training Squadron, Kansas Air National Guard, converted from F-100C Super Sabres into F-105D/Fs in March 1971. The mission of the 127th TFTS was as a Replacement Training Unit to train F-105 air crews for service with the US Air Force, Air Force Reserve and Air National Guard. In November 1979, the

127th TFTS was redesignated as a TFS and began conversion to the F-4D.

Markings on 127th TFTS F-105D/Fs included a red tail stripe with white trim, red canopy sills and radar reflector. The ANG badge was displayed in the middle of the vertical fin. Some aircraft had the 127th TFS squadron emblem painted on the fuselage under the cockpit.

AIR FORCE RESERVE

Three AFRES units operated Thunderchiefs between 1972 and 1984. All operated a mixture of F-105Ds and Fs; the 466th TFS had earlier employed F-105Bs between 1973 and 1981.

305TH TACTICAL FIGHTER SQUADRON (465TH TACTICAL FIGHTER SQUADRON)

On 20 May 1972, Air Force Reserve converted the 305th Military Airlift Squadron to a Tactical Fighter Squadron equipped with F-105D/Fs, the first squadron in Air Force Reserve to operate with the F-105. The first F-105D arrived at Tinker AFB, Oklahoma, on 14 April 1972. On 20 May 1973, the 305th TFS was renumbered as the 465th TFS.

10 January 1980 the 465th TFS completed transition from F-105Ds to F-4D Phantoms.

Aircraft markings applied to 305th TFS F-105s included a blue tail band with the legend 'Sooners' in white, and the tail code of 'UC'. When the 305th TFS was renumbered as the 465th, the code was changed to 'SH', other markings remaining unaltered.

The first AFRES unit to receive Thunderchiefs, the 305th TFS 'Sooners' was equipped with F-105Ds some eight months before the 466th TFS converted to F-105Bs passed down from the New Jersey ANG.

457TH TACTICAL FIGHTER SQUADRON

The 457th Tactical Fighter Squadron, Air Force Reserve, was activated at Carswell AFB, Texas, in July 1972. The 457th TFS was assigned 38 F-105D/F aircraft, including 29 of the advanced 'Thunderstick II' F-105Ds, the only unit to be equipped with the 'T-Stick II' systems. In October 1981, the 457th TFS began a transition to the McDonnell F-4D Phantom.

Markings included red canopy rails and a red band on the tail with white trim. Below the latter was a map of Texas in white. Most aircraft had 'AFRES' painted on the aft fuselage in either white or black, with codes letter 'TH' painted on the tail. Some aircraft had standard SEA camouflage with light grey undersides, while later aircraft had a wrap-around camouflage scheme.

466TH TACTICAL FIGHTER SQUADRON

The 466th TFS was organised at Hill AFB, Utah, on 1 January 1973, with 18 F-105Bs transferred from the 119th TFS, New Jersey ANG. In April 1980, the 466th TFS began the transition from F-105Bs to F-105D/Fs; the last flight by an F-105B took place on 5 January 1981. Initially equipped with 28 F-105Ds and four F-105Fs, the re-equipped 466th was to be the last unit to fly the F-105D/F, the final flight taking place on 25 February 1984; the 466th then flew F-16A/Bs.

Unit markings included a yellow

canopy rail, nose stripe and tail stripe, the latter with white trim. Initial camouflage was to T.O.1-1-4 standard, though some aircraft later wore a wrap-around camouflage. At least one aircraft was finished in a tan/brown scheme; another carried 'European One' green/green/grey. A rattlesnake emblem was painted in the tail of some aircraft; tail codes were 'HI'.

Pictured at Hill AFB in January 1974, 466th TFS F-105B 57-5814 was a veteran of the 'Thunderbirds' display team.

More than simply a refined version of the F-102 Delta
Dagger, Convair's F-106 encompassed state-of-the-art
technology when introduced in 1959, including
hands-off interception and a nuclear air-to-air missile.
Conceived as the '1954 Ultimate Interceptor', the
F-106 proved to be the last pure interceptor designed
as such for the USAF and the last to be retired.

Convair F-106
Delta Dart
The Ultimate Interceptor

ADC ★ FIS OPERATIONS 1959 TO 1988 ★ ANG
WHEN YOU'RE OUT OF SIXES, YOU'RE OUT OF INTERCEPTORS

F-106
DART

linked via its complex Hughes MA-1 'Digitaire' electronic fire control system through a digital datalink into the nation-wide SAGE (semi-automatic ground environment) as an integral component in a high-tech – for its era – air defence network. A technological achievement when it first entered service at McGuire AFB, New Jersey in May 1959, the 'Six' aged quickly and became a prime candidate for in-service upgrades. Improvements to the F-106 included the addition of a gun (in a neat installation in the missile bay, causing a slight bulge), a revised canopy and supersonic wing tanks. Always more than the sum of its 'black boxes' and missiles, the F-106 remained an unrepentant Cold Warrior until retirement of the last aircraft by the New Jersey Air National Guard in 1988. Even thereafter, it soldiered on as a chase plane, test ship, and unmanned target drone.

Design and development

The F-106 saga began on 8 October 1948 when a board of USAF officers recommended a design competition for a new all-weather interceptor to be available in 1954. From their recommendations came the F-102 and F-106 interceptors. As a result of their work, in January 1950 the USAF invited 50 electronics firms to submit bids for a fire control system (FCS) for the '1954 Interceptor'. On 1 September 1950, the USAF invited 19 aircraft contractors – about six times the number of manufacturers of combat aircraft in the US industry today – to submit bids for the '1954 Interceptor' under Project MX-1554.

On 2 October 1950, the Pentagon awarded Hughes the contract for the '1954 Interceptor' FCS. It was known then as Project 1179 but became the MA-1 fire control system that was to become the operational heart of the F-106 Delta Dart.

Convair had long ago designed a four-engined, delta-winged fighter called the XP-92 (which was never built) and a single-engined delta research ship called the XF-92A (flying at Muroc, California). The company became the USAF's choice on 11 September 1951 when it was awarded the contract for a prototype of the '1954 Interceptor'. The prototype was to exploit scientific work performed by Convair on delta-wing planforms. It eventually evolved into the F-102, which at the time was considered one of several 'interim' solutions to North American air defence.

It was a long route from the XF-92A test aircraft to the

Although it rarely ventured overseas, the Convair F-106 Delta Dart made an indelible mark on military history: it stood guard on North America and it advanced the science of aeronautics. It was a bulwark of the Cold War and a glimpse of the future. Sleek and beautiful, the 'Six' had an impact on the US Air Force totally out of proportion to the 340 airframes that were manufactured in Convair's Plant 2 in San Diego, California and fitted out for final delivery a few miles away at Palmdale. The F-106 was a 'Cadillac of the skies' to some pilots, the embodiment of elegance to others. Always, it was a pleasing sight to the eye despite its grim mission: to detect, identify, intercept and destroy Russian bombers – and later, air-launched missiles – carrying atomic weapons to American cities.

If it had been nothing more than an effective interceptor, the F-106 still would warrant a niche in history – but it also capped an era of unprecedented scientific advances. Its 'case 14' delta wing, replaced in due course by the 'case 29' version, was the apex of an engineering development process that encompassed great and not-so-great warplanes – XP-92, XF-92A, F-102, F-102A, Sea Dart and B-58 Hustler. Its area-ruled 'wasp waist' reflected an important leap forward in designing aircraft for supersonic flight. From its radar to its afterburner, from its nuclear-tipped air-to-air missilery to its cockpit flight instruments, the F-106 set a standard of progress and innovation that was unmatched in the late 1950s and early 1960s.

More than an aircraft, the F-106 was really a system,

operational F-106. Early progress with the MA-1 FCS was slow, and in November 1952 the USAF decided that the 'interim' F-102 would use the E-9 interim FCS instead of the MA-1. The long-sought MA-1 would be developed "patiently and gradually", as one document from the era described the unexpected delays, and would be put into the more advanced F-102B (company Model 8-21), the designation by which the F-106 was known at that time. Neither the 'interim' nor the 'eventual' version of the '1954 Interceptor' had been christened at the time and the popular names Delta Dagger (F-102) and Delta Dart (F-102B/F-106) came into use only in 1959.

In October 1953, the USAF leadership authorised the Air Research and Development Command (ARDC) to proceed with engineering work to make the forthcoming J75 engine compatible with the imminent F-102B (the future F-106). The J75 turbojet was chosen after plans to use the Bristol Olympus, which was to have been licence-built as the Wright J67, went awry due to technical problems. A Convair proposal to use the Rolls-Royce Conway as the powerplant for the F-102B appears to have attracted little interest. The J75 was based on the better-known J57, which at the time was the powerplant for several important warplanes, including the B-52 Stratofortress and the impending F-102A. Both were manufactured by Pratt & Whitney.

Delta genesis

A bare beginning, and a premature one, was made with the first flight of a YF-102 (Convair Model 8-80) prototype (52-7994) on 24 October 1953 with Richard L. 'Dick' Johnson at the controls. Although the 'Y' suffix indicated a service-test mission, the YF-102 lacked virtually all of the features that would be found on the operational F-102 to follow and had none of the refinements of the future F-106. A report on the YF-102 proclaimed succinctly, "Performance was lacking." One wag ignored the clean shape of its delta wings and tail, focused on its portly fuselage, and called it a "flying beer barrel with wings." The canopy had metal braces that resembled prison bars. And, of course, it carried no armament or FCS. There were plenty of problems: on 2 November 1953, the YF-102 crashed wheels-up on its seventh flight, severely injuring Johnson. Development of the FCS radar appeared to be proceeding so slowly that some wondered if any of this work on a new interceptor would ever bear edible fruit.

The YF-102A (Model 8-10) prototype (53-1787) that made its maiden flight more than a year later on 20 December 1954 had a different shape, including an 'area-ruled' or 'Coke bottle' fuselage based on the research of NASA's Richard Whitcomb and intended to facilitate supersonic flight. This aircraft was outwardly similar to the F-102A Delta Dagger which followed and which turned out to be more than an 'interim' in expectation of the eventual F-106.

The J57-powered F-102A Delta Dagger, or 'Deuce', (Convair Model 8) and its 'fat' TF-102A side-by-side cohort (the 'Tub') eventually played an enormous role in the defence of North America and NATO, and fought briefly in Vietnam, where one was shot down by a MiG-21. The F-102 equipped Air National Guard squadrons, served in Greece and Turkey, and ended its days as an unpiloted drone target. The operational F-102s used a fire control system called the MG-10 which included a radar element designated MG-3 (after the earlier E-9 FCS proved inadequate). The MG-10 system was the FCS of choice for proposed (but never built) export versions of the MA-1-equipped F-106. Convair manufactured 1,000 F-102s between 1953 and 1961, and this much-loved warplane justifies its own book. For our purposes, however, we will skip quickly past the long and valiant career of the

Above: The first YF-106A, 56-0451, left the ground at Edwards on its 20-minute maiden flight on 26 December 1956, narrowly meeting the stipulated deadline of the end of the year. At the time the aircraft was so secret that no photos or drawings had been released to the press. This photograph is believed to depict its first take-off.

Above left: The second aircraft flew exactly two months after the first, having also been trucked from San Diego to Edwards. The first three test aircraft wore 'FC' 'buzz numbers' as on the F-102A, reflecting the type's origins as the F-102B.

Top: 56-0461 was the ninth flying F-106 built (aircraft no. 3 was used for static tests) and is seen here over Edwards during the Category II test programme. It was one of the development aircraft later refurbished and issued to Air Defense Command. Finally leaving service with the 5th FIS in 1995, it is currently stored at AMARC.

The first F-106 is seen later in its career when adorned with high-visibility Dayglo trim. After a career of fewer than four years, it was retired and became part of the USAF Museum collection. Today it is displayed at Selfridge AFB, Michigan with a spurious serial number.

F-102 in order to relate the tale of the true '1954 Interceptor', alias the 'ultimate F-102B' (Model 8-24, formerly 8-21), which on 17 June 1956 was redesignated F-106A. This was also dubbed Weapon System WS-201B.

Navy Dart

While the earlier designation was still in effect (on 20 June 1955), Convair produced a report summarising its efforts to design and sell a US Navy carrier-based, high-altitude version of the F-102B (the future F-106). The company had earlier proposed a similar version of the F-102A, and the new proposal might have given the Navy a new aircraft contemporary with the McDonnell F4H-1 Phantom and Vought F8U-3 Crusader III. Convair tried to keep differences between the USAF and USN versions of the F-102B 'relatively few in number' and built a display model which retained most of the basic characteristics of the Air Force machine. The Navy model would have employed an Aero 11B fire control system including AN/APQ-50 radar, then much in favour with the Navy's Bureau of Aeronautics, together with a BuOrd Mk 16 combination sight and radar scope. Armament was four XAAM-N-2A (the future AIM-7A) Sparrow 1A missiles, which required a slight extension of the internal weapons bay. Alternate ordnance loads included two Ding Dong missiles (the future MB-1 Genie) or six XAAM-N-7 (the future AIM-9) Sidewinder missiles. The proposal was made with allowance for either the J67 (still then under consideration) or J75 engine.

The Navy's F-102B (the future F-106) would have had a strengthened wing to increase maximum g-load factor from 7.0 to 7.5. The empennage of the Navy fighter incorporated minor changes to accommodate Navy electronics antennas and to permit the tip of the fin to fold for shipboard stowage. The strengthened landing gear would have included dual independently-rotating nosewheels and a somewhat stronger main undercarriage. The tailhook envisioned for the seagoing F-102B was quite small, tucked at the extreme rear of the engine exhaust area. A Navy expert from the period remembers that, "Convair and their people were very eager but we had our eyes set on other fighters, so we said thanks, but no thanks." Had such an aircraft been built, using the naval aircraft designation system then in effect, it almost certainly would have become the Convair F3Y-1 Delta Dart. The term Sea Dart, of course, was already taken by the same builder's F2Y-1 flying-boat fighter which was then the subject of a vigorous research and development programme.

Production contract

Air Force officers and industry came together with a November 1955 contract for the first 17 aircraft (56-451/467), still using the original military designation F-102B. The contract was finalised and the F-102B construction order placed on 18 April 1956. Weeks later, the designation changed from F-102B to F-106A. On 3 August 1956, the USAF authorised a two-seat TF-106A (Convair Model 8-27) variant. The Pentagon changed the designation to F-106B by the end of that month.

Progress was slower than had been hoped. To develop the fire control system, initially called the MX-1179 FCS but soon redesignated the MA-1 FCS, Hughes Aircraft had acquired on bailment an NT-29B aircraft (Convair 340) in 1953 or 1954. At various times, two NT-29B aircraft (51-5164 and 51-7912) flew as airborne radar testbeds and it is unclear today which of them might have been in service as the Hughes testbed when, much later than originally hoped, the company began flight testing of the MA-1, in December 1956.

Test programme

The test programme for the F-106 was extensive and lengthy. The Edwards phase alone involved 12 aircraft and lasted until mid-1959. Although there were no problems of the magnitude that plagued the original F-102, supersonic acceleration in particular proved disappointing, and there were engine, fire control system and cockpit layout problems as well. The expensive modifications required nearly killed the whole programme when the USAF faced a funding crisis in 1957. Many changes were still required before the 'Six' could enter service.

Above: The eighth F-106 lifts off on a test flight. This aircraft tested the intake configuration fitted to production aircraft. The new, larger inlet with thinner duct lips improved the aircraft's range, ceiling and acceleration.

Left: A civilian, probably a Convair rep, briefs a test pilot before a hop from Edwards in the third test ship, which was delivered in August 1957, the scene being recorded by a company photographer. As the development programme progressed in parallel with production, aircraft diverged further from a common standard, causing the USAF many headaches as the F-106 entered service.

The first F-106A (Convair Model 8-24) aircraft (56-0451), sometimes referred to as a YF-106A with the 'Y' prefix indicating a service-test role, was completed in late 1956. One mystery revolving around the F-106 story is the question of why Convair apparently never held a roll-out ceremony or other celebration to mark the appearance of this new fighter for the Air Force. Possibly, officials believed that a ceremony would call attention to delays in the programme. Furthermore, photos of the F-106A were not yet cleared for release to the public. For whatever reason, the first aircraft did its first travelling on a flatbed truck. Meanwhile, the Air Force designated the F-106A as Weapon System 201B, a term intended to emphasise an integrated, well-orchestrated effort to develop aircraft, radar, electronics and armament as a co-ordinated 'package' – when, in fact, the entire developmental effort was proceeding in fits and starts.

Flight test

Taxi tests began at Edwards on 22 December 1956. On 27 December 1956, the *San Diego Tribune* reported the initial flight of an aircraft that had not yet been seen by press or public, and of which no drawings or artists' conceptions had yet been released. The pilot was Richard L. Johnson, the ex-Air Force test pilot (and veteran of combat in the Mediterranean) who had joined Convair's San Diego operation in 1953 and had previously made the premier flight of the F-102. The newspaper gave no reason why 26 December 1956 – as the day after Christmas, it was normally a quiet day – was chosen for Johnson to take off in his "hot new fighter-type jet" on the 20-minute maiden flight at 2:50 p.m. In fact, the manufacturer was struggling desperately to fulfil a contractual obligation to fly the aircraft by year's end.

Marty J. Isham, an Air Force civilian who is the leading expert on the F-106, remembers how time pressures affected the flight test effort. "As everyone in the programme knew, the '1954 Interceptor' was way behind the power curve. Weapon System 201B had to be operational and provide an all-weather air defence system for the period 1959 through 1962. This requirement was established by GOR No. 4 (ADI 51-1) dated 27 December 1951, and in accordance with ARDC System Requirement No. 82 dated 1 November 1955. To satisfy contract requirements, the now F-106A HAD to fly in 1956! Time had run out!"

In fact, although news reports missed it, pilot Johnson's maiden flight in the 'Six' was aborted due to air turbine

motor frequency fluctuation. Worse, the speed brakes opened and would not close. Glitches like this were not uncommon in an early test flight, but it was a contrast to an early success in another 'Century Series' programme: more than two years earlier, on 29 September 1954, McDonnell test pilot Robert C. Little had made the maiden flight of the F-101A Voodoo at Edwards in a flawless first outing that made the Voodoo the first aircraft to go supersonic on its debut. The contrast between the flawless start by the ugly, ungainly F-101A and a frustrating first flight by the 'Six' may not have attracted comment at the time, but in retrospect it puts in sharp relief the developmental problems that were dogging Convair and Hughes.

Nor would a Soviet intelligence analyst have gained much from the *Tribune*'s report on the first flight: "Electronic aiming devices in the F-106A and its armament are said to be improved over those in the F-102A," the newspaper ventured, "[but] no further information is available." In fact, the first two examples of the 'Model 8 Airplane', known to the builder as Prototypes 8-20-1 and 8-20-2 (F-106As 56-451/452), were aerodynamic test vehicles. (The Model 8-24 designation applied to the generic design.) The two prototypes had no provision for the Hughes MA-1 AWCIS (Aircraft & Weapons Control Interceptor System) and "no provision for installation or retrofit of any armament configuration except that the MB-1 armament bay doors [are] to be installed and operative." In fact, they carried ballast in the nose to preserve the design centre-of-gravity. MA-1 was, of course, the radar fire control system; MB-1 was the Douglas Genie nuclear-tipped missile.

Description

At this point, a description of the F-106A is in order. A 1957 US Air Force document sets forth basic facts about the F-106A Delta Dart, which lives today in the minds of many who see it as the most beautiful warplane ever built: "The F-106A was a single-place, delta-winged, supersonic airplane built by Convair to serve as an all-weather interceptor. Features of the airplane included an area-rule

Above: *Still showing evidence of intake modification, 56-0459 flies with a much later example (line number 160, delivered in November 1959). '459 is today displayed at McChord AFB, whereas '797 was shot down as a QF-106 drone out of Tyndall AFB in 1990.*

Far left: *After the first three aircraft, the 'buzz number' for the F-106 was changed from 'FC' to 'FE'. This code had previously been used on the F-47 Thunderbolt. Wing fences, as on the F-102, were fitted to the first 17 F-106As to fly, but were replaced by notches (as seen here) on most of the survivors.*

56-0453 was the third F-106 to fly and was delivered from the factory in August 1957. After a long career, it was converted to QF-106 configuration as AD111 and was lost in a crash at Holloman on 27 January 1995.

Speed record

On 15 December 1959, Major Joe Rogers broke the world absolute speed record in an F-106A with a flight measured at 1,525.93 mph (2455.68 km/h), eclipsing the 1491.3-mph (2399.95 km/h) mark set by Colonel G. Molosov of the USSR on 7 October of that year in the Mikoyan Ye-152-1. The flight was conducted on a straight-line course 11 miles (18 km) in length, at an altitude of 40,000 ft (12192 m). The flight was noteworthy for another reason – the aircraft used was not the one prepared for the record attempt (56-0459), which became unserviceable on the day, but another Air Force Flight Test Center aircraft (56-0467) which did not have a 'tweaked' engine. The record stood until 22 November 1961 when it was broken by an F4H-1F Phantom flown by Lieutenant Colonel R. B. Robinson. The F-106 flight was thought to remain a record for single-engined aircraft, but it appears that it was the Ye-152-1 (mislabelled E-166 by the Soviets) powered by one R-15, and again flown by Molosov, that recaptured the absolute record on 7 July 1962 at a speed of 1,665.89 mph (2680.92 km/h).

Top: Major Joe Rogers prepares to board 56-0459, the planned mount for the record attempt. In the event, this aircraft became unserviceable, and Rogers flew 56-0467 (above).

fuselage and a pressurised cockpit equipped with an ejection seat. The flight control system utilised elevons to give both aileron and elevator action." Here, the simplicity of the delta wing was a virtue. As company test pilot Dick Johnson put it, "There are no trailing- or leading-edge flaps, slots, or boundary layer bleeds or controls to lower, extend, turn on, or check [and] no trim changes to anticipate or correct for."

Wing design

The wing of the F-106A was developed from the planform employed by the F-102A. The original version, called the 'case 14' wing (or 'case XIV'), found on aircraft with Fiscal Year 1956 serial numbers, had outer-wing boundary layer fences as on the F-102A. The fences were replaced on the production-standard 'case 29' (or 'case XXIX') wing with leading-edge slots. The F-106 had a 'wet' wing with no fuel bladders, a characteristic later to be quoted as perfectly acceptable in the continental United States but a handicap if used in Vietnam (as was later considered). Fuel transfer was accomplished by low air pressure, bleeding off low-psi air pressure from engine into tanks. "A bullet hole in your wing and you'd lose air pressure," said pilot Lieutenant General Ranald Adams. "I don't know how many holes it would take, but ..." The delta-winged interceptor could outperform the F-4 Phantom above 20,000 ft (6096 m) but was not deemed effective in air combat manoeuvre down low because of its elevon load limit.

The simplicity of the delta wing was an enormous part of

its appeal. A conventional aircraft used movable ailerons, elevators and stabilisers for longitudinal control, and flaps, perhaps slots also, for lift augmentation – as contrasted with nothing more than elevons and a large wing for high lift on delta-winged aircraft. Having fewer control surfaces and actuating systems was a gift to maintainers. Convair noted that, "Pilots have more freedom with fewer controls to actuate [and] find the delta wing safer. The lack of movable surfaces and their operating mechanisms lends ruggedness to a delta-winged aircraft. The delta shape is not only ideal from an aerodynamic standpoint, but also approaches the ultimate shape for structural strength and stiffness. This precludes flutter and other forms of structural instability."

Automatic flight control

The F-106's AFCS (automatic flight control system) operated its elevons (aileron-elevator surfaces on the trailing edge of the delta wing) in response to commands received from the digital computer. Information received by the AFCS originated in the flight-sensing instruments, ground stations feeding intelligence to the MA-1, the Delta Dart's own radar system, and the computer's own memory drum. AFCS also functioned during the return portion of the mission.

Returning to the description from the 1957 document: "The tricycle landing gear was equipped with an electrically-controlled, hydraulically-powered nosewheel steering unit. An automatic fuel transfer system controlled the centre-of-gravity location during supersonic high-altitude flight. Engine variable inlet ramps [very much a new feature in 1957!] were provided to obtain optimum airplane performance at supersonic speeds with full engine power, and to maintain engine inlet airflow stability over a wide range of speed and altitude."

The Pratt & Whitney YJ75-P-1 twin-spool, axial-flow turbojet engine (company model JT4A) with afterburner (the initial model of the same engine that powered the F-105 Thunderchief) was rated in an AFFTC report at 15,000 lb (66.71 kN) static thrust at sea level at military power and 23,500 lb (47.41 kN) static thrust at sea level at maximum power. In time, the 'Six' was to progress to -9 and -17 versions of the engine.

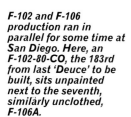

F-102 and F-106 production ran in parallel for some time at San Diego. Here, an F-102-80-CO, the 183rd from last 'Deuce' to be built, sits unpainted next to the seventh, similarly unclothed, F-106A.

In contrast to the F-102A, the F-106A fuselage was extensively modified with a more streamlined shape, having the variable ramp air intakes moved well aft of the nose, closer to the engine. The fin and rudder shape was changed markedly and a new landing gear installed with steerable, twin nosewheels. There were also numerous small measures designed to make the F-106A fast as well as formidable: the upper and lower rotating navigation beacon lights (immediately aft of the canopy in the dorsal position, and immediately behind the nosewheel on the belly of the aircraft) were designed on early F-106s so that they retracted when the aircraft went supersonic. In later years, this feature was disabled and the beacons no longer moved.

Cockpit design debate

The pilot of the F-106A sat far forward, well ahead of the engine intakes, but significantly back from the windshield. As will be noted below, early F-106As had both centre- and sidestick control columns, but the USAF settled eventually on a unique, two-handed grip for traditional control of the aircraft (right hand) and operation of the radar (left). This was for practical purposes the same as the 'yoke' used on most non-fighter aircraft. A button

between the two grips activated the left grip, giving the pilot control of the radar antenna; another button atop the left grip enabled the pilot to put a pipper on the target by following directions on the radar scope. Pilots were supposed to be encouraged to have radar and autopilot engaged simultaneously as much as possible, part of the lore of this being an 'automatic' aircraft ("a man-carrying guided missile," according to one publication), but most stuck to the old ways. Besides, if the radar had what was called a 'hot dot discrepancy' with the autopilot engaged (the image representing the F-106 at the centre of the radar scope), the aircraft would bounce the pilot about rather harshly. The pilot selected his missiles to be fired using a switch on the left console; the trigger to launch missiles was on the right-hand grip.

Design of the cockpit of the F-106A was influenced by experience with the F-102 Delta Dagger and initially featured a typical analog instrument display. (A USAF study in the mid-1950s showed that pilots were using 26 different instrument and flight-control arrangements in jet aircraft, leading to a call for standardisation that had not yet been made when the F-106 was designed.) The cockpit display had not been approved during the initial mock-up inspection of the aircraft, and the USAF demanded that further work be done. The MA-1 AWCIS in mock-up form made use of vertical-tape instruments (not initially adopted by production F-106s, though they came later), a side control stick (sidestick controller), a 10-in (25-cm) horizontal map display and a radar screen (not the Hughes MA-1 fire control display). Apart from the map display, these items marked a radical departure from customary Air Force cockpit instrumentation and resulted in a decision to develop two cockpit configurations simultaneously in the first 12 developmental aircraft. Six had the sidestick con-

The F-106 became the first fighter in the USAF to be fitted with a tailhook, although for land use only. It was designed by Bruce Sheaffer of the All American Engineering Company, which also provided the 'water squeezer' arrester cable system. The first F-106, by now belonging to AFFTC, undertook many tests, proving that the 'Sheaffer hook' met the air force's requirement of arrestment from 110 kt (204 km/h).

The MA-1 weapons system included the missiles, radar, computers and the F-106 airframe. All but the aircraft itself were manufactured by Hughes. This tableau shows AIM-4F (rear) and AIM-4G missiles, the radar scope (but not the scanner) and the many 'black boxes' in the system.

In this publicity shot from the 1950s, Hughes Aircraft Company test pilot James J. O'Reilly holds up a 36-in (91 cm) aluminium disc target pierced by a Hughes GAR-4A (AIM-4G) Falcon. The disc was suspended from a tower at Holloman AFB and heated to simulate a jet exhaust. O'Reilly's F-106A was "more than a mile away" when the missile was fired.

A trio of 'Geiger Tigers' F-106s poses for an early publicity shot. ADC felt that the Delta Dart as delivered was far short of being operationally ready, and niggling problems with generators, fuel flow, starters and canopies led to a temporary grounding in December 1959.

Above: This is a 539th FIS F-106A, one of the participants in William Tell 1961, the first in which the F-106 took part.

Below: While the 498th was working towards IOC, the 539th was carrying out the Category III test programme, involving proving of the weapons system at Tyndall AFB. The missile-firing phase ended in May 1960. The F-106B was declared operational in July of that year.

Into service

The first two units to receive the 'Six' were the 539th FIS at McGuire AFB, New Jersey and the 498th FIS at Geiger AFB, Washington on 30 May and 1 June 1959, respectively. Despite technically being the second Delta Dart operator, the 'Geiger Tigers' were undoubtedly first to stand and launch an alert – on 21 July 1959 – and declared initial operational capability (IOC) in October. This was five years later than originally planned for the '1954 Ultimate Interceptor'.

troller while six had a standard centre control stick with radar screen and some non-standard instruments, becoming known in flight test as the 'Sacred Six'. They had provisions for the sidestick controller to be installed.

The other six developmental aircraft had a Hughes MA-1 cockpit display, non-standard vertical tape instruments, radar screen display, horizontal map display and side-stick controller with provisions for a centre stick.

Some early F-106s with FY 1956 serial numbers had an additional fuel cell in the fin. It quickly became apparent that if this tank did not feed properly, the aircraft was almost impossible to land because of C of G problems. After the early flight test phase, this fuel tank was retained on the early aircraft but was never used in actual operations.

As a feature on newly-built aircraft, the vertical-tape instrument set, or IID (Integrated Instrument Display), was fitted on the production line with aircraft 58-0759. The first three squadrons of F-106As put into the field had analog, or 'round', instrument dials and, although some aircraft subsequently were upgraded with IID as indicated

below, many served their entire lives without ever getting the vertical tapes. In the case of the two-seat F-106B, the IID mod began at the factory apparently with aircraft 57-2525.

The 'brain' of F-106As was the MA-1 AWCIS 'Digitaire', the Delta Dart's airborne digital computer and fire control system created in what was little less than an engineering miracle by a young and vigorous Hughes company. A key sub-system was the TSD (Tactical Situation Display) that projected a map display onto a cockpit screen, permitting the pilot to follow the course of the mission pictorially. An automatic feature changed the

The 27th FIS at Loring AFB, Maine was the third squadron to convert to the Delta Dart (like the 498th, from F-102s). One of its aircraft is seen below with an unusual grey-painted radome.

maps along with the aircraft's location. Small symbols on the screen represented the aircraft, the position and movement, and the heading the F-106 needed to fly to reach the target.

The USAF viewed as extremely serious the business of the F-106A/MA-1 'weapon system' – the term was in vogue to emphasise that an airframe was meaningless – which was to intercept and destroy Soviet bombers, both subsonic and supersonic, operating from sea level to over 70,000 ft (21336 m). From the start, the armament of the F-106 was to include one Douglas MB-1 Genie, an unguided rocket projectile with a nuclear warhead. A number of sources which list the aircraft as being able to carry two Genies are incorrect. The single rocket was expected to assure a kill of an approaching bomber or bomber formation. (Initially known as the Ding Dong, the MB-1 Genie was redesignated AIR-2A on 1 October 1962. There was not an improved version called the AIR-2B, despite published references to the contrary.)

Super Falcon

In addition to the Genie, the armament of the F-106 included advanced versions of what had been the first US air-to-air missile, the Hughes Falcon. Although it was besmirched in later years by pilots who found it inadequate for fighter-versus-fighter combat in Vietnam, the Falcon was in every respect a scientific advance and an impressive achievement. It was originally known as the MX-904 Dragonfly but carried the USAF designation XF-98 until 20 August 1955. As developed for the F-106, these missiles totalled three variants: the GAR-3 and GAR-3A Super Falcon SARH (semi-active radar homing) missiles and the GAR-4A Super Falcon IR-homing missile. The designations of the three were changed, respectively, to AIM-4E, AIM-4F and AIM-4G on 1 October 1962. The F-106 was configured to fire Super Falcons in pairs and routinely fired one radar-guided and one IR-guided missile simultaneously. USAF pilots often grumbled, especially in later years, that the Super Falcon needed more range.

The GAR-3 (AIM-4E) was the first of the Super Falcons designed specifically for the F-106A. Hughes produced 300 before shifting to the GAR-3A (AIM-4F). The AIM-4E incorporated SARH with a contact-fused small HE (high-explosive) warhead deemed to be useful against a bomber only in attacks aft of beam. For example, attacks against a non-manoeuvring Myasischchev Mya-4 'Bison' bomber at 60,000 ft (18288 m) when made 30° aft of beam produced a Pk (probability of kill) of 8.4. From 135°, forward of beam, Pk dropped to 0.04.

The GAR-3A (AIM-4F), introduced in 1960, had improved radar guidance and hence greater accuracy, as well as greater reliability. It remained the standard radar missile for the F-106 throughout the interceptor's service career. The solid-fuel, bi-level thrust rocket engine of the 'F model' Super Falcon increased initial launch thrust. The missile proved successful under great extremes of temperature and in various manoeuvre regimes.

The GAR-4A (AIM-4G) Super Falcon was developed as an IR-seeking counterpart to the radar missiles. Pilots from the era say that they could get an infra-red track on some jet-powered vehicles (such as the widely-used Firebee drone) from the front, even though the concept of an 'all aspect' missile lay far in the future and the GAR-4A was

most effective in an 'ass end' attack. The pilot's radar display (which also displayed what was seen by the IR missile's seeker head, and in later years by an IR sensor installed in the nose) would show spikes to indicate heat sources. All Super Falcons were contact-fused, with the fuses located on the leading edge of all four fins, so that a direct hit on the target was needed to effect a kill. In fact, while a glancing blow could be lethal, if the missile struck a target straight-on it would have to penetrate in order to detonate.

Training missiles

In addition to 'real' Super Falcons, the F-106 carried inert AIM-4E/F/G missile rounds which could be fired for practice or in tests but which did not have a warhead. More frequently, the F-106 carried the Super Falcon WSEM (Weapons System Evaluator Missile), a dummy with a real seeker head that could track the target and simulate a real missile, but could not be launched from the aircraft. Because this was the routine way to practise missile firing – something which was rarely done, in any case – even an experienced pilot could go a number of years without firing a real Super Falcon. WSEMs were deemed essential to realistic training and practice because the pilot experienced most phases of an actual missile shoot, including opening the doors and extending the missile: they simulated everything except the real-world performance of the rocket motor.

The Genie, which also armed the Northrop F-89 Scorpion, reflected its era. Being an unguided, gyro-stabilised rocket, the Genie was a 'projectile', not a 'missile'

Above: 56-0462, the 11th F-106, appeared alongside its big brother, the B-58 Hustler, at a display at Andrews AFB in March 1960. Convair's Delta Dagger, Delta Dart and Hustler remain the only pure delta aircraft to have served with the USAF, apart from the SR-71.

Above left: The 5th F-106A later served with the Flight Dynamics Lab of the Aeronautical Systems Division at Wright-Patterson AFB, where it was seen in September 1966.

Convair put up this unique formation of F-106A, B-58A and 880 in 1959 to illustrate the fact that it made the world's fastest fighter, bomber and airliner. Of the three types, the F-106 was to be produced in the greatest numbers (340), compared to 116 Hustlers and 65 880s.

F-106 details

F-106A Delta Dart cutaway

1 Pitot head
2 Radome
3 Radar scanner dish
4 Radar tracking mechanism
5 Hughes MA-1 weapons system radar unit
6 Radar mounting bulkhead
7 Pulse generator units
8 TACAN aerial
9 Angle-of-attack transmitter
10 MA-1 weapons system electronics units
11 Electronics bay access door
12 Infra-red detector fairing
13 Retractable infra-red detector
14 Knife-edged windscreen panels
15 Central vision splitter
16 Instrument panel shroud
17 'Head-down' tactical display panel
18 Canopy external release
19 Rudder pedals
20 Cockpit front pressure bulkhead
21 Electrical relay panel
22 Nose undercarriage wheel bay
23 Nosewheel door
24 Taxiing lamp
25 Twin nosewheels
26 Torque scissor links
27 UHF aerial
28 Nose undercarriage leg strut
29 Oxygen filler point and gauge
30 Nosewheel leg pivot fixing
31 Liquid oxygen converter
32 Cockpit air conditioning ducting
33 Cockpit pressure floor
34 Control column
35 Two-handed control grip, radar and flight controls
36 Engine throttle lever

37 Pilot's ejection seat
38 Radar display
39 Optical sight
40 Cockpit canopy cover
41 Ejection seat headrest
42 Ejection seat launch rails
43 Cockpit rear pressure bulkhead
44 Side console panel
45 Ground power supply connections
46 Doppler navigation unit
47 Aft lower electronics compartment
48 Aft upper electronics equipment bays, port and starboard
49 Electronics bay door
50 Cockpit rear decking
51 Overpressurisation relief valve
52 Canopy pneumatic jack
53 Canopy hinge
54 Air exit louvres
55 Starboard engine air intake
56 Fuel tank access panel
57 Upper longeron
58 Fuselage fuel tank, total internal capacity, 1,514 US gal (5731 litres)
59 Fuselage frame construction
60 Ventral weapons bay
61 Missile pallet hinge arms
62 Bottom longeron
63 Boundary layer splitter plate
64 Port engine air intake
65 Variable-area intake ramp
66 Ramp bleed air louvres

67 Air conditioning system intake duct
68 Intake duct framing
69 Starboard side pressure refuelling connection
70 Forward missile pallet pneumatic jack
71 Air conditioning plant
72 De-icing fluid reservoir
73 Heat exchanger air exit duct
74 Air refuelling ramp door, open
75 Pneumatic system air bottles
76 Bifurcated intake ducting
77 Aft missile pylon pneumatic jacks
78 AIR-2 Genie air-to-air missile housing
79 Hydraulic accumulators
80 Hydraulic reservoirs, duplex systems
81 Intake trunking
82 Wing spar attachment fuselage main frames
83 Oil cooler air duct
84 Intake centre-body fairing
85 Engine intake compressor face
86 Bleed air ducting
87 Dorsal spine fairing
88 Fuel boost pump
89 Starboard main undercarriage pivot fixing
90 Wing forward fuel tank

91 Dry bay
92 Wing pylon mountings and connectors
93 Fuel system piping
94 Starboard wing main fuel tank
95 Leading-edge slot
96 Cambered leading edge
97 Wingtip fairing
98 Starboard navigation light
99 Outboard elevon
100 Elevon hydraulic jack
101 Elevon jack ventral fairing
102 Inboard elevon
103 Starboard wing aft fuel tank
104 Fuel system vent piping
105 Engine oil tank, 4.5 US gal (17 litres)
106 Pratt & Whitney J75-P-17 turbojet engine
107 Forward engine mounting
108 Ventral accessory equipment compartment
109 Cooling air ducting
110 Wing and fin spar attachment main frame
111 Inboard elevon hydraulic jack
112 Engine turbine section
113 Exhaust pipe heat shroud
114 Rear engine mounting
115 Aerial tuning units
116 Artificial feel system pitot intakes
117 Fin leading edge

118 Tailfin construction
119 Air-to-air identification (AAI) aerial
120 Fintip aerial fairing
121 UHF/TACAN aerial
122 Tail navigation light
123 Rudder
124 Rudder honeycomb construction
125 Split airbrake panels
126 Airbrake pneumatic jacks
127 Brake parachute housing
128 Rudder hydraulic jack
129 Rudder trim and feel force control units
130 Airbrake open position
131 Divergent exhaust nozzle
132 Variable-area afterburner exhaust nozzle
133 Detachable tailcone (engine removal)
134 Afterburner nozzle control jacks
135 Afterburner ducting
136 Sloping fin mounting bulkheads
137 Afterburner fuel spray manifold
138 Engine withdrawal rail
139 Port inboard elevon
140 Runway emergency arrester hook, lowered

141 Port outboard elevon
142 Elevon rib construction
143 Honeycomb trailing-edge panels
144 Port navigation light
145 Honeycomb wingtip fairing
146 Outboard elevon hydra jack
147 Port wing integral fuel tank bays
148 Machine wing spars
149 Machined main undercarriage mountin
150 Wing rib construction

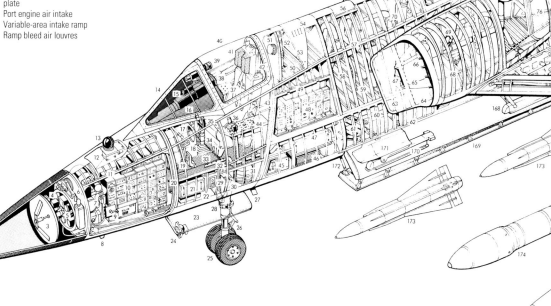

*t: F-106B 57-2530 of
th FIS is seen here
uire AFB in 1966
full set of IR-
AIM-4Gs on its
d rails.*

*he M61 gun
ation neatly filled
ce left between
r pair of Falcons,
he deletion of the
The prototype
ation is shown
he limited
y of the M61's
s hydraulic drive
e gun's rate of fire
0 rpm.*

*Douglas's **AIR-2 Genie** unguided nuclear rocket
was introduced on the F-89J and later equipped
both the F-101 and F-106. It had a top speed of just
over Mach 3, a range of 6 miles (10 km) and a
weight of 820 lb (372 kg). A broad blue band
around the centre of the rocket's body would
indicate a training round.*

Cambered leading edge
Leading-edge slot
Port wing pylon
connectors
Mainwheel leg door
Port mainwheel
Torque scissor links

157 Landing lamp
158 Main undercarriage leg
     strut
159 Drag brace and pneumatic
     brake reservoir
160 Main undercarriage leg
     pivot fixing
161 Breaker strut
162 Hydraulic retraction jack
163 Main undercarriage wheel
     bay

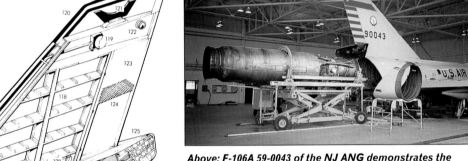

*Above: **F-106A 59-0043** of the **NJ ANG** demonstrates the
straightforward removal of its J75 for servicing.*

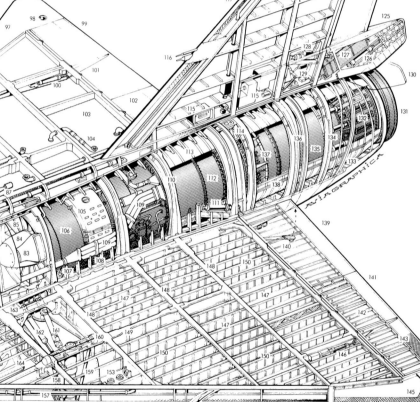

*Behind the F-106's open speed brake was the
braking parachute housing. This aircraft of the
49th FIS sports a colourful exhaust cover for
William Tell 1982.*

*The **QF-106A/EXD-01 Eclipse** tow-launch
demonstrator, 59-0130, sported this attachment
and release mechanism, modified from B-52G
drag chute release gear, for a 'tow rope' (actually
Vectran synthetic rope).*

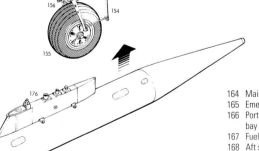

164 Mainwheel doors
165 Emergency ram air turbine
166 Port wing forward fuel tank
     bay
167 Fuel system vent pipe
168 Aft single missile pylon, port
     and starboard, lowered
     position
169 Weapons bay doors, open
170 Missile launch rail

171 Forward twin missile pallet
172 Weapons bay door
     pneumatic jack
173 AIM-4F Falcon air-to-air
     missile (4)
174 Single AIR-2A Genie air-to-
     air nuclear missile
175 Missile folding fins, deployed
     position
176 Port wing pylon
177 227-US gal (859-litre)
     external fuel tank

Two-seat 'Six'

The go-ahead for construction of a dual-place F-106 was given in August 1956, before the single-seater's first flight. Unlike the TF-102A with its side-by-side seating and inferior performance to the single-seater, the F-106B was designed to be as close to the F-106A in configuration as possible. The aircraft was not designated TF-106A, to reflect that it was more than a trainer and carried all the mission equipment of the basic interceptor. The first aircraft, 57-2507, did not fly until 9 April 1958 and was delivered four days later. The B suffered from the same development troubles as the A, and although nine aircraft were delivered by the end of 1958, none of them was assigned to operational units until the following year, the two-seater being declared operational in July 1960. The flyaway cost of an F-106B was estimated at $4.9 million, $200,000 more than an F-106A . The last of 63 F-106Bs was delivered in December 1960.

Above: The first F-106B was never assigned to ADC, being used for trials, principally ejection seat tests. Passing to NASA as '616' (later '816'), it was used for a variety of atmospheric and aerodynamic experiments. Retired from flight in 1981, it was cut in half lengthwise and used for wind tunnel tests at the Langley Research Center at Moffett Field where it was dubbed the 'F-53'.

Above right: Performance of the F-106B was very close to that of the F-106A. The basic dimensions were the same and the take-off weight of the B was 500 lb (227 kg) greater, giving a slightly longer take-off run, lower rate of climb and service ceiling, but the same maximum speed. Note the wing fences in this view of the first aircraft taking off from Edwards.

An open day in August 1960 gave the 94th FIS a chance to show off one of its newly-assigned F-106Bs.

With its 1.5-kT W-25 warhead, the Genie (much like the later AIM-26A Nuclear Falcon carried by the F-102 but not the F-106) imposed burdensome requirements on ADC. In order to operate nuclear weapons, ADC had to create and manage a PRP (Personnel Reliability Program) to exercise control over who had access to 'nukes'. Throughout the USAF, anyone who dealt with 'nukes' had to be screened for PRP and the access was made a part of the individual's medical records. Midway through its career, when it became an ANG aircraft, the F-106 retained its Genie capability but the weapons were no longer readily accessible at air base 'special munitions' facilities. The decision to use an atomic weapon projectile aboard an interceptor reflected the thinking of the time; under today's rules, nuclear weapons would not be released to ANG personnel.

Top secret

Apparently because of the Genie (though possibly with the advanced technology of the MA-1 system in mind, as well), the F-106 was for several years the only aircraft in USAF inventory having a cockpit layout and a flight manual (known in jargon as a 'Dash One') that was classified 'SECRET'. There were strict rules for the possession and handling of classified documents, which were rarely a problem when operating from home base (as the F-106 did most of the time), but which became a nightmare on even the most routine cross-country flight. Pilots were required to obtain special clearance before filing even the most

routine flight plan. These rules may have been placed into effect in the expectation that Delta Darts would travel around the country while carrying Genies; in fact, Genies were never carried on routine flights or on cross-country navigation trips. The PRP programme and the security rules were often more of a nuisance than a benefit.

The Genie, which Douglas Aircraft began developing in 1955, occupied a special place in the US arsenal. The Los Alamos, New Mexico National Laboratory designed the nuclear warhead. The Genie was unguided, relying on the power of its nuclear warhead to ensure a kill. It was powered by a 36,600-lb (162.78-kN) thrust Thiokol TU-389 rocket motor, also called the SR-49-TC-1. Launch weight was 822 lb (373 kg), and maximum velocity was about Mach 3.3. Flick-out fintips gave the Genie stability in flight and corrected for roll and gravity drop. Range of the Genie was about 6 miles (9 km). Lethal radius of the blast from the warhead was estimated at 1,000 ft (309 m).

Weapons bay

The F-106 carried its armament in the underside of the fuselage, housed in a single bay that was closed by pneumatically-operated double-folding doors. The bay had missile-launching mechanisms in both the forward and aft sections, from which the Super Falcon missiles were usually fired in pairs. A typical launch sequence consisted of the following actions: doors open; launchers extend; missiles fire; launchers retract; doors close. ADC doctrine held that the F-106 would be vectored to its target using the SAGE system and would make passes of the 'lead collision' type. "The intercept flight path and armament launching will be computed automatically in the execution of this type of attack," read a document of the 1950s. "If a lead-collision pass is not practical, the pilot may set up the fire control system for pursuit mode passes. In pursuit mode passes, the pilot must prepare and launch the armament by operating the trigger on the flight control stick." In an emergency, the pilot could select 'salvo' to jettison all missiles at once.

When the SAGE datalink system was in use, airspeed/altitude commands came up on the instrument

dials (later, on the vertical tape instruments). A Tactical Situation Display (TSD) showed a bird's eye view of the intercept situation. The MA-1's pulse radar system was difficult to use compared to the pulse-Doppler radar systems of today because it required a lot of tuning out ground return and short-range contacts, but it was a major advance in its time.

The combination of F-106 Delta Dart, MA-1 fire control system, and Super Falcon missiles and Genie rocket was viewed by ADC commanders as effective in all three combat regimes prescribed by ADC doctrine: Area Intercept (General Defence), Point Intercept (Local Defence), and Free-Lance Air Defence operations outside normal contiguous radar coverage. Pilots were expected to operate at the same level as their targets when possible. When the target – that is, the approaching enemy bomber – was too high either because of a late scramble or because it enjoyed better altitude capability (unlikely), the 'Six' pilot was expected to use a 'snap up' manoeuvre to fire his weapons. Much enamoured of their mission, ADC public information officers in the 1950s put out a brochure aimed at getting school children to memorise the command's mission in the form of an acronym, DIID (detect, identify, intercept and destroy). What most Americans and apparently many intelligence officers did not know at that time was that the Soviet Union's bomber force was less formidable than believed, while the ICBM (intercontinental ballistic missile) was soon to emerge as Moscow's strategic weapon of choice.

Exactly two months after the prototype F-106A began

Production line

Convair's Plant 2 at Lindbergh Field, San Diego built all 340 F-106s. During the war, the same factory churned out 7,500 examples of the B-24 Liberator and PB4Y Privateer series with a production rate that peaked at 270 aircraft *per month* in March and May 1944. Production of the F-102A did not finish until September 1958, well after F-106A volume production had begun. At the same time, the company was venturing into the civil market with the ill-starred CV-880 jetliner, all at the San Diego complex. The Delta Dart was the last military aircraft built at the plant, in a quantity of one-third that originally ordered. Deliveries peaked in Fiscal Year 1960 (1 July 1960 to 31 June 1961) when 150 F-106As and 36 F-106Bs were accepted by the Air Force at a flyaway cost (F-106A) of $4.9 million per aircraft. The cost could be broken down into: airframe, $2.2 million; engine (installed), $274,000; avionics $1.35 million; armament system, $1.09 million; and ordnance, $24,000.

Right: This view of the San Diego plant shows F-106 production in early 1958. The first aircraft fully visible is build no. 19, 57-0229, delivered in June 1958 and destroyed in a crash the following April while with Systems Command. Further along are some of the first F-106Bs, mixed in the production line with the single-seaters.

Below: The first F-106A to make its maiden flight from the factory, 56-0454, lifts off from Lindbergh Field on its delivery flight to Edwards in November 1957.

flying, the second ship (56-0452) made its initial flight at Edwards. The first flight of a 'Six' by an Air Force pilot occurred two months later, on 29 April 1957.

The test and developmental work on the F-106 was divided into no fewer than six 'Phases', which began with a rudimentary look at flying characteristics and continued all the way to transforming the new aircraft into a battle-ready, integrated weapon system. Phase I (described by one expert as little more than proving the F-106 airworthy) was to be conducted by the contractor and Phase II by the Air Force. The two prototype F-106As (56-0451/0542) assigned to the Phase II Flight Evaluation at Edwards differed from production Delta Darts in six ways:

– The test aircraft had YJ75-P-1 engines installed instead of the J75-P-9 engines scheduled for early production aircraft and the -17 engines found on late production F-106s and retrofitted to many early ones.

– The engine inlet duct of the test aircraft had a larger capture area (1,050 sq in/6774 cm^2 instead of 1,000 sq in/6451 cm^2). The inlet duct of the test aircraft was aligned

One of the early improvements to the F-106 weapons system, as with the F-102A, was the addition of an infra-red search and track (IRST) sensor. This was a retractable unit forward of the windscreen. The prototype unit was tested on 56-0457, seen here, and featured a prominent raised housing larger than that adopted for production.

Above and above right: Part of a sequence shows an ejection test of the Convair 'B' seat from an F-106B of AFFTC at Edwards. Note the seat rotation in the second photo.

The gas-operated stabilising arms can be seen attached to the seat frame following another test ejection. Clearance of the fin at supersonic speed was a goal of the designers, but one not always achieved, in the test programme at least.

Ejection Seat

The quest for an ejection seat suitable for the high-Mach, high-altitude flight regime for which the F-106 was designed occupied much energy at San Diego and Edwards. The original design was replaced by the 'B seat', which was overcomplicated and unreliable. Frustrated with the 'B seat', the USAF contracted Weber Aircraft, known for its spacecraft escape systems, to produce a 'zero-zero' F-106 seat. This it delivered in a remarkable 45 days, and the new seats served until the last F-106 was retired.

This is a rocket-sled test of the Convair 'B seat' at Holloman. Such tests propelled test seats to a high velocity for launch without risking an aircraft. Weber proved its F-106 seat with a live 'zero-zero' ejection test in 1965, the only one conducted in the US by an American company.

The Weber F-106 seat undergoes a test, apparently at a relatively low speed. A relaxation of the requirement for ejection at the high extremes of the flight envelope allowed the adoption of this effective seat, which was quickly fitted throughout the F-106 fleet.

with the fuselage reference whereas the duct of the production 'Six' would have an inclination 5° down from the fuselage reference line.

– The 'case XIV' wing of the prototype had the leading edge cambered to 10 per cent of the local semi-span with a design coefficient of 0.166 at Mach 1.0 where the production F-106 would have a 'case XXIX' wing with the leading edge cambered to 20 per cent of the semi-span and a design lift coefficient of 0.215 to Mach 1.0.

– The prototype was designed for a side stick installation (foreseeing the future F-16 Fighting Falcon) but a kit modification to a centre stick installation was made prior to the Phase II Evaluation. Production F-106s were to employ the traditional centre stick between the pilot's knees.

– The electrical system of the prototype was powered by an air turbine motor whereas the production F-106 would use a constant speed drive.

– The prototype F-106A during Phase II had its engine inlet pressure sensor, longitudinal control system trim servo, and automatic fuel transfer system (which controlled C of G during supersonic high altitude flight) disabled.

Even with their minor differences, all of the early F-106s were stellar performers. Convair pilot Johnson spoke of heading for the stratosphere in the aircraft: "A full-thrust climb is done on one's back – almost. During the early part of the climb, the feet are as high as the head. One needs to be doubly prepared when doing this on instruments. The F-106 will get to 35-40,000 ft about 30 seconds ahead of you, but with a maximum effort you can catch up by 50,0000." As for returning to earth, Johnson noted that,

The aircraft used for the majority of ejection trials was the first F-106B, 57-2507, seen here in 1970 at El Centro. At one time it also wore a predominantly white scheme.

A little-known user of the F-106 was the 6520th Test Group at Hanscom Field, Massachusetts, part of the Electronic Systems Division of ARDC. It operated a pair of F-106As between 1959 and 1961 alongside F-102s. One of its aircraft is seen above on a visit to Logan Field, Boston in 1959.

In 1963, these 438th FIS aircraft were seen overflying terrain uncharacteristic of their home state of Michigan. The configuration of the aircraft, however, is typical of early-period F-106s. At least three of the aircraft have the production IRST sensor and all carry the original subsonic fuel tanks. The aerial refuelling modification (which made a notch in the spine) is still several years in the future.

"the only let-down problem is to stay subsonic. Idle thrust and speed boards [the speed brakes located at the rear leading edge of the fin in the same enclosure as the drag chute, usually opened just before the downwind leg in the landing pattern] assure this with ease. The speed brakes can be used at all speeds and are quite effective."

No-one ever said the F-106 was easy to land, but Johnson set forth his rule for getting down safely in an aircraft that had a rapid sink rate and approached at a high angle of attack: "Fly the correct speed on a properly placed glide slope of 2.5-3°, day or night, foul or fair, and you will [land safely]." The F-106 employed a drag chute to retard roll rate on landing.

Phase II tests

The Air Force pressed ahead with Phase II flight evaluation between 22 May 1957 and 29 June 1957. Officially, the purpose of the test was "to obtain preliminary performance, stability, and control data and qualitative information on the handling characteristics of the airplane." Korean War ace Captain Iven C. Kincheloe was the project pilot. Phase II included nine flights (7 hours 5 minutes) on 56-452 to obtain performance data and five flights (5 hours) on 56-451 to obtain stability and control data. Ten additional flights were performed at Edwards for an evaluation of the new aircraft by pilots of the AFFTC (Air Force Flight Test Center), the Air Proving Ground Command (Eglin AFB), Air Materiel Command (Wright-Patterson AFB) and, of course, the intended user of the new interceptor, Air Defense Command (Ent AFB, Colorado).

The early test effort revealed a number of problems with the F-106 design, all minor in nature, including a need for

an engine inlet duct with sharper lips and thinner wall, and major changes to the ejection seat (a problem which was to resist solution for some time to come, perhaps in part because the original design had been undertaken as an off-shoot of the complex, ambitious seat design in the B-58 Hustler). Kincheloe and project engineer Willie L. Allan said in their summary of the test, among other things, that, "the F-106A performance is lower than that predicted by the contractor. The airplane is capable of approximately 1.8 Mach number in level flight at 36,000 ft [10972 m] under standard day conditions (as compared to a predicted Mach 2 capability). The maximum power combat ceiling is 53,000 ft [16154 m], 2,400 ft [732 m] lower than predicted, but an altitude of 60,000 ft [18288 m] was reached briefly from a zoom climb initiated from 1.7 Mach number at 40,000 ft [12192 m]."

Ejection seat

Kincheloe and Allan also said that, "the prototype cockpit is unsatisfactory and will require redesign. The ejection seat is inadequate for bail-out at supersonic speeds." Kincheloe's assessment reflected a misapprehension that became deep-rooted in the 1950s as supersonic 'Century Series' fighters entered inventory. Simply put, designers were trying to solve the problem of escaping from an aircraft at supersonic speed when, instead, they should have been looking at what happens 'low and slow' and developing zero-zero capability to allow a pilot to escape at low (or no) speed and altitude. This misunderstanding persisted during development of the Delta Dart.

Prototype F-106s were equipped with a Weber-built variation of the seat used on the Convair F-102 Delta Dagger. It was an open, catapult-only ejection seat which used an explosive charge to get out of the aircraft. The pilot wore a standard BA-18 parachute as a backpack. With this original, catapult-only seat, significant altitude and airspeed were needed to make the seat work. When it worked right, the pilot would be moving at 40 ft (12 m) per second at the top of the rail while exiting the aircraft. The original seat was not to last long, and production aircraft were scheduled to receive the Convair 'B' seat, itself soon to become

This view of the Tyndall ramp on a dull day in 1967 is notable for the single all-white F-106B among its grey brethren. It is thought that the aircraft was participating in high-altitude camouflage tests. At least one F-106A was similarly painted at the same time.

The first Delta Darts to venture outside North America were a pair of 48th FIS aircraft that visited the 25th Paris air show in June 1963 by way of Prestwick, Scotland. 59-0136 (above) was put in the static display at the show while 59-0124 remained out of sight. This was perhaps the only serious attempt by Convair to market the Dart to European nations.

F-106As of the 84th FIS based at Hamilton AFB, California take on fuel from a KC-135A, possibly as part of a White Shoes/College Shoes deployment to Alaska. The unit participated in two such deployments, in 1969 and 1970.

Air-to-air refuelling

Air refuelling capability came to the F-106 from September 1967 under the first modernisation phase carried out on the aircraft (as opposed to previous piecemeal modification programmes). Unlike other upgrade schemes then under consideration, the refuelling package was adopted quickly and the modification carried out 'in house' by the USAF. At the same time, 'supersonic' wing tanks were acquired and a new TACAN navigation system installed (under a separate contract). These changes, which had been applied to the aircraft of two squadrons by the end of 1967, were just in time to allow the deployment of ADC F-106s to Korea when the *Pueblo* crisis erupted in January 1968.

embroiled in controversy. Thus, Kincheloe – who would later lose his life in the downward ejection seat of an F-104 Starfighter – may have been complaining about the wrong seat.

This is how a New Jersey Guard F-106A appeared to the boom operator of a KC-135. The refuelling receptacle on the spine of the F-106A varied slightly in shape from that of the B. The new unit displaced none of the fuselage fuel capacity, which consisted of a single 227-US gal (859-litre) tank on the F-106A and a 177-US gal (670-litre) tank on the B.

Qualified approval

Test pilots had been trained to tell it like it was, and there appeared to be no strong reason why the F-106 could not evolve into an effective warplane. The Kincheloe/Allan remarks concluded, "Except for the lack of performance, the prototype airplane tested has the potential of being an excellent Air Defense Command interceptor. Satisfactory demonstration of stalls, spin recoveries, inertial coupling, and dead stick landings, as well as an operational fire control system, are required before the aircraft is delivered to operational units."

Kincheloe and Allan made 18 recommendations, ranging from minor changes to the canopy to improved brake pedals. Based on their findings, Convair's Phase III of the development effort included stall, spin and flame-out studies which exceeded those originally planned.

Convair was having difficulties fielding the F-106A and the imminent F-106B, but this did not prevent the company from proposing advanced versions. In 1954, company aerodynamicists R. C. Lingley and R. E. Craig

had laid out plans for a delta-winged interceptor powered by two General Electric J79 turbojets, the powerplant used by the company's B-58 Hustler bomber. A 5 November 1957 blueprint illustrates a version identified as the F-106C (no relation to a very real F-106C that was to come later) powered by a single Pratt & Whitney JT4B-22 turbojet, a variant of the J75, and offering a gross weight of 42,140 lb (19114 kg), about 28 per cent greater than the weight of the actual F-106. This was an innovative period for company designers, who were co-ordinating B-58 work in Fort Worth, Texas with F-106 work in San Diego, but none of the advanced F-106 variants was built. The task of manufacturing the F-106 required Convair to gear up with new tooling and fixtures on a separate production line while some F-102s were still being built. Final assembly still took place on the line in Building 3 at San Diego, and initially just 1,500 employees worked on the 'Six' while 7,000 continued to manufacture F-102s. The number of employees on the F-106 alone eventually rose to 11,851. During this era, as it nudged into the ballistic missile business, Convair employed 40,000 people and was dearly loved in southern California. General Dynamics had owned Convair (always officially known as the Consolidated Vultee Aircraft Corp.) since 15 May 1953, and in May 1961 the parent firm began using its own name in tandem with the Convair appellation.

ADC hoped at one juncture to acquire 1,000 F-106A fighters to equip no fewer than 40 combat squadrons. A decision was eventually reached (in September 1958) to

A 5th FIS Delta Dart taxis in at Buckley ANG Base in July 1971. As well as showing the early 5th FIS markings, this photograph reveals the IRST sensor in extended position and the optical sight for the Genie rocket mounted at the top of the windscreen. This device was later removed.

Convair F-106A-CO-105 Delta Dart
49th Fighter Interceptor Squadron
Griffiss AFB, New York, 1973

Super Falcon missiles

Originally designated XF-98 and then GAR-1, the AIM-4 Falcon was the first air-to-air guided missile to enter service with any air arm. The AIM-4E was the first of the 'Super Falcons', introduced in 1958 with a longer-burning motor and a larger warhead. F-106s could carry four Super Falcons, often a pair of radar-guided AIM-4Fs (in the front bay here) and a pair of infra-red-guided AIM-4Gs (rear bay). This only gave a two-shot capability, however, as the missiles were always ripple-launched in pairs. Unlike Soviet practice, the Falcons were not fired in mixed pairs (IR and radar) and the IR missiles were fired first so that they did not guide on the previous pair rather than the target. The F-106 was the last US fighter to carry AIM-4s, other platforms including the F-102, F-89 and F-4.

59-0021

Delivered on 8 February 1960 to the 319th FIS at Bunker Hill AFB, this particular F-106 was number 186 on the San Diego production line. On 9 March 1963, it was assigned to the 438th FIS at Kincheloe AFB, which relocated to Griffiss AFB in August-September 1968. On 30 September, the unit was redesignated the 49th FIS. The aircraft was assigned to the commander of the 21st NORAD Region, headquartered at Fort Lee, Virginia, which covered the eastern United States. On 15 May 1973, it crashed, following a lightning strike, killing Major General James D. Price. General Price was the instigator of the Six Shooter project, but his aircraft was one of the few that had not undergone the modifications by this date.

Windscreen and canopy

As with the F-102, the Delta Dart featured optically-flat windscreen panels which met at their forward edges. In order to prevent internal reflections, a 'vision splitter' was fitted. This was a blade-like metal structure protruding from the internal windscreen joint that stopped reflection but did not affect the pilot's forward vision. Vision through the canopy top was poor until the canopy with lengthways brace was replaced by the slightly-bulged clear-vision unit as part of Project Six Shooter, which came about once the F-106's potential as a dogfighter was recognised. The original F-106 canopy was tinted, unlike that on the F-102 or the later single-piece F-106 unit.

IRST

Hughes first tested an infra-red search and track system (as used on the F-102A) on the F-106 in 1960, and it proved so promising that it was included in the Project Broad Jump modifications instigated later that year. The unit retracted into a fairing in front of the cockpit, but is not often seen in the extended position in photographs.

Pueblo crisis

With increasing commitments in Vietnam, US air strength in South Korea was run down to the point that it was found severely lacking in 1968 when the North Koreans captured the USN spy ship USS _Pueblo_ on 23 January 1968, triggering the worst crisis since the end of the Korean War. This event, and the ongoing detention of the crew, led to the deployment of B-52s to Okinawa and F-100s, F-105s and RF-101s to bases in South Korea, as well as the stationing of USN carriers in Korean waters. Due to a particular lack of interceptor aircraft, F-106s of ADC were sent to Osan to bolster local air defences under the codename of College Cadence, beginning in February 1968 with the deployment of the 318th FIS. It was followed by the personnel of the 48th FIS in July 1968, who used the 318th's aircraft and flew home in them on 23 December (the day the _Pueblo_ crew were released) to be replaced by the 71st FIS. The 71st made way for the 94th FIS in June 1969. Further tension, including the shooting-down of an EC-121M of VQ-1, led to an extension of the deployment. The 94th handed the duty to the 95th FIS on 15 November 1969 and flew back to the US. Finally, the Joint Chiefs of Staff recommended an end to College Cadence deployments to Korea on 16 April 1970, and the 95th FIS returned home to Dover AFB, Delaware on 1 May 1970.

Above: A pair of 94th FIS aircraft patrols over the lush fields of South Korea. The threat from the North Korean Air Force in 1968 consisted of over 500 MiG-15s, -17s and -19s and 30 MiG-21s, as well as about 60 Il-28 bombers.

Right: The 318th FIS was the first F-106 unit to deploy to Korea, staging through Naha, Okinawa. Here, a 318th FIS F-106A stands guard at Osan as a Naha-based 815th TAS C-130A brings in more supplies. The Pueblo crisis stretched USAF resources as the bulk of tactical assets were at that time committed to the Vietnam conflict.

reduce this to about one-third. For much of the Delta Dart era, ADC operated a dozen squadrons, a figure that peaked briefly at 14. The TO&E (Table of Organisation & Equipment, i.e., authorised strength) of a squadron began at 18 aircraft but changed several times over the years, once reaching 24.

Built for two

The first two-seat F-106B (Model 8-27) aircraft (57-2507) flew at Edwards on 9 April 1958. The F-106B tandem, two-place Delta Dart was intended as a two-seat weapon system proficiency trainer and transitional trainer, although in later service it would sometimes be employed simply as an interceptor with two seats. The front cockpit duplicated the front cockpit of the F-106A. The idea was to duplicate all necessary flight controls for transition in the rear cockpit, and armament and other internal systems would be identical.

The B model was expected to have a somewhat reduced speed and ceiling because of its added weight, but it turned out to perform almost exactly like the F-106A. The first two-seater was used initially for spin tests and stall investigation, underwent minor modifications, and returned to Edwards on 29 June 1959 for further tests. On 30 September 1959, it underwent a high-speed taxi test to investigate nosewheel shimmy, during which the aircraft caught fire and sustained considerable damage. It was trucked to San Diego on 14 October 1960 for repair and returned to flying status on 29 April 1960. Beginning on 7 May 1960, F-106B 57-2507 was employed at Holloman

Left: The F-106 bomber: the Delta Dart never actually flew with dedicated air-to-ground ordnance, but one aircraft of the 48th FIS (still wearing 318th FIS marks) at Osan in 1968 was fitted with a pair of multiple ejector racks and a dozen Mk 82 bombs. It was all part of a joke for ADC CO General Agan, who was inspecting the farthest reach of his command.

Below: F-4Cs of the 80th TFS, 347th TFW share the ramp with 71st FIS F-106s. The Pueblo deployments were relatively uneventful for the tactical units involved, although the 95th FIS lost an aircraft and pilot in 1970.

Above: The 95th FIS arrived in November 1969 to take over the alert commitment. The operational tempo and environment of the Korean theatre was in contrast to that normally faced by ADC crews.

Above: Watched by the commanding officer of the 94th FIS, Lt Col Joe Olshefski, his counterpart in the 95th FIS, Lt Col Roy White, completes the paperwork for the handover of Osan alert duties to his unit on 15 November 1969.

AFB, New Mexico for ejection seat trials. This marked the beginning of difficult tests of the controversial Convair 'B seat'. On 29 June 1960, the first aft dummy seat ejection was made and resulted in damage to the vertical fin of 57-2507, one of many vicissitudes along the way.

Two-seat testing

The similarity between the F-106A and the F-106B meant that only a very limited Phase II programme was intended for the B model. Four F-106Bs were employed in this effort at the AFFTC (Air Force Flight Test Center) between January 1958 and about April 1959.

The number three F-106B (57-2509) was assigned to AFFTC for Phase IV testing (the intermittent Phase II also was performed by the contractor). This aircraft was the first F-106B incorporating the production wing ('case XXIX' delta) and the production longitudinal and lateral control system (centre stick). Tests consuming 60 hours of flying time began in May 1958.

A combined phase/test utilising both the F-106A and F-106B began in May 1958 with four F-106As and two F-106Bs assigned. The 10-month Phase VI effort consumed 150 flight hours and marked the first time the Delta Dart would be evaluated as an integrated weapon system rather than merely a flying airframe – replete with MA-1 AWCIS. This period marked the first loss of a 'Six' – on 27 May 1958 – when a JF-106A (57-0242) crashed at Edwards. Aircraft assigned to this phase were F-106As 57-229 (in May 1958), 57-231 (June 1958), 57-234 (July 1958), 57-235 (August 1958) and F-106Bs 57-2511 and -2512 (in August 1958). Phase VI included test firings of GAR-3A and GAR-4 Super Falcon missiles and MB-1 Genie projectiles at Holloman AFB, using two of the F-106As. Also included in this effort were runway barrier tests.

Included in Phase II development of the F-106 was the Armament and Airborne Weapon System Development (AAD) effort undertaken in 1959 at Holloman AFB, where tests were also conducted with the F-106 ejection seat. As part of the overall Delta Dart effort, numerous aircraft were to undergo 'testing to tactical' modification, transforming them from developmental to operational aircraft – and Holloman was also tasked with validating the results of these modifications.

Unbuilt Darts

Convair put in considerable work on an F-106 'fighter-bomber', with and without tactical reconnaissance capability. One proposal for a two-seater based on the eventual F-106B called for a set of three KA-8 cameras with 9x9-in (23x23-cm) film capacity for terrain identification, target identification, and bomb damage assessment. Several versions of an ECM (electronic countermeasures) pod were recommended for this Delta Dart variant.

Convair also proposed the F-106A 'Economy Fighter Bomber' capable of all-weather navigation and high-resolution radar bombing of fixed targets. This aircraft

95th FIS Darts sit on alert at a damp Osan. Note the different shade of blue used in the squadron markings.

Above: Towards the end of the 95th FIS's deployment to Korea, in April 1970, it looked like the 95th's six-month tour was going to be extended past the 1 May 1970 arrival home date – hence the 'screwed' patch.

Below: F-106s of the 94th top up with fuel on their return to the US following their Korean sojourn. The initial deployment of the 71st FIS to Korea in 1968 marked the first deployment of the F-106 using inflight refuelling.

Above: Live AIM-4s are unpacked for loading onto a 95th FIS aircraft. It is not thought that the AIR-2 Genie was taken to Korea, although USAF fighter-bomber units were at nuclear readiness.

A pair of 71st FIS F-106As is seen in 1967 with the minimal markings of a small fin badge worn for a time by this unit. This was about as 'low vis' as F-106 unit markings ever got, and the 71st later adopted a medium-blue chevron as a field for their badge.

would have had a new search and bombing radar and the capacity for a 'special weapon', a tactical nuclear bomb. This 'TAC Economy Model' (Tactical Air Command) would have had an inflight-refuelling 'socket' (receptacle) located forward of the pilot – more than a decade before real F-106s actually got one, in a different location behind the pilot – and would have carried a 2,000-lb (907-kg) 'special weapon' internally with an alternate load of two 90-US gal (340-litre) fuel tanks and a 1,000-lb (454-kg) conventional bomb. The 'Economy Model' was limited to a gross weight of 40,000 lb (18144 kg) to maintain the existing F-106 landing gear without redesign.

A higher-cost, two-seat version of the same concept would have had strengthened undercarriage, additional avionics, internal provision for a 2,000-lb (907-kg) 'special weapon' or two 65-US gal (246-litre) fuel tanks, one 1,000-lb (454-kg) conventional bomb, and two Sidewinder missiles. A Convair report noted that, "TAC pilots have performed LABS [low altitude bombing system] manoeuvres in this aircraft without difficulty."

Twin-engined Dart

Convair engineers also worked on a proposal for an F-106 powered by a single Pratt & Whitney J58 turbojet, and on a 'twin-engined version of the F-106-30 all-weather interceptor' which would be powered by two General Electric J93 (X-279E) engines. Both would have had gains in acceleration, rate of climb, and altitude capability as compared to the production F-106. The twin-engined F-106-30 had a two-man crew (pilot and radar operator/navigator) and had its engines slung under the wing in pods identical to those employed on the B-58 Hustler. A horizontal tail surface was also added. The fire control system was a conceptual Hughes # 5082 pulse-Doppler radar and armament was two GAR-9 missiles, an advanced version of the Super Falcon.

While the USAF was testing, developing and fielding the Delta Dart, Convair was trying to expand sales. The company considered the possibility of arranging an alternate production source (Lockheed or Canadair) for a Canadian version – not merely an interceptor variant, but an 'F-106 strike aircraft (RCAF)'.

There was also a detailed plan for F-106 final assembly and production in Germany, in partnership with Convair. A company memo dated 1 August 1959 talks of the difficulty of arranging F-106B orientation rides for Belgian and Netherlands pilots flying F-104s at Edwards. These

Air Defense Command practised dispersal of interceptors, and for many years one or two F-106s could be found in alert barns in some unlikely places. This 5th FIS F-106A was spotted at Davis-Monthan (later the temporary home of most of the surviving F-106s) in April 1979.

Below: To commemorate the feats of Eddie Rickenbacker 50 years before, a SPAD XIII was displayed at Andrews AFB with a 71st FIS F-106A in 1968. The Dart wears a William Tell special colour scheme and the pilots wear the flying gear of their respective periods.

pilots, the memo complained, were being "kept under wraps by Lockheed."

A different memo on the same date relates to preparing brochures for an F-106 version for Japan "with MG-10 fire control system [the system used on the F-102A Delta Dagger] and six Super Falcon missiles in lieu of the normal four-and-one (four Super Falcons and one Genie) armament." One company official, the memo reported, "has convinced everyone here that the sale is 95 per cent made."

'Multi-purpose' F-106

The manufacturer's efforts to snare Japan as a customer, as with Canada, included sketching out a version with air-to-ground attack capability. The Japanese concept had two pylons on each wing: the outer was capable of carrying on each side a 450-US gal (1703-litre) fuel tank, a 2,000-lb (907-kg) bomb, two 1,000-lb (454-kg) bombs mounted in tandem, or other weapons; the inboard would have accommodated on each side a 230-US gal (870-litre) fuel tank, a 1,000-lb (454-kg) bomb, two AIM-9 Sidewinder IR missiles or a gun pack. The Japanese multi-purpose F-106 would have had internal capacity for additional fuel or two 1,000-lb (454-kg) bombs, or three Sidewinders, or four Falcons, or two Falcons plus two Sidewinders, or a reconnaissance camera package. A separate document envisioned an armament package of 2.75-in Mighty Mouse unguided FFARs (folding-fin aircraft rockets) of the kind employed on the F-86D Sabre, F-89J Scorpion and F-94C Starfire. The planned export MG-10 fire control system would have been compatible with all of these weapons. A key sales point was that the MG-10 was a proven system (aboard 1,000 F-102s) and that the Japanese version would be interchangeable "with the fire control systems now being used in USAF F-102 interceptors now in Japan."

Below: Large formations were not part of the F-106's business, but this 16-ship from the 87th FIS was captured in 1969. Squadron establishment in the last years of the 'Six' was 15 aircraft; it was as high as 24 at one point.

Left and below: ADWC F-106Bs fly over Panama City, west of Tyndall AFB. The lower aircraft wears the fuselage stripes of the 2nd FITS squadron commander and the earlier type of fin markings worn by the ADWC.

ADWC-Tyndall

The Air Defense Weapons Center (ADWC) was formed at Tyndall AFB, Florida in November 1967. The base had been in ADC hands since 1957 with the 4756th ADW as the main flying unit, operating the F-101, F-102 and F-106 for transition training and the development of new weapons and tactics, tasks continued by the ADWC. In 1978 an Air Combat Manoeuvring (ACMI) range was opened, as was a new runway ('droneway') for drone operations. A large number of F-106s were assigned to the ADWC/4756th ADW at some point during their active careers, and many of them returned later as drones.

The Japanese sale never took place, however, and a few years later Japan manufactured F-4EJ Phantoms.

In May 1958, the USAF took delivery of two F-106Cs (57-0239/0240) with a 40-in (102-cm) nose radar dish (with no other change to the MA-1 system). The dish had been part of the initial MX-1179 concept but operational F-106s, which had a capacity for a dish of up to 28 in (71 cm), actually used 23-in (58-cm) examples. They were tested until October 1958, but the F-106C configuration was not chosen for a production contract. Had there been a production order, the proposed F-106C would have had a new engine, a new fuselage structure, and several technical changes. Convair was looking for a minimum purchase of 350 aircraft (10 more than the eventual F-106A/B buy, as it turned out). Of the two F-106Cs, only aircraft 57-0239 actually flew. This aircraft was subsequently destroyed in fatigue tests. Aircraft 57-0240 reverted in due course to standard F-106A configuration and later served with the New Jersey ANG and, still later, as a QF-106A drone.

The company was also working on a variant designated F-106D, which may simply have been a two-seat C model. Both the F-106C and the F-106D were deleted from the continuing Delta Dart developmental programme on 23 September 1958.

Rider on the storm

In 1959, the US Weather Bureau formed a National Severe Storms Project (NSSP) known colloquially as Project Rough Rider. This joint civilian/military project involved the USAF, NASA, FAA, and colleges and research centres in an ongoing investigation of the causes and effects of severe thunderstorms. Aircraft committed to the programme included a B-47 Stratojet, F-100F Super Sabre and T-33 Shooting Star. An F-106A (57-0234) was

supplied to the project and was modified with a metal nosecone for protection against hail, the intercept radar being removed from the aircraft. The nose pitot boom was modified with balsa vanes for measuring of air turbulence. The missile bay was filled with a special instrumentation package designed by NASA's Langley Research Center.

The USAF's interest in this weather study were not strictly meteorological: it wanted to evaluate the all-weather capability of its new interceptor and to assess the effects of water and ice ingestion in a jet engine at high Mach air speed. Beginning in May 1961, the F-106A flew 18 thunderstorm penetrations; during one, Major Jake Knight flew through the core of a thunderstorm at Mach 1.22. In September-October 1961, Rough Rider penetrations were mounted from MacDill and Homestead AFBs in Florida. It appears that the Delta Dart was used in this programme only during the 1961 season.

B for Bobsled

By the time operational service was on the horizon, the original ejection seat of the F-106 was gone and the aircraft was equipped with the Convair 'B seat'. The letter designation may have lacked special meaning, but pilots believed the seat was so-named because, when activated, the seat resembled a bobsled. It focused on ejection at supersonic speed (as recommended by the project test pilot and engineer), which was to prove, in due course, a worse choice

Above: F-106s of several ADC units are visible in the background, along with PQM-102s, on the ADWC flight line during William Tell 1972. The ADWC operated both F-106As and Bs, along with F-101Fs, as seen here.

Above left: This ADWC F-106B photographed in 1974 wears only minimal markings of an ADWC badge on the fin.

Convair F-106A Delta Dart
49th Fighter Interceptor Squadron 'Cavaliers'
24th Air Division
1st Air Force
Griffiss AFB, New York, 1986

'Missiles all' with the AIM-4

Because the aerodynamic range of the AIM-4F was greater than the range at which the seeker head radar could track a target, the IR-guided AIM-4G was the weapon of choice for high, fast targets. At high closure speeds, the MA-1 would actually present two missile-firing countdowns, the first for the -4G, and the second for the -4F. In a 'missiles all' armament selection, the -4Gs were fired first so they would not 'switch' lock-on to the radar-guided missiles. As a further precaution, the AIM-4F pair was carried in the aft bay.

AIM-4Fs and Gs were fired in 'like' pairs and ripple-fired so one would always be ahead of the other. Firing the missiles in pairs was not done primarily to increase Pk (kill probability); the pneumatic system had only enough stored high-pressure air for three cycles of the armament system – two cycles of the bay doors and missile rails, and one cycle for the AIR-2A. Therefore, there were essentially three shots: one AIR-2A, one pair of AIM-4Fs, and one pair of AIM-4Gs.

Fire-control system

Hughes's MA-1 (formerly MX-1179) Automatic Weapons Control System (AWCS), incorporating the first digital computer to be built into a fire-control system, remained at the heart of the F-106A's capability throughout its 29 years of service and was subject to over 60 different modifications and upgrades in that time (F-106Bs carried a similar AN/ASQ-25 system). A datalink with NORAD SAGE (Semi-Automatic Ground Environment) and AWACS controllers meant radio silence could be maintained during an intercept, while an autopilot allowed these controllers to 'fly' the aircraft from 'wheels up' until final approach to the target. A Tactical Situation Display (TSD) between the pilot's feet provided a moving map of the route relative to the ground, the pilot's aircraft and his target.

The various adjustments made to the MA-1 system during early production meant that successive production batches were completed to varying standards – a maintenance nightmare. In 1960/61, Project Wild Goose attempted to standardise mission-related avionics and airframes, and took a year to complete. Reliability problems plagued the MA-1 and ASQ-25 systems. Two programmes completed in 1963 attempted to rectify the situation, providing anti-chaff devices and enhancing detection and lock-on range by 30 per cent. In all, 314 F-106As and Bs received these modifications.

The 49th Fighter Interceptor Squadron

The 49th FIS had its origins in the 49th Pursuit Squadron (Fighter), activated on 15 January 1941 at Hamilton Field, California, as part of the 14th Pursuit Group. Equipped initially with a variety of aircraft types, including Curtiss P-40s, Republic P-43s and Vultee P-66s, the 49th was engaged in air defence patrols from San Diego during the days after the attack on Pearl Harbor. By the end of the year, the unit was re-equipping with Lockheed P-38s, and was preparing to transfer to Europe with the rest of the 14th PG as part of the 12th Air Force. Redesignated the 49th Fighter Squadron in May 1942, the unit moved to England and during October undertook missions over France from its base at Atcham. The group's move to North Africa came the following month, after the Torch landings, the 49th's P-38s spending most of the next two years in Algeria. By VE-Day, the squadron was in Italy, where it was inactivated in September.

Back in the States, the 49th FS/14th FG was activated again in 1946, for a three-year stint at Dow Field, Maine, equipped with Republic P-47s and the unit's first jet aircraft, Republic F-84s. In 1949 the 49th was once again inactivated; the unit's next incarnation in 1952. Based again at Dow Field, the unit was briefly equipped with Lockheed F-80s, but soon picked up much more capable North American F-86s for its air defence role within the 4711th Defense (later Air Defense) Wing, Air Defense Command. These it flew until 1959 (based at Laurence G. Hanscom Field, Massachusetts, from November 1955). After a few months with Northrop F-89s, the

49th picked up McDonnell F-101Bs, moving to Griffiss AFB in July. Voodoos flew air defence missions for most of the 1960s, alert stand-down coming in July 1968 with inactivation following on 30 September.

The 49th FIS was reactivated later that same day, having acquired the assets of the 438th FIS from Kincheloe AFB, Michigan. Officially nicknamed the 'Cavaliers' (as its emblem depicted a knight in shining armour), the unit was also unofficially referred to as the 'Green Eagles', the subject of its aircraft's artwork.

On 8 September 1969, the squadron deployed to Alaska to replace the 84th FIS. In William Tell competitions, the 49th FIS scored second in the F-106 category in 1974, second in 1976, first in 1978, fourth in 1980, and first again in 1982. On 1 October 1979 the 49th FIS transferred to Tactical Air Command, with the rest of Air Defense Command's interceptor squadrons. By the mid-1980s it was the last active-duty USAF squadron flying the F-106. During its period of F-106 deployment, the 49th operated 23 airframes and lost five on operations. (The F-106 had the lowest accident rate for single-engined aircraft in USAF history.) The first of the unit's F-106s to be retired was 59-0065, which arrived at the Davis-Monthan AFB 'boneyard' on 12 January 1982; the last two (59-0062 and 59-0136) arrived on 9 July 1987. Plans to re-equip the 49th with McDonnell Douglas F-15s were scrapped, the unit inactivating on 1 July 1987.

The 49th reappeared again in 1993 as the 49th Flying Training Squadron, a fighter 'lead-in' unit flying AT-38Bs from Columbus AFB, Mississippi.

Modifications and upgrades

Project Broad Jump, completed in 1963, saw the fitting of an infra-red search and track (IRST) ahead of the cockpit, while the concurrent Project Dart Board (completed in 1962) added thermal flash hoods, a new Convair ejection seat and an engine modification intended to eliminate engine flame-outs.

Other improvements, carried out during 1966/67, included the installation of a TACAN, zero-zero ejection seats, air-to-air refuelling gear and larger, 'supersonic' 360-US gal (1363-litre) underwing tanks, the latter permitting overseas deployments such as the *Pueblo* crisis deployment to South Korea. The original tanks were of 230-US gal (871-litre) capacity, as fitted to the F-102A.

This aircraft is seen in Project Sixshooter configuration, an upgrade programme approved in 1969, but not applied to F-106As until the early 1970s. The most obvious changes implemented under 'Sixshooter' were the fitting of a General Electric M61A1 20-mm, six-barrelled cannon in the rear half of the weapons bay (in the space otherwise occupied by the AIR-2A Genie rocket) and a new 'blown' canopy in place of the original framed example. The M61 installation, first tested in an F-106A in 1972, was a legacy of the USAF's experiences in Vietnam and a recognition of the F-106's dogfighting abilities. The gun was removable; aircraft so-equipped were identifiable by the bulged fairing under the fuselage which provided clearance for the gun's rotating barrels. In the F-106A the Vulcan had a maximum rate of fire of 4,500 rounds per minute, less than the 6,000 rpm when installed in an F-4E due to limitations in its hydraulic pump which rotated the weapon.

A lead-computing gunsight and a radar homing and warning (RHAW) set were also fitted, but a planned electronic counter-countermeasures (ECCM) equipment upgrade failed to gain funding. Missile armament was also updated at about this time, the AIM-4Es being replaced by AIM-4Fs with improved accuracy and ECCM capability. A weakness of the Super Falcon was its lack of a proximity fuse, impact being necessary for detonation.

The 'Sixes' that never were

Though the F-106 was subjected to a number of upgrade programmes during its service career, several particularly ambitious programmes planned were for the type, which either proceeded no further than a few test flights or were cancelled outright before 'hardware' was even contemplated.

In the late 1950s, a programme to improve the F-106's radar detection range was initiated, involving the fitting of a new parabolic radar scanner 40 in (102 cm) in diameter, in an extended radome some 5 ft (1.52 m) longer than that of the F-106A. Two aircraft (57-0239 and 57-0240) were modified to act as **YF-106C** radar systems and aircraft performance testbeds; after 10 flights by the first aircraft, the programme was cancelled. Had it proceeded, upgraded F-106As and Bs would have been re-engined with Pratt & Whitney JT4B-22 engines and redesignated **F-106C/D**, respectively. **F-106E/F** was another attempt to improve target detection capability, this time by fitting an entirely new radar set. Three antenna configurations were to be tested, housed in a new 9-ft (2.74-m) long radome, 4 ft (1.22 m) in diameter. This remained a paper project.

A proposal with much wider scope was the **F-106X**. This was an attempt to upgrade the entire aircraft as an alternative to purchasing the Lockheed YF-12, by fitting a new powerplant, avionics and 'look-down/shoot-down' radar and fire-control systems. Canard foreplanes were to be fitted aft of the cockpit, to improve handling.

Operators

On 30 May 1959, the first F-106As were delivered to Air Defense Command's 539th FIS at McGuire AFB, New Jersey (replacing the F-86L), but it was the the 498th FIS at Geiger Field, Washington (taking delivery of its first aircraft just two days later, to replace F-102s), that was the first operational 'Six' unit. Initially, plans existed for sufficient production to equip 40 squadrons with the interceptor, but successive cuts reduced this to 14 units. Even with this considerably reduced complement, it was necessary to refurbish a number of early test aircraft to operational standard.

A total of 18 fighter interceptor squadrons was initially equipped with the F-106A (and the F-106B two-seat conversion trainer), four more in 1959, as follows: the 84th, 27th (redesignated the 83rd in 1971), 95th, 456th (redesignated the 437th in July 1968 and the 460th in September). The balance were equipped with the F-106 in 1960: 319th, 5th, 318th, 94th (redesignated the 2nd in 1971), 438th (redesignated the 49th in 1968), 329th, 71st, 11th (redesignated 87th in 1968) and 48th.

Air National Guard units, the last to operate the 'Six', began to receive these aircraft in 1972, beginning with the Montana ANG's 186th FIS, which flew the type until 1987. Other ANG units were the 194th FIS/California, which was so-equipped between 1974 and 1984, the 101st FIS/Massachusetts (1972-87), 171st FIS/Michigan (1972-78), 159th FIS/Florida (1974-88) and the 119th FIS/New Jersey (1973-88). The 119th was the last F-106 unit of all, dispensing with its last machines on 1 August 1998.

Powerplant

Initially, the F-102B was to be powered by a Wright J67 turbojet (a licence-built Bristol Siddeley Olympus) in place of the F-102A's Pratt & Whitney J57, but development delays of over 12 months forced a change in 1955 to an afterburning version of Pratt & Whitney's J75, about to fly in prototypes of both the Republic F-105 and Lockheed U-2 (in the latter without an afterburner). This engine (the commercial derivative of which was known as the JT4 and powered the intercontinental Douglas DC-8s and Boeing 707s) was not without its teething problems, but was a safer bet than the British design.

The apparent indestructibility of the F-106's J75-P-17 (P-9 in early production aircraft) became the stuff of legend. It has been said that the engine would continue to function for as long as 15 minutes without lubricating oil, that it was immune to the effects of a bird strike and other FOD, and could lose compressor blades without apparent adverse effects.

Armament: hitting a flea with a sledgehammer!

The F-106 was conceived as an interceptor of Russian bombers and, as such, was originally equipped with an all-missile armament. All were carried within a fuselage weapons bay, thus cutting down on drag. The primary weapon in the Delta Dart's arsenal was the McDonnell Douglas AIR-2A Genie, equipped with a 1.5-kT nuclear warhead. Genie had a flight time of about 12 seconds and a blast radius of 1,000 ft (305 m), and was carried in the rear of the Dart's weapons bay. For the head-on engagement of Soviet bombers, a guided missile was required. To this end Hughes developed the conventional variant of their nuclear AIM-26A Falcon for the F-106. Conventional AIM-4 Super Falcons equipped F-106s, a pair of AIM-4Es with semi-active radar homing filling the forward half of the weapons bay (initially), and a pair of AIM-4Gs, with infra-red guidance, to the rear flanking the Genie. For many years this configuration (known as Standard Area Intercept IV) was typical of air defence '106s, and included 360-US gal (1363-litre) drop tanks.

F-106A-100-CO Delta Dart 58-0780

In a career that spanned over 33 years, 58-0780 served with the six ADC fighter interceptor squadrons and two ANG units, as well as the Air Defense Weapons Center. The aircraft's assignments were as follows:

4 November 1959	27th FIS, Loring AFB, Maine
22 June 1960	94th FIS, Selfridge AFB, Michigan
29 May 1969	71st FIS, Malmstrom AFB, Montana
7 June 1971	ADWC, Tyndall AFB, Florida
8 July 1971	319th FIS, Malmstrom AFB, Montana
10 Apr 1972	460th FIS, Grand Forks AFB, South Dakota
19 June 1974	171st FIS/191st FIG, Michigan ANG, Selfridge Field
26 July 1974	194 FIS/144th FIG, California ANG, Fresno Air Terminal
13 January 1984	49th FIS, Griffiss AFB, New York
22 June 1987	MASDC, Davis-Monthan AFB, Arizona (park code FN146 assigned)
13 December 1991	received for drone conversion (drone code AD166 assigned)
31 March 1992	accepted as QF-106A drone, Det 1, 82nd ATRS, Holloman AFB
9 March 1993	shot down on its first and only NULLO (Not Under Live Local Operation) mission by an AIM-7M missile

Above: The M61A1 gun package disturbed the clean lines of the F-106 but helped fulfil its potential for fighter vs fighter combat.

Right: The ADWC carried out the bulk of operational testing on the gun installation and other Six Shooter modifications. Seen with a BQM-34A is 58-0795, which sports 10 drone 'kill' marks.

Six Shooter

As early as 1967, the F-106 was recognised as having great potential in the fighter-vs-fighter role. Project Six Shooter, instigated by Lt Col Bob Archibald and managed by General James Price, centred around the installation of a 20-mm M61 Vulcan cannon in the rear of the F-106's weapons bay. Money for the Six Shooter modifications was authorised in 1969 following the Six Gun tests at Edwards. These trials, which cost $1.7 million, resulted in the adoption of a number of other improvements as well as the gun, including a lead-computing gunsight and a clear-topped canopy. The ECCM (electronic counter-counter measures) and RHAW (radar-homing and warning) gear requested by ADC were not funded and testing of the other modifications was not completed until mid-1972. Not all aircraft were fitted with the Six Shooter modification package, which effectively replaced the Genie capability, although the gun could be removed or replaced in about eight hours.

Above: One of the original F-106 'gunships' is seen at Edwards during the 1969 Six Gun tests. The clear-topped canopy was installed as part of these early tests.

than the original seat.

The Convair 'B seat' (manufactured in Denver and Colorado Springs, both in Colorado, by Stanley and Aircraft Mechanics, respectively) was a rocket-powered, open-type, upward ejection seat. It was designed (in 1957) to incorporate suggestions by a joint USAF/Industry Crew Escape System Committee. The seat was subsequently installed in F-106A/B aircraft to conform to "the original requirement for escape capability within the airplane mission profile" – bureaucratic language which means that planners seriously expected pilots to bail out without slowing down first. It was the first USAF ejection seat designed specifically for supersonic escape, so emphasis was placed on high-speed fintip clearance, windblast protection, packaging of the seat occupant, and retention of equipment. The seat's performance was demonstrated in 15 sled tests and 11 flight tests, mostly with dummies. One flight test (presumably using F-106B 52-7507 at Holloman) was conducted by ejecting an Air Force officer at 22,580 ft (6882 m) and 337 kt (388 mph; 624 km/h) IAS. Surviving records reveal that another test was made from 84,150 ft (25648 m) using a dummy, but do not disclose how that altitude was reached.

It quickly became apparent that one had to be 'a dummy' to want to eject from an F-106 using the 'B seat'. The 'ejection sequence' – actually using the seat to get out of the aircraft – was a nightmare. The pilot began the ejection sequence by pulling a D-ring; this jettisoned the canopy, retracted and locked the shoulder harness, retracted the occupant's feat, and raised the foot pans, seat pan, and leg guards. Thus, in the middle of the ejection sequence, the pilot was trussed into his seat with no use of his arms

and legs. Incredibly, the pilot then was expected to pull on the D-ring a second time to disconnect the seat actuator and fire the seat's vertical thruster. (On two-seat F-106Bs, the two seats were interconnected so that the rear seat had to complete all this before the front seat could eject.) Once the vertical thruster had propelled the seat up its rail, two rotational thrusters were supposed to fire, causing the seat to rotate into a horizontal position on top of the aircraft. Once horizontal, gas-operated stabilisation booms were to extend, four breakaway attachment bolts were to fire and the rocket was to ignite, propelling the seat away from the aircraft.

Live ejections

The first test ejection with the toboggan-like 'B seat' involving a live human being was made by Technical Sergeant James A. Howell of the 6511th Test Group at El Centro, California on 6 June 1961. Wearing a partial pressure suit, standard boots and an MA-3 helmet, Howell ejected from an F-106B piloted by Major James Hendrix at 558 mph (898 km/h). Shortly after Howell's live test of the 'B seat', First Lieutenant Win E. Depoorter became the first man to save his life in an emergency bailout using the rocket-powered seat.

During an inflight emergency on a flight from a base in the northwestern US (apparently in 1964), a pilot began the ejection sequence but the vertical thruster apparently failed to ignite. This left the pilot strapped immobile in his seat, watching helplessly while his F-106 plummeted from high altitude all the way to the ground – with him inside.

Because many F-106s had been used in many configurations during developmental work, the USAF placed great importance on the 'Test-to-Tactical' (T-to-T) modification programme aimed at bringing all F-106s up to a single standard – the configuration which would later be introduced on the production line with the 125th production aircraft.

Nearly 40 airframes were flying before the first 'Six' became operational, and they were in all kinds of 'testing' configurations that differed, usually in minor ways, from the service aircraft. No fewer than 28 F-106As and seven F-106Bs, therefore, underwent the 'Test-to-Tactical'

The old, the very old, and the new fly together in April 1975. The KC-97 was a descendant of the B-29 designed in 1940, and the F-15 will still be in US service in the 2020s. The last KC-97s were retired in 1978 (by the Texas ANG), by which time the F-15A had replaced the F-106 in most of the regular FIS squadrons.

The one true F-106 deployment to Europe was a participation by the 5th FIS in the NATO exercise Cold Fire in 1975. From 4 to 27 September, seven of the squadron's aircraft were deployed to Hahn AB. Until 1970, the F-102 had been a common sight in Europe, but the Delta Daggers were mainly replaced by F-4 Phantom squadrons.

September 1959), and 57-0239 (intentionally destroyed in fatigue tests ending on 4 April 1960). The final aircraft on the list of Delta Darts that never became operational is 56-0455, the fourth ship built. This aircraft was bailed to Convair for structural fatigue testing either at Edwards or Palmdale. The testing was completed on 31 March 1960 but the disposition of the airframe is not recorded.

An F-106A (left) and a B (above) of the 'Spittin' Kittens' participated in Cold Fire interception missions at Hahn during September 1975.

modification aimed at standardising their features for use in operational squadrons. Of these, 12 were temporarily designated JF-106A and eight two-seaters were called JF-106Bs, the 'J' prefix indicating a modification that could be 'undone' with subsequent changes. The other dozen aircraft did not go through the 'Test-to-Tactical' programme. The prototype (56-451) served briefly as a ground trainer at Amarillo AFB, Texas (beginning 27 January 1960), was assigned to the Air Force Museum on 23 March 1960, and was never equipped with radar, MA-1 system or armament. The second aircraft (56-452) was disposed of in an unknown way: its fate remains unknown and there is no report of it being lost in a mishap, yet it never reached ADC and never went on display.

Also not undergoing the 'Test-to-Tactical' brush-up were the following Delta Darts: 57-0242 (crashed on 27 October 1958), 57-0229 (crashed on 8 April 1959), 57-2511 (crashed on 5 January 1959 and had not been scheduled for 'T-to-T' anyway), 58-0762 (crashed on 23

Modifications

The 'T-to-T' modifications were identified by 'Mod' numbers and included: Mod T-1064, covering installation of the J75-P-17 engine, enlarged inlet ducts, increase in fuel capacity, raised pilots console and installation of the supersonic ejection seat (the 'B seat'); Mod T-1065, covering installation of automatic flight control system, air-to-air identification (AAI), and a recorder; Mod T-1066, covering the installation of vertical tape instruments. Among earlier aircraft not manufactured with the tapes from the start, some had the tapes installed at depot level but many never did. The first three operational squadrons of F-106As had round-dial instruments.

While testing, development work and uncommonly troublesome delays characterised the F-106 development effort, Air Defense Command moved to get the new warplane into service. It has been argued among those who were on the scene whether the 'first' F-106 squadron was the 539th FIS at McGuire AFB, New Jersey or the 498th

The 'Six' and the Navy

Despite the failure of Convair to persuade the US Navy to procure a version of the F-106, the USN maintained an interest in the Delta Dart over the years. Conversely, the USAF's evaluation of the Navy's new F4H-1 Phantom II against the F-106 in 1961 led to the purchase of a version of that aircraft for the Air Force. College Dart deployments in the 1970s gave both services the chance to practise dissimilar air combat training (DACT) against supersonic opponents. A USN Aggressor version of the F-106 was even proposed, but this idea came to nothing.

Above: A model of an 'aggressor' F-106A was displayed with that of an F-14A at a Joint Chiefs of Staff briefing in 1973. Note the pylon-mounted AIM-9s and the Israeli-style recognition triangles on the Delta Dart model.

Above: 48th FIS F-106s share the flight line with VF-301 F-4Ns. The idea of the F-106 as a dogfighter was far from that envisaged by Convair and ADC.

Left: 'Beat Navy' reads the inscription on the drop tank of this 49th FIS F-106A seen on a College Dart in October 1971. Note the F-4 'kills'.

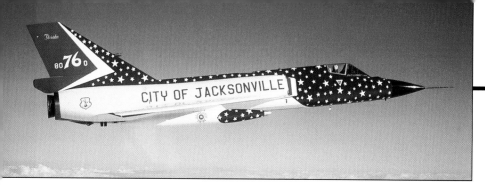

Bicentennial birds

The 1976 United States Bicentennial celebrations provided the excuse for some spectacular special colour schemes on US military aircraft. Many aircraft wore the Bicentennial 'pretzel' logo, but units were authorised to paint one aircraft in a special scheme. Three of the F-106 squadrons made a particular effort to commemorate the event, choosing aircraft with '76' in their serials.

Above: 58-0776 was the 318th FIS Bicentennial aircraft, which was inscribed with 'Freedom Bird' on the underwing tanks.

Left and above left: Certainly the most colourful F-106 – and perhaps the most colourful warplane of all time – was 58-0760, the Florida ANG's contribution to the 1976 celebrations, named 'City of Jacksonville'.

Above: 59-0076 of the 49th FIS was noted with several variations of its Bicentennial scheme in 1976. In September, when seen above, it sported red eagle's wings and lightning bolt as well as the coloured leading edge and 13-star flag.

Below: A pair of 318th FIS Darts breaks away from the camera. This view shows the degree of leading-edge camber on the superficially simple wing of the F-106.

vital and prestigious Strategic Air Command) and their 'detachment' and 'divert' locations were often nothing more than a couple of alert 'barn' hangars at a tiny civilian airstrip. ADC was armed to the teeth, enjoyed top priority for new equipment, and was expected to fight. Today, thousands of veterans of ADC believe that their vigilance contributed to preventing an atomic war in the era when the bombs were being tested in the atmosphere, existing nuclear weapons numbered in the tens of thousands, and President Eisenhower and Premier Khruschchev seemed to be in competition to publicly brandish the largest hydrogen bomb.

Nuclear age

It was taken for granted that nuclear weapons were part and parcel of warfare, including air defence. Every new USAF airman was issued a round, black plastic device to hang from a chain around his neck – a dosimeter, which would glow a different colour to tell him how much radiation he had absorbed. The US Army, in those days, was developing Nike (later Nike Ajax) and Nike Hercules air defence missiles, the latter with a nuclear warhead that was shown in tests to be dangerously unreliable – but nonetheless was fielded in a ring around US cities. The two ADC commanders in the 1950s, Generals Benjamin W. Chidlaw (after whom the command's headquarters building was later named) and Earl P. Partridge – who, between them, covered 1951 to 1956 – were gruff, tough combat veterans who regarded a 'nuke' as simply another tool to be employed in the aerial battlefield. Partridge said he would not hesitate to pull the trigger himself, and no-one doubted it: in Korea, he had spent three days flying around in a T-6 Texan dodging a hailstorm of gunfire in an unsuccessful effort to find and rescue a missing American.

No-one hesitated when a plan was developed several years later (in 1959) to provide an F-106 for Operation Trumpet, in which the aircraft would be flown close to an atmospheric nuclear detonation to measure its performance. In the late 1950s, a pilot's protective thermal curtain was routinely developed for the new interceptor, as for many other aircraft in inventory, to enable the flyer to minimise injury from a blinding atomic flash. It is unclear how the plan for Trumpet unfolded (no F-106 ever fired a 'live' nuclear round, although a Northrop F-89 Scorpion did, in the 'John' shot during Operation Plum Bob in the Nevada desert in July 1957). However, expecting USAF pilots to fly close to a nuclear detonation was not exceptional in this remarkable era.

It was also a time when the United States had a clear-cut

FIS at Geiger Field (now Spokane International Airport) in Washington. The best evidence seems to be that the 539th received its first 'Six' on 30 May 1959 and the 498th two days later. Press releases credited the latter squadron with being first, and there is no dispute that F-106s at Geiger Field were ready for combat before those at McGuire.

It would be almost impossible to exaggerate the importance of ADC at the time, or the real-world certainty with which American officers believed they were preparing for the largest air battles ever waged, over American soil. At the height of its efforts to defend North America, ADC had nearly 80 combat squadrons, more than 2,400 combat-ready warplanes, and principal or 'divert' operations at as many as 200 airfields. Nearly 100,000 Americans of all ranks served in ADC in the 1950s. Their flying squadrons were relatively small and were often 'tenant' units on air bases that belonged to other commands (such as the equally

foreign policy and had elected civilian leaders who were comfortable with military terms and ready to use military force. President Eisenhower was anything but a hawk, and is remembered today for counselling against some of the excesses of the era (as well as unsuccessfully warning Americans against developing a 'military industrial complex'). Still, 'Ike' routinely signed off plans for such measures as bomb shelters, a suitcase-sized nuclear device to be employed by Navy underwater demolition teams (the future Seals), an infantry weapon with nuclear capability, and just about anything that would help to defend American soil against the expected attack from the Soviet bomber fleet.

As far as the formidable and rather beautiful F-106 was concerned, little was said about its nuclear capability in print, but press releases otherwise reflected the tenor of the times. The F-106 was a "plane with a brain." It was "a marvel created by our hard-working scientists." The mission of the 539th was "the defence of the New York-Washington-Philadelphia triangle against attack by enemy H-bombers." The MA-1 system aboard the interceptor "literally thinks for the pilot, freeing him to make tactical decisions." The MA-1's 'Digitaire' computer was "capable of solving fantastic mathematical problems in a fraction of a second."

Members of the 539th went to Tyndall AFB – the base with which the F-106 would be associated longest – to assist with Category III developmental testing in July 1959. On 21 July the Geiger-based 498th FIS scrambled five F-106s on a simulated combat mission. The new interceptors found and 'destroyed' all targets within 10 minutes of the scramble. Very real F-102As were used as the targets. A historic moment came on 31 October 1959, when the 498th FIS began standing alert as part of ADC's fighting force. ADC practice was to keep interceptors ready to fly in flimsy metal 'barns' near runway's end, with the pilots suited up and ready to go.

Speed record and hands-off flight

It was clear all along that the F-106 was a speedster. This became more clear on 15 December 1959 when Major Joe W. Rogers piloted an F-106A (56-0467) to a world air speed record of 1,525.95 mph (2455.71 km/h). Within days, another F-106A (46-0466) went to Eielson AFB, Alaska to begin two months of cold-weather tests. The latter aircraft was painted in the familiar Arctic scheme of the era, with brilliant red on rear fuselage, wingtips and fin. (Eight months later, upgraded to operational status, Rogers's -0467 was assigned to the 329th FIS at George AFB, California.)

The ability to control the F-106 from the ground was dramatically demonstrated on 30 March 1960. An F-106A (59-0047) flew across the United States with the pilot, Major Frank Forsyth, onboard solely for the take-off and landing. Forsyth lifted off from Palmdale at 11:48 a.m. (EST), flew to Jacksonville, Florida, then landed at Tyndall at 3:46 p.m. (also EST). The flight involved 3 hours 12 minutes' work for the aircraft and five minutes' work for

Air refuelling greatly expanded the F-106's capabilities, although the unrefuelled combat radius with external tanks was not insignificant at 725 nm (1343 km). These 87th FIS jets were seen topping up from a KC-135 in May 1973.

Above: The 87th FIS adopted the 'Red Bulls' nickname and traditions of the 11th FIS. For a time, each aircraft even wore a bull's head marking on the nose, as seen in this 1978 view.

Left: Some FISs marked their T-33s in a 'mini' version of their F-106 scheme as seen on the 87th FIS's 'hack' in 1978.

the pilot. The *San Diego Evening Tribune* reported that, "the plane was piloted by a Hughes MA-1 navigation and fire control system. The system does everything except land and take off. The pilot is needed to monitor the system and take over if anything goes wrong." In fact, the USAF had planned an 'automatic' flight from Edwards to McGuire as far back as 4 June 1959, using the term Operation Longlegs, and aborted one attempt flown by Colonel William C. Clark, so Major Forsyth's achievement was nine months in coming.

Even then, Convair press relations employees argued over how to describe the aircraft. It was all right to call it 'automatic' (which it nearly was) but a company official worried that he might get into trouble "with Stan Sharp of security [at Convair]" if he said publicly that the aircraft could fly at Mach 2.0. This measurement of its speed had first appeared in a NORAD news release on 19 February 1959, but some internal flak bounced around San Diego

A pair of 'Crusaders' F-106As touches down at Griffiss in an unusual pairs landing, in June 1978. Note the ADC badges on the fins. In the latter period of F-106 operations, the command badge usually replaced the unit emblem.

Accidents and incidents

With an engine that was highly reliable (after some initial problems), and a high glide ratio, the F-106 achieved one of the best safety records for a single-engined aircraft in the USAF. Despite this, of a total production of 340 airframes, 112 (including 17 F-106Bs) were crashed, destroyed or lost in ground fires during the Dart's 29-year active career, a loss rate of 33 per cent. Others were lost in mishaps during the drone programme (27) and before acceptance by ADC (two). Many F-106s were involved in lesser incidents, requiring local repair or a journey to McClellan AFB for rebuild by the Air Materiel Area/Air Logistics Center there.

Above: This spectacular mishap happened on 1 July 1972 at Hamilton AFB. The damage caused to this F-106B of the 84th FIS was repairable.

Above: 58-0796 was the first F-106 to arrive for the 94th FIS – and the first to be written off, in this accident on 13 August 1961. The investigators have helpfully marked the final resting places of the landing gear components on the original photograph.

Above: This 71st FIS F-106A came to grief at King Salmon, Alaska in 1970.

Above and right: 59-0083 of the 49th FIS exceeded g limits on a 1978 Red Flag sortie and lost the outer leading edges of both wings. It made an emergency landing at Michael Auxiliary Airfield, Utah.

Left: Another F-106 that dropped into Michael AAF during a Red Flag that year was 59-0054 of the 318th FIS, which lost its nose and radar in a collision with an A-7. It was shot down as a QF-106 by an AIM-120 in February 1996.

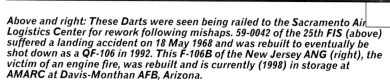

Above and right: These Darts were seen being railed to the Sacramento Air Logistics Center for rework following mishaps. 59-0042 of the 25th FIS (above) suffered a landing accident on 18 May 1968 and was rebuilt to eventually be shot down as a QF-106 in 1992. This F-106B of the New Jersey ANG (right), the victim of an engine fire, was rebuilt and is currently (1998) in storage at AMARC at Davis-Monthan AFB, Arizona.

Above: This trio of F-106As, two from the 48th FIS and one from the 11th FIS, was captured over Mt McKinley during a rotation of units at Elmendorf in April 1969.

White Shoes

F-106 Delta Dart

Perceived inadequacies of the F-102 then on Arctic duty led to the deployment of F-106s to Alaska under the name White Shoes in July 1963 when nine F-106As from McChord AFB, Washington – five from the 318th FIS and four from the 498th FIS – were sent to Elmendorf AFB. The first intercept of probing Soviet bombers took place on 8 September 1963 when two F-106s were scrambled from Galena AFS and intercepted two Tu-16 'Badgers' over the Bering Sea. There were 35 White Shoes (later College Shoes) deployments, the last in October 1970.

Above: A 94th FIS F-106A flies with an F-102A of the 317th FIS during a White Shoes rotation. The deployments to Alaska provided the spur for fitting the 'Six' with air-refuelling gear, which was to prove essential during the

Above: Carrying a pair of the original subsonic wing tanks, a 5th FIS Dart flies over Alaska during a February 1967 White Shoes deployment. The arrival of air-to-air refuelling on the F-106 fleet is thought to mark the change to College Shoes.

Above: The F-106s of the first White Shoes line up at Elmendorf on 15 July 1963. The 318th and 498th FISs took part, the latter unit's aircraft without tail markings.

when the term finally appeared in the manufacturer's house paper, *Convariety*, months later. Not for a long time thereafter did anyone acknowledge that Joe Rogers's speed record flight, which preceded Forsyth's robotic excursion by some months, had attained Mach 2.36.

The USAF wanted the F-106 to be largely automatic in actual military service and even pondered an unmanned version, but the interceptor never became the remote-controlled robot that Forsyth's flight implied. From the start, the intent was that the control system would guide the interceptor to the vicinity of its target, perform the air-to-air radar search for the target, and prepare selected armament for firing, but in practice the system was used in a way that left the pilot in command. When the F-106 was launched on a GCI (ground-controlled intercept) mission, a ground operator could use the SAGE system's datalink to the interceptor's MA-1 system to effect control movements on the aircraft, but the system was more routinely used simply to pass information to the pilot – with the datalink substituting for voice instructions from the ground operator.

SAGE ground control

Most noteworthy is the fact that the MA-1 included the first digital computer ever installed on an aircraft, and that the computer (and hence the aircraft) could be pre-programmed with information about the flight plan, conditions, weather and geography.

A ground crew member regarded the SAGE system and the MA-1 this way: "The SAGE system was supposed to be able to control the vectoring of the aircraft from ground stations on intercept mission of enemy aircraft formations. The system would receive controlling signals from the ground and these were coupled to the autopilot's analog computer system. The autopilot even then was capable of completely automatic interception in two modes of operation. These were Lead Collision (any attack from the front that allowed the autopilot to manoeuvre from the front of the enemy aircraft) and Auto Pursuit (any attack from the rear that allowed the autopilot to manoeuvre from the rear half of the enemy aircraft). With the autopilot engaged and attack mode selected, the weapons control

system – which included the autopilot, navigation and radar systems working together – would allow the aircraft to fly in and attack. The pilot selected the weapon he wanted to use and held the trigger down; when all the parameters were met, the weapon would launch automatically.

"On the funny side, we were always getting inflight write-ups from pilots that the autopilot system would not respond with rapid enough manoeuvres or that the autopilot responded too rapidly. We could adjust the system's response sensitivity, and did, but one pilot would want the aircraft to fly one way and the next pilot would feel differently. We did, however, know when the pilot came back with a bad headache or cracked helmet from bouncing his head off the canopy. The metal strip across the top of the canopy in the [early] F-106 was constantly colliding with the pilot's helmet."

As a new aircraft in service after an ambitious and rigorous test programme, the F-106 continued to have more teething troubles than it deserved. Part of the problem was the perception gaining favour that manned aircraft were on the way out and that a piloted interceptor like the F-106 could be replaced by an unpiloted one such as the Bomarc missile. In June 1960, the Senate deleted spending on F-106s from the defence money bill for FY 1961 and approved a spending measure that replaced the F-106 with the Bomarc. The Senate action ended plans to purchase 80 Delta Darts in addition to the 340 that became

During the Cuban missile crisis in October 1962, at least two squadrons were deployed to Florida – the 71st to Patrick and the 48th to Homestead – to provide air intercept capability, although there was little threat to the US from Cuban bombers. On 25 October, however, 11th FIS Darts, armed with live Genies, were scrambled in error from Volk Field, Michigan not knowing that SAC had quadrupled its airborne alert over the US. Thankfully, there were no 'blue on blue' incidents.

F-106A cockpit

Right: As built, the F-106A's cockpit was of so-called 'round eye' configuration with dial-type instruments. Under the hood above the instruments is the radar scope; the larger scope below is the tactical situation display (TSD). Note the two-handled control column, chosen by the USAF after conventional and sidestick combinations were evaluated on early production F-106s. The left-most of the two grips controlled the radar.

Far right: A redesigned instrument panel (the IID or integrated instrument display), with vertical tape instruments, was introduced on the production line beginning with aircraft 58-0759. Some (but by no means all) earlier aircraft were retrofitted to this standard. Here the cockpit of a QF-106A is shown. Note the absence of the TSD, and the Remote Flying Enable Box or 'NULLO Consent Panel' fitted in place of the radar scope, used by the safety pilot to switch control of various aircraft functions to ground controllers.

Left: The IRST (infra-red search and track) ahead of the cockpit was installed under Project Broad Jump in 1963. This aircraft also sports the clear-view bubble canopy introduced from October 1972 to improve all-round visibility.

'Six' nose art

Examples of colourful F-106 nose art are associated particularly with the William Tell competitions of the 1970s and 1980s. Designs often followed a squadron-related theme – for example, the 'red bulls' of the 87th.

48th FIS

59-0133, Broadway Byrd and artist.

Above: TAZ was seen on 59-0145 and other 48th FIS aircraft

Above: Patience adorned 59-0123

Above: 56-0458 of the 48th FIS

87th FIS

Above: 59-0089 was Lurch IV with the 87th FIS (known as 'The Red Bulls' after the 11th FIS) at William Tell '72.

Above: The City of Marquette was 59-0091, an 87th FIS machine in 1972, named for the city near the 87th's base, K. I. Sawyer AFB.

Left: 57-0230 of the 87th FIS displays another variation on the 'red bull' theme.

Above: Bones Crusher was 59-0094 of the 87th FIS, seen at Tyndall AFB in September 1972, just prior to that year's William Tell meet.

119th FIS

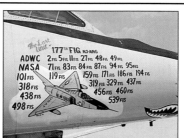

The last F-106 in service, 59-0043 of the 177th FIG (119th FIS/New Jersey ANG), sported an array of nose designs, including a list of F-106 units, a shark-mouth and a squadron insignia.

Left and above: The basic overall colour scheme for the F-106 was FS 16473 'ADC gray'. The line-up of glossy airframes being reworked at McClellan in 1962 (left) typifies the usual appearance of this scheme, in contrast to the worn appearance of this late New Jersey ANG without unit markings (above).

Left: At least two aircraft were seen at the SAALC at Kelly Field in gloss 'Air Superiority blue' (FS 15450) as used on early F-15 Eagles.

Right: A stripped F-106B seen after rework at Sacramento.

Left: NASA 607 (57-2507) is seen in the NASA house colours still in use today.

Below: The NF-106B used for the vortex flap programme was mainly flown in bare metal. The wings were painted black to help visualise the movement in the airflow of the tufts on the wing.

Left: Storm-hunting NF-106B NASA 816 is shown during in 1982. Paint spots were applied to mark lightning strike points.

Right: 57-2507 of the 6511th Test Group is seen in 1969 with a Dayglo radome.

Above: The fifth F-106A assigned to the test programme (56-0455) is seen in typical period high-visibility markings while assigned to the AFFTC for Category II testing.

Right: 56-0459 was painted over-all Dayglo while with the AFFTC. This colour scheme appears to have been unique to this aircraft.

Intercepts

The F-106 had fewer encounters with Soviet bombers than did the Iceland- and Alaska-based F-102s; however, the Delta Dart's longer endurance and air-refuelling capability allowed interception at greater ranges. The ANG units based on the Atlantic coast were the busiest units, mostly shepherding 'Bears' en route to Cuba, but the first interception of an intruder made by aircraft based in the continental US (ConUS) was carried out by F-106s of the 27th FIS based at Loring, in May 1969.

A historic benchmark was reached on 20 July 1961 when Convair delivered the 277th and last F-106A (59-0148) to ADC. The production run also included 63 F-106B two-seaters, for a total of 340 aircraft. The final example was accepted in a ceremony at San Diego by Lieutenant General Robert M. Lee, commander of ADC. (The final Delta Dart, 59-0148, put in only eight years of service when, while flying with the 318th FIS, it was lost in a mishap on 22 April 1969.) Average cost of a Delta Dart was about $2 million (then equivalent to about £500,000). This was the last military aircraft manufactured in San Diego by Convair, a firm that was even then making an ill-fated venture into the commercial jetliner market. The company had been a bulwark in San Diego and would continue missile work for another decade, but by the 1970s it would be gone – part of history, like so many in what had once been a great and vast industry.

the final production total. A newspaper report noted that, "recent Bomarc tests have proven the missile's ability to halt supersonic missiles more than 120 miles [193 km] away and a fighter plane 100 miles [161 km] away." This was an exaggeration, and the F-106, flown by real men, was to be around long after the Boeing-built Bomarc (designated F-99A until 15 August 1955, IM-99A until 1 October 1962, and CIM-10A thereafter) was gone from the inventory.

Matador 'kill'

The F-106 Delta Dart scored an aerial victory of sorts on 14 May 1960 when a TM-61 Matador surface-to-surface missile got away and had to be shot down during an Armed Forces Day air show at Holloman AFB. After an F-100 Super Sabre chase plane was unable to keep up with the Matador when it went wild, the Holloman test centre diverted an F-106A (57-0233) that had just taken off on a routine test flight, piloted by Major J. D. Fowler. The subsonic missile was at 27,000 ft (8230 m) and was 45 miles (72 km) in front of him when Fowler climbed to 32,000 ft (9753 m) and made a rear-end pursuit at Mach 1.5. Over an isolated area near Holloman, Fowler fired two GAR-3A Super Falcons, one an inert training round and the other a live missile without fuse. The Matador was struck solidly in the engine and spun to earth.

In September 1960, the USAF began Project Wild Goose, a modification programme aimed at standardising the fleet. This series of internal changes to most F-106s was completed a year later, on 18 September 1961. During this period, a separate programme to improve the fleet, Project Broad Jump, removed each F-106 from service for about 60 days for internal improvements. Yet another retrofit/modification programme, Project Dart Board, ended in April 1962.

Grounding

Despite the Delta Dart's successes, on 26 September 1961 ADC had to announce that the F-106 – still officially the world's fastest aircraft – was grounded. Repairs to the fuel system were needed, though the details are no longer apparent. The command had to take this embarrassing measure after two crashes, one of which killed a pilot at Geiger AFB. ADC, which at the time had 12 F-106 squadrons, later amended the order so that Delta Darts on alert were not affected but those used for training and transition flying were kept on the ground. It could not have happened at a worse time. The F-106 returned to normal flying after minor changes (the much-needed change to its flawed ejection seat would come later) and President Kennedy's newly-appointed Defense Secretary, Robert S. McNamara, spoke of reopening the production line (not for the 80 aircraft once contemplated for FY 1961, but for 36), but neither step could breathe new life into the Delta Dart and no further aircraft were built.

The grounding of the Delta Dart was still in effect on 23 October 1961, when the Pentagon launched an air-to-air competition – Project High Speed – between the Air Force's F-106A Delta Dart and the Navy's F4H-1 Phantom (soon to be redesignated F-4B). The test programme at Langley AFB and NAS Oceana, both in Virginia, was intended to evaluate the capabilities of the aircraft to perform similar missions. ADC had heard such glowing reports about the F4H that it asked for a comparative evaluation of the F-106 and F4H in the air defence mission. Even though reopening the F-106 production line was an on-again, off-again proposition (which ultimately stayed off), the USAF's position was that it needed 200 more interceptors. ADC was extremely interested in the new McDonnell fighter.

The test consisted of 153 sorties (77 by each aircraft, with one 'abort'), flown from 500 ft (152 m) to 62,000 ft (18897 m), during which 349 valid interceptions were completed. Due to the unavailability of a B-58 Hustler to stand in as a high-speed target, three planned intercept missions were not attempted. The Phantom's APQ-72

Genie rocket

The primary weapon of the F-106 as designed was the Douglas AIR-2A Genie. AIR stood for Air Intercept Rocket and the Genie was technically unguided, although the MA-1 system would track the target, arm and fire the missile, pull the aircraft into a turn away from the blast zone, and detonate the warhead at a predetermined point. Maximum flight duration was 12 seconds, and range was approximately 10 km (6.2 miles). The Genie had been developed under a project codenamed Ding Dong (later High Card), begun in 1955, with the first (inert warhead) firing taking place in July 1959. After launch, preferably at a formation of enemy bombers, the Genie's fintips flicked out for stability and to correct gravity drop, and the 36,600-lb (162.78-kN) Thiokol TU-289 solid-propellant motor kicked in and accelerated the missile to Mach 3. The lethal blast radius of the 1.5-kT warhead was estimated at 1,000 ft (305 m), which theoretically might have allowed the target(s) to evade, but it was calculated that electromagnetic pulse (EMP) from the detonation would knock out the target's electronics.

Above: Although 'special weapons' were not made as accessible to ANG personnel as to regular units, the Guard F-106 squadrons trained with the Genie until it was withdrawn from service in the mid-1980s. Here an inert round is launched from a Montana ANG F-106.

Left: The Genie dropped from the rear of the F-106's missile bay, as seen on this 5th FIS aircraft. A training round with a spotting charge was a 'Ting-a-Ling'.

radar demonstrated better reliability and maintainability, plus longer detection and lock-on ranges. Of these considerations, reliability was especially significant because the MA-1 system aboard the F-106 was said to have repeated technical glitches. By the end of December 1961, the USAF announced that the F4H/F-110 would be procured for Tactical Air Command. ADC would get no new interceptors.

One-sided competition

The conventional wisdom that the F4H won easily in this head-on contest with the F-106 did not appeal to Convair representatives, who had numerous complaints. "First," they concluded, "the F-4H [sic] system is about two years newer than the F-106. It has two men, a larger radar antenna, and a significant improvement in pilot display and radar lock-on capability. The armament launch characteristics are more versatile than the Falcon or the MB-1. This versatility promises better scoring in exercises, even though an actual firing might prove otherwise." (No missiles were launched in the competition.) But the real problem, complained Convair, was that the Air Force's F-106 pilots were asleep at the switch.

"The very best Navy squadron was paired against the worst or one of the worst F-106 squadrons. The Navy personnel had determination and enthusiasm as well as forced determination, i.e., 'beat the F-106s or out you go.' In contrast, there was an atmosphere of lethargy [among the Air Force participants]. No-one seemed to know how to get out of the slump they were in." Convair also complained that USAF maintainers were not adequately prepped to keep the equipment 'finely tuned'.

No detailed report comparing the two fighters has ever surfaced. Although the F4H clearly had superior radar and some other advantages, it appears that, in many sorties, F-106 pilots 'shot down' their Phantom adversaries. Contrary to myth, the men developing the F-106 knew from the beginning that it had enormous potential in the air-to-air, fighter-versus-fighter role. For this very reason, the 'Six' would later be considered for possible use in Vietnam and would appear in crisis-ridden Korea.

When the duel between the two fighters ended on 17 November 1961, the Phantom emerged with a technical edge – but, in many battles, the Delta Dart had roundly defeated the F-4.

In later years, an F-106 pilot looked at the comparison between Delta Dart and Phantom this way: "The F-4 had a longer range missile in the AIM-7 Sparrow but we [F-106 pilots] kicked F-4 butts each and every day in the visual arena. We owned the vertical on him, we got our energy back much, much quicker, had as good or better sustained turn most altitudes, and our instantaneous was also as good. He could never match our zoom when we hit the fight with any sort of knots. Our missiles had logic the early Sparrow AIM-7s were missing. In particular, the Falcon loved the beam intercept (early AIM-7 hated beam intercepts) and the Falcon loved ECM while the early AIM-7 hated ECM."

An important public appearance by the USAF's newest

Below: An F-106 pilot of the 95th FIS in Korea sports the type of flying equipment most commonly used in the later years of the Dart. Pressure suits were worn more often in the early days on flights planned for 55,000 ft (16764 m) and higher. For normal flights, home-based ADC crews normally wore high-conspicuity orange flight suits and standard helmets.

A delta of Delta Darts of the 5th FIS is led by the squadron commander in his specially marked jet. The colourful markings of the F-106 were, for a short while, carried on by the F-15s which replaced them in the fighter interceptor squadrons, but it seems that the days of instantly-identifiable, brightly-marked fighter squadrons are now gone forever.

259

Above and above right: *In April 1978, eight F-106As of the 87th FIS went to Keflavik NS, Iceland to supplement the 57th FIS, then in the process of converting from F-4Cs to F-4Es. At this time there was also increased Soviet activity around the Kola Peninsula, and ADC sent the 87th to cover the shortfall in capability. The 87th recorded three intercepts of Soviet aircraft during its Icelandic sojourn.*

interceptor occurred in May 1963 when an F-106A (59-0136) of the 48th FIS (Langley AFB) appeared at the 25th Paris air show at Le Bourget.

The F-106 Delta Dart became a defender of the ADIZ (Air Defense Identification Zones) surrounding Alaska from 1963. What became known as Project White Shoes (later, College Shoes) began amid a perception of failure. On 15 March 1963, a Soviet reconnaissance bomber overflew Nunivak Island and the west coast of Alaska. A pair of F-102A Delta Daggers of the 317th FIS at Elmendorf AFB was scrambled from the alert facility at King Salmon airfield but had to be recalled when only 20 miles (36 km) from their target because of low fuel. This failure to make contact led to a furious debate in which ADC officers demanded longer-legged F-4C Phantom IIs for their squadrons. They had an excellent precedent: years earlier, while war was raging in Korea, ADC had enjoyed priority for delivery of new fighters even over squadrons committed to battle during the Korean War. This time, however, ADC was told that the war in Southeast Asia would have priority for any assignments of the F-4C.

Rotations through Alaska

ADC then decided to keep up rotational deployments of eight F-106s at a time from continental US squadrons to assist in the air defence of Alaska. These deployments – White Shoes – began on 15 July 1963 with the arrival of nine F-106As from McChord AF, five from the 318th FIS and four from the 498th FIS. The 498th FIS then had no unit markings applied, while the 318th FIS aircraft had a North Star motif.

Two F-106s were scrambled from another alert facility at Galena, Alaska on 8 September 1963 and intercepted two Tupolev Tu-16 'Badgers' over the Bering Sea off the

northwest coast of Alaska. The White Shoes operation in Alaska also involved the permanent stationing of a support element of about 80 airmen. One of these veterans remembers that reconnaissance aircraft and bombers were not alone in drawing F-106 attention: "MiG-21s from Siberia routinely crossed into the ADIZ to test our defences and we often went after them." The long White Shoes/College Shoes commitment finally ended on 2 October 1970 after seven years and 35 deployments, when the 84th FIS returned to Hamilton AFB, California. Thereafter, F-106s travelled to Alaska only for brief appearances in summer and winter exercises.

Ejection seat revisited

The efforts to put the right ejection seat in the F-106 neared completion in 1965, as the USAF began to retrofit its Delta Dagger fleet with the Weber F-106 seat. This upward ejection seat used an M3A1 catapult initiator to send pilot, seat and BA-18 parachute into space. The Weber seat was frequently referred to as a 'zero-zero' seat, meaning that if necessary the pilot could safely eject while standing still on the ground. Actual tests showed it effective in about 95 per cent of realistic bailout scenarios.

Weber Aircraft carried out the only live 'zero-zero' test ever conducted by an American company in October 1965, using an F-106 seat occupied by Jim Hall, an experienced fighter pilot and parachutist. Weber delivered the first squadron's seats in only 45 days, and once they were installed in F-106s, the Convair 'B seat' was relegated to the scrap pile – where it belonged.

Goose Bay, Labrador was home to a fighter-interceptor commitment deemed vital to the defence of North America. Beginning in late 1966, ADC planned for the inactivation (in late 1967) of the F-102A-equipped 59th FIS at 'Goose' to fill an anticipated gap in the air defence of the northeastern United States. Soviet harassment of Labrador and Greenland airspace was on the increase. Interceptors would still need to fly from Goose Bay. The College Goose project called for six F-106As at a time to rotate through the base in the same way that other 'Sixes' had been operating in Alaska. The 27th FIS at Loring AFB, Maine, being the closest F-106 unit, drew the initial deployment.

By April 1967, ADC was re-evaluating the College Goose situation. For several reasons, availability of F-106s

Above: A Standard AAM is seen on the starboard fuel tank pylon of a 4750th Test Squadron F-106A. It is not clear if live firing tests were conducted with the Delta Dart or if actual XAIM-97 rounds were ever carried.

Right: The 4750th was the 'Skunk Works' of the ADWC, testing various air-to-air weapons concepts. This F-106 has a camera in the cannon housing.

Satellite killer

In October 1971 the Space and Missile Systems Office of AFSC informed USAF HQ that Project Spike, based on an AGM-78 Standard anti-radar missile, was a feasible anti-satellite (ASAT) weapon. Although this system was not adopted, the USAF and General Dynamics' Electro Dynamic Division developed an experimental missile under the codename Seekbat. The missile, also designated XAIM-97A, was intended for carriage by the F-4 – and possibly the F-106 – and was basically an AGM-78-6 with an IR seeker and a larger motor. Israel and Japan were particularly worried about the threat from the high-flying Mach-3 MiG-25 'Foxbat' interceptor, and the proposed AIM-97 would have been self-guiding to 80,000 ft (24384 m), the MiG-25's supposed operating altitude. The Standard airframe, already cleared for the F-4, was trialled on a Tyndall F-106. Reportedly, six Seekbats were available by the time of the 1973 Yom Kippur War, but there was no time to modify more Standards before it ended. Like the Navy's similar missile, the Brazo, Seekbat did not enter service,

William Tell

The biennial William Tell (WT) weapons meet was first held at Yuma, Arizona in 1954 for units of Air Defense Command concerned with defence of the contiguous US. In 1958, William Tell moved to Tyndall, Florida and in time broadened its scope to include air defence units of other commands and from Canada, as well as the Air National Guard. The competition element involved the various units flying a range of intercept profiles against other manned aircraft and live-firing against both BQM-type drones and 'droned' aircraft such as the QF-100 and QF-102. The competition was fierce in the air and on the ground, and traditions arose of decorating the aircraft – and everything else that did or did not move – with squadron motifs and other imagery. The F-106 first participated in WT '61 and for the final time in 1984.

Above: An F-106 of the 49th FIS is moved by an engineer into its parking spot alongside 'Sixes' of the 318th FIS and Canadian Armed Forces CF-101s at WT '82. The 'Green Eagles' pilots (left) had their own special ground transport in 1978.

Above: A 190th FIS, Idaho ANG F-102A flies with a 318th FIS F-106A and a CAF CF-101B over Tyndall circa 1968-74. The two US units were responsible for the defence of northwest North America, together with Canadian Voodoos.

Below: Various buildings used by the visiting squadrons received adornment, as well as aircraft and support equipment. 'Taz' dates from WT '78, and 'Florida's 'Fang' from 1976.

Above: Some of the humour displayed by William Tell participants was ever so slightly obscure to the outsider. These exhaust covers on Montana ANG F-106s in 1978 depicted a 'Swedish farmer' and a 'Swedish flagpole'.

Below: The 49th FIS brought this decorated T-33A to William Tell in 1974. Behind it can be seen the 'hacks' of other ADC squadrons.

The Florida ANG provided the 'target' aircraft for unarmed interception profiles in 1986. White, orange and yellow trim was applied to some of the 194th FIS aircraft.

was expected to be at a premium. ADC recommended that F-101B/F Voodoos be substituted for the F-106s, which would give the Voodoo squadrons mobility training they would not normally get. So, on 1 July 1967, when the 27th FIS F-106s rotated home, six F-101s from two squadrons took over the Goose Bay job.

The College Goose effort was eventually scrapped altogether but Soviet bomber flights persisted in 1967-68 and activity was heavy along the Greenland-Iceland-UK (GIUK) line. A new plan, College Shaft, was implemented on 20 November 1969. Again, the Loring-based 27th FIS

was selected for the job. On 13 May 1969, two F-106s were scrambled from Loring. Two hours and 33 minutes later, after landing and servicing at Goose Bay, they intercepted Russian bombers at a point 150 miles (241 km) from North America and 750 miles (1207 km) from Loring. This was the first time interceptors based in the continental US had intercepted Soviet aircraft. F-106s participated thereafter in College Shaft operations involving both brief appearances at Goose Bay and longer stays; they ended on 1 July 1970, after 14 deployments.

Installation of a gun on the F-106 was directly prompted

F-106 Colours

1st Fighter Interceptor Wing

In the early days of the F-106, squadron markings were based around this standardised design, usually with the squadron badge within the 'V'. The 94th FIS sometimes put its badge on the nose and the 1st FIW crest in the 'V'.

2nd FIS

The 'Horney Horses' unicorn badge was carried in this black-edged yellow band. The 94th FIS used this style until it transferred its aircraft to the 2nd.

5th FIS

The later markings of the 5th FIS featured a stylised lightning bolt with five stars. The 'Spittin' Kitten' faced to the rear.

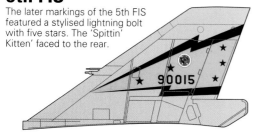

11th FIS

The first 'Red Bulls' placed its lightning-snorting charging bull above a red chevron. The 87th FIS later adopted the traditions and markings of the 11th, with a new design of bull.

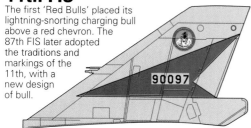

27th FIS

The 27th FIS tail markings were among the most spectacular seen on the F-106. The 'Fighting Falcon' squadron badge was the centrepiece.

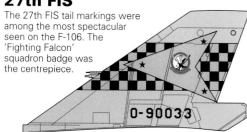

48th FIS

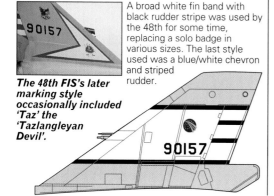

The 48th FIS's later marking style occasionally included 'Taz' the 'Tazlangleyan Devil'.

A broad white fin band with black rudder stripe was used by the 48th for some time, replacing a solo badge in various sizes. The last style used was a blue/white chevron and striped rudder.

49th FIS

The 'Crusaders' adopted a stylised green-and-white eagle marking. In common with most squadrons in the ADTAC era, the TAC crest replaced the unit badge on the fin from the late 1970s.

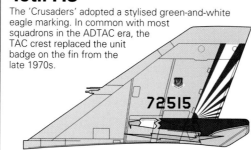

The 49th FIS 1776-1976 commemorative special scheme included the 13-star colonial flag and the 'crusader' squadron badge on the fin.

71st FIS

The 71st FIS's badge of a diving winged gauntlet was worn on a blue chevron.

83rd FIS

The ace of spades appeared at the points of the 83rd FIS tail chevron marking and on the badge, encircled by a golden horseshoe and pierced by a lightning bolt.

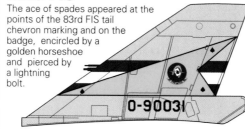

84th FIS

The 84th FIS took over the aircraft of the 498th FIS and applied its badge to the 498th's last markings. The black panther insignia later appeared on a red/white/black band.

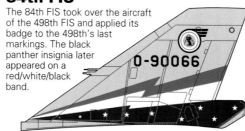

87th FIS

The 87th FIS initially adopted the markings of the 11th FIS with its own variation of the 'Red Bull' badge.

The 87th's stylised bull's head fin marking was probably the most original design used on the F-106. There were several variations in the shape of the head, and later the TAC insignia replaced the badge 'eye'.

94th FIS

One of numerous variations on the 94th FIS colour scheme was the placement of the 'Hat in the Ring' badge on a black/yellow band. The badge also appeared on the nose and in a disc on a plain tail.

95th FIS

The 95th FIS tail marking was originally a large disc containing the 'Mr Bones' squadron badge. Later this was incorporated in a diamond on a chordways band which was either medium or light blue.

318th FIS

The final and most elaborate form of 318th FIS tail marking was a large north star device, reaching to the edges of the fin, radiating from the squadron's green dragon-wielding-a-rocket insignia.

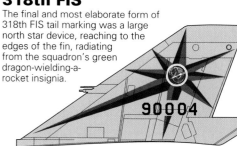

319th FIS

The 319th FIS's previous night-fighter/all-weather interceptor role (with P-61s, F-82, F-94 and F-89) was represented by its rocket-throwing tomcat badge and motto 'We get ours at night' on a blue chevron.

329th FIS

The 329th FIS placed its badge of a futuristic delta-winged aircraft within a red/white chevron. The 26th Air Division badge was displayed over horizontal bands at the base of the fin.

438th FIS

The 438th FIS's badge dated from World War II and depicted a machine-gun-toting Donald Duck running to the right, and a red lightning bolt. On the F-106 it usually appeared placed on a black-and-white chevron.

456th FIS

The 456th FIS placed its badge of a ferocious (six-legged) octopus on a yellow tail with black trim. The 456th was redesignated the 437th FIS, but it is not thought that the unit ever applied its badge to the base markings that it inherited.

460th FIS

The 460th FIS was a redesignation of the 437th FIS. Initially, it used the same yellow fin originated by the 456th FIS for its 'Cave Tigrim' (Beware of the Tiger) badge, but later changed to this design.

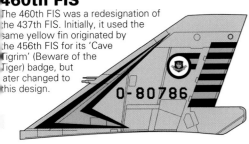

498th FIS

The 498th's 'Geiger Tiger' badge was initially displayed in a large disc on a fin with a red rudder. The design used for the longest time placed the badge in a disc with a 'swoosh' and had a giant lightning bolt across the base.

539th FIS

The 539th's lightning flash and star appeared with some variation in the shade of blue used. The star was sometimes even seen in a different shade to the lightning.

Air Defense Weapons Center

The first tail markings used on ADWC F-106s featured a large Center badge and a red/white/blue chevron at the forward end of the fin. The '0' for 'Obsolete' prefix was applied to the serials of aircraft over 10 years old.

The ADWC markings were later toned down slightly and the Tactical Air Command badge replaced the ADWC insignia. The '0' prefix was seen between 1956 and 1964, when it was removed.

101st FIS, Mass. ANG

The Massachusetts ANG kept essentially the same blue and white fin design throughout its F-106 period. The only significant difference was the replacement of the squadron badge (below) by the Air National Guard emblem (right).

119th FIS, New Jersey ANG

The first design used by the New Jersey ANG was quite simple and featured the 'Jersey Devil' badge of the 177th FIG rather than the squadron's own emblem.

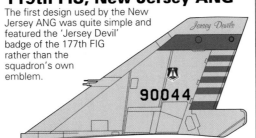

159th FIS, Florida ANG

The Florida ANG's F-106 squadron retained one marking, of a large lightning bolt on a blue band, through the Delta Dart era. This marking appeared on the 159th's F-16s and, in a smaller form, on its current F-15s.

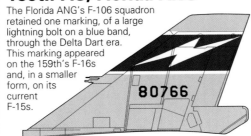

171st FIS, Michigan ANG

In the later F-106 years of the Michigan ANG, its aircraft sported a checked rudder and double yellow chevrons. Variations of these markings appeared on its F-4Cs and F-16s.

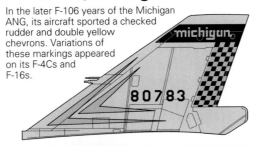

The original markings of the Michigan Air National Guard's F-106s included the 'Six Pack' nickname and the early-style circular ANG badge.

186th FIS, Montana ANG

Like most of the ANG F-106 units, the Montana Guard did not display its squadron badge on the aircraft. Instead, the state name and a local nickname were worn on blue bands throughout the F-106 era. The F-16s introduced in 1987 retained the 'Big Sky Country' titles.

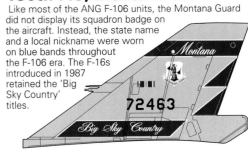

194th FIS, California ANG

California's Guard F-106s wore an all-white tail and the bear of the California Republic state flag. This popular marking was later changed to a simple blue band with 'California' titles.

B-1B Chase

The F-106s used by the USAF's Contract Management Division on B-1B bomber acceptance test flights wore this stylised representation of their mission. Black and red versions of the design also existed.

NASA

The QF-106s used by NASA for Project Eclipse had a high-visibility orange fin. As with most QF-106s, the rudder was left in its final service colours (in this case, those of the 5th FIS), for balance reasons.

An early F-106 used by NASA, 57-0235, was bailed to NASA between September 1958 and December 1959, for MA-1 fire control system and autopilot manoeuvre intercept tests. It was used at the Ames Research Center at Moffett Field. The Dayglo on the fin carried along the spine and onto the forward fuselage.

NASA F-106B N607NA (57-2507, the first two-seater) wore a predominantly white scheme with a blue cheatline for some time. The NASA 'worm' logo replaced the circular NASA badge design and the civil registration on the fin as seen at right. N607NA also wore this scheme with the large blue areas, but on a basically white airframe.

Above: A feature of ANG operations was (and is) the sharing of bases with civilian air traffic. The New Jersey ANG's 119th FIS shared Atlantic City's airport with 747s full of gamblers come to spend in the city's casinos.

Right: The Montana Guard was the first ANG unit to receive the 'Six'. It handed in its F-102s in the spring of 1972, and its F-106s 14 years later.

Far right: B-52s were a common intercept target for F-106s such as this 194th FIS, California ANG machine. Note the extended IR sensor.

The F-106 joined the Air National Guard in 1972, with the first delivery to the 186th FIS on 3 April. The aircraft were transferred from the 460th FIS, which traded up to upgraded aircraft. The 171st FIS (Michigan) and 101st (Massachusetts) also received their first Delta Darts that year. In all, six Guard units became F-106 users, the longest-lived of them being the 119th FIS from New Jersey, which flew the 'Six' from 1973 until 1988.

by Lieutenant General Arthur C. Agan, Jr, who commanded ADC from 1 August 1967 to 28 February 1970, and who felt that his command could contribute more to the ongoing war in Southeast Asia. Perhaps Agan remembered that, during the 1950-53 Korean conflict, ADC had enjoyed a high priority for receiving weapons and equipment but had contributed nothing to the fighting abroad. In any event, Agan asked for suggestions on how the F-106 could be employed for 'top cover' in Vietnam. A staffer, Lieutenant Colonel Bob Archibald, prepared a list of recommendations which included changes in training and equipment, a quick-shoot modification for the Falcon missiles, a clear-view canopy, tactical camouflage, and – above all – a gun. Air Force Systems Command, which was responsible for testing, looked at some of Archibald's suggestions and vetoed them, saying the F-106 had no mission with which the proposals could correspond.

Project Six Shooter

1967 was the year when North Vietnamese MiG-21s were scoring heavily against USAF F-4C Phantoms which had been built without guns; the MiGs scored a little-mentioned kill ratio of about 3:1 against the Americans. Archibald and others wanted a gun on the F-106 so badly that they bypassed AFSC and borrowed a pair of 20-mm gun pods from the Navy. Somehow, $1.7 million was scraped up to test a gun in what became known as Project Six Shooter, directed by Brigadier General James D. Price with help from Major George R. Hennigan. Price could hardly have been a better choice: as a wing commander, he had watched men die in Korea in June and July 1950 because they lacked weapons that were routinely going to ADC.

The gun was primarily intended to provide extra

firepower and a close-in kill potential for aircraft with a non-nuclear mission (the 'Six' would be able to carry gun or Genie, but not both), but interest in a gun also reflected the growing consensus that the F-106 might be useful in fighter-versus-fighter combat. The gun was also meant to augment the F-106's capability at low altitude, where the threat from bombers seemed increasingly concentrated. Convair set forth to re-equip the F-106 with a gun, an optical gunsight and a clear-view canopy in a programme that became known as Project Six Shooter. The arrangement came in the form of a 'kit' that could be installed by maintenance men at an operational airfield, but was not easily interchangeable: once the gun was installed, it took an experienced ground crew eight hours to remove it and restore Genie capability.

The weapon was a General Electric M61A1 20-mm Vulcan Gatling cannon with 650 rounds of standard electrically-primed HEI (high-explosive incendiary) or ball ammunition. The gun was to be located in an armament bay created by removing the Genie rocket. The gun came with a rounds-limit switch that gave the pilot the option of firing the gun until ammunition was depleted or using a counter to select the number of rounds to be fired. The gun was safetied on the ground: after engine start, the crew chief was to signal the pilot to raise his hands to a visible position, then remove gun safety devices and arm the gun for flight.

The Project Six Shooter gun installation was tried first on F-106A 58-0795 assigned to the Six Shooter programme on 10 February 1969, and subsequently on F-106A 59-0092 assigned on 29 March 1972. At Tyndall, an 'in-house' prototype gunsight was developed with a 'snap shoot' capability.

During contractor tests prior to releasing the gun-armed

Below: The 101st FIS, Massachusetts ANG (The 'Irish Guard') at Otis AFB (later ANGB) adopted 'Cape Cod' titles for its F-106s to reflect its location. The 101st received Darts in 1972 after a only a year on F-100s.

Below right: A peculiarity of Montana ANG F-106s was their blue cockpit interior, reportedly based on that of the MiG-25, part of which can be seen in this view of aircraft at William Tell.

Flying the F-106

Lieutenant Colonel Mike 'Buddha' Nelson, seen here at Tyndall AFB in 1975, rates the F-106 as his favourite of many fighter types flown. The 'alert' commitment at Tyndall at this time was filled by the Southern Air Defense Detachment (SADD), the 'Dixie Darts' employing ADWC aircraft and pilots attached to the Interceptor Weapons School. From 1976, the duty passed to the Florida ANG at Jacksonville.

"To quote Hemingway, 'A man has one virginity to lose in fighters, and if it's a lovely airplane, there will his heart remain forever.'

"I have flown several fighters and fighter trainers – T-38, T-33, A-37, F-101F, F-106A/B, F-4C/D/E (slatted), F-5E/F, F-15B and F-16D, and my heart lies forever with the 'Six'. Of all the fighters, I found the F-106 the lightest and most responsive on the stick. When flown by a skilled pilot, it could be safely flown from the deck to 80,000 ft, from (in some circumstances) zero airspeed to Mach 2. One could fill a small book on the fine points of manoeuvring the airplane, the techniques that the 'book' doesn't tell you (the difference between case 14 and case 29 wings, etc.).

"It was an honest bird. Without visual or audio prompts/cues, the 'Six' provided outstanding feedback to the pilot. Following the 'pebbles-rocks-boulders-sudden quiet' progression of buffet, the pilot could 'feel' the angle-of-attack. This was important, as differential elevon deflection caused adverse yaw, away from the direction of the turn. This, in turn, could lead to violent departures from controlled flight at the stall, and, if proper recovery procedures were not initiated, to a multi-axis or a flat spin. Spins, except for the dreaded flat spin, were eminently recoverable, given sufficient altitude. The airplane responded well to judicious application of forward stick (negative angle-of-attack), and could actually be flown to zero airspeed in a vertical climb, tail slide backwards, and turned with the rudder while falling backwards.

"In air-to-air combat with another fighter, the 'Six', due to its low (38 psi) combat wing loading, exhibited quick turning, quick recovery of energy, and outstanding 'nose authority'. Nose authority allowed the pilot to employ lag manoeuvres to gain position to fire the AIM-4Gs directly at the tailpipe, then pull the nose into a lead position to employ the AIM-4Fs and/or the gun. The altitude capability the 'Six' enjoyed over other period fighters meant that we could comfortably CAP at 45,000+ ft, perform a pincer front-to-stern attack with the IRST (radar in STBY) and slide in behind a flight of F-4s, etc. without notice.

"The responsiveness of the airplane, its capabilities of turn, speed and altitude, and its honesty in feedback, were the seeds of a life-long love affair. The F-106 never surprised me, everything it ever did was what was expected, given the conditions of flight. I never fully 'departed' the airplane, as it always responded immediately to recovery controls. In my capacity of weapons/flight instructor, I taught many fledgling 'Six' pilots to trust the airplane at low airspeeds and in high angle-of-attack manoeuvring. There have been many comments about the F-106 being a forgiving airplane – I disagree. Many a ham-handed aviator has come to grief with the airplane. However, in the hands of a skilled pilot, a pilot who listened when the airplane spoke, it was a real thoroughbred and an absolute joy to fly.

"A characteristic of the delta wing was a loss of elevon effectiveness above Mach 1 due to the shift in the centre of pressure on the wing. This shift was the reason for the installation of the 't-tanks' (transfer tanks) which shifted the centre of gravity in supersonic flight. Early aircraft had to keep trimming the stick aft as Mach increased, so that at Mach 2 the stick was virtually full aft. The 't-tanks' gave full range of stick movement, but did not make the elevons more effective.

"The F-106, like the F-4, fought best at around 0.92 Mach. Turns in the transonic/supersonic regime were handled better by the F-4, but pilots were not trained to fight supersonic in dogfights. Further, each of the airplanes had 'transonic tuck' problems. The F-106 suffered abrupt increase of elevon effectiveness coming subsonic, and the F-4 suffered a similar problem due to increased stabilator effectiveness, particularly in the birds with slotted stabilators.

"On the subject of cockpits: the early F-106s had the F-102 scope and required the use of a light shield or 'muff' for daytime use; the green multi-mode storage tube (MMST) came later, and eliminated the need for the 'muff'. (As an aside, the F-106 flight simulators retained the F-102-type scope at the instructor's console, while the simulator cockpit itself had an MMST.) As regards automatic flight, the autopilot could be coupled to the automatic navigation system 'Auto Nav' which used pre-set TACANs, the way points and profiles stored in the computer or the ILS localiser and glidepath, or it could be coupled to the SAGE, Back Up Interceptor Control (BUIC), or AWACS datalink. The datalink used was tactical time-division datalink, or TDDL. We used AWACS TDDL until the end. However, the autopilot did not have any throttle control. Regardless of the automatic flight mode, the pilot had to provide the throttle inputs.

"In the discussions of F-106 overseas deployments, there were several 'demonstration' deployments in the 1970s, to the Canal Zone and to Germany, for example. The 'Six' was favoured by the State Department because (1) it had no advertised air-to-ground capability, (2) no-one could tell whether or not it was loaded, and (3) [it introduced] the shadow of nuclear capability. College Tap was very real. As an instructor at Tyndall, I was expected to maintain full combat status and proficiency, even so far as to have the ADCOM IG give us a full-scale operational readiness inspection (ORI) to prove the point.

"I think the thing that does not come across is how advanced the F-106 was, even at the end of its life. The radar power and reliability problems had been long since conquered; contact ranges were up 100 per cent from where they were when I started flying it. The IRST was continually upgraded with new electronically cooled sensors and computer programmes (IR Prop), boresight lock-on capabilities, and angle-ranging. The Snapshoot gun systems was arguably the best air-to-air sight going. New MA-1 capabilities included Target Velocity Vector (TVV) which allowed us to sample lock a target to get his speed altitude and heading, break lock, and use the MA-1's dead-reckoning to track the target on the radar screen, the TSD, and the HSI. We were the bane of the early F-15s as we were better versed in radar tactics and could get in on them using the foibles of their system against them. We owned the low-level arena, as the F-15s needed drop tanks to fight for any time at all, and we had the only supersonic tanks (i.e., we could go faster and farther), and we could run down and shoot F-111s, F-105Gs – you name it.

"Our biggest foible was the AIM-4. The contact fuse and the lack of a blast-fragmentation warhead (ours was blast-overpressure) left us out of the modern arena, when it was decided by General Creech not to rearm the 'Six'. (Incidentally, the AIM-4G had essentially the same all-aspect seeker as the AIM-9L, and as studies of air combat in SEA were to reveal, the AIM-4D with the same basic seeker, when fired within parameters, was the most lethal of the air-to-air missiles carried by US forces.)"

Lieutenant Colonel Michael K. ('Buddha') Nelson

Like all good interceptors, the F-106 had a phenomenal climb rate – 41,200 ft (12558 m) per minute at sea level. This was eclipsed by its British contemporary, the Lightning, at 50,000 ft (15240 m) per minute. With its extremely low wing-loading, however, the 'Six' had the edge in air combat manoeuvring. Comparative production was 339 Lightnings and 340 Delta Darts, with service careers spanning 1960-88 and 1959-88, respectively.

Above: In the latter days of the F-106, air combat manoeuvring became an important part of its repertoire. Seen returning from a 1985 ACM mission off Florida are 159th FIS Darts and VA-72 A-7Es from Cecil Field.

Below: A B-52G leads an echelon of 119th FIS F-106s. Since 1981, when this scene was captured, the parent commands of these aircraft (SAC and ADTAC) have merged into Air Combat Command, and the 'Six' has gone, as has the B-52G. The only real link to the present is the 119th FIS, still flying fighters (F-16Cs) at Atlantic City.

The YF-106C was the only version other than the A and B to actually reach the hardware stage. Its only differences from the F-106A were a 40-in (102-cm) nose radar dish and a 5-ft (1.52-m) nose extension. Two were built, but only one flew with these modifications. The static test airframe (above) was later returned to standard configuration.

prototype (58-0795) to ADC, the aircraft was flown in the speed range of 165 KCAS to 1.9 Mach and from -3 g to +7 g, with no change in hinge moment due to gun firing. Thereafter, 58-0795 stopped briefly at Peterson AFB, Colorado (adjacent to ADC headquarters) where General Agan and other officials could look at it before it proceeded to Tyndall for Category III trials. After ADC assumed this test flight effort from Convair, the gun-armed prototype flew 20 sorties, including 18 against a TDU-10B Dart target towed by an F-100 Super Sabre and two against a Martin MQM-13A (TM-76A) Mace surface-to-surface missile. Missions against the Mace were flown at 10,000 ft (3048 m) and at 370 KCAS. Prior to the firing pass, the Mace was accelerated to 500 KCAS and put into a 45° banked turn. The F-106 pilot shot it down easily with HEI (high-explosive incendiary) ammunition but the aircraft sustained dents and 'dings' when it flew through the Mace explosion.

Tests showed that the Vulcan gun vibrations did not harm the AIM-4F/G Super Falcon missiles. Four missiles were carried on the gun sorties, then fired without a hitch on a subsequent mission.

The initial Six Shooter F-106A also evaluated the clear-top canopy sometimes referred to (not quite accurately) as a 'bubble' canopy. The new design eliminated the metal strip above the pilot's head that corresponded to the centreline of the aircraft. The new canopy was made from a single piece of ¾-in (1.9-cm) cast acrylic Plexiglas formed to

extend over the top, with the sides bowed out at the pilot's head. The Plexiglas piece was designed to fit in the existing canopy structure, with the canopy edges reinforced by an Orlon cloth laminate. The canopy apparently was tested primarily on the second Six Shooter aircraft (59-0092), initially with an air speed restriction of Mach 1.5 and a height restriction of 25,000 ft (7620 m), both of which were later lifted. No canopy defog was provided. Six pilots made 23 flights with the new canopy and reported a 100 per cent increase in visibility. By the time the flight test effort was completed, on 19 September 1972, the 20-mm cannon was scheduled for some F-106s (those which also received vertical tape cockpit instruments) and the canopy for all.

Gun package

The gun system was installed as a package into an enclosure which supported it in the F-106 missile bay and provided an aerodynamic shield for the portion of the gun protruding below the missile bay. Taking into account considerations which ranged from internal wiring to service-life expectancy, the USAF decided to install the gun only on those F-106s with vertical tape instruments, alias the Integrated Instrument Display system. Aircraft with analog instruments, no gun and Genie armament continued to serve. Nearly two decades later, the last units to fly these models were ANG squadrons at Otis AFB, Massachusetts, and Great Falls, Montana. (The nuclear commitment with the Genie ended in 1985.)

Tactics were designed to catch cruise missile carriers (Soviet bombers) 600-800 miles (966-1287 km) from shore (ADC did not believe the air-to-air radar on the F-106 would detect a cruise missile after launch). The addition of the gun gave the F-106 a powerful weapon from any angle – from behind, it could probably match the 6,000-ft (18280-m) reach of a Soviet tail gun despite the obvious advantage the latter enjoyed by shooting backward – and especially when an attack could be mounted forward of the bomber's 'gun line'. F-106 pilots practised group attacks on 'Bisons' and 'Bears' with one Delta Dart each in the two o'clock and 10 o'clock positions. By 'stitching' (firing cannon bursts from the side), the F-106 pilots could rip asunder the hydraulics and control lines of a large Soviet bomber. This, of course, was not the first method of attack – Falcon missiles had a reach of up to about 10 miles (16 km) – but it added flexibility to the job of intercepting attackers. Ironically, this was to prove useful at a time when bombers were acquiring stand-off capability and greater stress was placed on catching them farther from target, but the gun's capability was never to be used in actual fighter-versus-fighter action.

As for Archibald's suggestion that the F-106 receive tactical camouflage, no Delta Dart was ever painted in the green/brown T.-O. 114 camouflage employed by tactical aircraft in Vietnam. Archibald may have turned down the idea after talking to an Army helicopter pilot, freshly home

Convair F-106A-CO-100 Delta Dart
159th FIS, Florida Air National Guard
Jacksonville, circa 1981

Planform

YF-106s had the same boundary-layer fences as the F-102A, but production aircraft had a slot in the leading edge which performed the same function more efficiently. Apart from this, the wing shape of the Delta Dart was virtually the same as that of the Delta Dagger. The most noticeable difference in plan view was the more streamlined fuselage and the movement of the intakes aftward to a position closer to the leading edge of the wing.

ADC career

58-0786 served for nearly 40 years with the USAF. Delivered to the 4750th Air Defense Wing at MacDill AFB on 26 October 1959, it moved within Florida on 5 June 1960 to the 73rd Air Division at Tyndall AFB. It served there until 26 May 1969 when it was assigned to the 94th FIS at Selfridge AFB, Michigan. In July 1971, it went to the 71st FIS at Malmstrom AFB, Montana. The 319th FIS inherited the 71st's aircraft at Malmstrom in April 1972. 58-0786's final regular ADC assignment was to the 460th FIS at Grand Forks North Dakota on 6 April 1972.

Unit history

The 159th FIS (today the 159th FS) can trace its lineage to the 352nd FS based at Raydon with P-47s and P-51s as part of the 353rd Fighter Group. In 1946, the squadron was redesignated as the 159th FS and allocated to the Florida ANG at Jacksonville, equipped with P-51Ds and, later, F-80Cs. As the 159th FBS, the squadron took part in the Korean War flying F-84Es. On return to the US and State control, the unit flew Mustangs (F-51D and H) and P-80Cs again before converting to the F-86D in 1956 and taking on the interceptor role. The first F-102As arrived in July 1960 and F-106As in mid-1974. The F-106 era lasted until 1987 when the squadron converted to the F-16A/B, which it flew until transitioning to the F-15A/B in the mid-1990s.

Performance

Due to its bigger engine (50 per cent more thrust) and more refined shape, the F-106A had a top speed almost twice that of the F-102A; 1,525 mph (2454 km/h) at 40,000 ft (12192 m) versus 825 mph (1328 km/h) at 36,000 ft (10793 m). In initial tests, however, the acceleration of the Dart left something to be desired, the aircraft taking 4.5 minutes at 57,000 ft (17374 m) to go from from Mach 1.0 to Mach 1.7 and a further 2.5 minutes to reach Mach 1.8. This was cured by revising the intake configuration, enlarging the frontal area and thinning the lips.

With the Guard and beyond

'786 became a 'Guardsman' on 7 June 1974 when It joined the 119th FIS, New Jersey ANG. At some point after this, it went to the159th FIS, Florida ANG, although the date is unclear. On 29 December 1986, it returned briefly to the New Jersey Guard, leaving it on 24 February 1987 for storage at AMARC. On 11 October 1991, it was accepted as a QF-106 at Holloman AFB. On 25 September 1997, after nine unmanned flights (and numerous manned ones), it was terminated from the drone programme due to a cracked no. 3 spar on the right wing.

The ultimate F-106 squadron was the 119th FIS from New Jersey. Here, a quartet of 'Jersey Devils' promenades above the Atlantic City boardwalk. In 1988, the 119th bowed to the inevitable and sent the last active F-106s to the 'boneyard' at Davis-Monthan.

from 'Nam, who complained of flying a "big brown bug in a big blue sky," thereby inviting considerable attention from the Viet Cong. According to Archibald, one ship was camouflaged in a light blue air-to-air camouflage scheme at Tyndall, where everyone said it looked 'too white' compared to the standard ADC scheme. In due course, it was determined that this paint scheme offered no advantages. No-one knew it at the time, but the improvements that were adopted – gun, clear-top canopy, air-refuelling capability, supersonic tanks – never did reach Vietnam, although they would prove useful farther north on the Asian continent.

The original gun test ship (58-0795) was subsequently tested with a variation of the AGM-78 Standard ARM (anti-radiation missile) under the right wing in the Spike programme, which involved early attempts to create an anti-satellite weapon.

On 31 August 1967, after nearly a decade in the 'Six' business, the USAF inactivated its first Delta Dart squadron, the 539th FIS at McGuire AFB, New Jersey.

Infra-red seeker

It was about this time that the F-101B Voodoo, F-102A Delta Dagger and F-106A Delta Dart acquired a Hughes IRST device on the nose centreline in front of the windshield. Unlike those on the Voodoo and Dagger, the F-106's IRST was retractable. The device was always vulnerable to temperature and weather conditions, and would home in on the outline of a thundercloud, but it did give pilots an extra tool to locate a heat source from another aircraft. Pilots regarded this capability as valuable in

a situation where the adversary was dumping chaff to foil air-to-air radar. The device was initially fussy to prepare for a flight, since it was serviced with liquid nitrogen; in time, this arrangement was replaced by a closed-cycle cooler that generated nitrogen.

During this period, the F-106, which had always had the option of carrying external wing tanks, acquired newly-designed underwing tanks, often referred to as 'supersonic tanks', that could be carried by the aircraft at any speed. These 360-US gal (1362-litre) tanks carried on pylons beneath the centre wing had fully 50 per cent greater fuel capacity than the less frequently-used 227-US gal (859-litre) external containers originally designed for the Delta Dart. The 'supersonic tanks' were jettisonable, but the capability was rarely used; they were carried on any mission except the shortest-ranged intercepts.

Together with the new tanks, the USAF retrofitted inflight-refuelling capability to all surviving F-106s by installing a slipway receptacle in the dorsal position behind the pilot. This idea pre-dated General Agan, Archibald's suggestions, and the *Pueblo* incident (see next paragraph). Some three years earlier, a feasibility study (initiated on 4 October 1965 and concluded on 30 November 1965) determined the ideal location for the receptacle (at the location known as 'Station 364') based on mating with a flying boom refuelling device extended at 30° by a KC-135 Stratotanker. The study was apparently primarily a paper exercise, although mating test flights and a 'simulated hook-up' were carried out with a KC-135 and an unmodified F-106B. The Delta Dart fleet did not actually equip with refuelling receptacles (installed at depot level) until 1967,

Right: To protect stored aircraft from moisture and dust, a protective coating called Spraylat was used. This F-106B was trialled with an overall coat of Spraylat. It was found to be more cost-effective (in application and removal) to seal only canopies and joints where foreign matter might find its way in.

To the 'boneyard'

As the F-106 was phased out of the ADC squadrons, and then the ANG, most, if not all, surviving aircraft found their way to the Aerospace Maintenance and Regeneration Center (AMARC – known as MASDC until 1985) at Davis-Monthan AFB in the Arizona desert. The first F-106, a 48th FIS aircraft, arrived for storage on 12 January 1982, and more than 100 were parked in open storage by the end of 1985 when the USAF announced Pacer Six, a programme to convert more than 200 aircraft to pilotless drone configuration. The first aircraft left the 'boneyard' for conversion by Tracor Flight Systems at Mojave in October 1986.

Right and far right: Retired F-106s await conversion to aerial targets at AMARC in July 1987. Ex-5th FIS Dart 59-002 (far right) became a QF-106 in February 1991 and was shot down at Tyndall the following March. 59-0102, ex-87th FIS (right), lasted until 2 July 1997 when it was claimed by an AIM-120.

B-1B chase

One of the last users of the F-106 was the Contract Management Division of Air Force Systems Command, which used seven Delta Darts (four As and three Bs) as chase aircraft for the Rockwell B-1B acceptance test programme out of Palmdale, California. They replaced Edwards AFB F-111s in this role from October 1986 until June 1990, accompanying every bomber built in this period on its pre-delivery flights, as well as acting as support for flights out of Tinker AFB, Oklahoma. When B-1B production ended, the Darts became QF-106 drones.

Above left: The colour scheme used on the B-1B chase programme aircraft changed several times. Initially, it was this simple marking on a red tail fin.

Above: A typical four-hour B-1B acceptance flight required two F-106s, which switched at the half-way mark.

Left: One of the three F-106Bs used awaits its fate as a drone.

when General Agan was pondering a contribution to the Vietnam War. 20 November 1967 marked the first air-to-air refuelling of the F-106 when the 318th FIS, McChord AFB, Washington deployed to Tyndall with 10 F-106s. No-one predicted that the F-106's war contribution would occur, instead, in Korea.

Crisis in Korea

At the very time when 200 Americans per week were returning from Vietnam in body bags, tensions were high in Korea. There, an attempt to assassinate South Korean President Park Chung-hee on 21 January 1968 was followed two days later by North Korea's seizure of the spy ship USS *Pueblo* (AGER-2). It was a difficult and embarrassing time for the US, which has always argued that it can fight two wars at once, but has never been able to do so: the only tactical air power in Korea consisted of F-4 Phantoms on nuclear alert, and they were unable to alter their operations quickly enough to 'cap' the *Pueblo*. Overnight, a massive build-up of US air power in Korea began, marking the first and only time the F-106 would be employed overseas for a sustained period of time.

Fortunately, in the months before the *Pueblo* fiasco, ADC had been planning to apply lessons learned in Alaska by developing the potential to deploy its interceptors to other locations in an emergency. The College Cadence plan was developed by ADC in the spring of 1967, under which a force of 24 F-106As (consisting of six aircraft each from the 71st, 94th, 95th and 318th FIS) was tasked to be ready for worldwide deployment. All the F-106s of these four squadrons were equipped with new supersonic fuel tanks and inflight-refuelling capability.

College Cadence F-106 deployments to Osan Air Base, south of Seoul, began with the arrival of 318th FIS Delta Darts on 18 February 1968 after they had staged through Naha, Okinawa a week earlier. For a time, it had seemed that a new invasion of South Korea was imminent, at the very time when Americans were battling through the Tet Offensive in Vietnam. The invasion did not take place and, in due course, the *Pueblo* crew was released in December 1968, but tensions remained high. North Korean MiG-17 'Fresco' fighters shot down a US Navy EC-121 Constellation on 15 April 1969, killing all 31 on board. So the F-106 role in Korea continued until 1 May 1970. Over 27 months, more than half a dozen ADC squadrons contributed aircraft and/or airmen to the Delta Dart presence in Korea. At times, the F-106s were apparently in the air within minutes' flying time of North Korea's MiG-17s and MiG-21s, although neither side's fighters crossed the line.

ADC had a number of contingency plans for other F-106 deployments abroad. College South was aimed at Cuba. College Green was intended to provide an air defence of Ballistic Missile Early Warning System radar sites in Greenland. College Tap, which applied to 18-24 aircraft

at Tyndall, would have 'tapped' F-106s assigned to training duties to serve as combat interceptors in an emergency. College Key was a different measure aimed at Cuba and involved planned deployments to Key West, Florida. None of these was ever put into effect.

There was renewed interest in the ageing F-106 at this juncture, in part because Korea had reinforced pilots' long-standing contention that the aircraft had excellent potential for fighter-versus-fighter combat. The manufacturer was interested in exploiting this, but was also pushing for a more advanced interceptor version. In 1968, Convair, by then a division of General Dynamics, suggested a version known on paper as the F-106X, a basic F-106 that would feature a new radome and a larger radar antenna. It would also receive a modified fire control system (providing a look-down capability) and a new air-to-air missile (with shoot-down capability). Some illustrations from the era depict an aircraft with canard surfaces just forward of the delta wing, and significantly revised air intakes. The F-106X was a competitor to the long-range Lockheed YF-12 interceptor (itself a close cousin of the SR-71 Blackbird) which ADC wanted but which posed unparalleled technical and financial challenges.

F-106E/F

Later that year (on 3 September 1968), Convair made a detailed proposal for an F-106E/F 'improved interceptor' that was less ambitious than the F-106X but still quite versatile. The company was looking at "the post-1972 ConUS [Continental United States] aerospace defence environment" with an F-106E/F "compatible with the airborne warning and control system (AWACS) and over-the-horizon (OTH) radar defence network." Improvements in the F-106E/F would have included look-down/shoot-down radar and missile launch capability, a two-way UHF voice and datalink radio, and both nuclear and non-nuclear missiles including the AIM-26 Nuclear Falcon and/or the AIM-47.

On 9 February 1968, Defense Secretary McNamara (then serving under President Johnson) overruled the USAF, killed plans for a purchase of Lockheed F-12A interceptors and announced that the F-106 would remain the premier interceptor for the defence of the US. McNamara's announcement gave new impetus to plans to upgrade and improve the fleet of existing F-106s and also bolstered General Dynamics' hopes of selling the advanced

Above: This line-up of (mostly ex-5th FIS) aircraft was seen at Holloman in late 1996. 58-0793 was one of the lucky few, being retired to AMARC in February 1998.

Below: Ground crew prepare a QF-106B for a flight at Tyndall. In the background is a QF-100, the type that bridged the gap between the Pacer Deuce (PQM-102) and Pacer Dart (QF-106) programmes.

Top: A (manned) QF-106B trundles to the end of the Holloman runway, followed by the Manned Mobile Van, which provided back-up to the main control system at a remote site.

QF-106 FSAT

The last large-scale use of the F-106 was as an unmanned target drone or Full-Scale Aerial Target (FSAT). Four batches – of 46, 48, 48 and 31 aircraft – were converted to QF-106 FSATs, making a total of 173 production (and two prototype) aircraft. The first pre-production QF-106 was delivered in September 1989 and the last aircraft in December 1994. Responsibility for operating the drones fell to the 82nd Tactical Aerial Targets Squadron (TATS), later Aerial Targets Squadron (ATS), part of the 475th Weapons Evaluation Group (WEG). The 82nd was based at Tyndall with a permanent detachment at Holloman AFB, New Mexico and, in addition to providing unpiloted targets for live weapons engagements, carried out a wide range of test work, approximately 90 per cent of QF-106 flights being 'under live local operation' (i.e., manned). QF-106 operations ceased at Holloman in February 1997. The last QF-106 was shot down there on 28 January 1998.

Above: QF-106As and Bs line up on 'death row' at Tyndall in 1992. The rudders reveal numerous previous owners, including a Contract Management Division B-1 chase aircraft. Today this ramp is filling with QF-4 Phantoms.

Far right: One of the last Delta Dart pilots, Lt Col Robert 'Buzz' Sawyer (Ret) climbs into a QF-106B. A contract pilot with Lockheed Martin, Sawyer has over 1,800 F-106 hours, most of it with ADC squadrons. The blue 'horn' on the fuselage is part of the Airborne Electronic Threat Simulator (AETS), which was added to some aircraft. The 'high hour' pilot of the F-106 was Lieutenant Colonel Charles ('Chuck') Townsend, who logged 4,410.6 hours between 1968 and 1988. No other pilot exceeded 4,000 hours in the Dart.

F-106X. This led, among other things, to an exhaustive study of an F-106 variant armed with the AIM-47 missile developed for the YF-12A. In the end, expectations of a 'new-build' F-106 of the 1970s proved in vain.

The first ANG recipient of the F-106 was the 186th FIS of the Montana ANG at Great Falls, which took delivery of its first two aircraft (57-2485 and 57-2487) on 3 April 1972. The unit also became the first ANG squadron to lose an F-106 (57-2520), in a mishap on 3 October 1972.

An unusual overseas deployment by the F-106 occurred on 21 April 1978 when the 87th FIS went to Keflavik, Iceland to stand guard until 13 May 1978.

Replacement and (temporary) retirement

By this time, the F-15A Eagle was appearing as a potential replacement for the F-106 (on 14 August 1981, the 48th FIS at Langley became the first F-106 unit to receive an F-15) and it was apparent that the 1980s was the final decade for the Delta Dart. The first F-106 to go to the USAF's 'boneyard' in Arizona – the Aerospace Mainte-nance and Regeneration Center at Davis-Monthan AFB, nominally a storage facility, but in a sense a grave – arrived on 12 January 1982. The ex-48th FIS F-106A (59-0116) was assigned storage number FN001 – the first of many.

Another sign of the impending end was the final participation of the F-106 in the semi-annual William Tell gunnery competition, when the 119th FIS (New Jersey ANG) took part during 2-27 October 1984.

The end of the line came, finally, when the last three F-106s departed the Atlantic City-based 119th FIS on 1 August 1988. Many Delta Dart airframes were still far short of the 10,000 flight-hour lifetime that was official policy at this time (originally, the projected lifetime had been a mere 3,300 hours), but there was no longer a place for them in the interceptor world, by now populated with F-4 Phantoms and, soon, F-15 Eagles and F-16 Fighting Falcons. The F-106 story was not quite over, however, for there lay ahead duty as a chase aircraft, as an unpiloted

target drone, and ultimately as a towed stand-in for a future space vehicle.

In 1986, Flight Systems, Inc. (later Honeywell) began the Pacer Six programme to convert 194 F-106s stored at Davis-Monthan into target drones to replace the QF-100D/F Super Sabre and PQM-102 Delta Dagger. Initial work took place at Mojave, California and the first flight of a QF-106A occurred in July 1987. Following the completion of an initial batch of 10 QF-106As in 1990, responsibility for major portions of the work was shifted to the USAF itself. This was performed before the aircraft were removed from storage at the AMARC; further work was undertaken in East St Louis, Illinois. Commencement

of conversion of the 11th and subsequent aircraft was delayed from May 1991 to September 1991 by technical problems, then proceeded smoothly.

In late 1991, the QF-106A began operating as the USAF's FSAT (full-scale aerial target), first at the White Sands Missile Range, New Mexico and thereafter at the Eglin Gulf Test Range, Florida (based at Holloman and Tyndall). The 82nd Tactical Aerial Targets Squadron at Tyndall (with a detachment at Holloman) was the operator of the QF-106A, which was deemed better able to simulate an enemy aircraft for air-to-air missile engagements because of its higher speed and greater manoeuvrability.

As with earlier FSATs, a typical mission employed the QF-106A as a target for an air-to-air test of an infra-red missile and was flown 'nullo' (not under live local operation). The QF-106A was controlled by ground operators. The intention was for the QF-106A target drone to survive repeated engagements with air-to-air missiles. The QF-106A could, of course, be flown with a pilot aboard.

The delta wing of the QF-106A made it impossible for the aircraft to the employ wingtip propane burners used on earlier drones to create an IR source for heat-seeking missiles. The burners were placed on pylons located beneath the wing and rather far forward. This proved less than fully satisfactory, in part because in most test-range missile engagements the missile is fired down at the target.

The Holloman detachment alone flew more than 300 nullo QF-106 missions. Typical was 1996 when, of 367 missions flown at Holloman, 40 were unmanned and 14 drones were actually shot down at nearby White Sands. The final shoot-down of a Convair QF-106 Delta Dart drone at Holloman occurred on 20 February 1997. Det 1 of the 82nd ATS flew the terminal mission. The aircraft was a QF-106B (serial 57-2524). The mission was an IR countermeasures effort and the aircraft was shot down over the nearby White Sands Missile Range by a Russian-made SA-18 'Grouse' (9K-38 Igla) operated by the US Army. The last Tyndall-based drone flew the last nullo mission on 28 January 1998. QF-106A 59-0051 clung tenaciously to life – hit by an AIM-120 AMRAAM, it staggered on, and survived hits from 20-mm cannon. Finally it was brought down by an AIM-9M Sidewinder, thus effectively ending 39 years of unit-strength USAF operations with the Delta Dart. Today, the QF-106 has been replaced by QF-4 Phantom drones.

Delta dragger

The final mission assigned to the F-106 Delta Dart was to participate in Project Eclipse, a joint project of NASA and the USAF at Edwards. Using the final flyable QF-106A (59-0130), with a second aircraft (59-0010) as a back-up, the programme demonstrated technology for an RLV (reusable launch vehicle) to carry payloads into orbit. The F-106 was towed aloft by a NC-141A StarLifter (61-2775) belonging to the Air Force Flight Test Center's 418th Flight Test Squadron. The mechanism used to pull the QF-106A (designated EXD-1 during these tests, for Experimental Demonstrator) was a synthetic rope made of Vectran attached to a breakable link which, for safety reasons, was designed to snap if too much stress was placed on it. Nylon straps were attached, which were designed to help the spring tendencies of the link. The actual tow exercise was preceded by a test flight in which a NASA F/A-18 Hornet flew at various distances and angles behind the NC-141A to determine turbulence and collect wingtip vortex data. A similar flight followed with an unmodified QF-106A in July 1997.

The first towed flight in the Eclipse tests was made on 20 December 1997 and the tests continued until the final one on 6 February 1998, when the towed 'Six' (59-0130) was taken to an altitude of 24,684 ft (7524 m) with pilot Mark Stucky on board. (Kelly Space Technologies plans eventually to use a Boeing 747 to tow an RLV called the Astroliner to 45,000 ft/13176 m, where the Astroliner will ignite its rocket engine and achieve escape velocity, permitting a flight into orbit.) This marked the last time a Convair F-106 Delta Dart was flown for any reason than to enter retirement at the 'boneyard'. On 1 May 1998 this last flying F-106 made its final flight – from Edwards to the AMARC – and Mark Stucky made a few farewell passes over the base prior to going on his way. The NC-141A was also retired from service following the Eclipse tests.

As for the aircraft themselves, in 1998 there are 10 in museum collections and at least 21 in storage at Davis-Monthan. Many of the AMARC aircraft will probably be offered to museums, but there is a chance a civilian contractor might find a use for some. As a potential warbird, the F-106 offers fewer challenges than the English Electric Lightning, which now has provisional approval to fly in the US, but whether any operator has the enthusiasm (or money) to campaign a 'Six' on the warbird circuit is not known. If the story ends in 1998 with Project Eclipse, it is fitting that the 'ultimate interceptor', the 'plane with a brain' should crown its career by helping the next generation of spacecraft reach even higher. **Robert F. Dorr**

Above: The last (to date) and perhaps most extraordinary use of the F-106 has been as a demonstrator for the Eclipse Astroliner delta-winged reusable satellite launch platform. To validate the concept of towing a delta-winged platform to high altitudes, an ex-5th FIS QF-106 was modified for towing behind a Lockheed StarLifter at Edwards AFB. After eight towed flights in 1997/98, the two aircraft involved were flown to AMARC for storage and an unknown fate.

Above left: A second QF-106A (59-0010, also ex-5th FIS) was used by NASA Dryden as a back-up for the Eclipse project and as a crew proficiency trainer. It is seen in the hangar at Dryden a few days before it was flown for the last time – to AMARC.

Below: The last Delta Dart has now fallen silent, probably for the final time. The company that made it merged into one that no longer makes aircraft, and the fighter interceptor squadrons, too, are but a memory. Although it never fought an enemy aircraft and was built in the smallest numbers of any of the 'Century Series' fighters, the F-106 will always be remembered by pilots and enthusiasts alike as the 'ultimate interceptor'.

Left: The J85 pods fitted beneath the wings of NASA 616 are clearly visible in this view of the aircraft.

Right: B model 59-0158 provides the background for this portrait of the seven Mercury astronauts: (from left) Carpenter, Cooper, Glenn, Grissom, Schirra, Shepard and Slayton.

NASA's Dart test fleet

Though not as easily recognised as a NASA workhorse as its other 'Century Series' stablemate, the F-104, the Convair F-106 did indeed serve at most NASA centres in a wide variety of tasks – astronaut trainer, SST testbed, environmental programmes and space launch concepts, to name a few.

Astronaut Trainers

In the autumn of 1958 the Space Task Group (STG) was established at NASA Langley to implement the Project Mercury manned space flight programme. A small fleet of flight proficiency aircraft was assigned to the STG, initially consisting of USAF-loaned T-33s, two F-102A and two TF-102A. In 1961, F-106A 58-0782 and F-106B 59-0158 arrived at Langley. When the STG was renamed the Manned Spacecraft Center and moved to Houston in early 1962, these aircraft were relocated to nearby Ellington AFB, and the nucleus of NASA's future independent astronaut training fleet was formed. Astronauts would later fly F-106 chase missions from Patrick AFB, Florida in support of Mercury space launches at nearby Cape Canaveral.

Shortly thereafter, the USAF began formulating an astronaut training programme of its own. In July 1963 the Aerospace Research Pilots School (ARPS) at Edwards AFB, California modified its curriculum to increase its pool of candidates eligible for astronaut training on future NASA and military space programmes such as the X-15, X-20 Dyna-Soar and the all-USAF Gemini (later renamed the Manned Orbiting Lab). A number of dedicated aircraft were thus added, including one JF-106A (57-0238) to study variable lift-drag ratios (written-off, 6 Dec 1965), and two F-106Bs (57-2519 and 57-2529) to investigate variable stability. In 1968 X-24 side-stick controllers were added to the F-106Bs by Martin Aircraft but technical problems plagued the programme and little flying was done in this capacity. They were finally retired in October 1971.

NASA Ames F-106A 57-0235

In the 1950s the NACA (later NASA) Ames Flight Research Branch, at Moffett Field, was conducting work on automatic control systems for aircraft; a fairly large part of this effort involving the optimisation of missile guidance systems, computing gunsights for fighters and semi-automatic missile fire-control systems for interceptors. Between September 1958 and December 1959, F-106A 57-0235 arrived at Ames for MA-1 fire control system and autopilot manoeuvre intercept tests, often using a B-47 or Douglas F5D-1 as targets.

NASA Lewis NF-106B 57-2516/NASA 616

The most distinguished Delta Dart, F-106B 57-2516, spent its entire

Above: NF-106B NASA 816 is seen here with the vortex flaps installed during the late 1980s.

Below: This remarkable photograph shows NASA 816, in its later guise as a storm research airframe, experiencing one of the over 700 lightning strikes on the aircraft.

career as a test vehicle for a series of important USAF and NASA research projects. It was completed on 4 September 1958 and delivered to NASA's Lewis Research Center, Cleveland, Ohio on 31 October 1966, and registered NASA 616. On 31 May 1967 it was redesignated NF-106B, and finally withdrawn from the USAF inventory on 27 February 1970.

As part of a broad research effort in air-breathing propulsion, and in support of the US Supersonic Transport Program, the Lewis Research Center had begun studies in the mid-1960s on the effects of airframe flow on the performance of propulsion systems in the high subsonic and supersonic flight regimes. In order to further study installation effects in this flight envelope, as well as noise suppression in engine inlet and nozzle configurations, F-106B 57-2516 was acquired and modified to serve as a testbed. The F-106B was an ideal choice, since its delta wing planform was representative of those proposed for SSTs, and its excellent performance, high load-carrying capacity, and provision for a second crew member allowed monitoring and operation of test installations.

The most notable modification made to NASA 616 was the installation of two underwing nacelles, each housing a J85-GE-13 afterburning turbojet which served as the gas generator for the test inlets and nozzles.

The first flight of NASA 616 modified for propulsion system research took place on 3 June 1968, in a programme that encompassed over 300 flights and tested numerous inlet and nozzle configurations. Flights were made from Cleveland Hopkins Airport or Selfridge ANGB, Michigan using test corridors over Lake Erie or Lake Huron.

Chase support for this programme was provided by F-8A 141354/NASA 666. After it was lost in July 1969, it was replaced by F-102A 56-998/NASA 617 in June 1970 and, in September 1972, by NF-106B NASA 607 (see separate entry below).

At the conclusion of this programme at Lewis, NASA 616 was turned over to the NASA Dryden Flight Research Center and redesignated NASA 816. Research needs, however, resulted in it being transferred directly to the NASA Langley Research Center, Virginia on 29 January 1979.

NASA Lewis NF-106B 57-2507/NASA 607

On 26 September 1972, a second NF-106B (NASA 607) was added to the Lewis fleet, initially to provide chase support for NASA 616, but also used to support a number of other research programmes. Much of its USAF career had been spent as an ejection seat test aircraft with the AFFTC. Its first association with NASA was in connection with the final qualification tests for the Gemini spacesuit and spacecraft escape system designed by Weber. Following a static compatibility test on 15 October 1964, a subsonic ejection was conducted at El Centro on 12 January 1965 at Mach 0.65 and 15,700 ft (4785 m) altitude. Two weeks later a supersonic ejection was conducted at Mach 1.72 and 40,000 ft (12192 m), thus clearing the seat for the first manned Gemini mission on 23 March 1965.

At Lewis, NASA 607 was assigned to chase duties in support of the NF-106B SST testbed, NASA 616. It proved to be a versatile platform for a number of other research programmes, also, flown intermittently in this capacity until its transfer to Langley on 12 May 1981.

Starting in October 1974, NASA 607 took over a solar cell calibration task from Lewis's B-57B NASA 237 and later, as part of the Global Air Sampling Program (GASP), 607 was fitted with air sampling pods on each wing pylon. Between April and May 1977, NASA 607 was deployed for a 10-day GASP mission to Elmendorf AFB, Alaska. The last notable mission was flown to gather volcanic aerosols and ash in the wake of the eruption of Mount St Helens on 18 May 1980.

Under a separate environmental study, an ocean colour scanner was mounted on a wing pylon and used to monitor water quality and pollution levels in the Great Lakes and Lake Okeechobee, Florida (operating out of Patrick AFB). These missions were flown at altitudes below 1,000 ft (305 m). A test observer in the back seat gathered data for later correlation with samples taken from a surface vessel. At the end of its usefulness at Lewis, NASA 607 unfortunately met with a different fate as NASA 816. It was transferred to NASA Langley on 12 May 1981, where it was unceremoniously cut in half lengthways (as the 'F-53') and used in wind-tunnel tests.

NASA Langley NF-106B 57-2516/NASA 816

Following its arrival from Lewis on 29 January 1979, NF-106B NASA 816 was readied for the first of two major research programmes at Langley – Storm Hazards Research and Vortex Flap Research. F-106A 59-123 arrived at Langley on 19 March 1982 to provide spares for 816.

Storm Hazards Research 1979-1986: With the increased use of composite materials in aircraft construction, digital avionics, and electronic flight control systems came increased concerns over lightning protection for such features. To address these issues, NASA Langley initiated the Storm Hazards Research programme, for which NF-106B NASA 816 was prepared and 'hardened' against the effects of lightning. The majority of thunderstorm research flights were conducted in the vicinity of NASA Langley and the NASA Wallops Island Flight Facility, Virginia. Initial research flights in 1980 and 1981 were made in the vicinity of the National Oceans and Atmospheric Administration (NOAA) National Severe Storms Laboratory, Norman, Oklahoma.

During 195 Storm Hazards research flights, NASA 816 made 1,496 thunderstorm penetrations at altitudes ranging from 5,000-50,000 ft (1524-15240 m) and experienced 714 direct lightning strikes. The airborne data that was gathered provided the first verification that aircraft frequently trigger their own lightning strikes.

During the course of the Storm Hazards Program, NASA and the USAF Weapons Lab at Kirtland AFB, New Mexico conducted joint tests to compare the electromagnetic effects of lightning with those generated by nuclear detonations. A simulated electromagnetic pulse (EMP) test was conducted between January and March 1984 by mounting NASA 816 on a special dielectric test stand.

Vortex Flap Flight Experiment 1986-1991: Aircraft designed to cruise efficiently at supersonic speeds usually employ highly swept wings with relatively sharp leading edges which, under certain off-design conditions, produce strong vortices over the upper surfaces which increase lift but also increase drag. A special flap was developed at Langley to entrain the vortex spanways along the leading edge, thereby resulting in a significant improvement in lift-to-drag ratio. Verification of performance improvements provided by this 'vortex flap' required flight testing. Because its highly swept wing was representative of those that might employ a vortex flap, the F-106B was selected as the test vehicle.

Having just completed the Storm Hazards Program, NASA 816 was readied for this experiment and received modifications to evaluate a sharp, leading-edge vortex flap by gathering wing surface pressure distributions and flow visualisation data. Flight tests of the unmodified NF-106B were conducted in 1987 to establish a performance baseline. The wing leading edges were then removed and replaced with new leading edges incorporating ground-adjustable vortex flaps. The right wing was instrumented with pressure straps to measure surface pressures; the left wing was instrumented with accelerometers and strain gauges to monitor structural loads and deformations.

The first flight with the vortex flap took place on 2 August 1988. In all, 93 flights were conducted over the next two-and-a-half years, after which NASA 816 was ceremoniously retired on 17 May 1991 and the last manned F-106 passed from active service, except for a handful of QF-106s which continued to fly as target drones. NASA 816 was placed on permanent display along with other historic NASA and USAF aircraft in the Virginia Air and Space Center/Hampton Roads History Center.

NASA Dryden QF-106A/EXD-01 59-0130

In 1996 the NASA Dryden Flight Research Center began hosting Project Eclipse in support of a joint Kelly Space & Technology, Inc. (KST) and USAF project to tow in flight a modified F-106 using a C-141A. Data gathered would demonstrate the viability of towing delta-wing aircraft with high wing loading, validate simulation models, and develop operational and abort procedures. KST would use this data to develop its Eclipse family of low-cost, reusable tow-launch space vehicles.

The F-106 was an ideal candidate since its delta wing planform was representative of the Eclipse vehicles. Two aircraft were bailed from the USAF 475th WEG target drone inventory and delivered to NASA Dryden in the spring of 1997. QF-106 59-0130 was modified into the Eclipse eXperimental Demonstrator-01 by KST, and a second aircraft, 59-0010, served as a back-up and pilot proficiency aircraft.

Wake turbulence assessments and air data calibrations were conducted between the QF-106 and NC-141 between October 1996 and July 1997 as a prelude to the tow tests. On 20 December 1997 the two aircraft were staged on the Edwards runway and were prepared for their first tethered test flight. As a flight safety contingency, NASA Dryden research pilot Mark Stucky idled the J75 to 60 per cent thrust to facilitate rapid spool-up to full power if the need arose for a breakaway manoeuvre.

The tow train accelerated down the runway and, at 120 kt (138 mph; 222 km/h) airspeed, the StarLifter rotated and levelled off at 300 ft (91 m) to ensure that the QF-106 in tow stayed clear of any wake turbulence. Thirty seconds later Stucky rotated and took-off at 170 kt (195 mph; 315 km/h) for a smooth and uneventful climb to 10,000 ft (3048 m). Removal of the clamshell cargo doors on the C-141 imposed a tow speed limit of 200 kt (230 mph; 370 km/h). Throughout the flight, Stucky flew in a high-drag configuration with landing gear and speed brakes extended while maintaining a 'low tow' position at -20° elevation angle. A series of manoeuvres into the C-141 wake and vortex field was conducted and tow rope dynamics were investigated. The tow flight was concluded when Stucky released the rope, completed engine power-up and conducted an off-tow manoeuvre to clear the rope. The 18-minute test flight concluded with a normal landing at Edwards AFB. Three more tests were conducted on 21, 23 and 28 January 1998 and on 5 and 6 February, respectively, the two QF-106s were flown into storage at AMARC, ending NASA's nearly 40-year association with the type. **Terry Panopalis**

F-106 PRODUCTION

Here the USAF serial numbers, production line numbers, delivery dates and ultimate fates of all 340 F-106s are listed. Those aircraft marked '§' were still present at AMARC in early June 1998.

F-106As

56-0451	1	Dec 56	23 Mar 60	displayed, Selfridge AFB Museum (as '59-0082')
56-0452	2	Feb 57		not accepted by ADC; ground trainer, Amarillo AFB
n/a	n/a	Sep 57	?	? (static test airframe)
56-0453	3	Aug 57	27 Jan 95	to QF-106 (AD111); crashed, Holloman AFB
56-0454	11	Nov 57	4 Jun 96	QF-106 (AD102); cannibalised for parts, Holloman AFB
56-0455	4	Nov 57	16 May 67	written-off AFSC
56-0456	5	Oct 57	14 Jun 65	crashed on take-off 498th FIS
56-0457	14	Apr 58	13 Nov 91	QF-106 (AD116); shot down with AIM-7M, Tyndall AFB
56-0458	6	Nov 57	6 Sep 95	QF-106 (AD230); shot down with AIM-9M, Tyndall AFB
56-0459	7	Dec 57	?	displayed, McChord AFB
56-0460	8	Jan 58	?	displayed, Minot AFB
56-0461	9	Jan 58	2 Apr 85	AMARC§
56-0462	10	Mar 58	6 Jun 75	crashed 48th FIS
56-0463	12	Apr 58	21 Nov 95	QF-106 (AD235); shot down with 'ADP-1020', Holloman AFB
56-0464	15	Apr 58	4 Aug 64	crashed 318th FIS
56-0465	16	May 58	9 Nov 92	QF-106 (AD149); shot down with AIM-120, Holloman AFB
56-0466	17	May 58	12 Feb 97	QF-106 (AD247); shot down with AIM-120, Tyndall AFB
56-0467	18	Apr 58	14 Aug 61	crashed 329th FIS
57-0229	19	Jun 58	8 Apr 59	crashed AFSC
57-0230	20	May 58	1 Feb 85	written-off 87th FIS; displayed, Homestead AFB
57-0231	22	May 58	28 May 81	crashed 87th FIS
57-0232	23	May 58	12 Jun 92	QF-106 (AD151); crashed, Holloman AFB
57-0233	25	Jun 58	12 Apr 63	(Matador SSM kill, 1960); written-off 94th FIS.
57-0234	26	Jun 58	25 Oct 95	QF-106 (AD175); shot down with AIM-120, Tyndall AFB
57-0235	28	Jul 58	16 Nov 94	QF-106 (AD239); shot down with AIM-7M, Tyndall AFB
57-0236	30	Jul 58	29 Jan 97	QF-106 (AD248); shot down with AIM-120, Tyndall AFB
57-0237	32	Aug 58	8 May 74	crashed 5th FIS
57-0238	34	Aug 58	6 Dec 65	never assigned to ADC; crashed AFFTC
57-0239	36	Nov 58	4 Apr 60	YF-106C; destroyed in fatigue testing
57-0240	38	Dec 58	2 Dec 93	YF-106C; later QF-106 (AD251); shot down with AIM-9P, Tyndall AFB
57-0241	40	Oct 58	8 May 96	QF-106 (AD240); shot down with AIM-120, Tyndall AFB
57-0242	42	Nov 58	27 Oct 58	crashed AFFTC (Convair aircraft)
57-0243	43	Nov 58	10 Mar 93	QF-106 (AD114); shot down with AIM-7M, Tyndall AFB
57-0244	44	Nov 58	25 Apr 95	QF-106 (AD232); crash landing, Tyndall AFB
57-0245	45	Nov 58	17 Oct 91	QF-106 (AD117); shot down with AIM-120, Tyndall AFB
57-0246	46	Jan 59	29 Jun 93	QF-106 (AD161); ran off droneway, Tyndall AFB
57-2453	47	Feb 59	12 Dec 96	QF-106 (AD198); shot down with Patriot, Holloman AFB
57-2454	48	Feb 59	26 Jul 64	crashed 539th FIS
57-2455	49	Feb 59	2 Jun 93	QF-106 (AD214); shot down with AIM-7M, Tyndall AFB
57-2456	51	Mar 59	21 Jul 94	QF-106 (AD189); shot down with AIM-7M, Tyndall AFB
57-2457	52	Mar 59	22 Apr 69	crashed 460th FIS
57-2458	54	Mar 59	3 Sep 79	crashed 186th FIS
57-2459	55	Apr 59	4 Jun 96	QF-106 (AD103); cannibalised for spares, Holloman AFB
57-2460	56	Apr 59	9 Jun 79	crashed 186th FIS
57-2461	58	Apr 59	17 Apr 96	QF-106 (AD190); shot down with AIM-120, Tyndall AFB
57-2462	59	Apr 59	21 Dec 61	crashed 498th FIS
57-2463	61	Apr 59	6 May 94	QF-106 (AD193); crash landing, Tyndall AFB
57-2464	62	Apr 59	30 Jun 84	destroyed 186th FIS
57-2465	64	Jun 59	9 Jan 98	prototype ARDC instrument test aircraft; QF-106 (AD132); command destroyed, Tyndall AFB
57-2466	66	Apr 59	26 May 94	QF-106 (AD210); shot down with AIM-120, Holloman AFB
57-2467	67	May 59	9 Aug 96	QF-106 (AD209); shot down with ? (Army), Holloman AFB
57-2468	68	May 59	20 Jul 64	destroyed by fire 539th FIS
57-2469	70	May 59	7 Dec 67	crashed 456th FIS
57-2470	71	May 59	1 Feb 94	QF-106 (AD206); shot down with AIM-120, Holloman AFB
57-2471	72	May 59	4 May 65	destroyed in mid-air collision (57-2828) 539th FIS
57-2472	74	May 59	19 Jun 69	crashed 95th FIS
57-2473	75	May 59	6 Jun 83	crashed 101st FIS
57-2474	76	May 59	9 Jun 61	crashed 539th FIS
57-2475	78	Jun 59	9 Oct 96	QF-106 (AD203); control lost/command destroyed, Holloman AFB
57-2476	79	Jun 59	14 Sep 93	QF-106 (AD196); shot down with AIM-120, Tyndall AFB
57-2477	80	Jun 59	24 Apr 96	QF-106 (AD212); shot down with 20-mm fire, Tyndall AFB

F-106A 59-0047 was flown 'hands-off' between Palmdale and Jacksonville on 30 March 1960, using its Hughes MA-1 navigation/fire control system. Here it is seen, some years later, in the markings of the 95th FIS.

59-0043 was not only the ANG's last serving F-106, but went on to be one of the last two QF-106s. It was flown to AMARC in March 1998.

57-2478	81	Jun 59	22 Jun 95	QF-106 (AD195); shot down with AIM-120, Holloman AFB
57-2479	83	Jun 59	4 Feb 63	crashed 498th FIS
57-2480	84	Jun 59	2 Sep 94	QF-106 (AD211); shot down with AIM-120, Tyndall AFB
57-2481	85	Jun 59	25 Jul 95	QF-106 (AD185); shot down with AIM-120, Tyndall AFB
57-2482	86	Jul 59	20 Aug 96	QF-106 (AD191); shot down with AIM-7M, Tyndall AFB
57-2483	87	Jul 59	18 Dec 92	QF-106 (AD197); shot down with AIM-120, Tyndall AFB
57-2484	89	Jul 59	14 Sep 61	crashed 498th FIS
57-2485	90	Jul 59	26 Apr 93	QF-106 (AD192); written-off (broken wing spar), Tyndall AFB.
57-2486	91	Jul 59	14 Dec 72	crashed 186th FIS
57-2487	92	Jul 59	1 Mar 96	QF-106 (AD188); shot down with AIM-7M, Tyndall AFB
57-2488	93	Jul 59	10 Mar 61	destroyed 498th FIS
57-2489	94	Jul 59	19 Mar 63	crashed 456th FIS
57-2490	96	Jul 59	19 May 63	QF-106 (AD163); shot down with AIM-120, Tyndall AFB
57-2491	97	Jul 59	11 Jul 73	crashed 186th FIS
57-2492	98	Jul 59	20 Aug 97	QF-106 (AD199); shot down with AIM-120, Tyndall AFB
57-2493	99	Jul 59	10 Nov 94	QF-106 (AD208); shot down with 'ADP-1020', Holloman AFB
57-2494	100	Jul 59	27 Aug 96	QF-106 (AD200); shot down with Stinger, Holloman AFB
57-2495	101	Jul 59	2 Aug 94	QF-106 (AD165); crashed on take-off, Tyndall AFB
57-2496	103	Aug 59	8 May 96	QF-106 (AD186); inadvertently destroyed over range, Tyndall AFB
57-2497	104	Aug 59	21 Jan 93	QF-106 (AD194); shot down with AIM-120, Tyndall AFB
57-2498	105	Aug 59	5 May 64	crashed 95th FIS
57-2499	106	Aug 59	10 Jan 95	QF-106 (AD202); shot down with 'ADP-1020', Holloman AFB
57-2500	107	Aug 59	8 Jan 70	crashed 95th FIS (Osan AB)
57-2501	108	Aug 59	14 Aug 96	QF-106 (AD253); shot down with AIM-7M, Tyndall AFB
57-2502	110	Aug 59	29 Sep 70	Convair San Diego from 95th FIS; written-off in fatigue testing
57-2503	111	Aug 59	2 Apr 97	QF-106 (AD213); shot down with AIM-120, Tyndall AFB
57-2504	112	Aug 59	12 Aug 96	QF-106 (AD205); shot down with ? (Army), Holloman AFB
57-2505	113	Aug 59	28 Jul 93	QF-106 (AD204); shot down with AIM-7M, Tyndall AFB
57-2506	114	Aug 59	2 Aug 93	QF-106 (AD207); command destroyed (fatigue cracks), Tyndall AFB
58-0759	115	Aug 59	11 Apr 67	crashed 71st FIS
58-0760	117	Aug 59	2 Mar 93	QF-106 (AD136); shot down with AIM-7M, Tyndall AFB
58-0761	118	Aug 59	9 Jan 63	destroyed by fire 71st FIS
58-0762	119	Sep 59	30 Sep 59	crashed before delivery
58-0763	120	Sep 59	8 Jan 63	destroyed by fire 71st FIS
58-0764	121	Sep 59	19 Sep 94	QF-106 (AD179); shot down with AIM-120, Tyndall AFB
58-0765	122	Sep 59	18 Jan 71	crashed 48th FIS
58-0766	124	Sep 59	1 Feb 94	QF-106 (AD129); shot down with AIM-120, Tyndall AFB
58-0767	125	Sep 59	26 Aug 94	QF-106 (AD229); went out of control and crashed, Tyndall AFB
58-0768	126	Sep 59	2 Sep 69	crashed 94th FIS
58-0769	127	Sep 59	10 Mar 66	crashed after mid-air collision (T-33) 318th FIS
58-0770	128	Sep 59	9 Jan 61	crashed 71st FIS
58-0771	129	Sep 59	8 Jan 62	destroyed 71st FIS
58-0772	131	Sep 59	26 Sep 91	QF-106 (AD120); shot down with AIM-7M, Tyndall AFB
58-0773	132	Sep 59	13 Dec 95	QF-106 (AD234); shot down with 'ADP-1020', Holloman AFB
58-0774	133	Sep 59	4 Mar 98	QF-106 (AD146); AMARC§ after making last QF flight, Tyndall AFB
58-0775	134	Sep 59	20 Oct 92	QF-106 (AD138); shot down with AIM-120, Holloman AFB
58-0776	135	Oct 59	29 Aug 80	crashed 318th FIS
58-0777	136	Oct 59	18 Jul 79	crashed 194th FIS
58-0778	138	Oct 59	9 Jul 81	crashed ADWC
58-0779	139	Oct 59	9 Jan 98	QF-106 (AD141); shot down with AIM-9M, Tyndall AFB
58-0780	140	Oct 59	9 Mar 93	QF-106 (AD166); shot down with AIM-7M, Holloman AFB
58-0781	141	Oct 59	5 Apr 77	crashed 159th FIS
58-0782	142	Oct 59	13 Jul 93	QF-106 (AD147); shot down with AIM-120, Tyndall AFB
58-0783	143	Oct 59	21 Feb 92	QF-106 (AD108); shot down with AIM-120, Tyndall AFB
58-0784	145	Oct 59	3 Oct 86	crashed 159th FIS
58-0785	146	Oct 59	7 Feb 77	crashed 159th FIS
58-0786	147	Oct 59	25 Sep 97	QF-106 (AD154); written-off (cracked wing spar), Tyndall AFB
58-0787	148	Oct 59	15 Aug 86	to USAF Museum
58-0788	149	Oct 59	24 Sep 92	QF-106 (AD150); shot down with Patriot, Holloman AFB
58-0789	151	Oct 59	17 Mar 66	crashed 27th FIS
58-0790	152	Oct 59	30 Nov 93	QF-106 (AD228); ran off runway, Tyndall AFB
58-0791	153	Nov 59	10 Dec 97	QF-106 (AD121); shot down with AIM-120, Tyndall AFB
58-0792	154	Nov 59	26 Aug 93	QF-106 (AD153); command destroyed after lightning strike and flame out, Tyndall AFB
58-0793	155	Nov 59	23 Feb 98	QF-106 (AD242); AMARC§
58-0794	156	Nov 59	4 Nov 64	crashed 94th FIS
58-0795	158	Nov 59	11 May 94	QF-106 (AD180); shot down with AIM-7M, Tyndall AFB
58-0796	159	Nov 59	13 Aug 61	written-off 94th FIS
58-0797	160	Nov 59	20 Feb 90	QF-106 (AD104); shot down with AIM-7F, Tyndall AFB
58-0798	161	Nov 59	13 Jun 66	crashed 94th FIS
59-0001	162	Nov 59	12 Oct 66	crashed 5th FIS
59-0002	163	Nov 59	27 Mar 92	QF-106 (AD113); shot down with AIM-7M, Tyndall AFB
59-0003	165	Nov 59	24 Jan 85	AMARC; later Pima Air and Space Museum
59-0004	166	Nov 59	24 Jun 80	crashed 318th FIS
59-0005	167	Nov 59	8 Jun 95	QF-106 (AD238); shot down with AIM-120, Tyndall AFB

The trailing aircraft of this pair of 5th FIS F-106As, 59-0130, later served as one of the Project Eclipse aircraft, finally arriving at AMARC on 1 May 1998 as the last active 'Six'.

59-0006	168	Dec 59	9 Sep 91	QF-106 (AD110); shot down with AIM-120, Tyndall AFB
59-0007	170	Dec 59	5 Sep 97	QF-106 (AD215); shot down with 20-mm fire, Tyndall AFB
59-0008	171	Dec 59	5 Nov 96	QF-106 (AD167); shot down with AIM-120, Tyndall AFB
59-0009	172	Dec 59	13 Feb 78	crashed ADWC
59-0010	173	Dec 59	2 Aug 96	QF-106 (AD246) stored; 15 Jul 97 to NASA (Project Eclipse) 30 Apr 98 to AMARC**§**
59-0011	175	Dec 59	19 Sep 96	QF-106 (AD159); command destroyed after landing gear malfunction, Tyndall AFB
59-0012	176	Dec 59	3 Apr 85	AMARC**§**
59-0013	177	Dec 59	3 Oct 63	crashed 5th FIS
59-0014	178	Dec 59	10 Mar 69	crashed 5th FIS
59-0015	180	Dec 59	5 Mar 92	QF-106 (AD115); crashed on take-off, Tyndall AFB
59-0016	181	Dec 59	21 Nov 97	QF-106 (AD244); shot down with AIM-120, Tyndall AFB
59-0017	182	Dec 59	19 Dec 63	crashed 5th FIS
59-0018	183	Dec 59	16 Sep 74	destroyed in mid-air collision (59-0030) 5th FIS
59-0019	184	Jan 60	2 Dec 76	crashed 5th FIS
59-0020	185	Jan 60	15 Aug 95	QF-106 (AD172); shot down with AIM-120, Tyndall AFB
59-0021	186	Jan 60	15 May 73	crashed after lightning strike 49th FIS
59-0022	187	Jan 60	3 Oct 67	crashed 318th FIS
59-0023	188	Jan 60	20 Feb 98	QF-106 (AD218); Dover AFB for display
59-0024	190	Jan 60	10 Nov 93	QF-106 (AD182); shot down with AIM-120, Tyndall AFB
59-0025	191	Jan 60	8 Feb 94	QF-106 (AD233); crashed on landing, Tyndall AFB
59-0026	192	Jan 60	7 Sep 93	QF-106 (AD139); shot down with AIM-7M, Tyndall AFB
59-0027	193	Jan 60	1 Dec 94	QF-106 (AD183); crashed on take-off, Tyndall AFB
59-0028	194	Jan 60	19 Mar 74	crashed 49th FIS
59-0029	195	Jan 60	28 Jul 61	crashed 319th FIS
59-0030	196	Jan 60	16 Sep 74	destroyed in mid-air collision (59-0018) 5th FIS
59-0031	197	Jan 60	17 Jan 96	QF-106 (AD221); shot down with AIM-7M, Tyndall AFB
59-0032	198	Jan 60	11 Oct 94	QF-106 (AD231); shot down with 'ADP-1020', Holloman AFB
59-0033	199	Feb 60	19 Sep 94	QF-106 (AD220); shot down with AIM-120, Tyndall AFB
59-0034	200	Feb 60	8 Nov 96	QF-106 (AD223); shot down with Stinger, Holloman AFB
59-0035	202	Feb 60	1 Sep 92	QF-106 (AD124); shot down with AIM-7M, Tyndall AFB
59-0036	203	Feb 60	9 Jun 70	crashed 27th FIS
59-0037	204	Feb 60	17 Dec 93	QF-106 (AD243); shot down with AIM-120, Tyndall AFB
59-0038	205	Feb 60	10 Dec 93	QF-106 (AD171); shot down with AIM-120, Tyndall AFB
59-0039	206	Feb 60	8 Oct 63	crashed 27th FIS
59-0040	208	Feb 60	28 Feb 97	QF-106 (AD225); shot down with AIM-120, Tyndall AFB
59-0041	209	Feb 60	7 Sep 65	crashed 27th FIS
59-0042	210	Feb 60	15 Sep 92	QF-106 (AD122); shot down with AIM-9M, Tyndall AFB
59-0043	211	Feb 60	4 Mar 98	QF-106 (AD227); made last QF-106 flight (with 58-0774); later AMARC**§**
59-0044	212	Feb 60	27 Sep 94	QF-106 (AD226); crashed on landing, Tyndall AFB
59-0045	214	Feb 60	7 Jun 61	crashed 27th FIS
59-0046	215	Feb 60	10 Oct 96	QF-106 (AD224); shot down with Stinger, Holloman AFB
59-0047	216	Mar 60	23 Feb 98	QF-106 (AD219); written-off (cracked wing spar), Tyndall AFB
59-0048	217	Mar 60	5 Nov 96	QF-106 (AD217); crashed on landing, Tyndall AFB
59-0049	218	Mar 60	18 Apr 95	QF-106 (AD222); shot down with AIM-120, Tyndall AFB
59-0050	220	Mar 60	8 Apr 64	crashed 318th FIS
59-0051	221	Mar 60	28 Jan 98	QF-106 (AD255); shot down on last QF-106 mission with AIM-9M, Tyndall AFB
59-0052	222	Mar 60	11 Dec 73	crashed 84th FIS
59-0053	223	Mar 60	18 May 94	QF-106 (AD173); shot down with AIM-7M, Tyndall AFB
59-0054	224	Mar 60	14 Feb 96	QF-106 (AD201); shot down with AIM-120, Tyndall AFB
59-0055	226	Mar 60	30 Nov 65	destroyed by fire 318th FIS
59-0056	227	Mar 60	7 Jul 93	QF-106 (AD164); shot down with AIM-120, Tyndall AFB
59-0057	228	Mar 60	9 Apr 96	QF-106 (AD176); shot down with AIM-120, Tyndall AFB
59-0058	229	Mar 60	20 Jul 95	QF-106 (AD184); ran off droneway, Tyndall AFB
59-0059	230	Mar 60	6 Jul 90	QF-106 (AD105); crashed, Tyndall AFB
59-0060	232	Mar 60	16 Jun 95	QF-106 (AD127); shot down with AIM-120, Tyndall AFB
59-0061	233	Mar 60	3 Sep 93	QF-106 (AD156); shot down with AIM-9M, Tyndall AFB
59-0062	234	Apr 60	12 Nov 93	QF-106 (AD168); shot down with AIM-120, Tyndall AFB
59-0063	235	Apr 60	12 Feb 93	QF-106 (AD118); shot down with AIM-120, Tyndall AFB
59-0064	236	Apr 60	16 Jun 93	QF-106 (AD155); shot down with AIM-120, Tyndall AFB
59-0065	238	Apr 60	25 Feb 92	AMARC**§**
59-0066	239	Apr 60	22 Sep 95	QF-106 (AD187); shot down with AIM-120, Tyndall AFB
59-0067	240	Apr 60	20 Feb 73	crashed 49th FIS
59-0068	241	Apr 60	13 Sep 67	destroyed by fire 438th FIS
59-0069	242	Apr 60	?	displayed, Griffiss AFB
59-0070	244	Apr 60	22 Sep 61	'total loss' (crash?) 438th FIS
59-0071	245	Apr 60	4 Jun 81	crashed 49th FIS
59-0072	246	Apr 60	4 May 94	QF-106 (AD123); shot down with 'Brite Eye', Holloman AFB
59-0073	247	Apr 60	19 Nov 60	crashed 438th FIS
59-0074	248	Apr 60	2 Feb 93	QF-106 (AD133); shot down with AIM-7M, Tyndall AFB
59-0075	250	May 60	22 Aug 75	crashed 49th FIS
59-0076	251	May 60	12 Nov 93	QF-106 (AD169); control lost/command destroyed
59-0077	252	May 60	2 Jul 93	QF-106 (AD140); shot down with AIM-7M, Tyndall AFB
59-0078	253	May 60	27 Oct 78	crashed 49th FIS
59-0079	255	May 60	7 Jul 83	AMARC**§**
59-0080	256	May 60	8 Nov 81	QF-106 (AD126); shot down with AIM-9M, Tyndall AFB
59-0081	257	May 60	17 May 94	QF-106 (AD177); shot down with AIM-120, Tyndall AFB
59-0082	258	May 60	15 May 92	QF-106 (AD143); shot down with AIM-9M, Tyndall AFB
59-0083	260	May 60	18 May 93	QF-106 (AD143); shot down with AIM-120, Tyndall AFB
59-0084	261	May 60	25 Apr 73	crashed 49th FIS
59-0085	262	May 60	26 May 94	QF-106 (AD130); shot down with AIM-120, Holloman AFB
59-0086	263	May 60	4 Sep 85	AMARC**§**
59-0087	264	Jun 60	11 Oct 61	crashed 11th FIS
59-0088	266	Jun 60	5 Oct 72	crashed 87th FIS
59-0089	267	Jun 60	26 Nov 72	crashed 87th FIS
59-0090	268	Jun 60	3 Dec 87	QF-106 (AD254); shot down with AIM-7M, Tyndall AFB
59-0091	269	Jun 60	15 Jul 94	QF-106 (AD181); shot down with AIM-7M, Tyndall AFB
59-0092	270	Jun 60	22 Sep 92	QF-106 (AD112); shot down with AIM-7M, Tyndall AFB
59-0093	272	Jun 60	5 Jun 96	QF-106 (AD237); shot down with AIM-120, Tyndall AFB
59-0094	273	Jun 60	19 Sep 96	QF-106 (AD236); shot down with AIM-120, Tyndall AFB
59-0095	274	Jun 60	21 May 85	AMARC**§**
59-0096	275	Jun 60	20 May 94	QF-106 (AD160); shot down with AIM-120, Holloman AFB
59-0097	276	Jun 60	19 Nov 96	QF-106 (AD216); shot down with AIM-9M, Tyndall AFB
59-0098	278	Jun 60	19 Nov 62	crashed 11th FIS
59-0099	279	Jun 60	23 Apr 93	QF-106 (AD137); shot down with AIM-9M, Tyndall AFB
59-0100	280	Jul 60	1 Jul 94	QF-106 (AD174); shot down with AIM-120, Tyndall AFB
59-0101	281	Jul 60	18 Jul 79	crashed 87th FIS
59-0102	282	Jul 60	2 Jul 97	QF-106 (AD245); shot down with AIM-120, Tyndall AFB
59-0103	284	Jul 60	27 Nov 80	crashed ADWC
59-0104	285	Jul 60	5 Nov 93	QF-106 (AD142); shot down with AIM-120, Holloman AFB
59-0105	286	Jul 60	23 Feb 98	QF-106 (AD250); written-off (cracked wing spar), Tyndall AFB
59-0106	287	Jul 60	20 Dec 96	QF-106 (AD241); shot down with AIM-120, Tyndall AFB
59-0107	288	Jul 60	2 Jan 63	crashed 329th FIS
59-0108	290	Jul 60	4 Dec 97	QF-106 (AD249); shot down with AIM-120, Tyndall AFB
59-0109	291	Jul 60	19 Feb 92	QF-106 (AD148); shot down with AIM-120, Tyndall AFB
59-0110	292	Jul 60	19 Feb 93	QF-106 (AD125); shot down with AIM-120, Tyndall AFB

90165

725

FE-165 U.S. AIR FORCE

59-0165, the last B-model 'Six' off the line, became the personal mount of (and was accordingly named after) General 'Chappie' James, commander of Air Defense Command and CINCNORAD between 1 September 1975 and 6 December 1977.

59-0111	293	Aug 60	12 Oct 65	crashed 329th FIS
59-0112	294	Aug 60	9 Oct 73	crashed 48th FIS
59-0113	296	Aug 60	28 Jan 64	crashed 48th FIS
59-0114	297	Aug 60	4 Apr 63	crashed 48th FIS
59-0115	298	Aug 60	5 Mar 82	AMARC§
59-0116	299	Aug 60	12 Jan 82	AMARC
59-0117	301	Aug 60	3 Sep 63	crashed 498th FIS
59-0118	302	Aug 60	11 Jun 68	crashed ADWC
59-0119	303	Aug 60	13 Sep 91	QF-106 (AD106); shot down with AIM-120, Tyndall AFB
59-0120	304	Aug 60	14 Feb 61	crashed 329th FIS
59-0121	306	Aug 60	24 Apr 69	crashed 94th FIS
59-0122	307	Aug 60	25 Jan 82	AMARC
59-0123	308	Sep 60	9 Mar 83	NASA (for parts); later displayed, Warner Robins AFB
59-0124	309	Sep 60	9 Mar 64	crashed 48th FIS
59-0125	311	Sep 60	7 Nov 71	crashed 84th FIS
59-0126	312	Sep 60	13 Nov 96	QF-106 (AD158); broke-up in flight, Tyndall AFB
59-0127	313	Sep 60	25 Jun 92	QF-106 (AD131); shot down with AIM-9M, Tyndall AFB
59-0128	315	Sep 60	30 Apr 96	QF-106 (AD144); crashed over White Sands range, Holloman AFB
59-0129	316	Sep 60	30 Aug 94	QF-106 (AD162); written-off (T-tank ruptured), Tyndall AFB
59-0130	317	Sep 60	11 Sep 96	QF-106 (AD152) stored; 21 May 97 to NASA (Project Eclipse); 1 May 98 to AMARC§
59-0131	319	Sep 60	18 Oct 71	crashed 84th FIS
59-0132	320	Sep 60	21 Oct 92	QF-106 (AD135); shot down with Patriot, Holloman AFB
59-0133	321	Sep 60	8 Mar 94	QF-106 (AD252); crashed on take-off, Tyndall AFB
59-0134	323	Oct 60	2 Nov 95	displayed Peterson AFB
59-0135	324	Oct 60	12 Aug 93	QF-106 (AD170); control lost/command destroyed
59-0136	325	Oct 60	30 Mar 93	QF-106 (AD178); crashed, Tyndall AFB
59-0137	327	Oct 60	16 Oct 84	AMARC§
59-0138	328	Oct 60	11 Apr 95	QF-106 (AD157); crashed, Tyndall AFB
59-0139	329	Oct 60	17 May 61	crashed 456th FIS
59-0140	331	Oct 60	11 Jun 92	QF-106 (AD145); shot down with AIM-120, Tyndall AFB
59-0141	332	Oct 60	6 Nov 92	QF-106 (AD134); shot down with Stinger, Holloman AFB
59-0142	333	Oct 60	27 Aug 63	crashed 498th FIS
59-0143	335	Oct 60	24 Oct 84	crashed 49th FIS
59-0144	336	Oct 60	29 May 78	crashed 318th FIS
59-0145	337	Oct 60	?	displayed, Tyndall Air Park, Tyndall AFB
59-0146	338	Nov 60	?	displayed, Fresno Air Terminal, California
59-0147	339	Nov 60	17 Oct 83	AMARC§
59-0148	340	Nov 60	22 Apr 69	crashed 318th FIS

F-106Bs

57-2507	13	Apr 58	24 Feb 84	never assigned to ADC; written-off by NASA, Langley
57-2508	27	Aug 58	1 Nov 94	QF-106 (AD267); shot down with AIM-120, Tyndall AFB
57-2509	21	Jun 58	7 Oct 97	QF-106 (AD268); written-off after ground fire
57-2510	24	Jul 58	4 Apr 84	AMARC§
57-2511	29	Sep 58	5 Jan 59	crashed AFFTC
57-2512	31	Sep 58	3 Jun 94	QF-106 (AD263); shot down with AIM-7M, Tyndall AFB
57-2513	33	Apr 58	25 Jun 90	AMARC§
57-2514	35	Oct 58	23 Nov 87	AMARC§
57-2515	37	Nov 58	16 Dec 86	crashed 49th FIS
57-2516	39	Dec 58	17 May 91	retired by NASA (N816NA); displayed Virginia Air and Space Center, Hampton, Virginia
57-2517	41	Dec 58	21 Feb 97	QF-106 (AD256); crash landed, Tyndall AFB
57-2518	50	Jan 59	3 Dec 96	QF-106 (AD260); shot down with AIM-120, Tyndall AFB
57-2519	53	Feb 59	21 Apr 66	retired? (Sacramento ALC training aircraft)
57-2520	57	Mar 59	3 Oct 72	crashed 186th FIS
57-2521	60	Mar 59	2 Apr 85	destroyed in mid-air collision, 101st FIS
57-2522	63	Apr 59	21 Jan 98	QF-106 (AD259); shot down with AIM-120, Tyndall AFB
57-2523	65	Jul 58	4 Dec 92	prototype ARDC instrument test aircraft; later displayed, Atlantic City AP

The 25th Paris Air Salon in 1963 hosted two A-model Darts, 59-0124 and 59-0136, in the type's first trip across the Atlantic. Here the latter of the two is seen at Malmstrom AFB, Montana, in December 1969, while with the 71st FIS. In 1963, the aircraft was with the 48th FIS at Langley AFB, Virginia.

Prototype 56-0451, seen here while with the USAFM, later moved to Selfridge AFB, where it was displayed with a spurious serial number.

57-2524	69	Apr 59	20 Feb 97	QF-106 (AD258); shot down with 9K38 Igla (SA-18) SAM, Holloman AFB
57-2525	73	May 59	1 Nov 60	written-off (major damage) 95th FIS
57-2526	77	May 59	16 Oct 68	crashed ADWC
57-2527	82	Jun 59	9 Oct 73	crashed ADWC
57-2528	88	Jun 59	16 Oct 72	crashed ADWC
57-2529	95	Jul 59	21 Apr 66	retired? (Sacramento ALC training aircraft)
57-2530	102	Aug 59	24 Apr 97	QF-106 (AD257); shot down with AIM-120, Tyndall AFB
57-2531	109	Aug 59	30 Mar 66	crashed 539th FIS
57-2532	116	Sep 59	27 Mar 96	QF-106 (AD270); shot down with AIM-120, Tyndall AFB
57-2533	123	Sep 59	12 Dec 86	written-off (major damage); displayed Kelly AFB
57-2534	130	Sep 59	27 Jan 64	destroyed by fire 4756th ADW, Tyndall AFB
57-2535	137	Oct 59	1 Sep 93	QF-106 (AD109); shot down with AIM-9M, Tyndall AFB
57-2536	144	Oct 59	4 Mar 93	QF-106 (AD107); shot down with AIM-7M, Tyndall AFB
57-2537	150	Oct 59	28 Jan 98	QF-106 (AD276); shot down with AIM-120, Tyndall AFB
57-2538	157	Nov 59	19 Oct 72	crashed ADWC
57-2539	164	Nov 59	23 Aug 95	QF-106 (AD265); accidentally jammed by EF-111A/command destroyed, Tyndall AFB
57-2540	169	Nov 59	7 Jul 97	QF-106 (AD262); shot down with AIM-120, Tyndall AFB
57-2541	174	Dec 59	16 May 95	QF-106 (AD281); shot down with AIM-7M, Tyndall AFB
57-2542	179	Dec 59	27 Aug 64	crashed 4756th ADW, Tyndall AFB
57-2543	189	Jan 60	23 Feb 98	QF-106 (AD271); written-off (nose gear damaged on landing), Tyndall AFB
57-2544	201	Feb 60	29 Mar 71	crashed ADWC
57-2545	207	Feb 60	3 Jan 97	QF-106 (AD282); written-off (cracked intake duct), Tyndall AFB
57-2546	213	Mar 60	14 Jun 95	QF-106 (AD264); shot down with AIM-120/gun, Tyndall AFB
57-2547	219	Mar 60	15 Nov 96	QF-106 (AD279); shot down with AIM-120, Tyndall AFB
58-0900	226	Mar 60	10 Jul 95	QF-106 (AD274); crashed on landing, Tyndall AFB
58-0901	231	Apr 60	20 Dec 96	QF-106 (AD273); shot down with AIM-120, Tyndall AFB
58-0902	237	Apr 60	17 Jan 97	QF-106 (AD277); shot down with AIM-9M, Tyndall AFB
58-0903	243	Apr 60	3 Apr 84	AMARC§
58-0904	249	May 60	2 Apr 84	AMARC§
59-0149	254	May 60	6 Nov 97	QF-106 (AD261); shot down with AIM-120, Tyndall AFB
59-0150	259	May 60	4 Dec 97	QF-106 (AD278); shot down with AIM-9M, Tyndall AFB
59-0151	265	Jun 60	25 Nov 97	QF-106 (AD266); shot down with AIM-120, Tyndall AFB
59-0152	271	Jun 60	24 Jul 91	QF-106 (AD101); crashed after control loss, Tyndall AFB
59-0153	277	Jun 60	11 Sep 97	QF-106 (AD272); shot down with AIM-120, Tyndall AFB
59-0154	283	Jul 60	18 Dec 62	crashed 438th FIS
59-0155	289	Jul 60	16 Jul 97	QF-106 (AD269); shot down with AIM-120, Tyndall AFB
59-0156	295	Jul 60	1 Mar 64	crashed 11th FIS
59-0157	300	Aug 60	11 Feb 77	crashed 48th FIS
59-0158	305	Aug 60	23 Feb 98	QF-106 (AD275); later AMARC§
59-0159	310	Aug 60	5 Aug 93	QF-106 (AD119); shot down with AIM-9M, Tyndall AFB
59-0160	314	Sep 60	12 Jun 74	crashed 87th FIS
59-0161	318	Sep 60	22 Jan 97	QF-106 (AD280); shot down with AIM-120, Tyndall AFB
59-0162	322	Sep 60	9 Feb 71	crashed 84th FIS
59-0163	326	Oct 60	30 Sep 71	crashed ADWC
59-0164	330	Oct 60	4 Apr 84	AMARC§
59-0165	334	Oct 60	27 Feb 80	destroyed by fire ADWC

As the last F-106s bowed out with the New Jersey ANG in the summer/autumn of 1988, their place was taken by General Dynamics F-16A/Bs, which were upgraded to ADF standard during FY91. During the winter of 1994/95, they in turn were traded for F-16C/D aircraft.

F-106 Operators

Air Defense Command

The Air Force's F-106 fighter interceptor squadrons belonged to Air Defense Command (ADC, or ADCOM), headquartered at Ent AFB, Colorado. ADC was established on 21 March 1946 and, after numerous changes in the pre-Delta Dart era, was re-established as a major command on 1 January 1951. After Ent Field closed, ADC moved to new headquarters in the Chidlaw Building in Colorado Springs. ADC eventually became a component of NORAD (North American Air Defense Command) which combined US and Canadian efforts to defend against a trans-Polar bomber and missile attack. NORAD was established on 12 September 1957. For much of its existence, the ADC commander was also the NORAD commander-in-chief.

To reflect the growing importance of space, ADC's name was changed to Aerospace Defense Command on 15 January 1968. At the time, the term 'aerospace', devised by General Thomas D. White – who had been USAF chief of staff when the Soviet Union launched the first space satellite in October 1957 – was very much in vogue. White and others expected that the USAF would quickly be renamed the United States Aerospace Force and urged it repeatedly upon their bosses – the idea was revived during the service's 50th anniversary in 1997 – but it never happened. The term was all too apt to F-106 pilots who were expected to defend North American airspace against anything that came in, high or low.

The defence of North America, a top priority at the height of the Cold War, began to wane when it became evident there was no defence against ICBMs. It also became evident that the Soviet Union had a far less capable strategic bomber force than had been believed in the early days of the Cold War.

On 1 October 1979, ADC's F-106 squadrons were transferred to Tactical Air Command (TAC), which established a component called ADTAC, headquartered at Colorado Springs. All of the F-106 squadrons operated by the Air National Guard (ANG) were under state control for administrative purposes but were dedicated to ('gained' by) ADC and later TAC for the air defence mission. Under the 1979 reorganisation, the fighter interceptor squadrons were made subordinate to six air divisions – 20th, 21st, 23rd, 24th, 25th and 26th. A further change took place on 6 December 1985 when ADTAC was replaced by the newly-activated First Air Force. This command arrangement remained in effect until the last F-106s (operated by the New Jersey ANG) ended their career as fighter-interceptors and went to the boneyard.

Having given up its flying squadrons, ADC went out of business on 31 March 1980, inactivated as a major air command.

2nd FIS

On 1 July 1971 the 2nd Fighter Interceptor Squadron (FIS) was reactivated at Wurtsmith AFB, Michigan, equipping with

F-106 aircraft and personnel from the 94th FIS. (The 94th designation on that date was transferred from ADC to TAC.) The squadron had previously operated the F-101B/F Voodoo at Suffolk County, New York.

The 2nd FIS competed in the 1972 William Tell gunnery meet at Tyndall AFB, Florida and took second place in the F-106 category, with 13,761 points out of a possible 16,800. The squadron's Delta Dart era was brief, however, and it began transferring its aircraft to the 171st FIS/191st FIG, Michigan ANG on 29 December 1972. The squadron had operated a total of 20 F-106s and lost none in mishaps. The 2nd FIS was inactivated on 31 March 1973. In later years, it became a T-33 operator as the 2nd FITS at Tyndall.

The 2nd FIS was unofficially known as the 'Horney Horses'. The 'winged unicorn' from the unit's badge appeared in a white disc over a yellow tail band.

5th FIS

The 5th FIS 'Spittin' Kittens' at Minot AFB, North Dakota received its first F-106A (59-0019) on 30 January 1960, having previously been equipped with the F-102A Delta Dagger. The squadron's history dates to 20 November 1940. Its first aircraft was the P-40. The squadron badge is a lynx ('kitten') against an azure disc broken by two flashes of lightning. Its aircraft have typically been decorated with yellow or yellow-enclosed lightning bolts. The squadron had previously operated the F-102 Delta Dagger at Suffolk County, New York.

The squadron carried out three White Shoes deployments to Alaska, beginning respectively on 4 January 1967, 3 April 1968 and 10 July 1969. In William Tell competitions, the squadron scored second in 1965, fifth in 1972, and third in 1980. One of the squadron's better-known commanders was Lieutenant Colonel Jack Broughton, later the author of *Thud Ridge* and other books, from 16 April 1962 to 30 June 1964.

On a rare deployment to Europe in 1975, seven aircraft went to Hahn AB, Germany, to support NATO Exercise Cold Fire 75. The

F-106s arrived on 4 September 1975 and returned home on 27 September 1975. The 'Spittin' Kittens' was not the first squadron to operate the 'Six' in Europe, an honour that was claimed by the 48th FIS which had sent two aircraft to the 1963 Paris Air Show.

The squadron's last F-106A (59-0006) went to Davis-Monthan AFB, Arizona on 5 April 1985 to be converted to a QF-106A drone. During its F-106 tenure, the squadron operated 33 F-106s, nine of which were lost in mishaps. The 'Spittin' Kittens' in later years operated the F-15 Eagle, and subsequently became a training unit.

Right: The famous 'Spittin' Kittens' lightning bolt and stars appeared on later tail markings, as seen on these aircraft at William Tell '84.

Below: 'Spittin' Kittens' F-106s originally wore a large tail chevron as seen on this aircraft – the 5th FIS commanding officer's F-106 – seen in May 1974.

11th FIS

The 11th FIS 'Red Bulls' at Duluth Municipal Airport, Minnesota, part of the 30th Air Division, received the squadron's first F-106A (59-0080) on 23 June 1960. Previously, its aircraft had been the F-102 Delta Dagger. The 11th dates to 20 November 1940. The squadron badge depicts a charging red bull.

In William Tell 1961, the 11th FIS placed fourth, and two years later finished in second place. The 11th FIS made two White Shoes deployments to Alaska, beginning respectively on 6 September 1967 and 1 August 1968. The squadron frequently exercised at, and in wartime would have dispersed to, Volk Field, Wisconsin.

As a result of major changes that occurred throughout ADC on 30 September 1968, while four of its aircraft were away from Duluth on the squadron's second Alaskan deployment, the 11th FIS was discontinued at Duluth – a move that included the four aircraft in Alaska – where it was redesignated the 87th FIS. The latter squadron perpetuated the 'Red Bulls' nickname. During its tenure as a Delta Dart operator, the 11th FIS operated 33 F-106s and lost three.

Above right: A pair of 11th FIS F-106As drop in to Duluth IAP in the 1972 version of their markings. The nearer aircraft sports an ADC badge.

Right: Seen in May 1965 wearing an earlier form of 11th FIS markings and wing commander's stripes, this F-106A crashed in May 1981 while serving with the 87th FIS.

27th FIS

On 16 October 1959, an F-106A (58-0779) became the first Delta Dart to join the 27th FIS 'Fighting Falcons' at Loring AFB, Maine. The squadron patch depicts a red, yellow, and black falcon. This squadron had flown the F-102 Delta Dagger at Griffiss AFB, New York until officially relocated to Loring, effective 1 October 1959. Organised in 1917, the 27th is frequently described as the oldest American fighter squadron never to have been deactivated, although in fact it was briefly out of operation in 1945/46.

The 27th FIS had a detachment at Goose Bay, Labrador beginning in 1967 for about a year. For a brief period, the squadron also had a detachment at Dow AFB near Bangor, Maine. The 27th deployed five times to Alaska (on 4 May 1966, 1 November 1967, 29 January 1968, 30 August 1968, and 8 December 1969).

Under Operation College Shaft, the 27th FIS intercepted three Russian Tupolev Tu-95 'Bears' on 13 May 1969, using two F-106s scrambled from Loring. Two hours and 33 minutes from launch, the two F-106s caught up with the Russian bombers at a point within 150 miles (241 km) of North America and 700 miles (1126 km) from Loring. This was the first intercept of Soviet aircraft by interceptors based in the continental US.

During its Delta Dart tenure, the 27th FIS operated 49 F-106 airframes and suffered five losses. On 1 July 1971 the connection between the 27th FIS and the F-106 was severed when the squadron identity was moved to Langley AFB, Virginia as the 27th TFS. As a replacement, the 83rd FIS was reactivated at Loring.

Below: Tail markings were not confined to the single-seaters. F-106Bs were as capable an interceptor as the A model, most units having at least one example for continuation training purposes.

Above: This close-up of the tail of a 'Fighting Falcons' F-106 shows the tail marking design as it appeared in June 1969.

48th FIS

The 48th FIS was dubbed the 'Tasmanian Devils'. The squadron used a patch with an animated, Satan-like character before shifting to a less evocative starburst symbol. The 48th FIS at Langley AFB, Virginia received its first F-106, a B model, on 15 September 1960. Previously, the squadron operated the F-102 Delta Dagger.

In May 1963, the 48th became the first squadron to deploy an F-106 overseas when F-106A 59-0136 flew to the 25th Paris air show. On 7 September 1966, the squadron began the first of three White Shoes deployments to Elmendorf AFB, Alaska. Two further deployments began on 3 May 1967 and 7 April 1969.

The 48th FIS deployed to Korea in the wake of North Korea's seizure of the spy ship USS *Pueblo* (AGER-2). Beginning 11 July 1968, the 48th began standing alert at Osan AB, Korea, using aircraft left in place by the 318th FIS. The 48th FIS personnel left on 23 December 1968, the day the *Pueblo* crew was released, flying the 318th squadron's Delta Darts to McChord before returning home for Christmas.

Under Project College Sand, the 48th began standing alert at Homestead AFB, Florida on 3 June 1970. This deployment occupied six aircraft operating as a detachment at Homestead until May 1976.

On 1 October 1979, the 48th transferred from ADC to TAC. In February 1982, the squadron began retiring its F-106s to the 'boneyard' at Davis-Monthan AFB, Arizona. The 48th FIS had participated twice in the William Tell gunnery meet, scoring third in the F-106 category in 1963 and 1978. During its time as a Delta Dart operator, the squadron flew 45 airframes and sustained seven losses. The squadron continued to fly the air defence mission with the F-15A.

Right: From the mid-1960s until at least 1972, the 48th FIS used a comparatively simple broad white band, outlined in black, as its distinctive unit identifier.

Left: The last markings scheme applied to 48th Fighter Interceptor Squadron F-106s, seen here in March 1976, consisted of a white chevron with blue trim and alternating rudder stripes.

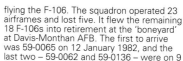
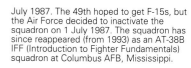

49th FIS

On 30 September 1968, the 438th FIS at Kincheloe AFB, Michigan was moved to Griffiss AFB, New York and redesignated the 49th; it acquired the assets of the discontinued 438th FIS. Previously, the 49th FIS appellation had belonged to the F-101B/F Voodoo squadron at Griffiss and was inactive for a time. The squadron was officially nicknamed the 'Cavaliers' because of its emblem depicting a knight in armour; the application of a large eagle with a green-white sunburst to its aircraft meant that the squadron was known less officially as the 'Green Eagles'.

On 8 September 1969, the squadron deployed to Alaska to replace the 84th FIS. In the William Tell competition, the 49th FIS scored second in the F-106 category in 1974, second in 1976, first in 1978, fourth in 1980, and first again in 1982.

Between 1983 and 1986, the squadron operated a detachment at Loring AFB, Maine.

On 1 October 1979, the 49th FIS – like all other interceptor squadrons in ADC – transferred to TAC. By the mid-1980s, it had become the last active-duty USAF squadron

flying the F-106. The squadron operated 23 airframes and lost five. It flew the remaining 18 F-106s into retirement at the 'boneyard' at Davis-Monthan AFB. The first to arrive was 59-0065 on 12 January 1982, and the last two – 59-0062 and 59-0136 – were on 9

July 1987. The 49th hoped to get F-15s, but the Air Force decided to inactivate the squadron on 1 July 1987. The squadron has since reappeared (from 1993) as an AT-38B IFF (Introduction to Fighter Fundamentals) squadron at Columbus AFB, Mississippi.

Above: During 1973, 49th FIS markings consisted of rudder stripes.

Right: By 1984, the full 'Green Eagle' had appeared. Yellow lightning bolts adorned fuel tanks.

71st FIS

The first F-106 assigned to the 71st FIS at Selfridge AFB, Michigan was F-106B 57-2532 on 17 October 1960. The Delta Dart era began after a long association by the 71st FIS with the F-102 Delta Dagger.

During the Cuban missile crisis in October 1962, the squadron deployed to Patrick AFB, Florida to provide air intercept capability. The squadron operated a detachment at Hulman Regional Airport in Terre Haute, Indiana, from the mid-1960s until the early 1970s. The squadron finished first in the F-106 category at William Tell gunnery meets in 1965 and 1970. The 71st had three deployments to Alaska in support of Operation White Shoes on 3 December 1965, 4 January 1968 and 2 February 1970. The 1968 move marked the first time air-to-air refuelling was used on a White Shoes deployment. In support of Project College Cadence deployments to Korea, the 71st arrived at Osan on 23 December 1968 and began standing alert until 17 June 1969.

The 71st FIS made two real moves, as distinguished from the 'paper' transfers that occurred when designations shifted: on 15

January 1967 the unit relocated to Richards-Gebaur AFB, Missouri (from which the first air-refuelled Alaskan deployment was launched) and on 1 July 1968 to Malmstrom AFB, Montana. On 1 July 1971, as part of the 1st FIW transfer to TAC, the 71st designation was transferred to Langley AFB, Virginia, losing its status as an air defence unit. The squadron at Malmstrom was

In 1970, not long after their return from Korea, 71st FIS Delta Darts could be seen with this smart blue chevron marking.

redesignated the 319th FIS. During its time as an F-106 operator, the 71st FIS flew 56 aircraft and sustained six losses.

83rd FIS

On 1 July 1971, the 83rd FIS was reactivated at Loring AFB, Maine, using the aircraft and crews left by the 27th FIS. In a previous life, the 83rd had been at Hamilton AFB, California flying F-101B/Fs and had inactivated on 1 July 1963.

The brief, new history of this squadron ended on 30 June 1972 when the 83rd FIS was inactivated, with its 17 F-106s being reassigned to the 95th FIS at Dover AFB, Nebraska. The squadron had operated a total of 20 aircraft during its F-106 era.

A rare photograph of a comparatively rare bird, this shot shows an F-106A of the short-lived 83rd FIS, seen here at McConnell AFB during October 1971. Darts equipped the 83rd in 1971, the unit having operated Voodoos eight years previously.

84th FIS

The 84th FIS 'Black Panthers' flew F-106s at Hamilton AFB, California and Castle AFB, California. Previously, this squadron had flown the F-101B/F Voodoo at Hamilton. On 30 September 1968, the 498th FIS moved from Paine Field, Washington with its F-106s to Hamilton AFB, California and was redesignated 84th FIS.

The 84th deployed twice to Alaska, on 5 June 1969 and 15 June 1970. In its only participation in the William Tell weapons meet, the squadron scored second in 1970. On 2 October 1970, the 84th returned to Hamilton, ending 11 years of White Shoes/College Shoes deployments to Alaska.

On 1 September 1973, the 84th FIS

The 84th FIS 'Black Panthers' initially adopted the markings of the 498th, whose aircraft it had taken over in 1968.

moved to Castle AFB, California. In 1977, the squadron deployed seven F-106s to Eielson AFB, Alaska for two weeks in support of the Jack Frost 77 winter exercise.

The squadron was redesignated 84th Fighter Interceptor Training Squadron on 3 June 1981. In this capacity, the squadron operated T-33A Shooting Stars as 'faker' or

aggressor aircraft for radar evaluation. Its F-106s were transferred to other units in the USAF/ANG. During its F-106 era, the squadron operated 39 F-106 aircraft and sustained four losses.

By 1974, a red/white/blue tail stripe and badge were seen on the tail of the 84th's Darts.

87th FIS

The 87th FIS became an F-106 operator at Duluth Municipal Airport, Minnesota on 30 September 1968. The squadron retained the 'Red Bulls' nickname of the former 11th FIS and adopted a similar patch with a differently styled bull. Formerly, the 87th had been an F-101 Voodoo squadron at Lockbourne AFB, Ohio, until deactivation in June 1968. In May 1971, the squadron moved to K. I. Sawyer AFB, Michigan, where it began full operations on 24 May 1971. For many years the squadron also maintained a detachment at Charleston AFB, South Carolina. The squadron also had a detachment at Volk Field in Camp Douglas, Wisconsin until 1974.

In April 1975, the 87th deployed F-106s to Luke AFB, Arizona for DACT (dissimilar air combat training) with the F-15 Eagle training unit.

On 21 April 1978, nine F-106s departed K. I. Sawyer for Keflavik AB, Iceland, one aborting en route. Soon afterward, the squadron's first intercept of a Soviet Tupolev Tu-95 'Bear' (of three) was made by Captains Gene Lutz and Bill Thomas. The eight F-106s arrived back at K. I. Sawyer on 13 May 1978.

On 1 October 1979, like other Delta Dart squadrons in the active force, the 87th FIS transferred from ADC to TAC.

The 87th FIS stood down from alert duty at K. I. Sawyer on 1 February 1985 and at Charleston on 1 July 1985. During its F-106 era, the squadron had operated 31 F-106s and suffered four losses. When the 87th FIS was inactivated on 1 October 1985, an F-106A (57-0230) was left behind at Charleston for display. This aircraft had been the YF-106C prototype.

Above right: An 87th FIS F-106A is seen at an air show at Rickenbacker AFB, Ohio in the early 1960s. The starboard side of the fin carried the ADC insignia. Note also the 'FE' 'buzz' code used during this period, but abandoned in the early 1960s.

Right: The 87th 'Red Bulls' adopted this stylised bull's head in the early 1970s and used it, with variations, until it gave up its 'Sixes'.

94th FIS

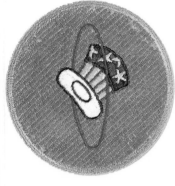

The 94th FIS 'Hat in the Ring' squadron took delivery of its first F-106A (58-0796) on 3 April 1960 at Selfridge AFB, Michigan. The USAF's second-oldest squadron, which claimed Captain Edward Rickenbacker as the American ace of aces in World War I, went directly into the Delta Dart from the

F-86L Sabre. The unit never took part in a William Tell competition. The 94th deployed to Alaska three times: 7 September 1966, 28 February 1968, and in July 1970.

In support of Project College Cadence deployments during the *Pueblo* crisis, the 94th deployed to Osan AB, Korea where it used aircraft of the 71st FIS to begin alert duty on 17 June 1969.

On 1 December 1969, the 94th designation was moved to TAC while the 2nd FIS was activated at Wurtsmith to replace the 94th. During its F-106 era, the 94th FIS operated 45 F-106s and experienced five losses. The relocated squadron became today's 94th FS operating the F-15C Eagle.

Left: The original 94th FIS markings featured the 'Hat in the Ring' in a blue 'V' cut into a band of red and white stripes. The final marking used was a narrow yellow fin band with the badge on a white disc.

Above: At least one 94th FIS F-106A, seen at Andrews in June 1967, wore a variation on the scheme with the tail band based on the elements of the 1st FW insignia.

95th FIS

The 95th FIS 'Mr Bones' was assigned its first F-106A (57-0246) on 17 July 1959 while stationed at Andrews AFB, Maryland. There, the squadron had previously operated the F-86D and F-102. On 1 July 1963, the 95th relocated from Andrews to Dover AFB, Delaware.

The squadron did not participate in any Alaskan deployments. The 95th was the last F-106 unit to deploy to Korea following the *Pueblo* crisis, arriving at Osan on 15 November 1969 to replace the 94th FIS. During the Korean deployment, the squadron lost one aircraft which is believed to have flown into the sea. The date of the end of the Korean operation is in dispute,

but a squadron member recalls that the 95th left Korea in May 1970.

The 95th FIS participated in the William Tell weapons meet just once, placing last among six teams in 1972.

On 31 January 1973, the 95th FIS was inactivated at Dover. Most of its F-106s were assigned to the 101st FIS, Massachusetts ANG, at Otis ANGB. Forty-nine F-106s had been operated by the 95th squadron, of which four were lost in mishaps. Today the squadron identity survives with the 95th FITS at Tyndall AFB.

The 95th FIS put its badge on a blue and yellow diamond. Seen in the background is a KC-97 of the Delaware ANG.

'Mr Bones' F-106s originally featured the squadron badge in a large disc on the tail, as seen on these examples photographed in 1963.

318th FIS

Left: The last markings worn on 318th FIS Darts were the full-size North Star as seen on these aircraft at Tyndall AFB.

Right: Earlier versions of the unit's marking were in the form of this two-tone blue, three-tailed dart shape. Note the '0' serial number prefix, indicating that the aircraft was over 10 years old.

The 318th FIS at McChord AFB, Washington was assigned its first F-106A (59-0055) on 21 March 1960. Like so many users of the 'Six', the 318th had flown the F-102 Delta Dagger. The 318th took the brunt of the first White Shoes deployments to Alaska. Five F-106s of the 318th arrived at Elmendorf AFB, Alaska, on 15 July 1963 along with four F-106s from the 498th FIS. In all, the 318th made seven deployments to Alaska.

The squadron also deployed to Tyndall AFB, Florida five times to participate in the William Tell competition, achieving first place in 1963, fourth in 1965, third in 1970, third in 1972 and third again in 1974. The squadron also initiated the Project College Cadence deployments to Korea during the *Pueblo* crisis. On 20 November 1967, 10 F-106As of the 318th flew non-stop from McChord to Tyndall with air-to-air refuelling. This was the first test of College Cadence.

In the spring of 1974, squadron F-106s deployed to Howard AFB in the Panama Canal Zone for Exercise Blackhawk '74.

With other surviving 'Six' squadrons, the 318th was transferred to TAC on 1 October 1979. On 2 November 1983, the squadron ended its Delta Dart era as the last F-106 departed McChord. One of the last active-duty air defence outfits, the 318th was an operator of the F-15A/B Eagle before being inactivated on 7 December 1989.

319th FIS

The 319th FIS flew the F-106 twice. The first period began at Bunker Hill AFB, Indiana with the arrival of the first aircraft (59-0020) on 2 February 1960. The 'Six' was, needless to say, an auspicious replacement for the squadron's F-89J Scorpions. This squadron's Delta Dart era ended for the first time in February 1963 as the F-106s began departing Bunker Hill in anticipation of the squadron's upcoming move to Homestead AFB, Florida and its transition to the F-104A/B Starfighter, beginning on 1 March 1963. Records show that F-106A 59-0021 was the last to leave Bunker Hill, on 9 March 1963. In three years, the squadron operated 26 F-106s, lost one in a crash, and had one damaged.

On 1 July 1971, the 319th was reactivated at Malmstrom AFB, Montana to take over the equipment and people of the departing 71st FIS. On 30 April 1972, the 319th was inactivated. The 18 F-106s it operated during this brief period were all ex-71st FIS aircraft. The last F-106A (59-0146) departed on 24 May 1972.

The markings of the 319th FIS, in its second incarnation (1971-72), came from the 71st FIS, whose aircraft it inherited.

329th FIS

At George AFB, California, the 329th FIS received its first F-106s on 29 July 1960. The squadron had operated the F-102 at George. In October 1964, the 329th was awarded the Hughes Trophy for air defence excellence. The squadron began to give up its F-106s in May 1967. An F-106A (59-0108) and an F-106B (59-0162) were the last Delta Darts to depart, on 9 June 1967. The squadron operated 31 F-106s and had three losses. The 329th FIS was inactivated on 31 July 1967.

The 329th FIS, a former Delta Dagger unit, adopted a squadron badge featuring a stylised delta-winged aircraft. It appeared in the centre of a three-pointed chevron on the unit's Darts in the 1960s.

437th FIS

On 18 July 1968, the 437th FIS came into existence at Oxnard AFB, California with the redesignation of the former 456th FIS. The squadron's former equipment was the McDonnell F-101B/F Voodoo. Equipping with the Delta Dart turned out to be a temporary measure, although, in its tenure of just two months, the squadron operated 21 F-106s. On 30 September 1968, the 437th FIS was discontinued. The aircraft and people remaining in place at Oxnard were redesignated the 460th FIS because the latter name was regarded as having a more distinguished history.

The 437th FIS was the shortest-lived F-106 squadron and used the markings of the 456th FIS, whose colours it inherited with the redesignation of that unit. This aircraft, seen refuelling from a KC-135 in September 1968, was lost in December 1972.

438th FIS

The 438th FIS began operation at Kincheloe AFB, Michigan (formerly Kinross AFB) on 12 May 1960 with the arrival of its first F-106A (59-0068). The squadron insignia was a copyrighted picture of Donald Duck in a flight jacket and dates to World War II when the 438th conducted replacement training at Kinross Field. Immediately prior to the 'Six', the squadron flew the F-102. The squadron maintained a detachment at Phelps-Collins Airport in Alpena, Michigan throughout much of the 1960s. It made two Alaskan deployments, replacing the 94th FIS on 1 March 1967 and 29 May 1968.

On 30 September 1968, the 438th FIS was relocated to Griffiss AFB, New York, discontinued, and redesignated the 49th FIS. This change also affected squadron F-106s that were then in Alaska on a White Shoes deployment. During its Delta Dart period, the 438th FIS operated 29 aircraft and had four losses.

Left: In this later variation of the unit's tail markings, the 'Donald Duck' design is facing to the right; on some aircraft this was reversed.

Above: Seen at Milwaukee in 1965, this 438th FIS Dart shows the first version of squadron markings.

456th FIS

F-106A 58-0761 arrived to join the 456th at Castle AFB, California on 16 September 1959, ushering in the squadron's Delta Dart era. The 456th competed in the William Tell weapons meet on three occasions, scoring first in 1961 (the first year the Delta Dart appeared), fourth in 1963 and third in 1965.

The 456th FIS had 64 F-106s assigned and sustained three losses. On 2 July 1968, the squadron was relocated to Oxnard AFB, California, and on 18 July 1968 the 456th was discontinued and redesignated the 437th FIS.

456th FIS F-106s wore the squadron badge on the starboard fin. The tail bands changed from black to blue in later years and the flash disappeared from the central badge.

460th FIS

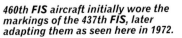

On 30 September 1968, the 460th FIS was reactivated as an F-106 user at Oxnard AFB, California through the redesignation of the 437th FIS. In a previous incarnation, the squadron had flown the F-102. The 460th FIS made its only White Shoes deployment to Alaska on 9 December 1968, replacing the 87th FIS. On 1 December 1969, the squadron relocated to Kingsley Field, Oregon as part of the 408th Fighter Interceptor Group. After a little more than a year there, the 460th FIS moved to Grand Forks, North Dakota on 16 April 1971.

In April 1972, the squadron transferred all of its F-106s to the Montana ANG's 186th FIS (these were to become the last Delta Darts in service with 'round' cockpit gauges, never receiving the taped instruments that were retrofitted to most examples) while taking charge of a new batch of F-106s formerly assigned to the 319th FIS. In 1972, the 460th FIS won first place in the F-106 category at the William Tell weapons competition.

When it went out of business in 1974, the 460th FIS had operated 42 F-106s and had sustained just one loss. The 460th FIS

460th FIS aircraft initially wore the markings of the 437th FIS, later adapting them as seen here in 1972.

was discontinued on 15 July 1974. Most of its F-106s from the second batch were transferred to the California ANG's 194th FIS at Fresno.

498th FIS

Aircraft history cards indicate that the first F-106 Delta Darts were assigned to the 498th FIS at Geiger Field, Washington on 2 June 1959. This airfield was renamed Spokane International Airport in August 1960. The 'Geiger Tigers' were among the most colourful squadrons in the Air Force

and made a dramatic movie about their days in the F-86D Sabre. A different historical record which appears less credible shows an F-106A (57-2462) being accepted on 27 May 1959 and delivered on 28 May 1959 to the 498th FIS at Geiger Field. The abundance of historical evidence now has it that the 539th FIS at McGuire became the first F-106 operator three days later. At the time, press releases credited the Geiger-based unit with being first with the 'Six'.

On 1 July 1963, the 498th FIS moved to McChord AFB, Washington after a swap of F-106s with the 456th FIS. On 15 July 1963, the 498th arrived at Elmendorf with the initial White Shoes deployment. A continuous rotation with the 318th FIS was maintained until 3 December 1965. The 498th FIS made two more deployments to Alaska on 4 May 1966 and 5 July 1967. On 14 June 1966, the 498th relocated to Paine Field, Washington. On 30 September 1968, the squadron relocated to Hamilton AFB, California, was discontinued, and was redesignated the 84th FIS. As the 498th FIS, it had operated 65 Delta Darts and experienced seven losses.

Above: When based at Geiger Field, the 498th proudly wore a large 'Geiger Tiger' badge on the fins of its F-106s.

Right: This 'compass' tail design appeared in the 1963-64 period when the 498th FIS was based at McChord AFB.

539th FIS

The 539th FIS (known unofficially as 'Iron Hand') had the distinction of being the first Air Defense Command unit to operate the F-106 Delta Dart. An operator of the F-86L Sabre, the 539th was fortuitously located at McGuire AFB, New Jersey, which was also the site of the East Coast SAGE (Semi-Automatic Ground Environment) air-intercept system. The squadron emblem, dating to its reactivation with F-86s in 1954,

depicts a mailed fist reaching down to destroy a bomber. At one time, the 539th had been scheduled to operate the F-102 Delta Dagger, but it moved directly to the F-106 instead.

Aircraft record cards show the first two F-106s arriving at McGuire on 30 May 1959. Other history records support this date, although maintenance records at ADC indicate that the date was 1 May 1959. Yet another historical record shows an F-106A (57-2457) being accepted by the USAF on 10 April 1959 and delivered on 17 April 1959 to the 539th FIS at McGuire AFB. In the absence of a way to reconcile the conflicting dates, the 30 May 1959 date is regarded as the most credible. It should be noted that the 539th did not become operational immediately in the F-106, and performed essentially as a field test unit for the early part of its existence. Thus, the first operational squadron was the 498th FIS at Geiger Field.

The 539th competed in the 1961 William Tell weapons meet, finishing in third place in the F-106 category. The 539th did not participate in any deployments outside the continental US. The squadron was discontinued on 31 August 1967. It operated 26 F-106s and suffered five losses.

Above: This 539th FIS F-106B, complete with a full load of AIM-4s, wears the last form of marking used by the unit before disbandment. A light blue colour was also used for the lightning bolt on some aircraft.

Below: The 539th FIS's first tail marking was a triangle pierced by a chevron.

Air National Guard

The ANG became a Delta Dart operator in April 1972 when the first aircraft were delivered to Montana's 186th FIS. Six Guard units flew the F-106 up to August 1988

when the 119th FIS, New Jersey ANG sent its last aircraft to AMARC at Davis-Monthan AFB, Arizona. All Air National Guard squadrons which operated the F-106 were

'ADC-gained' units which performed the Air Defense Command mission.

101st FIS Massachusetts ANG

The first two F-106s for the 101st TFS (57-2466 and 57-2524) were assigned on 28 April 1972. On 10 June 1972, the 101st TFS and its parent 102nd TFG were redesignated FIS and FIG. The squadron's initial batch of Delta Darts comprised 18 F-106As and one F-106B from the 95th FIS plus one F-106B from the ADWC.

The squadron made its first intercept of a Tu-95 'Bear' bomber off the coast of New York on 15 April 1975. The 101st FIS competed in three William Tell weapons events, scoring fourth place in 1978, second in 1980, and third in 1984. The squadron's Delta Dart era ended on 10 February 1988 when Lt Col Chuck Townsend flew out the last F-106 (57-2501/14). The squadron had operated 26 F-106s, suffering two losses.

Variations in the Massachusetts Guard's F-106 tail markings centred around the use of either the ANG badge or that of the 101st FIS.

119th FIS New Jersey ANG

The very last military operator of the Delta Dart was the 119th FIS/177th FIG, the 'Jersey Devils'. The squadron's first F-106A (59-0048) was assigned on 30 October 1972

at the Atlantic City, New Jersey airport. On 11 October 1974, F-106A 59-0044 collided in mid-air over Saxis, Virginia, with Piper PA-24-250 N6876P, but recovered safely. In

1984, at the final William Tell competition in which F-106s participated, the 'Jersey Devils' took first place and Major Lynn Robinson was named F-106 Top Gun.

Of the 20 aircraft initially assigned, 18 came from the 95th FIS, one from the 318th FIS, and one from AFLC. In all, the squadron operated 29 airframes and listed no losses.

The operational career of the F-106 Delta Dart came to an end on 1 August 1988 when the 'Jersey Devils' flew away their last three aircraft, two F-106As (59-0043, 59-0046) and one F-106B (59-0149).

A 'Jersey Devils' F-106 approaches the Jersey shore in 1981. These are the later markings as worn by the unit, retaining the red intake ramps of the earlier scheme.

In company with the unit's T-33, a pair of Jersey 'Sixes' displays the earlier, and less elaborate unit markings, with 'Jersey Devils' titles.

159th FIS Florida ANG

The 159th FIS/125th FIG in Jacksonville, calling itself the 'Fang' after the abbreviation

of its Guard status, became a user of the Delta Dart on 29 May 1974 with the arrival of the unit's first F-106B (57-2523). Of the first 15 aircraft received in 1974, three F-106As and one F-106B came from the 84th FIS, one F-106A and one F-106B from the 460th FIS, four F-106As from the 171st FIS, and five F-106As from the 119th FIS.

The squadron has always had a lightning bolt on the tail flash. The group patch has a palm tree with winged arm clutching a lightning bolt. The squadron patch shows an F-106 climbing out.

In the 1976 William Tell competition, the 159th FIS finished in fourth place. The squadron did not participate again, but at William Tell in 1986 F-106s from the 159th FIS were used as targets by other interceptors at the meet.

Beginning in 1984, the squadron operated a three-aircraft detachment at Homestead AFB, Florida which it maintained throughout the rest of the squadron's F-106 period. The squadron operated 43 F-106s and sustained two losses.

March 1987 marked the end of this squadron's Delta Dart period. The last large group of aircraft to depart was five F-106As plus one F-106B, on 3 March 1987. The final Delta Dart to leave the squadron, an F-106B (57-2509) which became a B-1B bomber chase aircraft, was late in departing because it was awaiting a vertical tail tip: it finally left the 159th FIS on 23 March 1987. The

Florida ANG Darts carried a simple unit marking of a blue band with thunderbolt during their 13-year career.

squadron converted to the F-16A/B Block 15 ADF in 1987, and has since become an operator of the F-15A/B Eagle.

171st FIS Michigan ANG

The 171st FIS/191st FIG 'Six Pack', at Selfridge Field, received its first F-106A (58-0767) on 29 December 1972. The squadron's initial batch of 18 aircraft came from the 2nd FIS and consisted of 18

F-106As and two F-106Bs. The squadron operated the Delta Dagger for fewer than six years, replacing them with McDonnell Douglas F-4C Phantoms. The last aircraft to depart this squadron was an F-106B (59-0150) which transferred to the 84th FIS on 16 August 1978. The squadron operated 24 Delta Darts in all, and experienced no losses.

Above right: In 1973, the Michigan ANG's aircraft carried simple markings, featuring the older-style circular ANG badge.

Right: A pair of 'Six Pack' two-seaters sits on the ramp at Selfridge. No squadron, wing or ANG badge was worn by the 171st, though the legend 'Michigan' appeared near the top of the fin and the squadron's nickname was sometimes applied to fuel tanks.

186th FIS Montana ANG

The first Air National Guard unit to operate the Delta Dart, the 186th FIS/120th FIG received its first two F-106As (57-2485 and 57-2487) on 3 April 1972. The squadron was located at the Great Falls airport. Its initial batch of 21 F-106s consisted of one F-106A from the 319th FIS, one F-106A and one F-106B from the ADWC, and 17 F-106As and one F-106B from the 460th FIS.

The 186th FIS did well in William Tell weapons meets: first place in 1974, first in 1976, second in 1978, and second in 1982. In 1985, the Montana ANG won the Hughes Trophy. The 186th FIS was the last F-106 squadron to participate in a Red Flag exercise at Nellis AFB, Nevada, in 1986. The squadron ended its F-106 era when its last two F-106Bs (57-2517 and 57-2530) left on

26 June 1987 for transfer to the 101st FIS. The squadron operated 27 F-106s and had six losses.

The unit designation and location is spelled out on the long fuel tanks of this F-106A at Andrews AFB in 1973.

194th FIS California ANG

The 194th FIS/144th FIG, located at Fresno airport, received its first F-106A (58-0774) on 8 May 1974. The squadron's initial complement of 16 F-106s included one F-106B from the 159th FIS, one F-106A from the 119th FIS, three F-106As and one F-106B from the 171st FIS, and one F-106B from the 460th FIS. The 194th competed at William Tell twice, ranking first in 1980 and fourth in 1982. The beginning of 1984 saw the end of the F-106 era for the 194th FIS. The last four F-106As (58-0780, 59-0011, 59-0038 and 59-0059) left on 13 January 1984 for reassignment to the 49th FIS.

Top: From 1974 to 1982, the 194th used this scheme, depicting the bear symbol of California on a white background, with the 'California' legend below on a red stripe.

Above: This much plainer scheme was in use in 1982. TAC and unit badges appeared on opposite sides of the fin.

Other operators

Edwards AFB special units

The Air Force Flight Test Center (AFFTC) performed much of the operational and

developmental work with the F-106. Throughout most of the F-106 era, AFFTC was part of ARDC (Air Research and Development Command). On 1 April 1961, this formation was renamed Air Force Systems Command (AFSC), the name it retained throughout the remainder of the service life of the F-106. On 1 July 1992, prior to the use of the F-106A as a tow subject, this formation became Air Force Materiel Command (AFMC), the name it uses today. The first Delta Dart assigned to Edwards was an F-106B (57-2507) sent to 'the Center' but not officially to any numbered unit for Category II tests, after the manufacturer performed the Category I phase. Among other things, this F-106B was used to test the Delta Dart's first and second ejection seat designs.

The 6510th Test Wing of the AFFTC at Edwards did much of the testing and developmental work on USAF aircraft, including the F-106. The 6511th Test Group conducted parachute tests.

The early developmental work on the

Delta Dart was performed by AFFTC. To maintain F-106 expertise, the 4786th Test Squadron was activated on 31 December 1969 at Edwards and for a prolonged period operated one F-106B (57-2512). On 1 March 1971, this unit was reassigned to the Air Defense Weapons Center at Tyndall; it was inactivated on 15 April 1972. F-106s were also operated by the Test Pilots School at Edwards. In addition, F-106s which remained on bailment to Convair were flown at Edwards.

Many years later (in 1997), an AFFTC NC-141A StarLifter wrote the final chapter of the F-106 story. The NC-141, belonging to the AFFTC's 418th FLTS, towed a NASA-owned F-106A (59-0130) in tests aimed at exploring reusable space vehicle

Speed-record-breaking aircraft 56-0467 is seen here at Edwards with ARDC and AFFTC badges.

technology. The tests were conducted between 20 December 1997 and 20 February 1998.

F-106 aircraft at AFFTC/Edwards included 56-0451/-0452 (programmed to be available to the Center by May 1957). Others were: 56-467, 57-234, 57-241/242; 57-245, 57-2507, 57-2509, and 57-2512.

F-106s that flew at Edwards while on bailment to Convair included 56-451, 56-459 (engineering support), 57-230 (structural demonstration) and 57-2509. Aircraft 56-455 was used for structural testing at either Edwards or Palmdale; records are unclear.

Tyndall AFB special units

F-106s were operated at Tyndall AFB for almost 25 years. From the arrival of the first F-106A (58-0778) on 26 October 1959 until the departure of the last two Delta Darts

(F-106Bs 58-0900 and 58-0902), the base in the Florida panhandle was "the mover and shaker for the F-106 fleet", as one expert described it. Tyndall operated 80 F-106s and sustained nine losses.

Tyndall units included the following: 73rd Air Division/Air Defense Weapons Center; 4756th Air Defense Group/Wing; USAF Interceptor Weapons School (IWS); 4756th Air Defense Sqn (Wpns); 4757th Air Defense Sqn (IWS); 62nd Fighter Interceptor Training Squadron (FITS); 319th FITS; 4756th Combat Crew Training Squadron (CCTS); 2nd FITS; 4750th Test Squadron (TS); 475th TS; 4786th TS (at Edwards AFB for YF-12 evaluation); and the Southern Air Defense Alert Scramble Section (SADASS) 'The Dixie Darts'.

The 73rd Air Division/Air Defence Weapons Center initially painted its F-106s as seen here, at Tyndall in 1963, prior to the removal of buzz numbers from USAF aircraft.

Right: Later in the 1960s, the red/white/blue trim seen at right was adopted. The ADWC badge on the tail was later replaced with its TAC equivalent.

Air Materiel Areas/Air Logistics Centers

Throughout the lifetime of the F-106, the USAF operated three depots for major aircraft maintenance and repair work. These were the Sacramento Air Materiel Area at McClellan AFB, California, the San Antonio Air Materiel Area at Kelly AFB, Texas, and the Oklahoma City Air Materiel Area at Tinker AFB, Oklahoma. These three depots were operated by AMC (Air Materiel Command) which became AFLC (Air Force Logistics Command) on 1 April 1961.

Today's successor to these major commands (since 1 July 1992) is AFMC (Air Force Materiel Command). In the 1970s, the Air Materiel Areas were redesignated ALCs (Air Logistics Centers).

Sacramento ALC was the depot-level maintenance and repair facility for the F-106. Here, the aircraft underwent periodic inspections, maintenance, and repair that could not be performed at the base level but which did not require a return to the

factory. Sacramento operated several of the aircraft (apparently without distinctive markings) throughout the type's career. At the time, the depot command did not follow the practice, adopted later, of having a numbered flying squadron. F-106s were operated by the Flight Test Branch, Quality Control Division, Directorate of Maintenance, SAMA.

Flight test: SA/OCF included an F-106A (57-2453) and an F-106B (57-2517) used in

the modification and maintenance programme, an F-106B (57-2512) used after 12 October 1959 for development and evaluation of technical data, and an F-106A (59-0061) used for pilot proficiency.

San Antonio ALC was the depot-level maintenance and repair facility for the complex Hughes MA-1 electronic fire-control system and operated at least one F-106A and one F-106B. Oklahoma City ALC was available as an alternate source of depot work for temporary periods but apparently did not have an ongoing F-106-related programme or any F-106s assigned.

San Antonio Logistics (SAL) F-106s did not wear a special colour scheme, although this one (59-0061) was tested in air superiority blue with a Dayglo tail and the unit's name on the drop tanks.

Hanscom Field units

Hanscom AFB, Massachusetts has long been a centre of USAF developmental work in radar and other electronic equipment, and was one location which tested the MA-1 fire-control system, the revolutionary datalink system, and the IFF kit on the F-106. Users of the Delta Dart at Hanscom Field included the 6520th Test Group and the AFCRC (Air Force Cambridge Research Center/Laboratories).

The 6520th TG was part of the Electronic Systems Division of ARDC (Air Research and Development Command), which became AFSC (Air Force Systems Command) on 1 April 1961. Today's equivalent command (since 1 July 1992) is AFMC. The designation of this flying group was unusual, in that units in the 65xx series were usually located at Edwards AFB, California. Furthermore, the 6520th was short-lived, eventually (by the late 1970s) being reorganised into the 3245th Maintenance and Supply Group. Its role as an operator of two F-106As (57-2490/2491) was connected with ongoing tests and operational evaluation of the MA-1, datalink system, and IFF system on the Delta Dart, all of which were quite advanced for the time.

AFCRC (Air Force Cambridge Research Center/Laboratories), also known as the Hanscom Complex after Hanscom AFB, Massachusetts, teamed with MITRE (a private company 'think tank' founded by Robert R. Everett in 1958) and Lincoln Laboratories to test the F-106 SAGE (Semi-Automatic Ground Environment) system in a way that would not interfere with FAA (Federal Aviation Administration) air traffic control operations. AFCRC operated two F-106A interceptors (57-244/245).

Detachment 15 (CMD), Palmdale

The Air Force maintained a detachment at Palmdale, California where F-106s manufactured in San Diego underwent a final fitting-out before delivery. Part of the purpose of the detachment was to complete final preparation for flyaway to an operational squadron.

Air Combat Command

Established only on 1 June 1992, Air Combat Command (ACC) is too recent to have fielded squadrons of manned F-106 Delta Dart interceptors. However, ACC sang the swan song for the F-106 with its drone squadron, which operated the aircraft until late 1997. ACC's 475th Weapons Evaluation Group headquartered at Eglin AFB, Florida is the parent command for the 82nd Aerial Target Squadron at Tyndall AFB and that squadron's Detachment 1, operating at Holloman AFB, New Mexico. The Tyndall and Holloman units employed the QF-106 drone through the early to mid-1990s for a variety of training and exercise missions.

In late 1991, the QF-106A began to replace the QF-100D/F Super Sabre as the USAF's FSAT (full-scale aerial target), first at the White Sands Missile Range, New Mexico and thereafter at the Eglin Gulf Test Range, Florida. The QF-106A is deemed better able to simulate an enemy aircraft for air-to-air missile engagements because of its higher speed and greater manoeuvrability.

As with earlier FSATs, a typical mission employs the QF-106A as a target for an air-to-air test of an infra-red missile and is flown 'nullo' (with no pilot aboard). The QF-106 is controlled by ground operators. The intent is for the QF-106A target drone to survive repeated engagements with air-to-air missiles.

The delta wing of the QF-106A made it impossible for the aircraft to employ the wingtip propane burners used on earlier drones to create an infra-red source for heat-seeking missiles. The burners were

Dayglo was applied to the tails of QF-106s; their rudders retained squadron markings to avoid control balance modifications.

placed beneath wing pylons, which are located beneath the wing and rather far forward. This proved less than fully satisfactory, in part because in most test range missile engagements the missile is fired down at the target.

Operation of Delta Darts at Holloman AFB, New Mexico and Tyndall AFB, Florida was managed by General Electric.

Civil contractors

In addition to operating aircraft at Edwards (separate entry), Convair was an 'F-106 operator' at Holloman AFB, New Mexico with three aircraft on bailment. An F-106A (56-460) and an F-106B (57-2514) were operated by the manufacturer at Holloman for armament separation tests. An F-106B (57-2507) undertook supersonic ejection tests.

Three Delta Darts were on bailment to Hughes, manufacturer of the fire-control system, at Holloman. One F-106A (56-457) was used for a general evaluation of characteristics of the aircraft. An F-106B (57-2508) was used to test the infra-red sight and chaff. A third aircraft (serial unknown) was used in engineering support.

The B-1 chase programme

The chase programme for the B-1B Lancer bomber got underway at Palmdale on 10 October 1986 with the arrival of the first chase aircraft, an F-106B (57-2513). F-106s accompanied every production B-1B during its check-out flight from Palmdale prior to delivery of the bomber to the USAF. The chase pilot's job was to provide an outside pair of eyes to spot any external problems on the B-1B about which the bomber's crew might not have known. The first flight of each of the 100 bombers final-assembled at Palmdale was of four hours' duration, requiring two F-106s that switched over at the two-hour mark.

F-106s were used to support test flights from Palmdale and Tinker AFB, Oklahoma. Eight 106s were assigned to the programme: 57-2509, 57-2513, 57-2535, 58-0795, 59-0008, 59-0060, 59-0061 and 59-0149. Initially, these chase aircraft had red tails. In time, black and blue tails also appeared, with a white 'B-1/F-106 CHASE' flash, designed by Jerry Roth, a crew chief with the B-1B programme. Following delivery of the final B-1B the last F-106 chase aircraft, an F-106A (59-0061), ended its role in the programme and departed for the 'boneyard' at Davis-Monthan AFB, on 6 July 1990.

The eight F-106s used for B-1B chase missions from 1986-90 wore a 'B-1/F-106 CHASE' logo.

NACA/NASA

The National Advisory Committee for Aeronautics (NACA) and its successor, NASA (the National Aeronautics and Space Administration), operated examples of the F-106 as early as 1961, when an F-106A joined the Ames fleet for use as an automated control systems test aircraft.

The Dart served almost continuously with NASA for nearly 40 years, supporting a diverse variety of programmes. NASA finished up as the last operator of the type, having employed nine airframes at various times. The busiest of these was NF-106B 57-2516 (NASA 616), which joined the NASA fleet in 1966. The last of the NASA Darts was a former drone, QF-106A 59-0130, used at NASA Dryden in Project Eclipse as the EXD-01.

NASA 616 wore a variety of colour schemes during its career with NASA, including this blue/grey one, while fitted with underwing J85 pods from 1966 to 1979.

INDEX

Picture acknowledgments

The publishers would like to thank the following individuals and organisations for their kind assistance in supplying photographs for this book.

6-7: Robert F. Dorr. **8:** Robert F. Dorr, Aerospace. **9:** Larry Davis Collection, USAF via Terry Panopalis, NAA. **10:** AFFTC via Terry Panopalis, Larry Davis Collection (two), Terry Panopalis. **11:** NASA Dryden via Terry Panopalis, Terry Panopalis (two). **12:** Larry Davis Collection (three), Terry Panopalis, Peter R. Foster. **13:** NAA, Larry Davis Collection (two). **14:** Larry Davis Collection, Curt Burns via Warren Thompson, Don Scott via Warren Thompson. **15:** Larry Davis Collection (three), Robert F. Dorr. **16:** Robert F. Dorr. **17:** Robert F. Dorr. **18:** Terry Panopalis (three), Larry Davis Collection. **19:** Larry Davis Collection, AFFTC via Terry Panopalis, NAA, Terry Panopalis. **20:** Larry Davis Collection (three), Don Scott via Warren Thompson, Bill Myers via Warren Thompson, Terry Panopalis, Chris Ryan. **22:** Larry Davis Collection, Terry Panopalis, USAF via David W. Menard via Terry Panopalis. **23:** Larry Davis Collection (three), Boeing via Terry Panopalis, Bob Terbet via Warren Thompson. **24:** Aerospace (two), Peter R. Foster, Larry Davis Collection (two). **25:** Larry Davis Collection, Aerospace (two), Terry Panopalis. **26:** Bob Terbet via Warren Thompson, Robert F. Dorr. **27:** Robert F. Dorr (three). **28:** Robert F. Dorr, USAF, USAF via Terry Panopalis, Terry Panopalis, Larry Davis Collection. **29:** Terry Panopalis, USAF (two), Larry Davis Collection. **32:** Larry Davis Collection (three). **33:** Terry Panopalis (four), Larry Davis Collection (two). **34:** Larry Davis Collection, Terry Panopalis (two), Peter R. Foster. **35:** Don Spering via Terry Panopalis, David Donald, Larry Davis Collection. **36:** Charles Hutchinson via Warren Thompson, Chris Ryan, EADS, Terry Panopalis (two). **37:** NASA Dryden via Terry Panopalis (three), Terry Panopalis. **38-41:** Larry Davis Collection. **42:** Terry Panopalis (four), AFFTC via Terry Panopalis. **43:** Larry Davis Collection (three), Peter R. Foster. **44-45:** McDonnell, USAF (two). **46:** Richard Burns via Warren Thompson, Peter R. Foster. **47:** USAF, Robert F. Dorr, USAF. **48-49:** McDonnell. **50:** USAF (two), McDonnell. **51:** McDonnell (two), USAF, C.A. Johnson. **52:** McDonnell (three), USAF. **53:** USAF (three), McDonnell, Robert F. Dorr. **54:** McDonnell (two), Aerospace, Robert F. Dorr. **55:** USAF (three), Peter R. Foster. **56:** RCAF (two), Aerospace, Peter R. Foster. **58:** Peter R. Foster (two), McDonnell (two). **59:** Robert F. Dorr, McDonnell, Roy Marsh via Warren Thompson, Richard Burns via Warren Thompson. **61:** Aerospace, USAF (two), via Peter R. Foster. **62:** Aerospace, USAF, Robert F. Dorr (two), Peter R. Foster. **64:** Peter R. Foster (three). **65:** Lockheed, Kentucky ANG, Aerospace. **66-67:** USAF via Marty Isham (MI), **68:** Convair, Convair via Terry Panopalis (TP). **69:** Bruce Chavis via Warren Thompson (WT), Convair, Aerospace. **70:** Aerospace, via Robert F. Dorr (RFD), Convair, AFFTC via TP. **71:** Convair, Harry Gann collection. **72:** AFFTC via TP, via RFD (three), Convair via RFD, Convair via TP. **73:** Convair (two), USAF, via RFD. **74:** Convair (three). **75:** Aerospace, AFFTC via TP, via RFD. **76:** Convair, Convair via TP, Aerospace. **77:** USAF, Convair, Convair via TP. **78:** Convair via Robert F. Dorr (two), R. E Kling. **79:** via Terry Panopalis (two), USAF, Don Spering, Convair. **80:** Lockheed Martin via TP (two), Convair via TP, via Larry Davis (LD). **81:** Convair via Bruce Robertson (two), B. Butcher via MI, via LD, LD. **82:** Lockheed Martin via TP, Preciado via LD, USAF via LD, D. Henderson via MI. **83:** Convair via Bruce Robertson, Aerospace, Convair, NASA Johnson via TP. **84:** R. L. Lawson via MI, B. Maleba via MI. **85:** Convair (six), Hughes via TP, USAF. **87:** Hughes via Terry Panopalis (six), via Terry Panopalis, Terry Panopalis. **88:** MI collection, J. Geer via MI, via Duncan Macintosh (two), via LD, Robert Mock via WT. **89:** Convair (two), Convair via TP (two). **90:** MI collection, Jack Morris via MI, USAF (three). **91:** USAF (three). **94:** via RFD, Budd Butcher via WT, R. Satterfield via MI, USAF, Bill McDonald via WT, Tom Hally via WT. **95:** via RFD, USAF, Bill McDonald via WT, Don Dickman via LD. **96:** via LD, Warren Bodie collection, via LD, Peter Mersky collection. **97:** E. John Raboin via WT, Clair Carling via WT, Charles Morden via WT, Bill Winkeler via WT, USAF. **98:** A. K. Smith via MI (two), Jim Monaco via WT, Don Spering, James Cobb via WT, MI collection. **100:** Aerospace, General Electric, via Chris Knott, via Bruce Robertson. **101:** Geoff Hughes via Chris Pocock, USAF via LD, USAF, MAP. **102:** USAF (two), Aerospace (two). **103:** S. Miller via LD, W. H. Strandberg Jr., via Bruce Robertson, B. Butcher via MI. **104:** Aerospace (four), KLu. **105:** via LD, Chris Ryan, USAF, Mike Hooks. **106:** A. R. Robinson, Chris Ryan. **108:** Aerospace (three), via RFD. **109:** Aerospace (two), René van Woezik (two). **110:** MI, Warren Bodie collection, Don Spering, via Chris Knott. **111:** Bill Curry via RFD, TP collection. **113:** Don Spering/AIR. **114:** Sperry via TP, Peter R. Foster, USAF. **115:** via Duncan Macintosh, NASA Dryden via TP, Aerospace, NASA via Johnson (two), USAF via TP. **116:** via RFD, Aerospace, Chris Pocock, Robert E. Kling. **117:** Sperry (five), Mike Herring via Chris Pocock. **118:** T. Cuddy via MI, K. Minert via MI, D. Menard via MI, Bill Curry via MI, D. Higbeg via MI. **119:** G. Wildt via MI, MI, via LD, M. Olsted via MI, Major P. Bracci via MI. **120:** via LD, B. Burgess via MI, via LD, B. Malerba via MI. **121:** Taylor via MI, Freeburg, Aerospace, J. Wogstad via MI, MI collection, B. Yocum via MI. **122:** Kaston via MI, MI collection, Malerba via MI, W. M. Jefferies via MI, via Larry Davis. **123:** Barry Miller via LD, Don Spering/AIR, Aerospace, MI collection. **124:** LD collection, Jim Winchester collection, Aerospace/Dave Menard, Aerospace, LD collection. **125:** via RFD, Aerospace, D. Dickman via MI, Aerospace. **126:** F. Retter via MI, Aerospace, Jim Monaco via WT. **127:** Dave Willis collection, Don Spering/AIR (three), Geoff Rhodes via Chris Pocock. **128:** via TP, D. Larsen via MI, MI collection, Don Spering/AIR (two). **129:** Don Spering/AIR (three), via Duncan Macintosh, J. Morris via MI, G. Brown via MI. **130:** via Chris Knott, J. Morris via MI, B. Strandberg via MI, Don Spering via Chris Pocock. **131:** Harry Gann, Freeburger, Peter Greve via Chris Pocock, NASA Lewis via TP, FAA, Aerospace (two). **132-133:** Lockheed. **134:** USAF (two), Lockheed. **135:** Lockheed (five). **136:** USAF (two). **137:** Lockheed (four), USAF, Aerospace. **138:** USAF (four), Aerospace. **139:** USAF (two), Lockheed (two), Phil Jarrett. **140:** John Fricker, Phil Jarrett, USAF. **141:** USAF, Lockheed (three), Peter R. Foster, John Fricker. **142:** Lockheed, via Terry Senior, USAF. **143:** Aerospace, USAF, Bob Burns (four), Ted Carlson/Fotodynamics. **144:** Aerospace (all). **145:** Lockheed (three). **146:** USAF (five). **147:** Lockheed (two), M.J. Hooks, Bob Mikesh, Chris Brooks/Aerophoto. **150:** G.A. Boymans, KLu, Hans Nijhuis, RDAF, Howard Levy, Lockheed (two). **151:** Lockheed (two), via Michael Stroud, RDAF. **152:** Stefan Petersen, Axel Ostermann, MBB, Luftwaffe. **154:** MBB (two), Fokker, Lockheed (two). **155:** Hans Nijhuis, KLu, CAF. **156:** Jeff Rankin-Lowe, Peter R. Foster, Jim Rotramel via Chris Brooks, Peter R. Foster. **157:** USAF, Lockheed, Canadair, Werner Münzenmaier, Ralf Hupfeld, Peter R. Foster. **158:** Axel Ostermann, Bruce Robertson, Mike Vines/Photolink, Stefan Petersen, Jelle Sjoerdsma, Marco Amatimaggio. **159:** Lockheed (two), Chris Ryan, Peter R. Foster, René van Woezik, Achille Vigna, Hans Nijhuis. **160:** Lockheed, Luftwaffe, Aerospace, USAF, Terry Senior, Ralf Hupfeld. **162:** Luftwaffe (two), Phil Jarrett, Lockheed, T. Malcolm English. **163:** Stefan Petersen, Werner Münzenmaier, Georg Mader, Axel Ostermann, Stefan Petersen, Peter R. March, Ralf Hupfeld (two), Chris Brooks/Aerophoto. **164:** Werner Münzenmaier, Peter R. Foster (two), Mike Vines/Photolink, Jelle Sjoerdsma. **165:** Stefan Petersen. **166:** US Air Force, Hans Nijhuis, Raffaele Mancini. **167:** Hans Nijhuis (five), Aerospace. **168:** Aerospace (three), Marco Amatimaggio, G.A. Boymans. **169:** Gert Kromhout, Aeritalia, Ralf Hupfeld, Ted Carlson/Fotodynamics, Werner Münzenmaier, Matthew Olaufsen. **170:** Aeritalia (two), Lockheed, Ralf Hupfeld. **172:** Mitsubishi, Chris Brooks/Aerophoto, Ralf Hupfeld, Lockheed (two). **173:** Herman J. Sixma (two), Hans Nijhuis, Peter R. March, Aeritalia, Martin Baumann. **174:** G.A. Boymans, Peter R. Foster, Marco Papisca, Achille Vigna (six), Claudio Toselli, Ralf Hupfeld (two), Jelle Sjoerdsma, M.Ottagalli and V. Marchetti/ITS (two), Carmine de Napoli. **175:** MBB (two), Hans Nijhuis, Peter Steinemann. **176:** Peter Steinemann, Hans Nijhuis (two), Carmine de Napoli. **177:** Stefan Petersen, Peter R. Foster, Jelle Sjoerdsma, Ian Black. **181:** Hendrik J. van Broekhuizen, Hans Nijhuis (two), Carmine de Napoli. **182:** Hans Nijhuis (two), M.J. Hooks, via Michael Stroud, Chris Brooks/Aerophoto. **183:** Jelle Sjoerdsma, Aerospace (two), Hans Nijhuis (two), Peter R. Foster, Chris Brooks/Aerophoto. **184:** via Terry Senior, Chris Brooks/Aerophoto, Martin Baumann, Stefan Petersen (two). **185:** Aerospace, Peter R. Foster, Raffaele Mancini, Enzo Maio, Bob Fischer. **186:** Stefan Petersen, Aerospace (two), Peter Steinemann. **187:** Aerospace (two), Peter Steinemann, Jelle Sjoerdsma (two). **188:** Aerospace, Hans Nijhuis, Chris Brooks/Aerophoto, John Fricker, Peter Steinemann. **189:** Aerospace (four), Hans Nijhuis. **190:** Aerospace, Herman J. Sixma (three), Hans Nijhuis. **191:** Peter Steinemann, US Air Force (two), USAF via Michael Stroud. **192-193:** Richard Kierbow via Larry Davis (LD). **194:** Republic via LD, Republic, AFFTC History Office via Terry Panopalis (TP). **195:** AFFTC History Office via TP, Aerospace, Republic. **196:** Aerospace (two), Mike Machat Collection via TP, San Diego Aerospace Museum via TP. **197:** Tom Brewer via LD, Aerospace, Republic. **198:** Republic via LD, Republic, via LD (three), Merle Olmsted via LD. **199:** USAF via LD (two), Cradle of Aviation Museum Collection via Ken Neubeck via TP. **200:** via LD, Warren Bodie via LD, Tom Brewer via LD. **201:** Cradle of Aviation Museum Collection via Ken Neubeck via TP, via Robert F. Dorr, San Diego Aerospace Museum via TP (two). **202:** via LD (two), David Donald. **203:** Jim Sullivan via LD. **204:** San Diego Aerospace Museum via TP, Mike Machat Collection via TP, Aerospace. **205:** via LD (two), Aerospace, Tom Brewer via LD. **206:** Dr J.G. Handleman via LD, H. Tate via LD, Republic via LD. **207:** Dave Graben via LD, Mick Roth Collection via TP, Dave Menard via LD, USAF, USAF via LD. **209:** Paul Freeburger via LD, via LD, Cradle of Aviation Museum Collection via Ken Neubeck via TP, Fairchild-Hiller. **210:** USAF via David Donald, USAF, Aerospace. **211:** Joe Bruchs via LD, Republic via TP (two). **212:** Robert Ames via LD, USAF (three). **213:** Aerospace, USAF via LD, Joe Bruchs via LD, via TP. **216:** Tom Brewer via LD (two), Duane Kasulka via LD. **217:** via LD (two), Dave Ostrowski via LD. **218:** Steven Miller via LD (two), Don Linn via LD. **219:** Ron Thurlow via LD (two), Robert Pickett via LD. **220:** Frank MacSorley via LD, Tom Brewer via LD, USAF, via LD. **221:** via LD, Tom Brewer via LD (two), Steven Miller via LD, Roger Warren via LD. **222:** USAF via LD, Tom Brewer via LD, Thomas Waller via LD. **223:** D. Jay via TP, Art Krieger via LD, Tom Brewer via LD, Fairchild-Hiller. **224:** Dave Hansen via LD, via LD, via TP, Nick Williams via LD. **225:** Frank MacSorley via LD, Lars Soldens via LD, Terry Love via LD, Tom Brewer via LD, B. Knowles via Robert F. Dorr. **226:** Don Spering/AIR (DS). **227:** Marty Isham (MI) collection. **228:** Convair/Aerospace, DS. **229:** Aerospace, Convair/Aerospace (two). **230:** Aerospace (two), Convair via Robert F. Dorr (RFD). **231:** Convair/Aerospace (three). **232:** Convair/Aerospace, Bob Cooper via A. D. Chong, Convair via RFD. **233:** All American Engineering/Aerospace, Hughes/Aerospace, Hughes via Terry Panopalis (TP). **234:** NORAD/Aerospace, DS collection (two), T. Cuddy via MI. **235:** MI collection via TP, DS, Convair via RFD. **236:** DS, USAF. **237:** via Larry Davis, DS (three), TP. **238:** Convair/Aerospace (two), R. Volker via MI. **239:** General Dynamics via TP, Convair/Aerospace (two). **240:** Convair via RFD (four), via Dave Macintosh (DM), via Larry Davis (LD). **241:** P. M. Paulsen via Dave Menard, Isham collection via Bob Burns, Mike Hooks, MI collection. **242:** MI collection, DS, Barry Miller via LD. **244:** via WT, Aerospace, MI collection, via WT, Joe Olshefski via WT (four), MI collection (two), USAF via MI. **246:** MI collection, USAF via LD, Chris Pocock. **247:** USAF/Aerospace, DS (two), via LD. **250:** Edwards History Office via A.D. Chong, DS, MI collection, D. Miller via MI. **251:** Chris Pocock (two), MI collection, D. Stultz via MI. C. Kaston via MI. **252:** via DM (two), Bob Mason via WT, MI, Aerospace. **253:** MI collection, Doug Barbier via MI, Robert E. Kling, G. Le Baron via MI. **254:** MI collection (two), D. Stultz via MI, Doug Barbier via MI (three), J. Shields via MI, via DM. **255:** USAF/Aerospace, USAF via MI (three), MI collection. **256:** Robert E. Kling, Ian Black, Chris Pocock, via DM, DS (11). **257:** MI collection via TP (three), DS (two), M.J. Delgado via DM, NASA via TP (two), NASA/Aerospace, AFFTC/HO via TP. **258:** USAF via MI, Aerospace, via DM (two). **259:** MI collection, via Enzo Maio, Aerospace, Joe Olshefski via WT, Aerospace. **260:** Baldur Sveinsson (two), MI collection (two). **261:** Aerospace, via DM (three), DS (three), via LD. **262:** MI, DS, MI collection, Jerry Geer via DS. **263:** DS, via DM. **264:** DS (three), via DM, Chris Ryan. **265:** M.K. Nelson, MI collection, DS. **266:** Hughes via TP, DS (two). **268:** DS, Don Logan via DM, WT (two). **269:** via Chris Knott, Aerospace, DS. **270:** Jack Callaway via RFD (two), MI collection, D. Adams, DS, Ian Black. **271:** Jim Winchester, NASA via TP, DS. **272:** NASA via TP (four), MI collection. **273:** DS, F. MacSorley via MI. **274:** via DM (three). **275:** Dave Menard, A. Swanberg via Warren Bodie, RFD collection. **276:** Aerospace, Jim Winchester, DS (two), WT, F. MacSorley via MI. **277:** MI, via DM, MI collection, Tim Maunder, via DM, J. Sandvik via MI, Jim Winchester, F. MacSorley via MI, DS. **278:** via MI, Jim Winchester, DS, MI collection, D. Miller via MI, MI collection, J. Geer via MI, WT, via DM. **279:** G. Bracken via MI, MI collection, Nick Williams via LD, via DM, MI collection, B. Balogh via MI, F. MacSorley via MI, via LD. **280:** Jim Winchester, USAF via MI, WT, Chris Ryan, Aerospace, Tim Maunder, B. Malerba via MI, MI collection, F. MacSorley via MI. **281:** MI collection, USAF via MI, WT, via DM (two), MI collection, K. Buchanan via MI, MI collection, J. Morris via MI. **282:** Tim Maunder, via MI (two), MI collection (two), R. Picciani via MI, B. Miller via LD, Aerospace (two), DS. **283:** Aerospace (two), DS (5), MI collection, WT. **284:** Aerospace, DS (two), MI collection, WT, Tom Brewer via MI, K. Buchanan via MI. **285:** via DM, David Donald, Jack Callaway via RFD, A. D. Chong, via A. D. Chong, Joe Zerbe.